# Teach Yourself VISUALLY™

## Microsoft® Office 2008 for Mac®

by Paul McFedries

Wiley Publishing, Inc.

# Teach Yourself VISUALLY™ Office 2008 for Mac®

Published by
**Wiley Publishing, Inc.**
10475 Crosspoint Boulevard
Indianapolis, IN 46256
www.wiley.com

Published simultaneously in Canada



Library of Congress Control Number: 2009925741

ISBN: 978-0-470-48503-3

Manufactured in the United States of America

10 9 8 7 6 5 4 3 2 1

## Trademark Acknowledgments



## Contact Us

For general information on our other products and services please contact our Customer Care Department within the U.S. at 877-762-2974, outside the U.S. at 317-572-3993 or fax 317-572-4002.

For technical support please visit www.wiley.com/techsupport.

Wiley Publishing, Inc.

**Sales**

Contact Wiley
at (877) 762-2974 or
fax (317) 572-4002.

# Praise for Visual Books

***"Like a lot of other people, I understand things best when I see them visually. Your books really make learning easy and life more fun."***

John T. Frey (Cadillac, MI)

***"I have quite a few of your Visual books and have been very pleased with all of them. I love the way the lessons are presented!"***

Mary Jane Newman (Yorba Linda, CA)

***"I just purchased my third Visual book (my first two are dog-eared now!), and, once again, your product has surpassed my expectations.***

Tracey Moore (Memphis, TN)

***"I am an avid fan of your Visual books. If I need to learn anything, I just buy one of your books and learn the topic in no time. Wonders! I have even trained my friends to give me Visual books as gifts."***

Illona Bergstrom (Aventura, FL)

***"Thank you for making it so clear. I appreciate it. I will buy many more Visual books."***

J.P. Sangdong (North York, Ontario, Canada)

***"I have several books from the Visual series and have always found them to be valuable resources."***

Stephen P. Miller (Ballston Spa, NY)

***"Thank you for the wonderful books you produce. It wasn't until I was an adult that I discovered how I learn — visually. Nothing compares to Visual books. I love the simple layout. I can just grab a book and use it at my computer, lesson by lesson. And I understand the material! You really know the way I think and learn. Thanks so much!"***

Stacey Han (Avondale, AZ)

***"I absolutely admire your company's work. Your books are terrific. The format is perfect, especially for visual learners like me. Keep them coming!"***

Frederick A. Taylor, Jr. (New Port Richey, FL)

***"I have several of your Visual books and they are the best I have ever used."***

Stanley Clark (Crawfordville, FL)

***"I bought my first Teach Yourself VISUALLY book last month. Wow. Now I want to learn everything in this easy format!"***

Tom Vial (New York, NY)

***"Thank you, thank you, thank you...for making it so easy for me to break into this high-tech world. I now own four of your books. I recommend them to anyone who is a beginner like myself."***

Gay O'Donnell (Calgary, Alberta, Canada)

***"I write to extend my thanks and appreciation for your books. They are clear, easy to follow, and straight to the point. Keep up the good work! I bought several of your books and they are just right! No regrets! I will always buy your books because they are the best."***

Seward Kollie (Dakar, Senegal)

***"Compliments to the chef!! Your books are extraordinary! Or, simply put, extra-ordinary, meaning way above the rest! THANK YOU THANK YOU THANK YOU! I buy them for friends, family, and colleagues."***

Christine J. Manfrin (Castle Rock, CO)

***"What fantastic teaching books you have produced! Congratulations to you and your staff. You deserve the Nobel Prize in Education in the Software category. Thanks for helping me understand computers."***

Bruno Tonon (Melbourne, Australia)

***"Over time, I have bought a number of your 'Read Less - Learn More' books. For me, they are THE way to learn anything easily. I learn easiest using your method of teaching."***

José A. Mazón (Cuba, NY)

***"I am an avid purchaser and reader of the Visual series, and they are the greatest computer books I've seen. The Visual books are perfect for people like myself who enjoy the computer, but want to know how to use it more efficiently. Your books have definitely given me a greater understanding of my computer, and have taught me to use it more effectively. Thank you very much for the hard work, effort, and dedication that you put into this series."***

Alex Diaz (Las Vegas, NV)

# Credits

**Senior Acquisitions Editor**
Jody Lefevere

**Project Editor**
Jade L. Williams

**Technical Editor**
Dennis Cohen

**Copy Editor**
Kim Heusel

**Editorial Director**
Robyn Siesky

**Editorial Manager**
Cricket Krengel

**Business Manager**
Amy Knies

**Senior Marketing Manager**
Sandy Smith

**Vice President and Executive Group Publisher**
Richard Swadley

**Vice President and Executive Publisher**
Barry Pruett

**Project Coordinator**
Patrick Redmond

**Graphics and Production Specialists**
Carrie A. Cesavice
Andrea Hornberger
Jennifer Mayberry

**Quality Control Technician**
Amanda Graham

**Proofreading and Indexing**
Cindy Ballew
Christine Karpeles

**Screen Artist**
Jill A. Proll

**Illustrators**
Rhonda David-Burroughs
Cheryl Grubbs

## About the Author

**Paul McFedries** is a technical writer who has been authoring computer books since 1991. He has more than 60 books to his credit, which together have sold more than three million copies worldwide. These books include the Wiley titles *Teach Yourself VISUALLY Mac* and *The Unoffical Guide to Microsoft Office 2007*. Paul also runs Word Spy, a Web site dedicated to tracking new words and phrases (see www.wordspy.com). Please visit Paul's personal Web site at www.mcfedries.com.

## Author's Acknowledgments

The book you hold in your hands is not only an excellent learning tool, but it is truly beautiful as well. I am happy to have supplied the text that you will read, but the gorgeous images come from Wiley's crack team of artists and illustrators. The layout of the tasks, the accuracy of the spelling and grammar, and the veracity of the information are all the result of hard work performed by project editor Jade Williams, copy editor Kim Heusel, and technical editor Dennis Cohen. Thanks to all of you for your excellent work. My thanks, as well, to acquisitions editor Jody Lefevere for asking me to write this book.

# Table of Contents

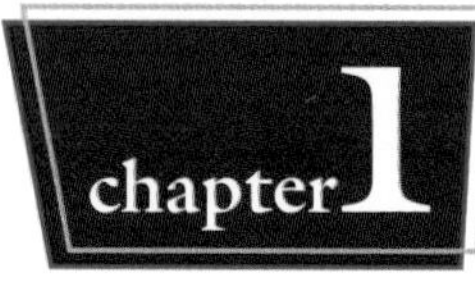


## Working with the Office Programs

chapter 2

## Working with Office Documents

## chapter 3 Formatting Office Documents

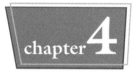

## chapter 4 Adding and Editing Graphics

# Table of Contents

## Inserting Text and Other Items

chapter 6

## Formatting Word Documents

## Working with Microsoft Word's Features



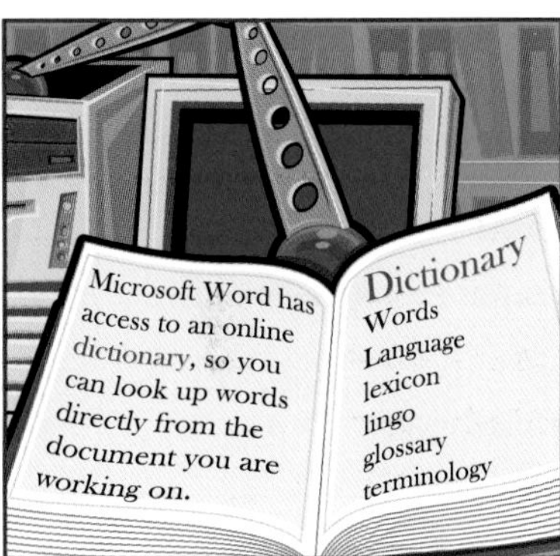


chapter 8

## Building Word Tables

# Table of Contents

## Adding Document Elements

chapter 10

## Building an Excel Spreadsheet

# Working with Excel Ranges

chapter 12

# Formatting Excel Data

# Table of Contents

## chapter 13 Manipulating Formulas and Functions

## chapter 14 Visualizing Data with Excel Charts



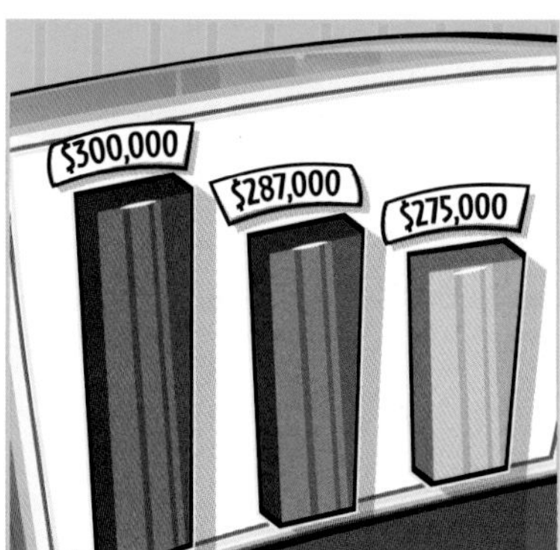

# chapter 15 Building a PowerPoint Presentation

# chapter 16 Formatting PowerPoint Slides



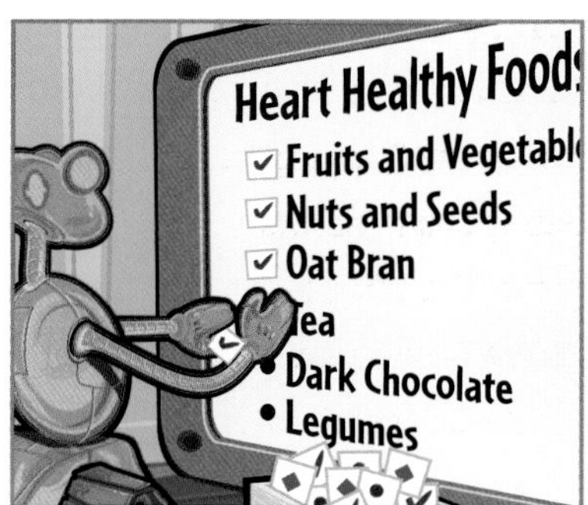

# Table of Contents

## Setting Up and Running a Slide Show

chapter 18

## Sending and Receiving E-Mail

## Working with Appointments and Tasks



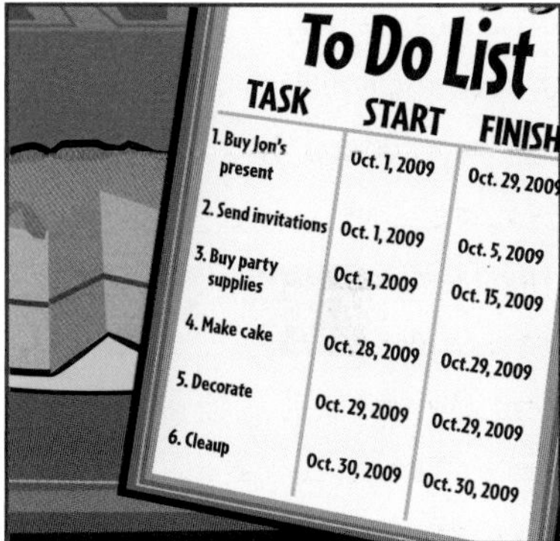


chapter 20

## Working with Contacts

# Working with the Office Programs

Are you ready to learn about Microsoft Office for Mac? You begin in this chapter by learning how to work with the Office programs, including starting and quitting programs, and working with windows, toolbars, and preferences.

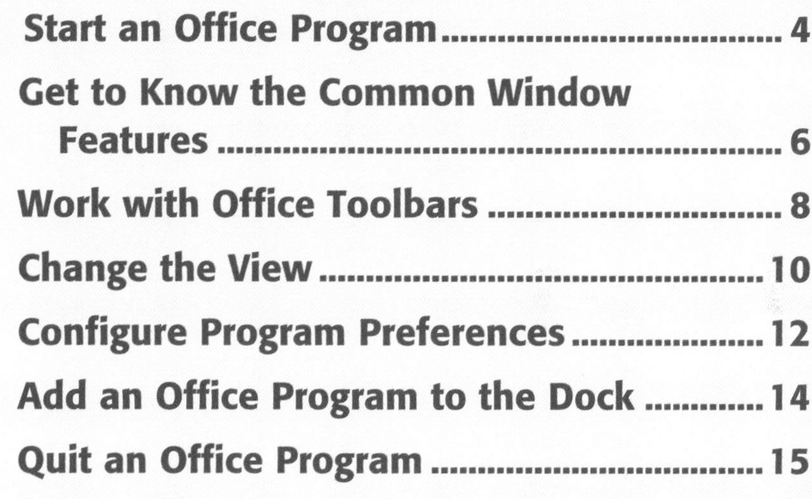

# Start an Office Program

**To work with any Office program, you must first tell OS X which program you want to run. OS X then launches the program and displays it on the desktop.**

## Start an Office Program

1. Click the **Finder** button (![]).

*Note: If the Office application that you want to start has a button in the Dock, you can click the button to start the program and skip the rest of these steps. See "Add an Office Program to the Dock" later in this chapter.*

The Finder window appears.

2. Click **Applications**.

*Note: You can navigate to the Applications folder in any Finder window by pressing* Shift + ⌘ + A.

The Applications window appears.

3. Double-click **Microsoft Office 2008**.

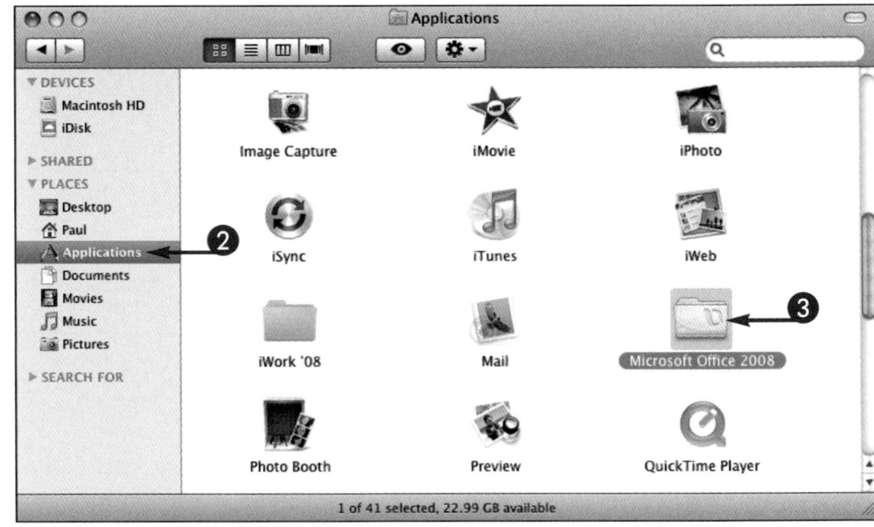

The Microsoft Office 2008 window appears.

4 Double-click Office program you want to start.

***Note:*** *The first time you start an Office program you see the Microsoft Office Setup Assistant, which takes you through the process of setting up Office for your Mac.*

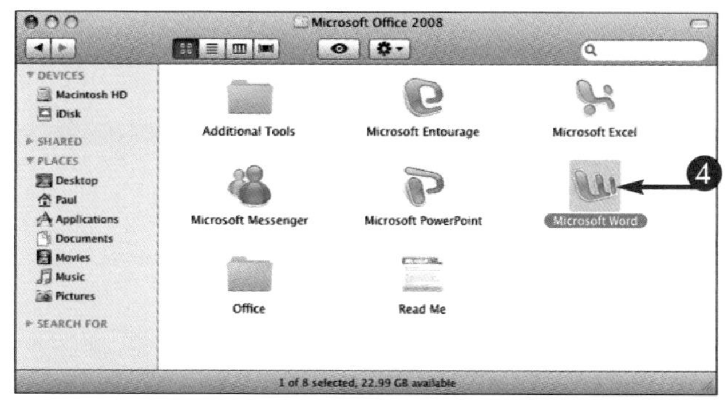


- The program appears on the desktop.

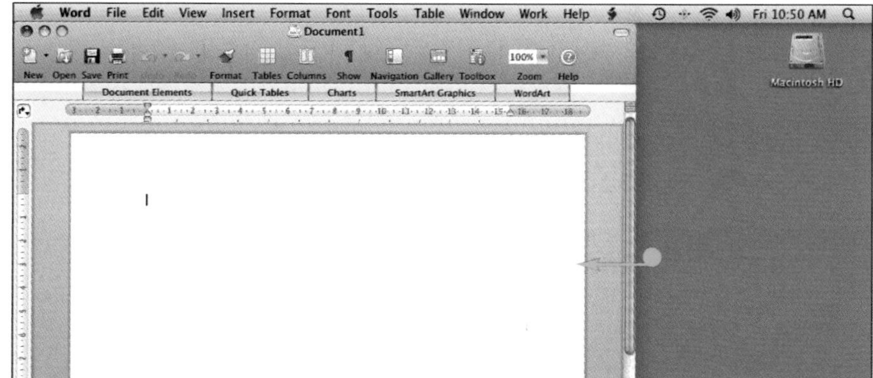


## TIP

### Can I open an Office application automatically when I start my Mac?

Yes. You can set up the application as a login item for your user account:

1. Click **System Preferences** ( ) in the Dock.
2. Click **Accounts**.
3. Click your user account.
4. Click the **Login Items** tab.
5. Click **Add** (+).
6. Click **Applications**.
7. Click **Microsoft Office 2008**.
8. Click the Office application you want to run at startup.
9. Click **Add**.

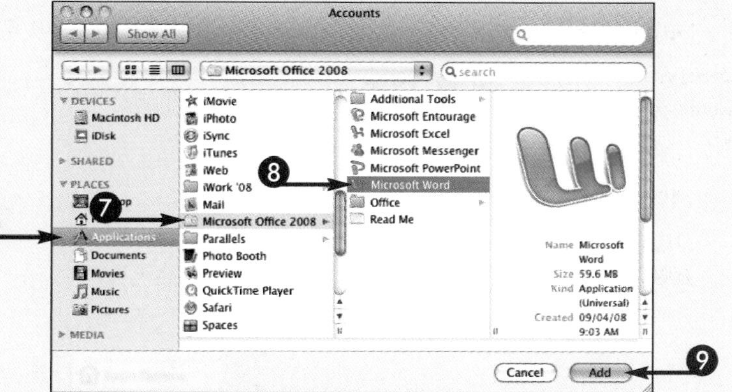

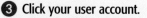

# Get to Know the Common Window Features

**Before you can get productive with Microsoft Office, you need to get comfortable with the layout of the Office windows, particularly common features such as the toolbar, status bar, and Elements Gallery.**

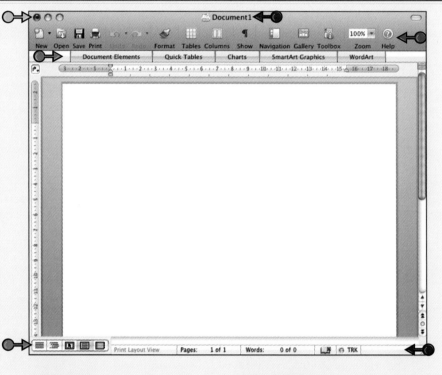

### Window Controls

Click these buttons to close (), minimize (), and zoom () the current window.

### Title Bar

This bar displays the name of the current document. You can also click and drag the title bar to move the window.

### Standard Toolbar

This offers a collection of buttons, lists, and other controls that give you quick access to common program features.

### Elements Gallery

This displays a collection of tabs that represent various objects — called *elements* — that you can add to your Office documents.

### Status Bar

This displays information about the current document.

### View Buttons

Click these buttons to change the current document view.

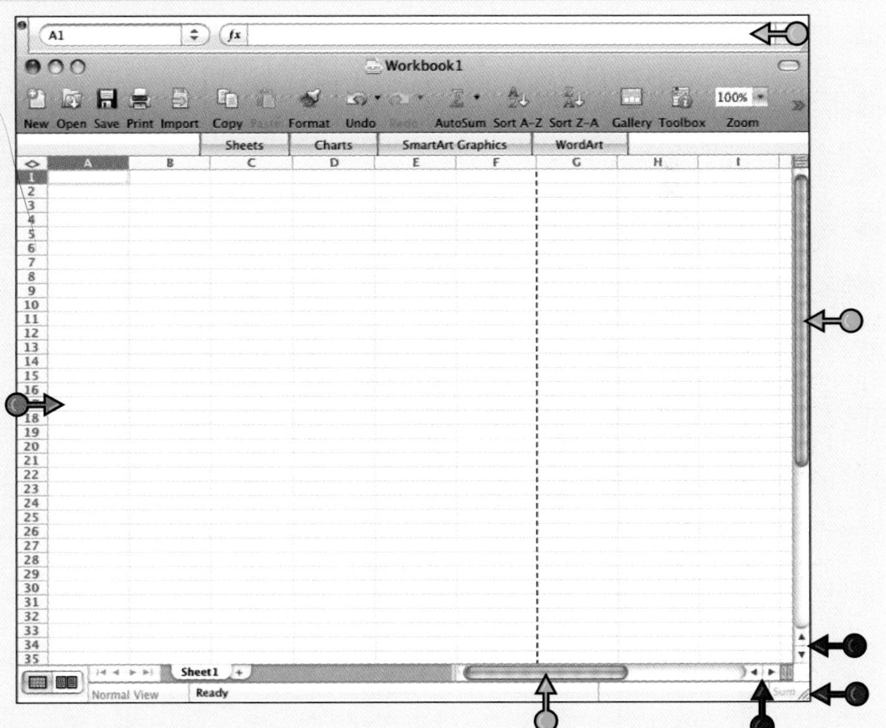

### Work Area

You use this area to add and edit data in your Office files. In Word, the work area shows a word processing document; in Excel, you see a worksheet; in PowerPoint, you see a slide.

### Scroll Bars

Click and drag the vertical scroll bar to scroll the current document up or down; click and drag the horizontal scroll bar to scroll the current document left or right.

### Scroll Buttons

Click these buttons to scroll up (▲), down (▼), left (◄), or right(►) one line at a time.

### Formula Bar

In Excel, you use this area to insert text and formulas into worksheet cells and to edit cell contents.

### Window Size Control

Click and drag the lower-right corner to change the window size.

# Work with Office Toolbars

**In the Office applications, the Standard toolbar gives you quick access to commonly used commands. However, all the Office programs come with multiple toolbars, so you need to know how to display the toolbar you want to work with.**

**If you want more room to work on an Office document, you can also hide all the toolbars.**

## Work with Office Toolbars

### DISPLAY A TOOLBAR

❶ Click **View**.

The View menu appears.

❷ Click **Toolbars**.

❸ Click the toolbar you want to display.

- If a toolbar is currently displayed, the program shows a check mark (☑) beside the toolbar name.

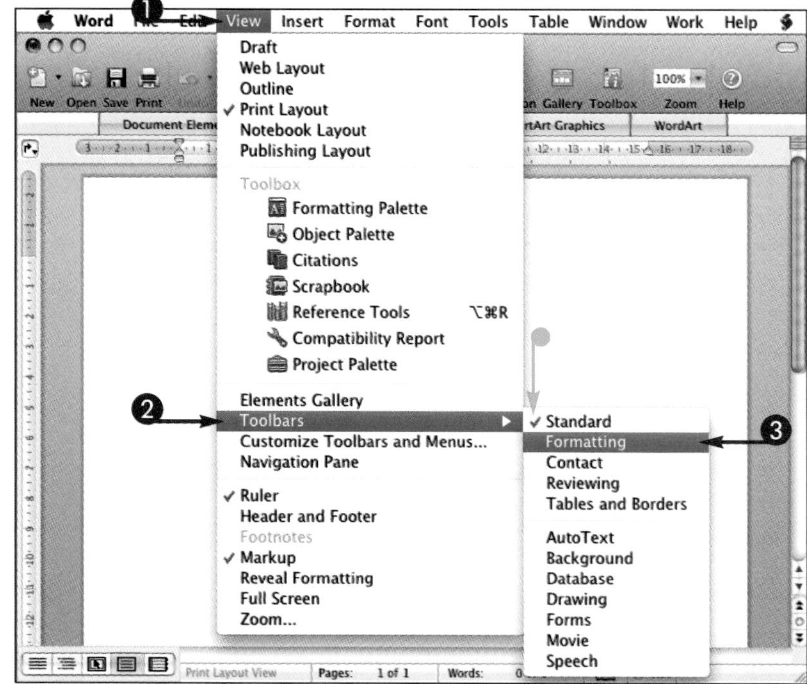


***Note:*** *Another way to display the list of toolbars is to right-click (or* Ctrl *+click) the Standard toolbar, and then click* ***Toolbars****.*

- The application displays the toolbar.

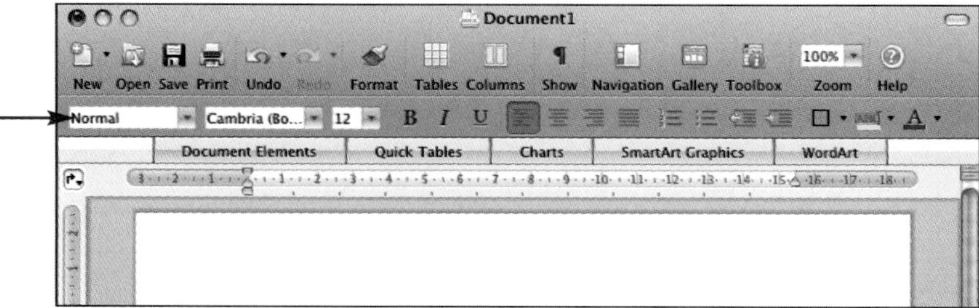

### HIDE ALL TOOLBARS

1. Click the **Show/Hide Toolbar** button (▭).

- The application hides all the displayed toolbars.
- To show the toolbars again, click ▭.

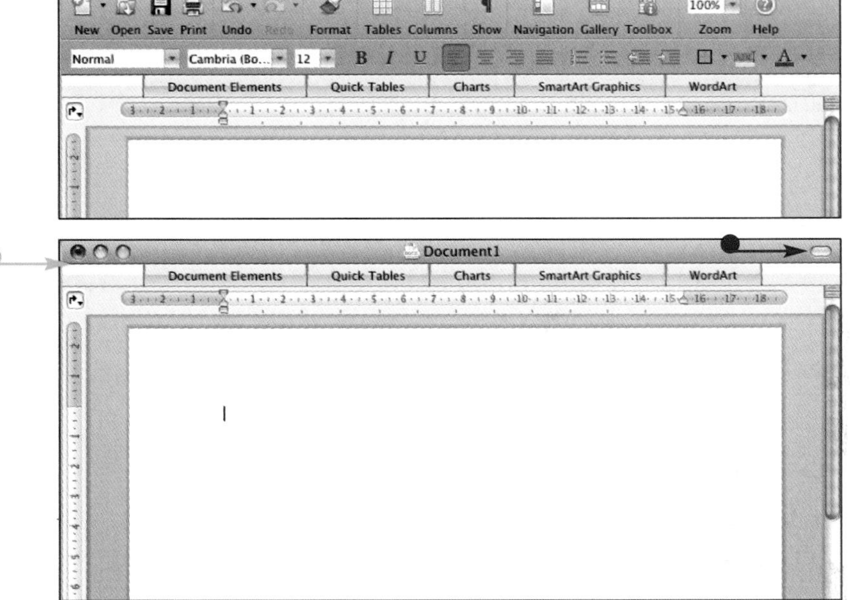

TIP

**Can I customize the buttons that appear on a toolbar?**

Yes. Follow these steps:

1. Click **View**.
2. Click **Customize Toolbars and Menus**.

   The Customize Toolbars and Menus dialog appears.
3. Click the **Commands** tab.
4. Click an item in the **Categories** list.
5. Click and drag a command and drop it on the toolbar.

   The program adds the command to the toolbar.
6. Click **OK**.

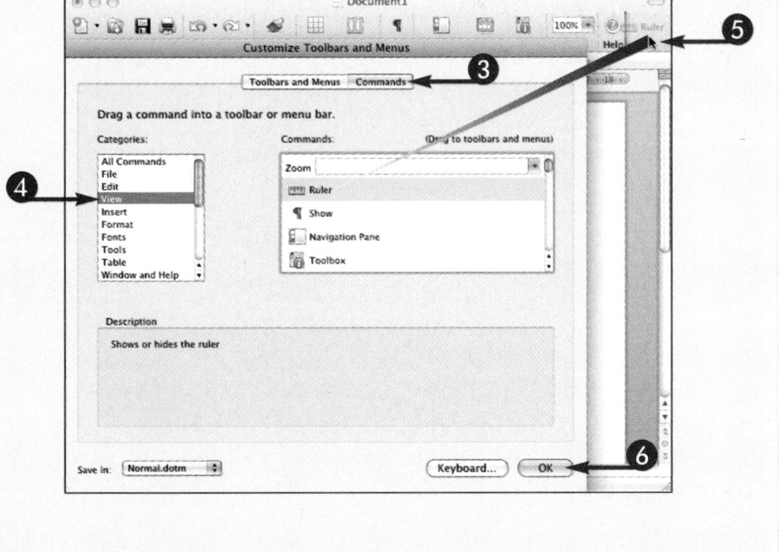

# Change the View

Depending on what you are doing in an application, you might need to select a different view. For example, to see what a Word document will appear when printed, switch to Print Layout view.

**You can also change the view by choosing a different magnification. For example, choose a higher magnification to zoom in on a document.**

## Change the View

### SELECT A VIEW

1. Click **View**.
2. Click the view you want to use.

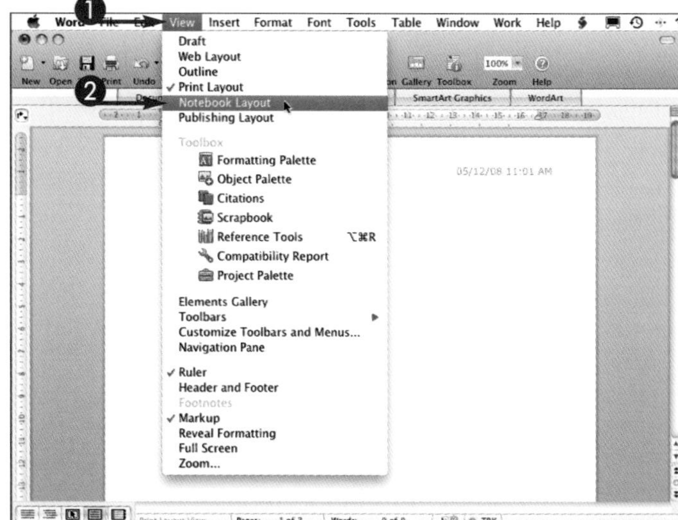


- The application switches to the new view.
- The application displays the name of the current view in the status bar.
- You can also change the view by clicking the view buttons.

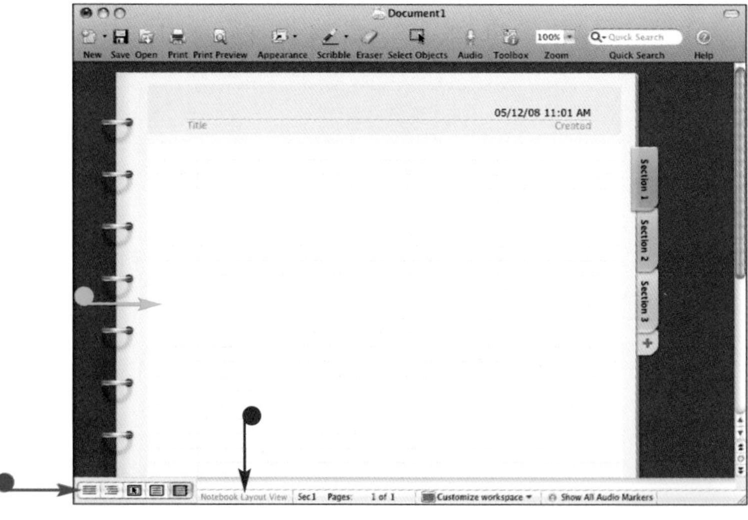

### CHANGE THE ZOOM MAGNIFICATION

1. Click **View**.
2. Click **Zoom**.

   The Zoom dialog appears.

3. Select a magnification option (◯ changes to ◉).

- You can also select the **Custom** option (◯ changes to ◉) and then type the magnification value.

4. Click **OK**.

The application redisplays the document using the new magnification.

- You can also use the **Zoom** control in the Standard toolbar to set the magnification.

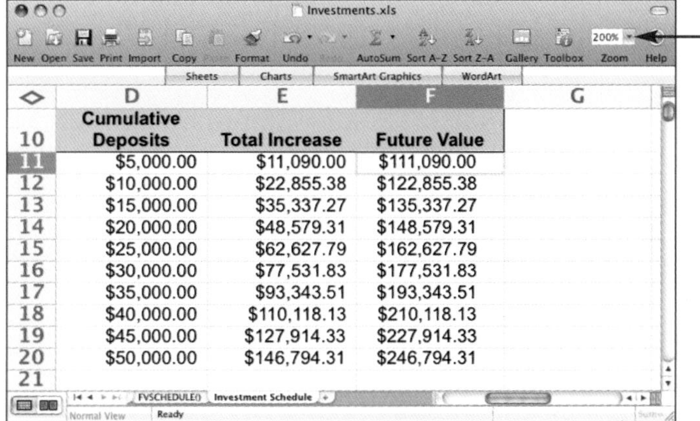

Investments.xls
200%
Cumulative Deposits
Total Increase
Future Value
$5,000.00
$11,090.00
$111,090.00
$10,000.00
$22,855.38
$122,855.38
$15,000.00
$35,337.27
$135,337.27
$20,000.00
$48,579.31
$148,579.31
$25,000.00
$62,627.79
$162,627.79
$30,000.00
$77,531.83
$177,531.83
$35,000.00
$93,343.51
$193,343.51
$40,000.00
$110,118.13
$210,118.13
$45,000.00
$127,914.33
$227,914.33
$50,000.00
$146,794.31
$246,794.31

### What's the difference between the various Word views?

| | |
|---|---|
| **Draft** | Displays the document without images for faster viewing. |
| **Web Layout** | Shows how the document appears when viewed in a Web browser. |
| **Outline** | Displays a document as an outline where you can collapse and expand sections based on the headings in the document. |
| **Print Layout** | Shows how the document appears when printed. |
| **Notebook Layout** | Displays the document using a notebook metaphor that enables you to add and edit data using different notebook tabs. |
| **Publishing Layout** | Displays the document in a mode that enables you to apply publication templates for things like newsletters and brochures. |

# Configure Program Preferences

**Each Office program offers a number of customization features in the Preferences dialog, a collection of settings and options that control the overall look and operation of the program. To use these settings, you must know how to display the program's Preferences dialog.**

## Configure Program Preferences

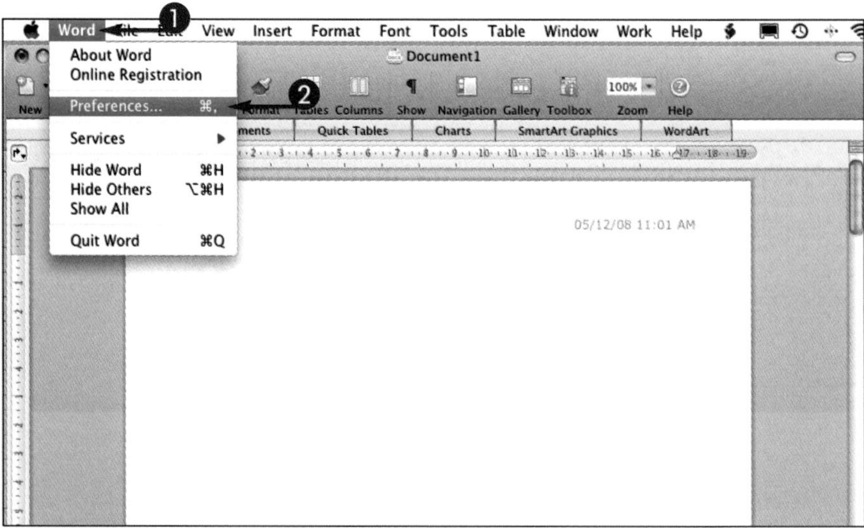


1. Click the program's application menu.

***Note:** This menu uses the same name as the program: Word, Excel, PowerPoint, or Entourage.*

2. Click **Preferences**.

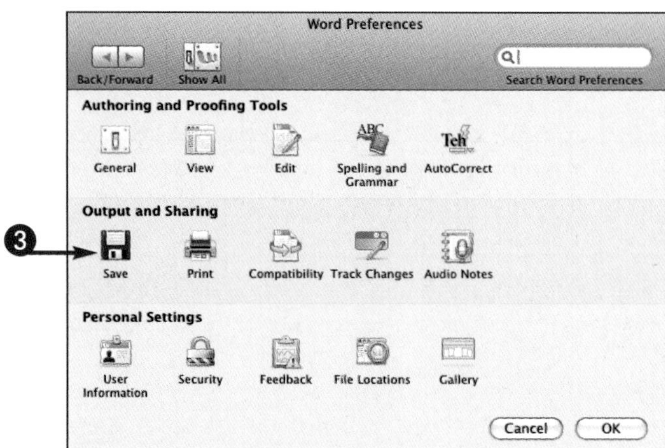


The program's Preferences dialog appears.

3. Click the button for the preference category you want to work with.

The preferences in that category appear.

4 Make your changes to the options and settings you want to modify.

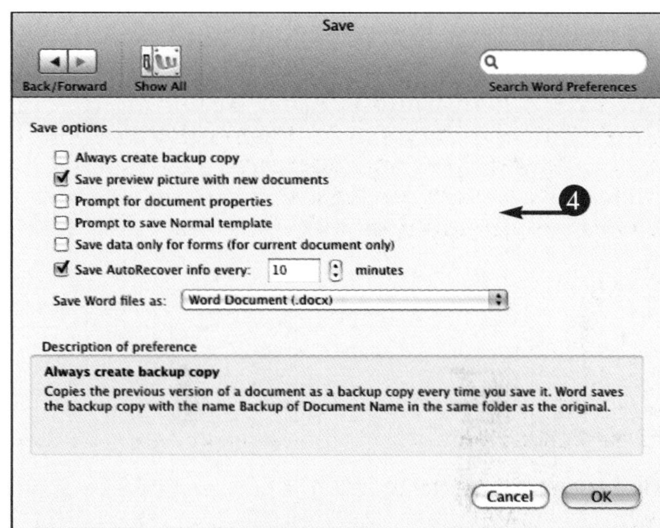

5 Click **OK**.

The program puts the new settings into effect.

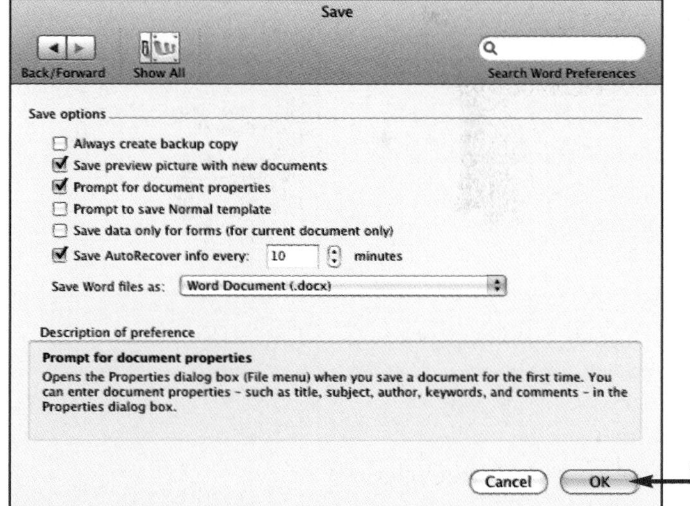


## TIPS

### Are there faster methods I can use to open and close the program preferences?

The fastest way to open the program preferences is to press ⌘+, (comma). Probably the fastest method you can use to quit the program preferences and put your new settings into effect is to press Return; to close the program preferences without putting any changed settings into effect, press Esc.

### When I open the program preferences, how can I restore the original icons?

To return to the main System Preferences window, you have two choices:

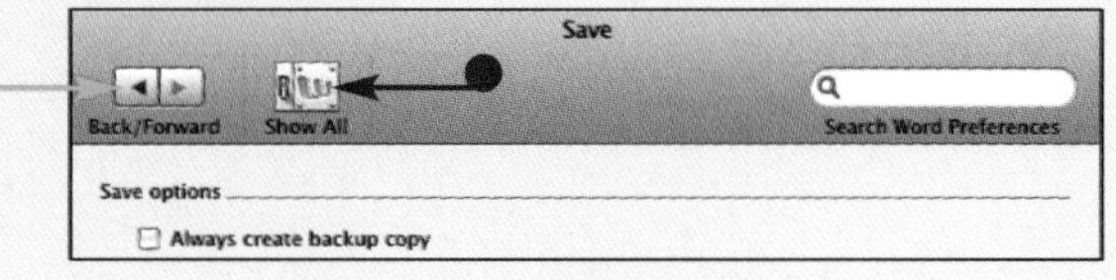

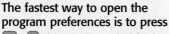

- Click ◀ until the main window appears.
- Click **Show All**.

# Add an Office Program to the Dock

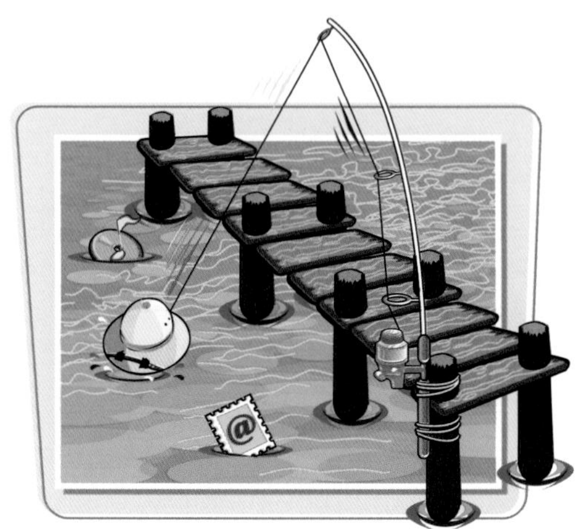

**If there is an Office program that you use frequently, you can launch that program faster by adding the program's button to the Dock. This enables you to start the program just by clicking its Dock button.**

**Some Office installations add buttons for all the Office programs to the Dock by default, so you may not need to follow these steps.**

## Add an Office Program to the Dock

1. Click the **Finder** button ( ).

   A Finder window appears.

2. Click **Applications**.
3. Click the **Microsoft Office 2008** folder.

   The folder opens.

4. Click and drag the button of the Office program you want to start and drop it on the Dock.

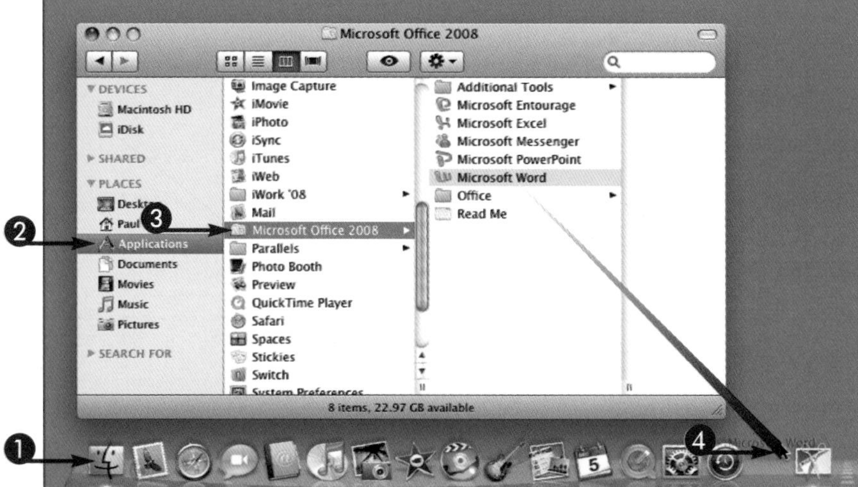


- Mac OS X adds the program button to the Dock.

***Note:*** *If the Office program is already running, you can also right-click (or* Ctrl *+click) the program's Dock button and then click* ***Keep in Dock****.*

# Quit an Office Program

**When you complete your work in an Office program, you should shut down that program. This reduces clutter on the desktop and in the Dock, and it also conserves memory and other system resources.**

## Quit an Office Program

### QUIT AN OFFICE PROGRAM USING THE MENUS

1. Click the program's application menu.

   Word is shown in this example.

2. Click **Quit *Program***, where *Program* is the name of the Office program.

***Note:*** *If you have any open documents with unsaved changes, the program prompts you to save your work.*

***Note:*** *Another way to run the Quit command is to press* ⌘+Q.

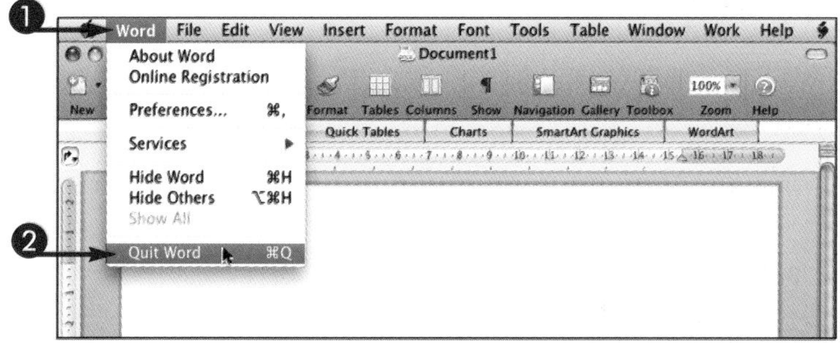


### QUIT AN OFFICE PROGRAM USING THE DOCK

1. Right-click the Office program's Dock button.

   You can also Ctrl+click the button.

2. Click **Quit**.

***Note:*** *If you have any open documents with unsaved changes, the program prompts you to save your work.*

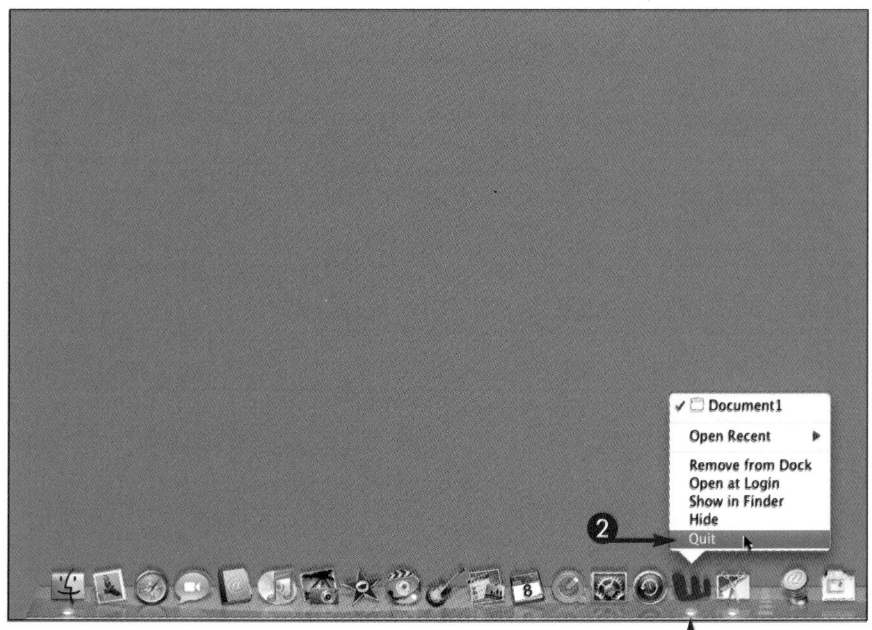

# Working with Office Documents

The three main Office for Mac programs — Word, Excel, and PowerPoint — work with documents in similar ways. Whether you need to create a new document, save or print a document, or edit document text, the techniques you use are the same in all three programs.

# Create a New Document

To perform new work in an Office program, you need to first create a new Word document, a new Excel workbook, or a new PowerPoint presentation.

## Create a New Document

### CREATE A NEW DOCUMENT IN WORD

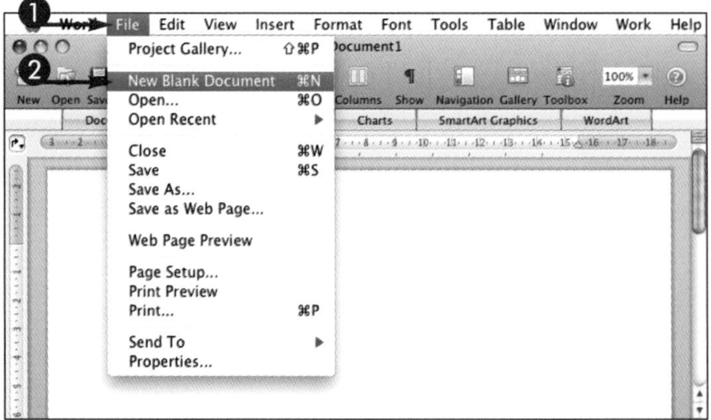


1. Click **File**.
2. Click **New Blank Document**.

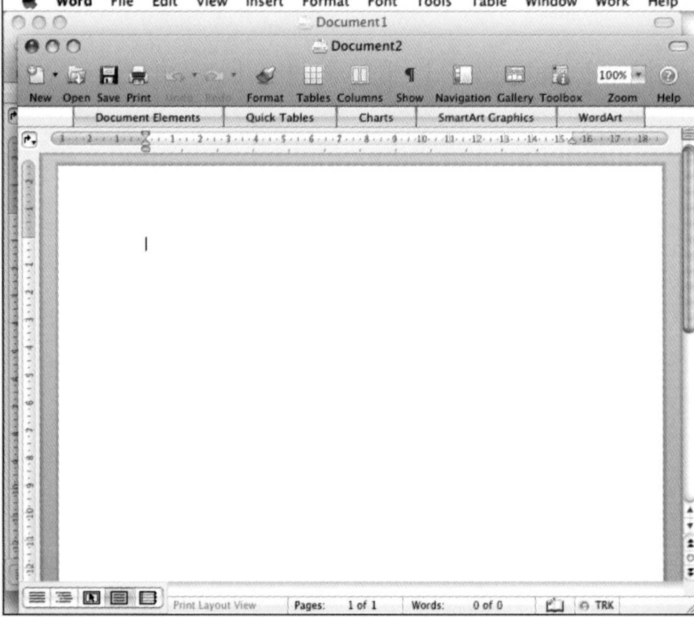


Word displays the new document.

## CREATE A NEW DOCUMENT IN EXCEL

1. Click **File**.
2. Click **New Workbook**.

   Excel displays the new workbook.

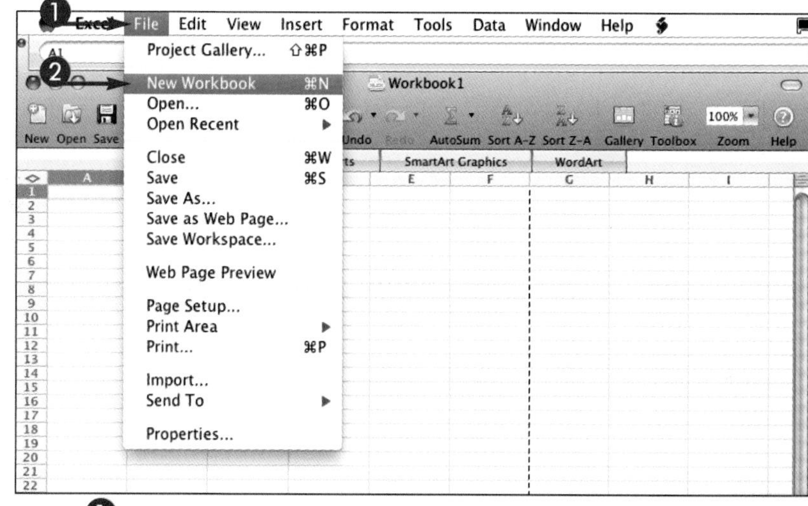


## CREATE A NEW DOCUMENT IN POWERPOINT

1. Click **File**.
2. Click **New Presentation**.

   PowerPoint displays the new presentation.

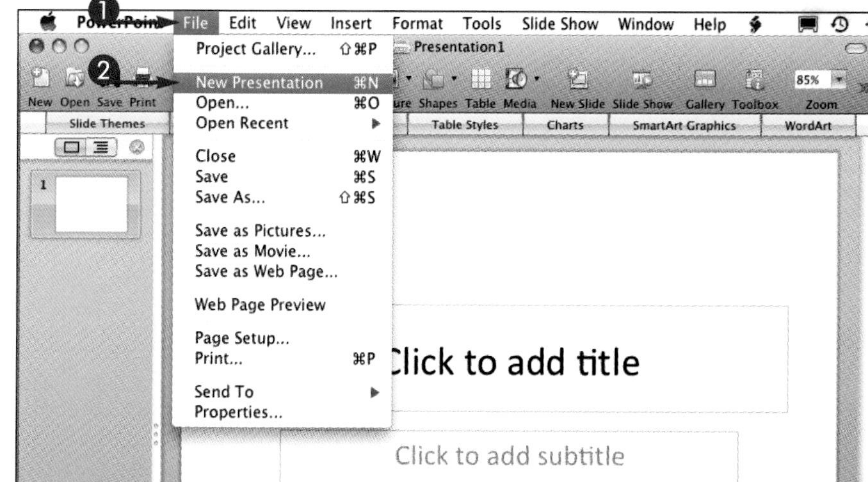


## TIPS

**Does Word offer other options for creating new documents?**

Yes. Word also enables you to start a new document using either the Notebook layout or the Publishing layout:

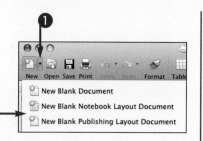

1. Click ▾ beside the **New** button (📄).
2. Click either **New Blank Notebook Layout Document** or **New Blank Publishing Layout Document**.

**Are there faster methods I can use to create a new document, workbook, or presentation?**

Yes. Word, Excel, and PowerPoint each offer a keyboard shortcut and toolbar button for faster document creation. From the keyboard, press ⌘ + N; in the Standard toolbar, click the **New** button (📄).

# Create a New Document Using Project Gallery

Office 2008 for Mac comes with a program called Project Gallery that you can use to create new documents based on a template. Each template includes preformatted colors, fonts, styles, and more, which saves you time when creating your documents.

**Office 2008 for Mac offers more than a dozen template categories, including Brochures, Business Cards, Newsletters, and Resumes.**

## Create a New Document Using Project Gallery

1. Click **File**.
2. Click **Project Gallery**.

***Note:*** *You can also launch Project Gallery by pressing* Shift + ⌘ + P.

***Note:*** *You can also run Project Gallery as a stand-alone program. In Finder, click* ***Applications****, open the* ***Microsoft Office 2008*** *folder, open the* ***Office*** *folder, and then double-click* ***Microsoft Project Gallery****.*

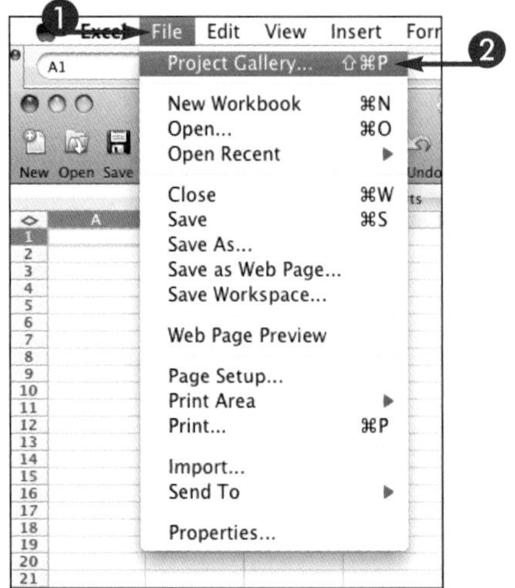


The Project Gallery dialog appears.

3. Click the **New** tab.
4. Click a category.

- If the category offers subcategories, click ▶ to expand the list (▶ changes to ▼).

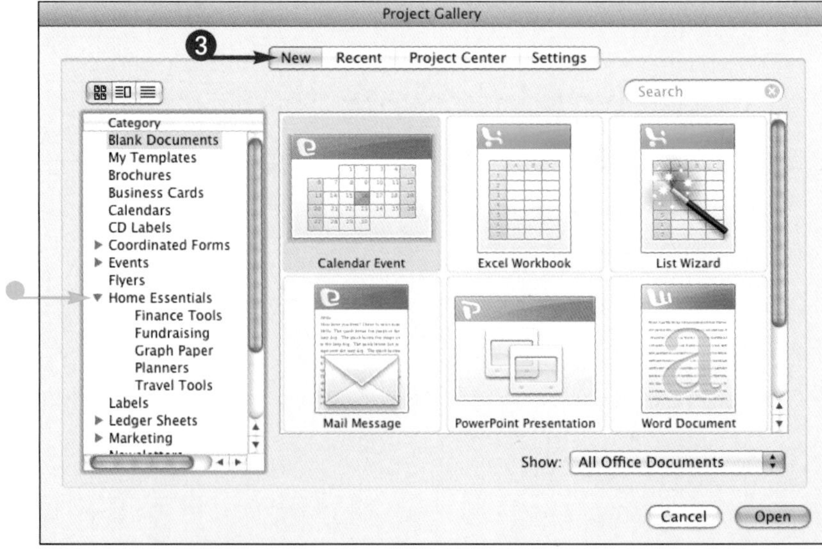

- The Project Gallery displays the available templates in the category.

5 Click the template you want to use.

6 Click **Open**.

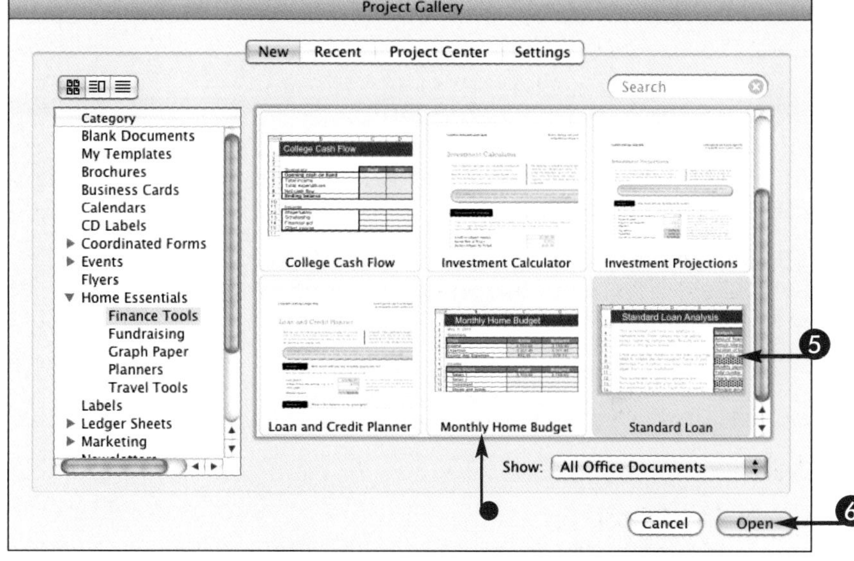


The program creates a new document based on the template.

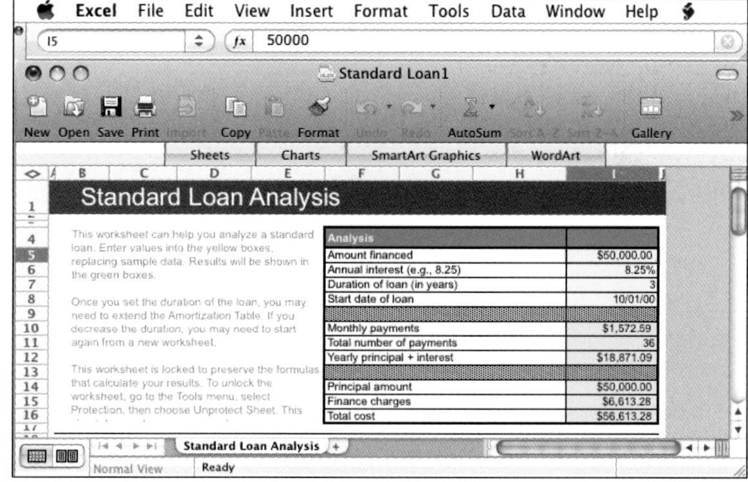


TIP

**Can I make the Project Gallery appear automatically at startup?**

Yes, by following these steps:

1 Click **File**.

2 Click **Project Gallery**.

3 Click the **Settings** tab.

4 Select the **Show Project Gallery at startup** option (☐ changes to ☑).

5 Click **OK**.

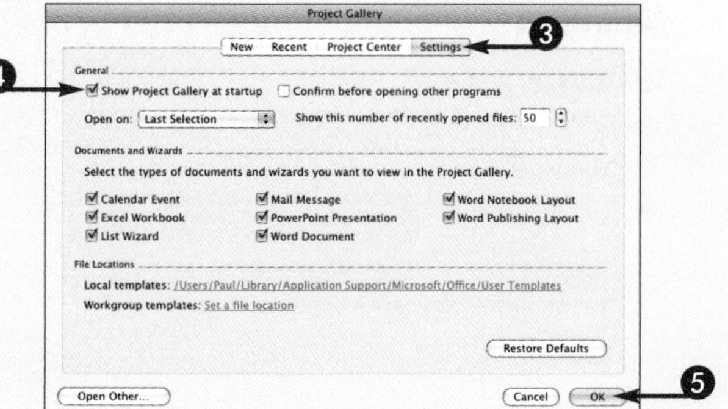

# Save a Document

After you create a document in Word, Excel, or PowerPoint and make changes to it, you can save the document to preserve your work.

**When you work on a document, Office stores the changes in your computer's memory, which is erased each time you shut down your computer. Saving the document preserves your changes on your Mac's hard drive.**

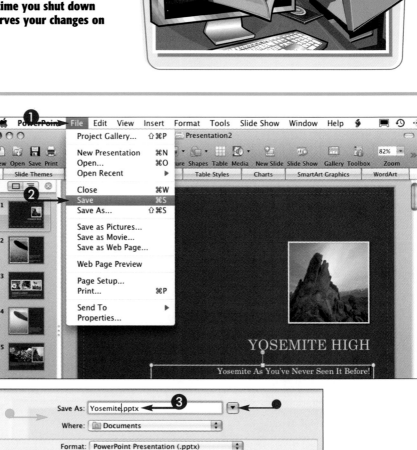

## Save a Document

1. Click **File**.
2. Click **Save**.

   You can also press ⌘ + S or click the **Save** button ( ) in the Standard toolbar.

   If you have saved the document previously, your changes are now preserved, and you do not need to follow the rest of the steps in this section.

- If this is a new document that you have never saved before, the Save dialog appears.

3. Click in the **Save As** text box and type the name that you want to use for the document.

- To select a different folder in which to store the file, you can click ▾ beside the Save As box and then click the location that you prefer.

4. Click **Save**.

   The program saves the file.

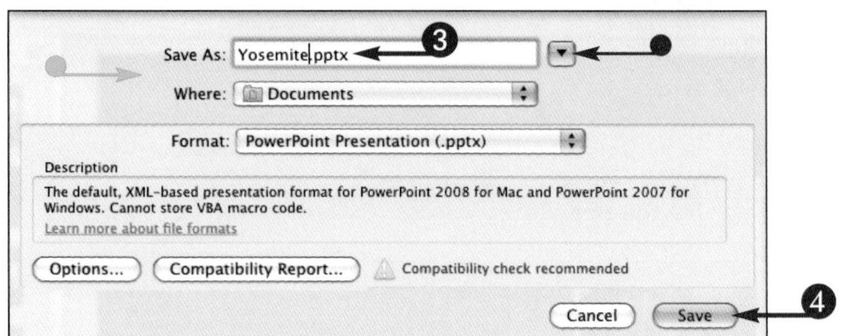

# Open a Document



**To work with an Office document that you have saved in the past, you can open it in the same Office program that you used to create it.**

## Open a Document

1. Start the Office program that you want to work with.
2. Click **File**.
3. Click **Open**.

   You can also press ⌘+O, or click the **Open** button in the Standard toolbar.

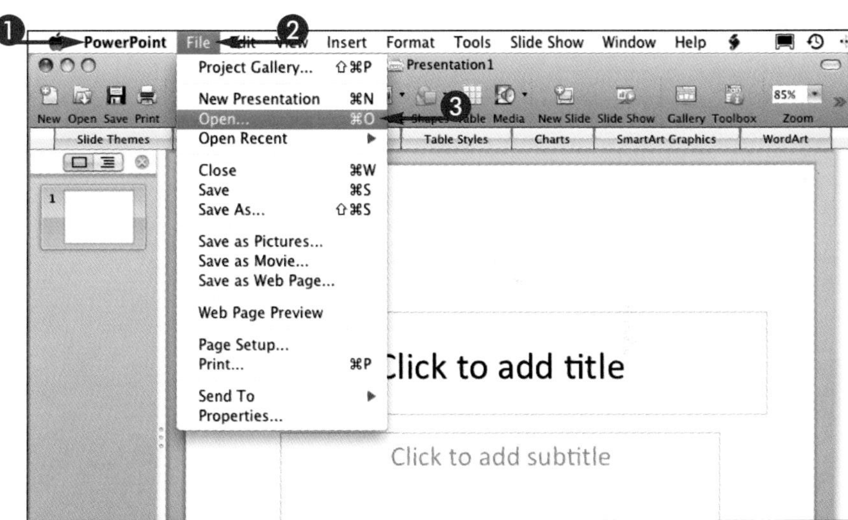


The Open dialog appears.

4. Click the folder that contains the document you want to open.

- To select a different folder from which to open the file, you can click the arrows in the From list and then select the location that you prefer.

5. Click the document.
6. Click **Open**.

   The document appears in a window.

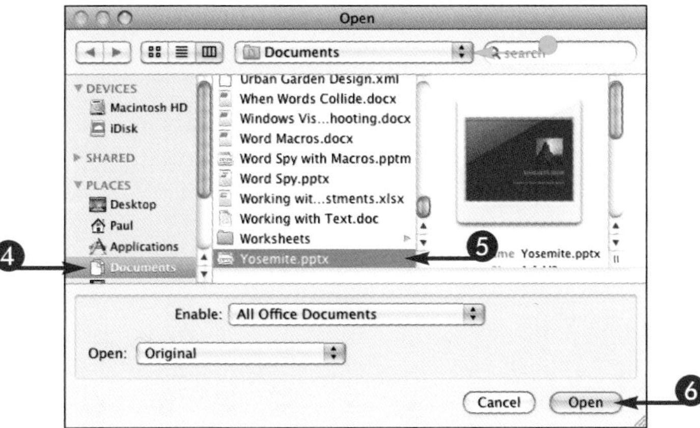

# Edit Document Text

When you work with a character-based file, such as a text or word-processing document or an e-mail message, you need to know the basic techniques for editing, selecting, copying, and moving text.

## Edit Document Text

### DELETE CHARACTERS

1. In a text document, click immediately to the right of the last character that you want to delete.

   The cursor appears after the character.

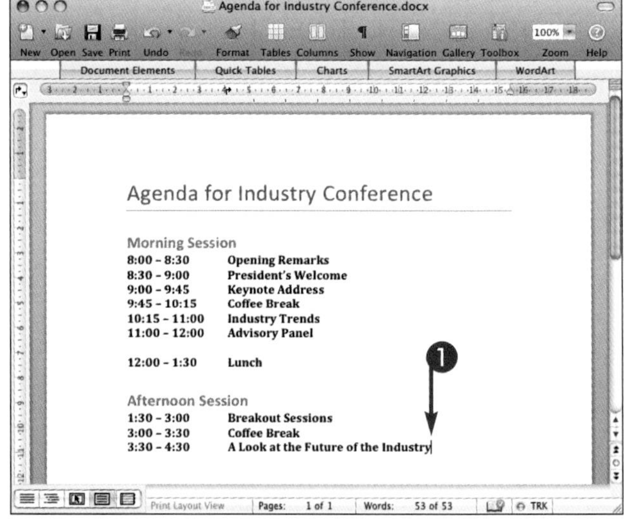


2. Press Del until you have deleted all the characters you want.

***Note:** You can press ⌘+Del to delete the entire word to the left of the cursor.*

   If you make a mistake, immediately click **Edit**, and then click **Undo**. You can also press ⌘+Z or click the **Undo** button (↶) in the Standard toolbar.

## SELECT TEXT FOR EDITING

❶ Click and drag across the text that you want to select.

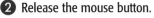

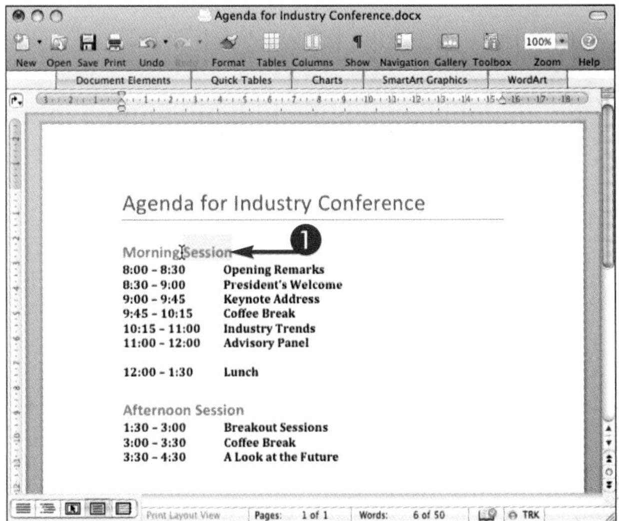


❷ Release the mouse button.

- The program highlights the selected text.

**Are there any shortcut methods for selecting text?**

Yes. There are several shortcuts you can use. Here are the most useful ones:

- Double-click a word to select it.
- Triple-click inside a paragraph to select it.
- Click to the left of a line to select it.
- Press ⌘ + A to select the entire document.

# Edit Document Text *(continued)*

**After you select text, you can copy or move the text to another location in your document.**

## Edit Document Text *(continued)*

### COPY TEXT

1. Select the text that you want to copy.
2. Click **Edit**.
3. Click **Copy**.

   You can also press ⌘+C.

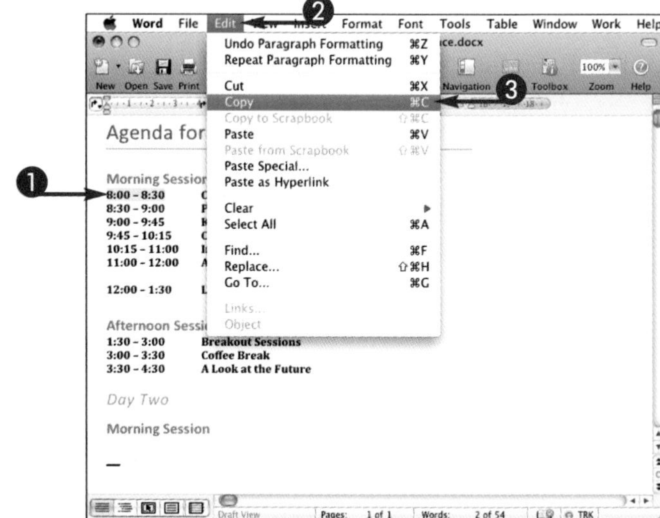

4. Click inside the document at the position where you want the copy of the text to appear.

   The cursor appears in the position where you clicked.
5. Click **Edit**.
6. Click **Paste**.

   You can also press ⌘+V.

- The program inserts a copy of the selected text at the cursor position.

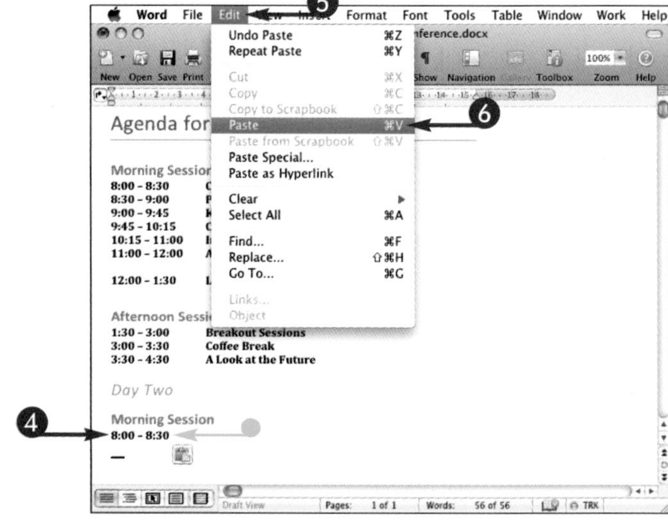

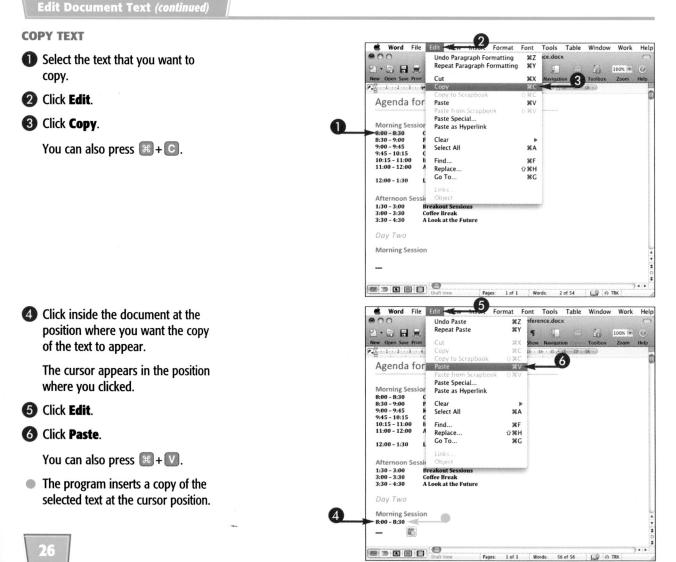

## MOVE TEXT

1. Select the text that you want to move.
2. Click **Edit**.
3. Click **Cut**.

   You can also press ⌘ + X.

   The program removes the text from the document.

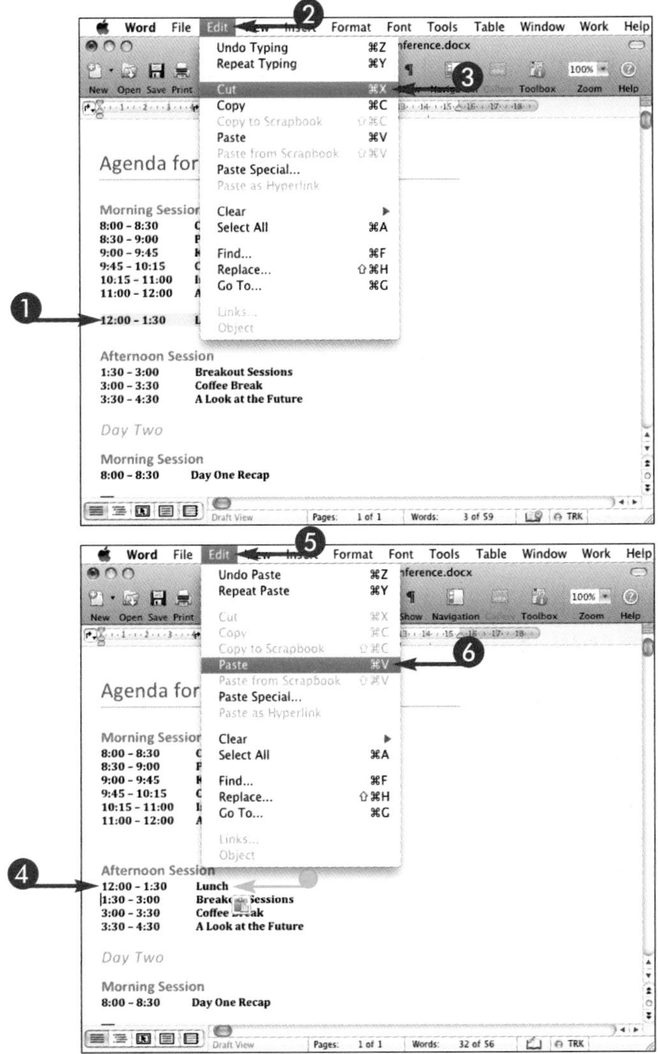

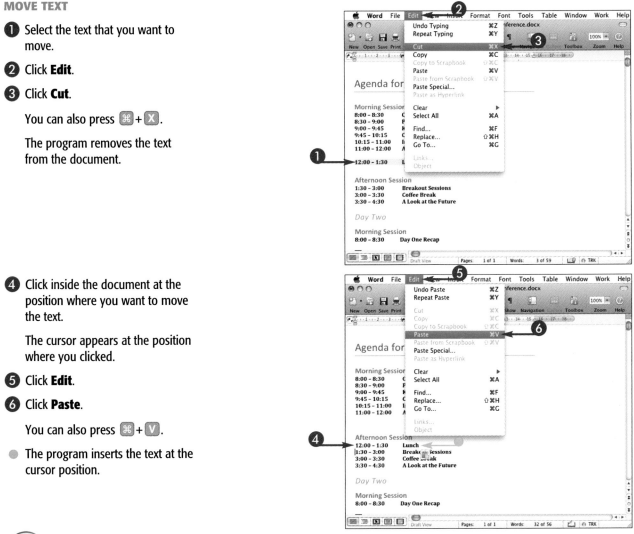

4. Click inside the document at the position where you want to move the text.

   The cursor appears at the position where you clicked.

5. Click **Edit**.
6. Click **Paste**.

   You can also press ⌘ + V.

- The program inserts the text at the cursor position.

### How do I move and copy text with my mouse?

First, select the text that you want to move or copy. To move the selected text, position the mouse pointer over the selection and then click and drag the text to the new position within the document.

To copy the selected text, position the mouse pointer over the selection, press and hold Option, and then click and drag the text to the new position within the document.

# Find Text in a Document

In large documents, when you need to find specific text, you can save a lot of time by using the program's Find feature, which searches the entire document in the blink of an eye.

**This section uses Word as an example, but finding text in Excel and PowerPoint is similar.**

## Find Text in a Document

❶ Click **Edit**.

❷ Click **Find**.

***Note:*** *You can also run the Find command by pressing* ⌘ + F.

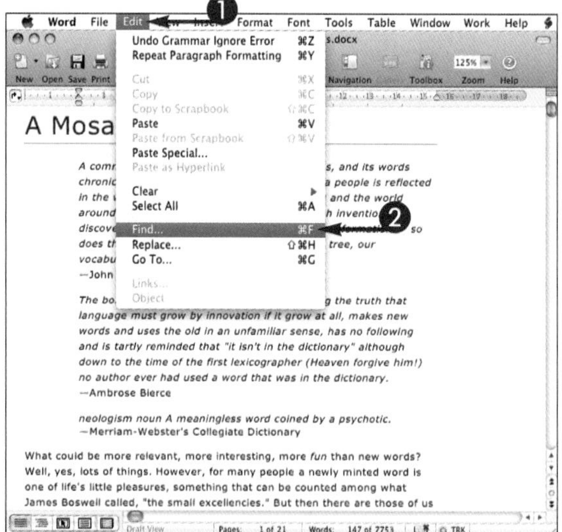


The Find dialog appears.

❸ Click in the **Find what** text box and type the text you want to find.

❹ Click **Find Next**.

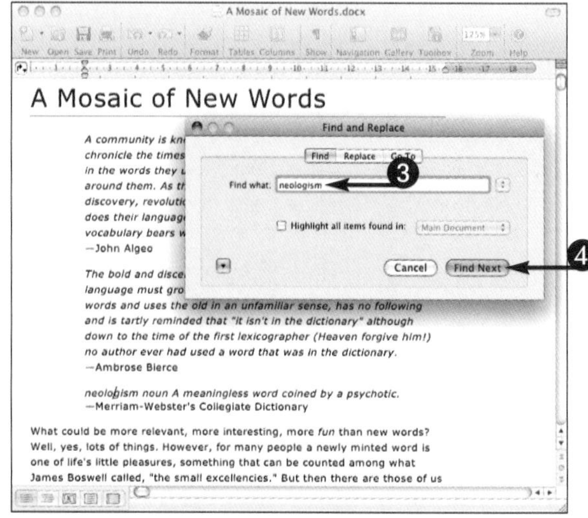

- The program selects the next instance of the search text.

***Note:** If the search text does not exist in the document, the program displays a dialog to let you know.*

5. If the selected instance is not the one you want, click **Find Next** until the program finds the correct instance.

6. Click **Cancel** to close the Find dialog.

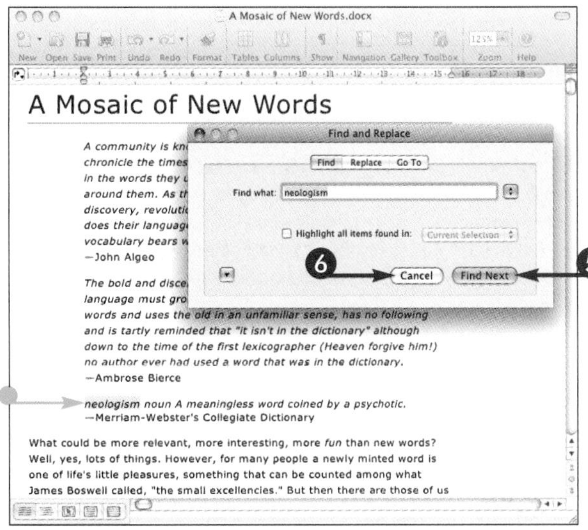

- The program leaves the found text selected.

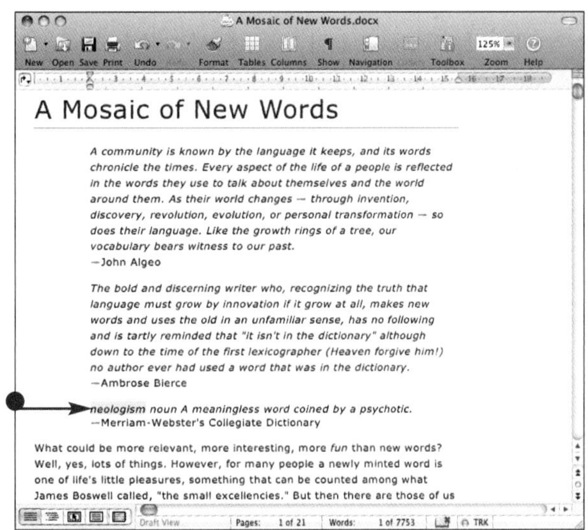

TIPS

**When I search for a small word such as *the*, the program matches it in larger words such as *theme* and *bother*. How can I avoid this?**

In Word's Find dialog, click ▾ to expand the dialog. Select the **Find whole words only** option (☐ changes to ☑). This option — which is only available in Word and PowerPoint — tells the program to match the search text only if it is a word on its own and not part of another word.

**When I search for a name such as *Bill*, the program also matches the non-name *bill*. Is there a way to fix this?**

In Word's Find dialog, click ▾ to expand the dialog. Select the **Match case** option (☐ changes to ☑). This option tells the program to match the search text only if it has the same mix of uppercase and lowercase letters that you specify in the **Find what** text box. If you type **Bill**, for example, the program matches only *Bill* and not *bill*.

# Replace Text in a Document

Do you need to replace a word or part of a word with some other text? If you have several instances to replace, you can save time and do a more accurate job if you let the program's Replace feature replace the word for you.

**This section uses Word as an example, but replacing text in Excel and PowerPoint is similar.**

## Replace Text in a Document

1. Click **Edit**.
2. Click **Replace**.

*Note: You can also run the Replace command by pressing Shift + ⌘ + H.*

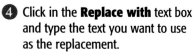

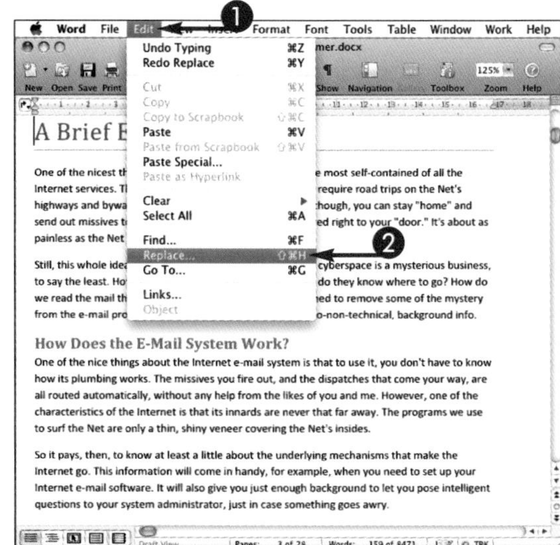

The Replace dialog appears.

3. In the **Find what** text box, type the text you want to find.
4. Click in the **Replace with** text box and type the text you want to use as the replacement.
5. Click **Find Next**.

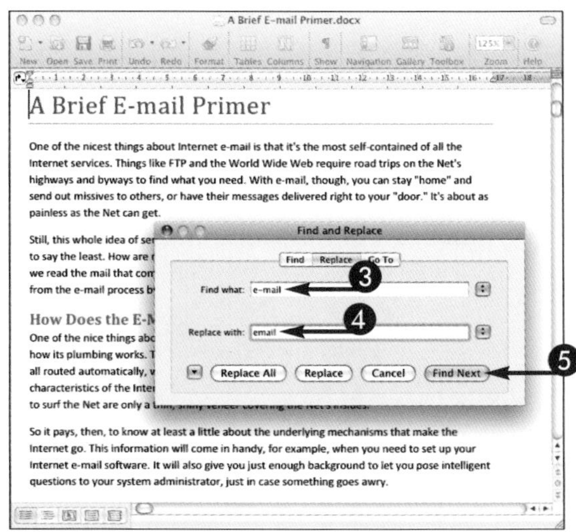

- The program selects the next instance of the search text.

***Note:*** *If the search text does not exist in the document, the program displays a dialog to let you know.*

6. If the selected instance is not the one you want, click **Find Next** until the program finds the correct instance.

7. Click **Replace**.

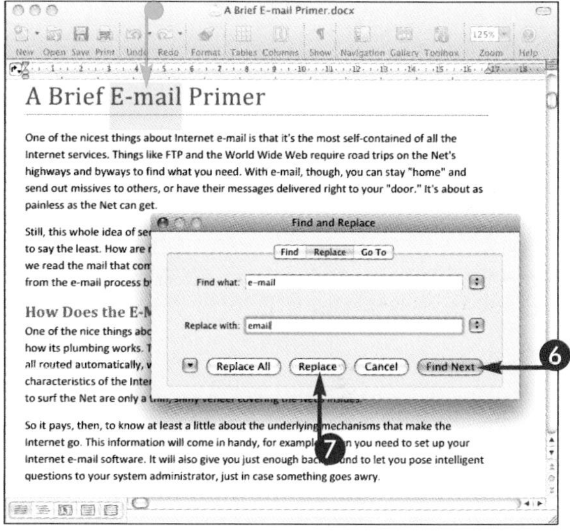


- The program replaces the selected text with the replacement text.
- The program selects the next instance of the search text.

8. Repeat Steps **6** and **7** until you have replaced all of the instances you want to replace.

9. Click the **Close** button to close the Replace dialog box.

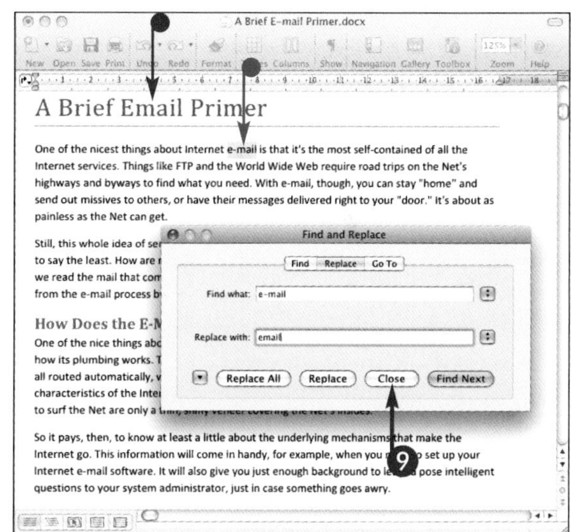

**Is there a faster way to replace every instance of the search text with the replacement text?**

Yes. In the Replace dialog, click **Replace All**. This tells the program to replace every instance of the search text with the replacement text. However, you should exercise some caution with this feature because it may make some replacements that you did not intend. Click **Find Next** a few times to make sure the matches are correct. Also, consider selecting the **Find whole words only** and **Match case** options (☐ changes to ☑), as described in the section "Find Text in a Document."

# Check Spelling and Grammar

You can reduce the number of errors in your Office documents by taking advantage of the spell checker in Word, Excel, and PowerPoint, and the grammar checker in Word.

**You can either handle individual errors — spelling errors are underlined in red, while grammar problems are underlined in green — or you can run the Spell Checker tool.**

## Check Spelling and Grammar

### FIX INDIVIDUAL ERRORS

1. Right-click a spelling or grammar error.

   You can also Ctrl+click.

2. Click the correction you want to use.

- Click **Ignore** to skip this instance of the error.
- Click **Ignore All** to skip all instances of the error.
- Click **Add** to add the word to the dictionary.

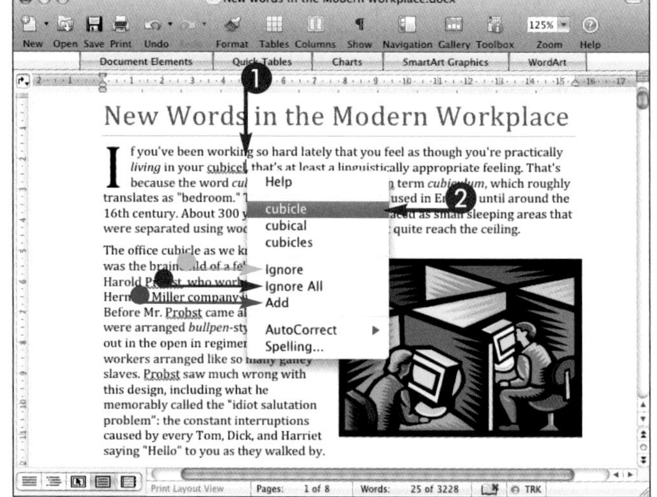

### CHECK THE ENTIRE DOCUMENT

1. Click **Tools**.
2. Click **Spelling and Grammar**.

***Note:*** *In Excel and PowerPoint, click the* ***Spelling*** *command.*

***Note:*** *You can also press* Option + ⌘ + L.

- The Spelling and Grammar dialog appears and displays the first error.

3 Click the correction you want to use.

4 Click **Change**.

- Click **Change All** to correct every instance of the error.
- Click **Ignore** to skip this instance of the error.
- Click **Ignore All** to skip all instances of the error.
- Click **Add** to add the word to the dictionary.

5 When the check is complete, click **OK**.

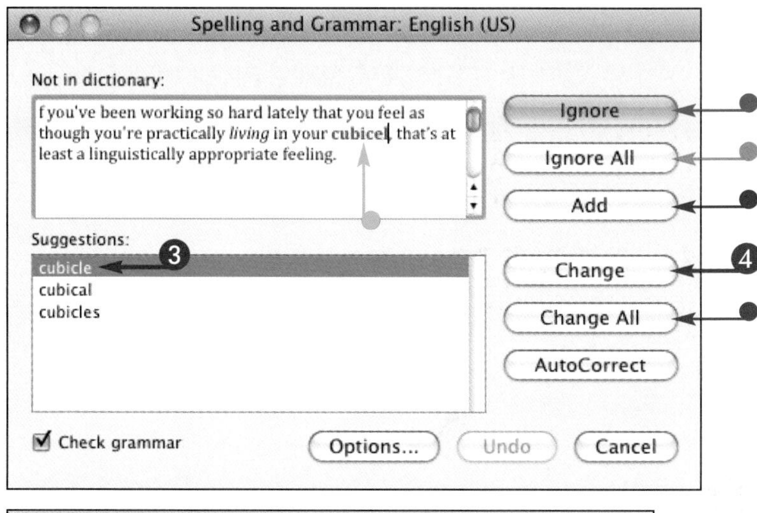


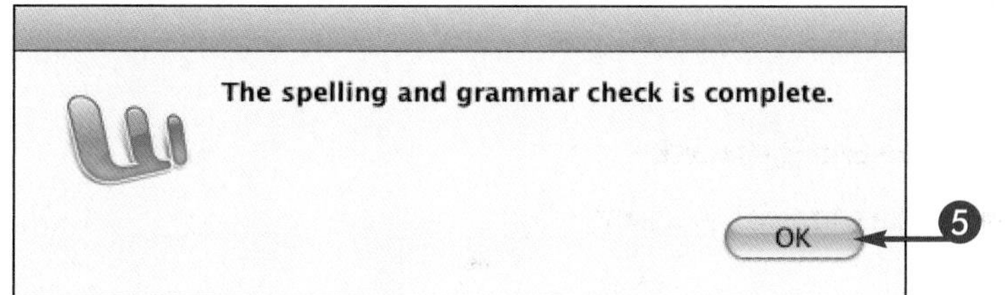

### Can I hide the red and green underlining that indicates spelling and grammar errors?

Yes. Follow these steps:

1 Click **Word**.

2 Click **Preferences**.

3 Click **Spelling and Grammar**.

4 Select the **Hide spelling errors in this document** option (☐ changes to ☑).

5 Select the **Hide grammatical errors in this document** option (☐ changes to ☑).

6 Click **OK**.

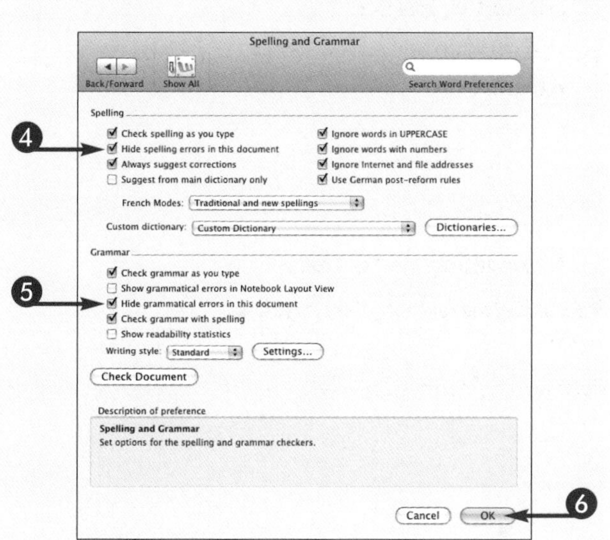

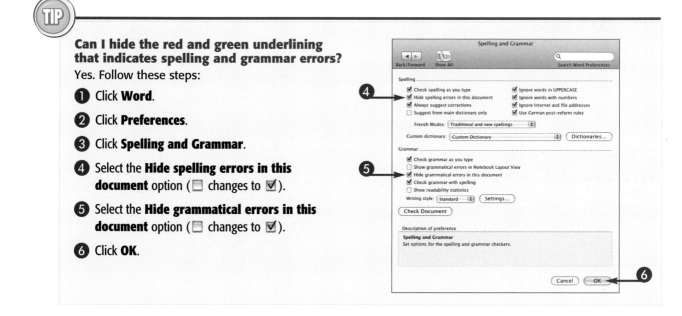

# Save a Document as a Web Page

If you have a Word document, Excel spreadsheet, or PowerPoint presentation that you want to share on the Web, you can save that file as a Web page.

**When you save a document as a Web page, you can also specify the title text that appears in the browser's title bar and the keywords that search engines use to index the page.**

## Save a Document as a Web Page

1. Open or create the document you want to save as a Web page.
2. Click **File**.
3. Click **Save as Web Page**.
4. Type a name for the Web page file in the Save As text box.
   - To select a different folder in which to store the file, you can click ▾ beside the Save As box and then click the location that you prefer.
5. Click **Web Options**.

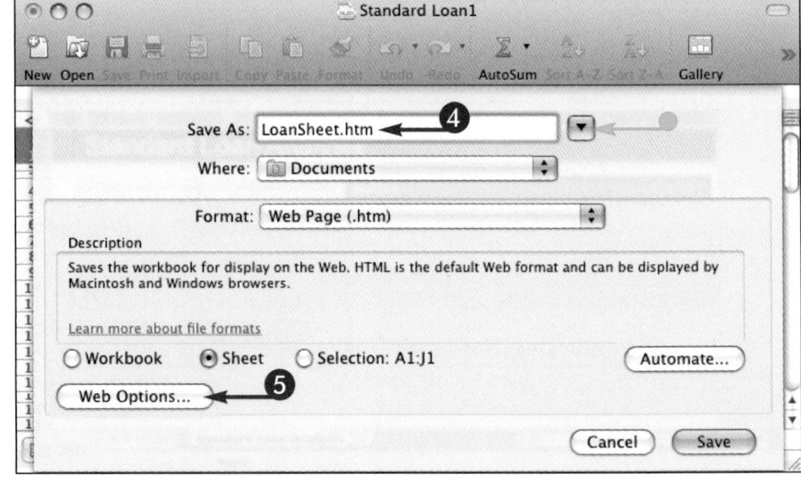

The Web Options dialog appears.

6 Click the **General** tab.

7 Type the page title in the Web page title text box.

8 Type the page keywords in the Web page keywords text box.

9 Click **OK**.

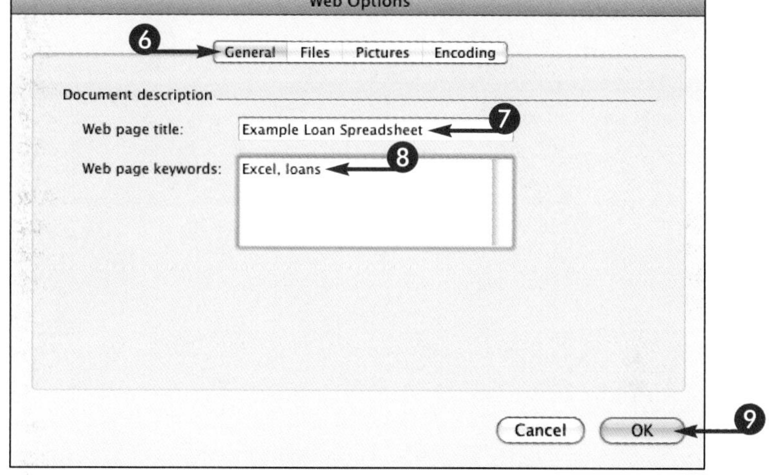


10 In Excel, choose which part of the file you want to save.

You can select the entire workbook, just the current worksheet, or just the selected cells (○ changes to ◉)

11 Click **Save**.

The program saves the document as a Web page.

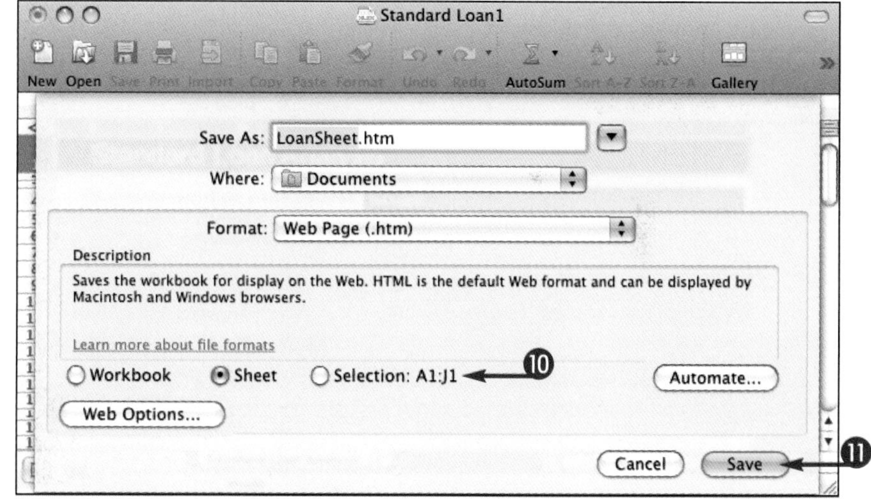

### How do I get my page on the Web?

Assuming you already have an account with a Web hosting provider, first check to see if the host offers some sort of file upload tool. Most hosts offer such a tool, and that is often the easiest way to get a file from your Mac to your site.

FileManager Tool Box
Select Files/Directories to:
Rename Delete
Move to: Home/
Copy to: Home/
Create in: home/blog
Enter file name to upload:
Choose File index.html Upload
Enter folder name to create:
New Folder

Alternatively, you need to install an FTP (File Transfer Protocol) program on your Mac. Here are some good programs to check out:

- Fetch (see http://fetchsoftworks.com/)
- CyberDuck (see http://cyberduck.ch/)
- Interarchy (see www.nolobe.com)
- Transmit (see www.panic.com)

# Print a Document

When you need a hard copy of your document, either for your files or to distribute to someone else, you can send the document to your printer.

## Print a Document

1. Turn on your printer.
2. Open the document that you want to print.

3. Click **File**.
4. Click **Print**.

***Note:*** *You can also press ⌘ + P.*

***Note:*** *To send the document to the printer immediately, click the **Print** button (🖶) in the Standard toolbar.*

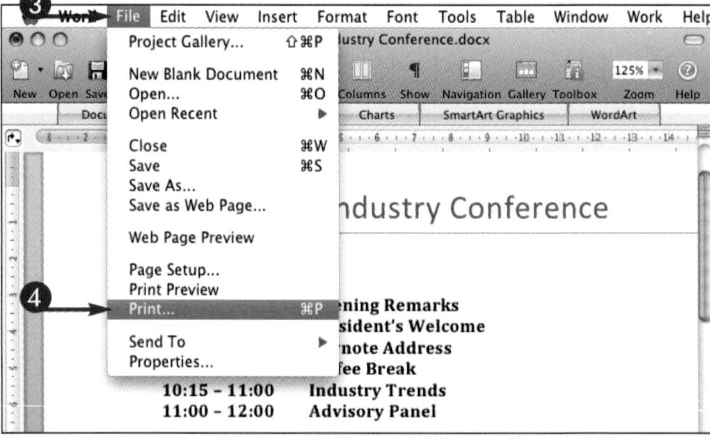

The Print dialog appears.

5. If you have more than one printer, click ⬍ in the Printer pull-down menu to select the printer that you want to use.

- To print more than one copy, type the number of copies to print in the Copies text box.

6. Click **Print**.

OS X prints the document.

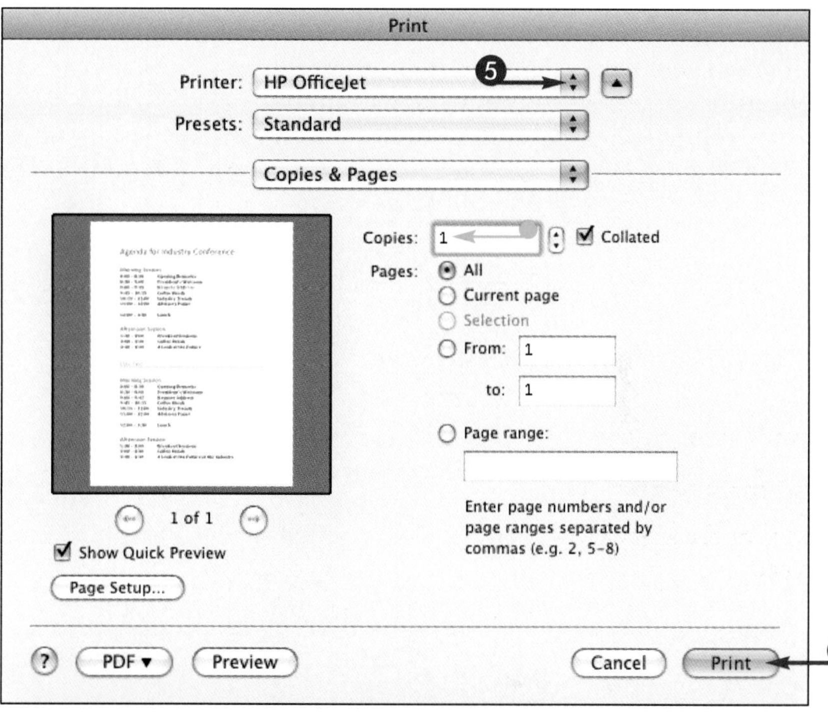


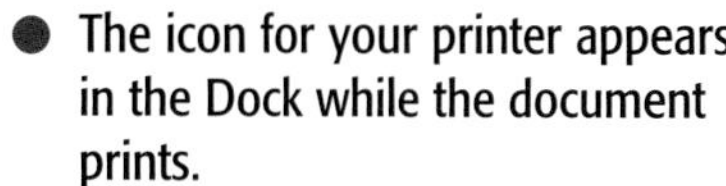

- The icon for your printer appears in the Dock while the document prints.

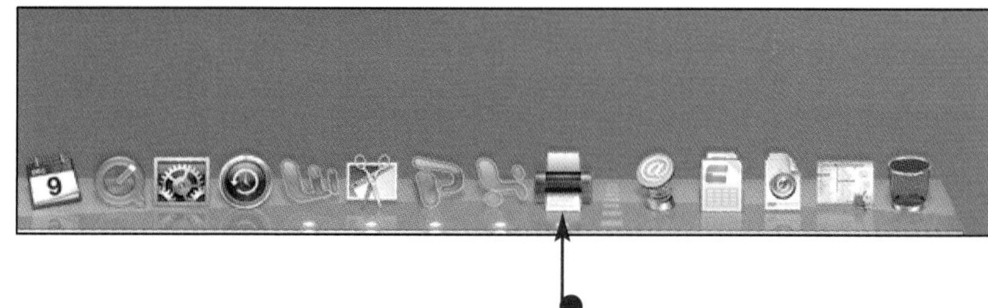

**Can I preview my document before I print it?**

Yes. It is a good idea to preview the document before printing it to ensure that the document layout looks the way you want. To preview the document, follow Steps **1** to **4** in this section to display the Print dialog box and then use the Quick Preview controls to scroll through the document. If you want a closer look at the document, click **Preview** to display the document in the Preview application. When you finish, click **Preview** and then click **Quit Preview**.

# Close a Document

**When you finish working on a document, you should close it to reduce desktop clutter. If the document is very large or contains many images, closing the file also frees up memory and other system resources.**

## Close a Document

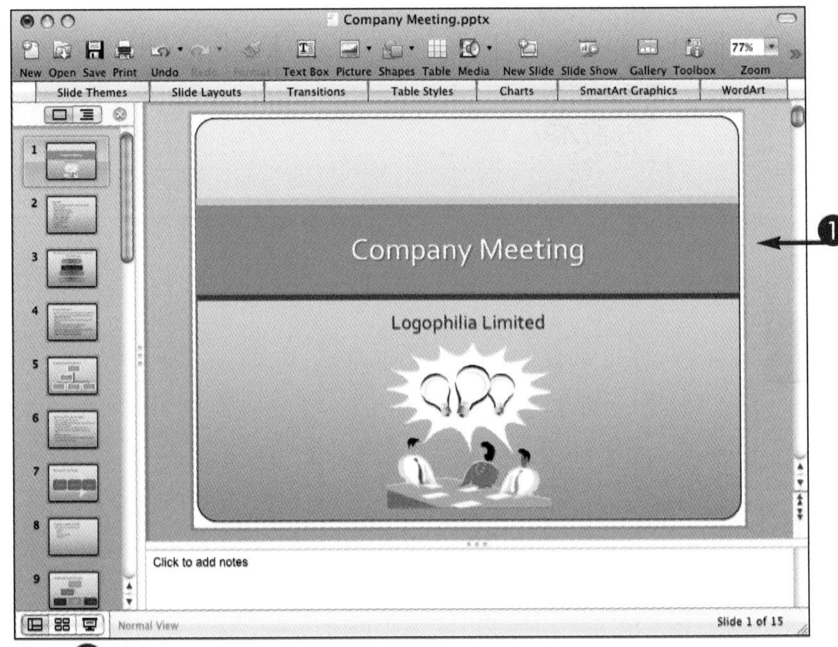


1. Display the document you want to close.

2. Click **File**.

❸ Click **Close**.

If you have unsaved changes in the document, the Office application asks if you want to save your work.

❹ Click **Save**.

- If you do not want to preserve your changes, click **Don't Save**.
- If you decide to keep the document open, click **Cancel**.

The program saves your work and then closes the document.

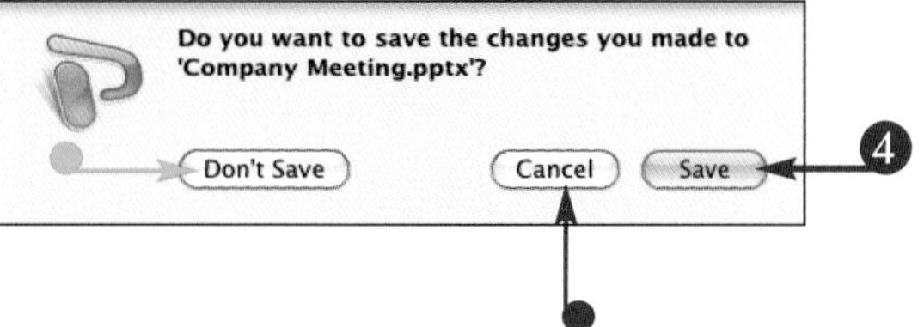

**Are there faster methods I can use to close a document?**

Yes. You can also close a document using a keyboard shortcut or with a mouse click. From your keyboard, press ⌘+W to close the current document; with your mouse, click the **Close** button (◉) in the upper-left corner of the document window.

# Make a Document Compatible with Earlier Versions of Office

You can save your documents in a special format that makes them compatible with earlier versions of Microsoft Office. This enables you to share your documents with other Office users.

**If you use an earlier version of Office on another computer, or if the people you work with use earlier Office versions, those programs cannot read documents in the standard Office 2008 format.**

## Make a Document Compatible with Earlier Versions of Office

1. Open or create the document you want to make compatible.
2. Click **File**.
3. Click **Save As**.

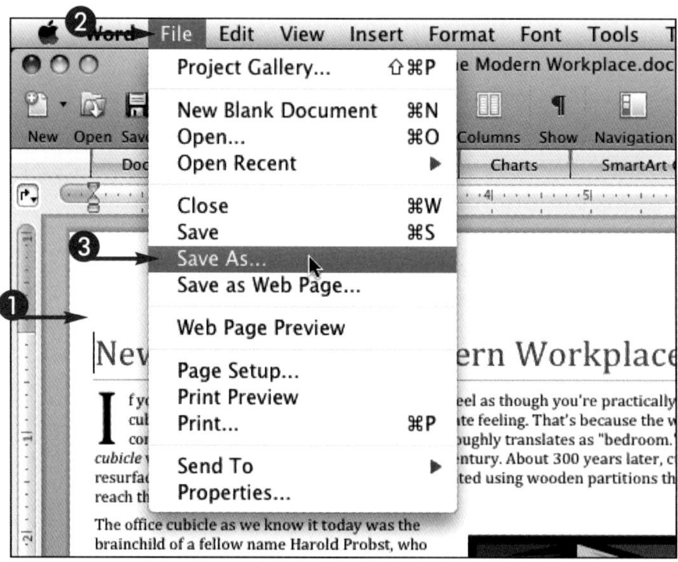


The Save dialog appears.

4. Click in the **Save As** text box and type the name that you want to use for the document.

- To select a different folder in which to store the file, you can click ▾ beside the Save As box and then click the location that you prefer.

5. Click ▾ beside the Format box

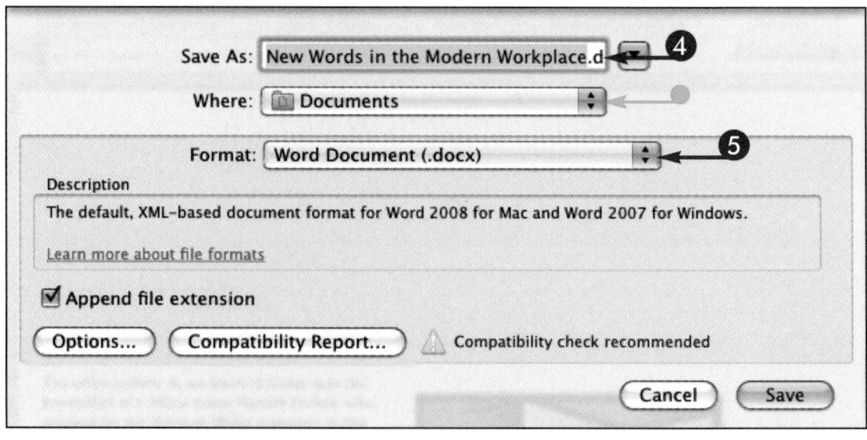

6 Click the **97-2004** file format (such as the Word 97-2004 Document (.doc) format shown here).

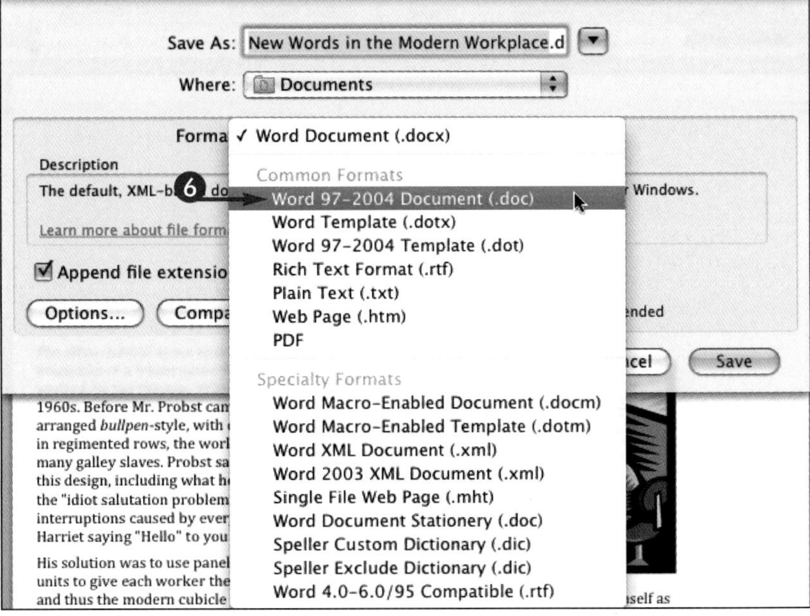


7 Click **Save**.

The program saves the file using the 97-2004 format.

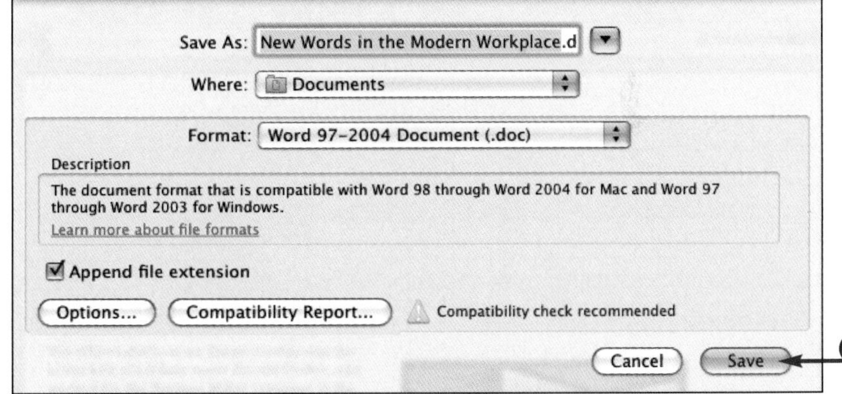


TIPS

### Can people using Microsoft Office 2007 for Windows open my Office documents?

Yes. The file format used by both Office 2008 for Mac and Office 2007 for Windows is the same. If you only work with people who use either or both of these Office versions, then you should stick with the default file format because it offers many benefits in terms of Office features.

### Which versions of Office are compatible with the 97-2004 file format?

For the Mac, the 97-2004 file format is compatible with Office 98, Office 2001, and Office 2004. For Windows, the 97-2004 file format is compatible with Office 97, Office 2000, Office XP, and Office 2003. In the unlikely event that you need to share a document with someone using either Office 4.0 for Mac or Office 95 for Windows, use the 4.0-6.0/95 file format, instead.

CHAPTER 3

# Formatting Office Documents

The Office programs offer many commands and options for formatting documents, spreadsheets, slides, and e-mail messages. Some of these formatting options are specific to each program, but many are universal, including the font, text color, and text alignment.

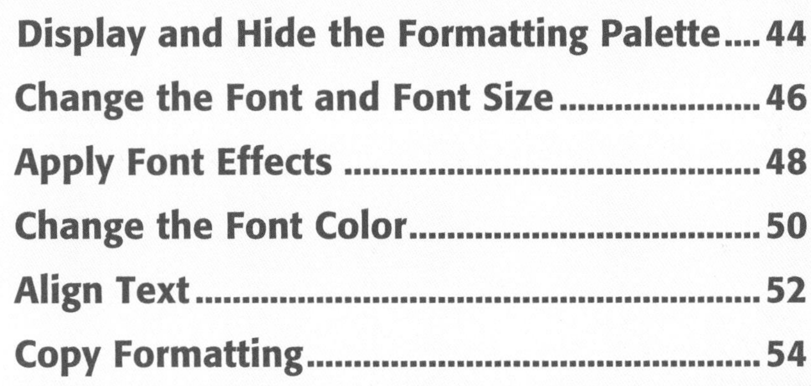

# Display and Hide the Formatting Palette

The Office for Mac programs offer quick access to many popular formatting options via the Formatting Palette, which is part of the Office Toolbox.

**The options you see in the Formatting Palette vary from program to program, and even within each program they vary depending on what you are formatting. In the sections that follow, you learn the specific steps required to apply these formatting options.**

## Display and Hide the Formatting Palette

### DISPLAY THE FORMATTING PALETTE

1. Click **View**.
2. Click **Formatting Palette**.

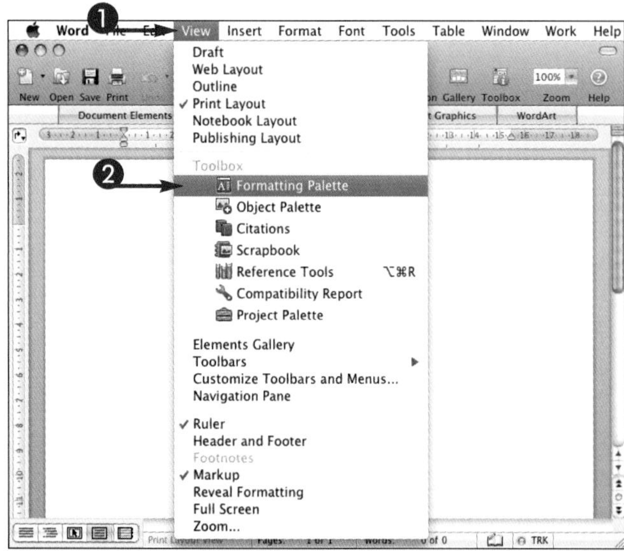


- The Formatting Palette appears.
- You can also click the Toolbox button ( ) in the Standard toolbar, and then click the Formatting Palette button ( ).
- Click ▶ to expand a panel and see its formatting options (▶ changes to ▼).

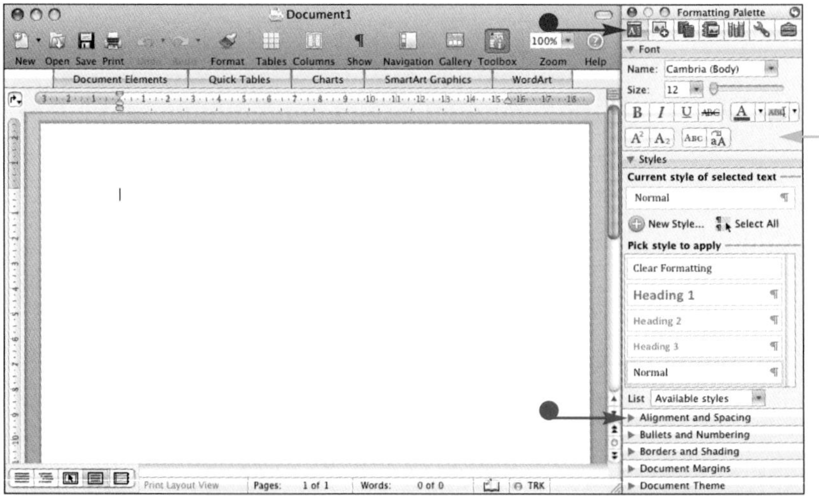

## HIDE THE FORMATTING PALETTE

1. Click **View**.
2. Click **Formatting Palette**.

- You can also click the **Close** button (◉) in the Toolbox.

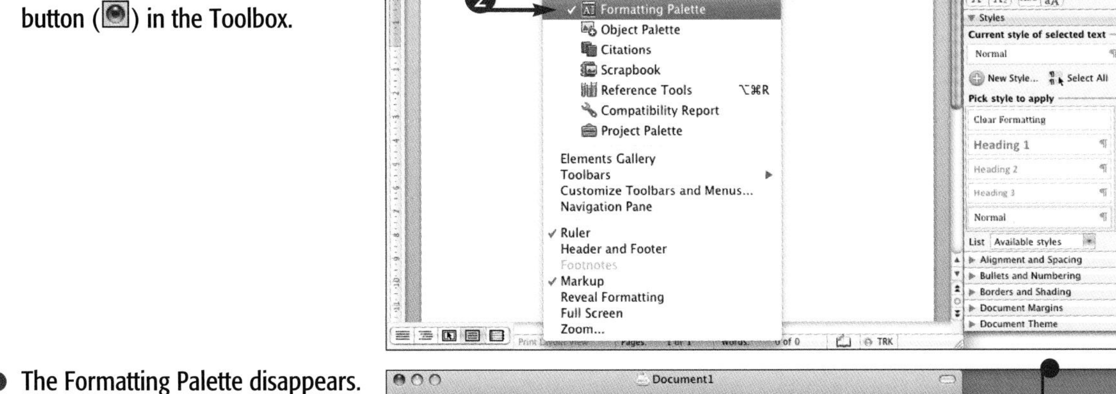

- The Formatting Palette disappears.

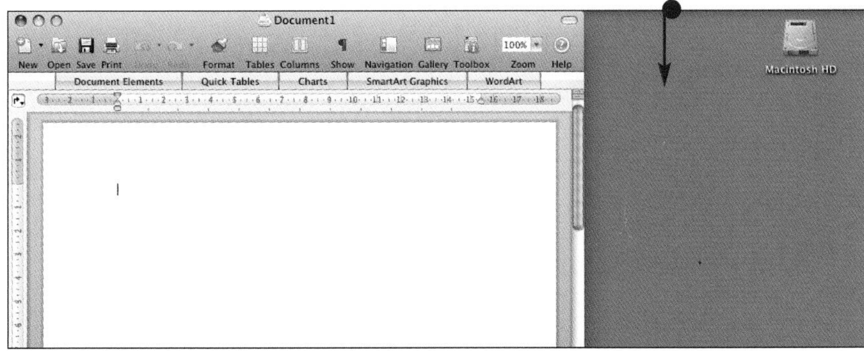

TIP

**There are panels on the Formatting Palette that I never use. Can I hide them?**

Yes. Follow these steps:

1. Click the **Toolbox Settings** button (◎) in the upper-right corner of the Toolbox.

   The Toolbox Settings dialog appears.

2. In the Show Panels list, select each option that you want to hide (☑ changes to ☐).
3. Click **OK**.

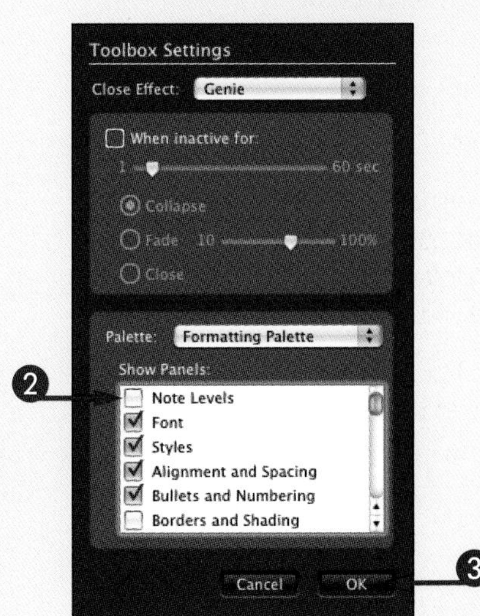

# Change the Font and Font Size

When you work in a Word document, Excel worksheet, PowerPoint slide, or Entourage e-mail message, you can add visual appeal by changing the font and font size.

**In this section, the term *font* is synonymous with *typeface*, and both refer to the overall look of each character. Also, the font size is measured in *points*, where there are roughly 72 points in an inch.**

## Change the Font and Font Size

1. Select the text you want to format.
2. Display the Formatting Palette.

***Note:*** *See the section "Display and Hide the Formatting Palette" earlier in this chapter.*

3. Open the Font panel.

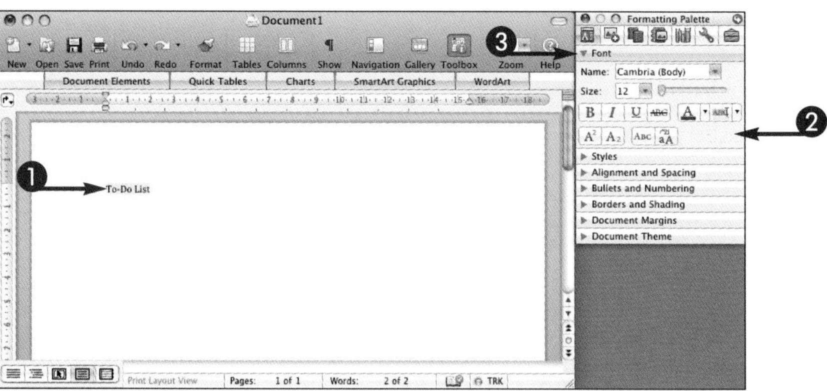


4. To change the typeface, click ▾ in the Name list and then click the typeface you want to apply.

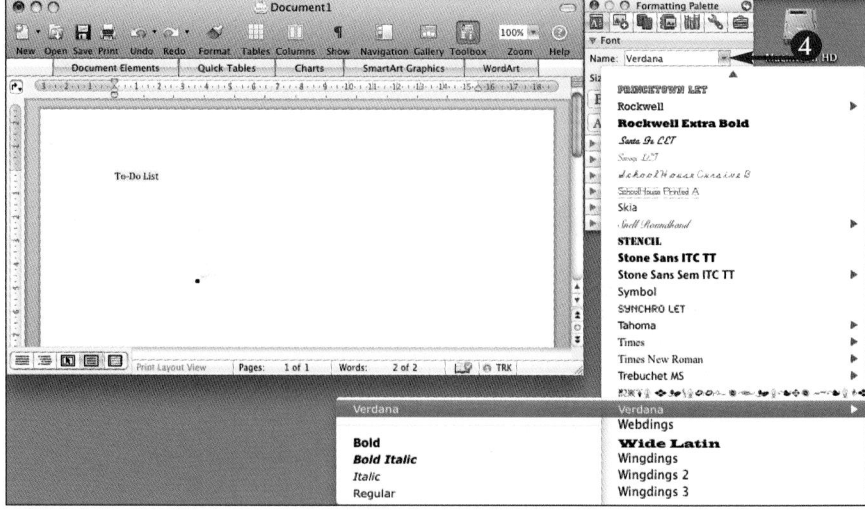

- The Office application applies the font to the selected text.

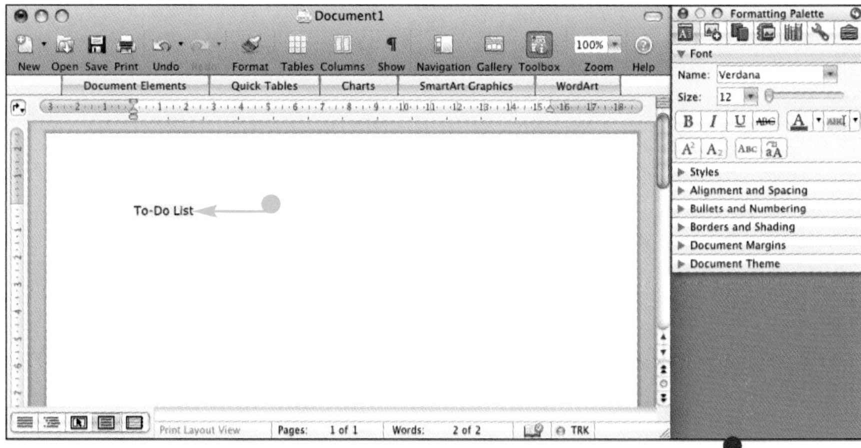

5 To change the font size, click ▾ in the Size list and then click the size you want to apply.

- You can also type the size you want in the Size text box.
- You can also click and drag the **Size** slider ( ) to set the font size.
- The Office application applies the font size to the selected text.

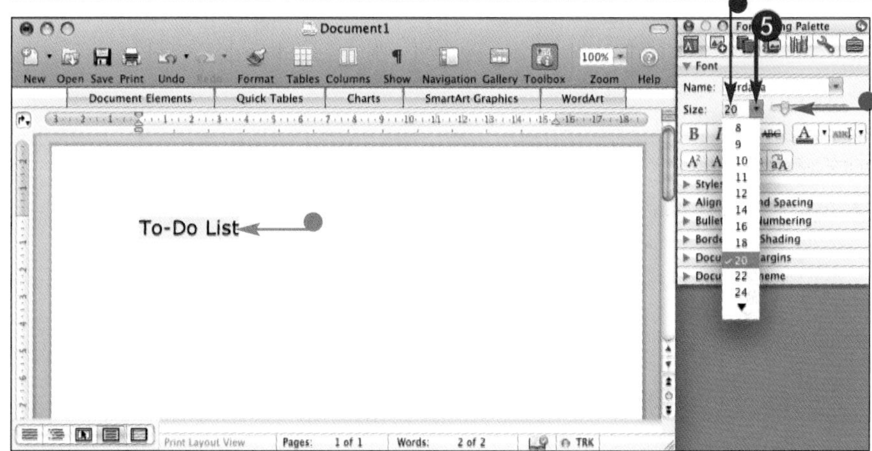

TIPS

### Are all the fonts in Office for Mac compatible with Office for Windows?

No. There are many fonts available in the Mac version of Office that are not available in the Windows version. If you use any of these incompatible fonts, Windows users may not see your document as you intended. To avoid this, follow steps **1** to **4** to open the Font list, click **Font Collections**, click **Windows Office Compatible**, and then use only the fonts in the menu that appears.

### How do I change the default font in Word?

Word's default font is the font associated with the Normal template. To change this font, first apply the font formatting you want to use as described in this section and in the next two sections. Click **Format** in the menu bar and then click **Font** (or press ⌘+D). In the Font dialog, click **Default** and when Word asks you to confirm, click **Yes**.

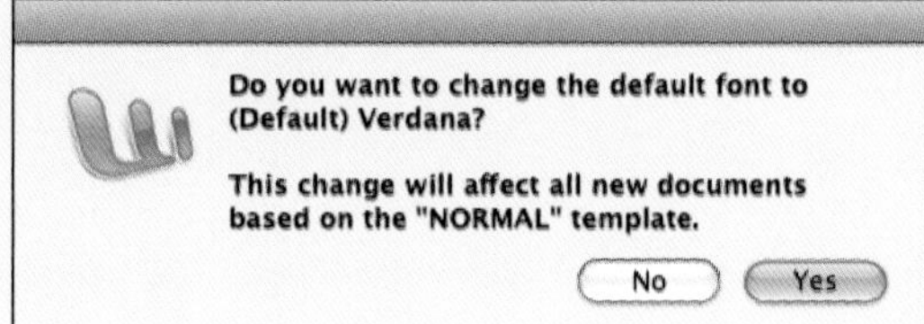

Do you want to change the default font to (Default) Verdana?
This change will affect all new documents based on the "NORMAL" template.
No
Yes

# Apply Font Effects

You can improve the look and impact of text in a Word document, Excel worksheet, PowerPoint slide, or Entourage e-mail message by applying font effects.

**Font effects include common formatting such as bold, italic, and underline, as well as special effects such as strikethrough, superscripts, subscripts, and small caps. The available font effects vary depending on the Office application you are using.**

## Apply Font Effects

1. Select the text you want to format.
2. Display the Formatting Palette.

*Note: See the section "Display and Hide the Formatting Palette" earlier in this chapter.*

3. Open the Font panel.

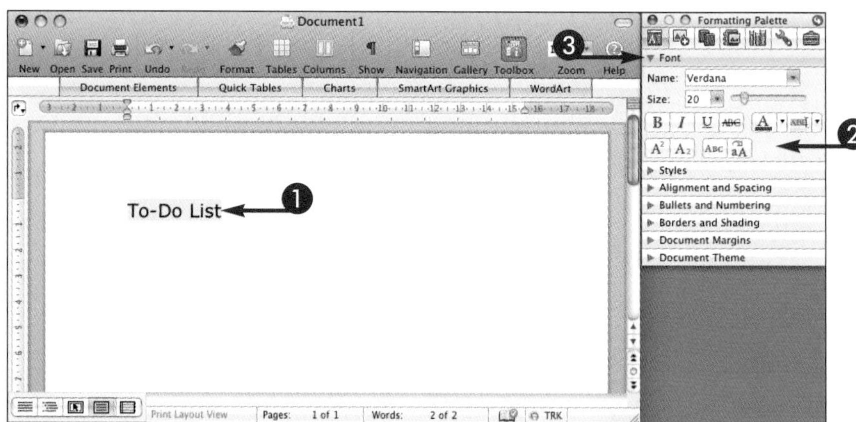


4. To format the text as bold, click the **Bold** button (B).
5. To format the text as italic, click the **Italic** button (I).
6. To format the text as underline, click the **Underline** button (U).
7. To format the text as strikethrough, click the **Strikethrough** button (ABC).

8. To format the text as a superscript, click the button **Superscript** (A²).

9. To format the text as a subscript, click the **Subscript** button ($A_2$).

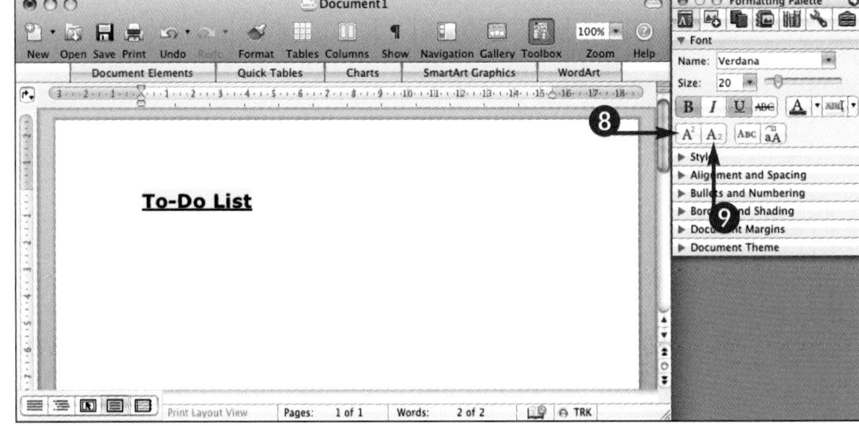

10. To format the text as small caps, click the **Small Caps** button (ABC).

11. To format the text as all uppercase characters, click the **All Caps** button (aA).

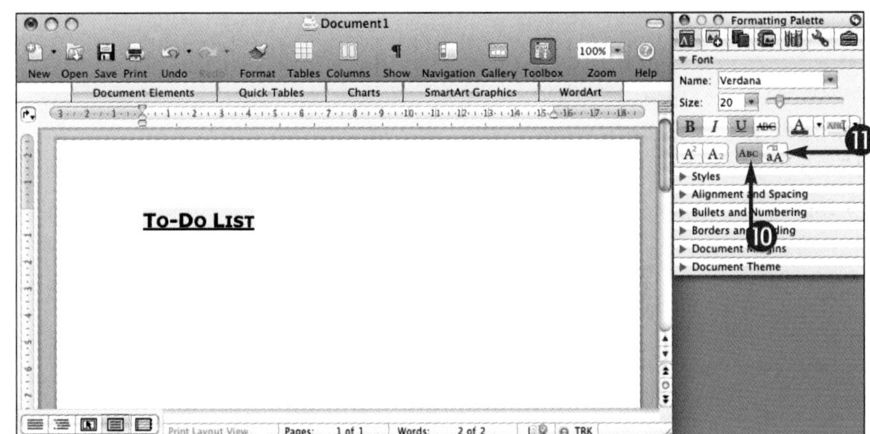

TIP

**Are there any font-related keyboard shortcuts I can use?**

Yes. All Office applications support the following font shortcuts:

| ***Press*** | ***To*** |
|---|---|
| ⌘+B | Format the selected text as bold |
| ⌘+I | Format the selected text as italic |
| ⌘+U | Format the selected text as underline |
| Shift+⌘+> | Increase the font size |
| Shift+⌘+< | Decrease the font size |

# Change the Font Color

When you work in a Word document, Excel worksheet, PowerPoint slide, or Entourage e-mail message, you can add visual interest by changing the font color.

**You can change the font color in two ways: you can change the color of the text, and you can apply a highlight color to the text background. Note, however, that only Word supports changing the highlight color.**

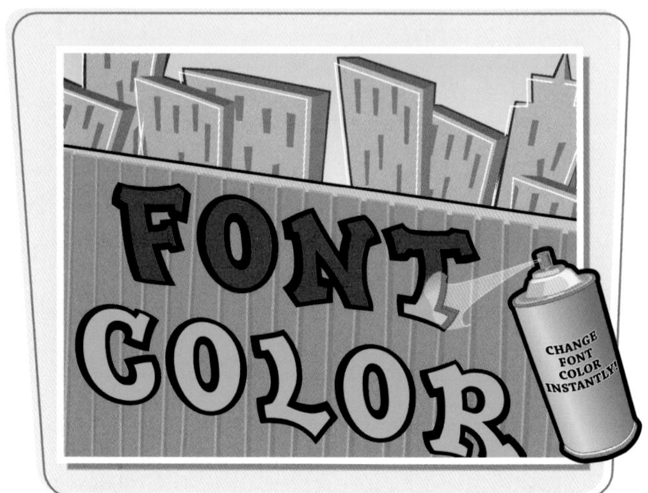


## Change the Font Color

1. Select the text you want to format.
2. Display the Formatting Palette.

*Note:* *See the section "Display and Hide the Formatting Palette" earlier in this chapter.*

3. Open the Font panel.

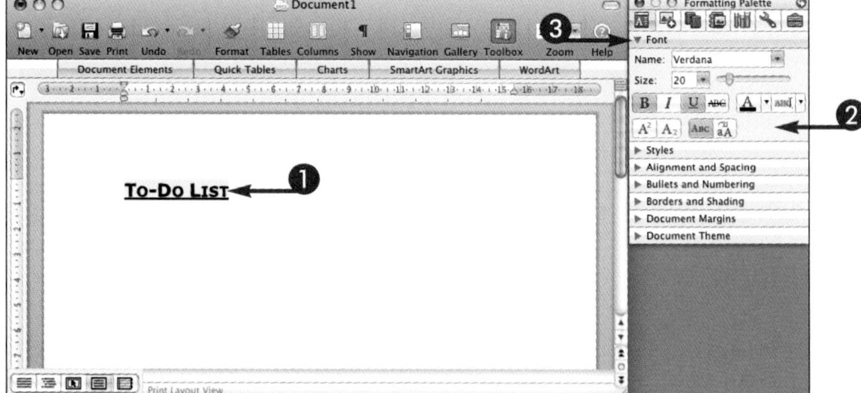


4. To format the font color, click ▾ in the **Font Color** control and then click the color you want to apply.

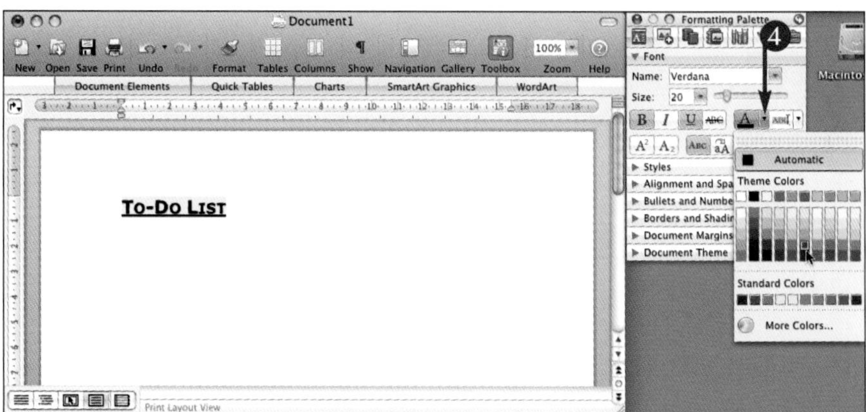

5 To format the highlight color, click ▾ in the **Highlight** control and then click the color you want to apply.

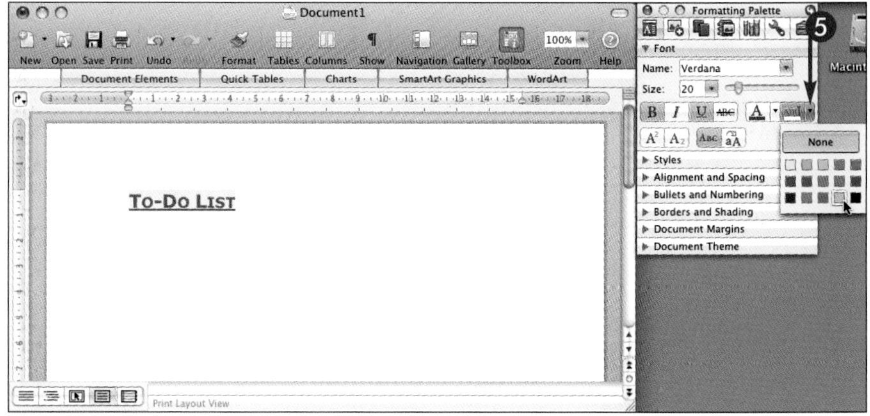

● The Office application applies the colors to the selected text.

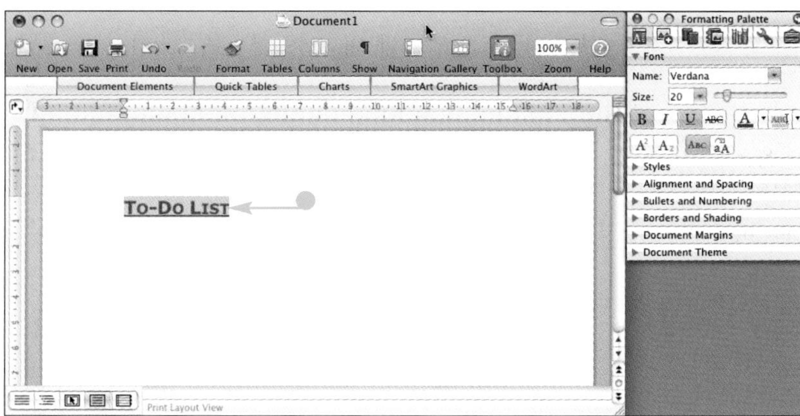

TIP

**How can I make the best use of fonts in my documents?**

- Do not use many different typefaces in a single document. Stick to one, or at most two, typefaces to avoid the ransom note look.
- Avoid overly decorative typefaces because they are often difficult to read.
- Use bold only for document titles, subtitles, and headings.
- Use italics only to emphasize words and phrases, or for the titles of books and magazines.
- Use larger type sizes only for document titles, subtitles, and, possibly, the headings.
- If you change the text color, be sure to leave enough contrast between the text and the background. In general, dark text on a light background is the easiest to read.

# Align Text

You can make a Word document, Excel worksheet, or PowerPoint slide easier to read by aligning the text.

**You can align text horizontally and vertically, and you can change the text orientation, which determines the direction the text runs.**

## Align Text

1. Select the text or data you want to format.
2. Display the Formatting Palette.

*Note: See the section "Display and Hide the Formatting Palette" earlier in this chapter.*

3. Open the Alignment and Spacing panel.

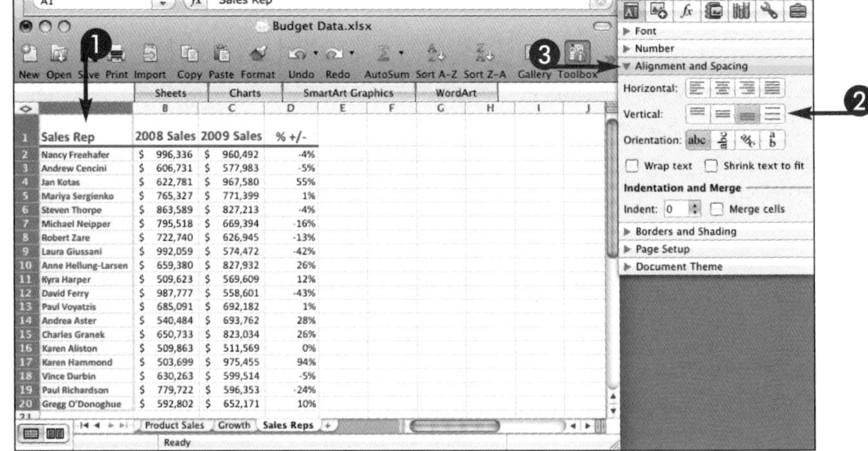


4. Click the **Horizontal** options buttons to set the horizontal text alignment: **Align Text Left** (▤); **Align Center** (▤); **Align Text Right** (▤); or **Justify** (▤).

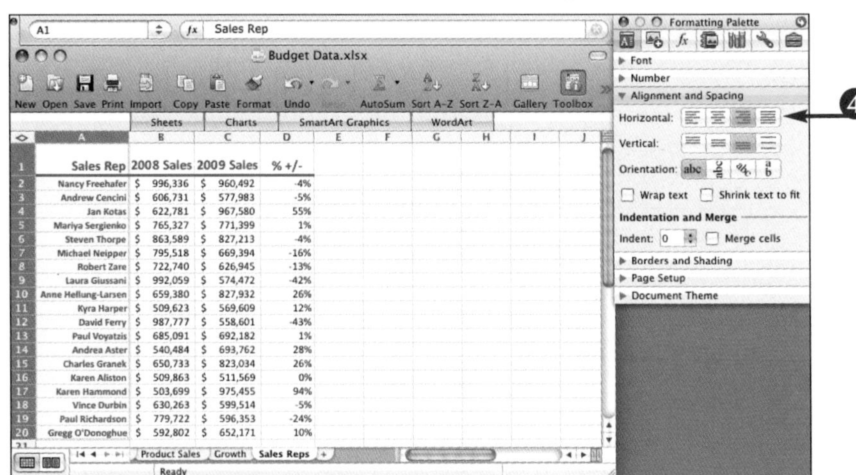

5 Click the **Vertical** options buttons to set the vertical text alignment: **Top** ( ); **Center** ( ); **Bottom** ( ); or **Justify** ( ).

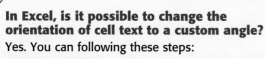

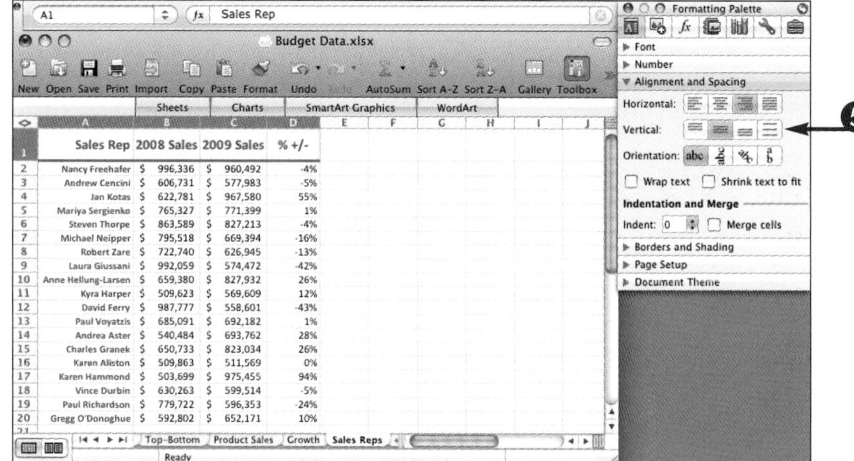


6 Click the **Orientation** options buttons to set the text direction: **Horizontal Text** ( ); **Rotate Text Up** ( ); **Angle Text Downward** ( ); or **Vertical Text** ( ).

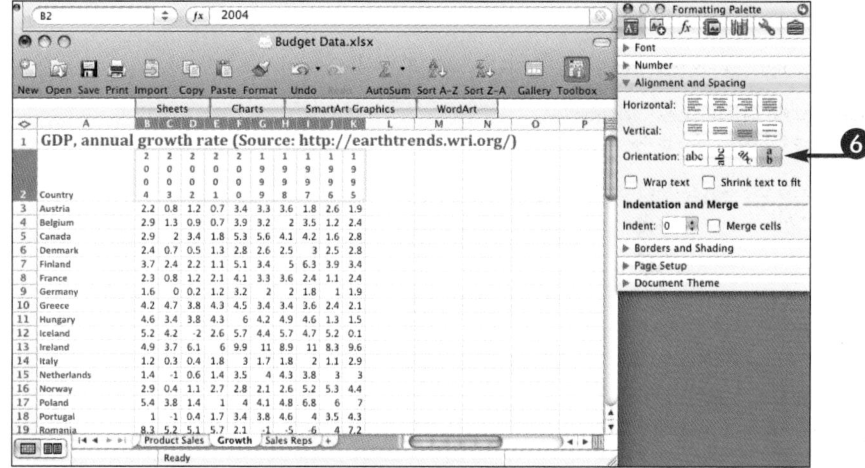


## TIP

**In Excel, is it possible to change the orientation of cell text to a custom angle?**

Yes. You can following these steps:

1. Select the cell or range you want to format.
2. Click **Format** in the menu bar.
3. Click **Cells**, or press ⌘+1 to open the Format Cells dialog.
4. Click the **Alignment** tab.
5. Type the number of degrees you want for your custom orientation in the Degrees text box.
6. Click **OK**.

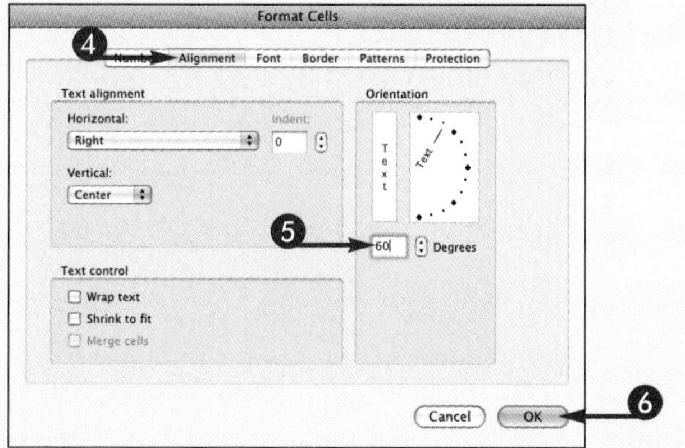

# Copy Formatting

**You can save yourself a great deal of time by copying existing formatting to other areas of a document. After you spend time formatting text or data, rather than spending time repeating the steps for other data, you can use the Format Painter tool to copy the formatting with a couple of mouse clicks.**

## Copy Formatting

### COPY FORMATTING ONCE

1. Select the text or data that has the formatting you want to copy.
2. Click the **Format Painter** button (![]).
3. Select the text or data you want to format.

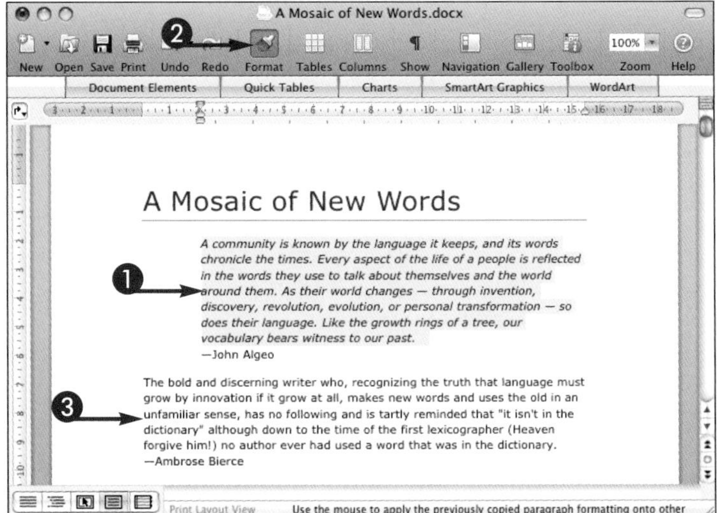


- The Format Painter applies the copied formatting to the selected text.

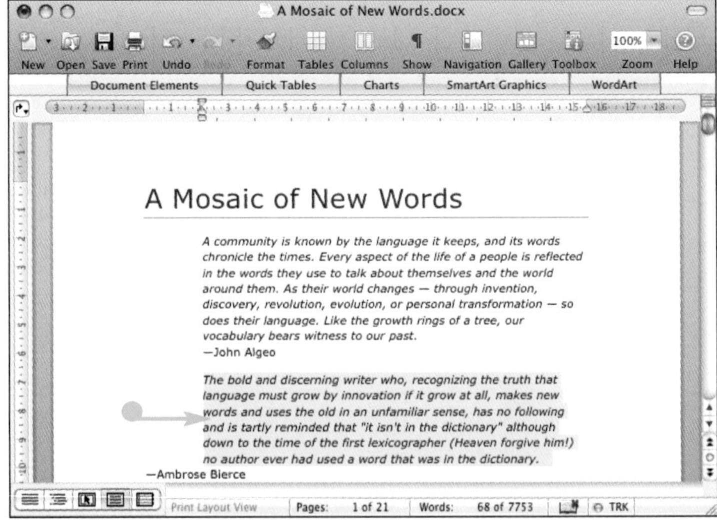

### COPY FORMATTING MULTIPLE TIMES

1. Select the text or data that has the formatting you want to copy.
2. Double-click the **Format Painter** button ().
3. Select the text or data you want to format.

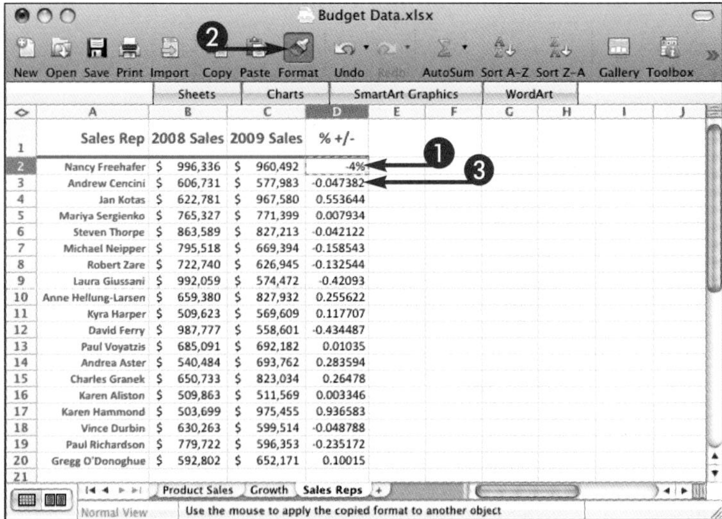


- The Format Painter applies the copied formatting to the selected text.
- The Format Painter remains activated.

4. Repeat Step **3** to copy the formatting to other text or data.
5. Click to deactivate the Format Painter.

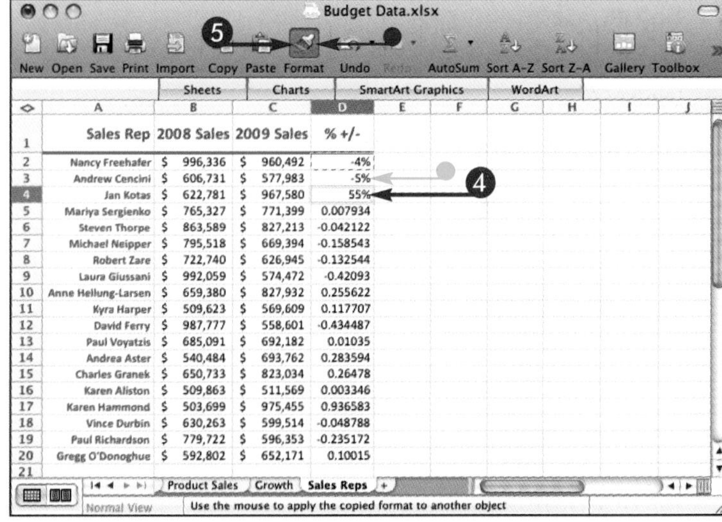

**Do I always have to select text in Word before using the Format Painter?**

It depends on what type of formatting you want to copy. If you want to copy text formatting such as bold or italic, then you must select some text that has the formatting applied. However, if you want to copy paragraph formatting such as alignment, then you do not need to select the entire paragraph. Instead, you can just click inside the paragraph that has the formatting applied. After you do that, click to activate the Format Painter, and then click inside another paragraph to copy the formatting.

# Adding and Editing Graphics

You can enhance the visual appeal and effectiveness of your Word documents, Excel worksheets, and PowerPoint slides by incorporating graphic objects such as shapes, clip art, pictures, or WordArt and SmartArt images. This chapter shows you how to insert graphics and also how to edit and format graphics.

# Display and Hide the Object Palette

The Office for Mac programs offer a Toolbox pane called the Object Palette, which enables you to quickly choose and insert shapes, clip art, symbols, or photos.

**In the next few sections you learn the specific steps required to draw a shape and to insert a clip art image or picture.**

## Display and Hide the Object Palette

### DISPLAY THE OBJECT PALETTE

1. Click **View**.
2. Click **Object Palette**.

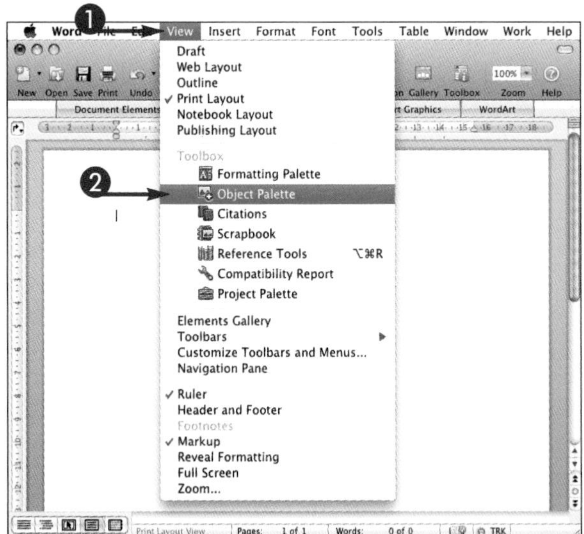

- The Object Palette appears.
- You can also click the Toolbox button ( ) in the Standard toolbar, and then click the Object Palette button ( ).
- Click these buttons to see the different objects available for insertion.

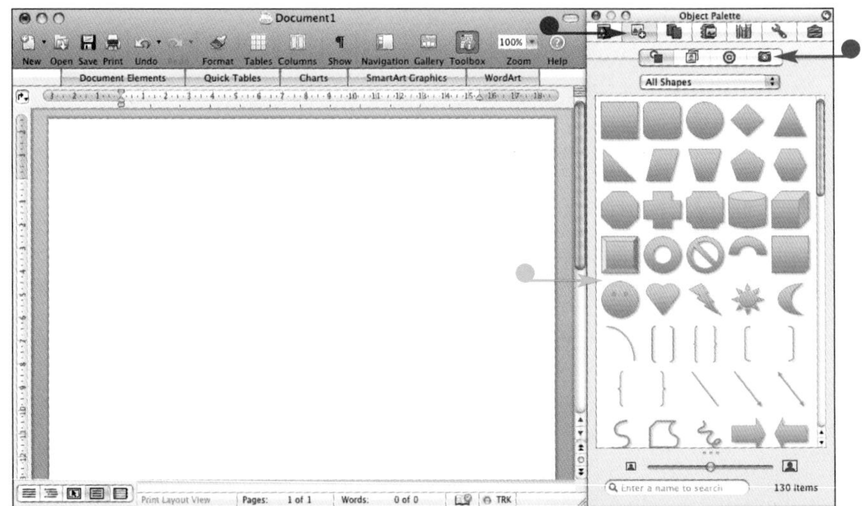

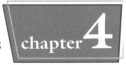

## HIDE THE OBJECT PALETTE

1. Click **View**.
2. Click **Object Palette**.

- You can also click the **Close** button (●) in the Toolbox.

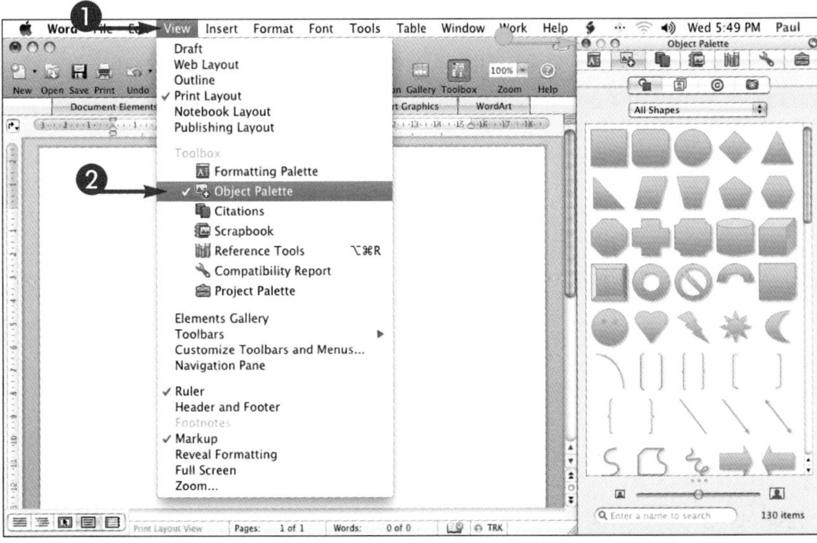

- The Object Palette disappears.

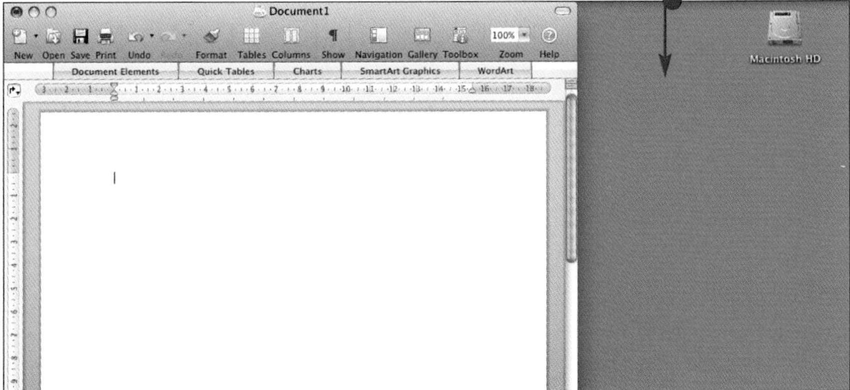

TIP

### Can I change the layout of the Object Palette?

Yes. Office gives you two methods for changing the layout:

- Click and drag here to make the Object Palette bigger or smaller.
- Click and drag the **Thumbnail Size** slider (⊙) to change the size of the displayed objects.

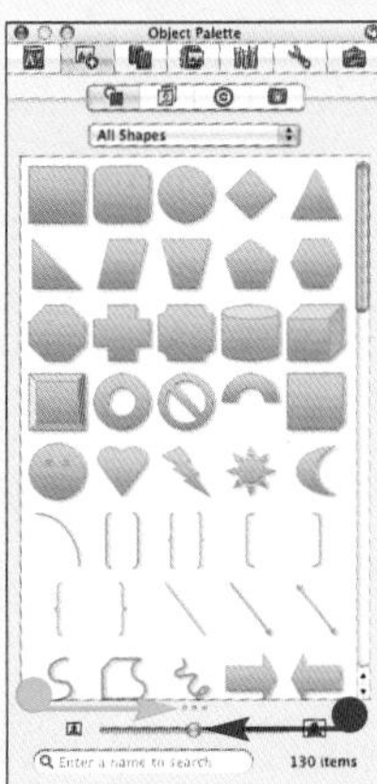

# Draw a Shape

The Office Object Palette comes with 130 predefined objects called *shapes* (or sometimes *AutoShapes*) that enable you to quickly and easily draw anything from simple geometric figures such as lines, rectangles, and ovals, to more elaborate items such as starbursts, flowchart symbols, and callout boxes.

## Draw a Shape

1. Open the document where you want to draw the shape.
2. Display the Object Palette.

***Note:*** *See the section "Display and Hide the Object Palette" earlier in this chapter.*

3. Click the **Shapes** button ( ).

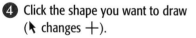

4. Click the shape you want to draw (pointer changes +).

5 Click and drag the mouse + to draw the shape.

6 When the shape is the size you want, release the mouse button.

- The program draws the shape and adds edit handles around the shape's edges.

***Note:*** *If you need to move or size the shape, see the section "Move or Resize a Graphic" later in this chapter.*

TIPS

**Is there an easy way to draw a perfect circle or square?**

Yes. The Office programs offer an easy technique for drawing circles and squares: Hold down the Shift key as you click and drag the shape to constrain the shape into a perfect circle or square. When you finish drawing the shape, release Shift.

**Can I add text to a shape?**

Yes. You can add text to the interior of any 2-D shape (that is, any shape that is not a line). After you draw the shape, right-click (or Ctrl+click) the shape, click **Add Text**, and then type your text inside the shape. You can use the Formatting Palette (see Chapter 3) to format the text. When you finish, click outside of the shape.

# Insert a Clip Art Image

You can improve the look of a Word document, Excel worksheet, or PowerPoint slide by adding a clip art image to the file.

***Clip art* refers to small images or artwork that you can insert into your documents. Office for Mac ships with over 300 clip art images that you can use without charge.**

## Insert a Clip Art Image

1. Open the document where you want to insert the clip art image.
2. Display the Object Palette.

***Note:*** *See the section "Display and Hide the Object Palette" earlier in this chapter.*

3. Click the **Clip Art** button ( ).

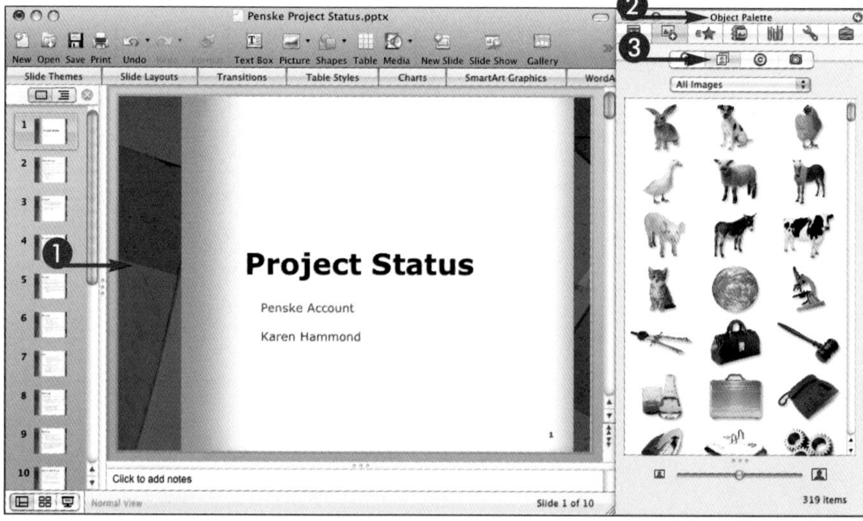

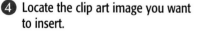

4. Locate the clip art image you want to insert.

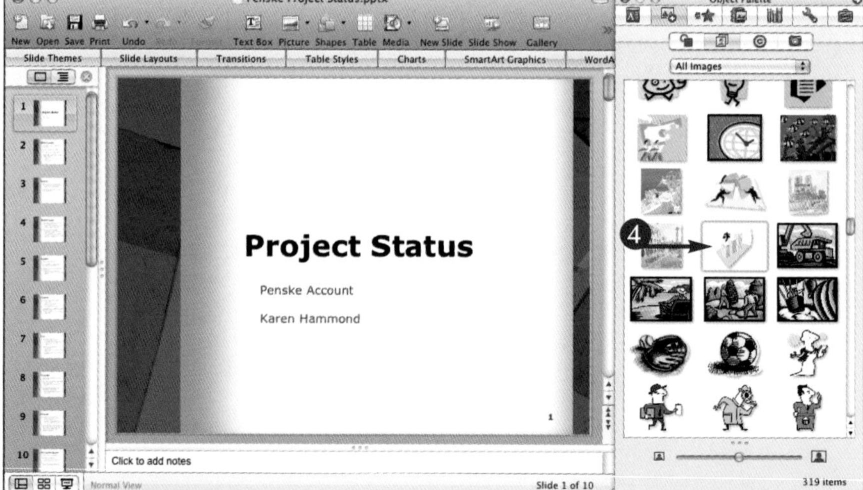

5 Click and drag the clip art image from the Object Palette (↖ changes to ↖+) and drop it inside the document.

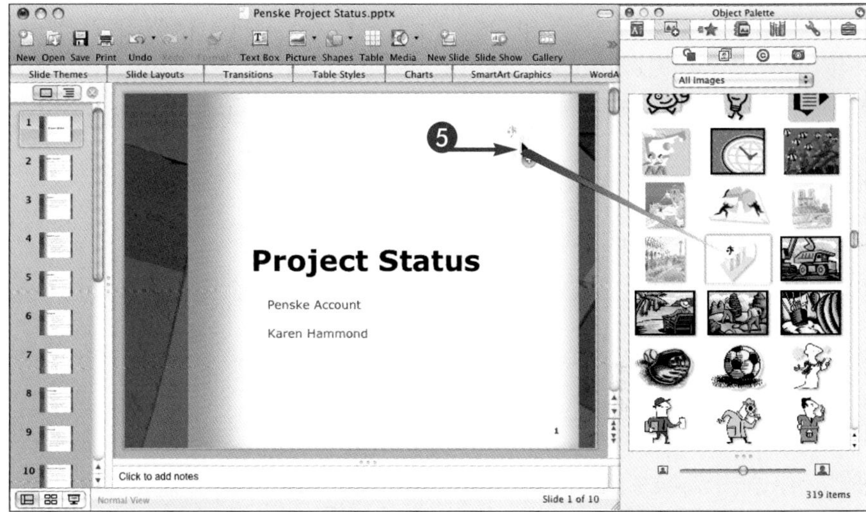


- The program inserts the clip art.

***Note:*** *If you need to move or size the clip art, see the section "Move or Resize a Graphic" later in this chapter.*

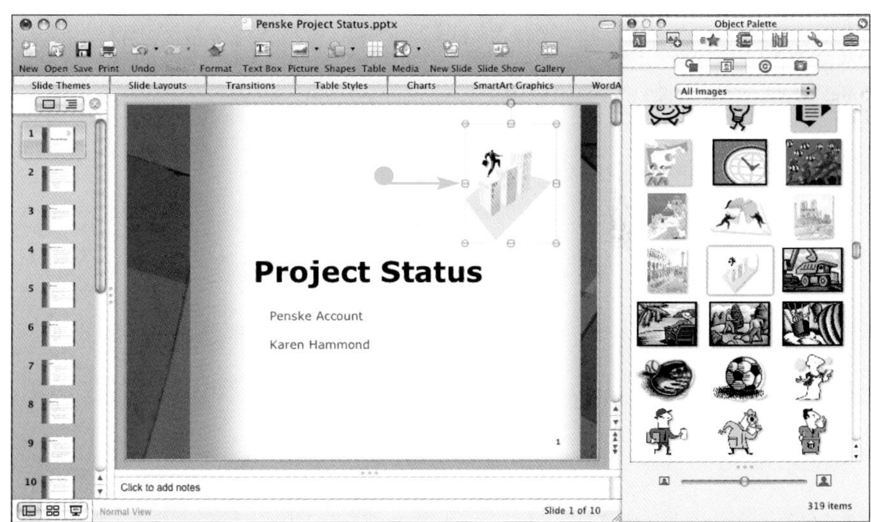


TIP

**Is there an easier way to locate the clip art image that I want?**

Yes. You can filter the clip art list to show only those images from a particular category, such as Animals or People:

1. Display the Object Palette.
2. Click ▣.
3. In the **Categories** pop-up menu, click ⬍.
4. Click the category you want to work with.

   The Object Palette displays only the clip art images in the category you choose.

# Insert a Photo

You can enhance the visual appeal and strengthen the message of a Word document, Excel worksheet, or PowerPoint slide by adding a photo to the file.

**The Office programs can work with the most popular picture formats, including JPEG, TIFF, PNG, and GIF.**

## Insert a Photo

1. Open the document where you want to insert the photo.
2. Display the Object Palette.

***Note:*** *See the section "Display and Hide the Object Palette" earlier in this chapter.*

3. Click the **Photos** button (📷).

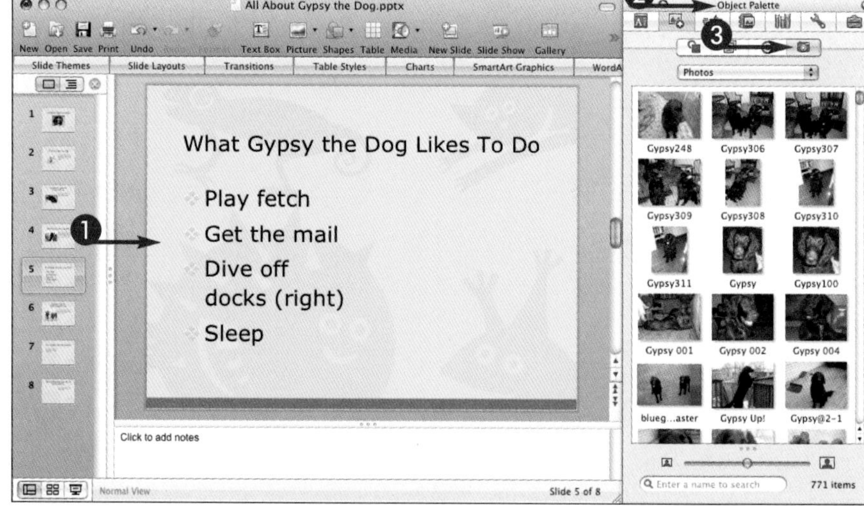


4. Locate the photo you want to insert.

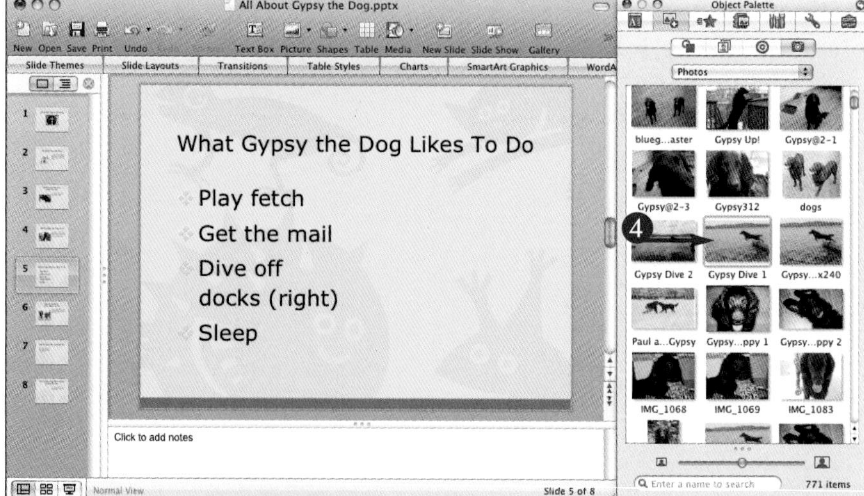

5 Click and drag the photo from the Object Palette (changes to ) and drop it inside the document.

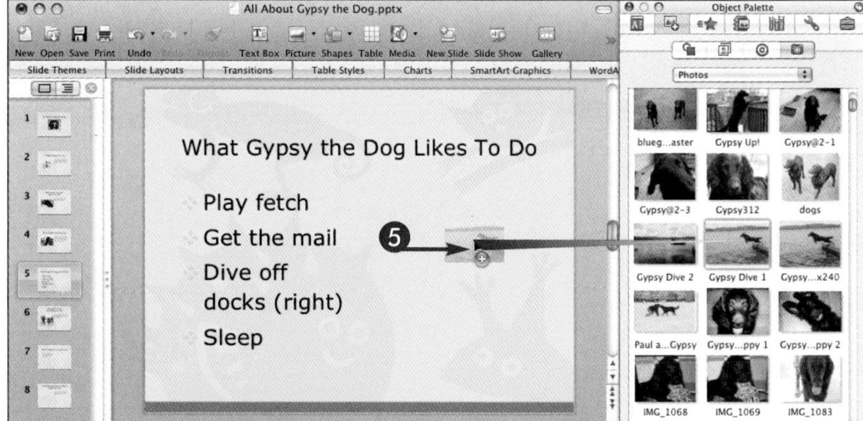


- The program inserts the photo.

***Note:*** *If you need to move or size the photo, see the section "Move or Resize a Graphic" later in this chapter.*

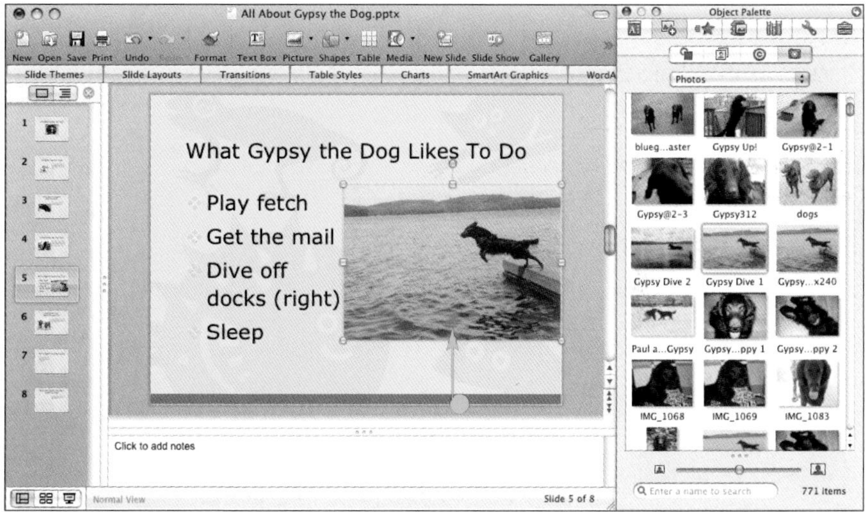


TIP

## Is there an easier way to locate the photo I want?

Yes. You can filter the Photos list to show only those images from a particular iPhoto album, iPhoto event, or folder:

1. Display the Object Palette.
2. Click .
3. In the **Categories** pop-up menu, click .
4. Click **Albums**.
5. Click the item you want to work with.

   The Object Palette displays only the images in the category you choose.

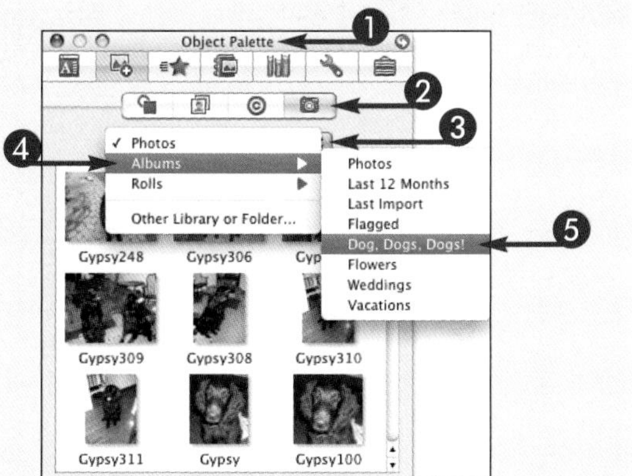

# Insert a WordArt Image

You can add some pizzazz to your Office documents by inserting a WordArt image. A WordArt image is a graphic object that contains text stylized with shadows, outlines, reflections, and other predefined effects. Some WordArt images display the characters in a curve or circle.

**WordArt images enable you to apply sophisticated and fun effects to text with just a few mouse clicks.**

## Insert a WordArt Image

1. Open the document where you want to insert the WordArt image.
2. Click **WordArt**.

   The WordArt gallery appears.
3. Click and to locate a WordArt style that interests you.
4. Click the WordArt style you want to use.

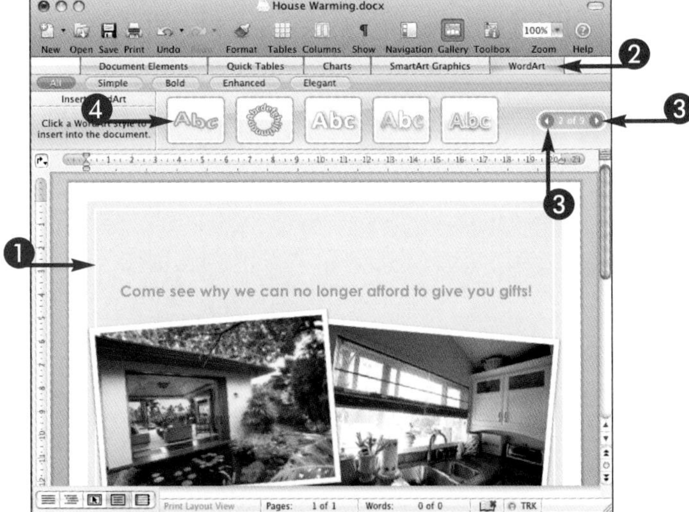


- The WordArt image appears in the document.

***Note:** You will likely have to move the WordArt image into position; see the section "Move or Resize a Graphic" later in this chapter.*

5. Double-click the WordArt image.

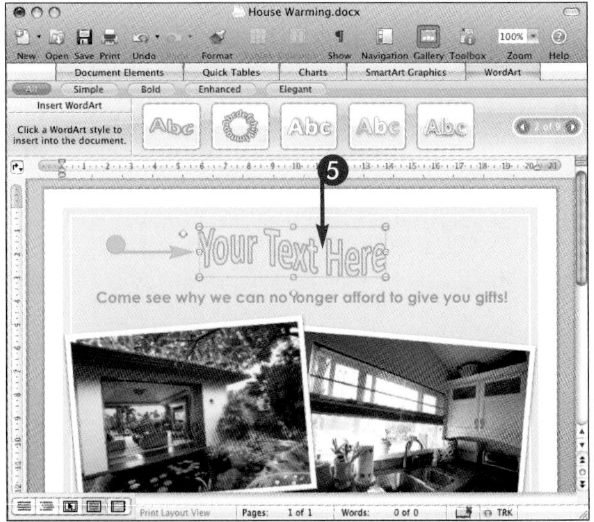

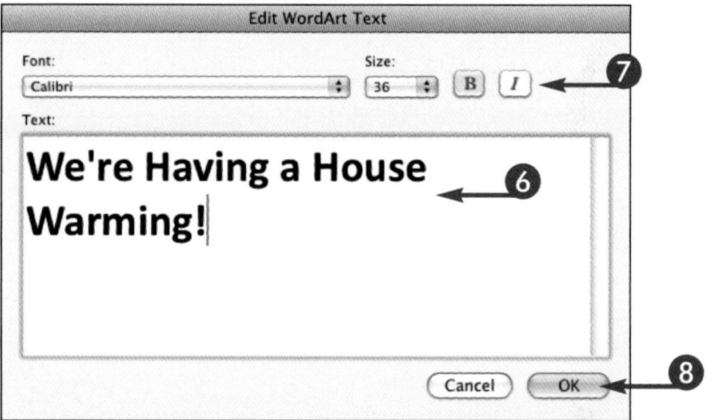


The Edit WordArt Text dialog appears.

6. Type the text that you want to appear in the WordArt image.
7. Use the font controls to set the font for the WordArt text.
8. Click **OK**.

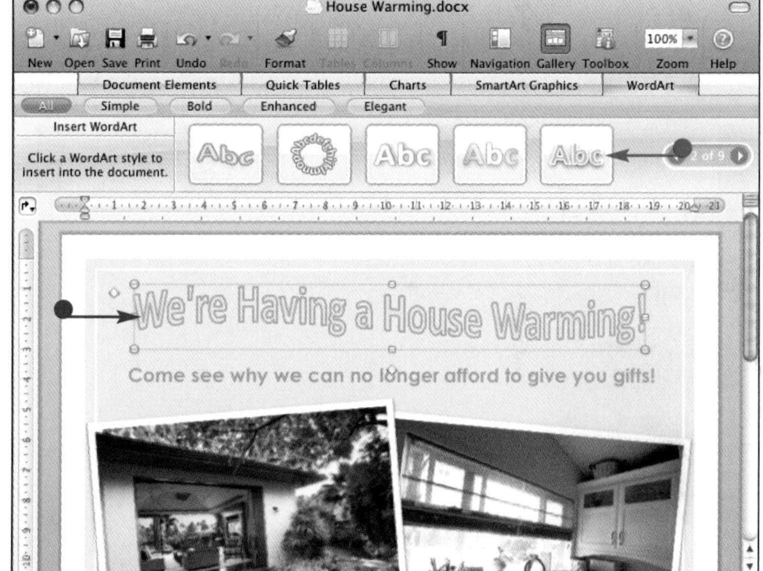


- The Office program updates the WordArt text.
- To change the WordArt style, use the Gallery to display and then click the style you prefer.

## TIP

### Can I make my WordArt text run vertically?

Yes. Follow these steps:

1. Follow Steps **1** to **8** to insert your WordArt image and set the text.
2. From the menu, click the **Toolbox** button ( ).
3. Click **Formatting Palette**.
4. Select ▶ to expand the WordArt panel.
5. Click the **Stack Text Vertically** button ( ).

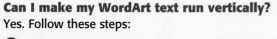

- The Office program displays the WordArt text vertically.

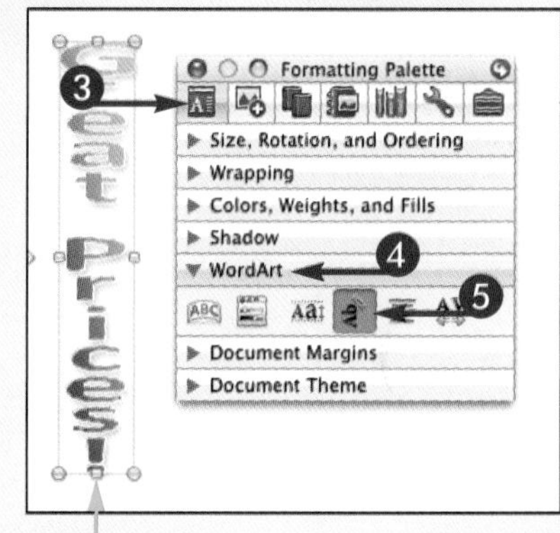

# Insert a SmartArt Graphic

You can add a SmartArt graphic to a document to help present information in a compact, visual format. A SmartArt graphic is a combination of text and shapes that enables you to convey information visually.

**For example, you can use a SmartArt graphic to present a company organization chart, the progression of steps in a workflow, the parts that make up a whole, and much more.**

## Insert a SmartArt Graphic

1. Open the document where you want to insert the SmartArt graphic.
2. Click **SmartArt Graphics**.

   The SmartArt Graphics gallery appears.
3. Click ◀ and ▶ to locate a SmartArt style that interests you.

- You can also click these buttons to filter the SmartArt styles by category.

4. Click the SmartArt style you want to use.

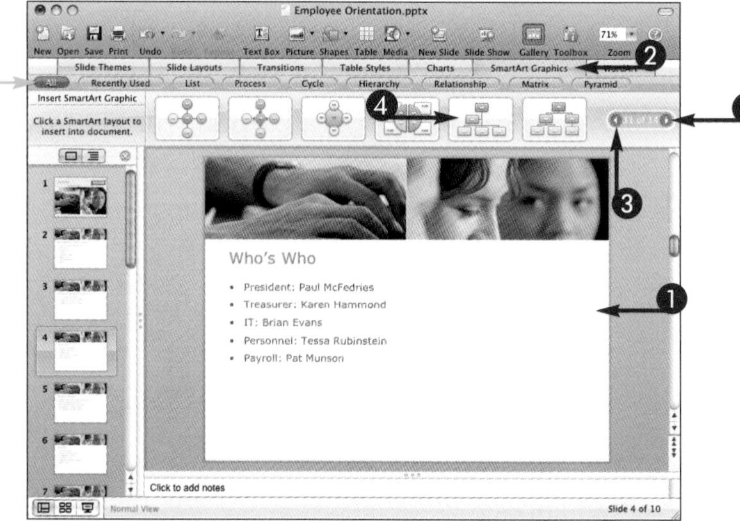


- The SmartArt graphic appears in the document.

***Note:** You will likely have to move the SmartArt graphic into position; see the section "Move or Resize a Graphic" later in this chapter.*

- You use the Text Pane to type the text for each node and to add and delete nodes.

5. Click a node in the Text Pane.
6. Type the text that you want to appear in the node.

- The text appears automatically in the associated shape.

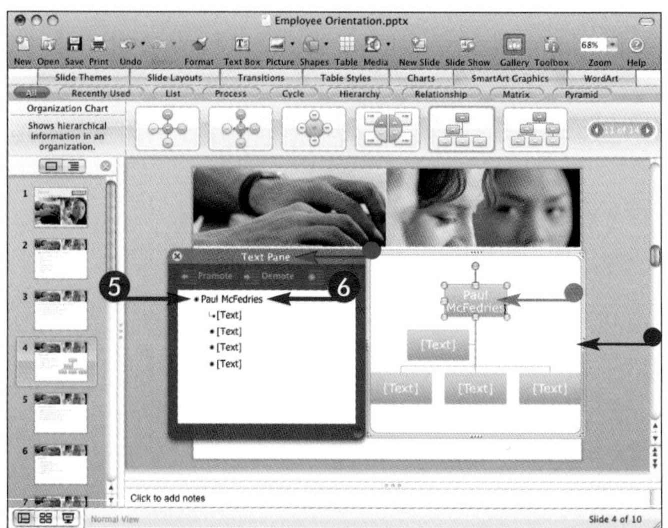

7. Repeat Step **5** to fill in the other nodes in the SmartArt graphic.

- Click the **Add** button (▪) to add a new node.
- Click the **Delete** button (▪) to remove the current node.

8. Click outside the SmartArt graphic.

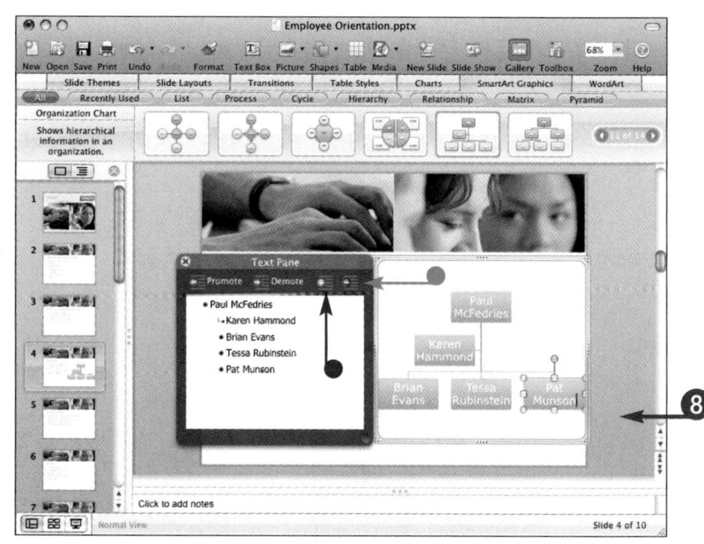


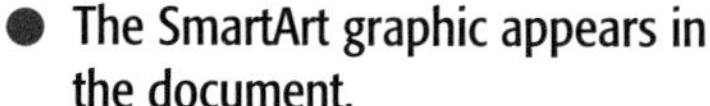

- The SmartArt graphic appears in the document.

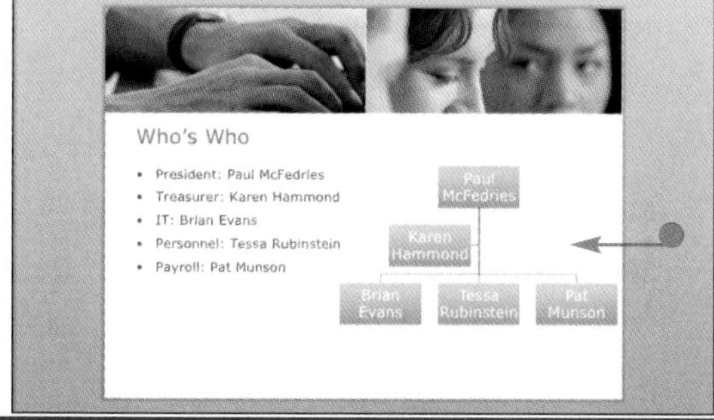


TIP

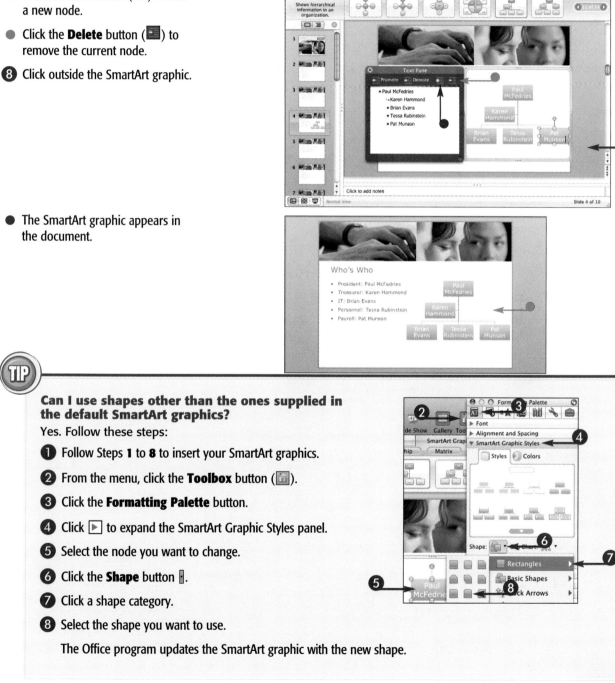

**Can I use shapes other than the ones supplied in the default SmartArt graphics?**

Yes. Follow these steps:

1. Follow Steps **1** to **8** to insert your SmartArt graphics.
2. From the menu, click the **Toolbox** button (▪).
3. Click the **Formatting Palette** button.
4. Click ▶ to expand the SmartArt Graphic Styles panel.
5. Select the node you want to change.
6. Click the **Shape** button ▪.
7. Click a shape category.
8. Select the shape you want to use.

The Office program updates the SmartArt graphic with the new shape.

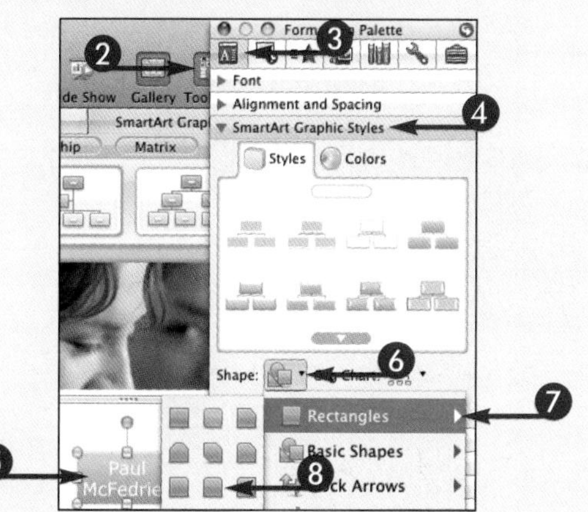

# Move or Resize a Graphic

To ensure that a graphic is ideally placed within an Office document, you can move the graphic to a new location, or you can resize the graphic in its current location. You can move or resize any graphic, including shapes, clip art, pictures, WordArt images, and SmartArt graphics.

## Move or Resize a Graphic

### MOVE A GRAPHIC

1. Click and drag the graphic you want to move.

   The mouse ↖ changes to ✥.

2. Drop the graphic in the location you prefer.

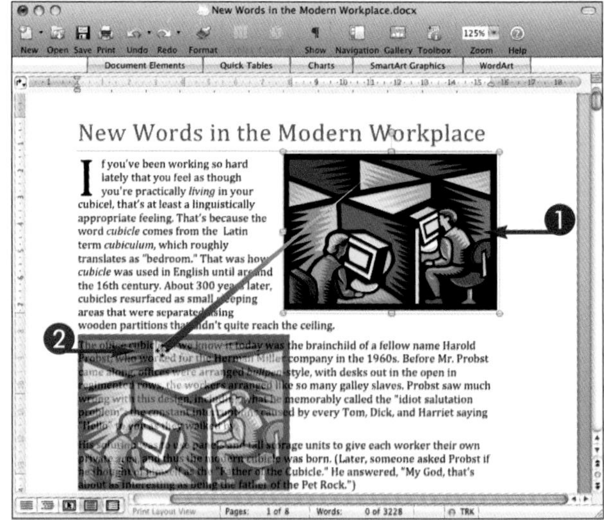


- The Office program moves the graphic to the new location.

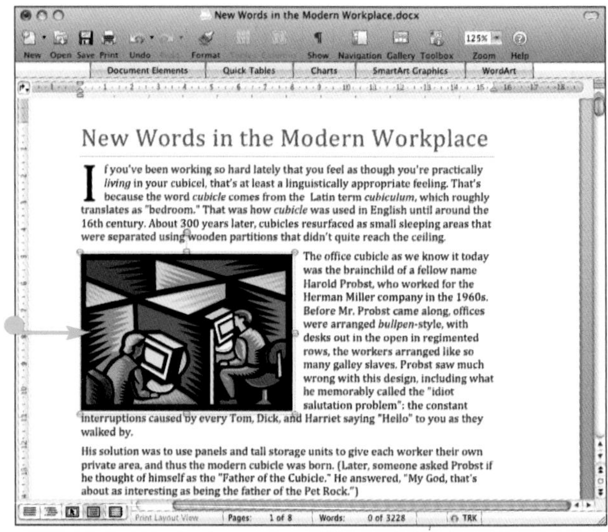

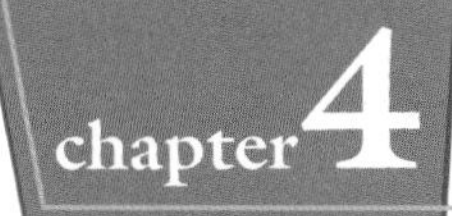


## RESIZE A GRAPHIC

1. Click the graphic you want to resize.

- Sizing handles appear around the graphic's edges.

2. Click and drag a sizing handle.

   The mouse changes to +.

- Drag a side handle to adjust that side.
- Drag a corner handle to adjust the two sides adjacent to the corner.

3. Release the mouse button when the handle is in the position you want.

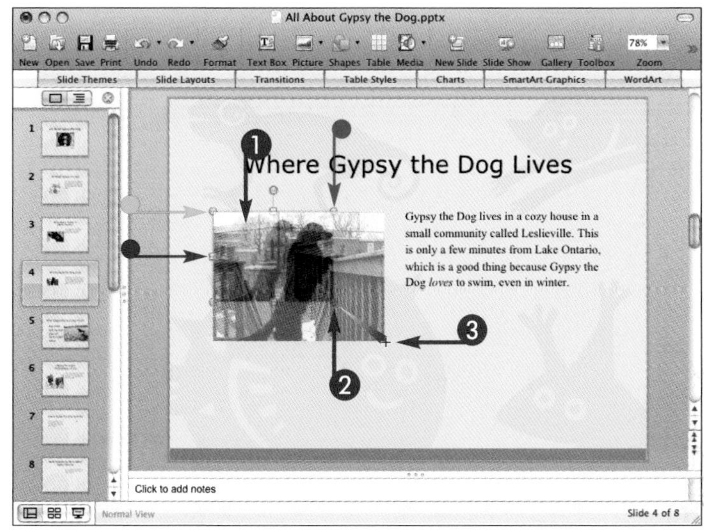


- The Office program resizes the graphic.

4. Repeat Steps **2** and **3** to resize other sides of the graphic, as necessary.

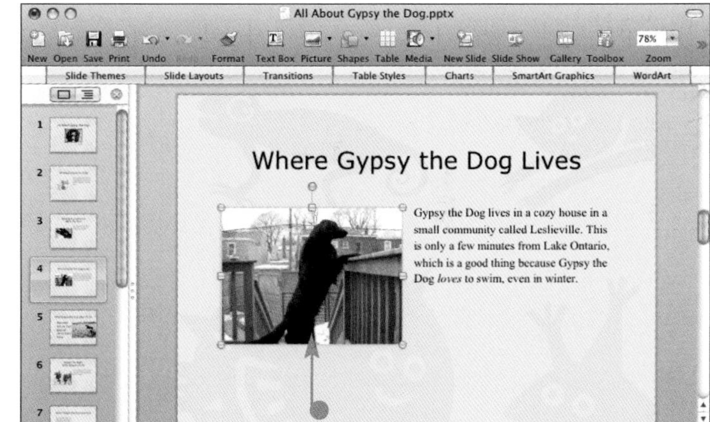

### Can I rotate a graphic?

Yes. Most graphic objects come with a green rotate handle. Follow these steps:

1. Move the mouse over the rotate handle (changes to ).
2. Click and drag the rotate handle clockwise or counterclockwise to rotate the graphic.
3. Release the mouse button when the graphic is in the position you want.

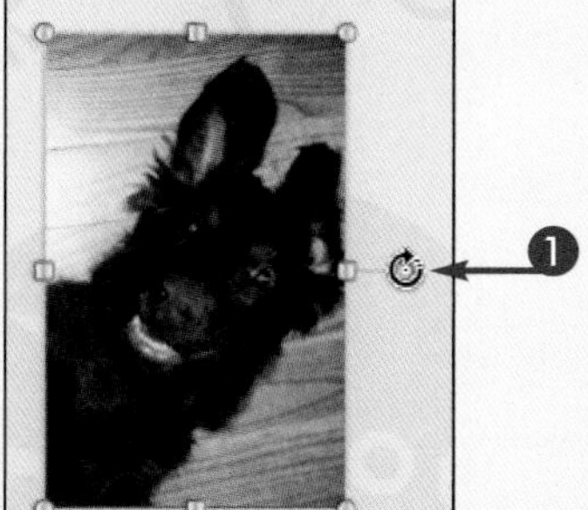

### Is it possible to resize a graphic in all directions at once and keep the proportions the same?

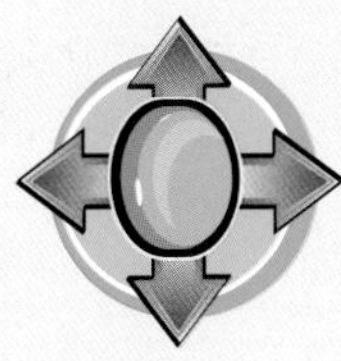

Yes. You normally resize one side at a time by dragging a side handle, or two sides at a time by dragging a corner handle. To resize all four sides at once, hold down the Option key and then click and drag any corner handle.

# Crop a Picture

**If a picture contains extraneous material near the outside edges of the image, you can crop the picture to remove that material. This not only reduces the size of the picture in the document, but it also serves to focus more attention on the remaining part of the image.**

## Crop a Picture

1. Select the picture you want to crop.
2. Display the Formatting Palette.

***Note:*** *See Chapter 3 to learn how to display the Formatting Palette.*

3. Open the Picture panel.

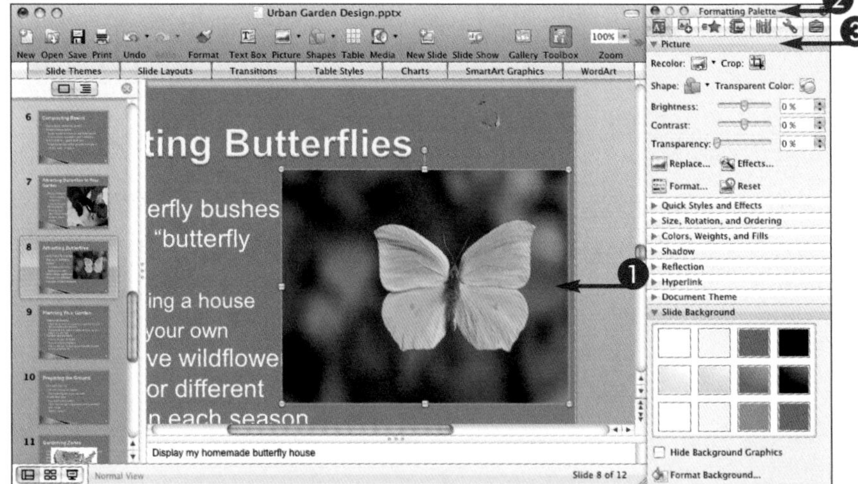


4. Click the **Crop** button (⧉).

- Crop handles appear around the picture.

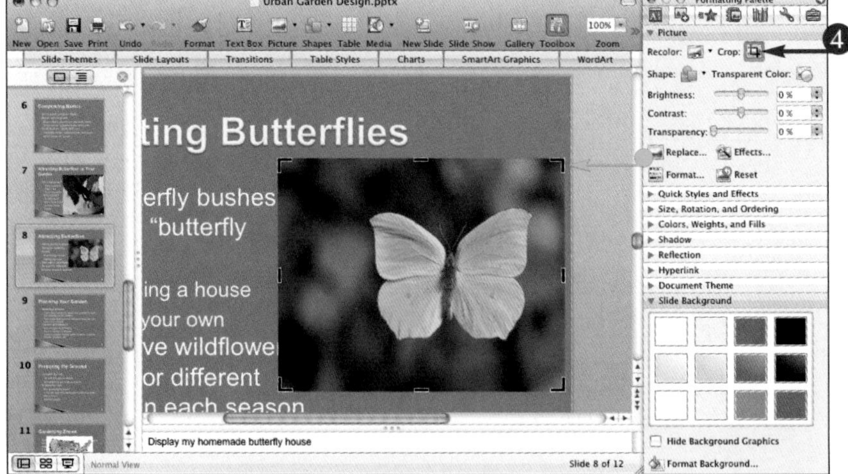

5 Click and drag a crop handle.

The mouse ↖ changes to +.

- Click and drag a side handle to crop that side.
- Click and drag a corner handle to crop the two sides adjacent to the corner.

6 Release the mouse button when the handle is in the position you want.

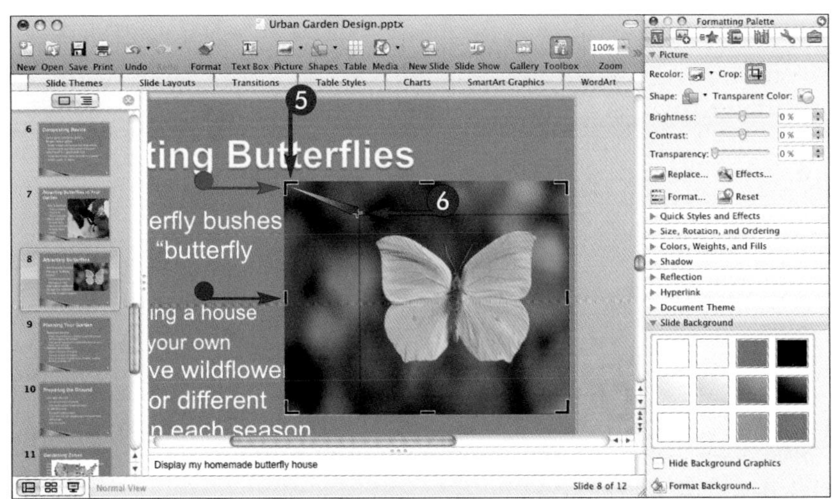

- The Office program crops the picture.

7 Repeat Steps **5** and **6** to crop other sides of the picture, as necessary.

8 Click ⊡ to deactivate the crop handles.

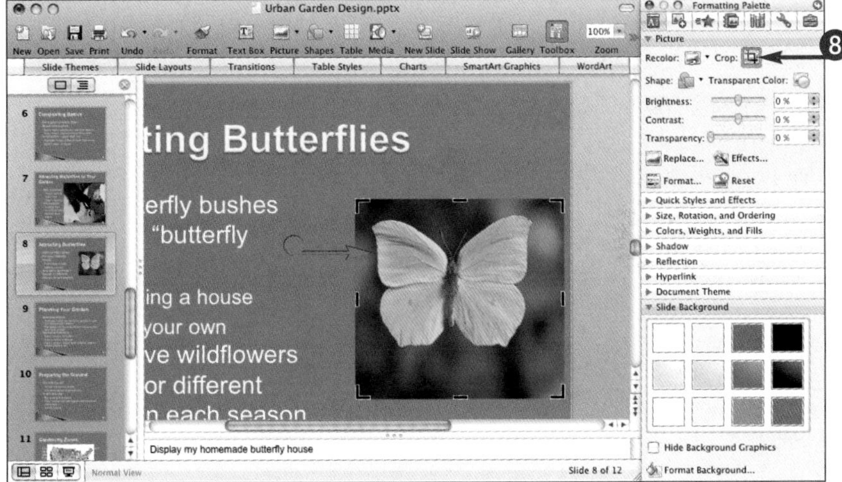

**If I have a picture with the main element in the middle, is it possible to crop in all directions at once to keep just that middle element?**

Yes. You normally crop one side at a time by clicking and dragging a side crop handle, or two sides at a time by clicking and dragging a corner crop handle. To crop all four sides at once, hold down the Option key and then click and drag any corner crop handle.

**Can I control how text flows around a graphic in Word?**

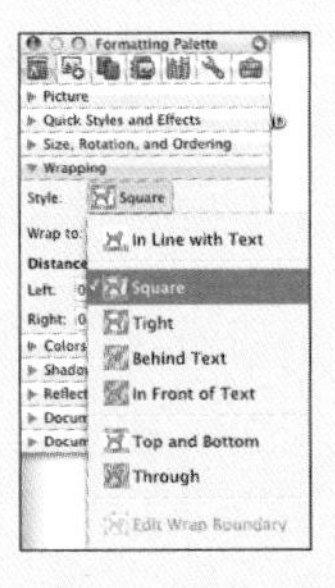

Yes. Word offers several wrapping options. For example, Square wrapping flows text around the rectangular frame of the graphic, while Tight wrapping flows text around the contours of the graphic. Click the graphic, display the Formatting Palette, open the Wrapping panel, click **Style**, and then click the wrapping style you want to use.

# Format a Picture

You can enhance your clip art and pictures by formatting the images. For example, Office for Mac offers a number of Quick Styles, which are predefined formats that apply shadows, reflections, borders, and 3-D effects. You can also apply a wide variety of special effects such as distortions and blurs.

## Format a Picture

### APPLY A QUICK STYLE

1. Select the picture you want to format.
2. Display the Formatting Palette.

*Note:* *See Chapter 3 for information on how to display the Formatting Palette.*

3. Open the Quick Styles and Effects panel.

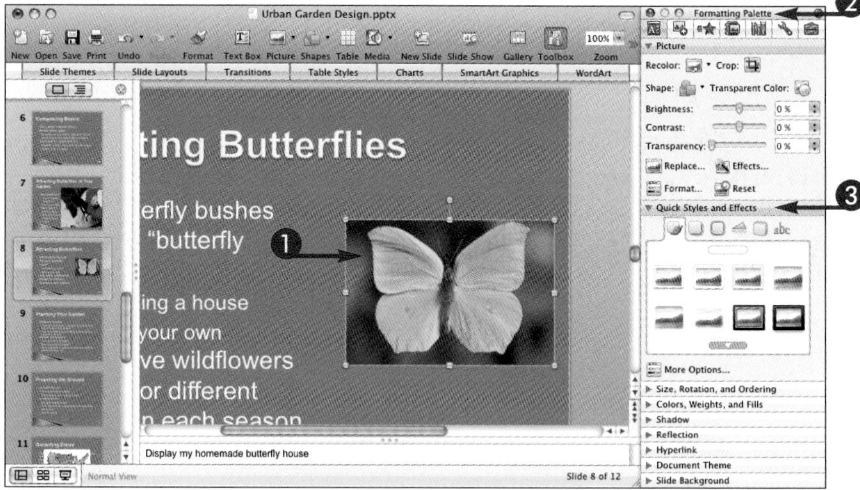


4. Click the **Quick Styles** button ( ).
5. Click the Quick Style you want to use.

- The Office program applies the Quick Style to the picture.

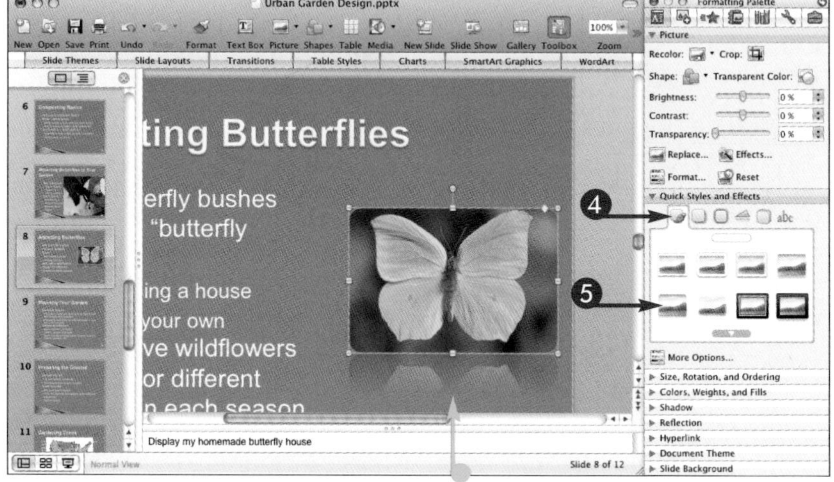

## APPLY AN IMAGE EFFECT

1. Select the picture you want to format.
2. Display the Formatting Palette.

*Note: See Chapter 3 for information on how to display the Formatting Palette.*

3. Open the Picture panel.
4. Click the **Effects** button (![]).

   The Image Effects dialog appears.

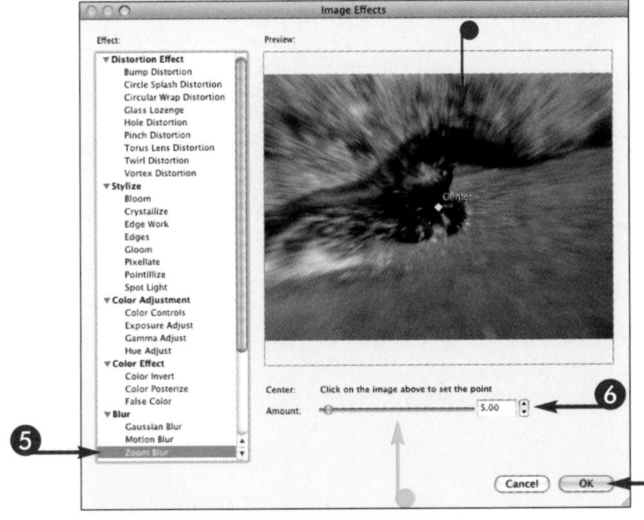


5. In the Effects list, click the effect you want to apply.

- The effect's controls appear here.

*Note: The controls that appear depend on the effect.*

6. Adjust the controls to get the effect you want.

- The Preview area shows what the effect will look like.

7. Click **OK**.

   The Office program applies the effect to the picture.

### I applied a Quick Style to a picture, but now I want to change the picture to something else. Do I have to start over?

No. You can simply replace the existing picture with the other picture, and the Office program preserves the Quick Style so you do not have to repeat your work. Click the existing picture, and then follow Steps **1** to **3** to open the Picture panel. Click the **Replace** button (![]), click the new picture you want to use, and then click **Insert**.

### I am using an image that has a solid background color that clashes with my document. Can I hide the background?

Yes. You can make the background transparent so that your document shows through. Click the picture, and then follow Steps **1** to **3** to open the Picture panel. Click the **Transparent Color** button (![]), and then click any part of the picture's background. The background changes to transparent.

# Add a Shadow or Glow to a Picture

You can give your clip art and pictures more prominence by enhancing them with either a shadow effect or a glow effect. Office 2008 for Mac offers a number of predefined shadow and glow effects, and you can apply them with just a few mouse clicks.

## Add a Shadow or Glow to a Picture

### ADD A SHADOW TO A PICTURE

1. Select the picture you want to format.
2. Display the Formatting Palette.

***Note:*** *See Chapter 3 for information on how to display the Formatting Palette.*

3. Open the Quick Styles and Effects panel.
4. Click the **Shadows** button (▢)

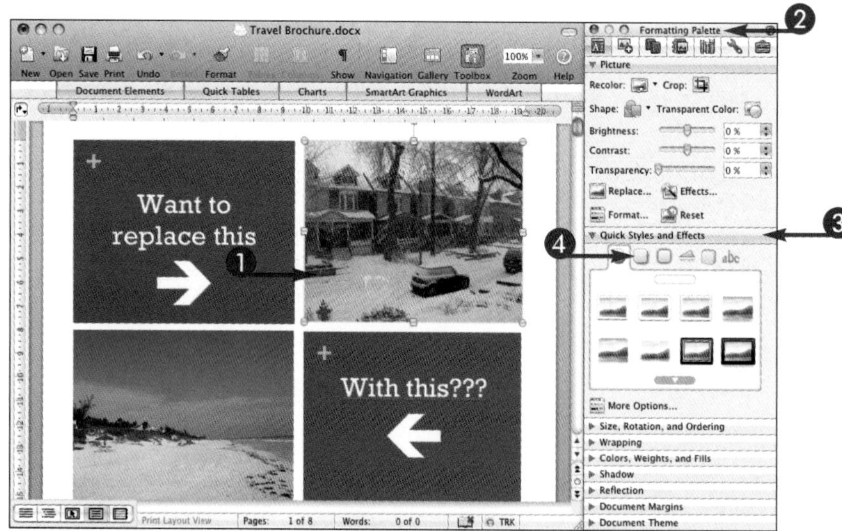

5. Click the shadow effect you want to use.

- The Office program applies the shadow to the picture.

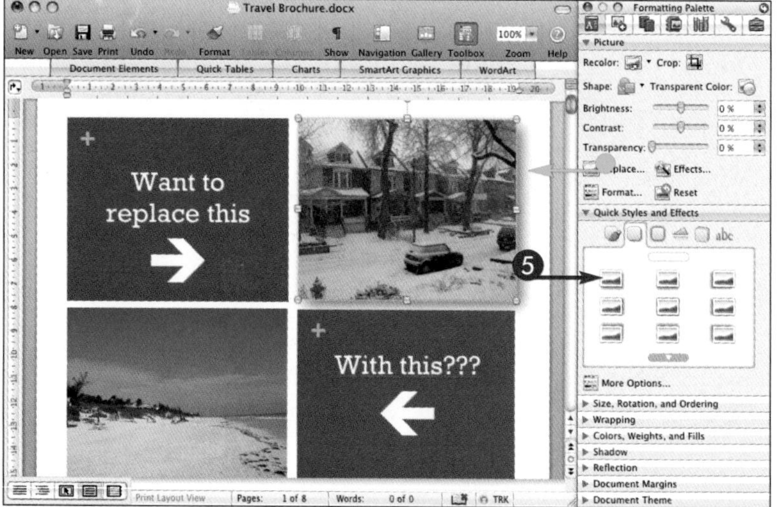

## ADD A GLOW TO A PICTURE

1. Select the picture you want to format.
2. Display the Formatting Palette.

***Note:*** *See Chapter 3 for information on how to display the Formatting Palette.*

3. Open the Quick Styles and Effects panel.
4. Click the **Glows** button (▢)

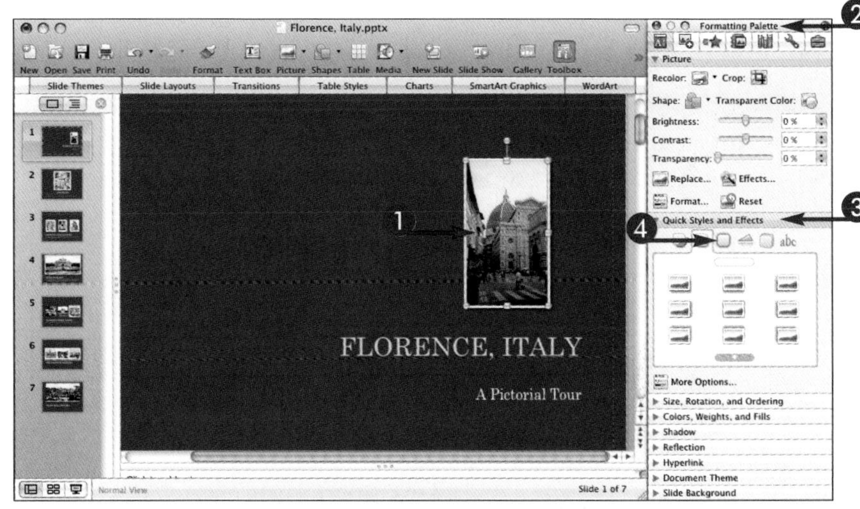

5. Click the glow effect you want to use.

- The Office program applies the glow to the picture.

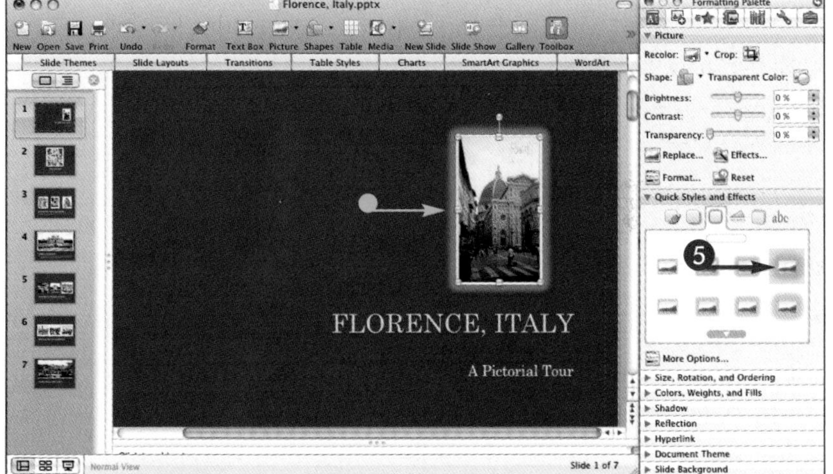

### Can I manually adjust the shadow to get the exact effect I want?

Yes. Office for Mac offers several controls that enable you to manually adjust various aspects of the shadow. Follow Steps **1** and **2** to display the Formatting Palette, and then open the Shadow panel. Use **Angle** to adjust the angle of the shadow; click **Color** to change the shadow color; use the Distance text box to set the shadow size; and click and drag the **Blur** and **Transparency** sliders to set the look of the shadow.

### How do I remove a shadow or glow from a picture?

If you no longer require a shadow or glow effect, you can remove it. If the effect was the last thing you did, click **Undo** in the Standard toolbar to reverse it. Otherwise, to remove a shadow, follow Steps **1** to **4** in the section "Add a Shadow to a Picture," and then click the **No Shadow** button. To remove a glow, follow Steps **1** to **4** in the section "Add a Glow to a Picture," and then click the **No Glow** icon.

# Add a Reflection or 3-D Effect to a Picture

You can make your clip art and pictures stand out by enhancing them with either a reflection effect or a 3-D effect. Office 2008 for Mac offers a number of predefined reflection and 3-D effects, and you can apply them with just a few mouse clicks.

## Add a Reflection or 3-D Effect to a Picture

### ADD A REFLECTION TO A PICTURE

1. Select the picture you want to format.
2. Display the Formatting Palette.

***Note:*** *See Chapter 3 for information on how to display the Formatting Palette.*

3. Open the Quick Styles and Effects panel.
4. Click the **Reflections** button (  ).

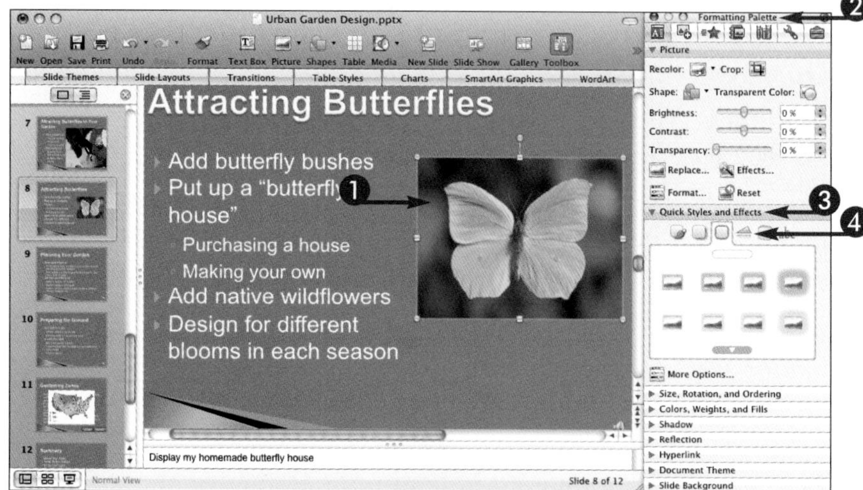


5. Click the reflection effect you want to use.

- The Office program applies the reflection to the picture.

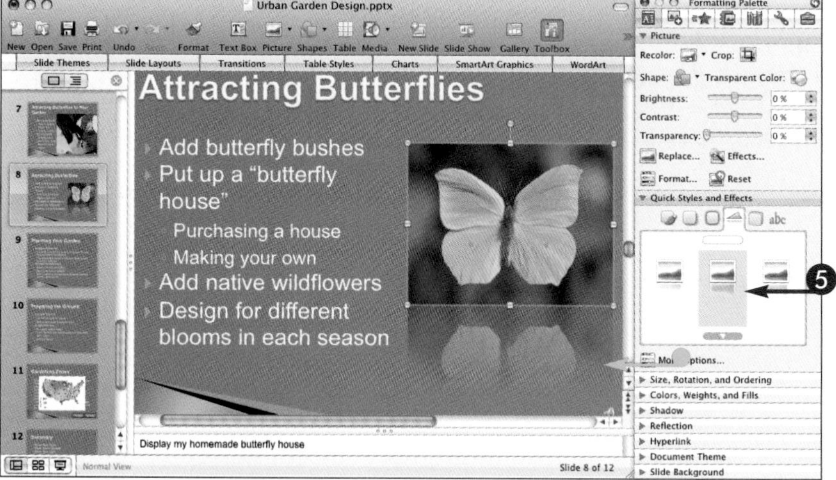

## ADD A 3-D EFFECT TO A PICTURE

1. Select the picture you want to format.
2. Display the Formatting Palette.

*Note:* *See Chapter 3 for information on how to display the Formatting Palette.*

3. Open the Quick Styles and Effects panel.
4. Click the **3-D Effects** button (▢)

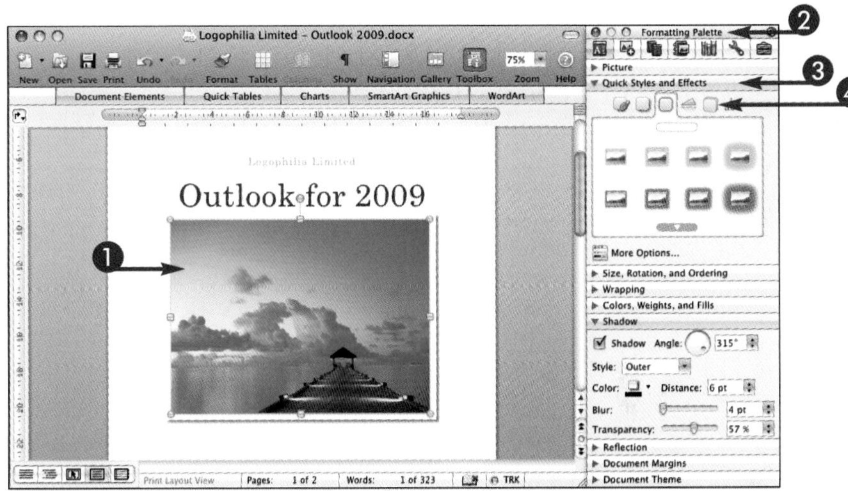

5. Click the 3-D effect you want to use.

- The Office program applies the 3-D effect to the picture.

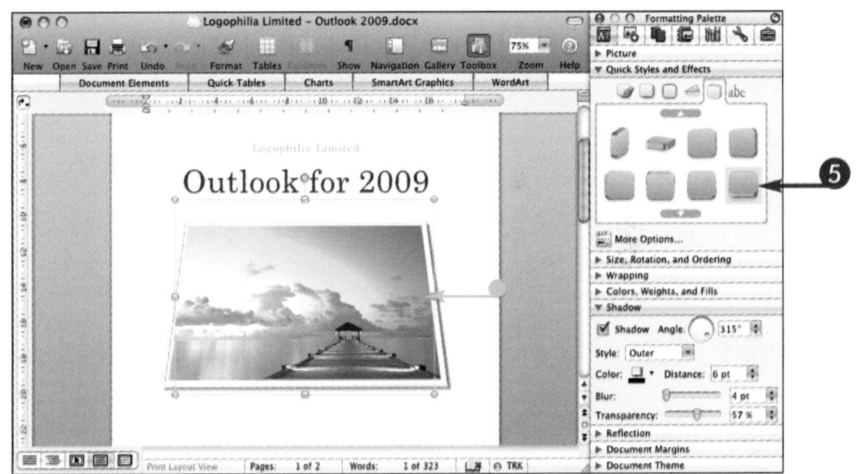

## TIPS

### Can I manually adjust the 3-D settings to get the exact effect I want?

Yes. Office for Mac offers several controls that enable you to manually adjust various aspects of a 3-D effect. Follow Steps **1** to **3** to display the Quick Styles and Effects panel, and then click **More Options**. In the Format Picture dialog, click the **3-D Format** tab to set the location and size of the bevel, and click the **3-D Rotation** tab to adjust the 3-D angle and perspective.

### How do I remove a reflection or 3-D effect from a picture?

If you no longer need to use a reflection or 3-D effect, you can remove it. If the effect was the last thing you did, click the **Undo** button in the Standard toolbar to reverse it. Otherwise, to remove a reflection, follow Steps **1** to **4** in the section "Add a Reflection to a Picture," and then click the **No Reflection** button. To remove a 3-D effect, follow Steps **1** to **4** in the section "Add a 3-D Effect to a Picture," and then click the **No 3-D** button.

# Recolor an Image

You can modify the colors in an image to get the effect you want. For example, you can change a picture to black and white or you can apply a sepia effect to make the photo look older. You can also apply one of the document's theme colors to help get the image to match the document. This is known as *recoloring* the image.

## Recolor an Image

1. Select the image you want to recolor.
2. Display the Formatting Palette.

***Note:*** *See Chapter 3 for information on how to display the Formatting Palette.*

3. Open the Picture panel.

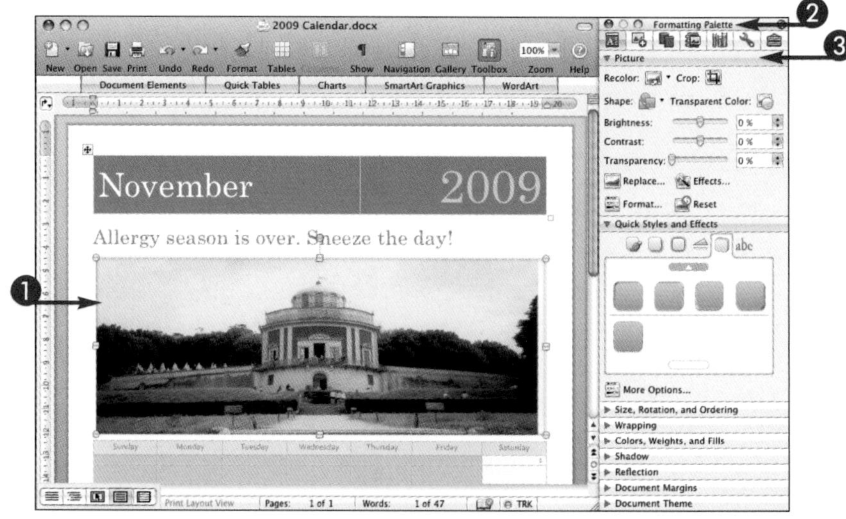


4. Click the **Recolor** button.

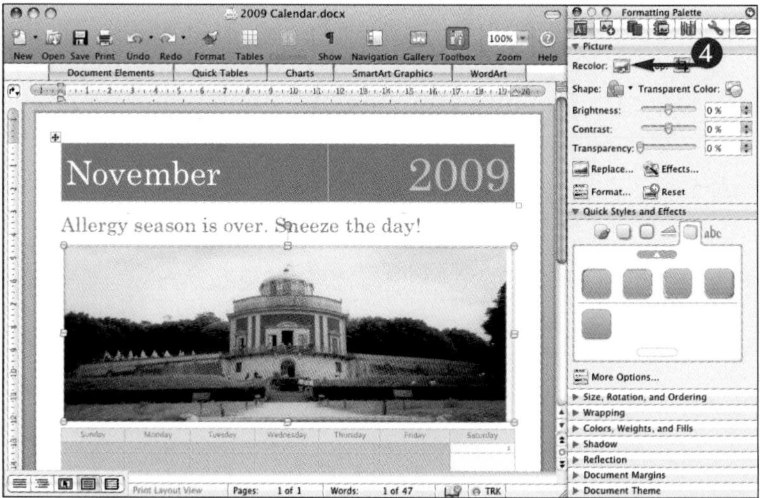

5. Click the color effect you want to apply.

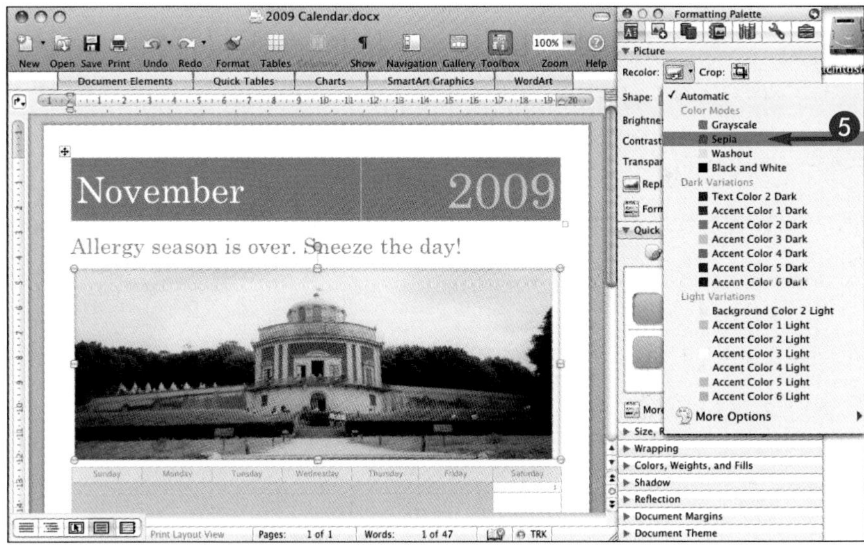

- The Office application recolors the image.

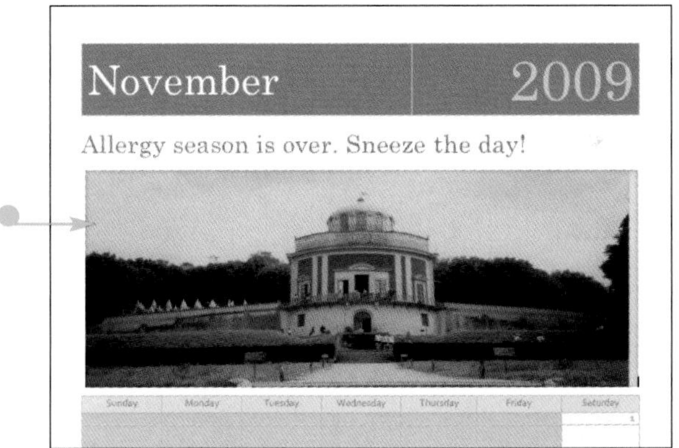

## TIP

**Can I use the Washout option to format a picture for use as a watermark?**

Yes. Remember, first, that Word has a Watermark command that does this automatically. However, if you want to add an image watermark to a PowerPoint slide, follow Steps **1** to **4** and then click **Washout** in the Color Modes list.

To make the image a true watermark, follow Steps **1** to **3**, open the **Size, Rotation, and Ordering** panel, click **Arrange**, and then click **Send to Back**.

# CHAPTER 5

# Inserting Text and Other Items

Microsoft Word is a simple program in the sense that it is easy to get started: You just create a new document and then start typing. Of course, not all Word documents consist of basic text. For example, you might require a bulleted or numbered list, special symbols such as © or ™, or document elements such as page breaks and page numbers. This chapter shows you how to insert these and other items into your Word documents.

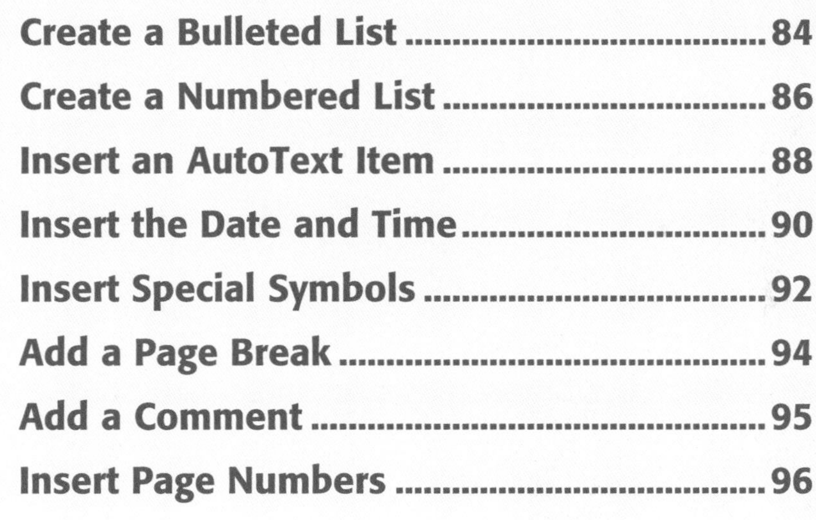

# Create a Bulleted List

You can make a list of items more prominent and more readable by inserting those items as a bulleted list. This tells Word to format the items slightly indented from the regular text, with a small character — called the *bullet*, which is usually a black dot — in front of each item.

**Word enables you to convert an existing list of items to a bulleted list. Also, you can customize the amount each item is indented and the bullet character used in the list.**

## Create a Bulleted List

1. If you want to convert existing text to a bulleted list, select the text.

**Note:** *The text must be a series of items, of any length, each in its own paragraph.*

2. Display the Formatting Palette.

**Note:** *See Chapter 3 for information on how to display the Formatting Palette.*

3. Open the Bullets and Numbering panel.
4. Click the **Bullets** button.

- If you selected your text in advance, Word converts the text to a bulleted list.

5. To choose a different bullet style, click in the Style list and then click a bullet style.
6. To change the bullet indentation, click the **Decrease Indent** button or the **Increase Indent** button.

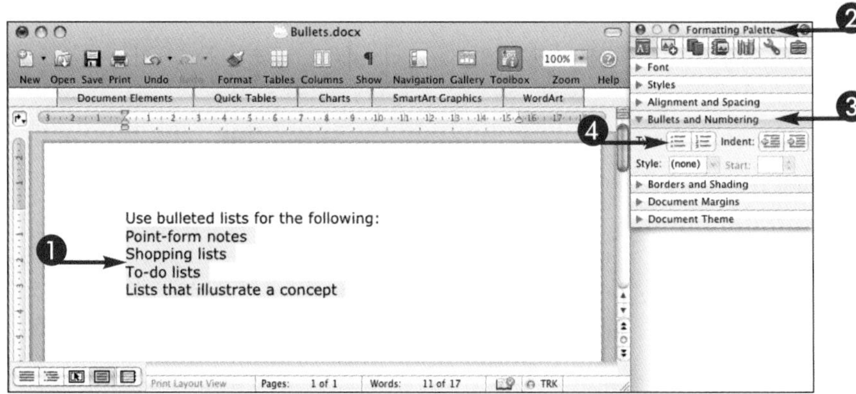


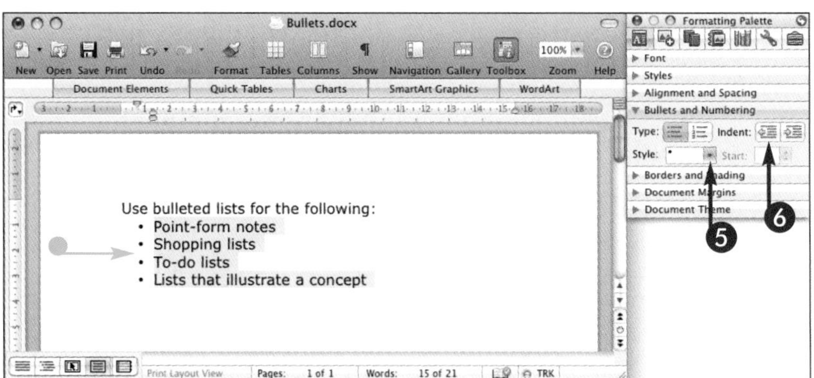

7. If you selected text in advance, click at the end of the last item.
8. Press Return.

- Word creates a new item in the bulleted list.

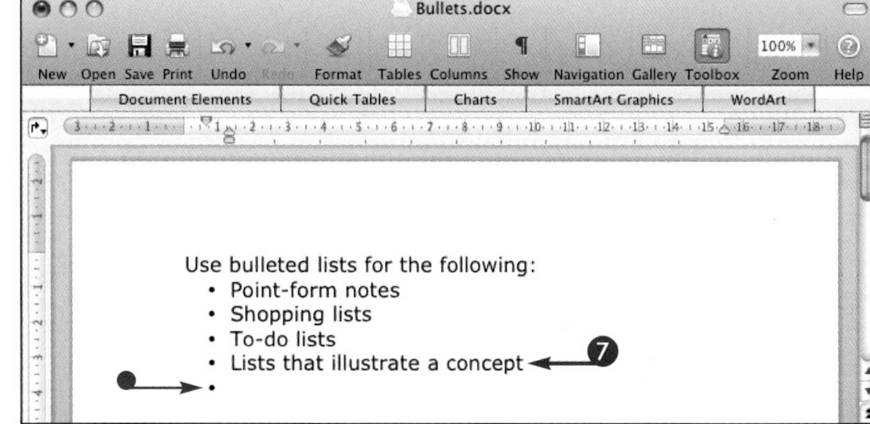


9. Type the text for the new list item.
10. Repeat Steps **8** and **9** to complete the bulleted list.
11. Press Return twice.

Word ends the bulleted list.

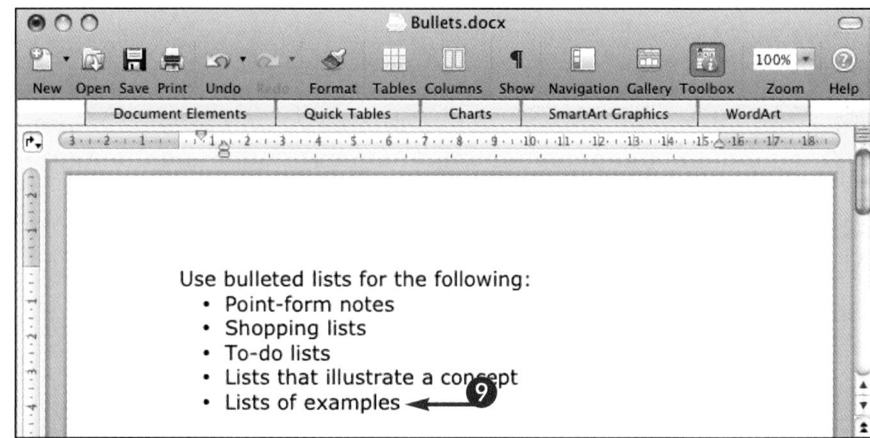

### How can I use a custom character or picture as the bullet?

If you require a custom character or image, follow these steps:

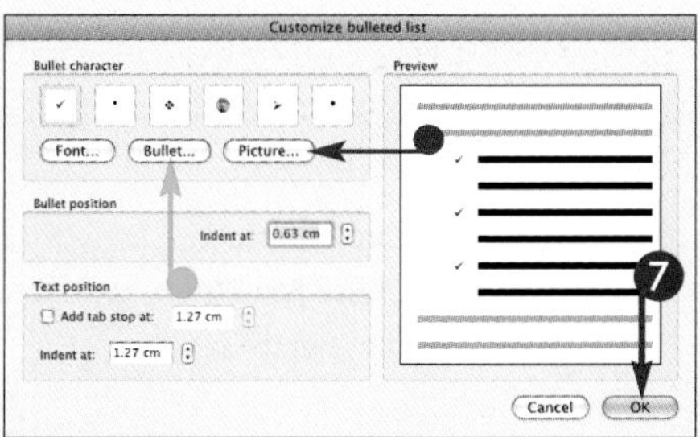


1. Select the bulleted list.
2. Click **Format** in the menu bar.
3. Click **Bullets and Numbering**.
4. In the Bullets and Numbering dialog, click the **Bulleted** tab.
5. Click the built-in bullet style that you want to customize.
6. Click **Customize**.

   The Customize Bulleted List dialog appears.

- To choose a custom character, click **Bullet**, use the Symbol dialog to click the character, and then click **OK**.
- To choose a custom image, click **Picture**, use the Choose a Picture dialog to click the image, and then click **Insert**.

7. Click **OK**.

# Create a Numbered List

You can make a set of steps or an ordered list more readable and easier to follow by creating those items as a numbered list. This tells Word to format the items slightly indented from the regular text, with a number in front of each item. The numbers increase sequentially, usually from 1 to the total number of items in the list.

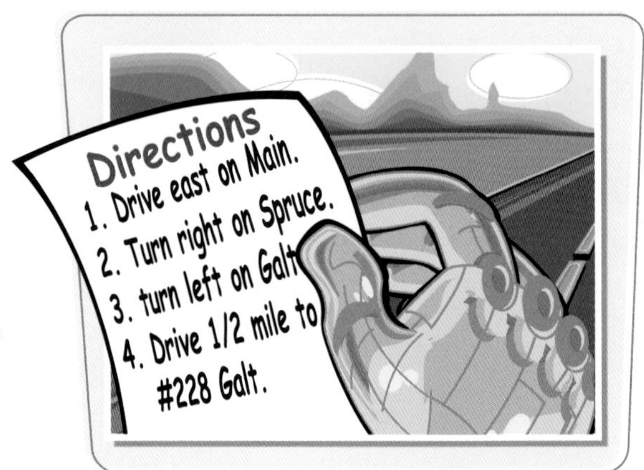


**Word enables you to convert an existing list of items to a numbered list. Also, you can customize the amount each item is indented, the style of the numbers, and the starting value of the numbers.**

## Create a Numbered List

1. If you want to convert existing text to a numbered list, select the text.

***Note:*** *The text must be a series of items, of any length, each in its own paragraph.*

2. Display the Formatting Palette.

***Note:*** *See Chapter 3 for information on how to display the Formatting Palette.*

3. Open the Bullets and Numbering panel.
4. Click the **Numbering** button.

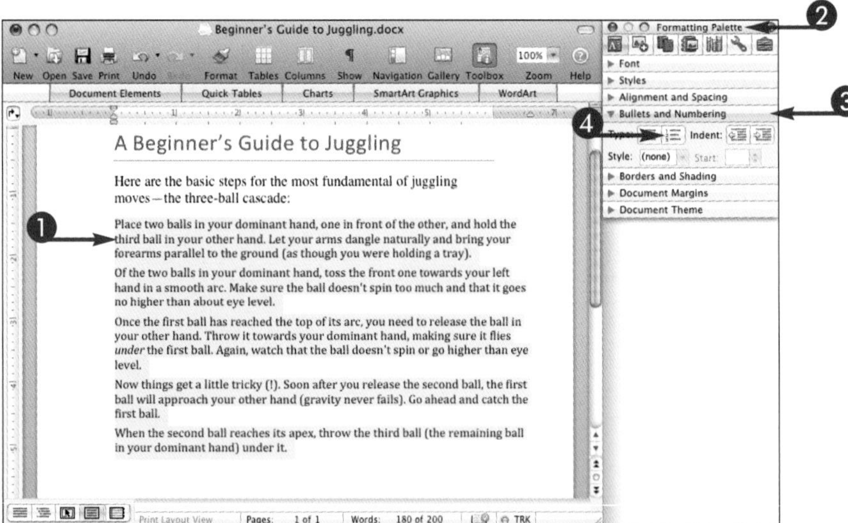


- If you selected text in advance, Word converts the text to a numbered list.

5. To choose a different number style, click ▾ in the Style list and then click a bullet style.
6. To change the starting number, type the value in the Start text box.
7. To change the indentation, click the **Decrease Indent** button or the **Increase Indent** button.

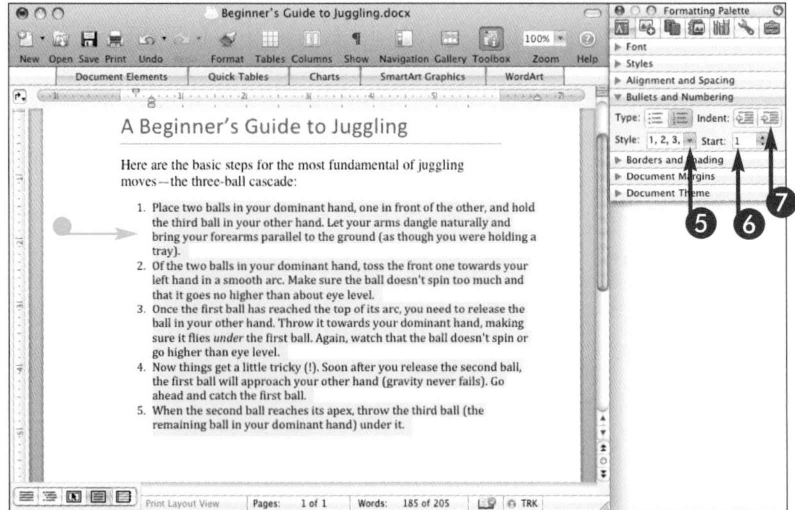

8. If you selected text in advance, click at the end of the last item.
9. Press Return.

● Word creates a new item in the numbered list.

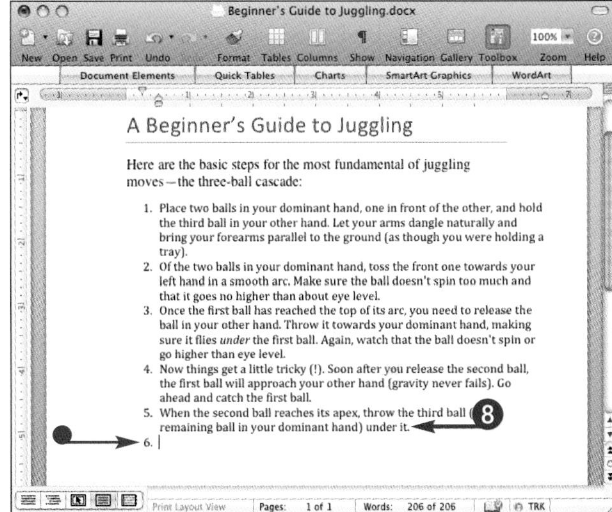


10. Type the text for the new list item.
11. Repeat Steps **8** and **9** to complete the numbered list.
12. Press Return twice.

Word ends the numbered list.

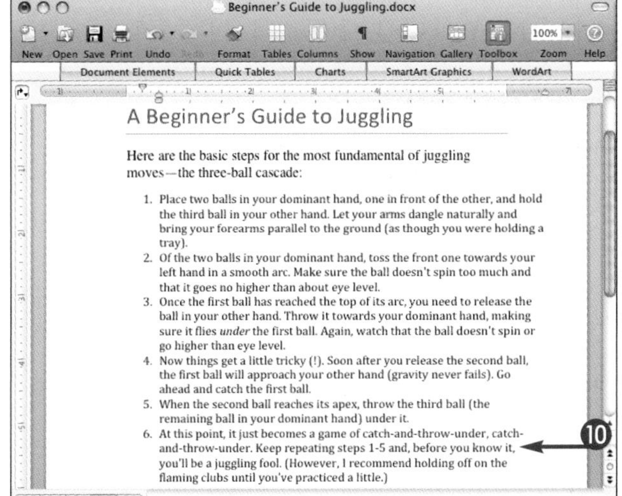

**If I interrupt my numbered list with some text or an image, how do I continue the numbering in the second part of the list?**

1. Select the second part of the bulleted list.
2. Click **Format** in the menu bar.
3. Click **Bullets and Numbering.**
4. Click the **Numbered** tab.
5. Select the **Continue previous list** option (○ changes to ◉).
6. Click **OK.**

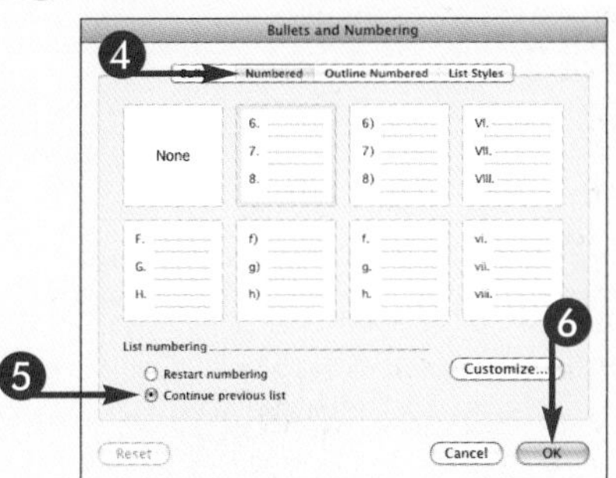

# Insert an AutoText Item

You can save yourself time and finger fatigue when typing by taking advantage of Word's AutoText feature. This feature enables you to insert certain predefined phrases just by typing a few characters.

**If you have certain phrases that you type repeatedly, you can create your own AutoText entries for those phrases.**

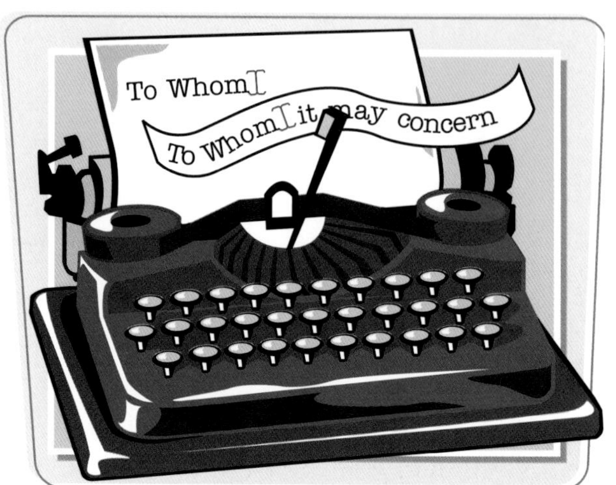


## Insert an AutoText Item

### INSERT AN AUTOTEXT ENTRY

1. Begin typing the AutoText entry.

- Word displays a banner that shows the rest of the AutoText entry.

***Note:*** *Depending on the entry, Word displays the AutoText banner after you type between three and five characters.*

2. Press Return.

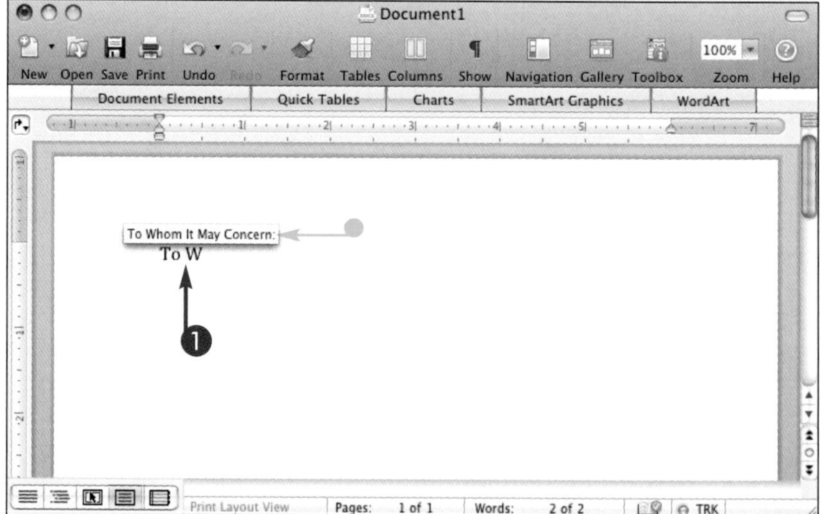


- Word inserts the full AutoText entry.

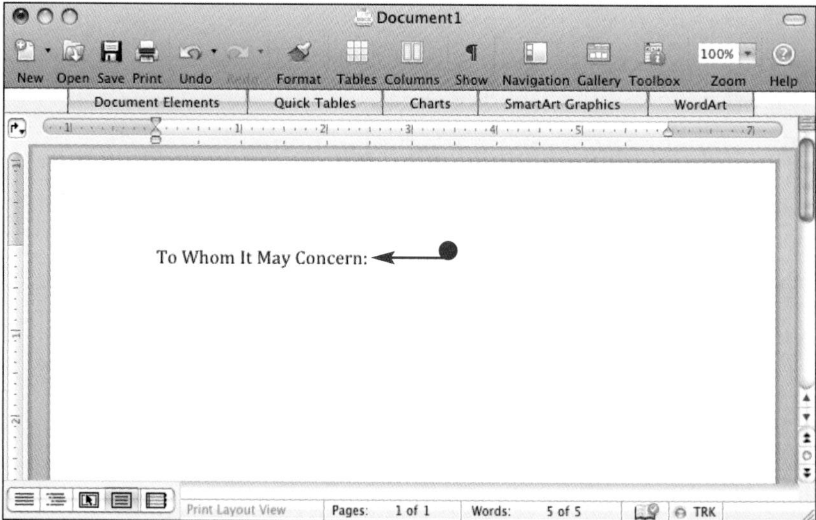

#### CREATE AN AUTOTEXT ENTRY

1. Select the text that you want to define as an AutoText entry.
2. Click **Insert**.
3. Click **AutoText**.
4. Click **New**.

The Create AutoText dialog appears.

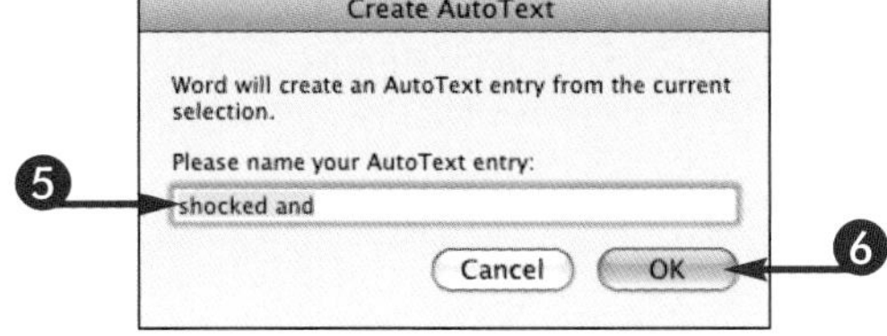


5. Edit the text in the Please name your AutoText entry text box, if desired.
6. Click **OK**.

Word saves your AutoText entry.

The next time you type the first few characters of the AutoText entry name, Word displays the entry in an AutoText banner.

### Can I insert AutoText entries from a list?

Yes. Word maintains a list of all the predefined and custom AutoText entries, and that list is available via the menu system. Click **Insert**, click **AutoText**, click a category such as **Salutation** or **Closing**, and then click the entry you want to insert. You can also choose entries from the AutoText toolbar. Click **View**, click **Toolbars**, and then click **AutoText**.

### How do I delete AutoText entries?

You can delete any of the predefined AutoText entries or any of the custom entries you create. Click **Insert**, click **AutoText**, and then click **AutoText** to display the AutoCorrect dialog. Click the **AutoText** tab. Select the entry you want to remove from the Enter AutoText entries here list and then click **Delete**.

# Insert the Date and Time

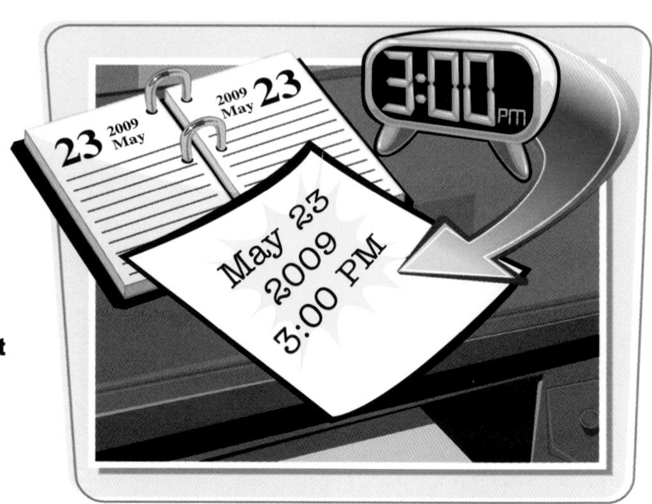


If you are writing a letter, memo, or other document that requires the current date, the current time, or both, you can save a bit of time by having Word insert that data for you.

**You can tell Word to enter the date or time as a special object called a *field*, which Word updates automatically to the current date and time whenever you open the document.**

## Insert the Date and Time

1. Click inside the document at the spot where you want the date and time to appear.

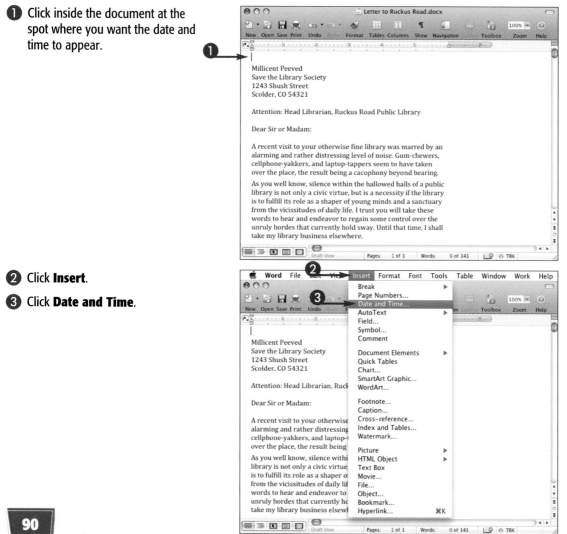

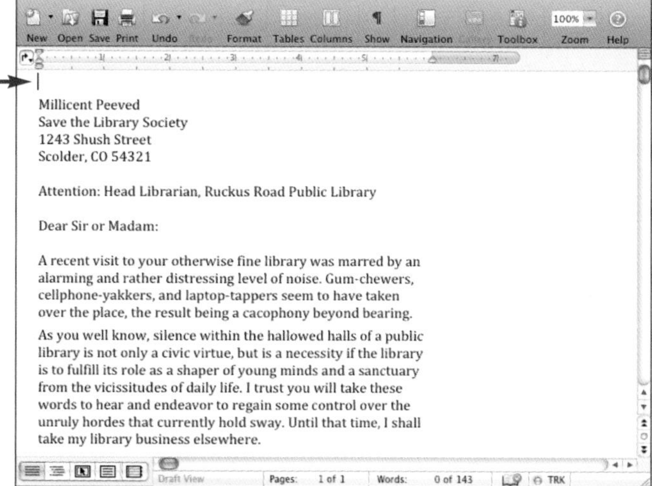


2. Click **Insert**.
3. Click **Date and Time**.

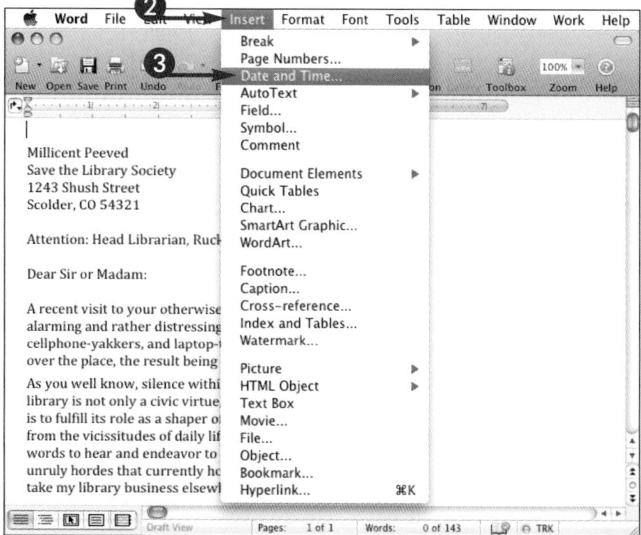

The Date and Time dialog appears.

4. Select the date and time format you want to use in the Available formats list.

- If you always want Word to use this format, click **Default** and then click **Yes**.

5. If you want Word to update the date and time whenever you open the document, select the **Update automatically** check box (☐ changes to ☑).

6. Click **OK**.

- Word inserts the date and time using the format you choose.

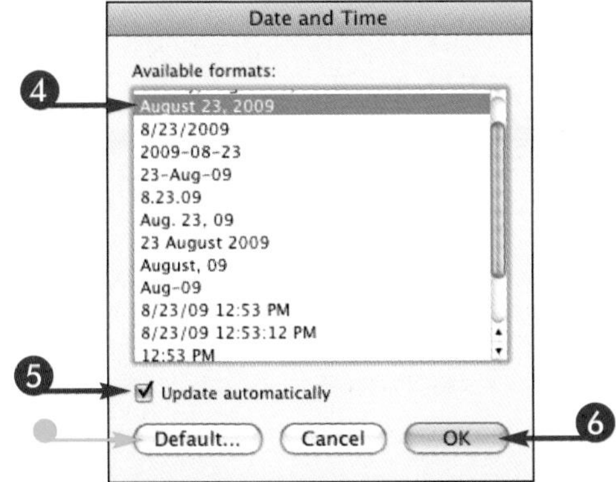


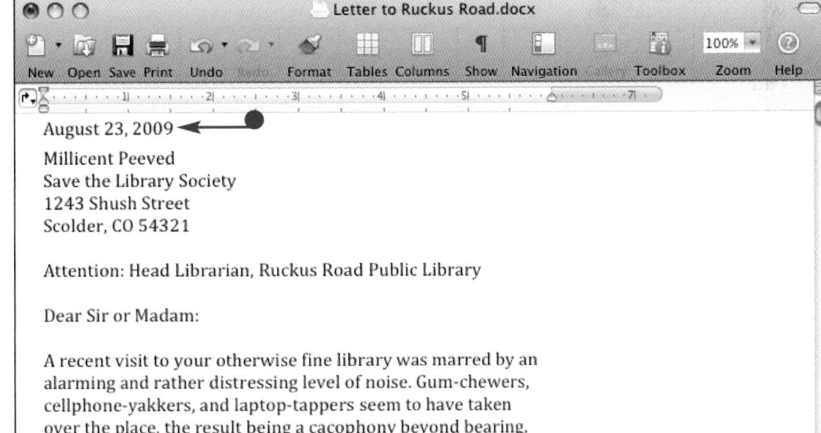

### Are there any keyboard shortcuts I can use to insert the current date or time?

Yes. For the date, type the first few characters of the current month name (such as **augu** for August), and then press Return when Word displays the month name in an AutoText banner. (Note that this does not work for short month names, such as May and June.) Press ‘ace and then press Return when Word displays the current date in an AutoText banner. To insert the current date as a field, press Ctrl + Shift + D; to insert the current time as a field, press Ctrl + Shift + T

### How can I update a date field manually?

Normally Word only updates the field the next time you open the document. If you need to update the date and time after opening the document, Word gives you a couple of methods to use. You can either right-click (or Ctrl +click) the field and then click **Update Field**, or you can click inside the field and then press Option + Shift + ⌘ + U.

# Insert Special Symbols

You can make your Word documents more readable and more useful by inserting special symbols that are not available via your keyboard's standard keys.

**These special symbols include foreign characters such as ö and é, mathematical symbols such as ÷ and ∞, financial symbols such as ¢ and ¥, commercial symbols such as © and ®, and many more.**

## Insert Special Symbols

1. Click inside the document at the spot where you want the symbol to appear.

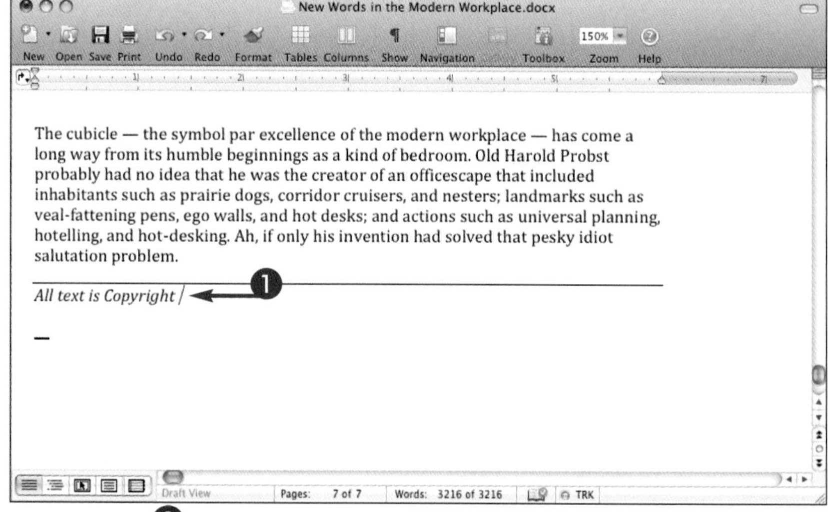


2. Click **Insert**.
3. Click **Symbol**.

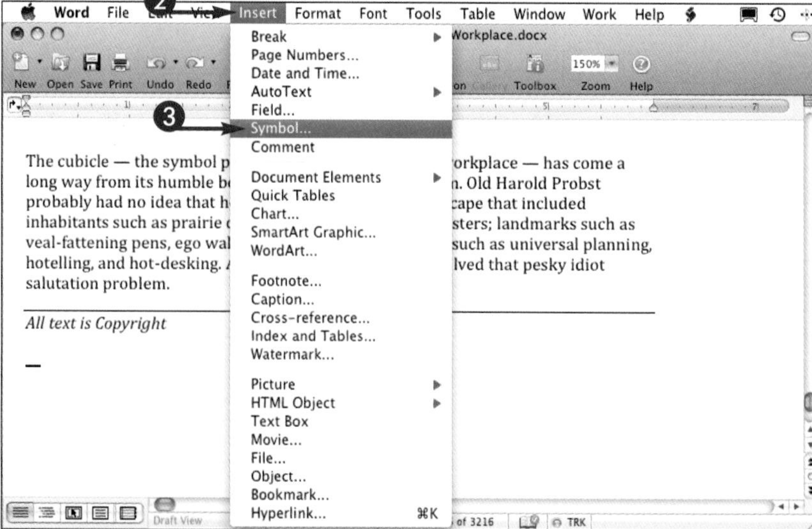

The Symbol dialog appears.

4. Click the **Symbols** tab.
5. In the **Font** pop-up menu, click ⬍, and then click **(normal text)**.
6. Click the symbol you want to insert.

***Note:*** *Many other symbols are available in the Webdings and Wingdings fonts. To see these symbols, click the* ***Font*** ⬍*, and then click either* ***Webdings*** *or* ***Wingdings****.*

7. Click **Insert**.

- Word inserts the symbol.

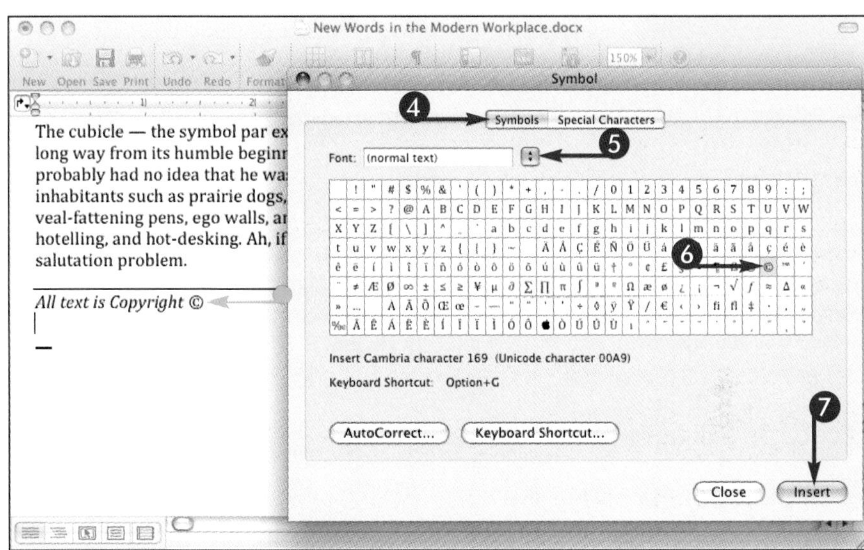


8. Repeat Steps **6** and **7** to insert any other symbols you require.
9. Click **Close**.

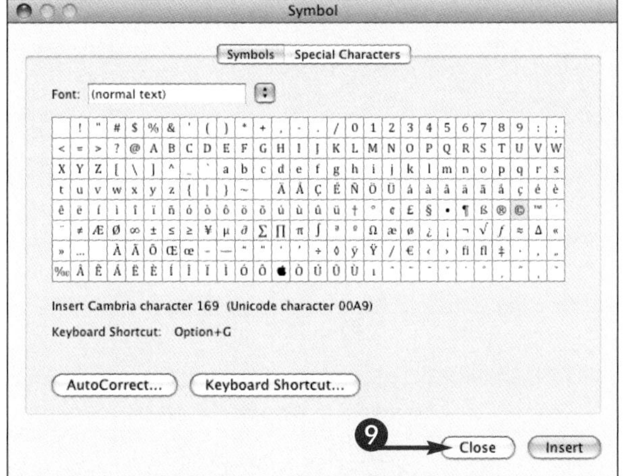

## Is there an easier way to insert symbols that I use frequently?

Yes. Your Mac offers keyboard shortcuts for many symbols. When you click a symbol in the Symbol dialog, examine the Keyboard Shortcut area, which tells you whether a shortcut is available. Here are some examples:

| To Insert This | Press This | To Insert This | Press This |
|---|---|---|---|
| © | Option + G | £ | Option + 3 |
| ® | Option + R | ¢ | Option + 4 |
| ™ | Option + 2 | ÷ | Option + / |
| ¥ | Option + Y | ∞ | Option + 5 |

# Add a Page Break

You can often gain more control over your document text by adding a page break. Word normally starts a new page when the current page is full of text or other data. A page break is a special symbol that tells Word to start a new page, even if the previous page is not full.

**Use a page break when you want to force a particular part of your document to start on a new page. For example, if you start a major new section of your document, you might want that section to start on a new page.**

## Add a Page Break

1. Position the insertion point cursor at the beginning of the paragraph that you want to appear at the top of the new page.
2. Click **Insert**.
3. Click **Break**.
4. Click **Page Break**.

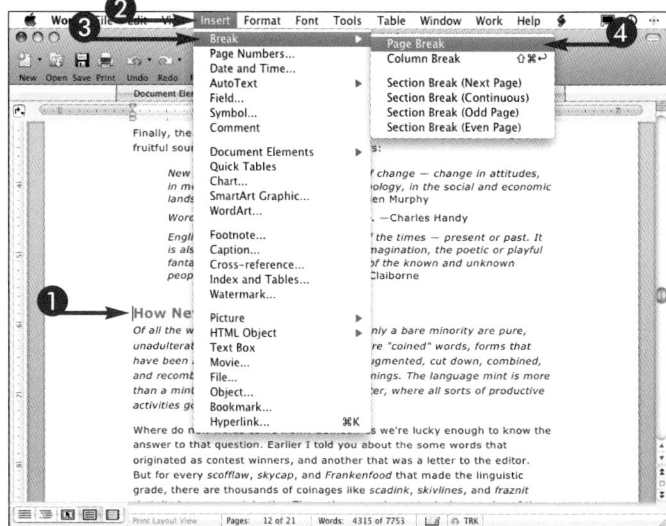

- Word inserts the page break.

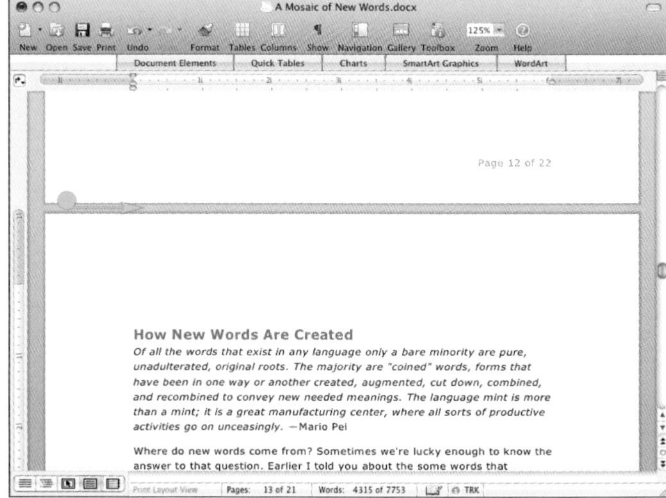

# Add a Comment

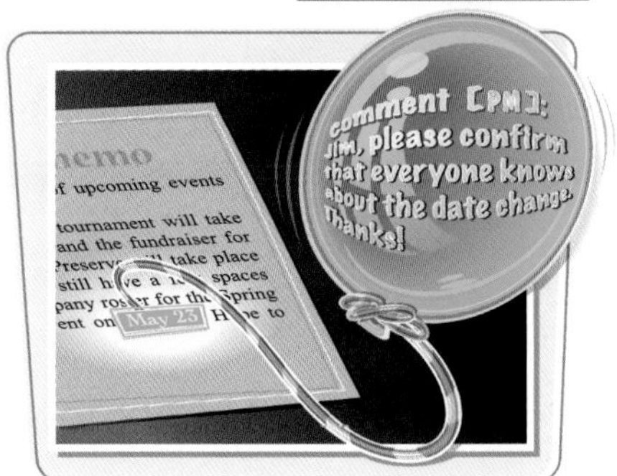


To add notes, commentary, questions, and other feedback to a document without modifying the document text, use Word's Comments feature. The comment text appears off to the side, so it does not affect the existing document text.

**Use comments when you want to remind yourself to edit a section or look up a fact. Comments are also very useful when you collaborate with other people, because they enable you or others you collaborate with to provide feedback on a document.**

## Add a Comment

1. Select the text you want to comment on.
2. Click **Insert**.
3. Click **Comment**.

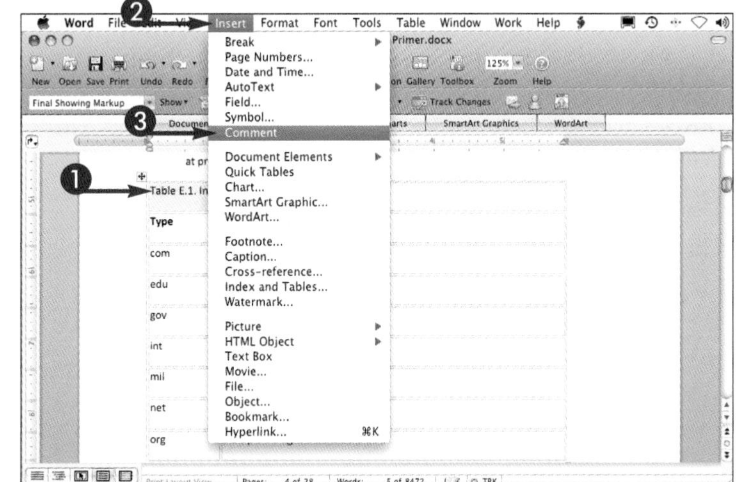


- Word inserts a comment balloon.
- Word displays the Reviewing toolbar.

4. Type your comment.

- With the Reviewing toolbar displayed, you can add another comment by selecting the text and then clicking **New Comment**.

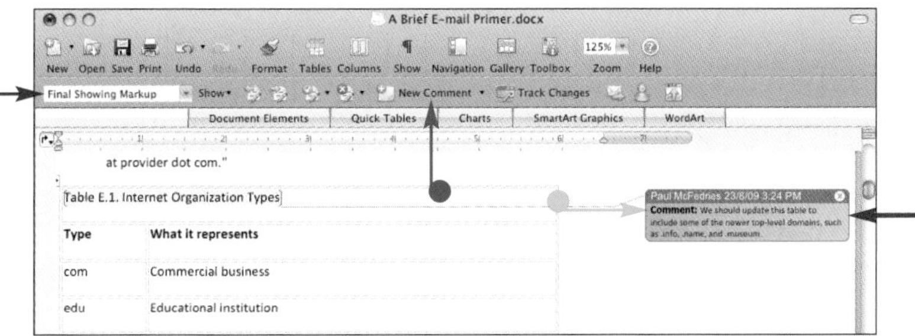

# Insert Page Numbers

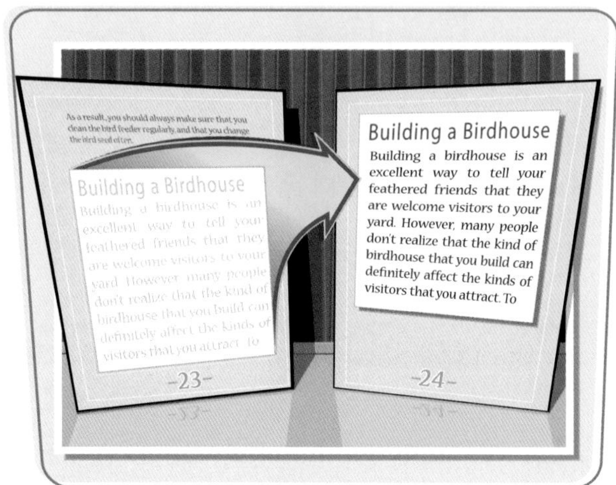


You can make it easier to navigate a long document by inserting page numbers at the top or bottom of each page. Page numbers are also useful if you print a long document, because they help you keep the printed pages in order.

**Page numbers are also useful if you share a long document with another person. By having page numbers, the other person can refer to specific pages, which enables you to more quickly locate the relevant part of the document.**

## Insert Page Numbers

1. Click **Insert**.
2. Click **Page Numbers**.

   The Page Numbers dialog appears.

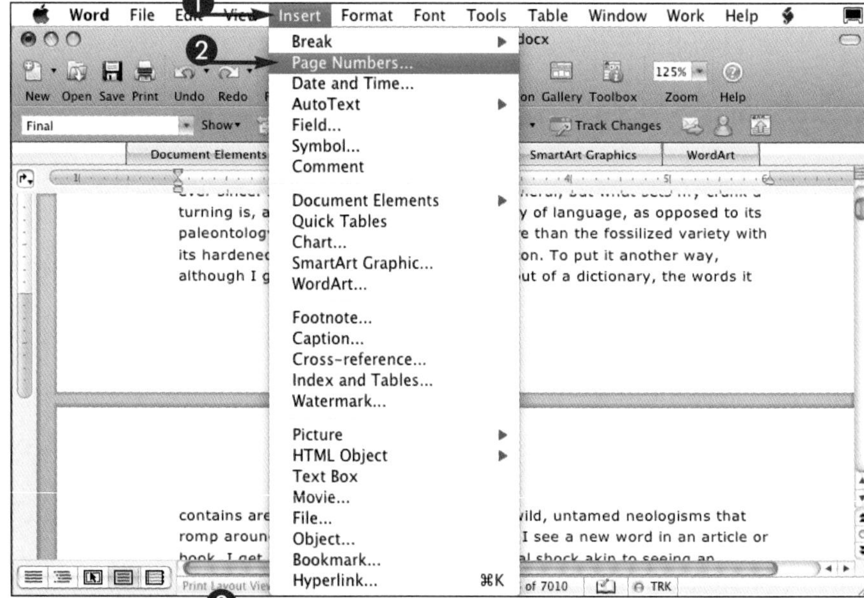


3. Click ⬍ in the Position pop-up menu, and then select where you want the page numbers to appear.

   You can select **Bottom of page (Footer)** or **Top of page (Header)**.

4. Click ⬍ in the Alignment pop-up menu, and then select where you want the page numbers aligned within the header or footer.

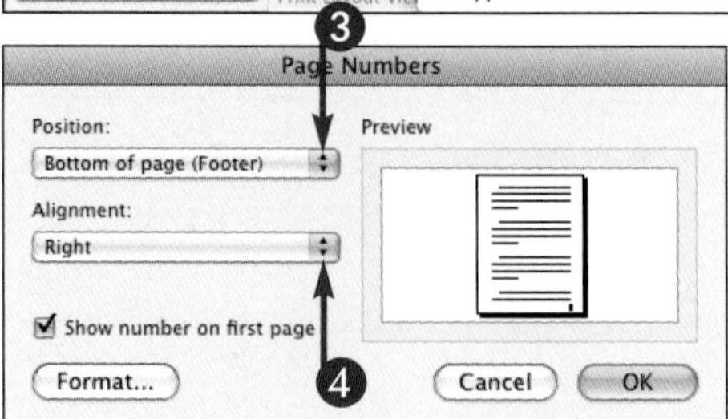

5 If you want the page number to appear on the first page of the document, select the **Show number on first page** option (☐ changes to ☑).

6 Click **OK**.

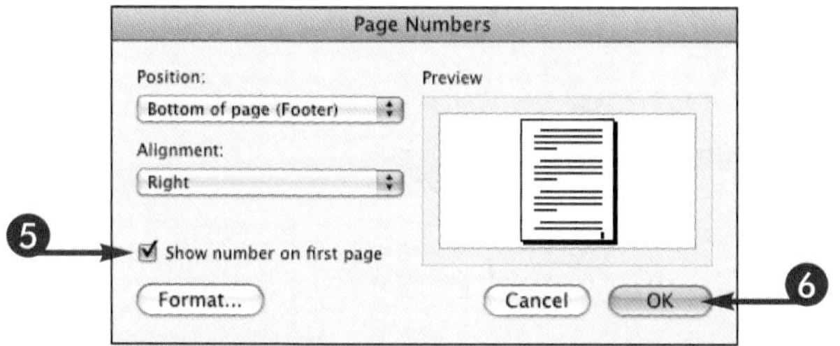


- Word inserts the page numbers.

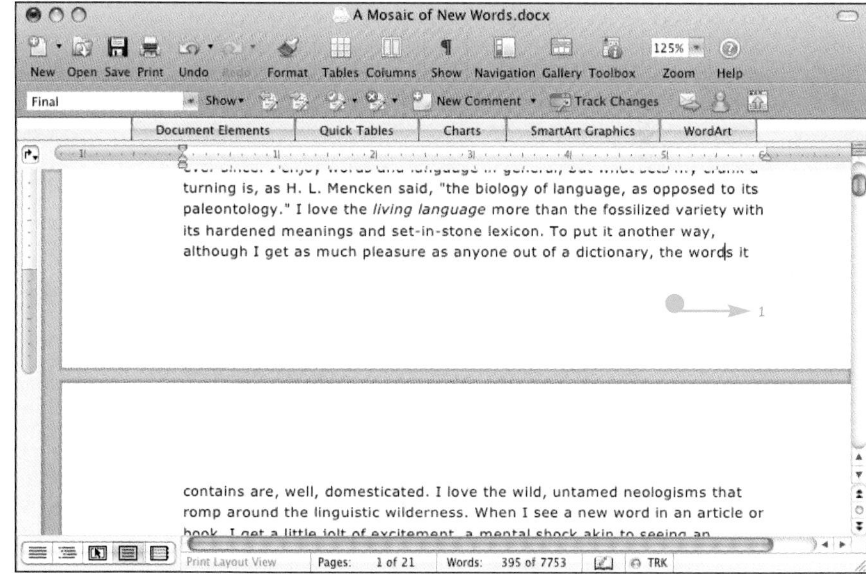

## TIPS

### How can I change the format used by the page numbers?

Word offers several page number formats. To change the format, follow Steps **1** and **2** to display the Page Numbers dialog. Click **Format** to display the Page Number Format dialog. In the Number format pop-up menu, click ⬍, and then click the format you want to use. Click **OK** to return to the Page Numbers dialog, and then click **OK**.

### Can I also show the total number of pages along with each page number?

Yes. You can insert a Page *X* of *Y* element into the footer, where *X* is the current page number and *Y* is the total number of pages in the document. Click **View** and then click **Header and Footer** to activate the document's headers and footers. Click inside any footer. Click **Insert**, click **AutoText**, and then click **Page X of Y**. Word inserts the element into each footer. Click the footer's **Close** tab.

# CHAPTER 6

# Formatting Word Documents

It's a 50th
Birthday
Celebration
honoring Louise !
May 26th, 2pm
in the Breakroom.


Plain documents are often useful, but most of the time you will need to improve the look and readability of your Word documents by formatting them. In this chapter you learn how to apply text effects, set paragraph spacing and indents, add borders, set tabs and margins, apply styles and themes, and more.

# Apply Text Effects

You can add visual interest to your Word documents by taking advantage of Word's various text effects. These effects include common formatting such as strikethrough and subscripts, but also fancier looks such as shadows, outlines, embossing, and engraving.

**Embossing formats the text to look as though it is raised slightly from the document; engraving formats the text to look as though it is etched into the document.**

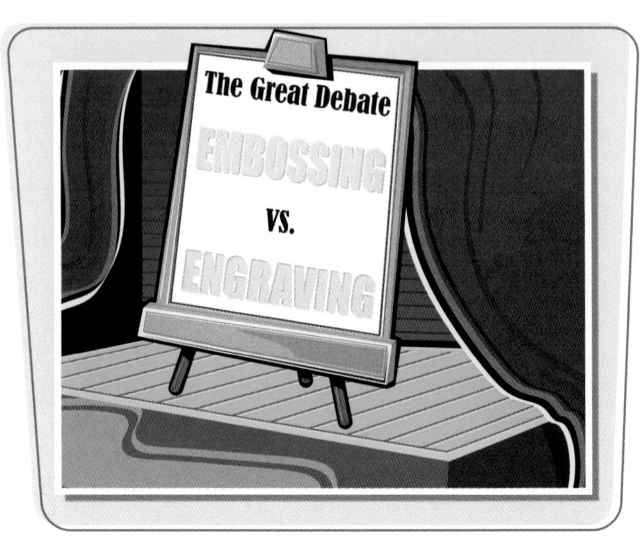


## Apply Text Effects

1. Select the text you want to format.
2. Click **Format**.
3. Click **Font**.

***Note:*** *You can also press* ⌘ + D.

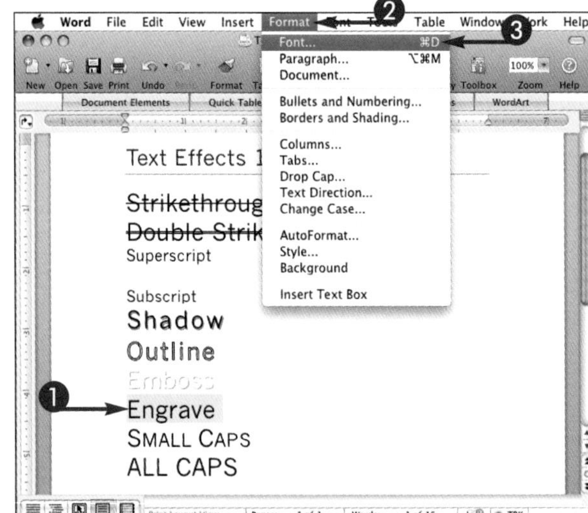

The Font dialog appears.

4. In the Effects section, select the options for each text effect you want to apply (☐ changes to ☑).

***Note:*** *Some of the effects are mutually exclusive and so cannot be applied together. For example, you cannot apply both the Emboss and the Engrave effects.*

- The Preview area shows what the text effect will look like.

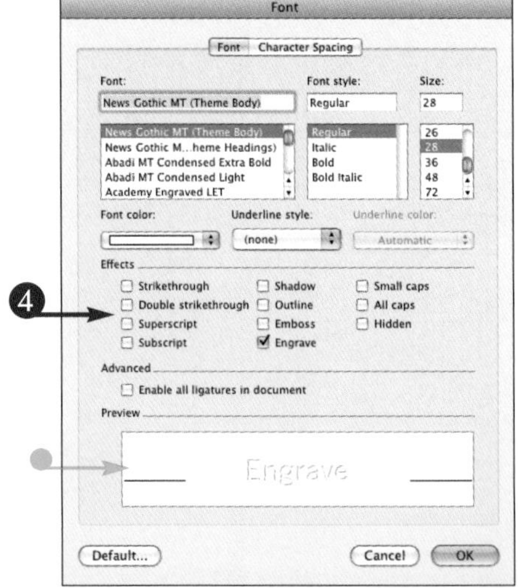

5. Apply any other font formatting that you require.
6. Click **OK**.

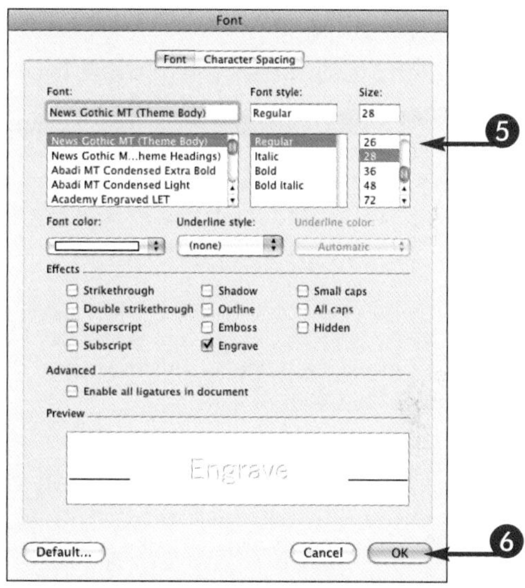

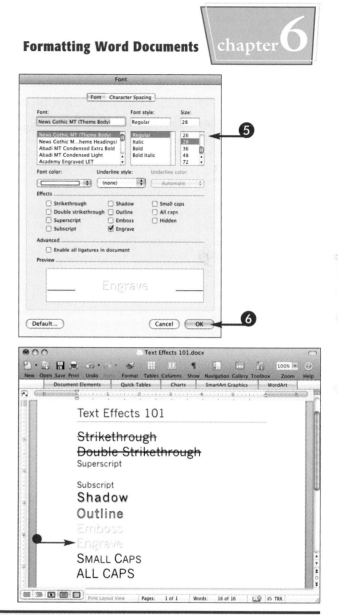

- Word applies the formatting to the selected text.

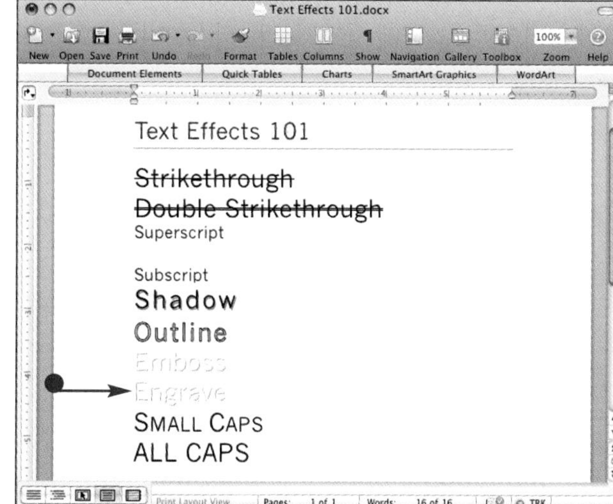

TIP

**Are there faster ways to apply text effects?**

Yes. Many of the effects have Toolbox buttons in the Formatting Palette, and some of them also have keyboard shortcuts:

| *Effect* | *Toolbox Button* | *Keyboard Shortcut* |
|---|---|---|
| Strikethrough | ABC | None |
| Subscript | A2 | ⌘ + = |
| Superscript | A2 | Shift + ⌘ + = |
| Small Caps | ABC | Shift + ⌘ + K |
| All Caps | aA | Shift + ⌘ + A |

# Set a Tab

You can easily align your document text by setting one or more *tab stops,* or just *tabs.* A tab means that when you press the Tab key, Word advances the cursor to the tab location and subsequent text begins there. By applying tabs to multiple paragraphs, you can create columns of text that are aligned vertically.

**By default, text is left-aligned with each tab. However, you can have text right-aligned on the tab or centered on the tab. If you have a column of numbers, a *decimal tab* aligns the numbers on the decimal point. A *bar tab* adds a vertical bar at the tab position.**

## Set a Tab

### SET A TAB

1. Select the paragraphs to which you want to add the tab.
2. Click the **Tab marker** button.
3. Click the type of tab you want to set.

   You can select Left, Center, Right, Decimal, or Bar.

4. Click inside the ruler at the location where you want to set the tab.

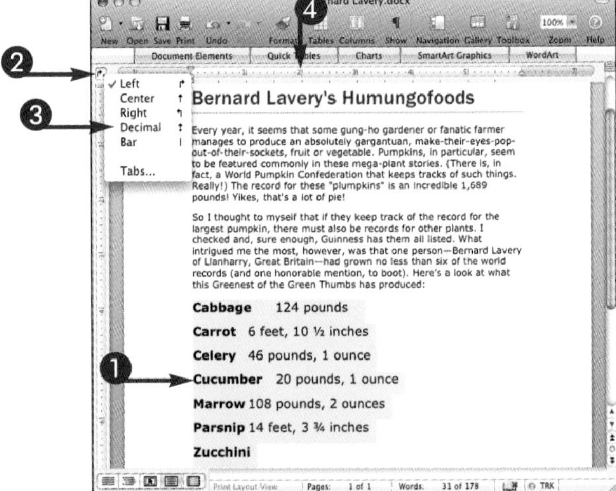


- Word adds a tab marker to the ruler.
- Selected text with existing tabs is aligned on the new tab.

5. Click at the end of a paragraph that has the tab set.
6. Press Tab.

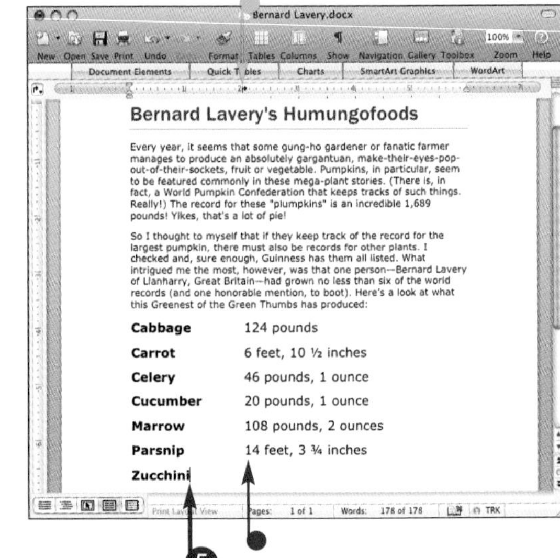

- The insertion point cursor advances to the tab location.
- If the tab is not in the correct location, select the text, move ↖ over the tab, then click and drag the tab left or right to set the new location.

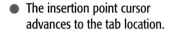

Bernard Lavery.docx

## Bernard Lavery's Humungofoods

Every year, it seems that some gung-ho gardener or fanatic farmer manages to produce an absolutely gargantuan, make-their-eyes-pop-out-of-their-sockets, fruit or vegetable. Pumpkins, in particular, seem to be featured commonly in these mega-plant stories. (There is, in fact, a World Pumpkin Confederation that keeps tracks of such things. Really!) The record for these "plumpkins" is an incredible 1,689 pounds! Yikes, that's a lot of pie!

So I thought to myself that if they keep track of the record for the largest pumpkin, there must also be records for other plants. I checked and, sure enough, Guinness has them all listed. What intrigued me the most, however, was that one person—Bernard Lavery of Llanharry, Great Britain—had grown no less than six of the world records (and one honorable mention, to boot). Here's a look at what this Greenest of the Green Thumbs has produced:

| | |
|---|---|
| **Cabbage** | 124 pounds |
| **Carrot** | 6 feet, 10 ½ inches |
| **Celery** | 46 pounds, 1 ounce |
| **Cucumber** | 20 pounds, 1 ounce |
| **Marrow** | 108 pounds, 2 ounces |
| **Parsnip** | 14 feet, 3 ¾ inches |
| **Zucchini** | |

### REMOVE A TAB

1. Move ↖ over the tab.
2. Click and drag the tab off the ruler.
3. Release the mouse button.

Word removes the tab from the ruler.

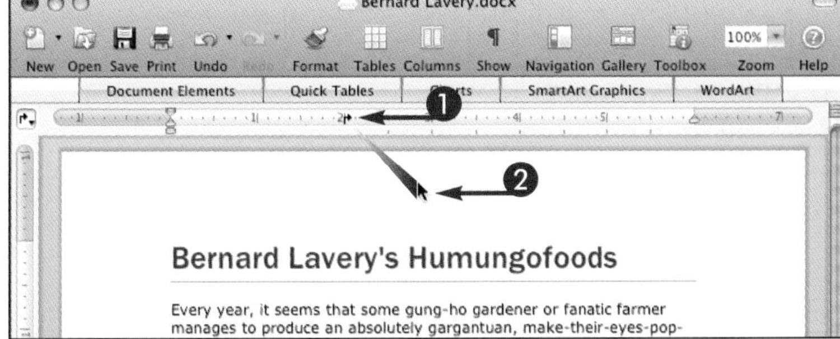

### Can I change the position of the default tabs?

Yes. By default, Word sets an automatic tab every 0.5 inches, which means that when you press Tab, Word advances the cursor to the next half-inch marker on the Ruler. To change this, click **Format**, and then click **Tabs** to open the Tabs dialog. In the Default tab stops text box, type the default tab width in inches and then click **OK**.

### Can I add dots to separate my tab columns?

Yes. You can do this by creating a *leader tab*, which fills the empty space between the tabs with dots (.), dashes (-), or underscores (_). Select the text that has the tabs set, click **Format**, and then click **Tabs** to open the Tabs dialog. In the Leader group, click the option for the type of leader tab you want (**2** for dots; **3** for dashes; **4** for underscores; ○ changes to ◉). Click **OK**.

# Set Line and Paragraph Spacing

You can improve the look of your Word documents by adjusting the line and paragraph spacing. For example, by increasing the spacing, you produce more white space, which can make a document easier to read.

**The line spacing determines the amount of space between each line in a paragraph. For example, double spacing uses twice as much space between the lines as the standard single spacing. Paragraph spacing determines the amount of space, measured in points, before and after a paragraph.**

## Set Line and Paragraph Spacing

### SET LINE SPACING

1. Select the text you want to format.
2. Display the Formatting Palette.

*Note: See Chapter 3 for information on how to display the Formatting Palette.*

3. Open the Alignment and Spacing panel.

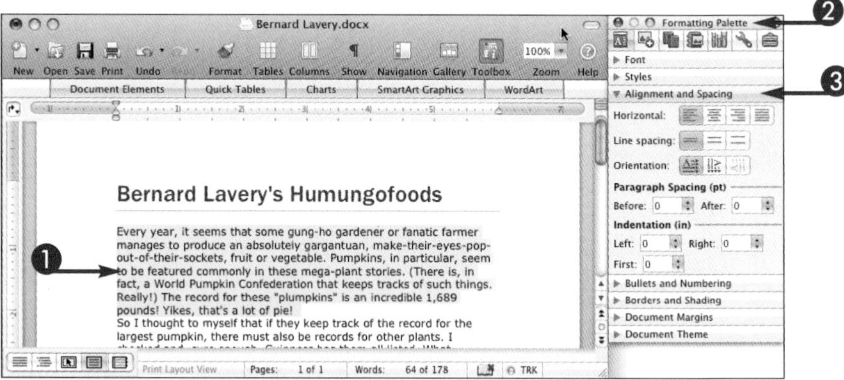


4. Click the line spacing you want.

   You can click for single spacing.

   You can click for 1.5-line spacing.

   You can click for double spacing.

- Word applies the spacing to the selected text.

## SET PARAGRAPH SPACING

1. Select the paragraphs you want to format.
2. Display the Formatting Palette.

**Note:** *See Chapter 3 for information on how to display the Formatting Palette.*

3. Open the Alignment and Spacing panel.

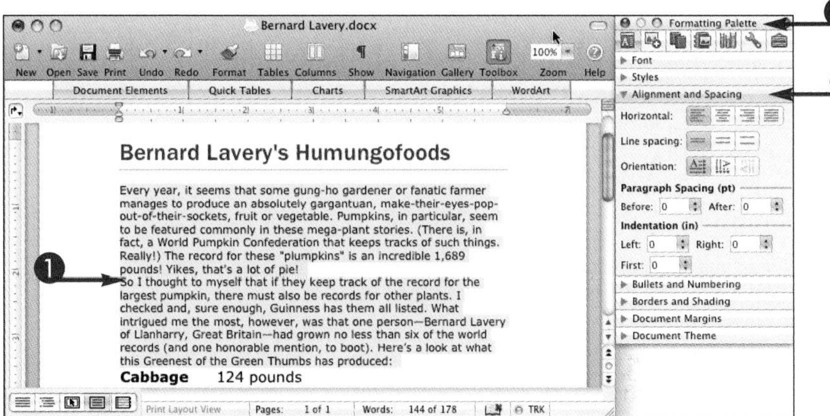

4. Type the number of points of space you want before each paragraph in the Before text box.
5. Type the number of points of space you want after each paragraph in the After text box.

- Word applies the spacing to the selected paragraphs.

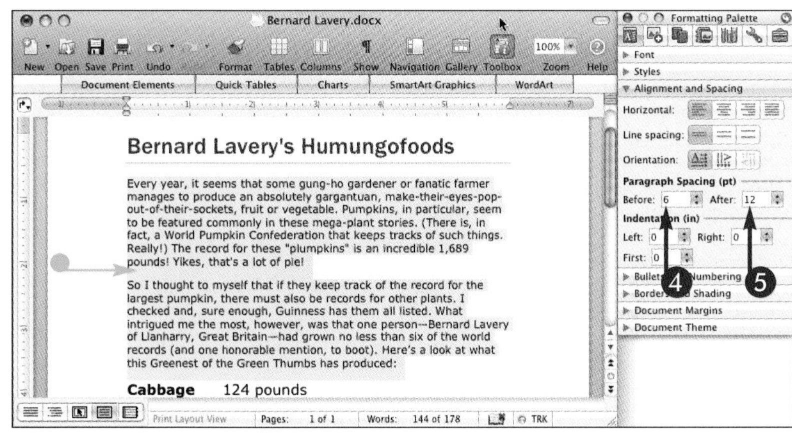

## TIPS

### Word increased the spacing in a single line that includes a large font. How do I make the line spacing even throughout the paragraph?

You must set a line spacing value for the entire paragraph that is equal to (or, ideally, a bit larger than) the number of points in the largest font size in the paragraph. For example, if the paragraph includes a 20-point font, set the paragraph's line spacing to 20 points (or more).
Click **Format** and then click **Paragraph** (or press Option + ⌘ + M). Click the **Line spacing** ⬍, click **Exactly**, type a value in points in the At text box, and then click **OK**.

### Can I adjust the spacing between characters?

Yes. You can increase the spacing to open up the text, which often makes a document easier to read. Similarly, you can decrease the spacing as a special effect or to squeeze more text on a line.

Click **Format**, click **Font** (or press ⌘ + D), and then click the **Character Spacing** tab.
Type a percentage value in the Scale text box. Alternatively, click the **Spacing** ⬍, click either **Expanded** or **Condensed**, and then type a value in the By text box.
Click **OK**.

# Indent a Paragraph

You can set a paragraph off from the rest of the text by indenting the paragraph. You can indent the paragraph from the left, from the right, or from both sides. For example, if your document includes a lengthy quotation, indent the quotation to make it stand out.

**You can also indent just the first line in a paragraph, which is a standard format in many types of writing.**

## Indent a Paragraph

### INDENT USING THE TOOLBOX

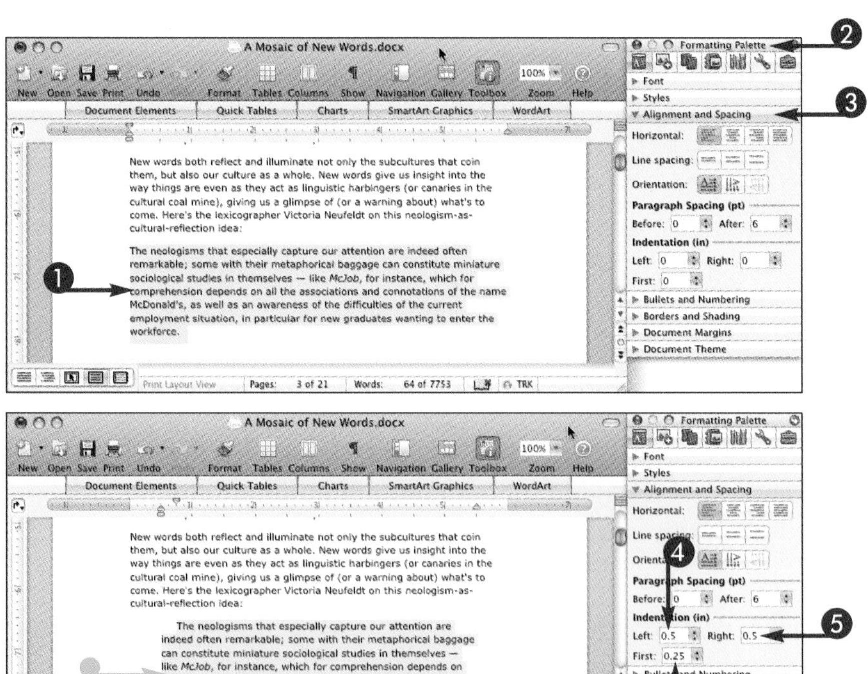

1. Select the paragraph you want to indent.

**Note:** *If you are indenting a single paragraph, you can click anywhere inside the paragraph instead of selecting the entire paragraph.*

2. Display the Formatting Palette.

**Note:** *See Chapter 3 for information on how to display the Formatting Palette.*

3. Open the Alignment and Spacing panel.
4. In the Left text box, type the number of inches you want the paragraph indented from the left margin.
5. In the Right text box, type the number of inches you want the paragraph indented from the right margin.
6. In the First text box, type the number of inches you want the first line of the paragraph to be indented.

- Word applies the indents to the selected paragraph.

### INDENT USING THE RULER

1. Select the paragraph you want to indent.
2. Click and drag the **Left Indent** marker ( ) left or right to set the distance you want the paragraph indented from the left margin.
3. Click and drag the **Right Indent** marker ( ) left or right to set the distance you want the paragraph indented from the right margin.

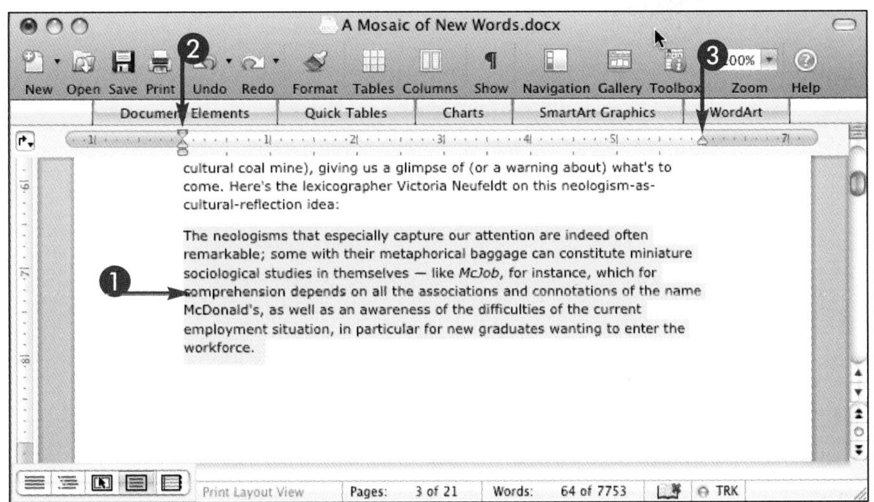


4. Click and drag the **First Line Indent** marker ( ) to the right to set the distance you want the first line of the paragraph to be indented.

- Word applies the indents to the selected paragraph.

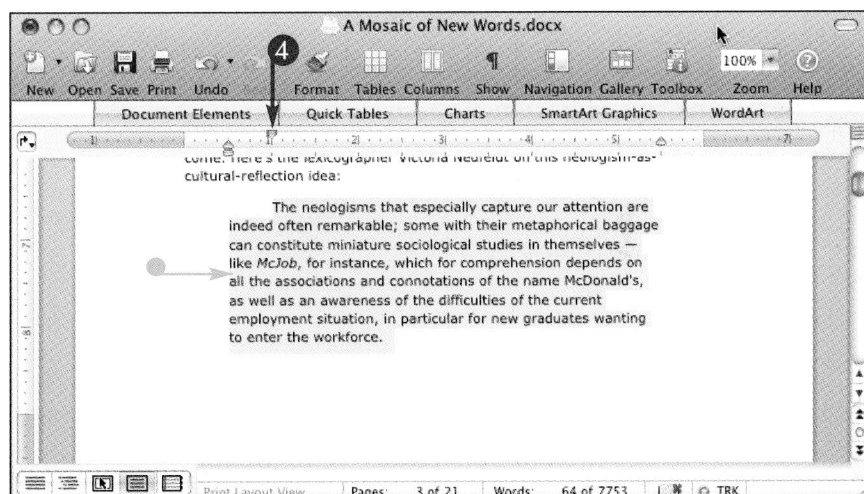


TIP

### How do I create a hanging indent?

A *hanging indent* is when the first line of a paragraph is indented to the left of the rest of the lines in the paragraph.

To set a hanging indent using the Toolbox, follow Steps **1** to **3** in the section "Indent a Paragraph." In the Alignment and Spacing panel, type a negative value, in inches, in the First text box.

To set a hanging indent using the Ruler, click and drag the **Hanging Indent** marker ( ) to the left.

# Add a Drop Cap

You can use a drop cap to add emphasis to your text or to create a dramatic effect. A drop cap is a large initial or capital letter that appears at the beginning of a paragraph.

**By default, a drop cap is set up to drop three lines. This means that the height of the drop cap is equivalent to three lines of text. You can specify how many lines down to set the drop cap. You can also specify a distance from the text. By default, the drop cap appears at zero distance from, or directly next to, the paragraph text.**

## Add a Drop Cap

1. Select the paragraph to which you want to add the drop cap.

*Note: You can also click anywhere inside the paragraph instead of selecting the entire paragraph.*

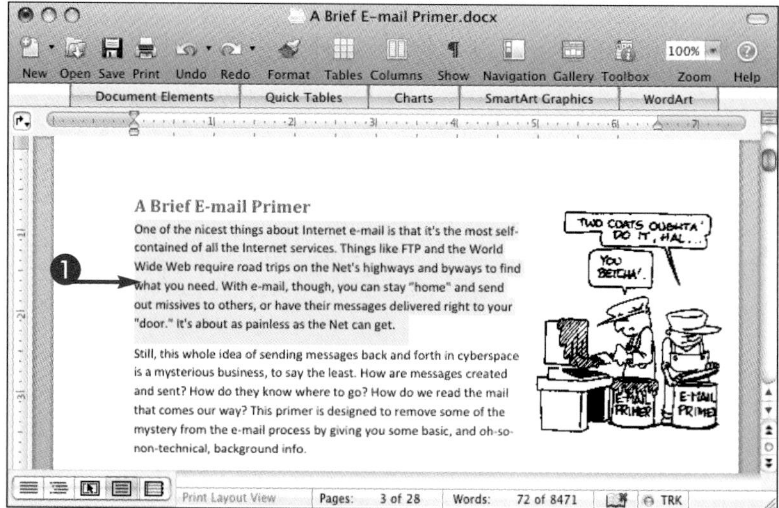


2. Click **Format**.
3. Click **Drop Cap**.

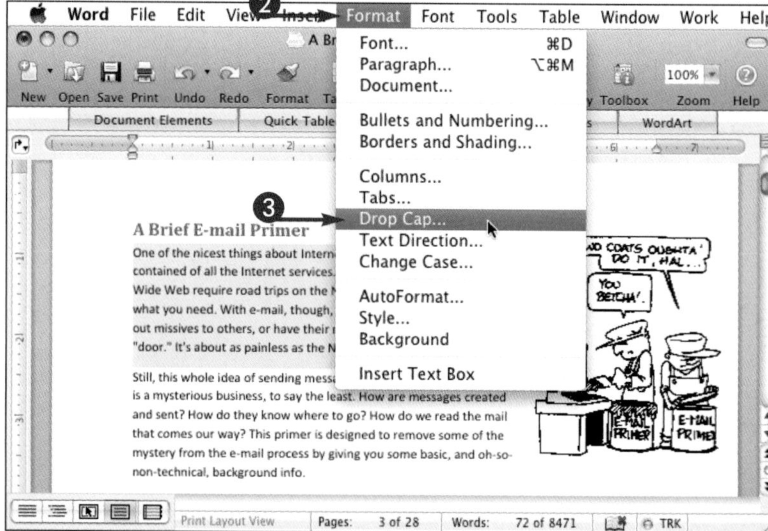

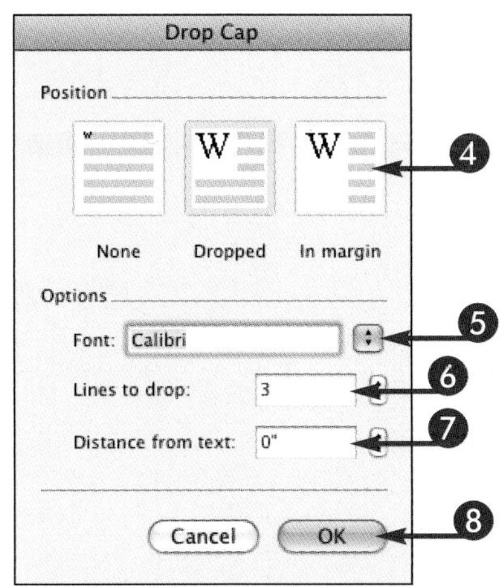


The Drop Cap dialog appears.

4. Click the drop cap position you want to use.

   You can select **Dropped** or **In margin**.

5. Click the **Font** ⬍ and then click the font you want to use for the drop cap letter.

6. In the Lines to drop text box, type the height of the drop cap in lines.

7. In the Distance from text text box, type the space you want between the drop cap and the text.

8. Click **OK**.

- Word replaces the first character in the paragraph with a drop cap.

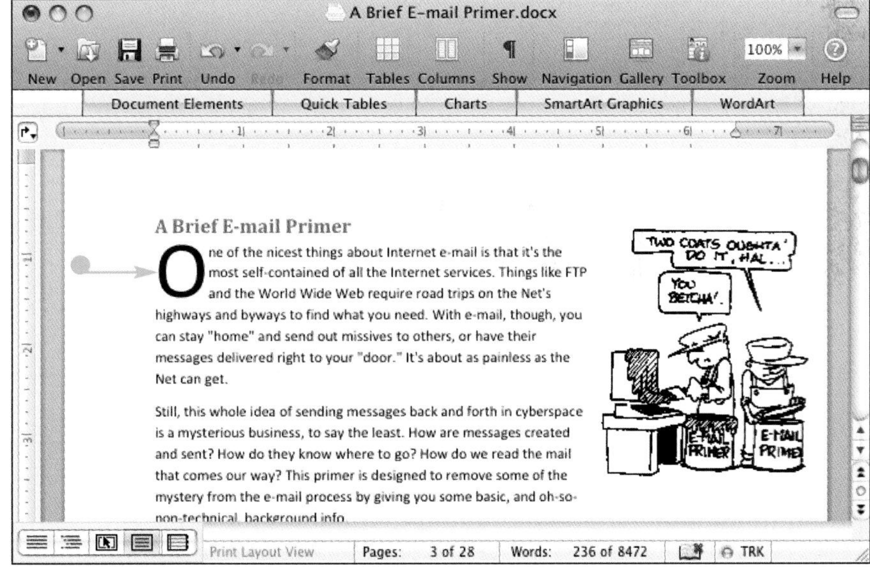


*__Note:__ Because Word places drop caps in text boxes, you can move, resize, and apply formatting to the text box, such as a background color or a border.*

*__Note:__ To return a drop cap to normal character text, follow Steps __1__ to __3__, click __None__, and then click __OK__.*

### How can I get the most out of drop caps?

First, remember that a drop cap is a special effect, which means you should use it sparingly. Avoid the temptation of adding a drop cap to every paragraph in a document. Instead, only use a drop cap for the first paragraph in the document, and perhaps also for the first paragraph in each major section of the document.

Also, do not be afraid to create eye-catching drop caps. For example, rather than using the same font as the document text, use a decorative font, such as Matura M7 or Mistral.

# Add Borders and Shading

You can emphasize document text, or you can make that text more visually appealing by applying a border around the text. Word offers a number of border types, and you can format each border with various styles, colors, and weights.

**You can also add emphasis or aesthetic appeal to some document text by shading the text with a background pattern.**

## Add Borders and Shading

### ADD A BORDER

1. Select the text you want to format.
2. Display the Formatting Palette.

*Note: See Chapter 3 for information on how to display the Formatting Palette.*

3. Open the Borders and Shading panel.
4. Click the **Type** ▾ and then click the border type you want to apply.

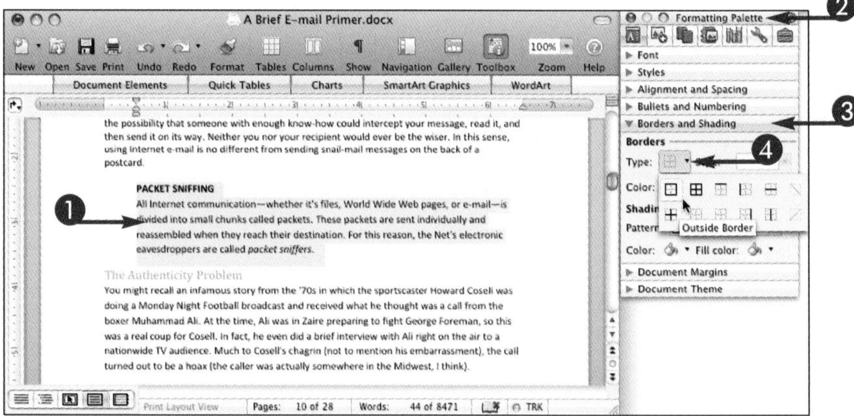


- Word applies the border to the selected paragraphs.

5. Click the **Style** ▾ and then click the border style you prefer.
6. Click the **Color** ▾ and then click the border color you prefer.
7. Click the **Weight** ▾ and then click the border thickness you prefer.

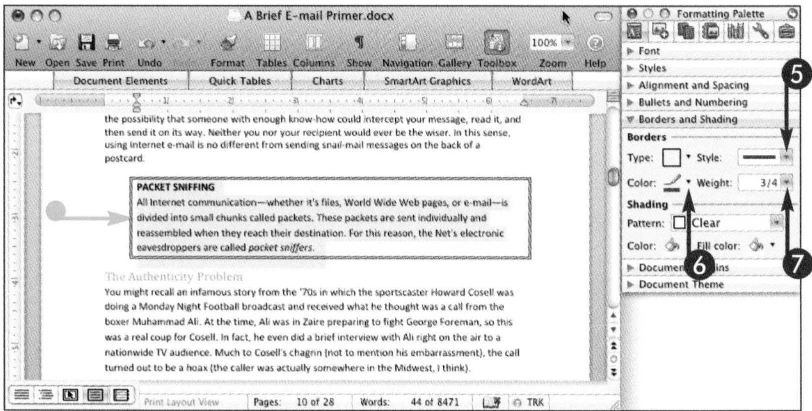

## ADD SHADING

❶ Select the text you want to format.

❷ Display the Formatting Palette.

***Note:** See Chapter 3 for information on how to display the Formatting Palette.*

❸ Open the Borders and Shading panel.

❹ Click the **Pattern** and then click the shading pattern you want to apply.

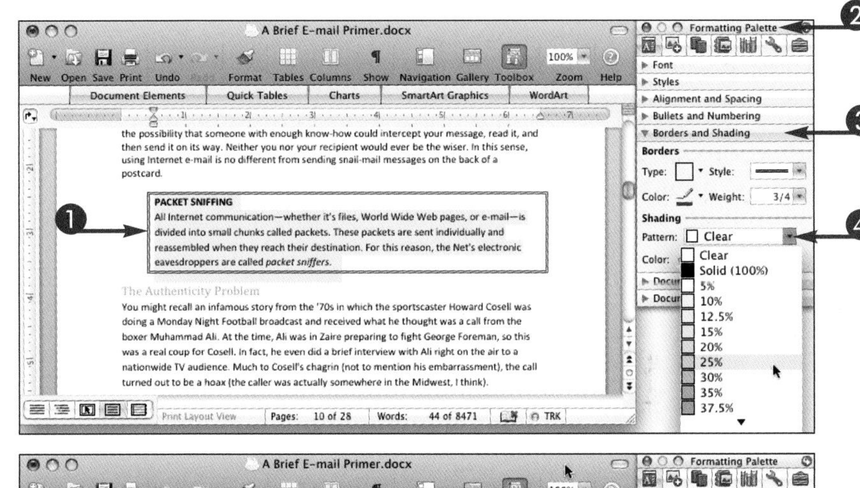


- Word applies the shading to the selected paragraphs.

❺ Click the **Color** and then click the pattern color you prefer.

❻ Click the **Fill color** and then click the background color you prefer.

***Note:** Be sure to choose a shading pattern and color that do not interfere with the text. For example, using a complex pattern with a dark fill color can make black text impossible to read.*

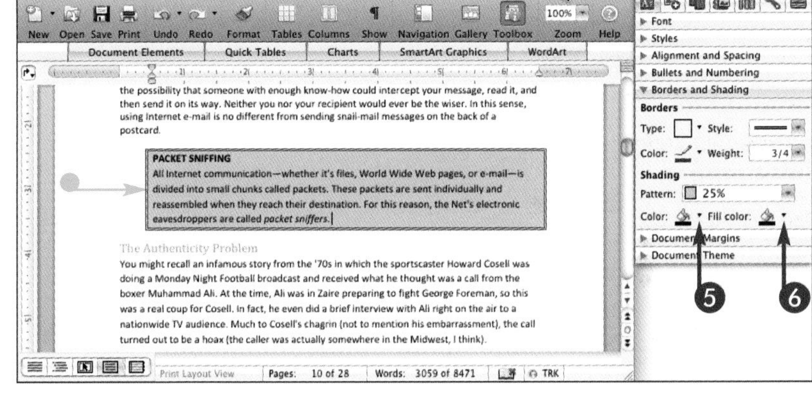

### Is it possible to display a paragraph with a drop shadow?

Yes. Word offers a drop shadow as an option in the Borders and Shading dialog. To display this dialog, select the paragraph, click **Format**, and then click **Borders and Shading**. Click the **Borders** tab, click the **Shadow** setting, and then click **OK**.

### How do I highlight a word or phrase?

Word has a Highlight tool that enables you to apply a highlight color to a word or phrase, which makes it appear as though the text has been marked with a highlighter. Select the text you want to highlight and then display the Formatting Palette.

Open the Font panel, click the **Highlight**, and then click the highlight color you want to use. Word applies the highlight to the selected text.

# Set the Document Margins

You can control the size of a document's text area by setting the document's *margins*, the blank space that surrounds the document text. Decreasing the margins allows more text to fit on each page, which is useful when printing a long document. Increasing the margins decreases the amount of text that can fit on each page, but the added white space can make the document look more appealing.

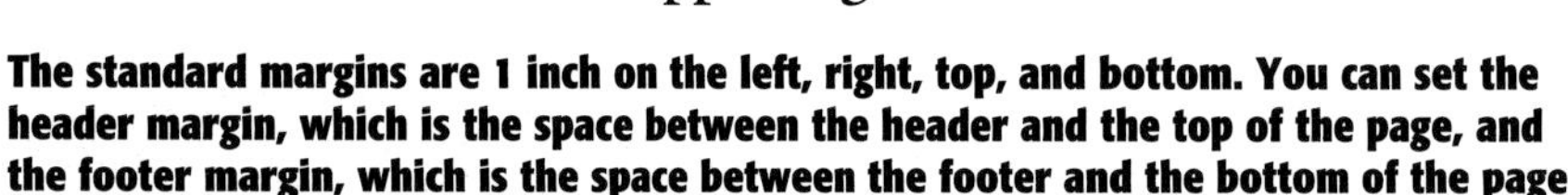

**The standard margins are 1 inch on the left, right, top, and bottom. You can set the header margin, which is the space between the header and the top of the page, and the footer margin, which is the space between the footer and the bottom of the page.**

## Set the Document Margins

### SET MARGINS USING THE TOOLBOX

1. Open the document you want to format.
2. Display the Formatting Palette.

*Note: See Chapter 3 for information on how to display the Formatting Palette.*

3. Open the Document Margins panel.
4. In the Margins section, use the text boxes to specify the margin sizes in inches.

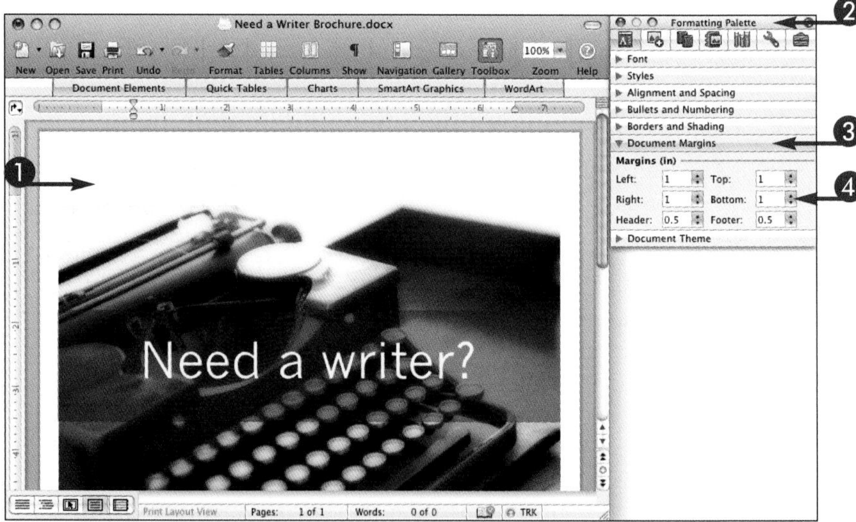


- Word adjusts the document margins.

*Note: If you plan on printing the document, do not make the margin too small or your document may not print properly. Most printers cannot handle margins smaller than about 0.25 inches, although see your printer manual to confirm this. In particular, see if your printer offers a "borderless" printing option.*

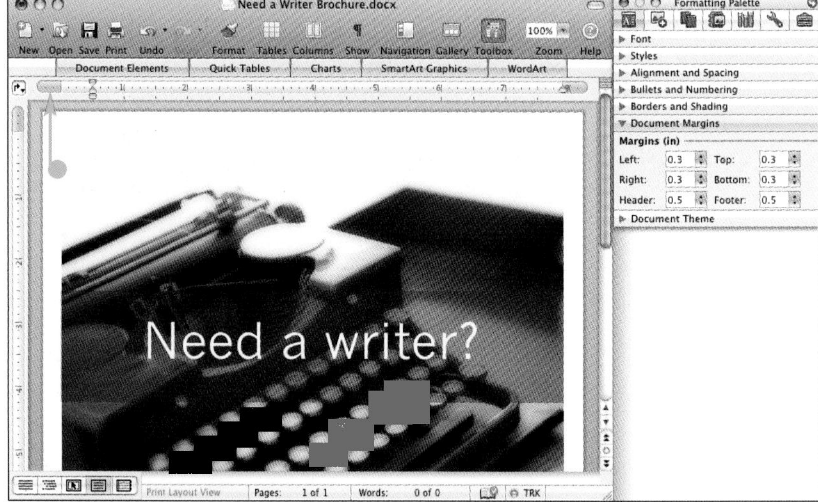

## SET MARGINS USING THE RULER

1. Open the document you want to format.
2. Move the ↖ over the right edge of the ruler's left margin area (↖ changes to ↔).
3. Click and drag the edge of the margin to set the margin width.

- Word adjusts the margin.

4. Move the ↖ over the left edge of the ruler's right margin area (↖ changes to ↔).
5. Click and drag the edge of the margin to set the margin width.

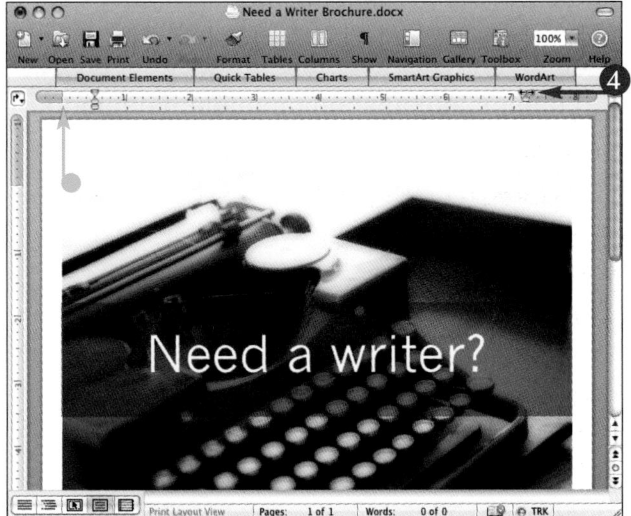

### Can I change the default margins?

Yes. The default margins are defined in Word's Normal template, which is the template used for most Word documents. To change the margins in the Normal template, click **Format** and then click **Document** to display the Document dialog. Click the **Margins** tab and then set the margins you want to use. Click **Default**, and when Word asks you to confirm the changes to the Normal template, click **Yes**. Click **OK** to close the dialog.

### I am going to print and bind my document. Do I need to increase my left and right margins to allow for the binding?

No. Remember that the bound part of the page appears on the right for some pages and on the left for others, so your text will appear offset on all pages if you adjust both margins. It is better to set the size and position of the *gutter*, extra white space added to the inside margin to handle document binding. Click **Format** and then click **Document** to display the Document dialog. Click the **Margins** tab, type the width of the gutter in the Gutter text box, and then click **OK**.

# Apply a Style

You can save time and effort when formatting your Word documents by taking advantage of Word's predefined styles. A *style* is a collection of formatting options, such as fonts, colors, borders, shading, and alignment. When you apply a style to some text, Word applies all of the style's formatting at once.

**Word offers dozens of predefined styles, the look of which depends on the document theme (see the section "Apply a Document Theme"). You can modify the predefined styles and create your own styles.**

## Apply a Style

1. Select the text you want to format.
2. Display the Formatting Palette.

***Note:*** *See Chapter 3 for information on how to display the Formatting Palette.*

3. Open the Styles panel.

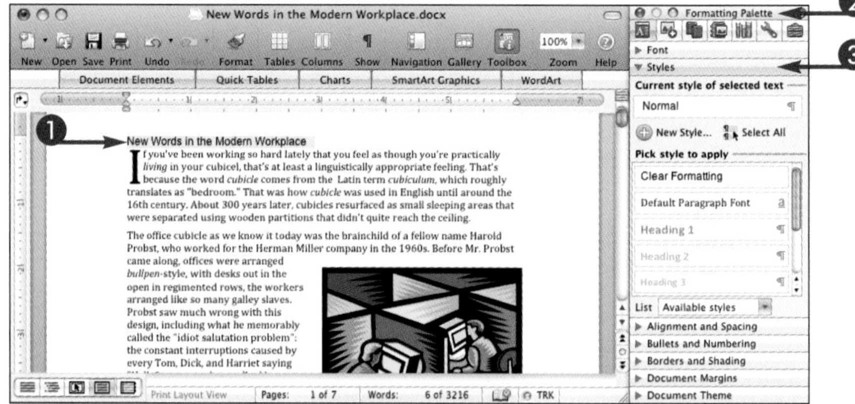


4. Click the **List** ▾ and then click **All styles**.

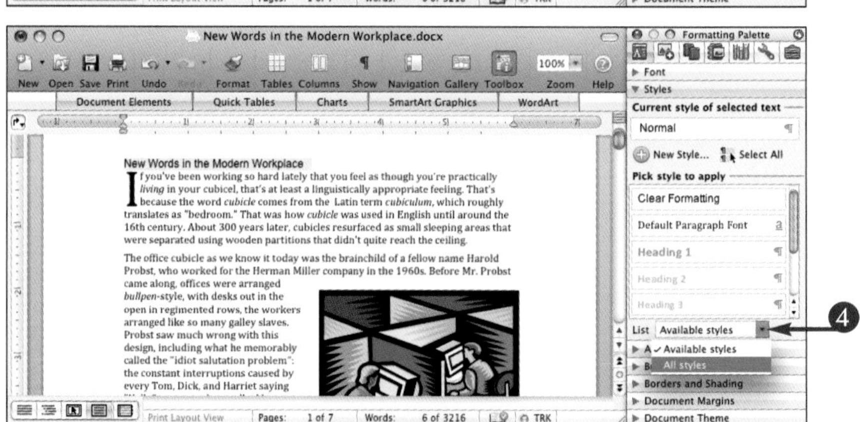

- Word displays all the available styles.
- The icons on the right tell you the type of style:

  [a] applies text formatting.

  [¶] applies paragraph formatting.

  [⊞] applies table formatting.

***Note:** To see the formatting in the style, hover the ↖ over the style.*

5. Click the style you want to apply.

- Word applies the style to the selected text.

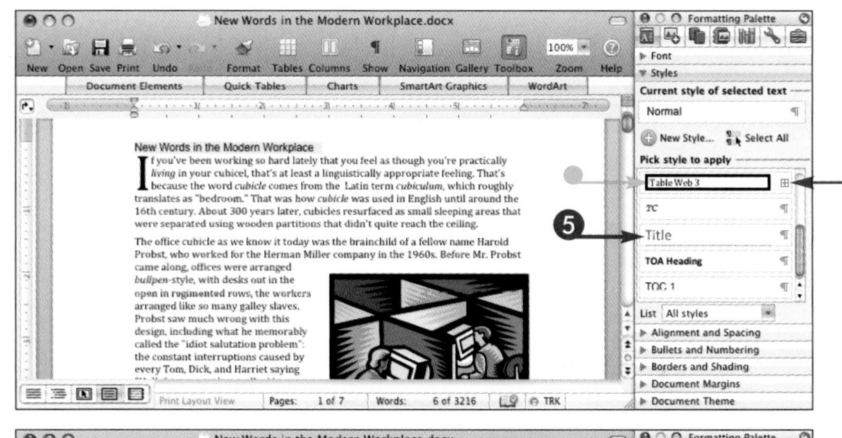

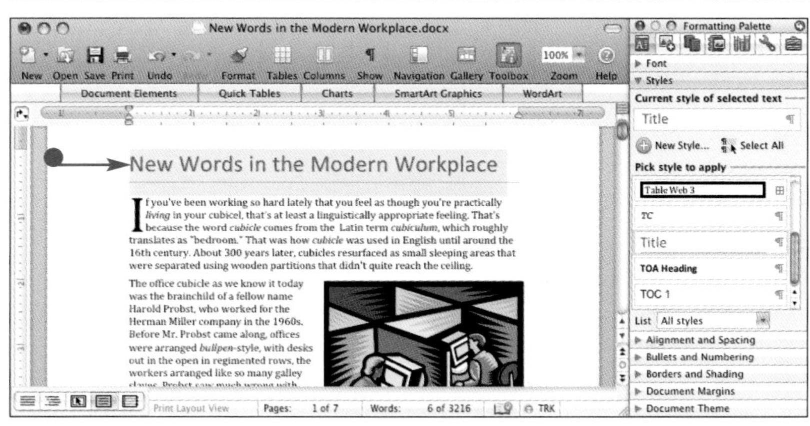

TIPS

## Can I modify an existing style?

Yes. You can modify any aspect of Word's predefined styles to suit your needs. Follow Steps **2** to **4** to display all the styles. Hover the ↖ over the style you want to work with, click the ▾ that appears, and then click **Modify Style**. In the Modify Style dialog, use the Formatting controls to edit the style's text formatting. You can also click the **Format** ⬍ and then click a format category, such as Paragraph or Border. Click **OK**.

## Can I create my own style?

If none of Word's predefined styles is exactly right for your needs, you can create a new style from scratch. Follow Steps **2** and **3** to display the Styles panel, and then click **New Style** to display the New Style dialog. In the Name text box, type a name for the new style, and use the Formatting controls to edit the style's text formatting. You can also click the **Format** ⬍ and then click a format category, such as Paragraph or Border. Click **OK**.

# Apply a Document Theme

You can save time and add aesthetic appeal to your Word documents by applying a document theme. A *theme* is a collection of formatting options that controls the document fonts, color scheme, and background. When you apply a theme, Word automatically changes the fonts, colors, and background for the entire document.

**Each theme includes a pair of fonts: The first font applies to the document headings, and the second font applies to the document text.**

## Apply a Document Theme

❶ Open the document you want to format.

❷ Display the Formatting Palette.

***Note:** See Chapter 3 for information on how to display the Formatting Palette.*

❸ Open the Document Theme panel.

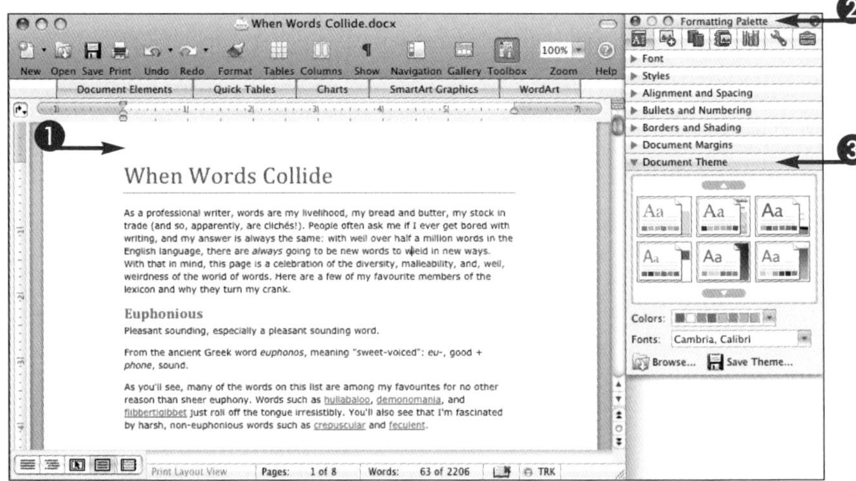


❹ Click the theme you want to use.

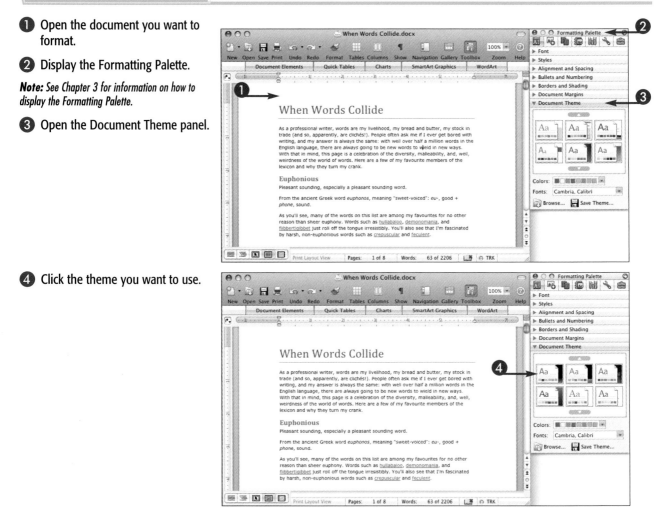

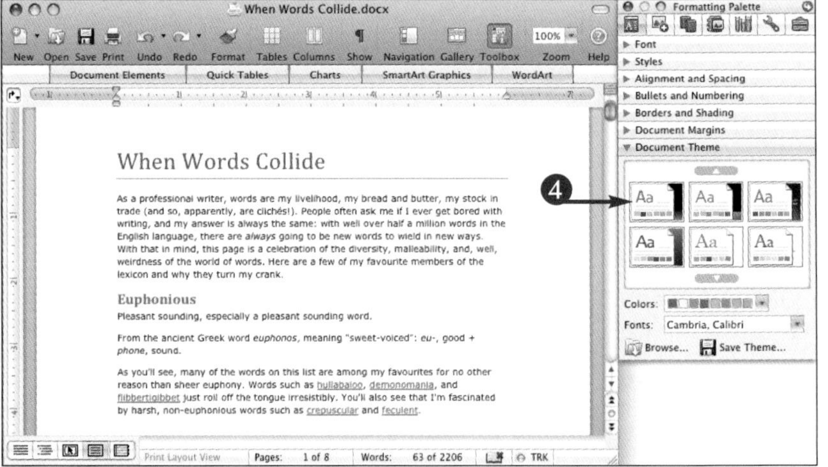

- Word applies the theme fonts, colors, and background.

5. To change just the document colors, click the **Colors** and then click a color scheme.

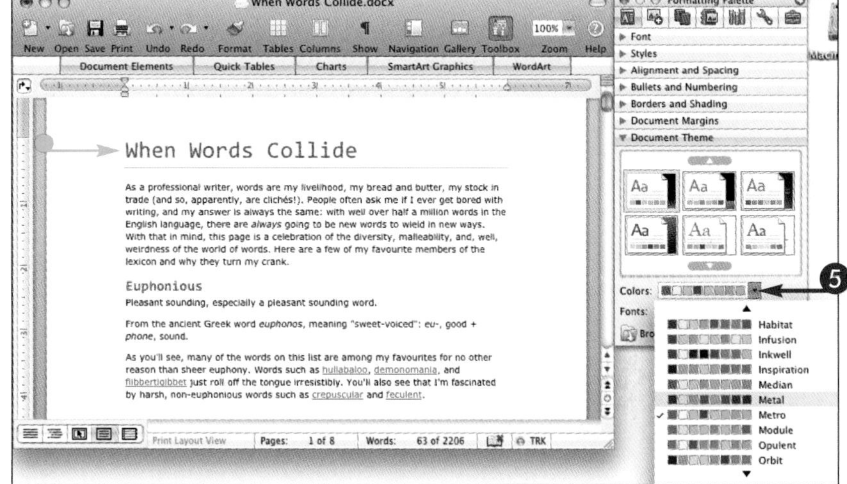


- Word applies the color scheme to the document.

6. To change just the document fonts, click the **Fonts** and then click a font pair.

   Word applies the fonts to the document.

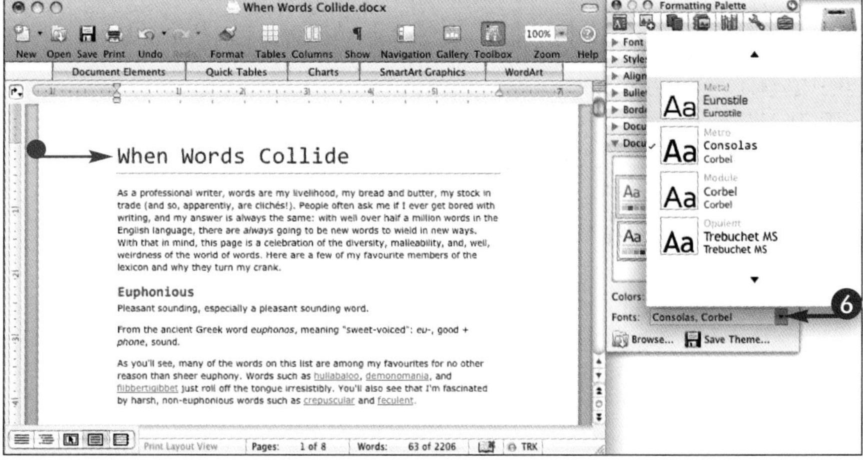


TIPS

### When I apply a theme, why does Word not change the background color?

Word only applies the theme's background color if you have set the document background. To do this, click **Format** and then click **Background** to display the Background dialog. Click the color you want to apply. If you want to use a non-theme color, click **More Colors**, although note that this color overrides the theme background color. You can also click **Fill Effects** to apply an effect such as a gradient or texture.

### Can I create my own document theme?

Yes, although you cannot create a theme from scratch. Instead, follow Steps **1** to **4** to select a predefined scheme, and then follow Steps **5** and **6** to modify the theme to suit your needs. In the Document Theme panel, click **Save Theme**, type a name for your theme in the Save As text box, and then click **Save**. Word adds the custom theme to the top of the list of document themes.

# Display Text in Columns

If you are putting together a brochure, newsletter, or any document where you want to mimic the layout of a newspaper or magazine, you can configure the text to appear in two or more columns.

**When you use columns, as the text in the first column reaches the bottom of the page, it continues at the top of the next column. It is only when the text reaches the bottom of the last column that it continues on the next page.**

## Display Text in Columns

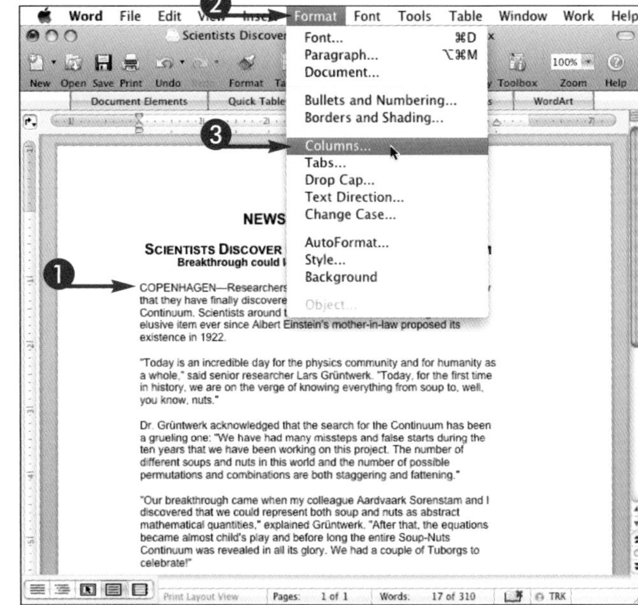


❶ Position the cursor at the beginning of the text you want to convert to columns.

*Note:* *If you want to display only part of the document in columns, select the text you want to convert.*

❷ Click **Format**.

❸ Click **Columns**.

The Columns dialog appears.

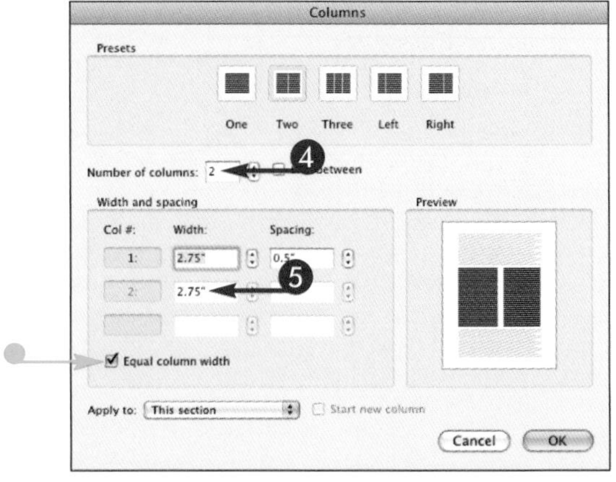


❹ In the Number of columns text box, type the number of columns you want to use.

❺ In the Width text box, type the width of each column in inches.

- If you do not want all your columns to be the same width, deselect the **Equal column width** option (☑ changes to ☐).

6. In the Spacing text box, type the amount of space in inches you want between the columns.

- The Preview area shows what the columns will look like.
- You can also click a **Presets** button to select a column configuration.

7. Click the **Apply to** ⬍ and then click **This point forward**.
8. Click **OK**.

- Word converts the selected text to columns.

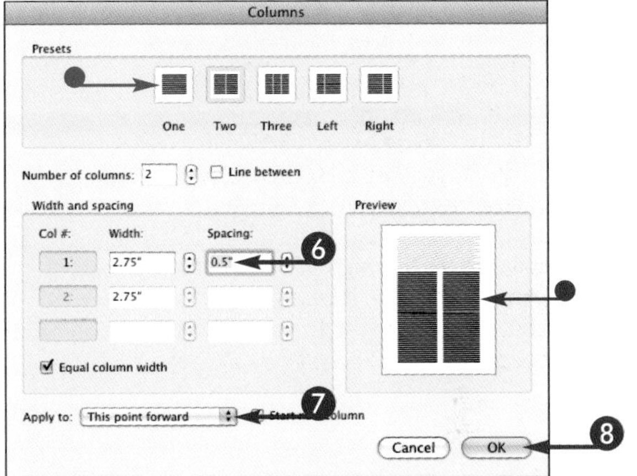


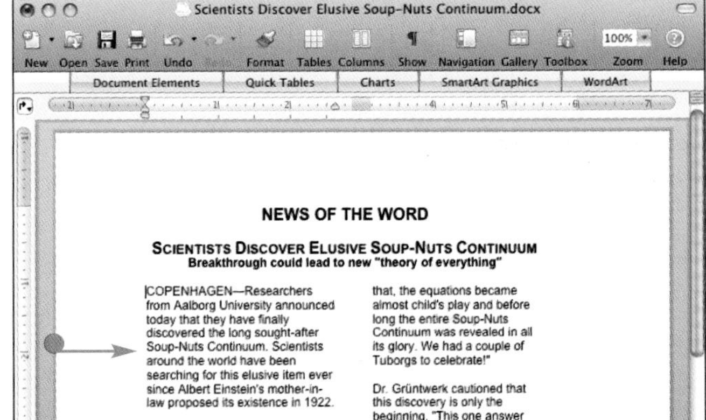

**Is there a faster way to create basic columns?**

Yes. You can click the **Columns** button on the Standard toolbar:

1. Select the text you want to display in columns.
2. Click the **Columns** button (▥).
3. Click the number of columns you want.

   Word converts the selected text into columns.

**How do I get the text to jump to the next column before reaching the bottom of the current column?**

You can do that by inserting a *column break*. In the same way that a page break tells Word to continue the text at the top of the next page, a column break tells Word to continue the text at the top of the next column. Position the cursor at the spot where you want the column break to occur, and then press Shift + ⌘ + Return.

CHAPTER 7

# Working with Microsoft Word's Features

To help you work faster, smarter, and better, Word offers a large collection of tools that you can use. For example, you can look up synonyms, definitions, and translations; you can track the changes made to a document and protect a document from changes; you can calculate the total number of words, create new AutoCorrect entries, and more.

# Find a Synonym

You can make your writing more interesting and more vivid, and you can improve your vocabulary, by looking up synonyms for some words. Microsoft Word has a built-in thesaurus, so you can look up synonyms and also antonyms without having to leave the program or even the document you are working on.

## Find a Synonym

❶ Select the word you want to work with.

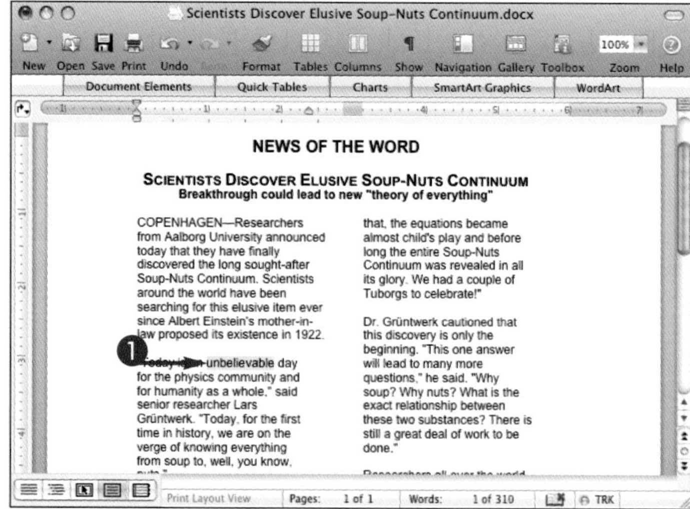


❷ Click **Tools**.

❸ Click **Thesaurus**.

***Note:*** *You can also press* Ctrl + Option + ⌘ + R.

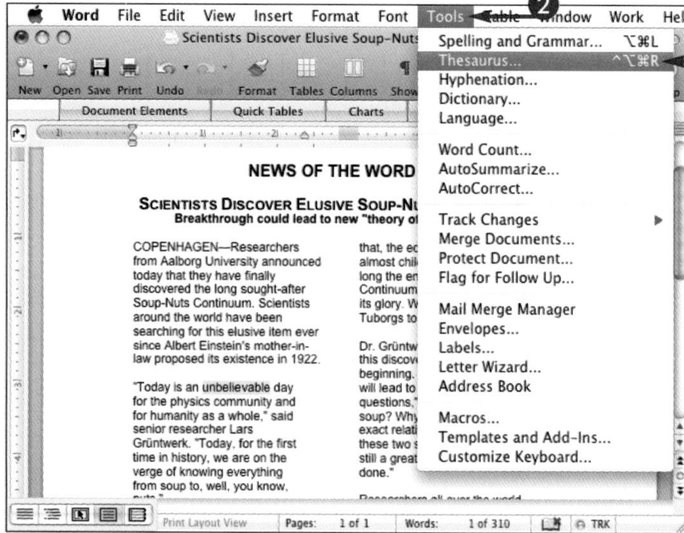

- Word opens the Toolbox, selects the Reference Tools palette, and opens the Thesaurus panel.

4 If the word has multiple senses, click the sense you are using in the Meanings list.

- Word displays the synonyms.

5 Click the synonym you want to use.

6 Click **Insert**.

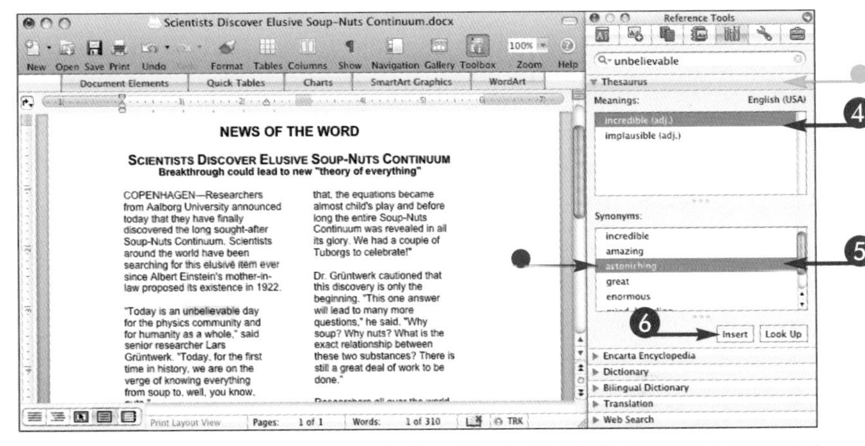

- Word replaces the selected word with the synonym.

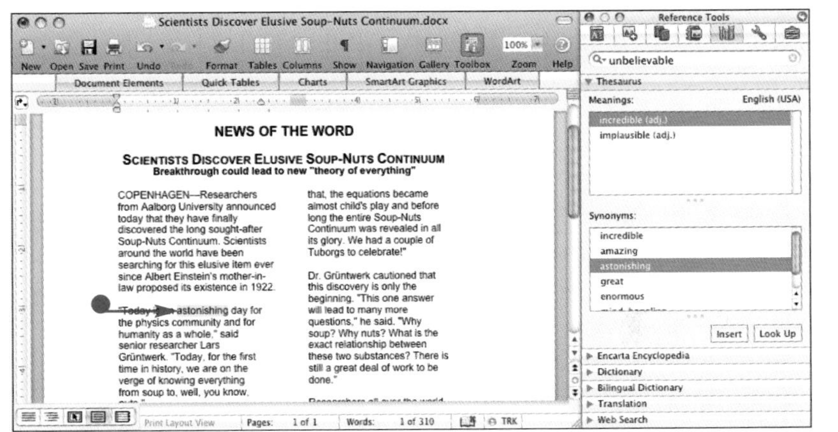

## TIP

### Can I look up synonyms for a word that is not in a document?

Yes. The Reference Tools palette has a search feature you can use:

1 If the Reference Tools palette is not displayed, click **Toolbox** ( ) and then click the **Reference Tools** button ( ). You can also press Option + ⌘ + R.

2 Open the Thesaurus panel.

3 Type the word you want to look up and then press Return.

- Word displays the meanings and synonyms.

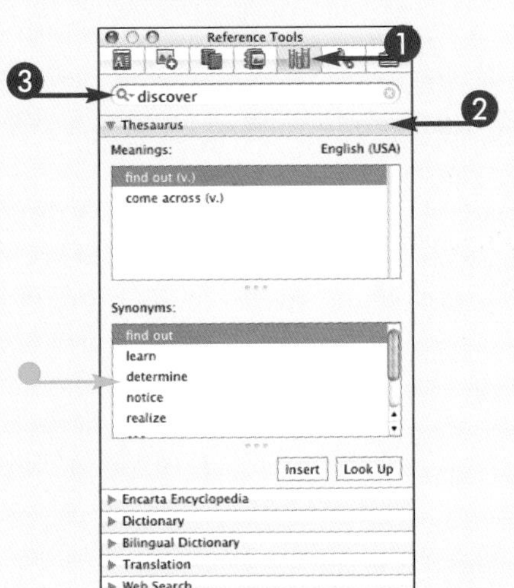

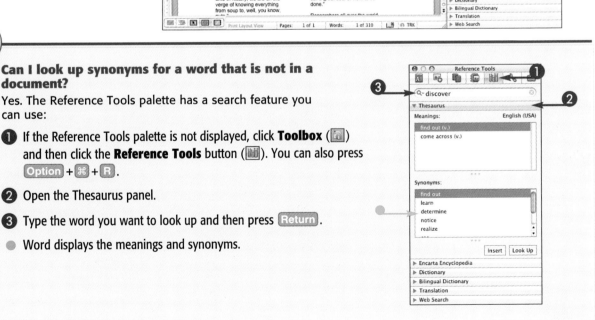

# Look Up a Word in the Dictionary

You can make your writing more accurate by looking up the definitions of words you use to ensure you are using them correctly. Microsoft Word has access to an online dictionary, so you can look up words directly from the document you are working on.

**Word's dictionary is also useful if you are reading a document written by someone else and you encounter an unfamiliar word.**

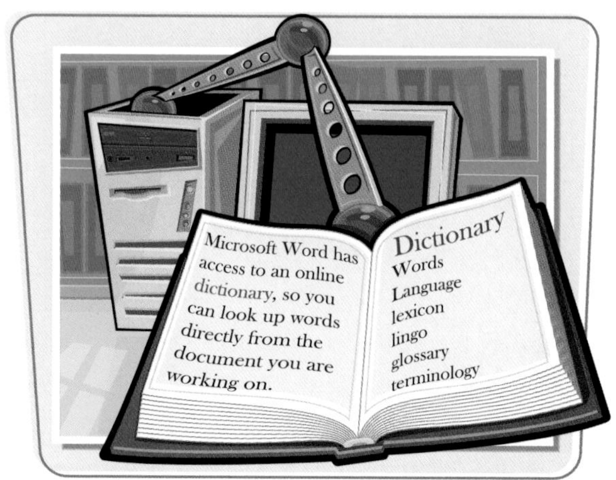


## Look Up a Word in the Dictionary

1. Select the word you want to look up.

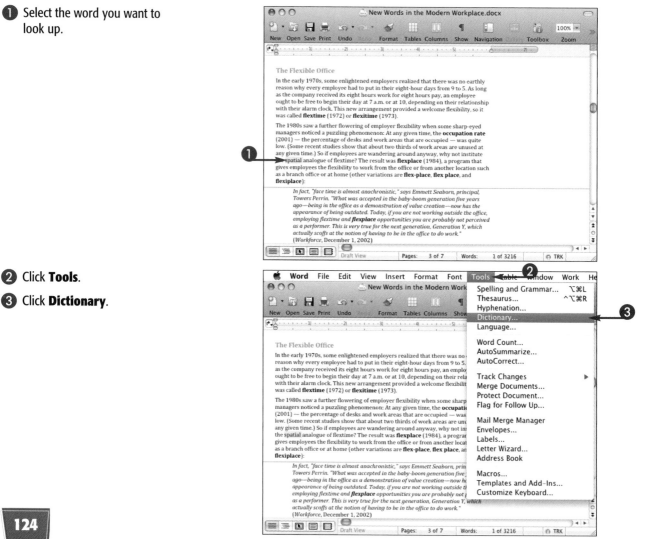

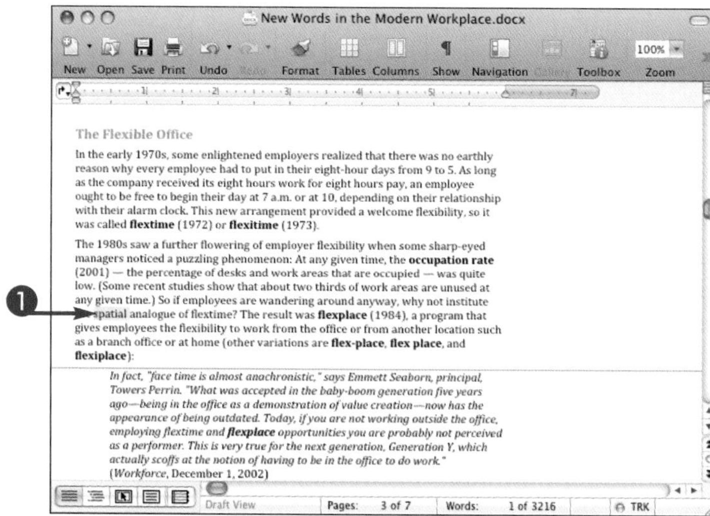


2. Click **Tools**.
3. Click **Dictionary**.

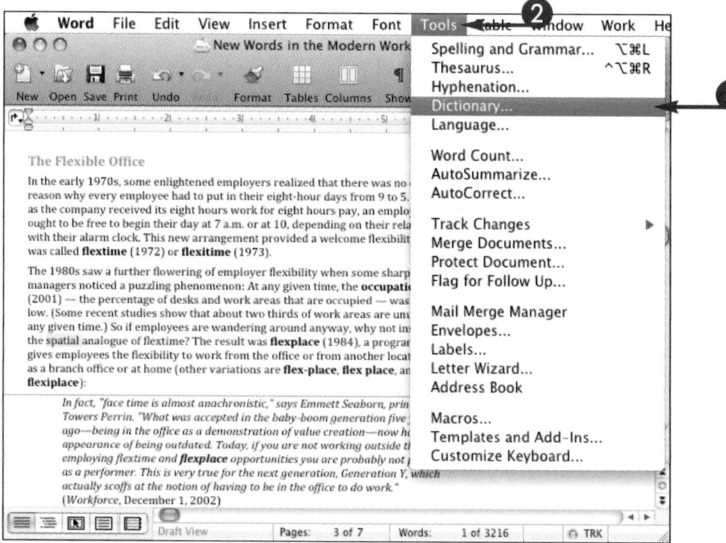

- Word displays the Toolbox, selects the Reference Tools palette, and opens the Dictionary panel.
- The first time you look up a definition, Word may tell you that the online Reference Tools are turned off.

4. Click the link to activate the online Reference Tools.

- Word displays the definition.

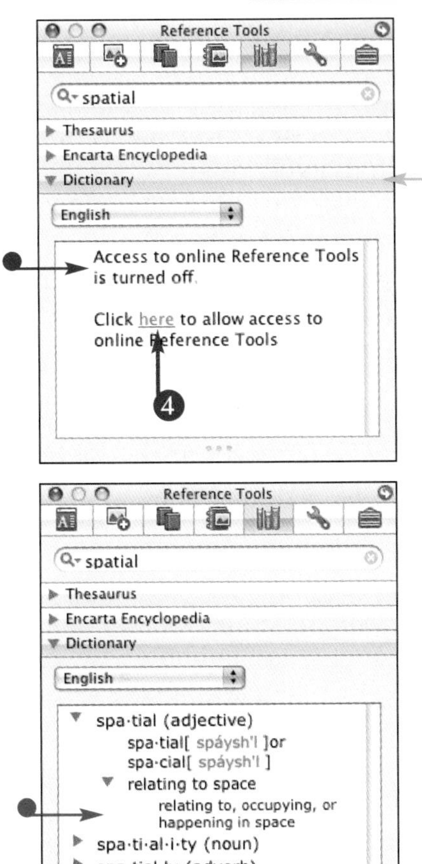

**Can I look up a definition for a word that is not in a document?**

Yes. You can use the Reference Tools palette's search feature to look up any word:

1. If the Reference Tools palette is not displayed, click **Toolbox** (▣) and then click the **Reference Tools** button (▣). You can also press Option + ⌘ + R.
2. Open the Dictionary panel.
3. Type the word you want to look up and then press Return.

- Word displays the word's definitions

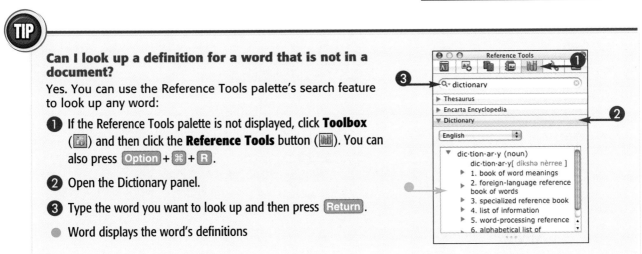

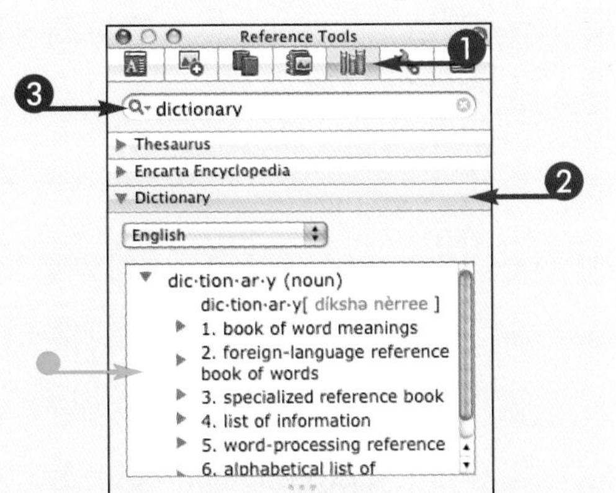

# Translate a Word

If you encounter a non-English word that you do not understand, you can use Word's Translation tool to translate that term into English.

**Word's Translation tool supports several languages, including French, German, Italian, Spanish, Japanese, and Chinese, so you can also translate an English word into another language.**

## Translate a Word

❶ Select the word you want to translate.

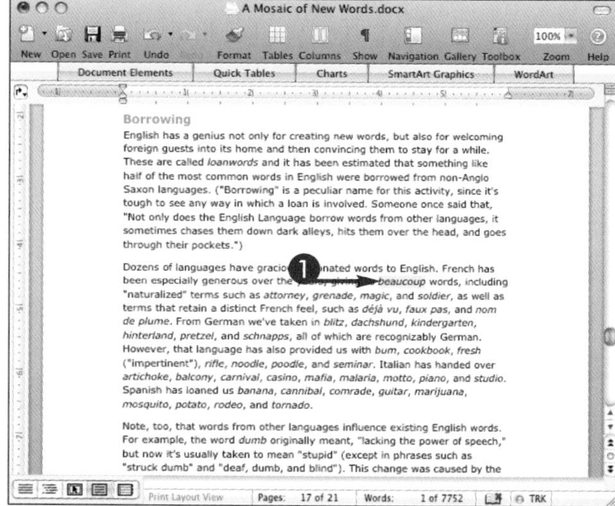


❷ Click **View**.

❸ Click **Reference Tools**.

***Note:*** *You can also press* Option + ⌘ + R.

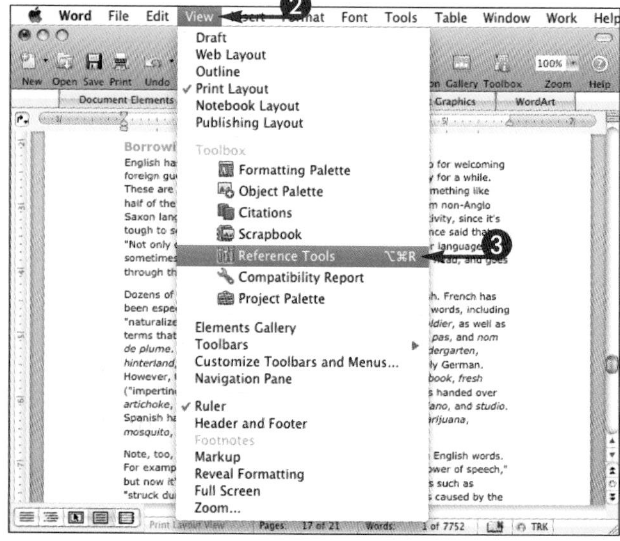

- Word opens the Toolbox and selects the Reference Tools palette.

4 Click the **Translation** panel.

5 Click the **From** and then click the language of the selected word.

6 Click the **To** and then click the language you want to use for the translation.

- Word displays the translation.

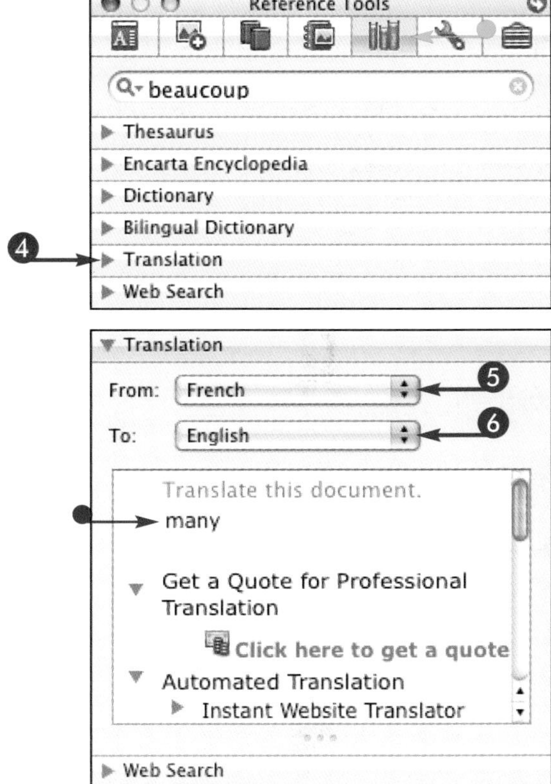


TIP

**Can I translate a word that is not in a document?**

Yes. You can use the Reference Tools palette's search feature to translate any word:

1 If the Reference Tools palette is not displayed, click **Toolbox** ( ) and then click the **Reference Tools** button ( ). You can also press Option + ⌘ + R.

2 Open the Translation panel.

3 Click the **From** and then click the language of the selected word.

4 Click the **To** and then click the language you want to use for the translation.

5 Type the word you want to translate and then press Return.

- Word displays the word's translation

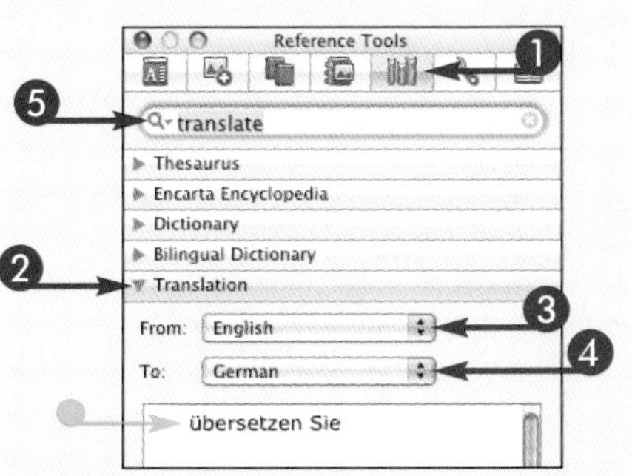

# Hyphenate a Document

You can improve the overall look of a long document by hyphenating the document. Word's hyphenation feature looks for longer words that occur at the ends of lines and automatically adds hyphens to those words rather than wrapping them onto the next line.

## Hyphenate a Document

1. Open the document you want to hyphenate.
2. Click **Tools**.
3. Click **Hyphenation**.

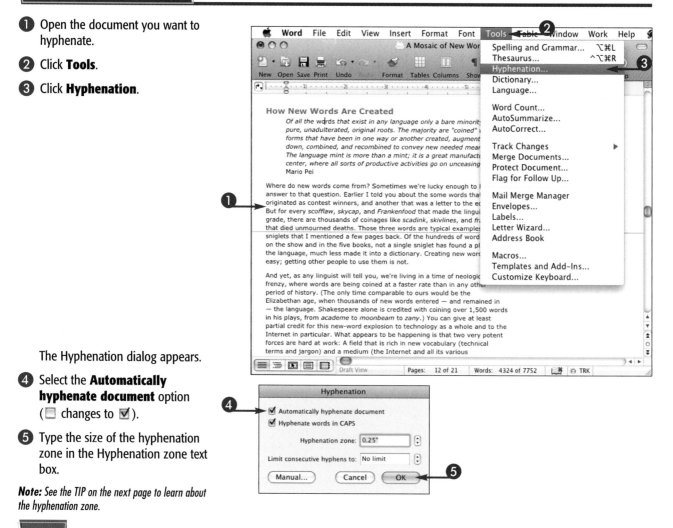

The Hyphenation dialog appears.

4. Select the **Automatically hyphenate document** option (☐ changes to ☑).
5. Type the size of the hyphenation zone in the Hyphenation zone text box.

***Note:*** *See the TIP on the next page to learn about the hyphenation zone.*

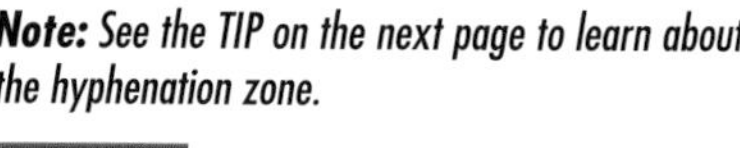

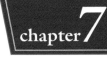

6. Type the maximum number of consecutive lines that can end with hyphens in the Limit consecutive hyphens to text box.

7. Click **OK**.

***Note:** If you use a small hyphenation zone to reduce raggedness, you run the risk of having hyphens ending too many lines, which is a visual distraction for the reader. In this case, you should set the maximum number of consecutive hyphenated lines.*

- Word hyphenates the document.

***Note:** If you have words that always use hyphens — for example, CD-ROM or e-mail — you probably do not want lines to break at such hyphens. In that case, replace the regular hyphen with a nonbreaking hyphen by pressing Shift + ⌘ + –.*

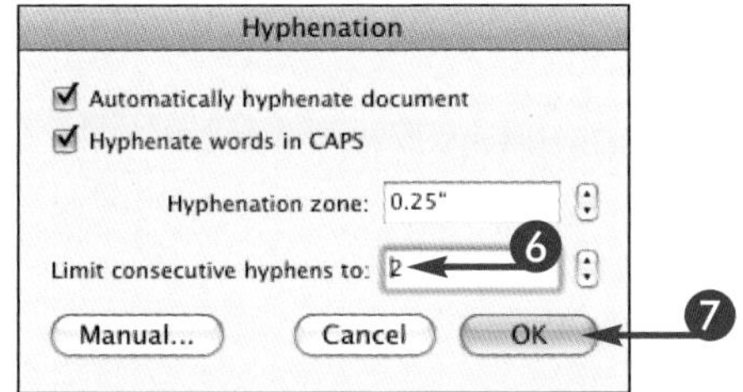


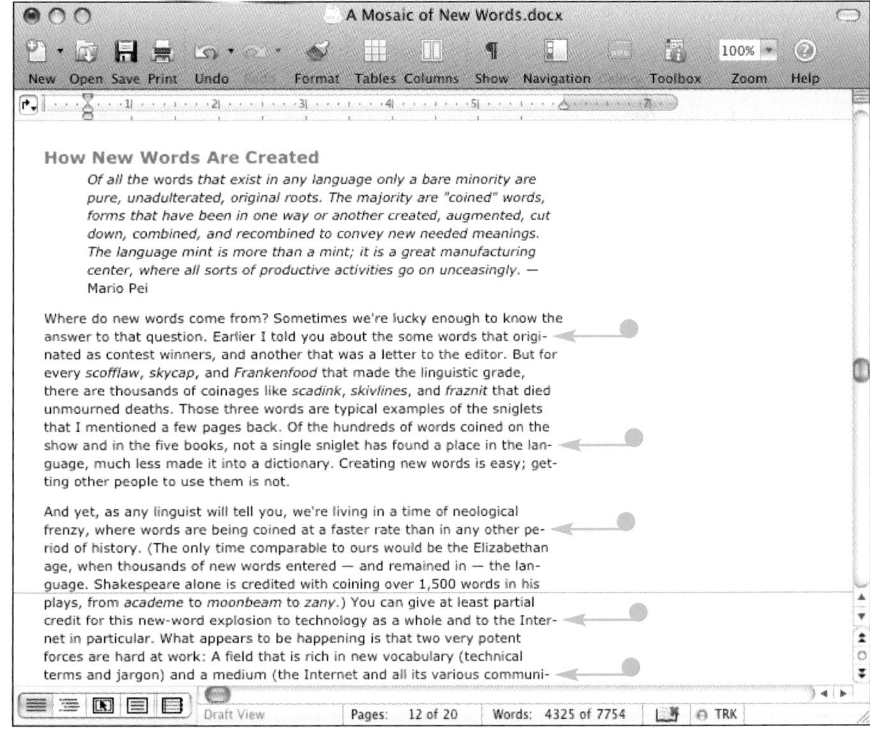

A Mosaic of New Words.docx
New
Open
Save
Print
Undo
Format
Tables
Columns
Show
Navigation
Toolbox
100%
Zoom
Help
How New Words Are Created
Of all the words that exist in any language only a bare minority are pure, unadulterated, original roots. The majority are "coined" words, forms that have been in one way or another created, augmented, cut down, combined, and recombined to convey new needed meanings. The language mint is more than a mint; it is a great manufacturing center, where all sorts of productive activities go on unceasingly. — Mario Pei
Where do new words come from? Sometimes we're lucky enough to know the answer to that question. Earlier I told you about the some words that origi-nated as contest winners, and another that was a letter to the editor. But for every scofflaw, skycap, and Frankenfood that made the linguistic grade, there are thousands of coinages like scadink, skivlines, and fraznit that died unmourned deaths. Those three words are typical examples of the sniglets that I mentioned a few pages back. Of the hundreds of words coined on the show and in the five books, not a single sniglet has found a place in the lan-guage, much less made it into a dictionary. Creating new words is easy; get-ting other people to use them is not.
And yet, as any linguist will tell you, we're living in a time of neological frenzy, where words are being coined at a faster rate than in any other pe-riod of history. (The only time comparable to ours would be the Elizabethan age, when thousands of new words entered — and remained in — the lan-guage. Shakespeare alone is credited with coining over 1,500 words in his plays, from academe to moonbeam to zany.) You can give at least partial credit for this new-word explosion to technology as a whole and to the Inter-net in particular. What appears to be happening is that two very potent forces are hard at work: A field that is rich in new vocabulary (technical terms and jargon) and a medium (the Internet and all its various communi-
Draft View
Pages: 12 of 20
Words: 4325 of 7754
TRK

### What is the purpose of the hyphenation zone?

The *hyphenation zone* is the amount of space that it is okay for Word to leave between the last word in a line and the right margin. You control hyphenation by designating the size of this zone. For left-aligned text, a smaller hyphenation zone reduces the raggedness of the right margin by hyphenating more words; a larger hyphenation zone decreases the number of hyphenated words but increases the right margin's raggedness.

### Can I prevent Word from hyphenating a paragraph?

Yes. If you have a paragraph that you do not want hyphenated, you can tell Word to avoid that paragraph during the hyphenation process. Click anywhere inside the paragraph, click **Format**, and then click **Paragraph** to open the Paragraph dialog. Click the **Line and Page Breaks** tab, select the **Don't hyphenate** option (☐ changes to ☑), and then click **OK**.

# Track Changes Made to a Document

When you collaborate on a document with other people, you can use Word's Track Changes tool to see the revisions that the other people have made, including adding, editing, deleting, and formatting the text. Track Changes shows you not only the document revisions, but also who made each change and when.

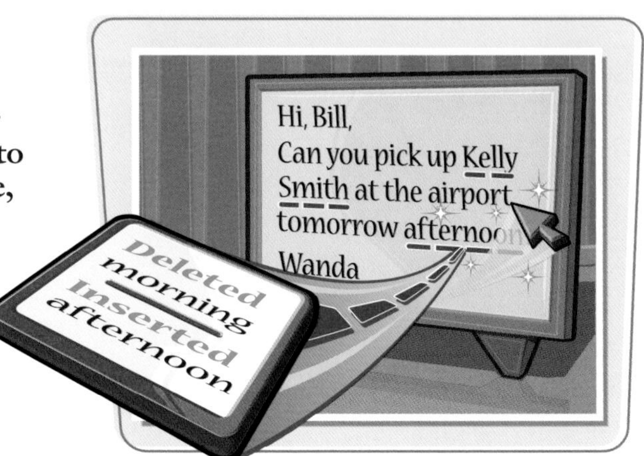


**With the Track Changes tool activated, you can review each change that the other users have made to the document, and you can then accept or reject each change.**

## Track Changes Made to a Document

### ACTIVATE TRACK CHANGES

1. Open the document you want to work with.
2. Click **View**.
3. Click **Toolbars**.
4. Click **Reviewing**.

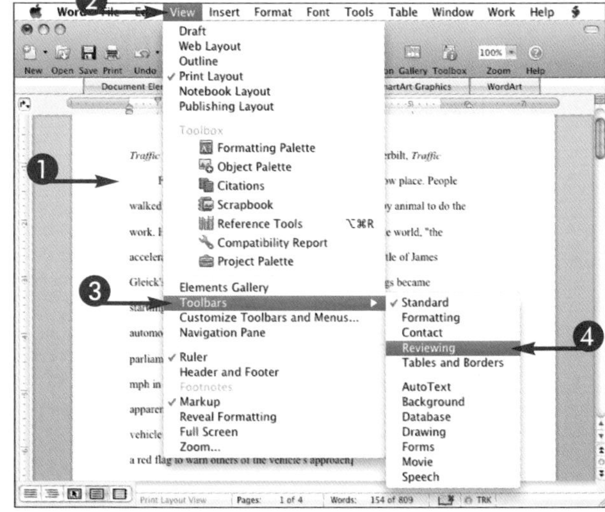


- The Reviewing toolbar appears.

5. Click **Track Changes** (▣).

- You can also click **Track Changes** in the status bar or press Shift + ⌘ + E.

   Word activates the Track Changes tool.

6. Click the **Display for Review** ▾ and then click **Final Showing Markup**.

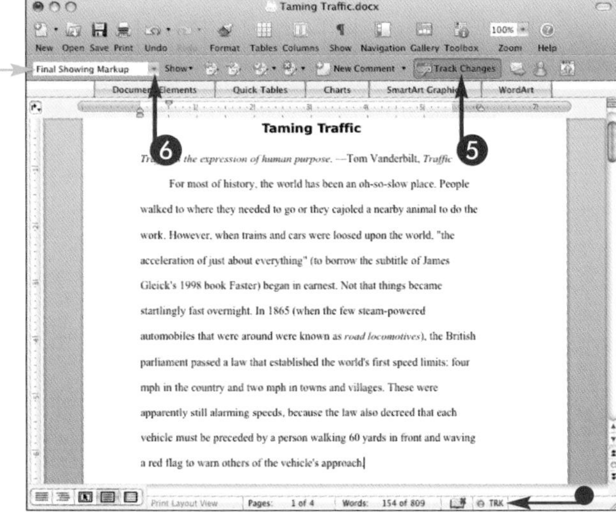

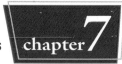

- New text appears in the document underlined and in a different color.
- Each deletion or formatting change appears in a balloon.
- Hover the pointer over the change to see the name of the reviewer and when the change was made.

***Note:** You need to be in Print Layout View (click **View** and then click **Print Layout**) to see the balloons.*

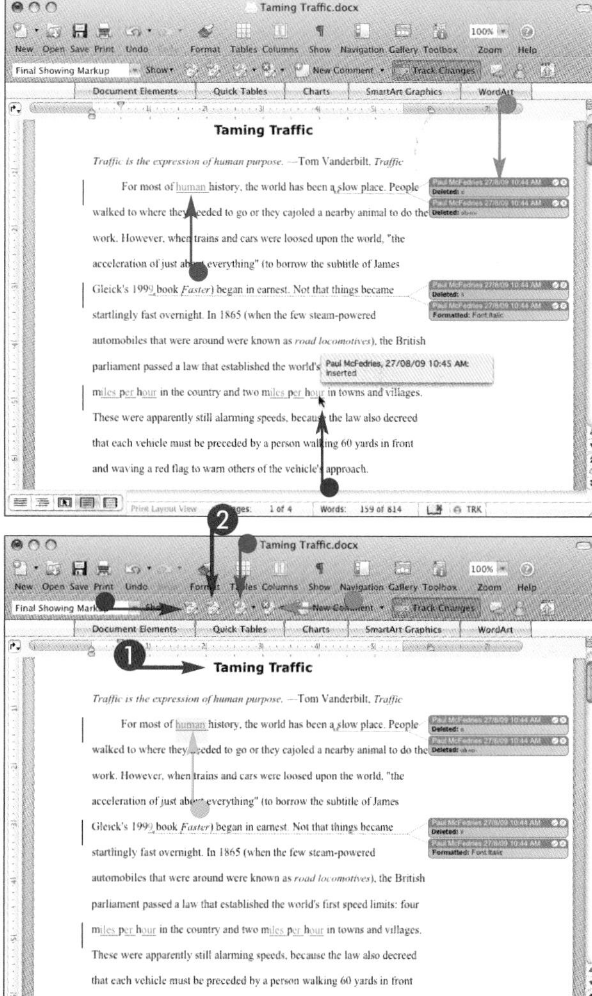

## ACCEPT OR REJECT CHANGES

1. Click at the beginning of the document.
2. In the Reviewing toolbar, click the **Next** button.

- Word selects the next change in the document.
- To return to an earlier change, click the **Previous** button.
- To accept the change, click the **Accept** button.
- To reject the change, click the **Reject** button.

### Are their faster ways to review a document's changes?

Yes. Word offers a few shortcut methods that you can use. For example, if you want to accept most of the changes, you do not need to go through them individually. Instead, make your rejections, click the **Accept** ▾, and then click **Accept All Changes in Document**. Similarly, to reject all the remaining changes click the **Reject** ▾ and then click **Reject All Changes in Document**.

### Is it possible to see only the changes made by a single person?

Yes. Word enables you to show the changes made by individual users — who are called *reviewers*. In the Reviewing toolbar, click the **Show** ▾, click **Reviewers**, and then click **All Reviewers** to hide the changes made by all the reviewers. Click the **Show** ▾, click **Reviewers**, and then click the name of the reviewer whose changes you want to see.

# Protect a Document

If you have a document that you want to share with other people and where it is important that you keep track of all the changes made to the document, you can configure the document to prevent untracked changes, and even to enforce this option with a password.

**It is easy to turn off the Track Changes tool — either accidentally or on purpose — so you can never be sure whether your document contains any untracked changes. Protecting the document prevents this from happening.**

## Protect a Document

1. Open the document you want to protect.
2. Click **Tools**.
3. Click **Protect Document**.

   The Protect Document dialog appears.

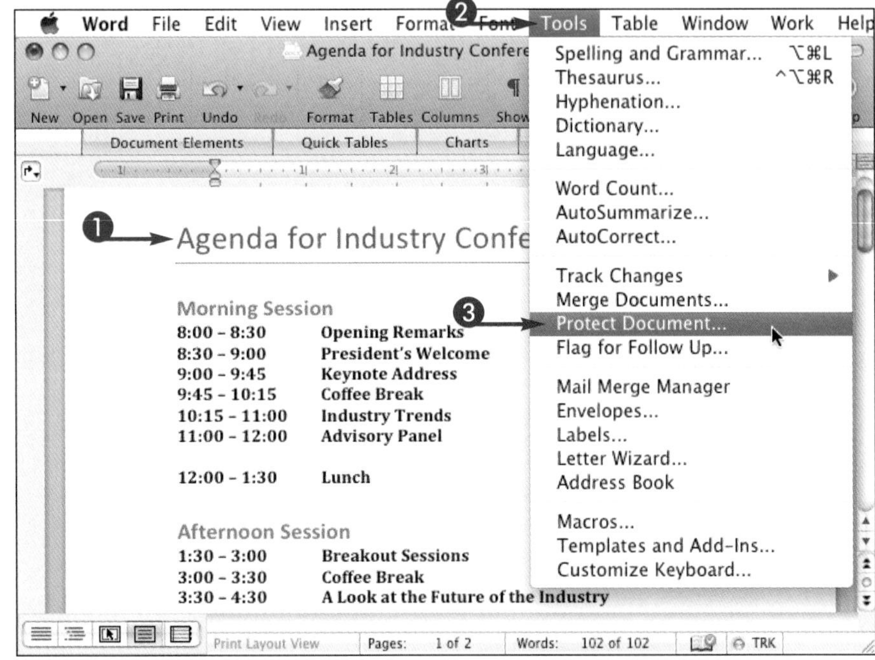


4. Select the **Tracked changes** option (○ changes to ◉).
5. Type a password.
6. Click **OK**.

   The Confirm Password dialog appears.
7. Type the password again.
8. Click **OK**.

***Note:** To turn off document protection, click **Tools**, click **Unprotect Document**, type the password, and then click **OK**.*

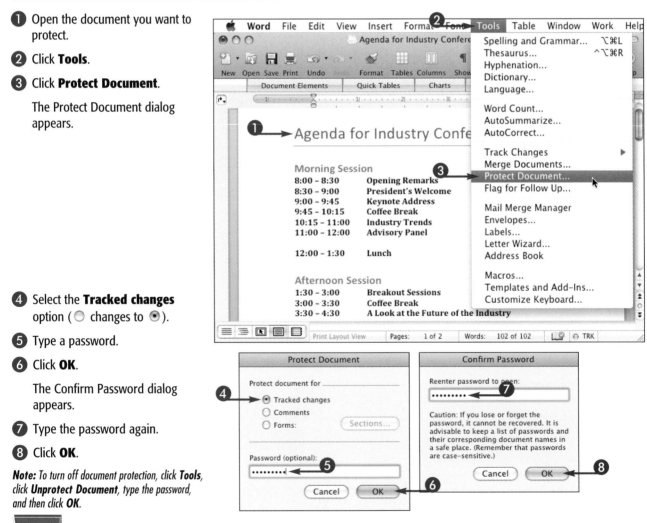

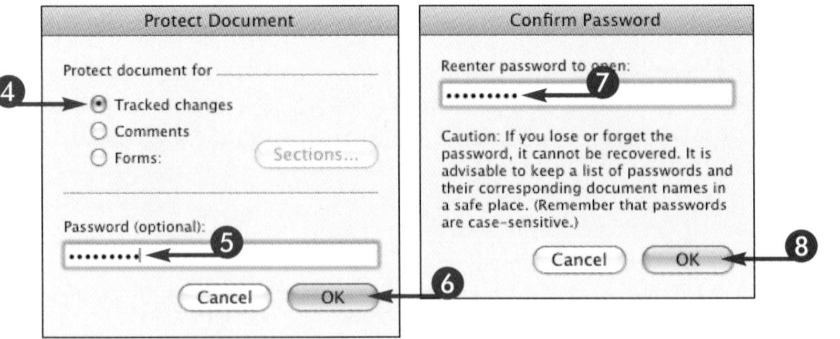

# Calculate the Word Count

You can use the Word Count tool to calculate not only the number of words in a document, but also the number of pages, characters, paragraphs, and lines.

## Calculate the Word Count

1. Open the document you want to work with.
2. Click **Tools**.
3. Click **Word Count**.

- This value tells you the total number of pages.
- This value tells you the total number of words.
- You can also click anywhere in the status bar's Word Count section to run the Word Count tool.

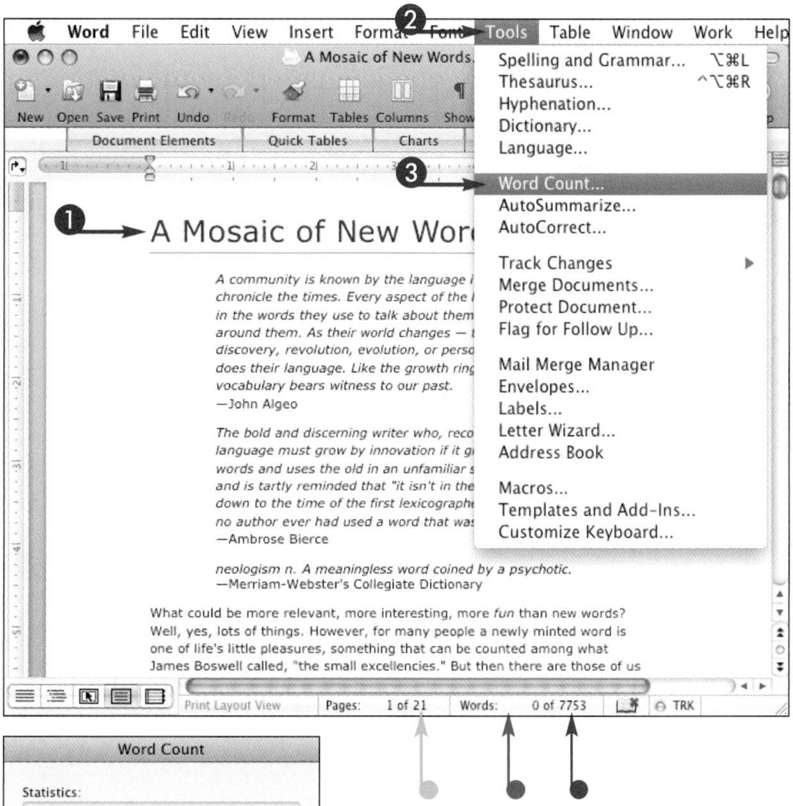

Word · File · Edit · View · Insert · Format · Font · Tools · Table · Window · Work · Help

A Mosaic of New Words

Spelling and Grammar... ⌥⌘L
Thesaurus... ^⌥⌘R
Hyphenation...
Dictionary...
Language...
Word Count...
AutoSummarize...
AutoCorrect...
Track Changes
Merge Documents...
Protect Document...
Flag for Follow Up...
Mail Merge Manager
Envelopes...
Labels...
Letter Wizard...
Address Book
Macros...
Templates and Add-Ins...
Customize Keyboard...

Print Layout View · Pages: 1 of 21 · Words: 0 of 7753 · TRK

The Word Count dialog appears.

- Word displays the document's statistics.

4. When you finish, click **OK**.

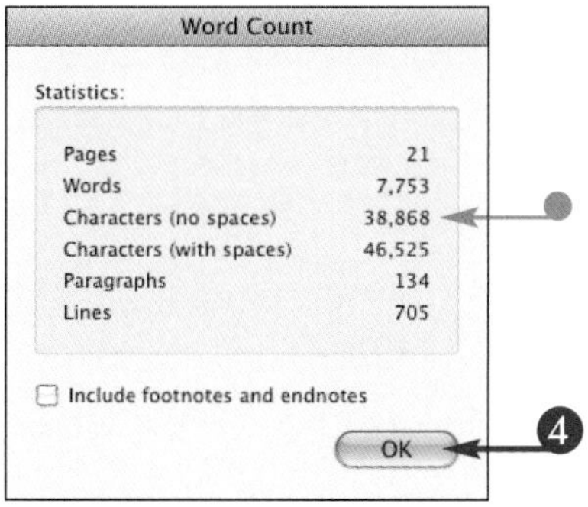

**Word Count**

Statistics:

| | |
|---|---|
| Pages | 21 |
| Words | 7,753 |
| Characters (no spaces) | 38,868 |
| Characters (with spaces) | 46,525 |
| Paragraphs | 134 |
| Lines | 705 |

☐ Include footnotes and endnotes

OK

# Add a Document to the Work Menu

If you have a document that you use frequently, you can make it easier and faster to open that document by adding it to Word's Work menu. This enables you to open the document with just a couple of mouse clicks.

## Add a Document to the Work Menu

### ADD A DOCUMENT TO THE WORK MENU

1. Open the document you want to add to the Work menu.

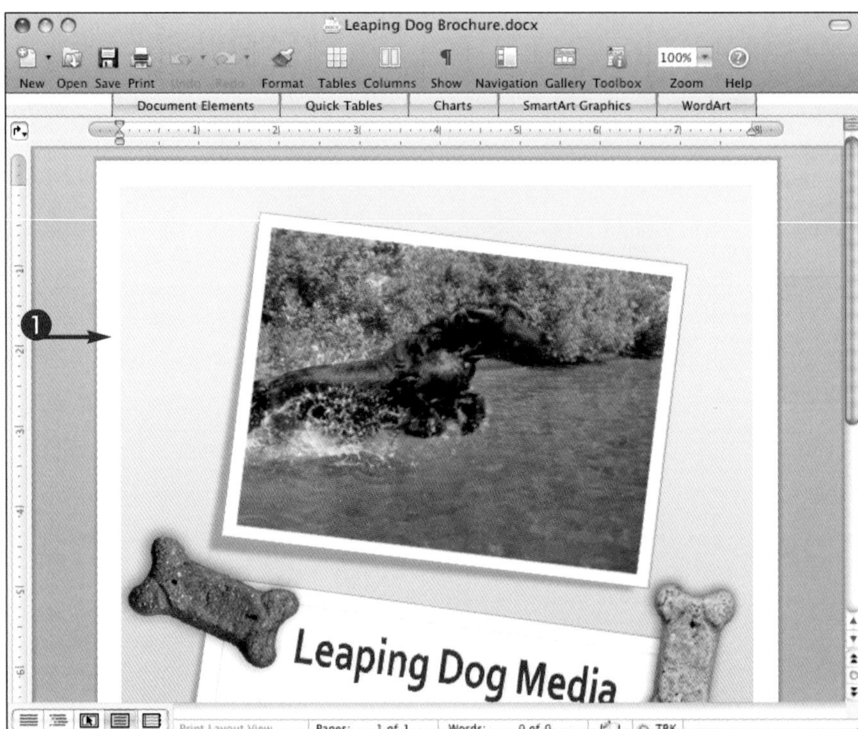


2. Click **Work**.
3. Click **Add to Work Menu**.

   Word adds the document name to the Work menu.

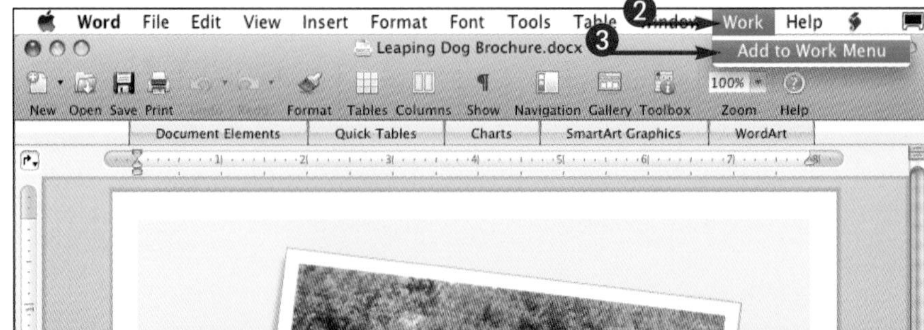

## OPEN A DOCUMENT FROM THE WORK MENU

1. Click **Work**.
2. Click the document you want to open.

- Word opens the document.

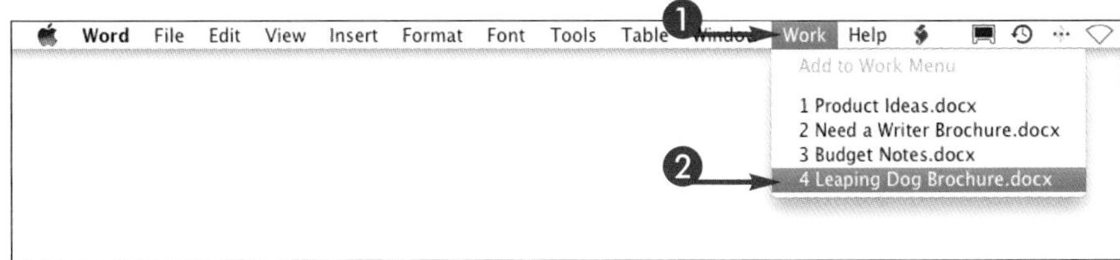

TIP

### How can I remove documents from the Work menu?

Unfortunately, Word does not offer an easy way to do this. Follow these steps to add a command to the Work menu:

1. Click **View**.
2. Click **Customize Toolbars and Menus**.
3. Click the **Commands** tab.
4. In the Categories list, click **All Commands**.
5. In the Commands list, click and drag **ToolsCustomizeRemoveMenuShortcut** and then drop the command inside the Work menu.
6. Click **OK**.

To remove a document from the Work menu, click **Work**, click **Tools Customize Remove Menu Shortcut** (changes to –), click **Work** again, and then click the document you want to remove.

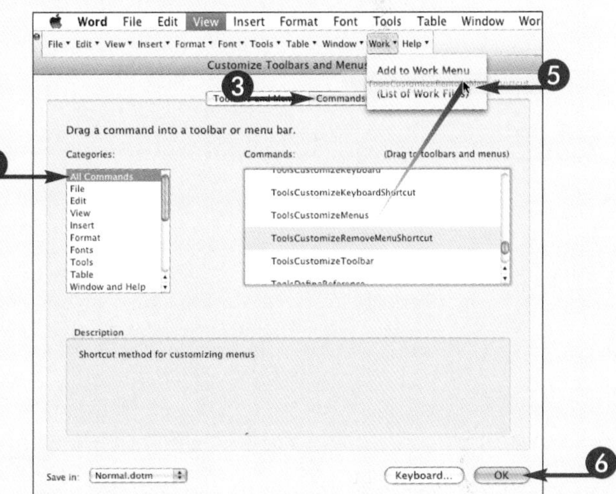

# Add an AutoCorrect Entry

You can speed up your text entry chores and make your Word documents more accurate by adding your own entries to Word's AutoCorrect tool.

**The AutoCorrect tool looks for common misspellings as you type, and automatically corrects those errors. If there is a word that you often misspell that is not recognized by AutoCorrect, you can add your own entry for that term to enable AutoCorrect to fix the error for you in the future.**

## Add an AutoCorrect Entry

1. Click **Word**.
2. Click **Preferences**.

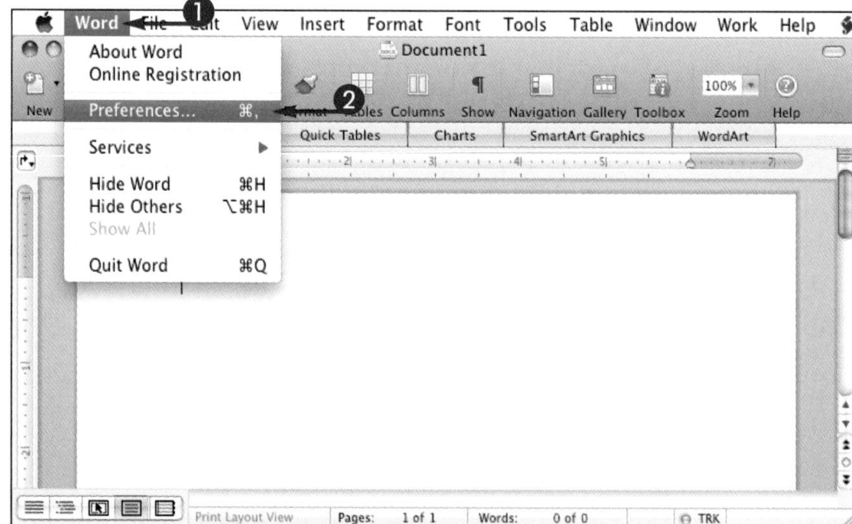


The Word Preferences dialog appears.

3. Click **AutoCorrect**.

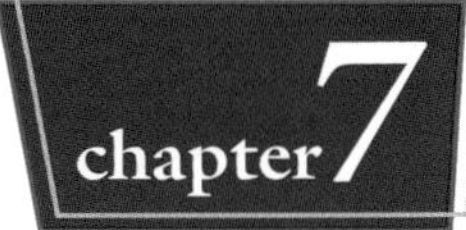


The AutoCorrect preferences appear.

4. Click the **AutoCorrect** tab.
5. Type the misspelling that you want corrected in the Replace text box.
6. Type the correction in the With text box.
7. Click **Add**.

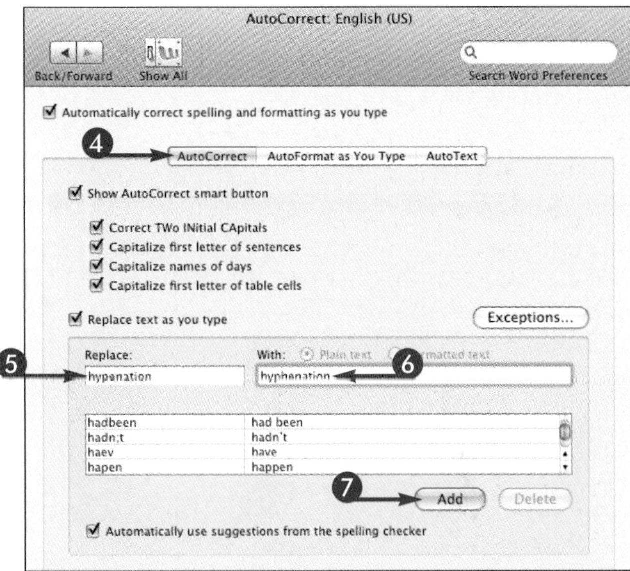


- Word adds the misspelling and correction to the list of entries.

8. Click **OK**.

The next time you type the misspelling that you specified in Step **5**, Word automatically corrects it to the text that you specified in Step **6**.

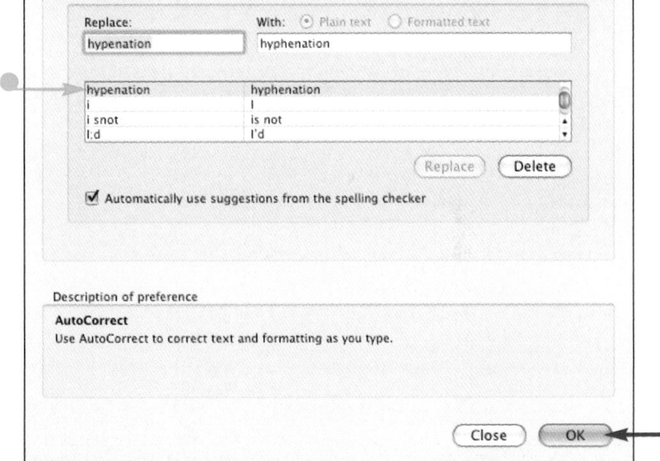

### Can I reverse an AutoCorrect correction?

Yes. If you have not performed any other actions in Word since the correction, press ⌘ + Z to undo the change. Otherwise, position the pointer over the corrected text until you see an underline appear. Move the mouse over the underline to reveal the AutoCorrect Smart Tag. Click the Smart Tag and then click Undo Automatic Correction.

### Is AutoCorrect only for correcting spelling errors?

No. You can use it as a shortcut for typing frequently used text. Such frequently used bits of text are called *boilerplate*, and having to type them constantly can be tedious and time-wasting. To fix this, select the boilerplate text and follow Steps **1** to **7**. In Step **4**, type a short abbreviation or code. When you later type that code, Word replaces it with the boilerplate text.

CHAPTER

# Building Word Tables

**If you have data that consists of a list of items, each with several details — for example, a parts list or class roster — you can display that data in an organized fashion by using a *table*. This is a rectangular structure where each item in the list gets its own horizontal rectangle called a *row*; each set of details in the list gets its own vertical rectangle called a *column*; and the rectangle formed by the intersection of a row and a column is called a *cell*, and you use the table cells to hold the data. A Word table is similar to an Excel worksheet or a database table.**

# Insert a Quick Table

## You can insert a table quickly and easily by using Word's Quick Tables. A Quick Table is a table that has a predefined layout and style, so you can add a table with just a few mouse clicks.

**Word offers nearly two dozen predefined Quick Tables. After you insert the Quick Table, you add your own data into the existing cells. You can also customize the table by adding rows and columns and by applying different formatting.**

## Insert a Quick Table

1. Position the cursor where you want the table to appear.
2. Click **Quick Tables**.
3. Click either **Basic** or **Complex**.
4. Use ◀ and ▶ to locate the Quick Table style you prefer.
5. Click the Quick Table that you want to insert.

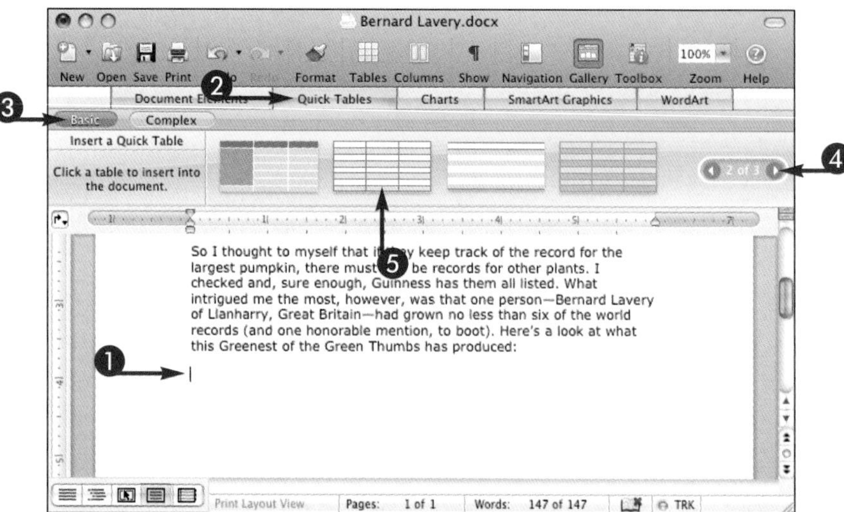


- Word adds the Quick Table to the document.
- Click in a cell to add data to that cell.

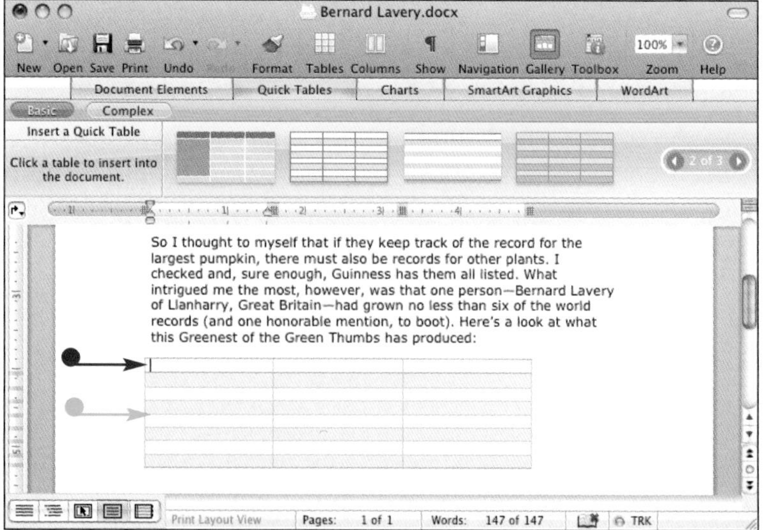

# Insert a Table

**If none of Word's Quick Tables is suitable, or if you just need a simple table without any formatting, you can use Word's Tables features to insert a plain table.**

**See the section "Insert a Quick Table" to learn about Quick Tables.**

## Insert a Table

1. Position the cursor where you want the table to appear.
2. Click **Tables**.
3. Move the ↖ into the grid that appears.

- Word displays the size of the table represented by the box under the ↖.

4. Click the box that represents the table size you want.

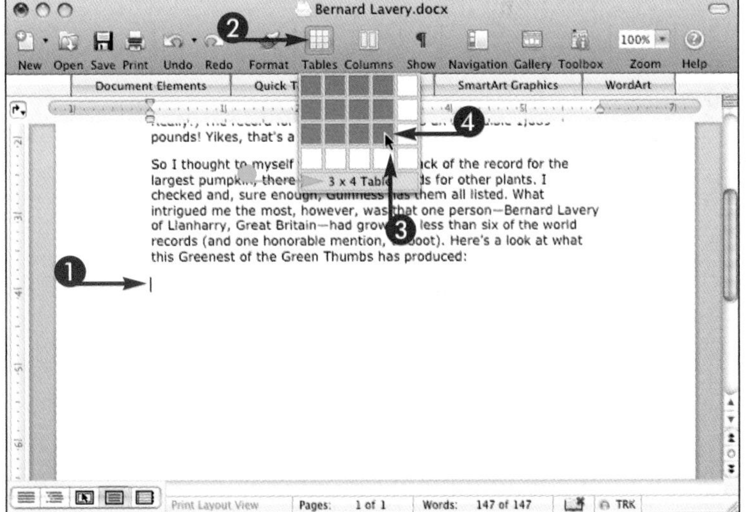

- Word inserts the table.
- Click in a cell to add data to that cell.

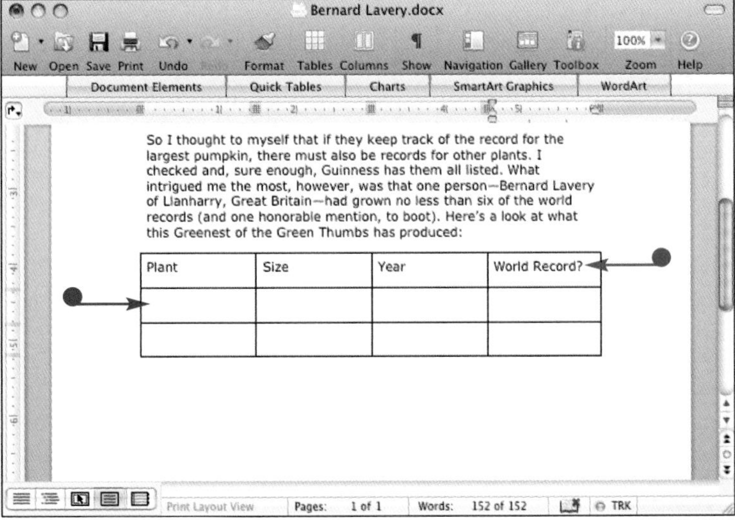

# Draw a Table

If you require an unusual table configuration, or if you want complete control over the layout of your table, you can use Word's Draw Table feature. This feature enables you to use your mouse to draw a table and all of its rows and columns.

## Draw a Table

❶ Click **Table**.

❷ Click **Draw Table**.

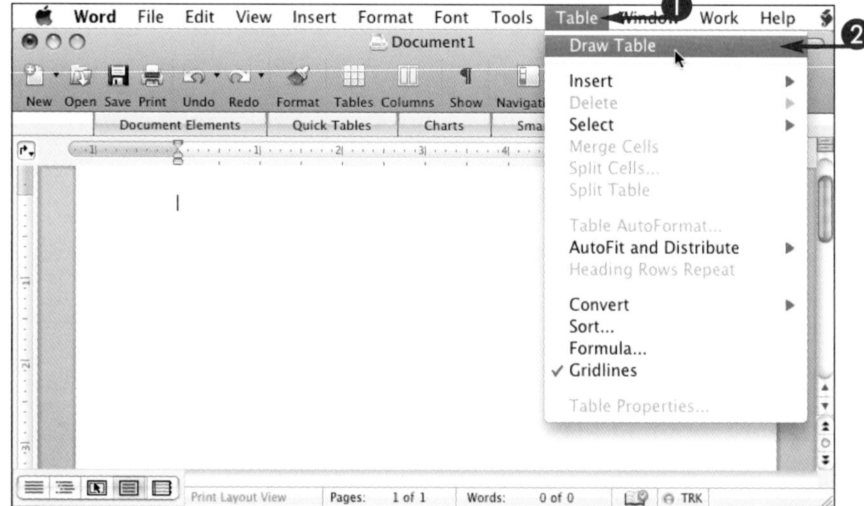


● ↖ changes to ✎.

❸ Click and drag ✎ to create the borders of your table.

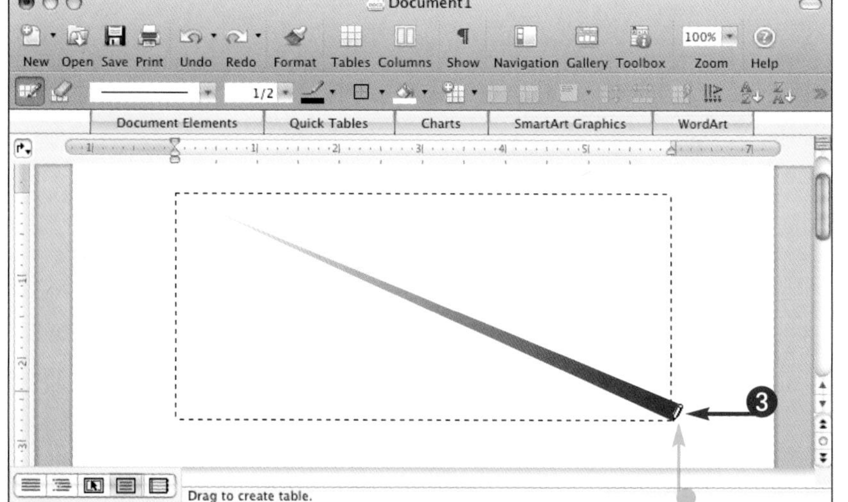

4 Click and drag horizontally.

- Word displays a dotted line.
- When you drag past the halfway point, Word completes the line.

5 Release the mouse button.

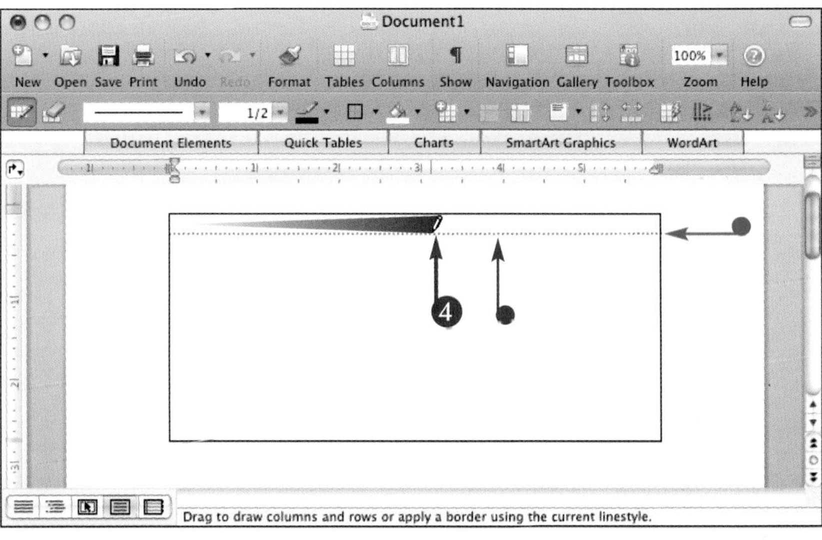


- Excel adds a horizontal line to define a row.

6 Click and drag vertically to define a column.

7 Repeat steps **4** to **6** to draw your table's rows and columns.

***Note:*** *Your rows and column do not have to be a uniform size and shape.*

8 When you finish, click **Draw Table** ( ) to turn off the Draw Table feature.

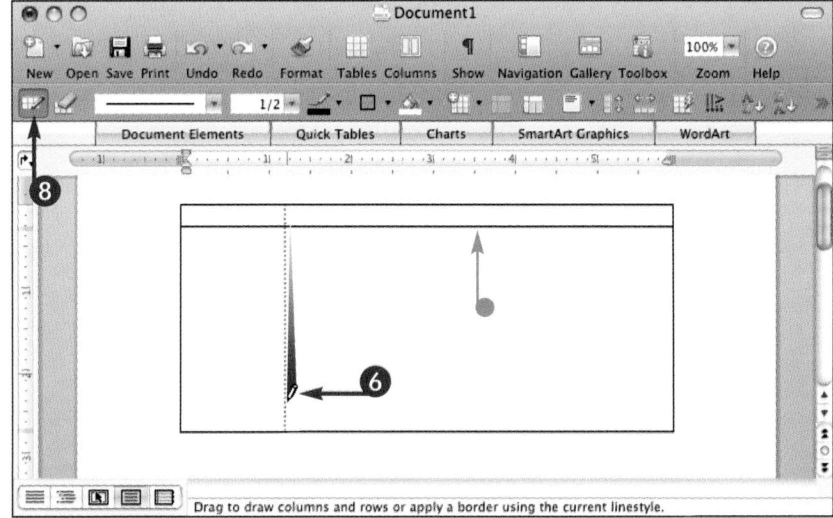

TIPS

**I have a list of items where I have used tabs to create columns. Can I convert that data to a table?**

Yes. This is often a good idea because then you can apply Word's many table tools to the data. Select the text, click **Table**, click **Convert**, and then click **Convert Text to Table**. In the Convert Text to Table dialog, adjust the number of rows and columns, if necessary. Select the **Tabs** option ( changes to ) and then click **OK**.

**Can I insert an Excel worksheet in a Word document?**

Yes. You can insert a sheet from an existing Excel workbook, or you can insert a blank Excel worksheet. To insert an existing worksheet, click **Insert**, click **File**, click the Excel file, click **Insert**, and then click **OK**. Select a worksheet, type a range, and then click **OK**. To insert a blank sheet, click **Insert**, click **Object**, click **Microsoft Excel Sheet**, and then click **OK**.

# Select Table Cells

To perform most table operations, such as formatting cells, adding and deleting rows and columns, and merging and splitting cells, you must first select a cell, row, column, or even the entire table.

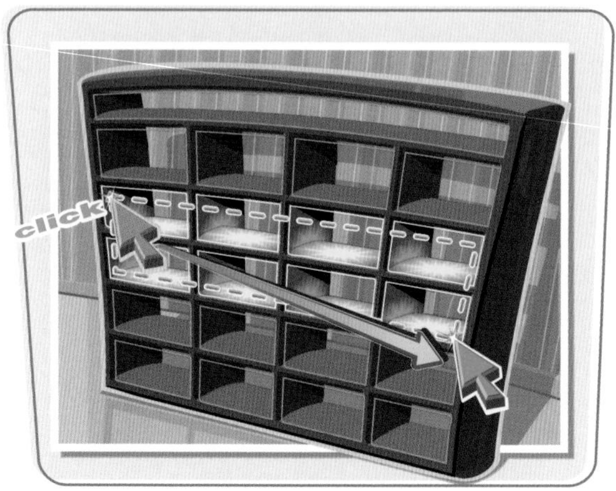
click

## Select Table Cells

1. Click inside the table. Where you click depends on what you want to select:

   If you want to select a cell, click the cell.

   If you want to select a row, click any cell in that row.

   If you want to select a column, click any cell in that column.

   If you want to select the entire table, click any cell.

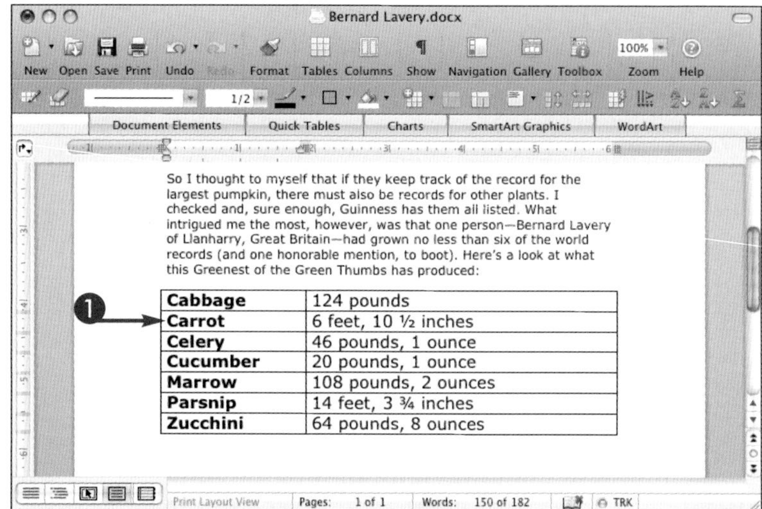

Bernard Lavery.docx
New
Open
Save
Print
Undo
Redo
Format
Tables
Columns
Show
Navigation
Gallery
Toolbox
Zoom
Help
100%
Document Elements
Quick Tables
Charts
SmartArt Graphics
WordArt
So I thought to myself that if they keep track of the record for the largest pumpkin, there must also be records for other plants. I checked and, sure enough, Guinness has them all listed. What intrigued me the most, however, was that one person—Bernard Lavery of Llanharry, Great Britain—had grown no less than six of the world records (and one honorable mention, to boot). Here's a look at what this Greenest of the Green Thumbs has produced:
Cabbage 124 pounds
Carrot 6 feet, 10 ½ inches
Celery 46 pounds, 1 ounce
Cucumber 20 pounds, 1 ounce
Marrow 108 pounds, 2 ounces
Parsnip 14 feet, 3 ¾ inches
Zucchini 64 pounds, 8 ounces
Print Layout View
Pages: 1 of 1
Words: 150 of 182
TRK

2. Click **Table**.
3. Click **Select**.

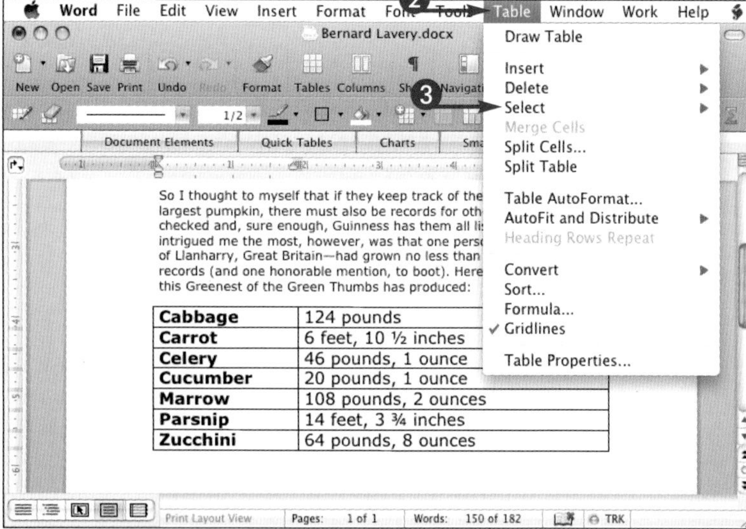

Word
File
Edit
View
Insert
Format
Table
Window
Work
Help
Draw Table
Insert
Delete
Select
Merge Cells
Split Cells...
Split Table
Table AutoFormat...
AutoFit and Distribute
Heading Rows Repeat
Convert
Sort...
Formula...
Gridlines
Table Properties...
Cabbage 124 pounds
Carrot 6 feet, 10 ½ inches
Celery 46 pounds, 1 ounce
Cucumber 20 pounds, 1 ounce
Marrow 108 pounds, 2 ounces
Parsnip 14 feet, 3 ¾ inches
Zucchini 64 pounds, 8 ounces
Print Layout View
Pages: 1 of 1
Words: 150 of 182

Word displays a menu of select options.

4 Click the object you want to select.

You can select Table, Column, Row, or Cell. This example shows Row selected.

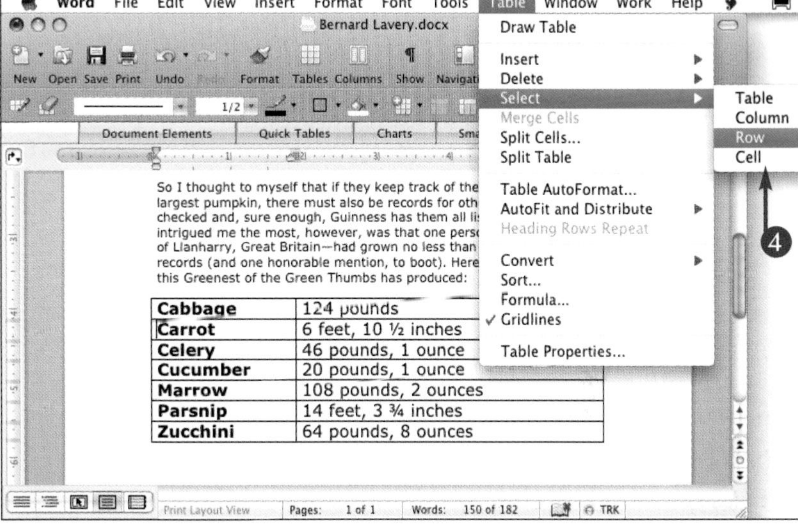

- Word selects the object.

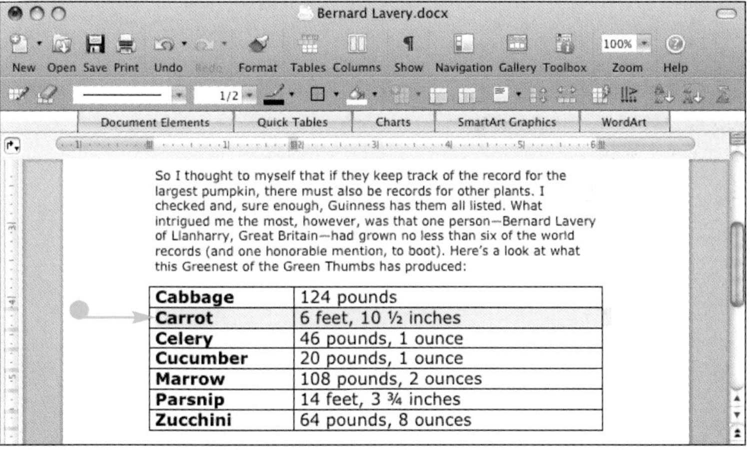

TIP

**Are there mouse methods I can use to select table cells?**

Yes. You can select any cell, row, column, or even the entire table with a single click:

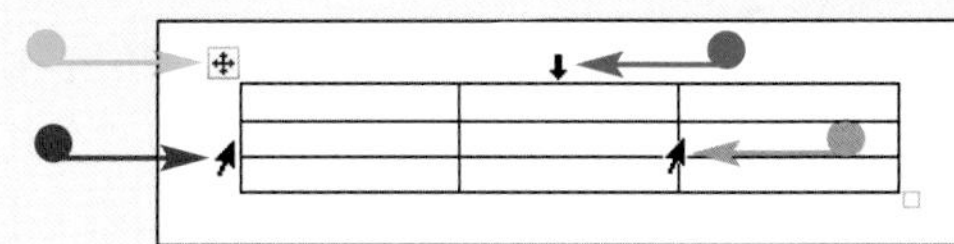

- To select the entire table, move the ↖ over the table and then click the table select icon (⊞).
- To select a row, move ↖ to the left of the row (↖ changes to ↗) and then click.
- To select a column, move ↖ above the column (↖ changes to ⬇) and then click.
- To select a cell, move ↖ to the left margin of the cell (↖ changes to ↗) and then click.

To select multiple, rows, columns, or cells, click and drag over the objects you want to select.

# Insert and Delete Rows or Columns

If you need to add more items to your Word table, you can add rows either at the end of the table or within the table. Similarly, if you need to record extra details about each item, you can add more columns to the table.

**If you have items or details that you no longer need, you can delete one or more rows or columns to keep the table uncluttered.**

## Insert and Delete Rows or Columns

### INSERT A ROW OR COLUMN

1. Select an existing row or column.

   To insert multiple rows or columns, select the same number of existing rows or columns.

2. Click **Table**.
3. Click **Insert**.
4. Click a command.

   You can click **Rows Above** or **Rows Below** to insert a row above or below the current row.

   You can click **Columns to the Left** or **Columns to the Right** to insert a column left or right of the current column.

- Word inserts the row or column.
- Another way to add a row to the end of the table is to click in the bottom-right cell, position the cursor after any text in the cell, and then press Tab.

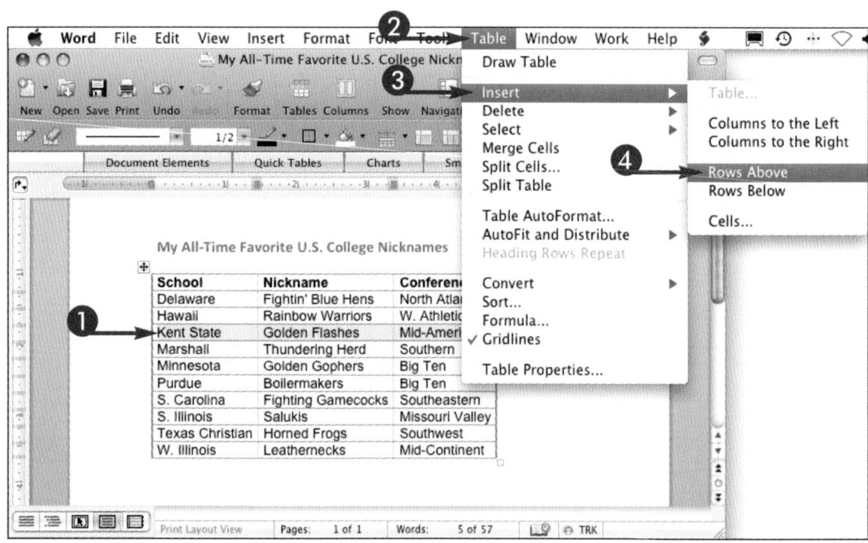

## DELETE A ROW OR COLUMN

1. Select the row or column you want to delete.
2. Click **Table**.
3. Click **Delete**.
4. Click the object you want to delete: Rows or Columns.

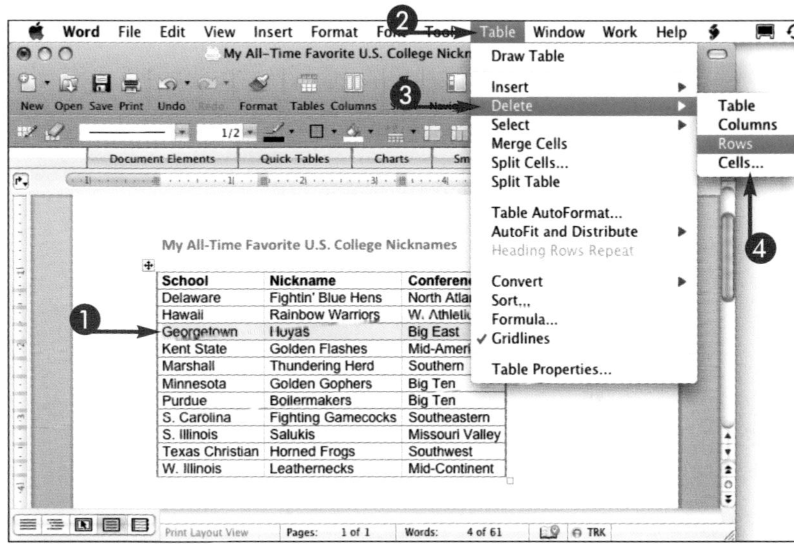

- Word deletes the row or column.

### TIP

**Can I insert rows and columns using the toolbar?**

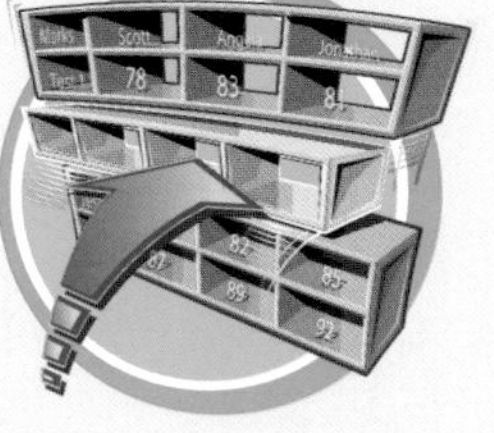

Yes. First, make sure the table tools are visible: click **View**, click **Toolbars**, and then click **Tables and Borders**. Find the **Insert Table** tool (⇹), click ▾, and then click one of the following:

| | |
|---|---|
| ⇕ | Click to insert a column to the left. |
| ▦▾ | Click to insert a column to the right. |
| ▤ | Click to insert a row above. |
| ▤ | Click to insert a row below. |

# Change the Column Width or Row Height

If you have a long line of text in a cell, Word may wrap the text onto a second line. To avoid the wrapping, you can increase the width of the column. Similarly, if a column only contains a few characters in each cell, you can decrease the width to fit more columns on the page.

**Word also enables you to change the row height. This is useful if you want to insert an image, WordArt, or SmartArt graphic in a cell.**

## Change the Column Width or Row Height

### CHANGE THE COLUMN WIDTH

❶ Move ↖ over the right border of any cell in the column you want to resize (↖ changes to ↔).

❷ Click and drag the border to the right to increase the width or to the left to decrease the width.

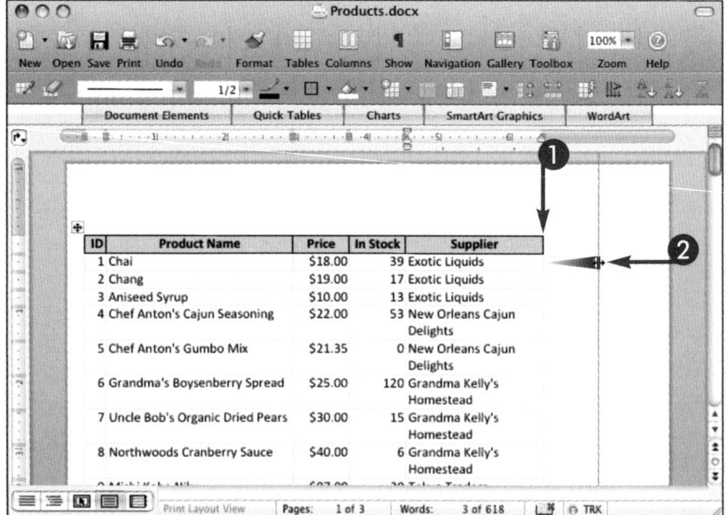


| ID | Product Name | Price | In Stock | Supplier |
|---|---|---|---|---|
| 1 | Chai | $18.00 | 39 | Exotic Liquids |
| 2 | Chang | $19.00 | 17 | Exotic Liquids |
| 3 | Aniseed Syrup | $10.00 | 13 | Exotic Liquids |
| 4 | Chef Anton's Cajun Seasoning | $22.00 | 53 | New Orleans Cajun Delights |
| 5 | Chef Anton's Gumbo Mix | $21.35 | 0 | New Orleans Cajun Delights |
| 6 | Grandma's Boysenberry Spread | $25.00 | 120 | Grandma Kelly's Homestead |
| 7 | Uncle Bob's Organic Dried Pears | $30.00 | 15 | Grandma Kelly's Homestead |
| 8 | Northwoods Cranberry Sauce | $40.00 | 6 | Grandma Kelly's Homestead |

❸ Release the mouse.

- Word changes the column width.

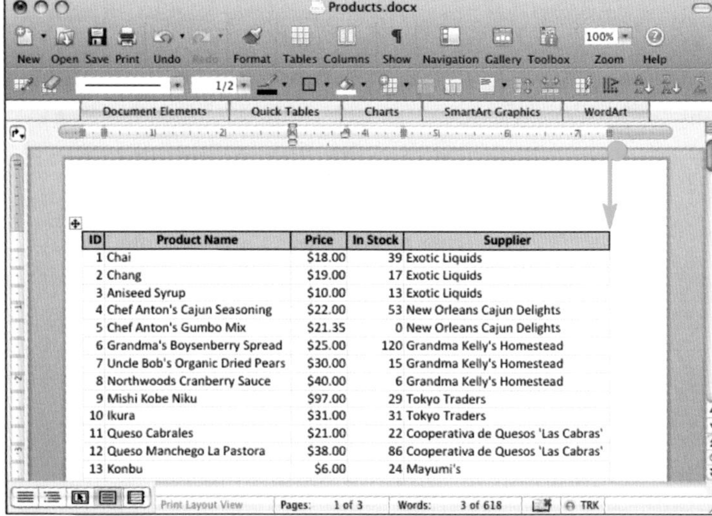


| ID | Product Name | Price | In Stock | Supplier |
|---|---|---|---|---|
| 1 | Chai | $18.00 | 39 | Exotic Liquids |
| 2 | Chang | $19.00 | 17 | Exotic Liquids |
| 3 | Aniseed Syrup | $10.00 | 13 | Exotic Liquids |
| 4 | Chef Anton's Cajun Seasoning | $22.00 | 53 | New Orleans Cajun Delights |
| 5 | Chef Anton's Gumbo Mix | $21.35 | 0 | New Orleans Cajun Delights |
| 6 | Grandma's Boysenberry Spread | $25.00 | 120 | Grandma Kelly's Homestead |
| 7 | Uncle Bob's Organic Dried Pears | $30.00 | 15 | Grandma Kelly's Homestead |
| 8 | Northwoods Cranberry Sauce | $40.00 | 6 | Grandma Kelly's Homestead |
| 9 | Mishi Kobe Niku | $97.00 | 29 | Tokyo Traders |
| 10 | Ikura | $31.00 | 31 | Tokyo Traders |
| 11 | Queso Cabrales | $21.00 | 22 | Cooperativa de Quesos 'Las Cabras' |
| 12 | Queso Manchego La Pastora | $38.00 | 86 | Cooperativa de Quesos 'Las Cabras' |
| 13 | Konbu | $6.00 | 24 | Mayumi's |

## CHANGE THE ROW HEIGHT

1. Move ➘ over the bottom border of any cell in the row you want to resize (➘ changes to ÷).
2. Click and drag the border down to increase the height or up to decrease the height.

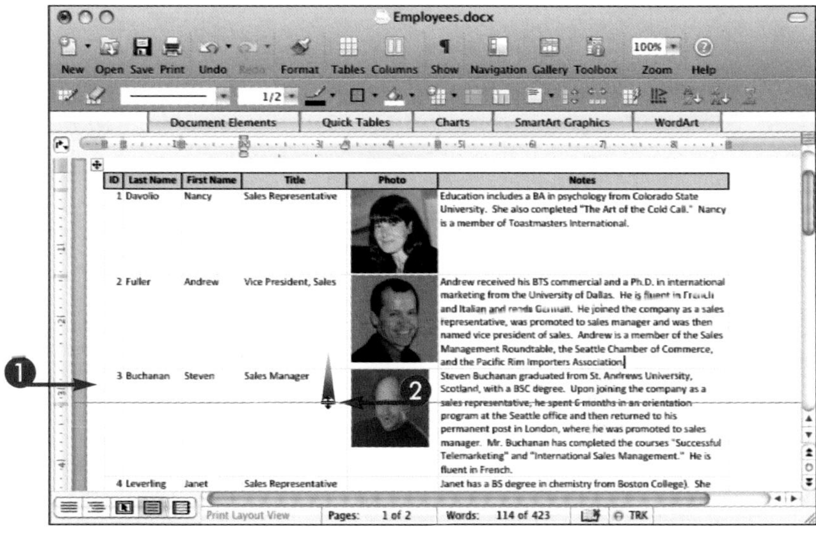

3. Release the mouse.

- Word changes the row height.

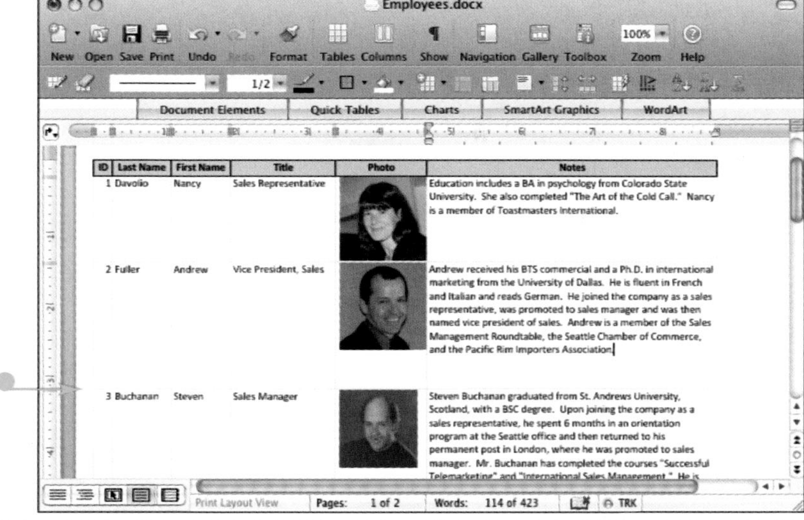

## TIPS

### Is there an easier way to adjust the column width to fit the contents of a column?

Yes. You can use Word's AutoFit feature, which automatically adjusts the column width to fit the widest item in a column. Select the row or column, click **Table**, click **AutoFit and Distribute**, and then click **AutoFit to Contents**. Alternatively, move ➘ over the right edge of any cell in the column (➘ changes to ◂||▸) and then double-click.

### Why does Word prevent me from making a row height any smaller than a certain size?

The most likely explanation is you have text or an image in that row that would no longer fit in the row if you made the height any smaller. In general, the row height can be as small as possible to fit all the text and images in the row, but no smaller.

# Apply an AutoFormat to a Table

**You can save time and effort by formatting your Word table using the AutoFormat feature. AutoFormat offers more than 40 predefined table styles that apply formatting for the table borders, cell backgrounds, and cell fonts.**

**You can apply the entire AutoFormat to your table, or you can choose which formats you want to apply.**

## Apply an AutoFormat to a Table

1. Click anywhere inside the table you want to format.
2. Click **Table**.
3. Click **Table AutoFormat**.

   You can also click the **Table AutoFormat** button ( ) in the Tables and Borders toolbar.

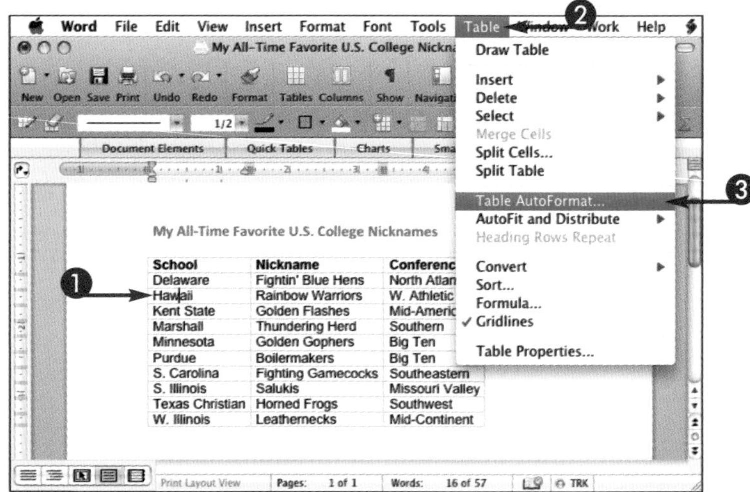


The Table AutoFormat dialog appears.

4. In the Formats list, click the AutoFormat you want to apply.

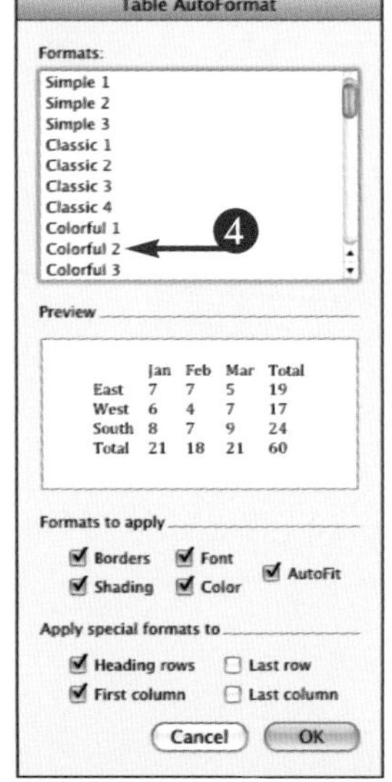

- Word shows a preview of the formatting.

5 To prevent a format from being applied, click its check box (☑ changes to ☐).

6 Click **OK**.

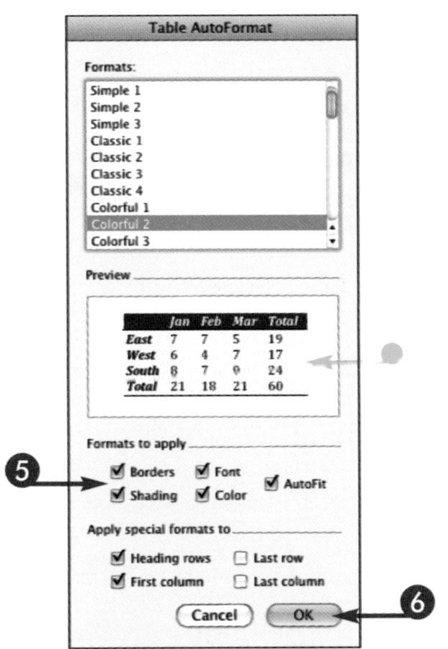


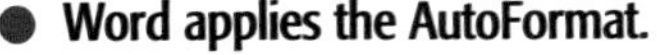

- Word applies the AutoFormat.

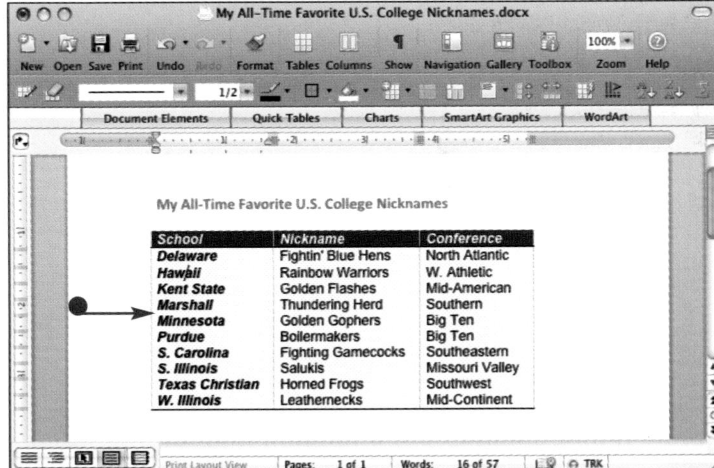


| School | Nickname | Conference |
|---|---|---|
| Delaware | Fightin' Blue Hens | North Atlantic |
| Hawaii | Rainbow Warriors | W. Athletic |
| Kent State | Golden Flashes | Mid-American |
| Marshall | Thundering Herd | Southern |
| Minnesota | Golden Gophers | Big Ten |
| Purdue | Boilermakers | Big Ten |
| S. Carolina | Fighting Gamecocks | Southeastern |
| S. Illinois | Salukis | Missouri Valley |
| Texas Christian | Horned Frogs | Southwest |
| W. Illinois | Leathernecks | Mid-Continent |

**TIP**

## How can I apply an AutoFormat from the Formatting Palette?

1 Click anywhere inside the table you want to format.

2 Click the **Toolbox** button.

3 Click the **Formatting Palette** button.

4 Click the **Styles** panel.

5 Use the Pick style to apply list to click a table style.

- The table styles display the ⊞ icon.

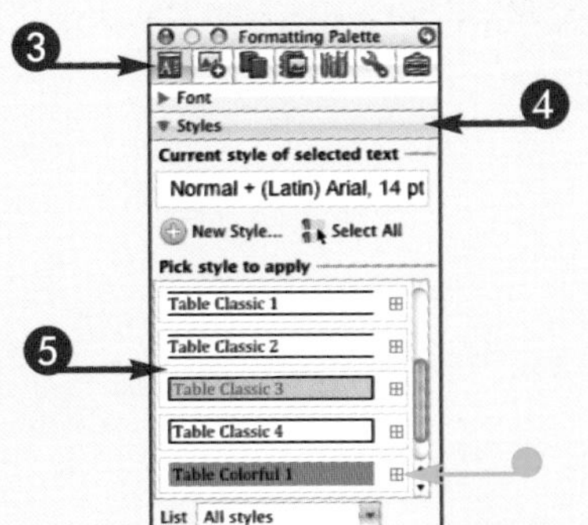

# Merge Table Cells

You can create more room for text or graphics by merging two or more cells into a single cell. For example, it is common to merge some or all of the top row of cells to use as a table title.

## Merge Table Cells

### MERGE CELLS HORIZONTALLY

1. Select two or more cells in a row.

*Note:* *To learn how to select cells, see the section "Select Table Cells" earlier in this chapter.*

2. Click **Table**.
3. Click **Merge Cells**.

- You can also click the **Merge Cells** button (▤) in the Tables and Borders toolbar.

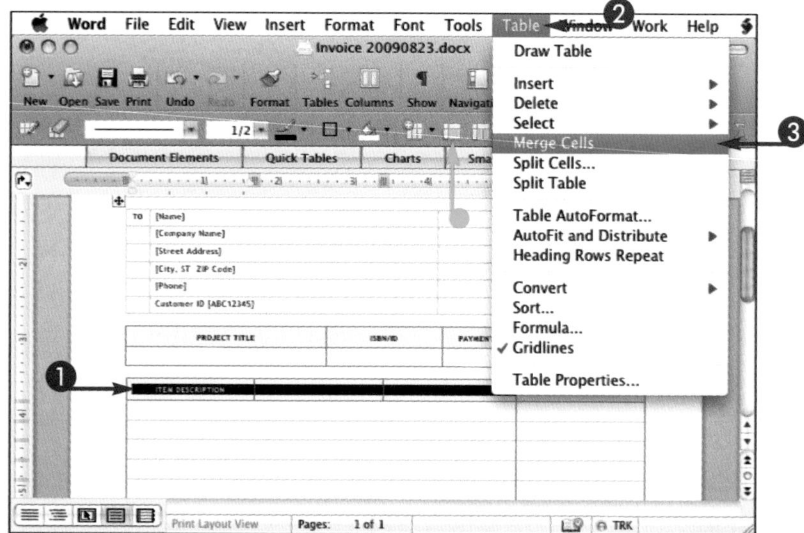


- Word merges the selected cells into a single horizontal cell.

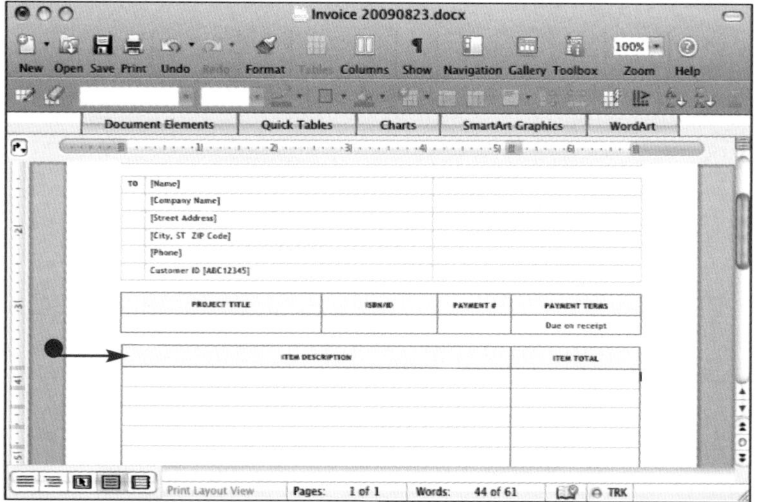

## MERGE CELLS VERTICALLY

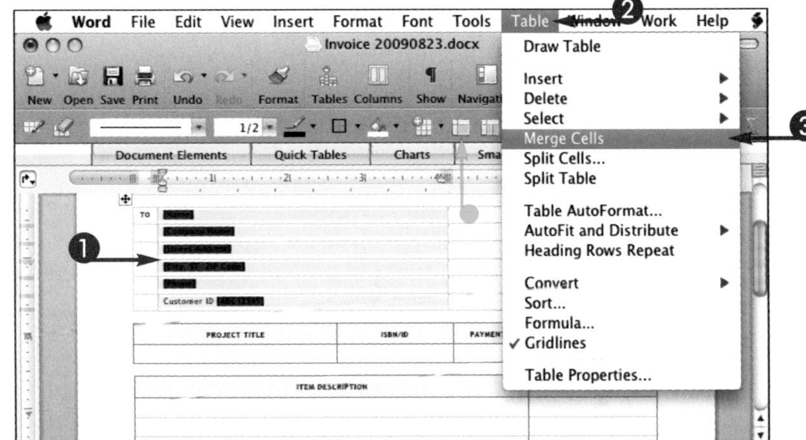


1. Select two or more cells in a column.

**Note:** *To learn how to select cells, see the section "Select Table Cells."*

2. Click **Table**.
3. Click **Merge Cells**.

- You can also click the **Merge Cells** button ( ) in the Tables and Borders toolbar.

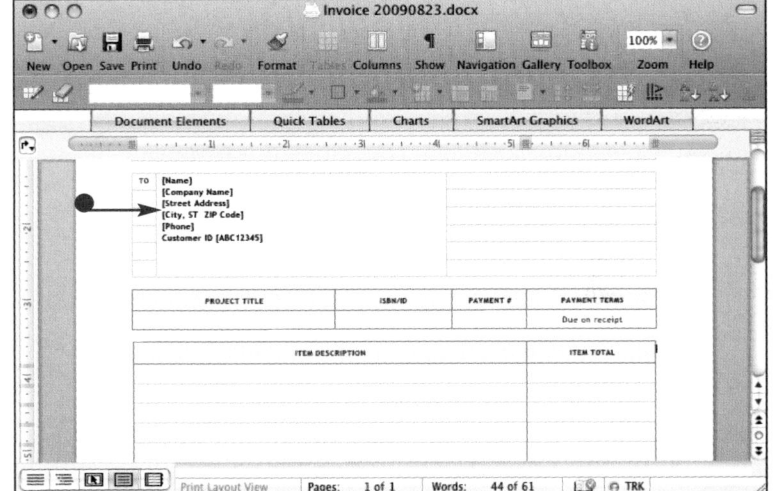


- Word merges the selected cells into a single vertical cell.

**I selected my cells, but the Merge command is disabled. Why?**

First, check to make sure that the cells you selected are not in fact a single cell that you merged previously. Second, Word only allows you to merge cells that you have selected by clicking and dragging the mouse. If your selection includes one or more cells that you selected individually by clicking the left margin of the cell, Word disables the Merge command.

**Can I merge cells horizontally and vertically in a single operation?**

Yes. However, for this to work, there are two things you need to do. First, all the cells must be adjacent to each other; you cannot merge cells from different parts of the table. Second, the cells you select must form a complete rectangle, which means you must select an equal number of cells horizontally, and an equal number of cells vertically. For example, it is okay to select a 3x4 rectangle of cells (three cells horizontally and four cells vertically).

# Split a Cell into Two or More Cells

You can create more detailed data by splitting a cell into two or more cells. For example, if you currently use a single cell to record an entire address, you can split that cell into multiple cells that each hold part of the address, such as the street name and number, city, and postal code.

**You can also split a cell if you want to add a different type of data to the cell, such as a graphic.**

## Split a Cell into Two or More Cells

❶ Select the cell you want to split.

***Note:*** *To learn how to select a cell, see the section "Select Table Cells."*

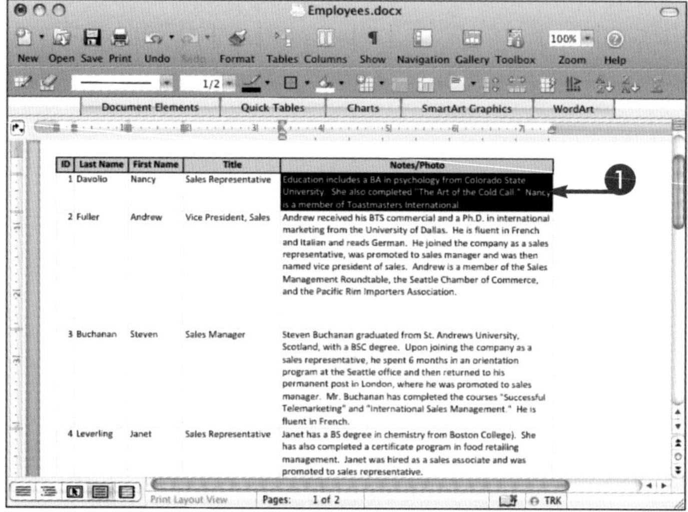


❷ Click **Table**.

❸ Click **Split Cells**.

- You can also click the **Split Cells** button (▤) in the Tables and Borders toolbar.

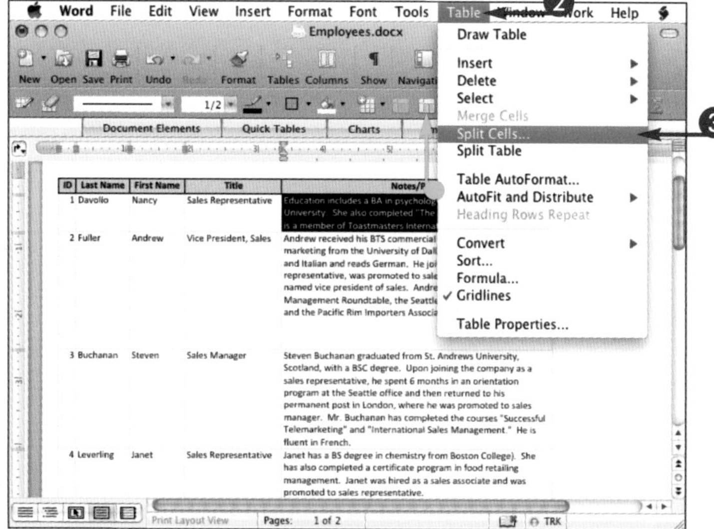

The Split Cells dialog appears.

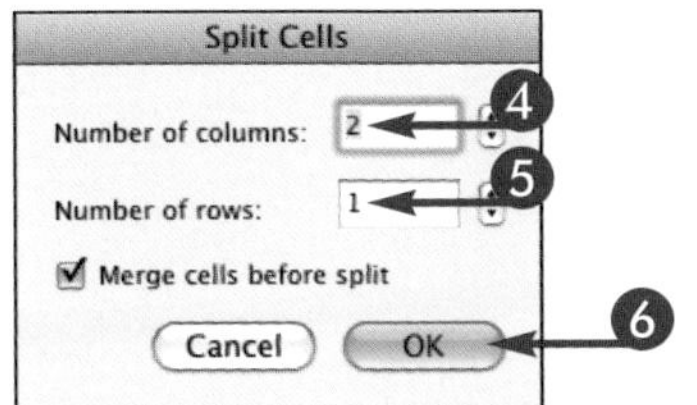


4. In the Number of columns text box, type the number of columns you want to create within the selected cell.
5. In the Number of rows text box, type the number of rows you want to create within the selected cell.
6. Click **OK**.

- Word splits the cell into the number of columns and rows that you specified.

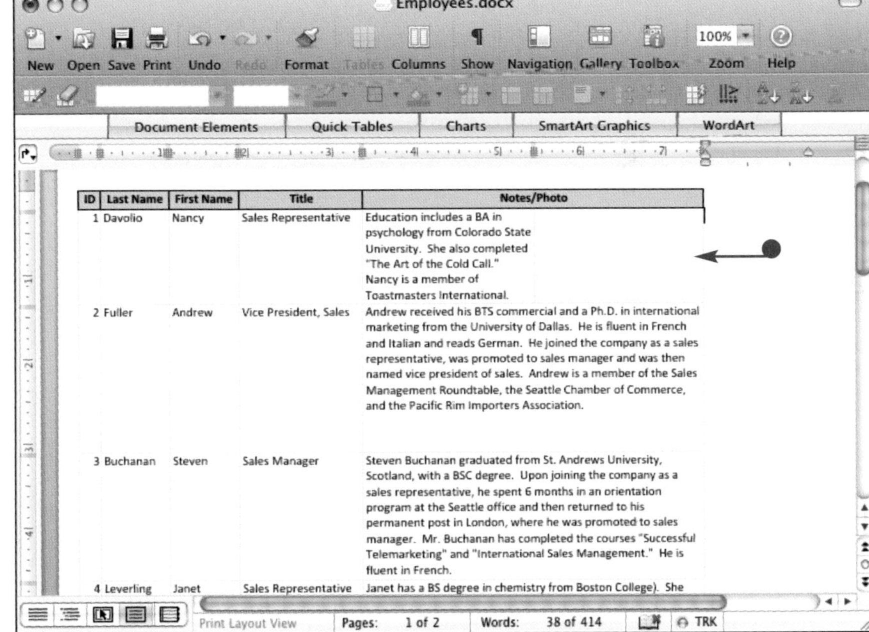

Employees.docx
New
Open
Save
Print
Undo
Redo
Format
Tables
Columns
Show
Navigation
Gallery
Toolbox
Zoom
Help
100%
Document Elements
Quick Tables
Charts
SmartArt Graphics
WordArt
ID
Last Name
First Name
Title
Notes/Photo
1 Davolio
Nancy
Sales Representative
Education includes a BA in psychology from Colorado State University. She also completed "The Art of the Cold Call." Nancy is a member of Toastmasters International.
2 Fuller
Andrew
Vice President, Sales
Andrew received his BTS commercial and a Ph.D. in international marketing from the University of Dallas. He is fluent in French and Italian and reads German. He joined the company as a sales representative, was promoted to sales manager and was then named vice president of sales. Andrew is a member of the Sales Management Roundtable, the Seattle Chamber of Commerce, and the Pacific Rim Importers Association.
3 Buchanan
Steven
Sales Manager
Steven Buchanan graduated from St. Andrews University, Scotland, with a BSC degree. Upon joining the company as a sales representative, he spent 6 months in an orientation program at the Seattle office and then returned to his permanent post in London, where he was promoted to sales manager. Mr. Buchanan has completed the courses "Successful Telemarketing" and "International Sales Management." He is fluent in French.
4 Leverling
Janet
Sales Representative
Janet has a BS degree in chemistry from Boston College). She
Print Layout View
Pages: 1 of 2
Words: 38 of 414
TRK


## TIPS

### Can I split multiple cells at once?

Yes, but you need to be a bit careful to avoid messing up your data. Select the cells that you want to split, and then follow steps **2** to **5** to specify the number of rows and columns you want to use in the split. Deselect the **Merge cells before split** option (☑ changes to ☐) to ensure that Word does not merge all the data in the selected cells before it performs the split. Click **OK**.

### Can I split an entire table into two separate tables?

Yes. This is useful if you need to track part of the table data separately or if you need to modify the layout of one part of a tale differently from the rest of the table. Note, however, that Word only enables you to split a table horizontally, not vertically. First, select the row above which you want to split the table. Click **Table** and then click **Split Table**.

# Move and Resize a Table

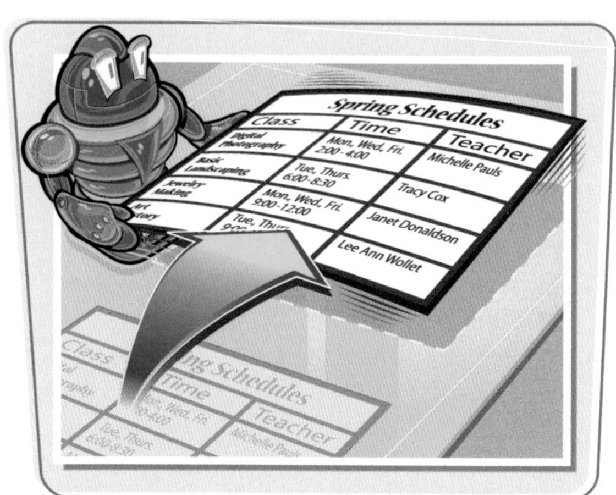

Spring Schedules
Class
Time
Teacher
Michelle Pauls
Tracy Cox
Janet Donaldson
Lee Ann Wollet

You can move an entire table to a better position within your document. For example, you can move a table so that it is closer to the document text that discusses the table data.

**If a table is too large or too small, you can resize the entire table. This enables you to resize all of the table's column widths and row heights in a single operation.**

## Move and Resize a Table

### MOVE A TABLE

1. Move the mouse pointer over the **Table Select** icon (⊞).
2. Click and drag ⊞ to move the table.
   - The pointer changes to ✥.
   - A dotted outline shows the table location as you drag.

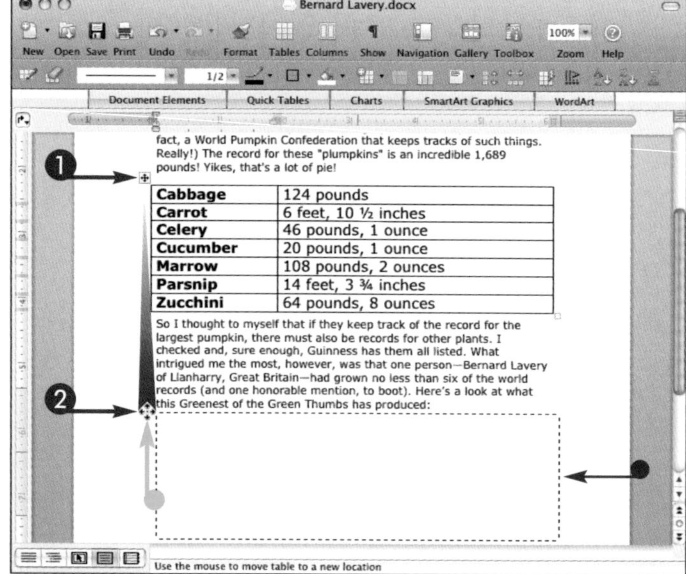

Bernard Lavery.docx
New Open Save Print Undo Redo Format Tables Columns Show Navigation Gallery Toolbox Zoom Help
Document Elements Quick Tables Charts SmartArt Graphics WordArt
fact, a World Pumpkin Confederation that keeps tracks of such things. Really!) The record for these "plumpkins" is an incredible 1,689 pounds! Yikes, that's a lot of pie!
Cabbage 124 pounds
Carrot 6 feet, 10 ½ inches
Celery 46 pounds, 1 ounce
Cucumber 20 pounds, 1 ounce
Marrow 108 pounds, 2 ounces
Parsnip 14 feet, 3 ¾ inches
Zucchini 64 pounds, 8 ounces
So I thought to myself that if they keep track of the record for the largest pumpkin, there must also be records for other plants. I checked and, sure enough, Guinness has them all listed. What intrigued me the most, however, was that one person—Bernard Lavery of Llanharry, Great Britain—had grown no less than six of the world records (and one honorable mention, to boot). Here's a look at what this Greenest of the Green Thumbs has produced:
Use the mouse to move table to a new location

3. Release ⊞.
   - Word moves the table to the new location.

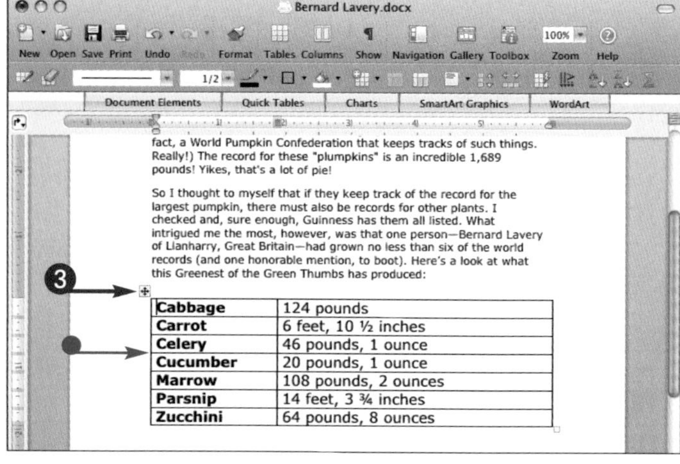

Bernard Lavery.docx
New Open Save Print Undo Redo Format Tables Columns Show Navigation Gallery Toolbox Zoom Help
Document Elements Quick Tables Charts SmartArt Graphics WordArt
fact, a World Pumpkin Confederation that keeps tracks of such things. Really!) The record for these "plumpkins" is an incredible 1,689 pounds! Yikes, that's a lot of pie!
So I thought to myself that if they keep track of the record for the largest pumpkin, there must also be records for other plants. I checked and, sure enough, Guinness has them all listed. What intrigued me the most, however, was that one person—Bernard Lavery of Llanharry, Great Britain—had grown no less than six of the world records (and one honorable mention, to boot). Here's a look at what this Greenest of the Green Thumbs has produced:
Cabbage 124 pounds
Carrot 6 feet, 10 ½ inches
Celery 46 pounds, 1 ounce
Cucumber 20 pounds, 1 ounce
Marrow 108 pounds, 2 ounces
Parsnip 14 feet, 3 ¾ inches
Zucchini 64 pounds, 8 ounces

## RESIZE A TABLE

1. Click inside the table you want to resize.
   - Word displays a resize handle in the lower-right corner of the table.
2. Move ↖ over the resize handle.
3. Click and drag the resize handle.

   ↖ changes to +.
   - A dotted outline shows the table size as you drag.

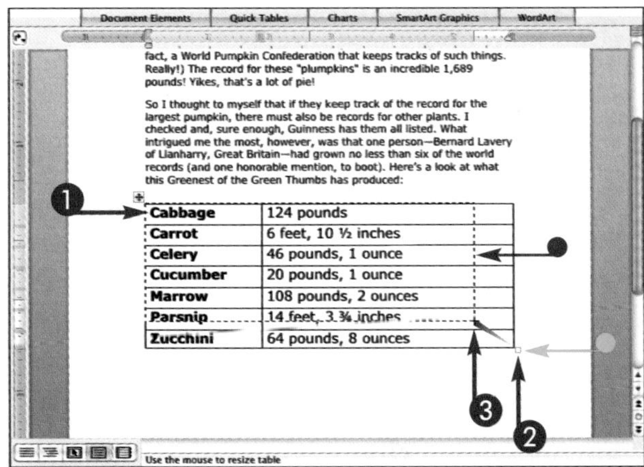

4. Release the +.
   - Word resizes the table.

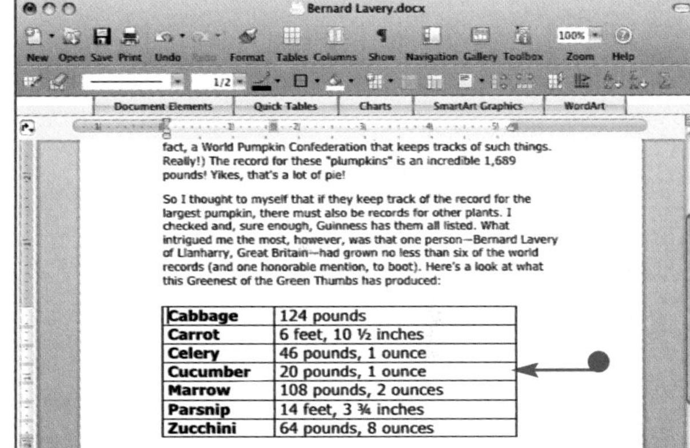

## TIP

**When I move or resize my table, the document text does not wrap around the table. How can I fix this?**

Follow these steps:

1. Click inside the table.
2. Click **Table**.
3. Click **Table Properties**.
4. In the Table Properties dialog, click the **Table** tab.
5. In the Text wrapping section, click **Around**.
6. If you want to modify the table position relative to the surrounding text, click **Positioning** and use the Table Positioning dialog to make your changes.
7. Click **OK**.

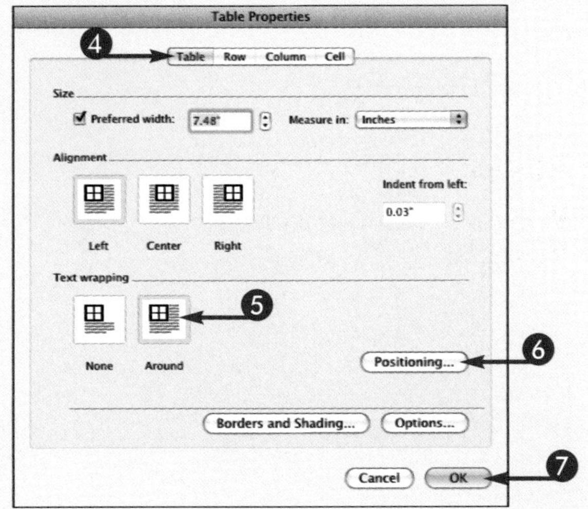

# Add a Sum Formula to a Table

**If your table includes numeric values, you can add a sum formula to a cell to display the total of those values. For example, if you are using a table to display an invoice, you can create a sum formula that displays the invoice total.**

**Word's AutoSum feature enables you to add a sum formula with just a couple of mouse clicks. You can sum either a column of values or a row of values.**

## Add a Sum Formula to a Table

### ADD A SUM FORMULA

1. Click inside the cell where you want the sum to appear.
2. Click the **AutoSum** button (Σ) in the Tables and Borders toolbar.

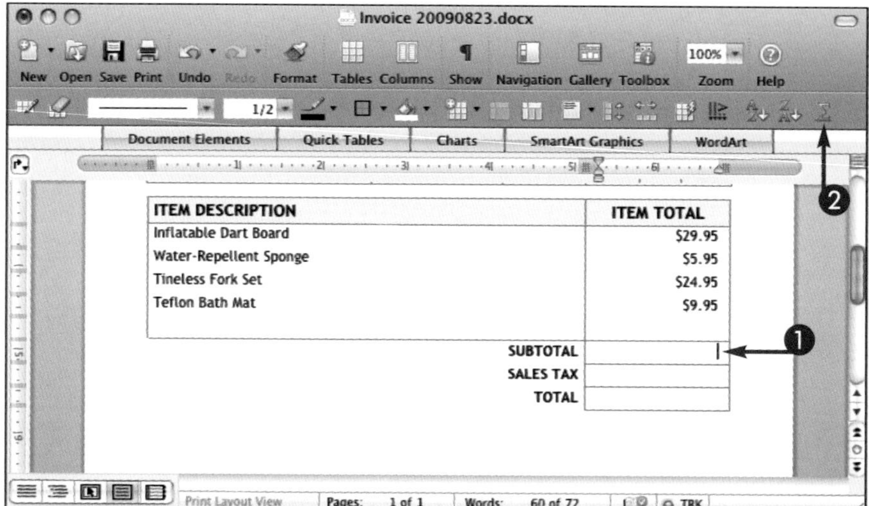


- Word displays the sum.

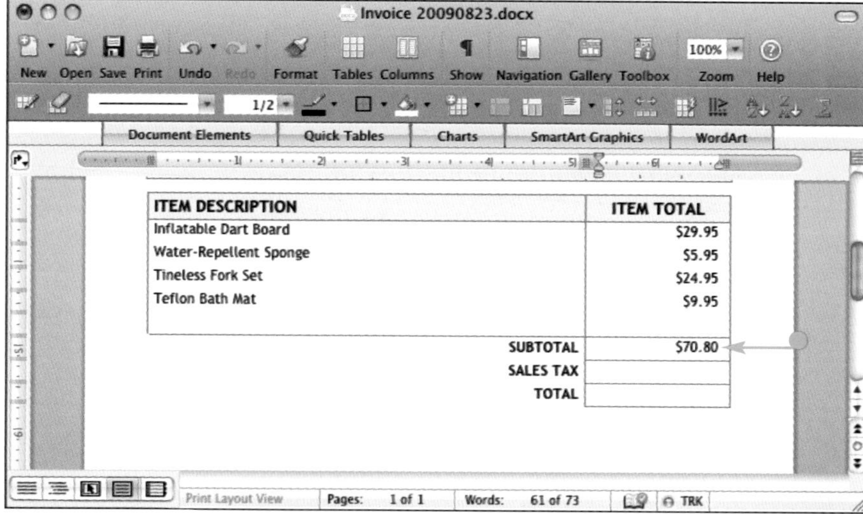

## UPDATE A SUM FORMULA

1. Right-click the sum.

   You can also Ctrl+click.

2. Click **Update Field**.

   You can also position the cursor within the sum and then press Shift + Option + ⌘ + U.

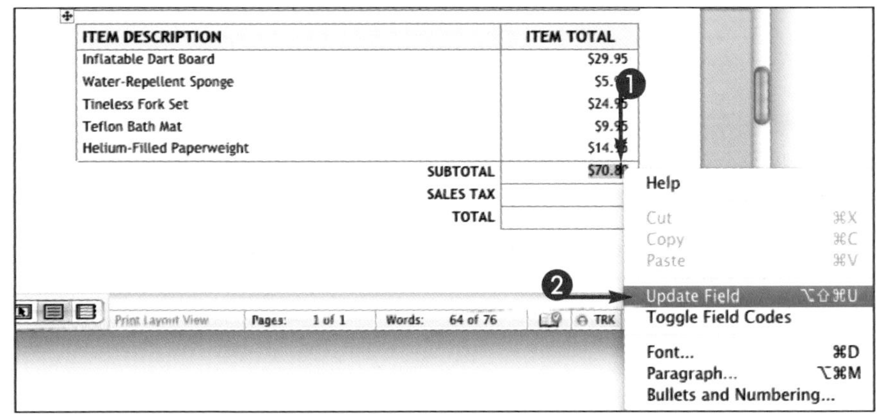


- Word recalculates the sum.

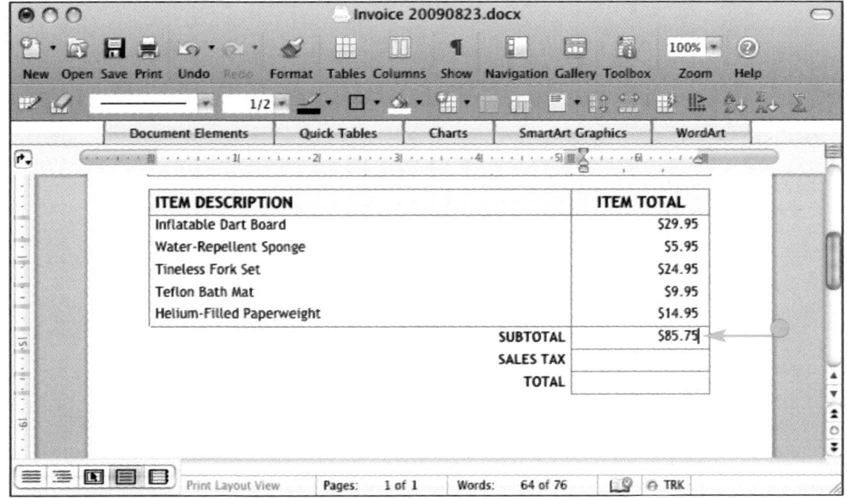

Invoice 20090823.docx
New Open Save Print Undo Redo Format Tables Columns Show Navigation Gallery Toolbox Zoom Help
Document Elements
Quick Tables
Charts
SmartArt Graphics
WordArt
ITEM DESCRIPTION
ITEM TOTAL
Inflatable Dart Board
$29.95
Water-Repellent Sponge
$5.95
Tineless Fork Set
$24.95
Teflon Bath Mat
$9.95
Helium-Filled Paperweight
$14.95
SUBTOTAL
$85.75
SALES TAX
TOTAL
Print Layout View
Pages: 1 of 1
Words: 64 of 76


## TIPS

**AutoSum is summing the values above the current cell. How do I get it to sum the values to the left of the current cell, instead?**

{=SUM(LEFT)}

To sum the values to the left of the current cell, right-click or Ctrl+click the sum and then click **Toggle Field Codes**. You see the following formula: { = SUM(ABOVE) }. Edit the formula to read as follows: {= SUM(LEFT) }. Right-click or Ctrl+click the formula and then click **Toggle Field Codes**.

**Can I add a formula for a different calculation, such as taking the average of the values?**

Formula

Formula:

=AVERAGE(ABOVE)

Number format:

Paste function: Paste bookmark:

Cancel OK

Yes. Click inside the cell you want to use, click **Table**, and then click **Formula**. In the **Formula** text box, type =, click the **Paste function** ⬍, click a function, type **ABOVE** (or **LEFT**) between the parentheses, and then click **OK**.

# Adding Document Elements

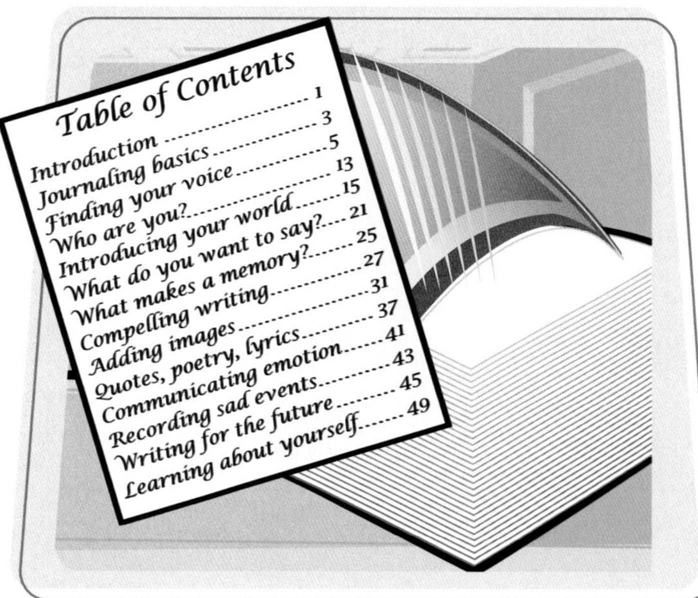


You can add more value to your documents by including one or more of the various document elements that Word provides. These elements include cover pages, headers and footers, footnotes or endnotes, envelopes or mailing labels, a table of contents, or an index. This chapter shows you how to add each of these elements to your documents.

# Add a Cover Page

**You can give your document a professional look by adding a cover page that displays the document title, subtitle, and author's name, along with a graphical design.**

**Word comes with 17 predefined cover pages, each of which you can add to a document with just a few mouse clicks.**

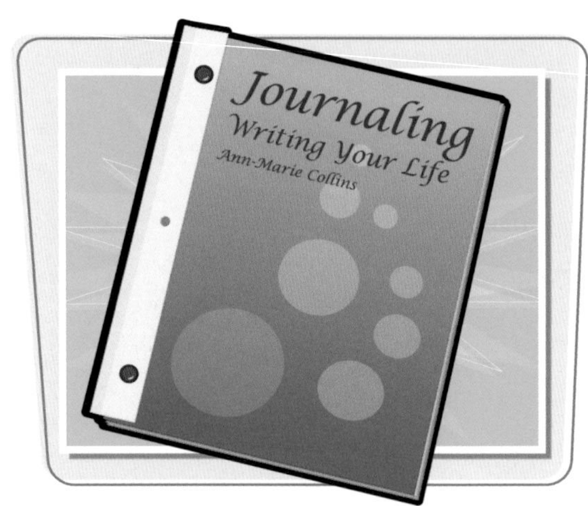


## Add a Cover Page

1. Open the document to which you want to add the cover page.
2. Click **Print Layout View**.
3. Click **Document Elements**.

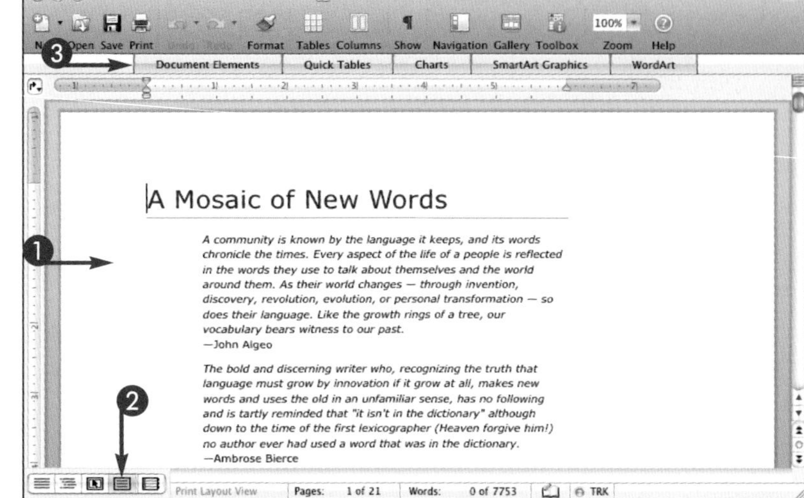


4. Click **Cover Pages**.
5. Click ▶ and ◀ to review the predefined cover pages.

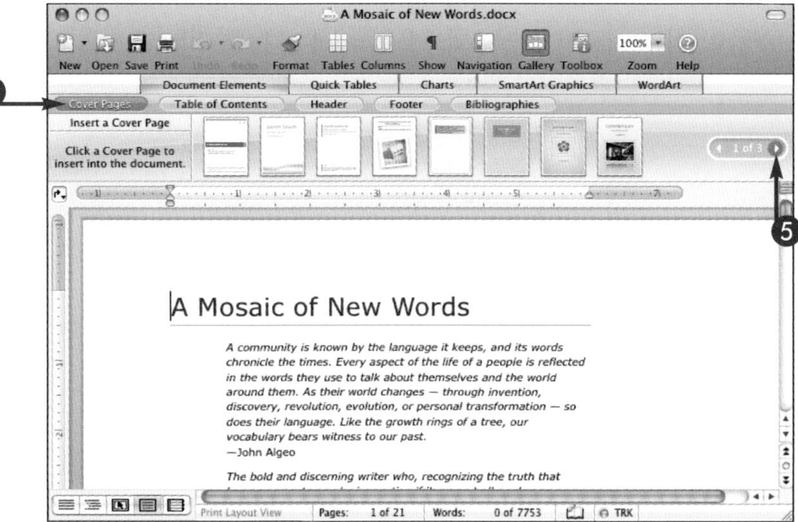

6 Click the cover page you want to use.

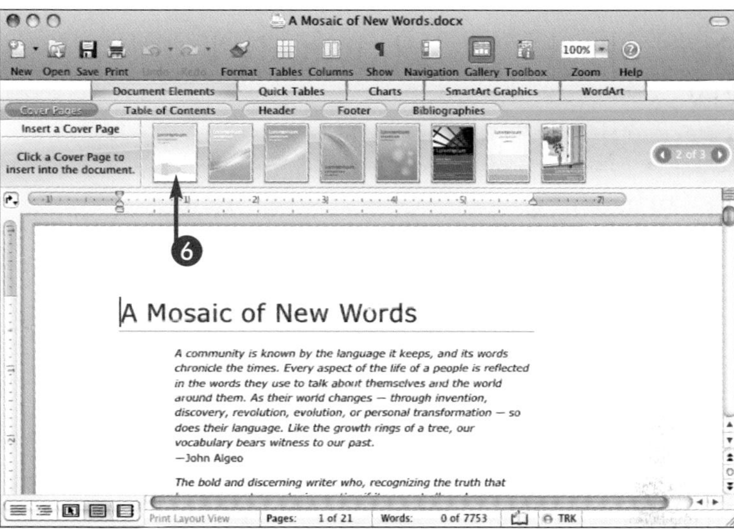

- Word inserts the cover page.

7 Click the **[Document Title]** field and then type the title of your document.

8 Click the **[Document Subtitle]** field and then type the subtitle of your document.

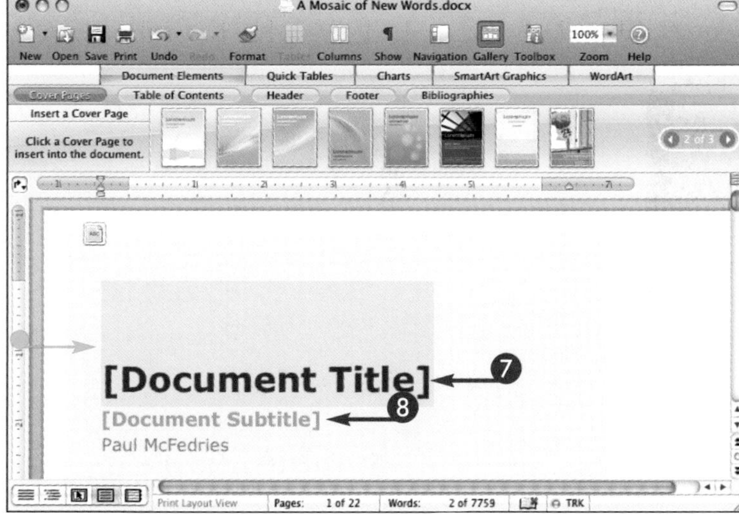

**How do I remove a cover page?**

If you no longer need a cover page, removing it reduces the file size and makes the document easier to navigate. Follow these steps:

1 Scroll to the top of the document and look for the Cover Page icon ( ).

2 Click ▾ in the Cover Page icon.

3 Click **Remove Cover Page**.

Word removes the cover page from the document.

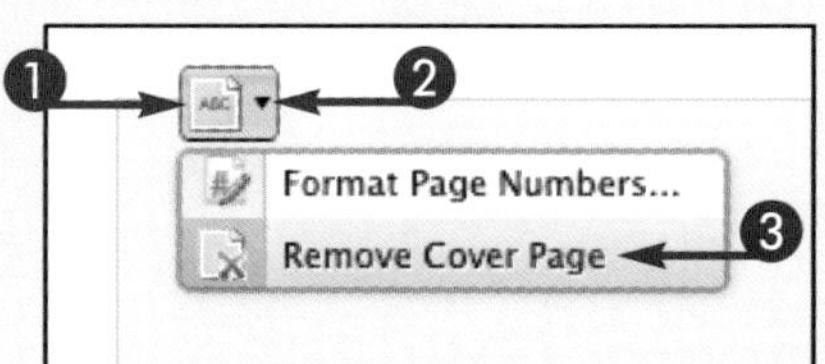

# Insert a Header

If you have text that you want to appear on every page of your document, you can add a header to the document. The header appears between the top of the document text and the top margin, and you can use it to add text such as the document title, page numbers, current date, or custom text.

**You can configure your header to appear on every page in the document, or on just the even or odd pages.**

## Insert a Header

1. Open the document to which you want to add the header.
2. Click **Print Layout View**.
3. Click **Document Elements**.

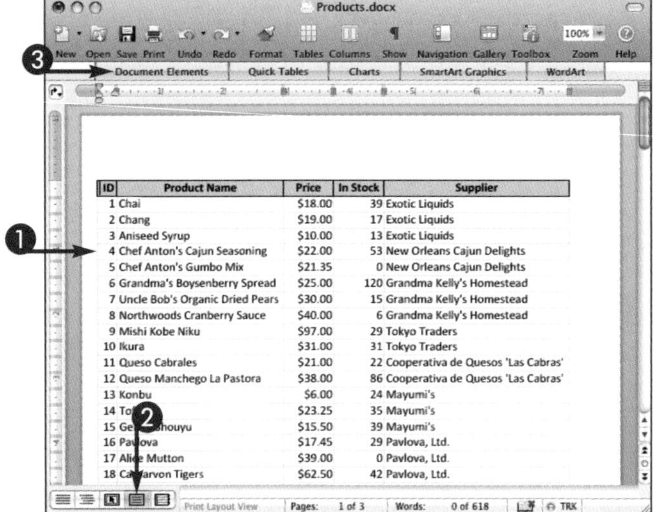


4. Click **Header**.
5. Click the **Insert as** ⬍ and then click where you want the header to appear.
6. Click ▶ and ◀ to review the predefined header layouts.

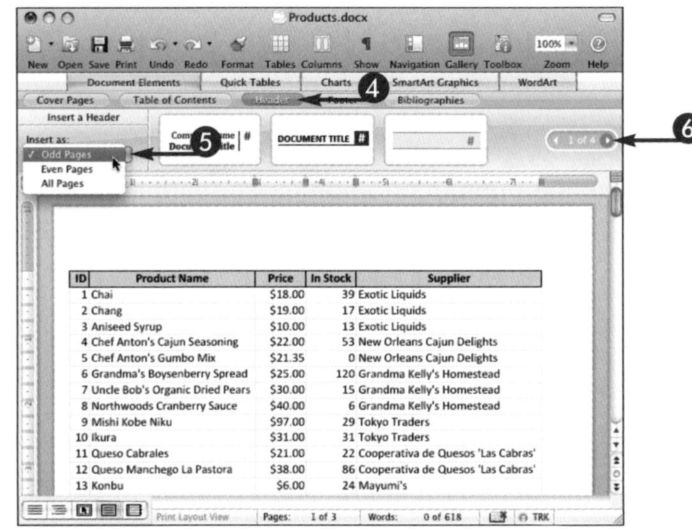

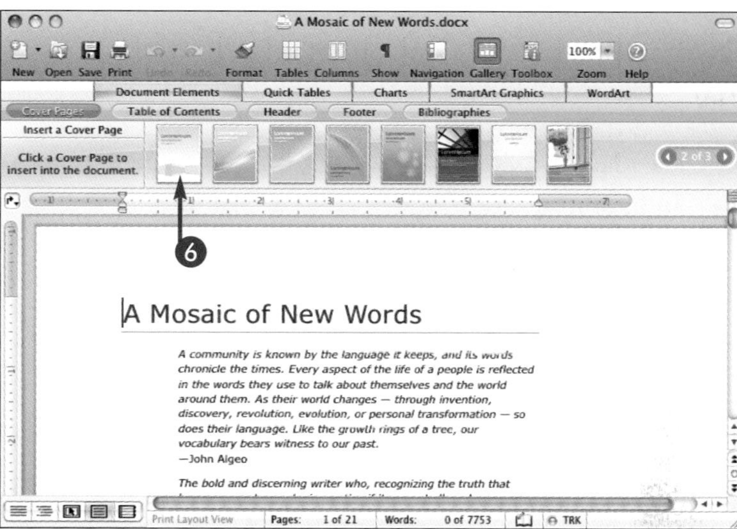


6 Click the cover page you want to use.

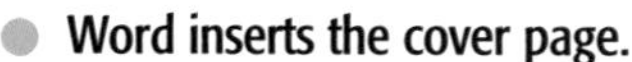
Word inserts the cover page.

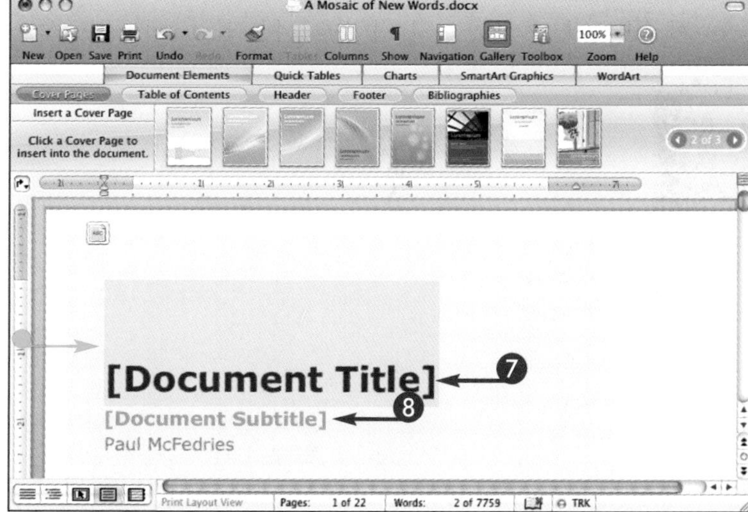


7 Click the **[Document Title]** field and then type the title of your document.

8 Click the **[Document Subtitle]** field and then type the subtitle of your document.

### How do I remove a cover page?

If you no longer need a cover page, removing it reduces the file size and makes the document easier to navigate. Follow these steps:

1 Scroll to the top of the document and look for the Cover Page icon ( ).

2 Click ▾ in the Cover Page icon.

3 Click **Remove Cover Page**.

Word removes the cover page from the document.

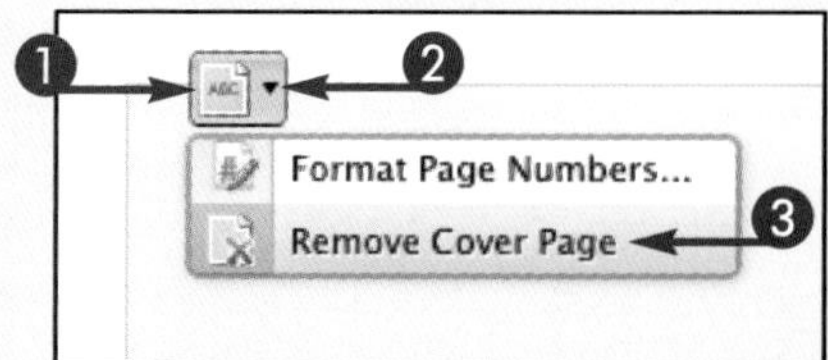

# Insert a Header

If you have text that you want to appear on every page of your document, you can add a header to the document. The header appears between the top of the document text and the top margin, and you can use it to add text such as the document title, page numbers, current date, or custom text.

**You can configure your header to appear on every page in the document, or on just the even or odd pages.**

## Insert a Header

1. Open the document to which you want to add the header.
2. Click **Print Layout View**.
3. Click **Document Elements**.

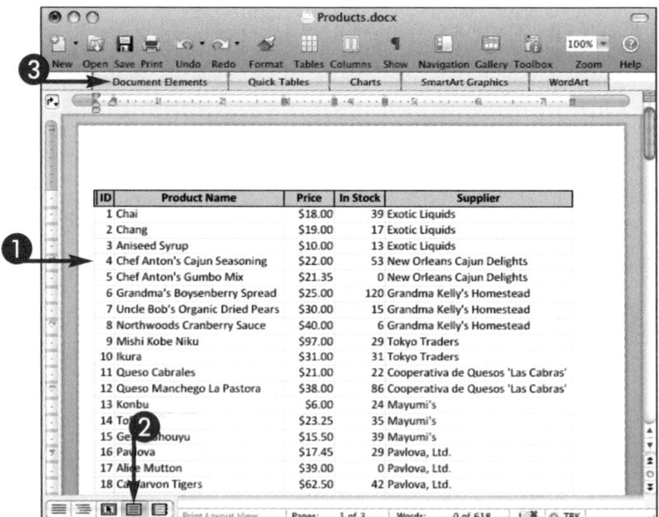


| ID | Product Name | Price | In Stock | Supplier |
|---|---|---|---|---|
| 1 | Chai | $18.00 | 39 | Exotic Liquids |
| 2 | Chang | $19.00 | 17 | Exotic Liquids |
| 3 | Aniseed Syrup | $10.00 | 13 | Exotic Liquids |
| 4 | Chef Anton's Cajun Seasoning | $22.00 | 53 | New Orleans Cajun Delights |
| 5 | Chef Anton's Gumbo Mix | $21.35 | 0 | New Orleans Cajun Delights |
| 6 | Grandma's Boysenberry Spread | $25.00 | 120 | Grandma Kelly's Homestead |
| 7 | Uncle Bob's Organic Dried Pears | $30.00 | 15 | Grandma Kelly's Homestead |
| 8 | Northwoods Cranberry Sauce | $40.00 | 6 | Grandma Kelly's Homestead |
| 9 | Mishi Kobe Niku | $97.00 | 29 | Tokyo Traders |
| 10 | Ikura | $31.00 | 31 | Tokyo Traders |
| 11 | Queso Cabrales | $21.00 | 22 | Cooperativa de Quesos 'Las Cabras' |
| 12 | Queso Manchego La Pastora | $38.00 | 86 | Cooperativa de Quesos 'Las Cabras' |
| 13 | Konbu | $6.00 | 24 | Mayumi's |
| 14 | To[illegible] | $23.25 | 35 | Mayumi's |
| 15 | Ge[illegible]houyu | $15.50 | 39 | Mayumi's |
| 16 | Pa[illegible]ova | $17.45 | 29 | Pavlova, Ltd. |
| 17 | Ali[illegible] Mutton | $39.00 | 0 | Pavlova, Ltd. |
| 18 | Ca[illegible]arvon Tigers | $62.50 | 42 | Pavlova, Ltd. |

4. Click **Header**.
5. Click the **Insert as** ⬍ and then click where you want the header to appear.
6. Click ▶ and ◀ to review the predefined header layouts.

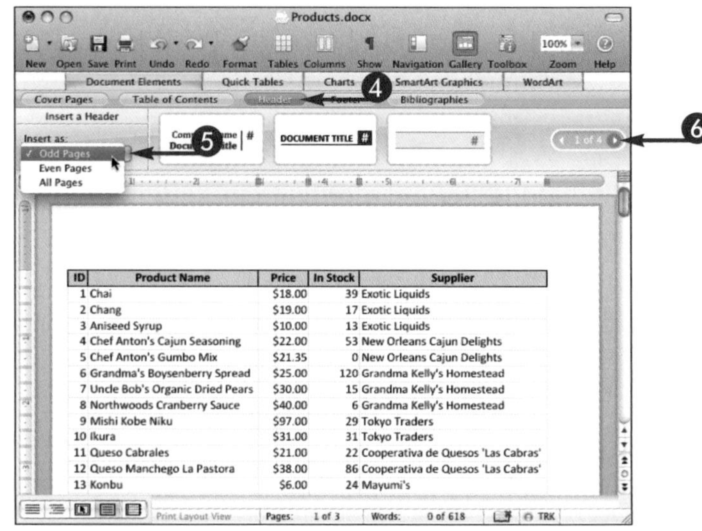


| ID | Product Name | Price | In Stock | Supplier |
|---|---|---|---|---|
| 1 | Chai | $18.00 | 39 | Exotic Liquids |
| 2 | Chang | $19.00 | 17 | Exotic Liquids |
| 3 | Aniseed Syrup | $10.00 | 13 | Exotic Liquids |
| 4 | Chef Anton's Cajun Seasoning | $22.00 | 53 | New Orleans Cajun Delights |
| 5 | Chef Anton's Gumbo Mix | $21.35 | 0 | New Orleans Cajun Delights |
| 6 | Grandma's Boysenberry Spread | $25.00 | 120 | Grandma Kelly's Homestead |
| 7 | Uncle Bob's Organic Dried Pears | $30.00 | 15 | Grandma Kelly's Homestead |
| 8 | Northwoods Cranberry Sauce | $40.00 | 6 | Grandma Kelly's Homestead |
| 9 | Mishi Kobe Niku | $97.00 | 29 | Tokyo Traders |
| 10 | Ikura | $31.00 | 31 | Tokyo Traders |
| 11 | Queso Cabrales | $21.00 | 22 | Cooperativa de Quesos 'Las Cabras' |
| 12 | Queso Manchego La Pastora | $38.00 | 86 | Cooperativa de Quesos 'Las Cabras' |
| 13 | Konbu | $6.00 | 24 | Mayumi's |

7 Click the header you want to use.

- Word inserts the header.

8 If the header has any fields that require you to add information manually, click the field and then type the data.

9 Click **Close**.

***Note:** If you want to have different headers on your document's odd and even pages, perform Steps **5** to **9** twice, first by choosing **Odd Pages** in Step **5**, and then again by choosing **Even Pages** in Step **5**.*

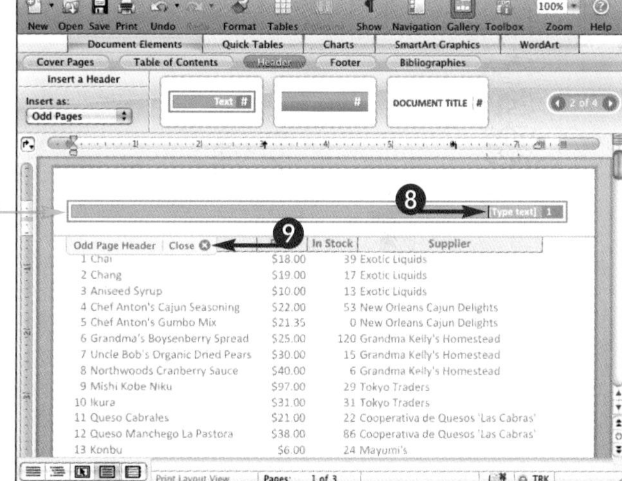

## How do I remove the header from the first page of my document?

First, if you chose **Even Pages** in Step **5**, then you do not need to do anything because no header appears on page 1. If you chose either **Odd Pages** or **All Pages**, instead, then a header appears on page 1. To remove it, click **Format** and then click **Document** to display the Document dialog. Click the **Layout** tab, select the **Different first page** option (☐ changes to ☑), and then click **OK**.

## How do I remove all the headers from my document?

If you no longer require the headers, you can delete them. First, double-click any header to activate it. Click **Edit** and then click **Select All** or press ⌘+A to select all the header text. Press Del to remove the header, and then click **Close**. If you added separate headers for the odd and even pages, you need to repeat this procedure for the other header.

# Insert a Footer

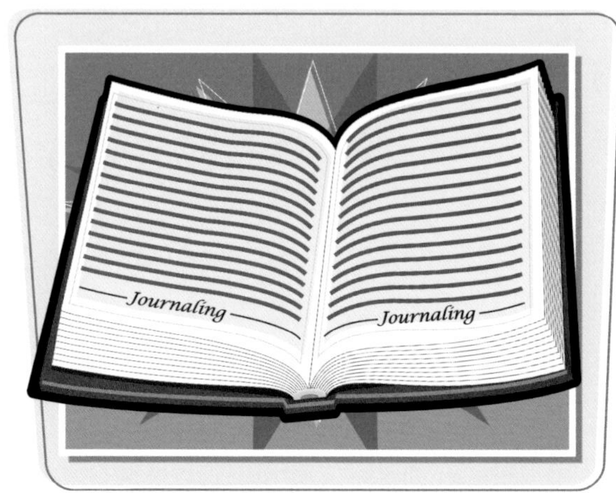


If you have text that you want to appear on every page of your document, you can add a footer to the document. The footer appears between the bottom of the document text and the bottom margin, and you can use it to add text such as the document title, page numbers, current date, or custom text.

**You can configure your footer to appear on every page in the document, or on just the even or odd pages.**

## Insert a Footer

1. Open the document to which you want to add the footer.
2. Click **Print Layout View**.
3. Click **Document Elements**.

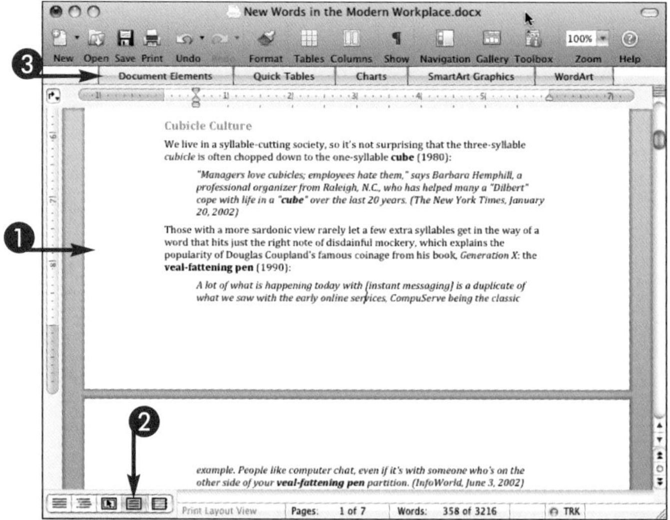


4. Click **Footer**.
5. Click the **Insert as** ⬍ and then click where you want the footer to appear.
6. Click ▶ and ◀ to preview the predefined footer layouts.

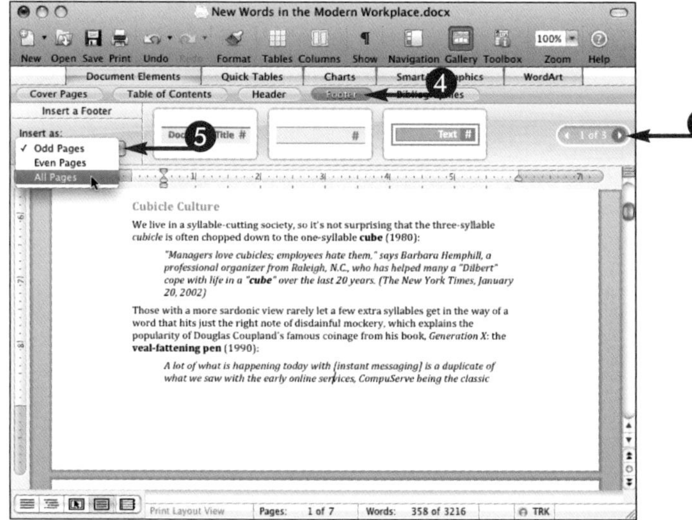

7 Click the footer you want to use.

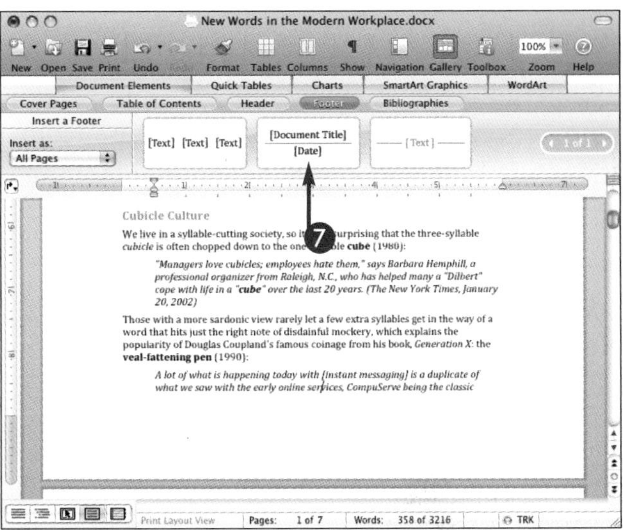

- Word inserts the footer.

8 If the footer has any fields that require you to add information manually, click the field and then type the data.

9 Click **Close**.

***Note:** If you want to have different footers on your document's odd and even pages, perform Steps **5** to **9** twice, first by clicking **Odd Pages** in Step **5**, and then again by clicking **Even Pages** in Step **5**.*

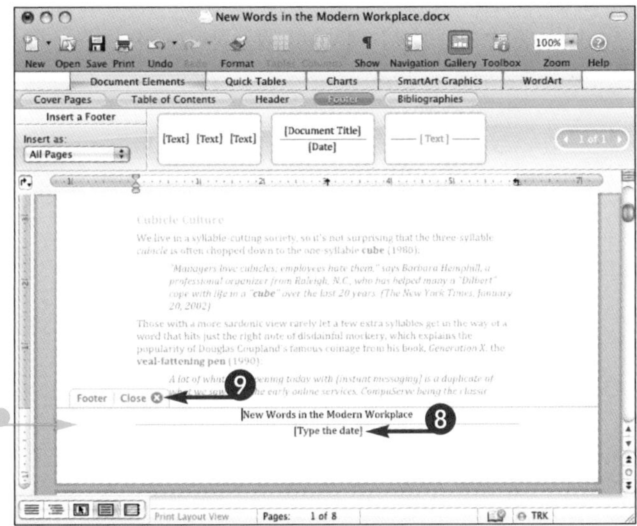

TIPS

**When I insert a footer that includes a Document Title field, how do I get Word to insert the document title automatically?**

You need to specify the Title property for the document before adding the footer. Click **File** and then click **Properties** to open the document's Properties dialog. Click the **Summary** tab, and in the Title text box type the document title. Click **OK**. When you insert a footer (or header) that includes the Document Title field, Word adds the title automatically.

**How do I remove all the footers from my document?**

If you no longer require the footers, you can delete them. First, double-click any footer to activate it. Click **Edit** and then click **Select All** or press ⌘+A to select all the footer text. Press Del to remove the footer, and then click **Close**. If you added separate footers for the odd and even pages, you need to repeat this procedure for the other footer.

# Create a Table of Contents



You can make a long document easier to navigate by adding a table of contents (TOC). The TOC gives the reader a good sense of the overall structure of the document, and it includes page numbers, which enables the reader of a document printout to easily find a particular section.

**Word generates the entries that comprise a TOC from a document's Heading styles, so you should first format your document's headings with the appropriate Heading styles.**

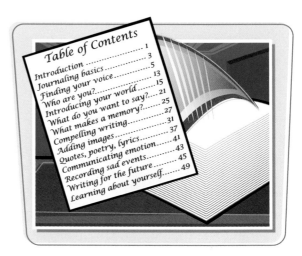

## Create a Table of Contents

1. Open the document to which you want to add the TOC.
2. Position the cursor at the beginning of the document.

   If you prefer to add the TOC elsewhere in the document, position the cursor at the spot where you want the TOC to appear.
3. Click **Print Layout View**.
4. Click **Document Elements**.

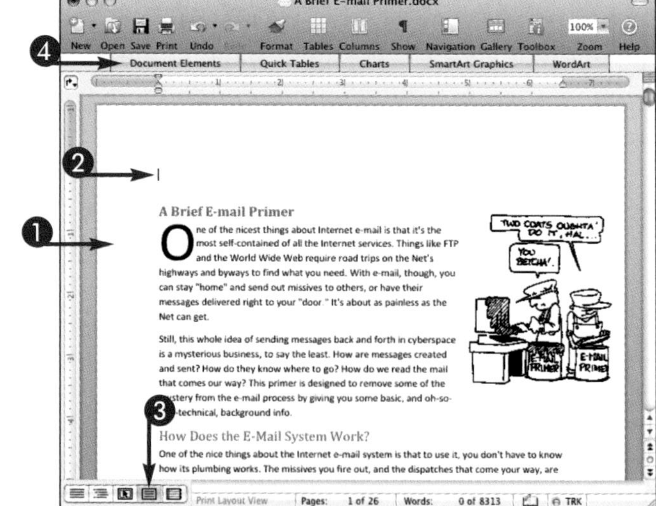


5. Click **Table of Contents**.
6. Select the **Heading Styles** option (○ changes to ⊙).
7. Click ▶ and ◀ to preview the predefined TOC layouts.

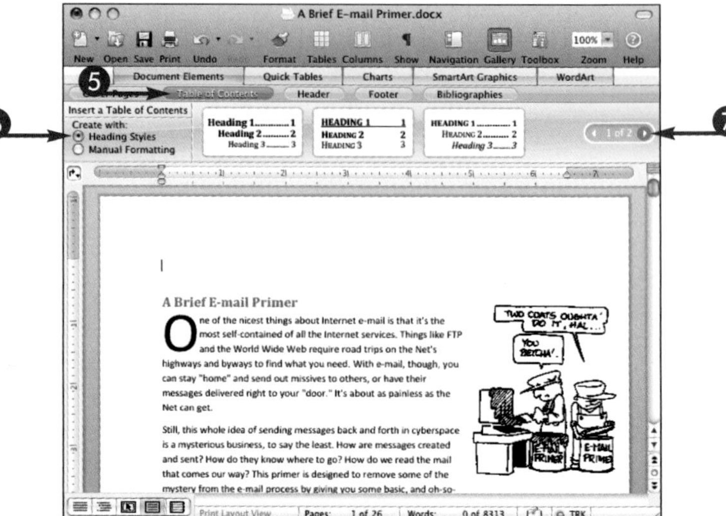

8 Click the TOC you want to use.

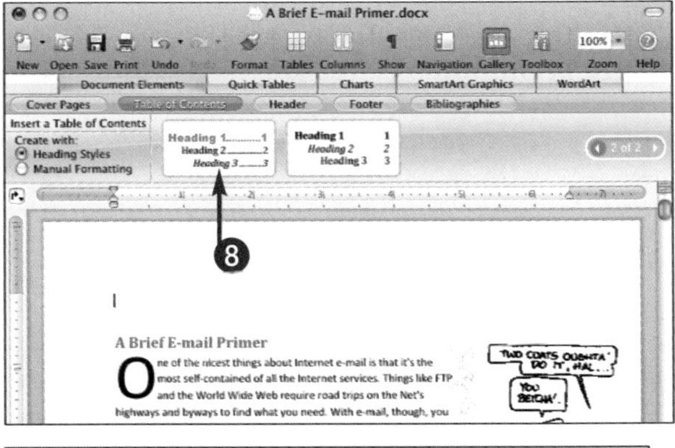

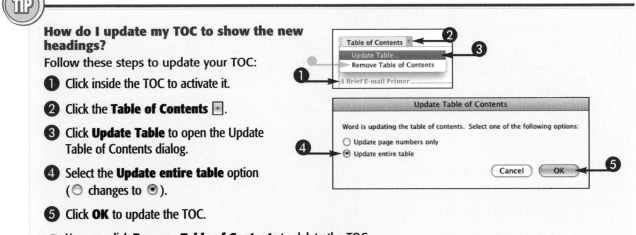

- Word inserts the TOC.

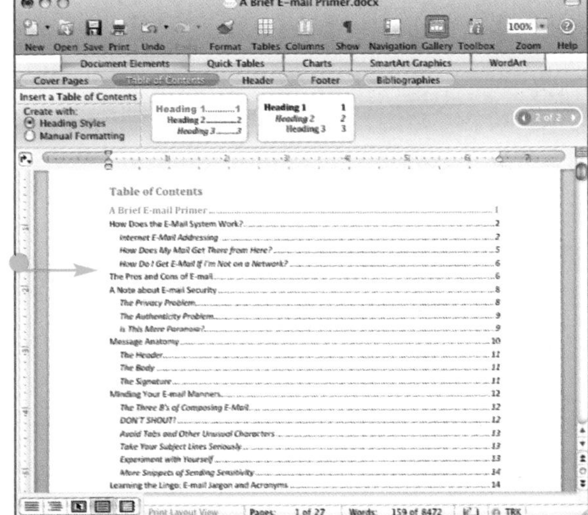


## TIP

### How do I update my TOC to show the new headings?

Follow these steps to update your TOC:

1. Click inside the TOC to activate it.
2. Click the **Table of Contents** ▾.
3. Click **Update Table** to open the Update Table of Contents dialog.
4. Select the **Update entire table** option (○ changes to ◉).
5. Click **OK** to update the TOC.

- You can click **Remove Table of Contents** to delete the TOC.

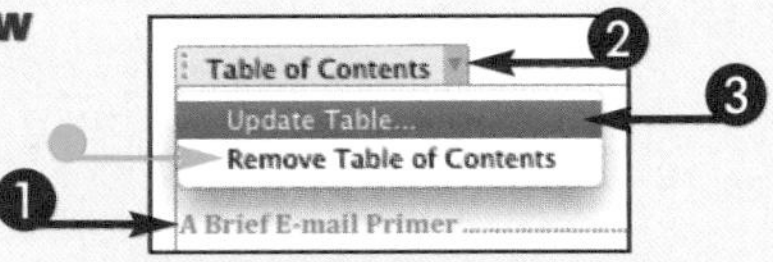

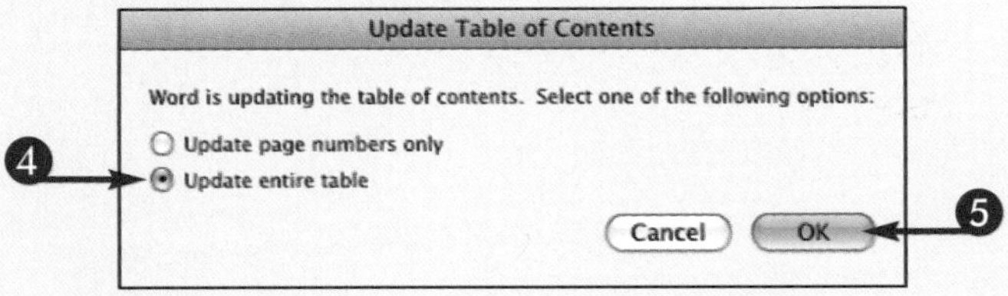

# Insert a Footnote or Endnote

You can add authority to a document by adding footnotes or endnotes. A *footnote* is a short note at the bottom of a page that provides added data about something mentioned in the regular text on that page. You can use footnotes to specify sources, point out references, or add extra information.

**You can also place all of your footnotes at the end of a section or document, in which case they are called *endnotes*.**

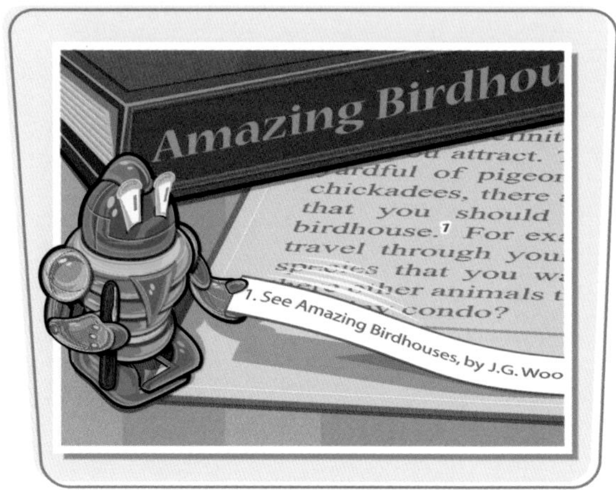


## Insert a Footnote or Endnote

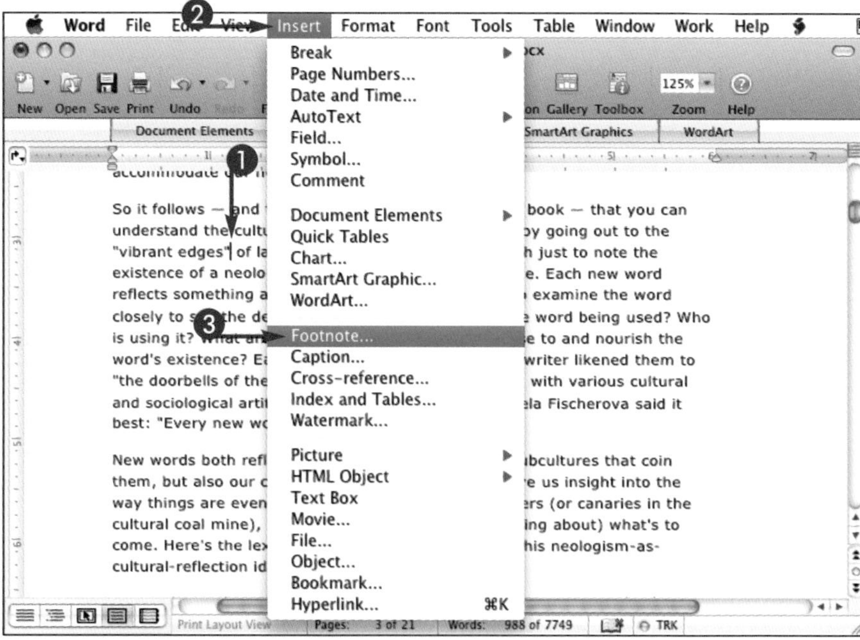


1. Position the cursor where you want the footnote or endnote number to appear.
2. Click **Insert**.
3. Click **Footnote**.

The Footnote and Endnote dialog appears.

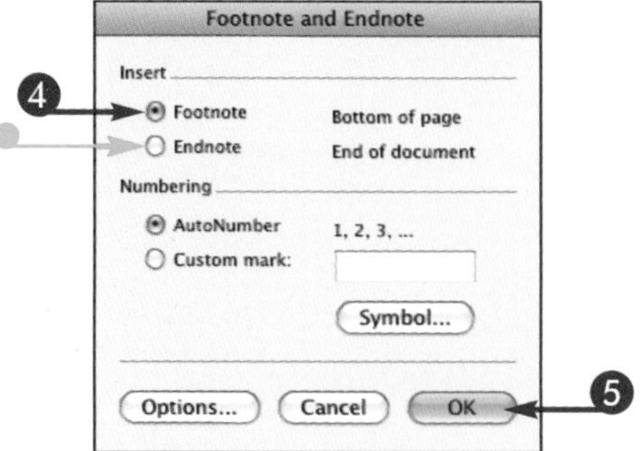


4. Select the **Footnote** option (○ changes to ◉).

- If you want to insert an endnote, select the **Endnote** option (○ changes to ◉).

5. Click **OK**.

8 Click the TOC you want to use.

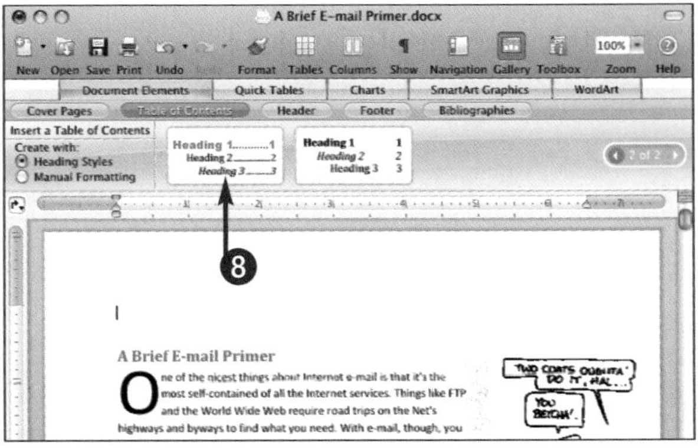


- Word inserts the TOC.

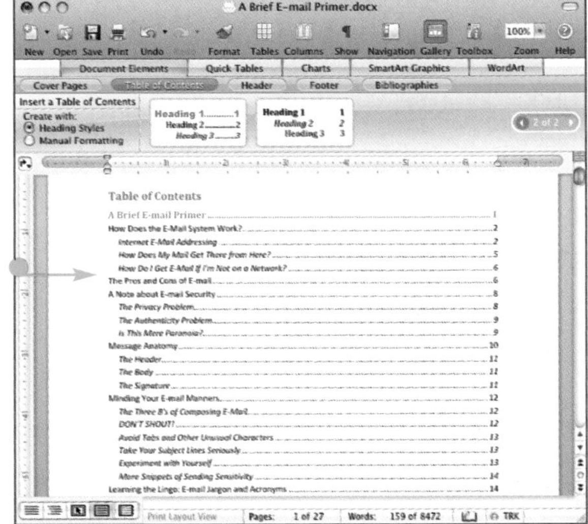


## TIP

**How do I update my TOC to show the new headings?**

Follow these steps to update your TOC:

1. Click inside the TOC to activate it.
2. Click the **Table of Contents** ▾.
3. Click **Update Table** to open the Update Table of Contents dialog.
4. Select the **Update entire table** option (○ changes to ◉).
5. Click **OK** to update the TOC.

- You can click **Remove Table of Contents** to delete the TOC.

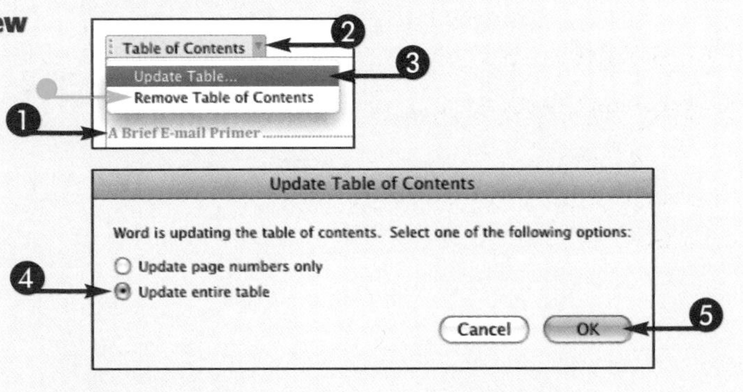

# Insert a Footnote or Endnote

You can add authority to a document by adding footnotes or endnotes. A *footnote* is a short note at the bottom of a page that provides added data about something mentioned in the regular text on that page. You can use footnotes to specify sources, point out references, or add extra information.

**You can also place all of your footnotes at the end of a section or document, in which case they are called *endnotes*.**

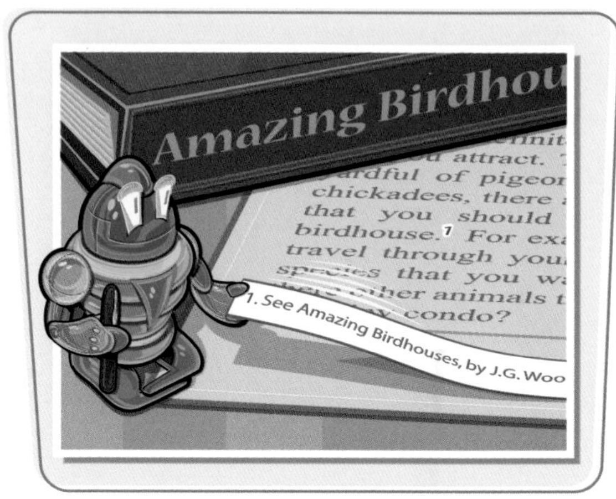


## Insert a Footnote or Endnote

1. Position the cursor where you want the footnote or endnote number to appear.
2. Click **Insert**.
3. Click **Footnote**.

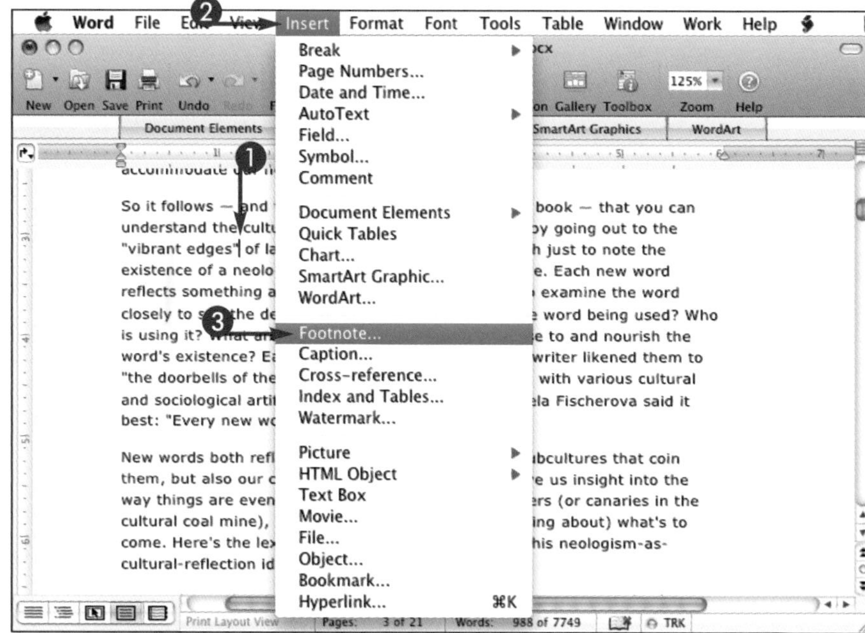

The Footnote and Endnote dialog appears.

4. Select the **Footnote** option (○ changes to ◉).

- If you want to insert an endnote, select the **Endnote** option (○ changes to ◉).

5. Click **OK**.

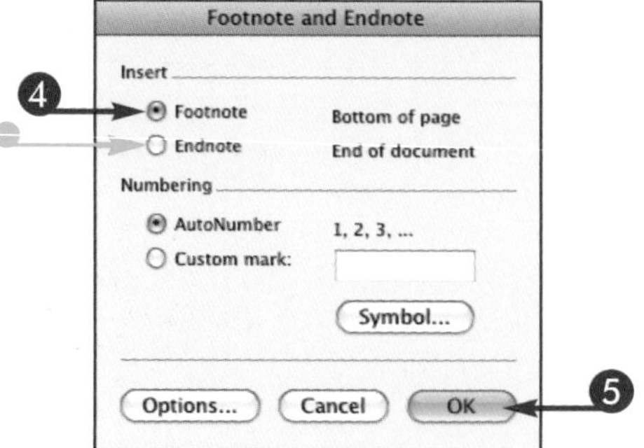

- Word creates the footnote.

6. Type the footnote text.
7. Double-click the footnote number to return to the regular document text.

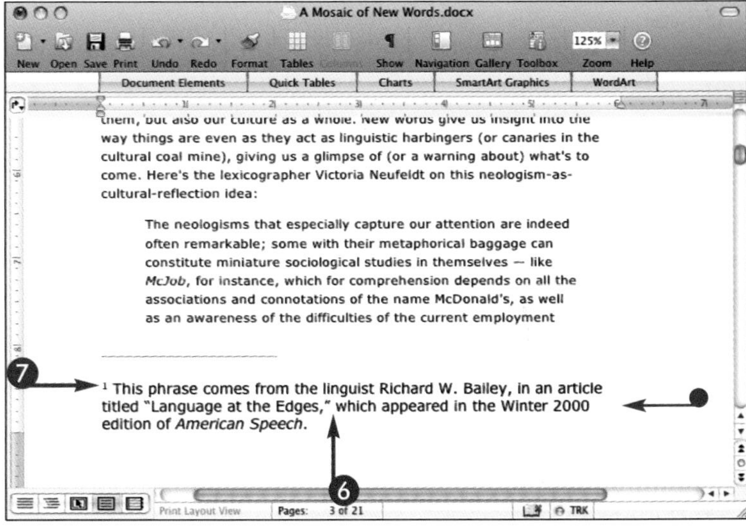


- The footnote number appears in the text. You can double-click this number to jump to the footnote text.

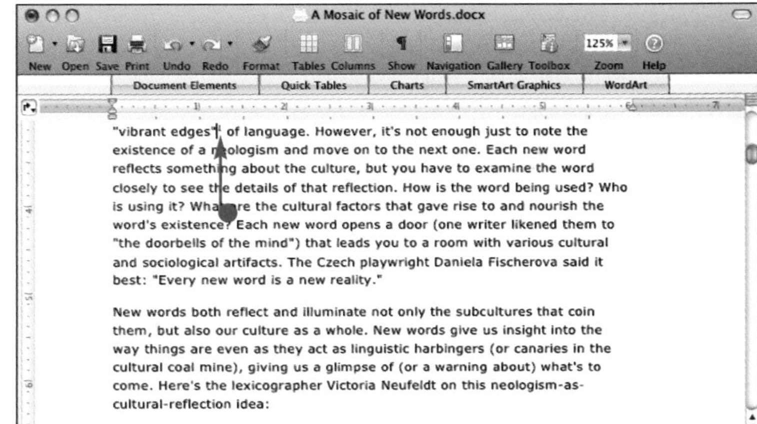


## TIPS

### Can I use symbols instead of numbers as the footnote reference marks?

Yes. You can apply a custom format that uses letters, Roman numerals, or symbols such as *, †, ‡, and §, or you can use a specific symbol for all footnotes. Follow Steps **1** to **3**. If you want to use a different number format, click **Options**, click the **Number format** ⇕, click the format you want to use, and then click **OK**. To use a specific symbol instead, select the **Custom mark** option (○ changes to ◉) and then either type the symbol or click the **Symbol** button.

### Is it possible to convert my footnotes to endnotes?

Yes. You can convert individual footnotes to endnotes, or you can convert all your footnotes to endnotes. To convert a single footnote, display the footnote, right-click or Ctrl+click the footnote number, and then click **Convert to Endnote**. To convert all footnotes, click **Insert**, click **Footnote**, click **Options**, and then click **Convert** to display the Convert Notes dialog. Select the **Convert all footnotes to endnotes** option (○ changes to ◉), and then click **OK**.

# Create an Envelope

You can use Word to create and print an envelope that displays both the recipient's address and your return address. If the address is already in the document, Word automatically uses the address for the envelope.

**Using Word to create an envelope is a good idea because it reduces the chance that the post office might misread the address, and it also looks more professional than a handwritten address.**

## Create an Envelope

1. Select the recipient's address if it appears in the document.

*Note: If no other address appears in the document, you can skip Step 1 because Word picks up the address automatically.*

2. Click **Tools**.
3. Click **Envelopes**.

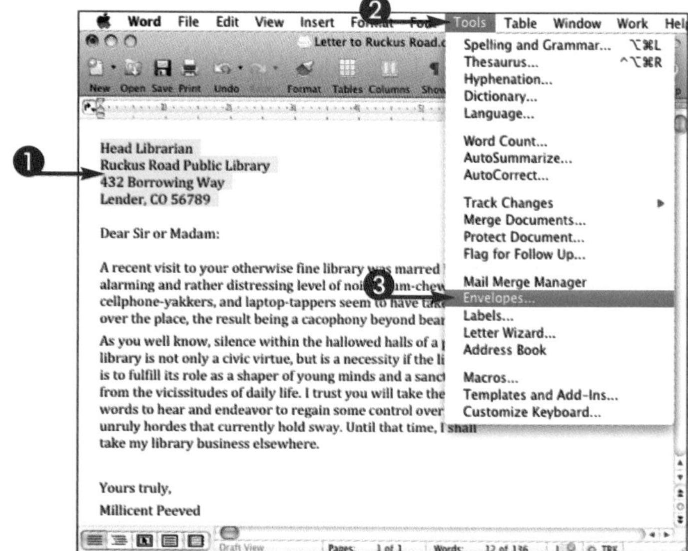

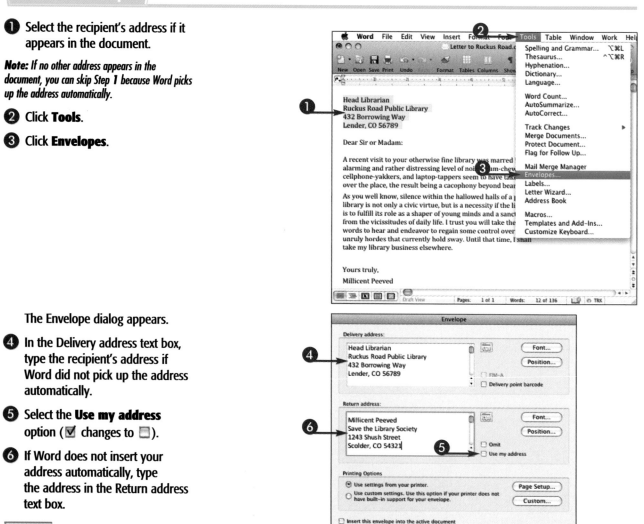

The Envelope dialog appears.

4. In the Delivery address text box, type the recipient's address if Word did not pick up the address automatically.
5. Select the **Use my address** option (☑ changes to ☐).
6. If Word does not insert your address automatically, type the address in the Return address text box.

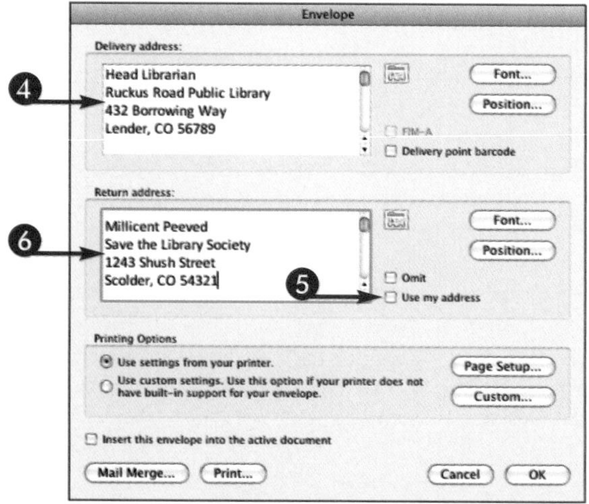

- You can click the **Font** buttons to format the address text.
- You can click the **Position** buttons to change where the addresses appear on the envelope.

7. Click **Print**.

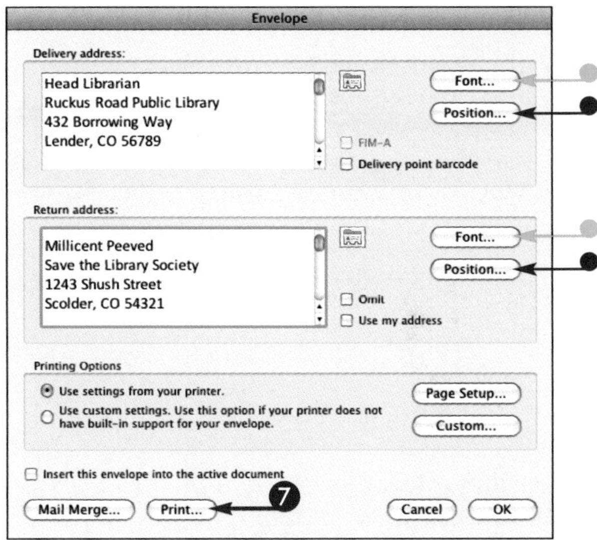


The Print dialog appears.

8. Click **Print**.

Word sends the envelope to the printer.

***Note:** See your printer manual to learn how to print an envelope.*

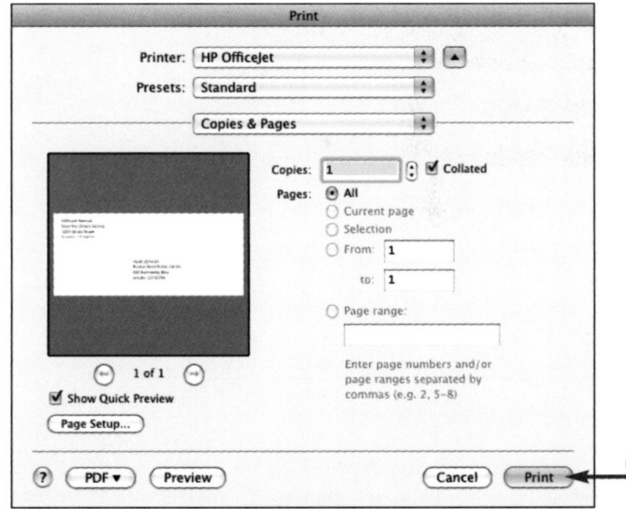


## TIPS

**I want to customize my label with a graphic. Is there a way to avoid printing the envelope right away?**

Yes. You can tell Word to insert the envelope into the document. Follow Steps **1** to **6** to open the Envelope dialog and set up the addresses. Select the **Insert this envelope into the active document** option (☐ changes to ☑), and then click **OK**. Word inserts the envelope at the top of the document, and you can then add your image.

**How do I tell Word that I am using a nonstandard envelope?**

Follow Steps **1** to **6** to open the Envelope dialog and set up the addresses. Click **Custom** to open the Custom Page Options dialog. Click the **Envelope size** ⬍ and then click the envelope size you are using. You can also use this dialog box to tell Word how your printer requires you to feed the envelope. When you finish, click **OK**.

# Create Mailing Labels

You can use Word to create and print mailing labels that display an address that you can then affix to an envelope or package. You can create labels either for a destination address or for your own address.

**Using Word to create mailing labels is better than using handwritten addresses because the labels are easier to read and look more professional.**

## Create Mailing Labels

1. Select the label address if it appears in the document.

*Note: If no other address appears in the document, you can skip Step 1 because Word automatically picks up the address.*

2. Click **Tools**.
3. Click **Labels**.

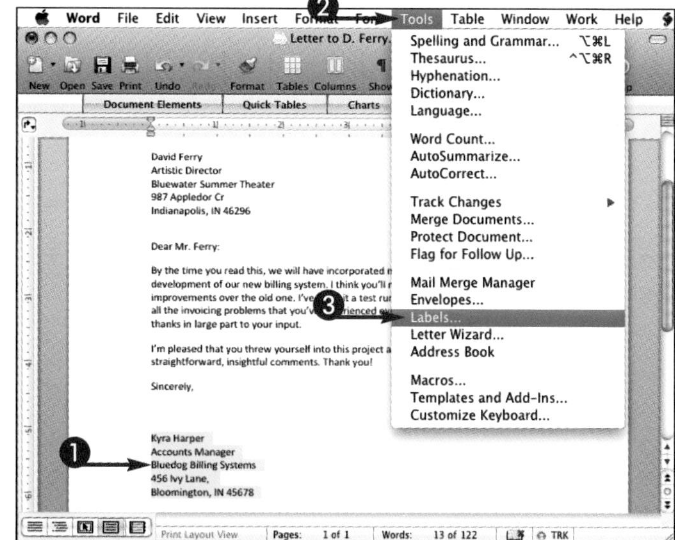

The Labels dialog appears.

4. In the Address text box, type the recipient's address if Word did not pick up the address automatically.

- If you want to create a label for your own address and you have entered your information into the Entourage Contacts database, select the **Use my address** option (☐ changes to ☑).

- This area shows the type of label Word will create.

5. To choose a different label, click **Options**.

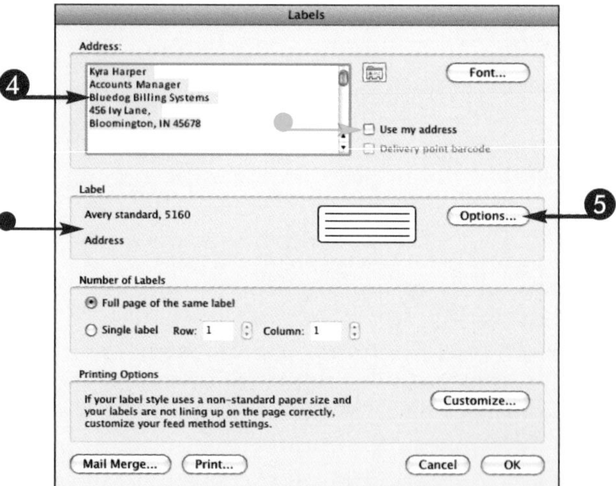

The Label Options dialog appears.

6. Click the **Label products** ⬍ and then click the label style you are using.

7. In the Product number list, click the label type you are using.

8. Click **OK**.

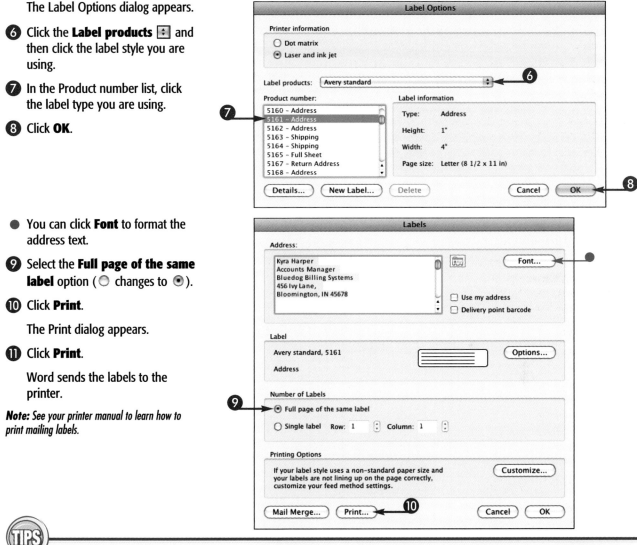

- You can click **Font** to format the address text.

9. Select the **Full page of the same label** option (○ changes to ◉).

10. Click **Print**.

    The Print dialog appears.

11. Click **Print**.

    Word sends the labels to the printer.

***Note:** See your printer manual to learn how to print mailing labels.*

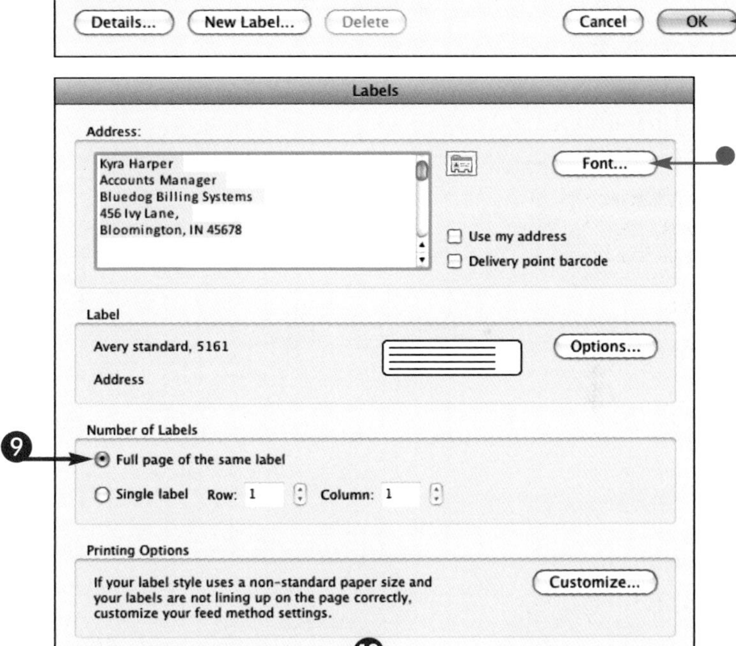

**Is there a way to store my address in Word to avoid typing it each time I print my labels?**

Yes. Click **Word** and then click **Preferences** to open the Word Preferences dialog. Click **User Information** to open the User Information preferences. In the First and Last text boxes, type your first and last names; in the Company text box, type your company name; and in the Address, City, State, and Zip text boxes, type your address. Click **OK**.

**Can I print just one label?**

Yes. Word treats a page full of labels as though they were organized in rows and columns. When you print a single label, you need to point out which one to print by specifying its row number and column number. Follow Steps **1** to **8** to set up your address and labels. Select the **Single label** option (○ changes to ◉). In the Row and Column text boxes, specify the position of the label on the page.

# Create an Index

You can make the information in a Word document easier to find by including an index with the document. An index is a list of the various terms and topics in the document, with references to the page numbers where those topics appear within the document.

**Although Word offers several useful tools for creating an index, creating an index in most documents is tedious, time-consuming, and finicky work. Do not make the decision to include an index lightly.**

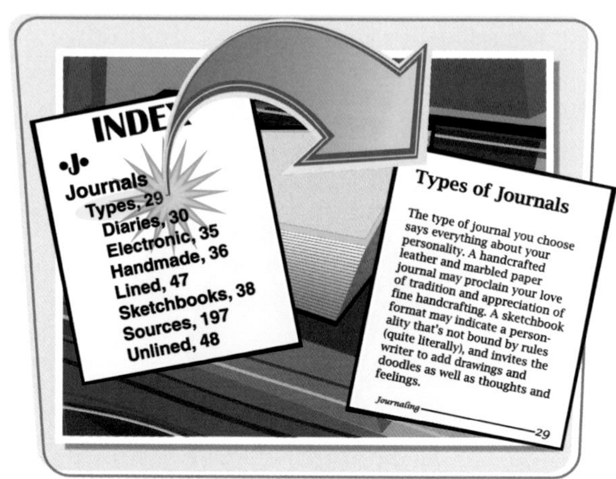


## Create an Index

### MARK INDEX ENTRIES

1. Select the text that you want to use as an index entry.
2. Press Shift + Option + ⌘ + X.

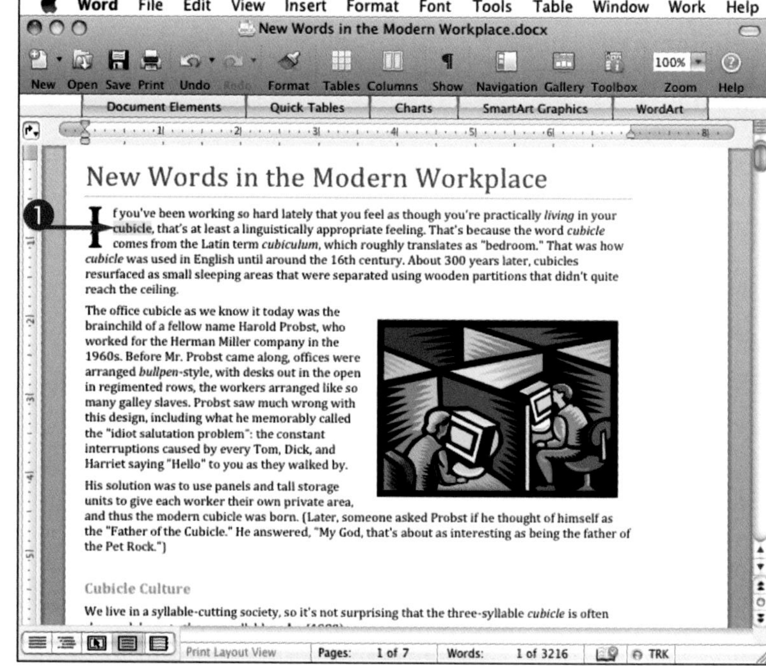


The Mark Index Entry dialog appears.

- The selected text appears here.

3. Edit the Main entry text, if necessary.
4. Click **Mark**.

- If the topic appears in multiple places and you want to mark all instances, click **Mark All**.

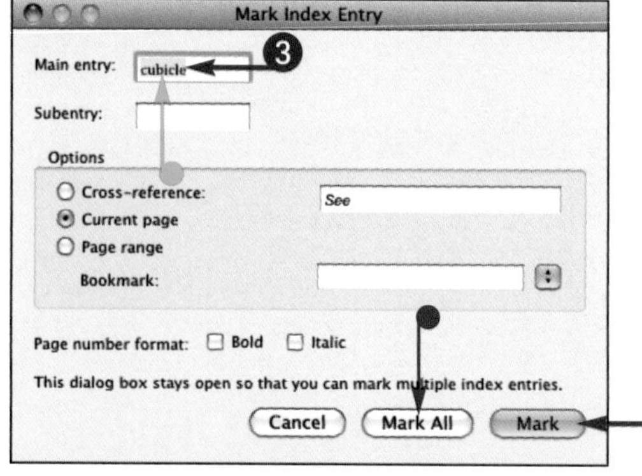

- Word adds a field to indicate an index entry.

5. Select the next text that you want to use as an index entry.

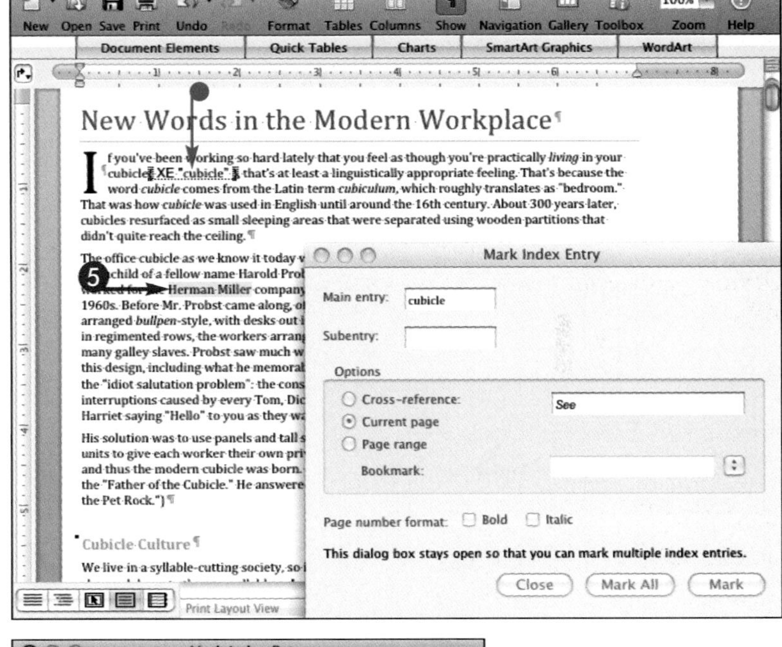

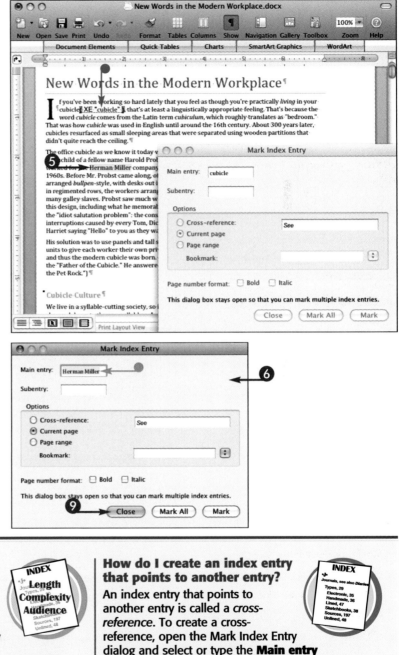

6. Click the Mark Index Entry dialog.
- The selected text appears here.
7. Repeat Steps **3** and **4** to mark the index entry.
8. Repeat Steps **5** to **7** to mark all the index entries for your document.
9. Click **Close**.

### When should I add an index to a document?

The decision to add an index depends on several factors. For example, the longer the document, the more likely an index is necessary or expected. Similarly, the more complex a document's subject matter, the more likely an index helps cut through that complexity and enables your readers to find what they want. Finally, consider the document's intended audience.

### How do I create an index entry that points to another entry?

An index entry that points to another entry is called a *cross-reference*. To create a cross-reference, open the Mark Index Entry dialog and select or type the **Main entry** text. Select the **Cross-reference** option (○ changes to ◉), and in the Cross-reference text box, type **See** followed by the name of the other entry. Click **Mark** or **Mark All** to set the entry.

continued

# Create an Index *(continued)*

**After you mark all the entries for your index, your next step is to create the index itself. In most cases, the index appears at the end of the document.**

## INSERT THE INDEX

1. Position the cursor where you want the index to appear.

2. Click **Insert**.

3. Click **Index and Tables**.

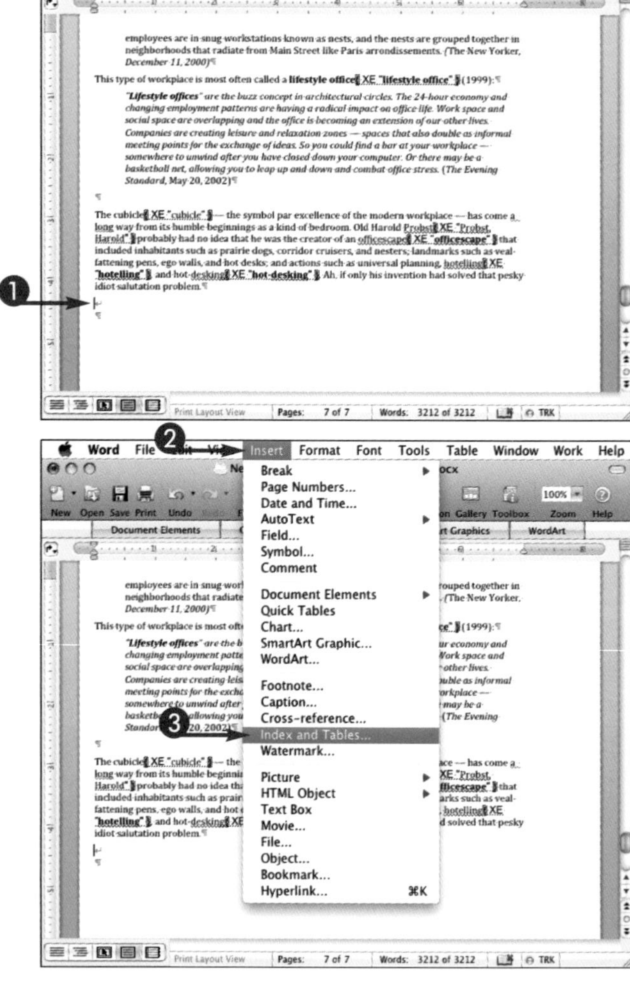

The Index and Tables dialog appears.

4. Click the **Index** tab.
5. In the Formats list, click the index format you want to use.
   - The Preview area shows you what the index will look like.
6. In the Columns text box, specify the number of entry columns you want to use.
7. Click **OK**.
   - Word inserts the index.
   - If you do not want to see the indexing fields, click **Show** (¶).

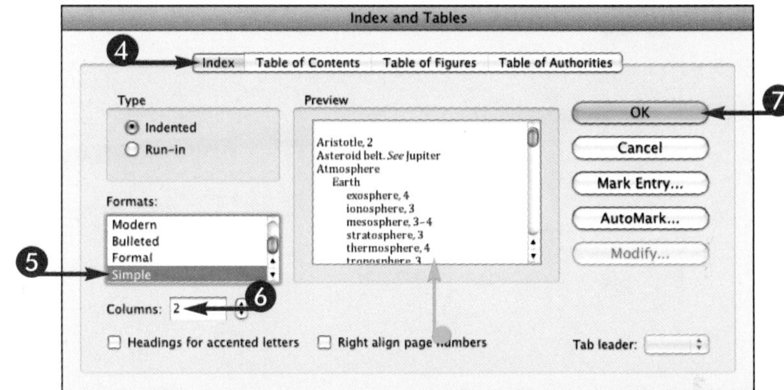


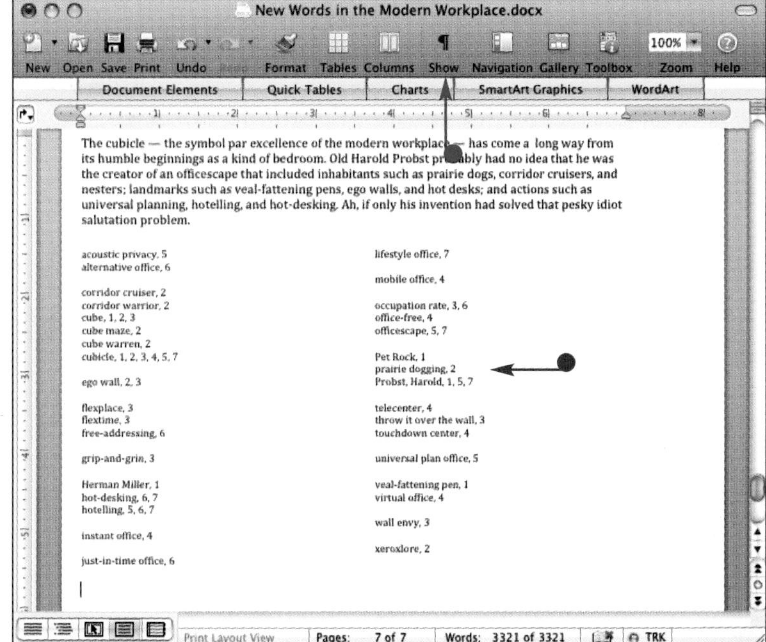


TIP

**Is there an easier way to create an index?**

Yes. As long as you have a good idea of the words and phrases you want to include in your index, you can set up a separate *concordance file*, a Word document that includes these words and phrases. To create this file, start a new Word document and insert a two-column table. Use the left column to type the words or phrases that you want Word to look for in the document you are indexing, and use the right column to type the words or phrases that you want Word to use as the index entries.

With the concordance file completed and saved, switch to the document you want to index and then follow Steps **1** to **6** to set up the index. Click **AutoMark**, use the Choose an Index AutoMark File dialog to select the concordance file, and then click Open. Word marks all the concordance items as index entries.

CHAPTER 10

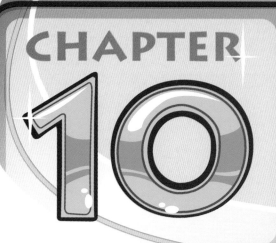

# Building an Excel Spreadsheet

You use Microsoft Excel to create *spreadsheets*, which are documents that enable you to manipulate numbers and formulas to quickly create powerful mathematical, financial, and statistical models. In this chapter you learn about Excel worksheets, how to enter and edit data, and how to manipulate worksheets.

# Understanding the Layout of a Worksheet

In Excel, a spreadsheet file is called a *workbook*, and each workbook consists of one or more *worksheets*. These worksheets are where you enter your data and formulas, so you need to know the layout of a typical worksheet.

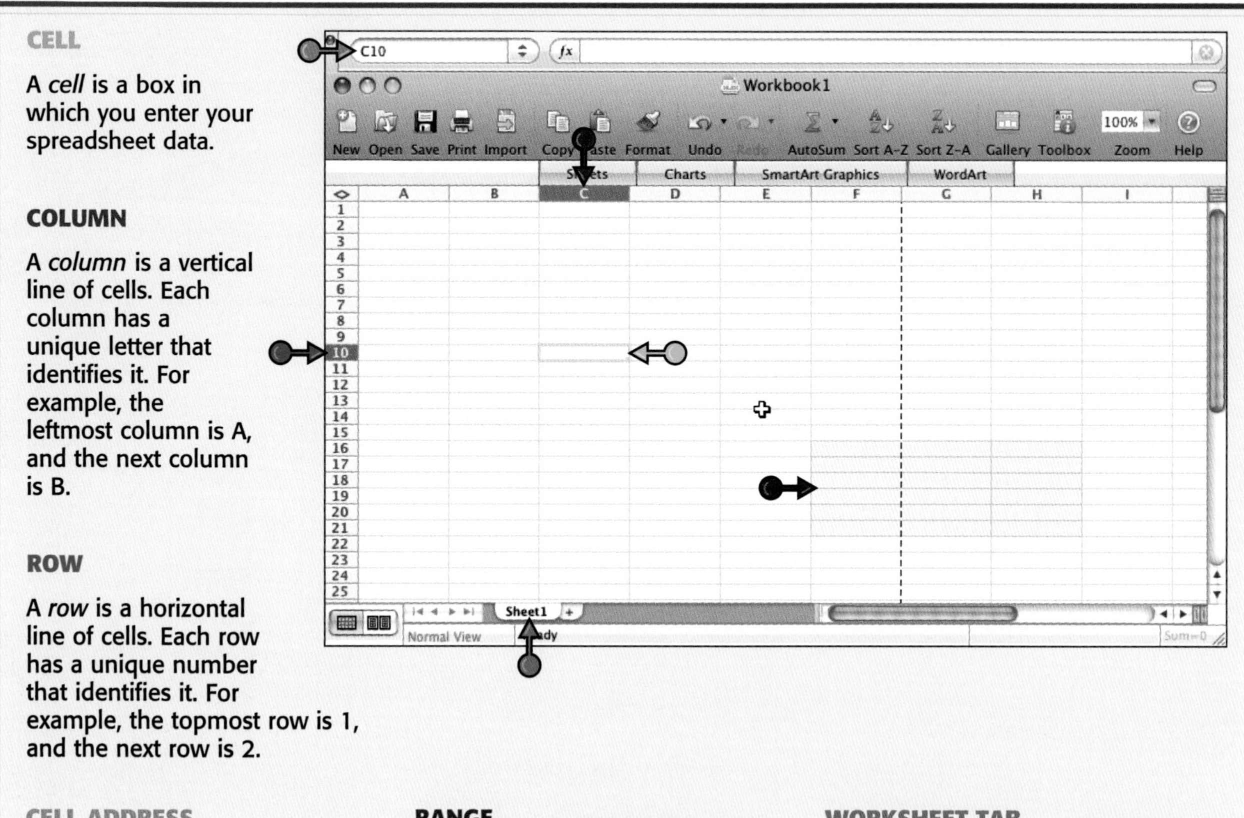


### CELL

A *cell* is a box in which you enter your spreadsheet data.

### COLUMN

A *column* is a vertical line of cells. Each column has a unique letter that identifies it. For example, the leftmost column is A, and the next column is B.

### ROW

A *row* is a horizontal line of cells. Each row has a unique number that identifies it. For example, the topmost row is 1, and the next row is 2.

### CELL ADDRESS

Each cell has its own *address,* which is determined by the letter and number of the intersecting column and row. For example, the cell at the intersection of column C and row 10 has the address C10.

### RANGE

A *range* is a rectangular grouping of two or more cells. The range address is given by the address of the top-left cell and the address of the bottom-right cell. F16:H21 is an example of a range of cells.

### WORKSHEET TAB

The worksheet tab displays the worksheet name. If your workbook contains multiple worksheets, you use the tabs to navigate between the worksheets.

# View the Formula Bar

**You can make many Excel spreadsheet-building chores easier by using the Formula bar to enter and edit cell data. Excel does not display the Formula bar by default, so you must follow these steps to display it.**

## View the Formula Bar

1. Click **View**.
2. Click **Formula Bar**.

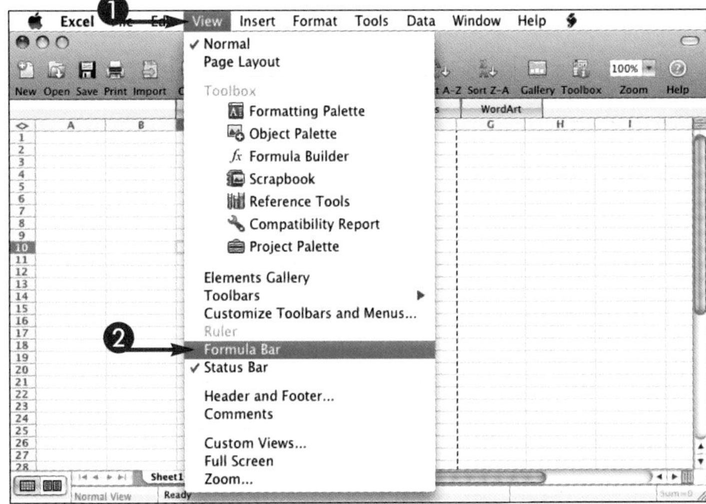


- Excel displays the Formula bar.

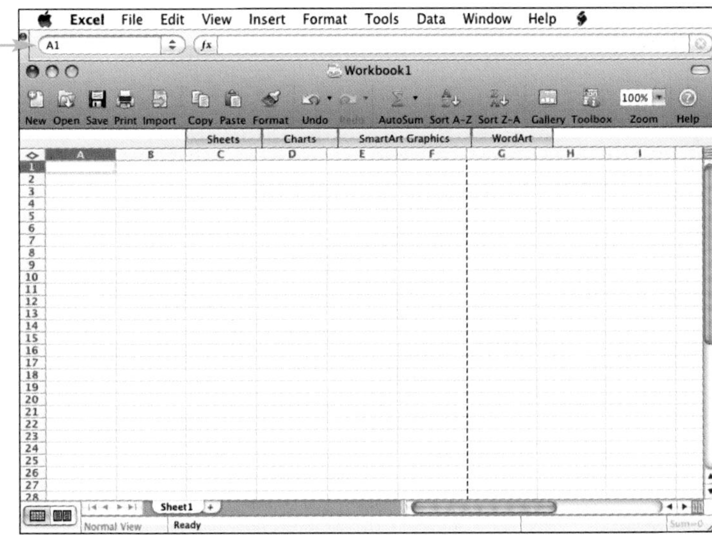

# Enter Data into a Cell

You build a spreadsheet by entering data into the worksheet cells, and then using formulas and functions to manipulate the cell data. So your first step when building a spreadsheet is to enter the data you require.

**Excel data is usually numbers, dates, or times, but you can also enter text into a cell, which is useful for labeling data or adding headings.**

## Enter Data into a Cell

1. Click in the cell that you want to use to enter the data.
   - Excel marks the current cell by surrounding it with a thick, light blue border.

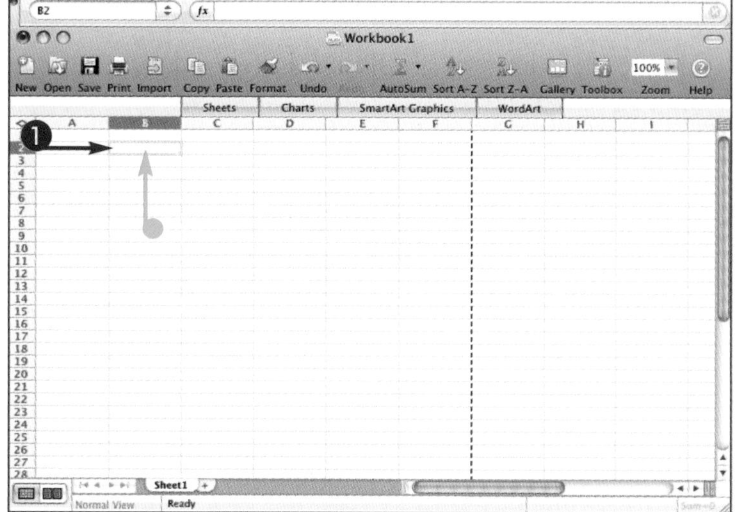


2. Start typing your data.
   - Excel opens the cell for editing and displays the data as you type.
   - Your typing also appears in the Formula bar.

*Note:* *Rather than typing the data directly into the cell, you can also type the data into the Formula bar.*

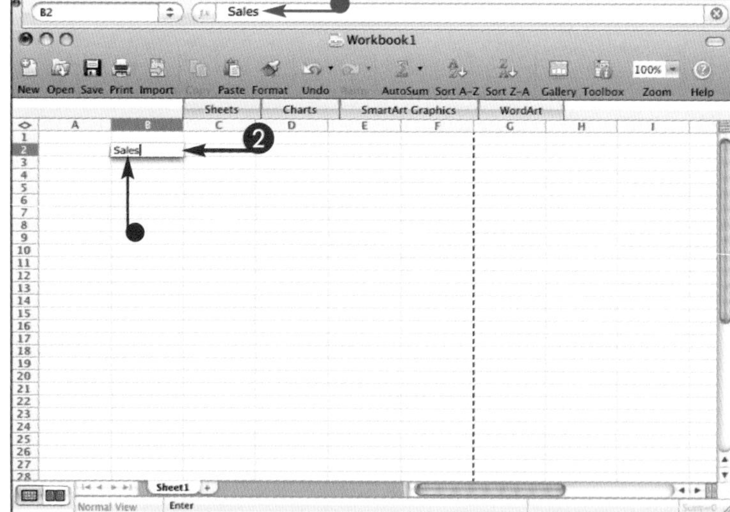

❸ When your data is complete, press Return.

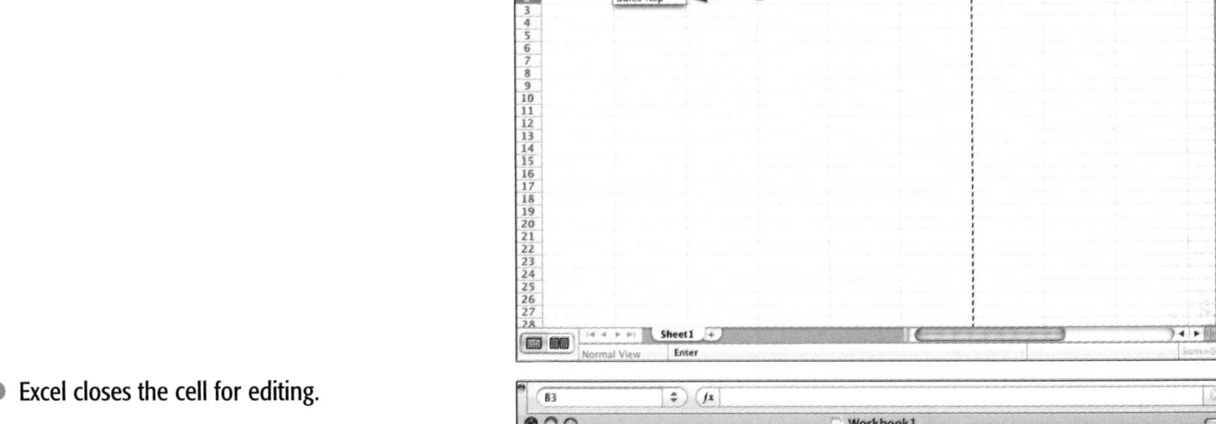


- Excel closes the cell for editing.
- Excel moves the selection to the cell below.

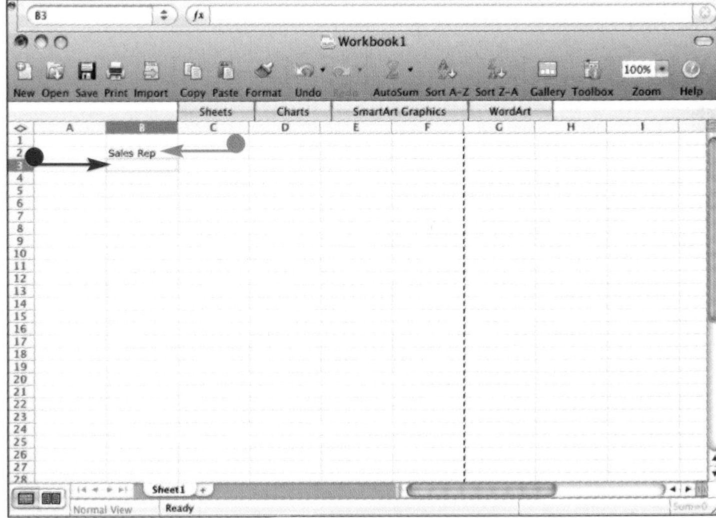

**Are there any shortcuts I can use to enter data?**

Yes. Excel offers a few keyboard shortcuts that you can use:

| Press | To |
|---|---|
| ⌘+; | Insert the current time |
| Ctrl+; | Insert the current date |
| Shift+⌘+' | Copy the value from the cell above |
| ⌘+' | Copy the formula from the cell above |

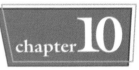

# Edit Cell Data

**If the data you entered into a cell has changed or is incorrect, you can edit the data. You can edit cell data either directly in the cell or by using the Formula bar.**

## Edit Cell Data

1. Click in the cell that you want to edit.
2. Press Ctrl + U.

   You can also double-click the cell you want to edit.

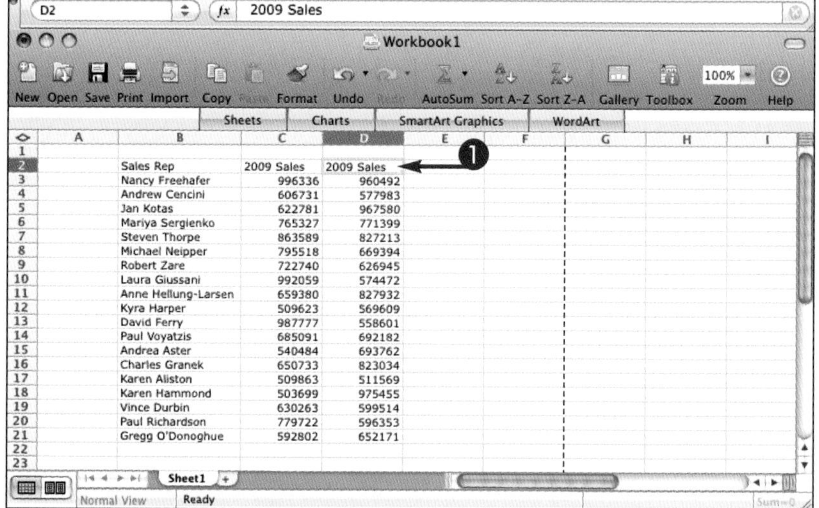

D2
2009 Sales
Workbook1
New Open Save Print Import Copy Paste Format Undo Redo AutoSum Sort A-Z Sort Z-A Gallery Toolbox Zoom Help
100%
Sheets Charts SmartArt Graphics WordArt
A B C D E F G H I
Sales Rep 2009 Sales 2009 Sales
Nancy Freehafer 996336 960492
Andrew Cencini 606731 577983
Jan Kotas 622781 967580
Mariya Sergienko 765327 771399
Steven Thorpe 863589 827213
Michael Neipper 795518 669394
Robert Zare 722740 626945
Laura Giussani 992059 574472
Anne Hellung-Larsen 659380 827932
Kyra Harper 509623 569609
David Ferry 987777 558601
Paul Voyatzis 685091 692182
Andrea Aster 540484 693762
Charles Granek 650733 823034
Karen Aliston 509863 511569
Karen Hammond 503699 975455
Vince Durbin 630263 599514
Paul Richardson 779722 596353
Gregg O'Donoghue 592802 652171
1
Sheet1
Normal View
Ready


- Excel opens the cell for editing and moves the cursor to the end of the existing data.
- Excel displays Edit in the status bar.
- You can also click inside the Formula bar and edit the cell data there.

3. Make your changes to the cell data.

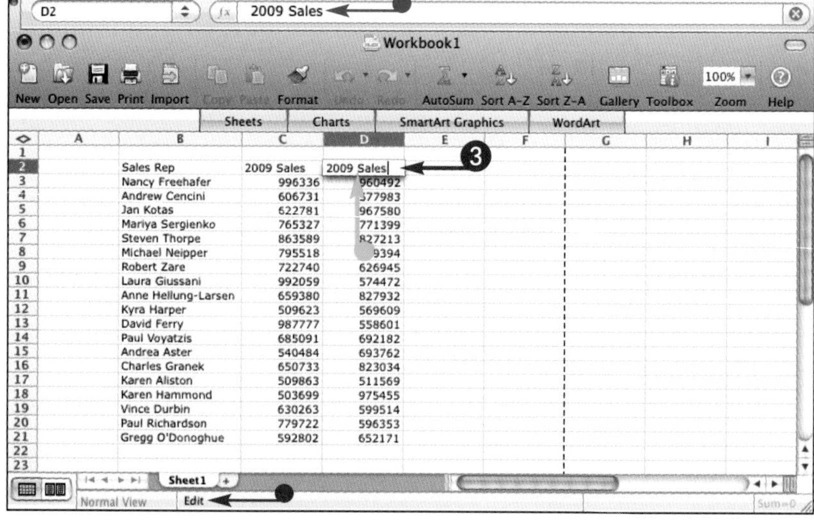

D2
2009 Sales
Workbook1
New Open Save Print Import Copy Paste Format Undo Redo AutoSum Sort A-Z Sort Z-A Gallery Toolbox Zoom Help
100%
Sheets Charts SmartArt Graphics WordArt
A B C D E F G H I
Sales Rep 2009 Sales 2009 Sales
Nancy Freehafer 996336 960492
Andrew Cencini 606731 577983
Jan Kotas 622781 967580
Mariya Sergienko 765327 771399
Steven Thorpe 863589 827213
Michael Neipper 795518
Robert Zare 722740 626945
Laura Giussani 992059 574472
Anne Hellung-Larsen 659380 827932
Kyra Harper 509623 569609
David Ferry 987777 558601
Paul Voyatzis 685091 692182
Andrea Aster 540484 693762
Charles Granek 650733 823034
Karen Aliston 509863 511569
Karen Hammond 503699 975455
Vince Durbin 630263 599514
Paul Richardson 779722 596353
Gregg O'Donoghue 592802 652171
3
Sheet1
Normal View
Edit

4 When you finish editing the data, press Return.

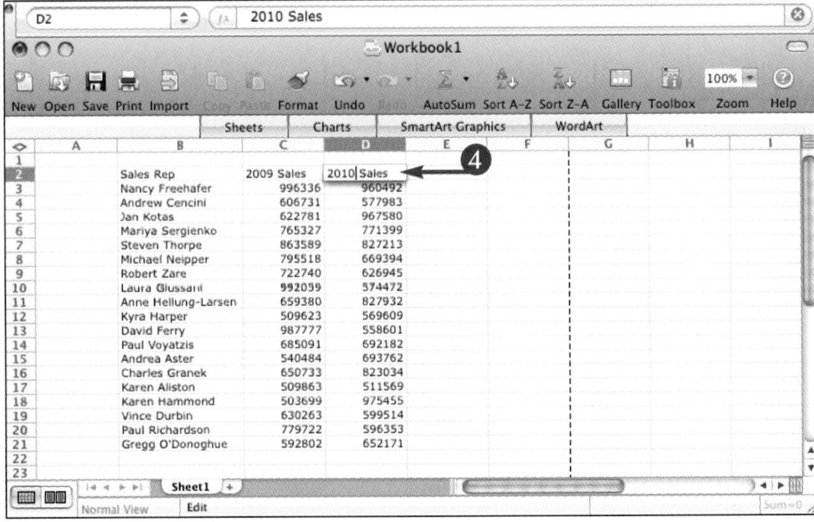


- Excel closes the cell for editing.
- Excel moves the selection to the cell below.

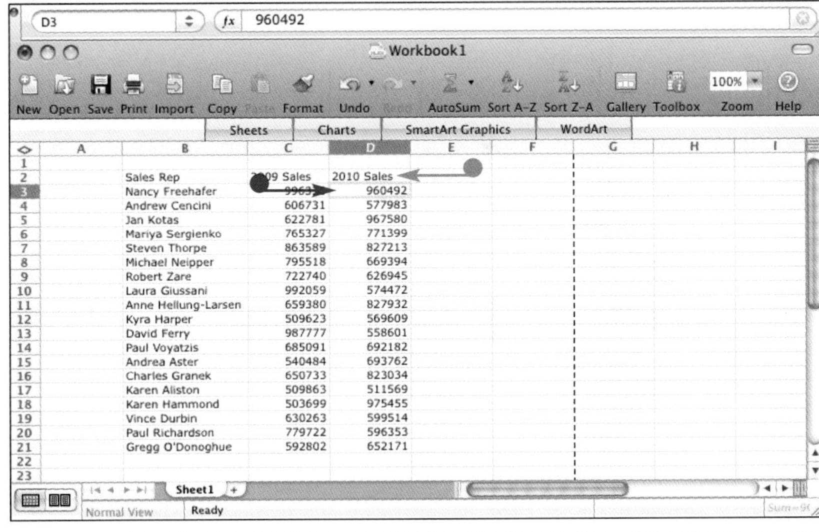

### Is there a faster way to open a cell for editing?

Yes. Move ✚ over the cell you want to edit, and center ✚ over the character where you want to start editing. Double-click the mouse. Excel opens the cell for editing and positions the cursor at the spot where you double-clicked.

### Is there a way to configure Excel to move the selection to the right after I press Return?

Yes. By default, Excel moves the selection down when you press Return after entering or editing cell data. However, you can change this using Excel's preferences. Click **Excel** and then click **Preferences** to open the Excel Preferences dialog. Click **Edit**, click the **Direction** ⬍, and then click the direction you prefer (Right, Left, Up, or Down). Click **OK**. You can also press Tab to move to the cell to the right.

# Navigate a Worksheet

You can use a few keyboard techniques that make it easier to navigate data after it is entered in a worksheet.

**It is usually easiest to use your mouse to click in the next cell you want to work with. However, if you are entering data, then using the keyboard to navigate to the next cell is often faster.**

| Keyboard Techniques for Navigating a Worksheet | |
|---|---|
| ***Press*** | ***To move*** |
| ← | Left one cell |
| → | Right one cell |
| ↑ | Up one cell |
| ↓ | Down one cell |
| Home | To the beginning of the current row |
| Page down | Down one screen |
| Page up | Up one screen |
| Option + Page down | One screen to the right |
| Option + Page up | One screen to the left |
| ⌘ + Home | To the beginning of the worksheet |
| ⌘ + End | To the bottom right corner of the used portion of the worksheet |
| ⌘ +arrow keys | In the direction of the arrow to the next non-blank cell if the current cell is blank, or to the last non-blank cell if the current cell is not blank |

# Rename a Worksheet

You can make your Excel workbooks easier to understand and navigate by providing each worksheet with a name that reflects the contents of the sheet.

**Excel provides worksheets with generic names such as Sheet1 and Sheet2, but you can change these to more descriptive names such as Sales 2009, Amortization, or Budget Data.**

## Rename a Worksheet

1. Display the worksheet you want to rename.
2. Double-click the worksheet's tab.

   You can also click **Format**, **Sheet**, and then click **Rename**.

- Excel creates a text box around the name and selects the text.

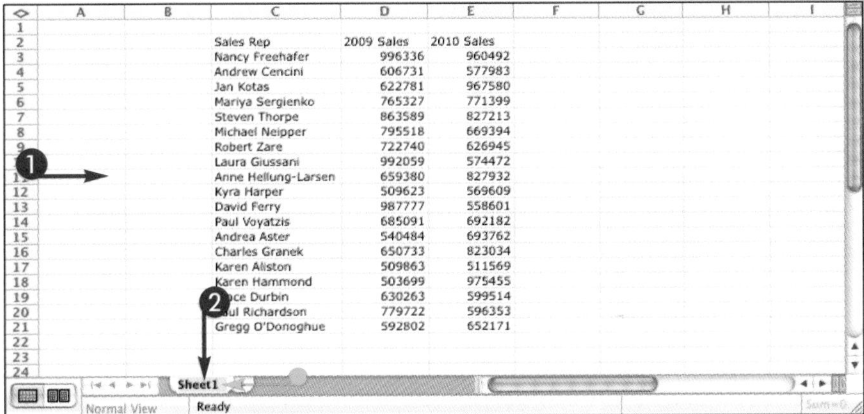

| Sales Rep | 2009 Sales | 2010 Sales |
|---|---|---|
| Nancy Freehafer | 996336 | 960492 |
| Andrew Cencini | 606731 | 577983 |
| Jan Kotas | 622781 | 967580 |
| Mariya Sergienko | 765327 | 771399 |
| Steven Thorpe | 863589 | 827213 |
| Michael Neipper | 795518 | 669394 |
| Robert Zare | 722740 | 626945 |
| Laura Giussani | 992059 | 574472 |
| Anne Hellung-Larsen | 659380 | 827932 |
| Kyra Harper | 509623 | 569609 |
| David Ferry | 987777 | 558601 |
| Paul Voyatzis | 685091 | 692182 |
| Andrea Aster | 540484 | 693762 |
| Charles Granek | 650733 | 823034 |
| Karen Aliston | 509863 | 511569 |
| Karen Hammond | 503699 | 975455 |
| Vince Durbin | 630263 | 599514 |
| Paul Richardson | 779722 | 596353 |
| Gregg O'Donoghue | 592802 | 652171 |



3. If you want to edit the existing name, press either ← or → to deselect the text.
4. Type the new worksheet name.
5. Press Return.

   Excel assigns the new name to the worksheet.

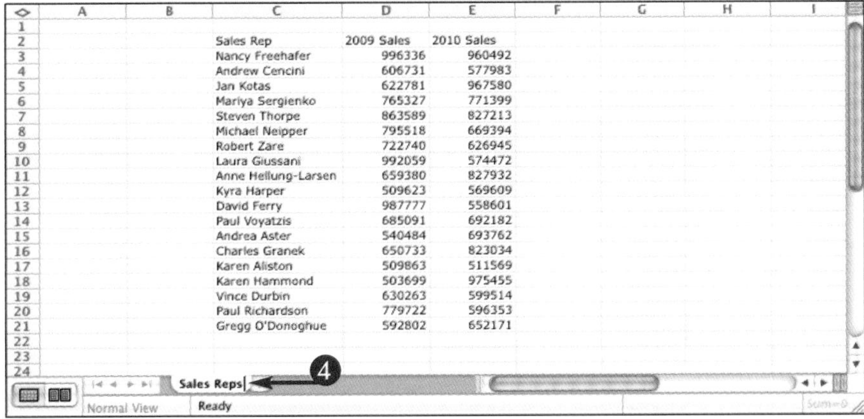

| Sales Rep | 2009 Sales | 2010 Sales |
|---|---|---|
| Nancy Freehafer | 996336 | 960492 |
| Andrew Cencini | 606731 | 577983 |
| Jan Kotas | 622781 | 967580 |
| Mariya Sergienko | 765327 | 771399 |
| Steven Thorpe | 863589 | 827213 |
| Michael Neipper | 795518 | 669394 |
| Robert Zare | 722740 | 626945 |
| Laura Giussani | 992059 | 574472 |
| Anne Hellung-Larsen | 659380 | 827932 |
| Kyra Harper | 509623 | 569609 |
| David Ferry | 987777 | 558601 |
| Paul Voyatzis | 685091 | 692182 |
| Andrea Aster | 540484 | 693762 |
| Charles Granek | 650733 | 823034 |
| Karen Aliston | 509863 | 511569 |
| Karen Hammond | 503699 | 975455 |
| Vince Durbin | 630263 | 599514 |
| Paul Richardson | 779722 | 596353 |
| Gregg O'Donoghue | 592802 | 652171 |

# Create a New Worksheet

Excel supports multiple worksheets in a single workbook, so you can add as many worksheets as you need for your project or model.

**In most cases, you will add a blank worksheet, but Excel also comes with more than 30 predefined worksheet templates that you can use.**

## Create a New Worksheet

1. Open the workbook to which you want to add the worksheet.
2. Click **Sheets**.

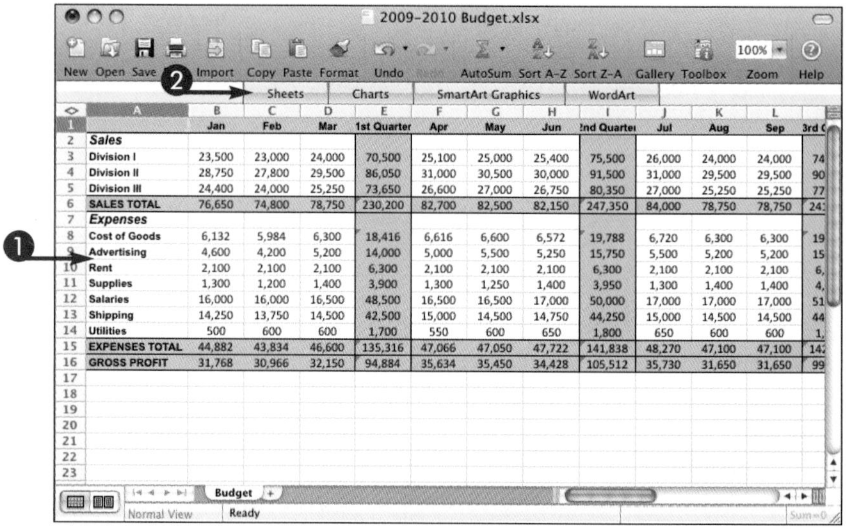


3. Click the type of worksheet you want to add.
4. Click ▶ and ◀ to preview the predefined worksheets.
- Move ↖ over the template icon.
- The name of the template appears here.

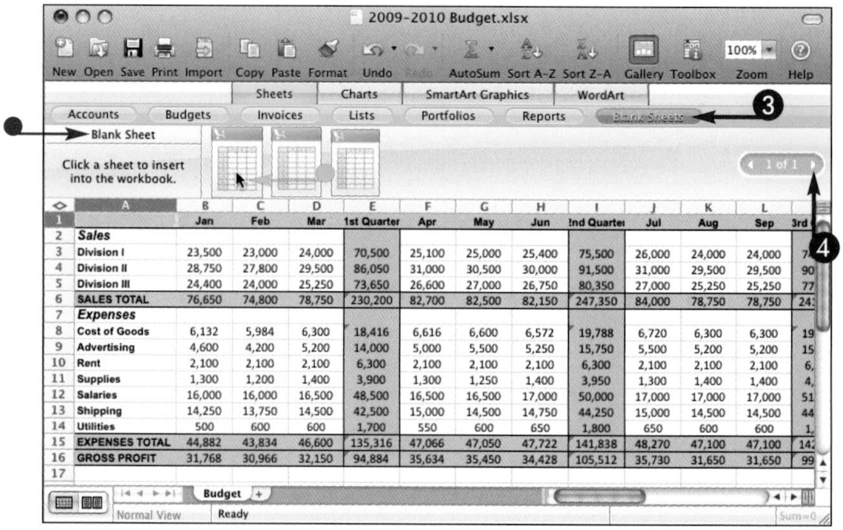

❺ Click the worksheet you want to add.

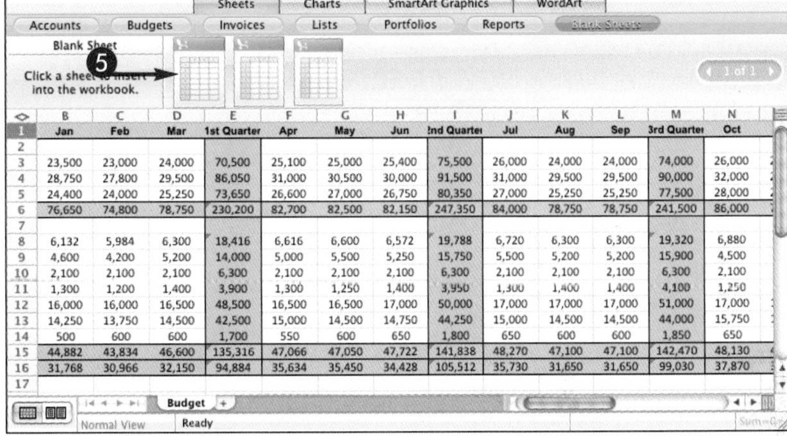


- Excel inserts the worksheet.

❻ Click **Sheets** to hide the Gallery.

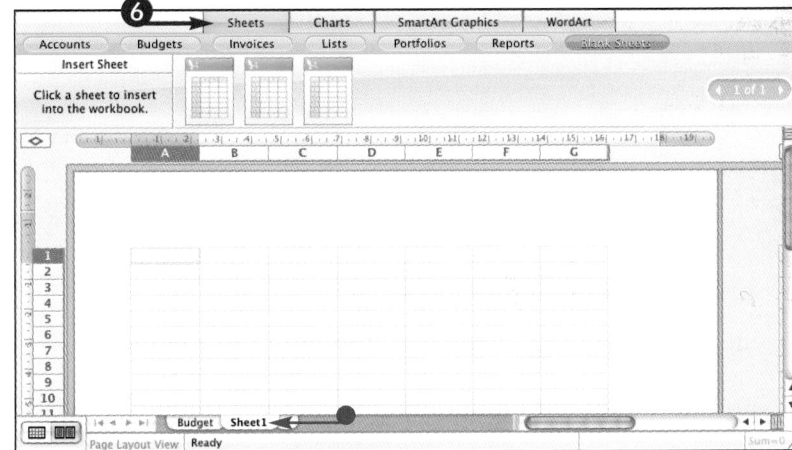


## TIPS

### Is there an easier way to add a blank worksheet?

Yes. Open the workbook to which you want to add the worksheet, and then click the **Insert Sheet** button (+).

- Click +.

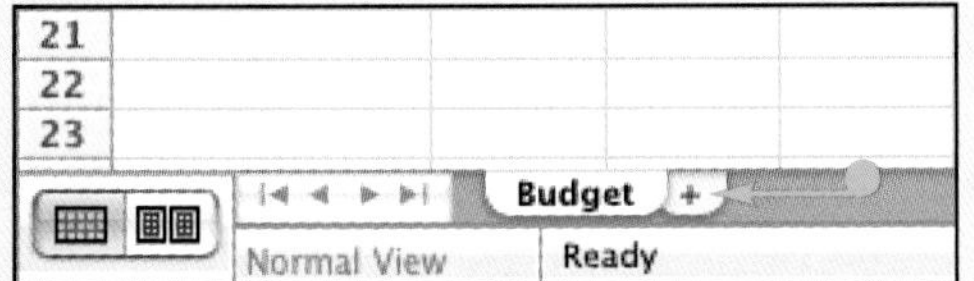


### How do I navigate from one worksheet to another?

The easiest way is to click the tab of the worksheet you want to use.

From the keyboard, press Ctrl + Page down to move to the next worksheet, and press Ctrl + Page up to move to the previous worksheet. You can also click the following controls:

| | |
|---|---|
| \|◄ | Move to the first worksheet. |
| ◄ | Move to the previous worksheet. |
| ► | Move to the next worksheet. |
| ►\| | Move to the last worksheet. |

# Move or Copy a Worksheet

You can make an Excel workbook more organized and easier to navigate by moving your worksheets to different positions within the workbook. You can also move a worksheet to another workbook.

**Excel also enables you to make a copy of a worksheet, which is a useful technique if you require a new worksheet that is similar to an existing worksheet. You can copy the sheet to the same workbook or to another workbook.**

## Move or Copy a Worksheet

1. If you want to move or copy the worksheet to another workbook, open that workbook and then return to the current workbook.
2. Click the tab of the worksheet you want to move or copy.

2009-2010 Budget.xlsx

| | A | B | C | D | E | F | G | H | I | J | K |
|---|---|---|---|---|---|---|---|---|---|---|---|
| 1 | | Jan | Feb | Mar | 1st Quarter | Apr | May | Jun | 2nd Quarter | Jul | Aug |
| 2 | Sales | | | | | | | | | | |
| 3 | Division I | 21,620 | 21,160 | 22,080 | 64,860 | 23,092 | 23,000 | 23,368 | 69,460 | 23,920 | 22,080 |
| 4 | Division II | 26,450 | 25,576 | 27,140 | 79,166 | 28,520 | 28,060 | 27,600 | 84,180 | 28,520 | 27,140 |
| 5 | Division III | 22,448 | 22,080 | 23,230 | 67,758 | 24,472 | 24,840 | 24,610 | 73,922 | 24,840 | 23,230 |
| 6 | SALES TOTA | 70,518 | 68,816 | 72,450 | 211,784 | 76,084 | 75,900 | 75,578 | 227,562 | 77,280 | 72,450 |
| 7 | Expenses | | | | | | | | | | |
| 8 | Cost of Good | 5,924 | 5,781 | 6,086 | 17,790 | 6,391 | 6,376 | 6,349 | 19,115 | 6,492 | 6,086 |
| 9 | Advertising | 4,830 | 4,410 | 5,460 | 14,700 | 5,250 | 5,775 | 5,513 | 16,538 | 5,775 | 5,460 |
| 10 | Rent | 2,205 | 2,205 | 2,205 | 6,615 | 2,205 | 2,205 | 2,205 | 6,615 | 2,205 | 2,205 |
| 11 | Supplies | 1,365 | 1,260 | 1,470 | 4,095 | 1,365 | 1,313 | 1,470 | 4,148 | 1,365 | 1,470 |
| 12 | Salaries | 16,800 | 16,800 | 17,325 | 50,925 | 17,325 | 17,325 | 17,850 | 52,500 | 17,850 | 17,850 |
| 13 | Shipping | 14,963 | 14,438 | 15,225 | 44,625 | 15,750 | 15,225 | 15,488 | 46,463 | 15,750 | 15,225 |
| 14 | Utilities | 525 | 630 | 630 | 1,785 | 578 | 630 | 683 | 1,890 | 683 | 630 |
| 15 | EXPENSES T | 46,611 | 45,523 | 48,401 | 140,535 | 48,864 | 48,848 | 49,556 | 147,268 | 50,119 | 48,926 |
| 16 | GROSS PRO | 23,907 | 23,293 | 24,049 | 71,249 | 27,220 | 27,052 | 26,022 | 80,294 | 27,161 | 23,524 |

Budget | 2008-2009 Final | Assumptions | Projections

3. Click **Edit**.
4. Click **Move or Copy Sheet**.

   The Move or Copy dialog appears.

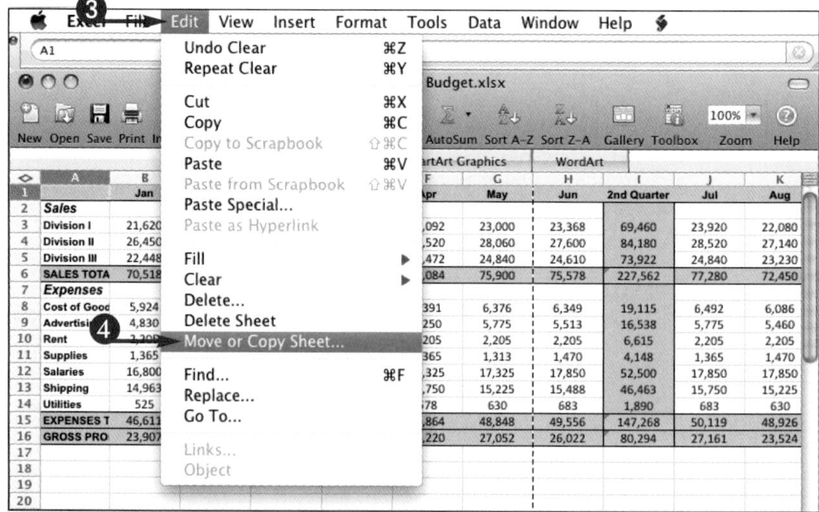

5. If you want to move or copy the sheet to another workbook, click the **To book** and then click the workbook.
6. Use the **Before sheet** list to click the worksheet before which you want the sheet moved or copied.
7. To create a copy of the worksheet, select the **Create a copy** option (☐ changes to ☑).
8. Click **OK**.

- Excel moves or copies the worksheet.

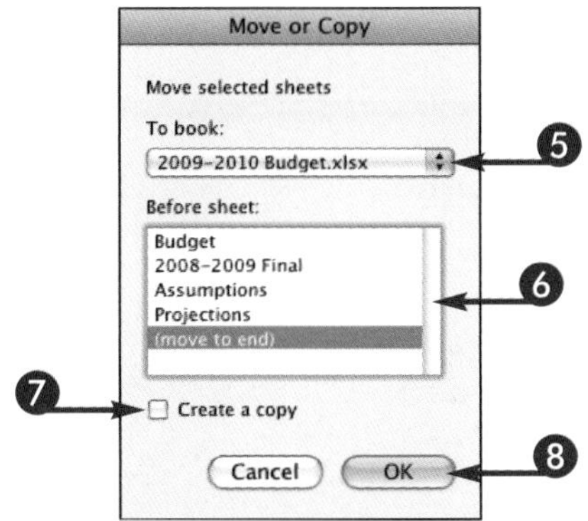


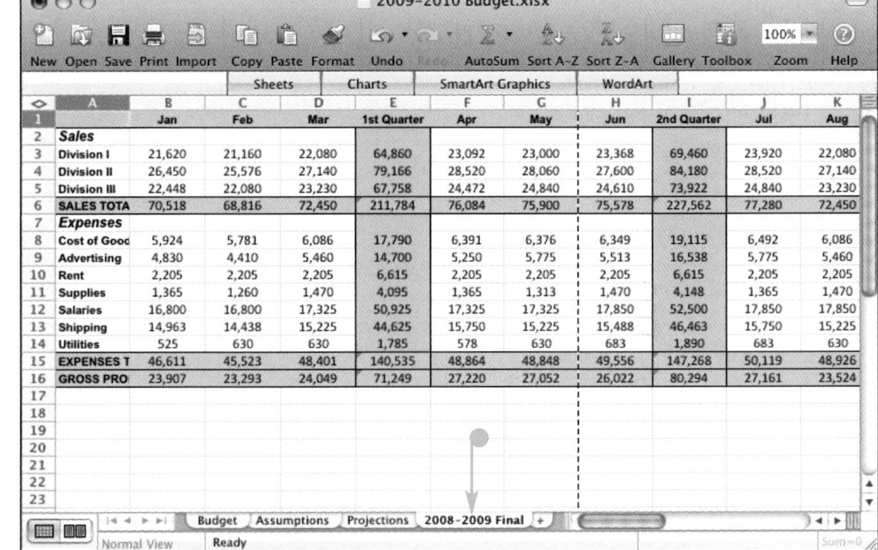


| | A | B | C | D | E | F | G | H | I | J | K |
|---|---|---|---|---|---|---|---|---|---|---|---|
| 1 | | Jan | Feb | Mar | 1st Quarter | Apr | May | Jun | 2nd Quarter | Jul | Aug |
| 2 | Sales | | | | | | | | | | |
| 3 | Division I | 21,620 | 21,160 | 22,080 | 64,860 | 23,092 | 23,000 | 23,368 | 69,460 | 23,920 | 22,080 |
| 4 | Division II | 26,450 | 25,576 | 27,140 | 79,166 | 28,520 | 28,060 | 27,600 | 84,180 | 28,520 | 27,140 |
| 5 | Division III | 22,448 | 22,080 | 23,230 | 67,758 | 24,472 | 24,840 | 24,610 | 73,922 | 24,840 | 23,230 |
| 6 | SALES TOTA | 70,518 | 68,816 | 72,450 | 211,784 | 76,084 | 75,900 | 75,578 | 227,562 | 77,280 | 72,450 |
| 7 | Expenses | | | | | | | | | | |
| 8 | Cost of Good | 5,924 | 5,781 | 6,086 | 17,790 | 6,391 | 6,376 | 6,349 | 19,115 | 6,492 | 6,086 |
| 9 | Advertising | 4,830 | 4,410 | 5,460 | 14,700 | 5,250 | 5,775 | 5,513 | 16,538 | 5,775 | 5,460 |
| 10 | Rent | 2,205 | 2,205 | 2,205 | 6,615 | 2,205 | 2,205 | 2,205 | 6,615 | 2,205 | 2,205 |
| 11 | Supplies | 1,365 | 1,260 | 1,470 | 4,095 | 1,365 | 1,313 | 1,470 | 4,148 | 1,365 | 1,470 |
| 12 | Salaries | 16,800 | 16,800 | 17,325 | 50,925 | 17,325 | 17,325 | 17,850 | 52,500 | 17,850 | 17,850 |
| 13 | Shipping | 14,963 | 14,438 | 15,225 | 44,625 | 15,750 | 15,225 | 15,488 | 46,463 | 15,750 | 15,225 |
| 14 | Utilities | 525 | 630 | 630 | 1,785 | 578 | 630 | 683 | 1,890 | 683 | 630 |
| 15 | EXPENSES T | 46,611 | 45,523 | 48,401 | 140,535 | 48,864 | 48,848 | 49,556 | 147,268 | 50,119 | 48,926 |
| 16 | GROSS PRO | 23,907 | 23,293 | 24,049 | 71,249 | 27,220 | 27,052 | 26,022 | 80,294 | 27,161 | 23,524 |

TIP

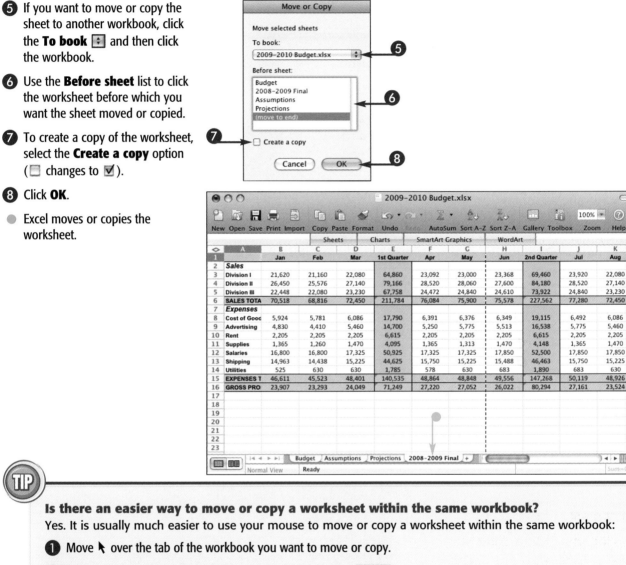

**Is there an easier way to move or copy a worksheet within the same workbook?**

Yes. It is usually much easier to use your mouse to move or copy a worksheet within the same workbook:

1. Move the pointer over the tab of the workbook you want to move or copy.
2. If you want to create a copy of the worksheet, hold down Option.
3. Click and drag the worksheet tab left or right to the new position within the workbook.

   The pointer changes to the drag pointer.

- As you drag, an arrow shows the position of the worksheet.

4. Drop the worksheet tab.

   Excel moves or copies the worksheet.

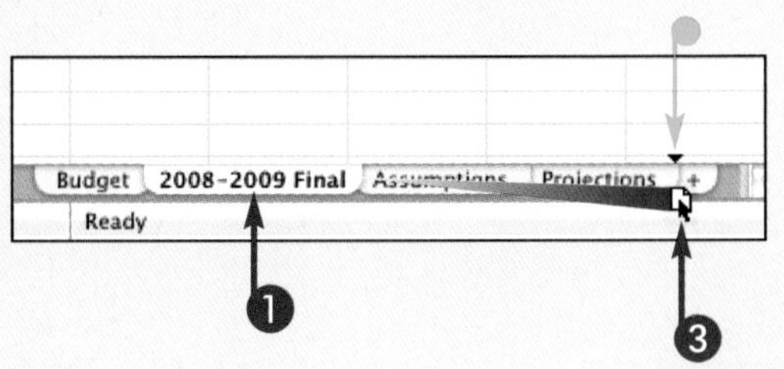

# Delete a Worksheet

**If you have a worksheet that you no longer need, you can delete it from the workbook. This reduces the size of the workbook and makes the workbook easier to navigate.**

**You cannot undo a worksheet deletion, so check the worksheet contents carefully before proceeding with the deletion.**

## Delete a Worksheet

1. Click the tab of the worksheet you want to delete.

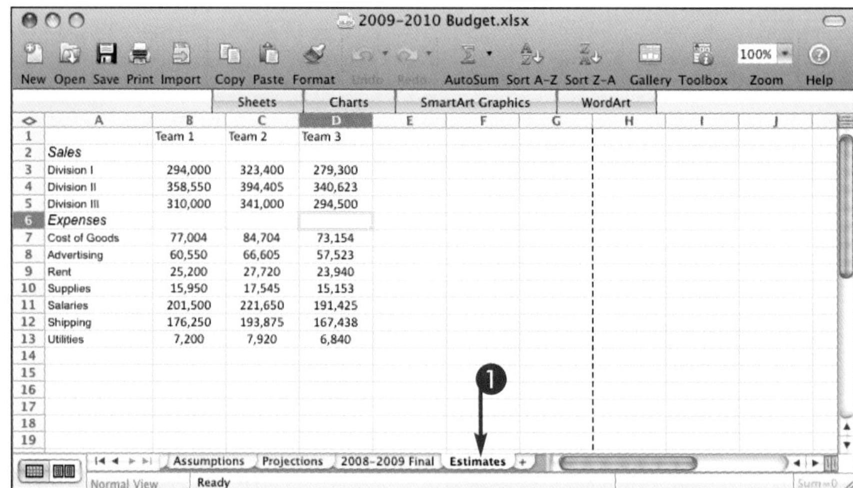


2. Click **Edit**.
3. Click **Delete Sheet**.

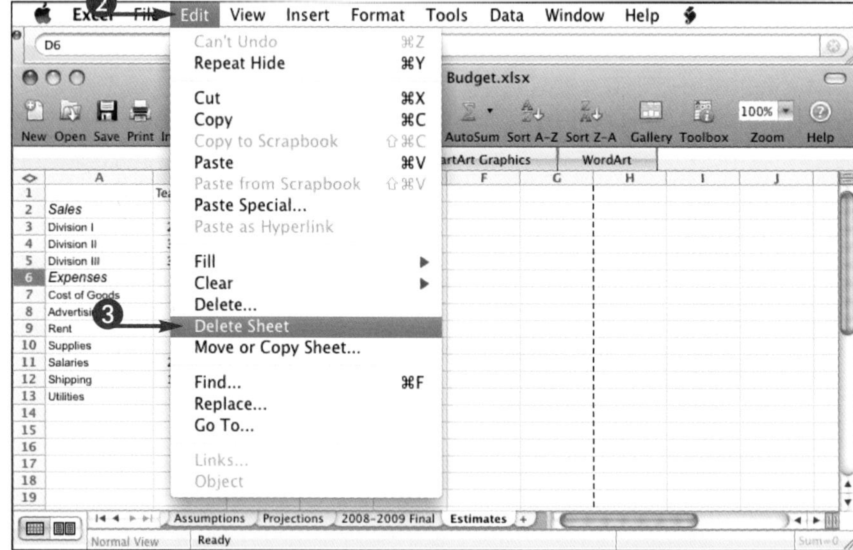

Excel asks you to confirm that you want to delete the worksheet.

4. Click **OK**.

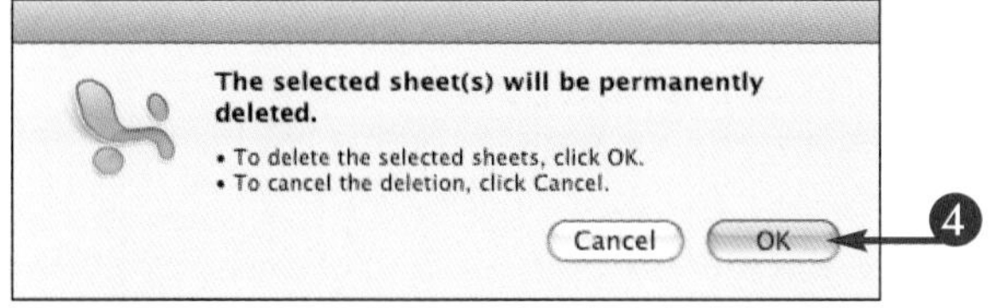

The selected sheet(s) will be permanently deleted.
• To delete the selected sheets, click OK.
• To cancel the deletion, click Cancel.
Cancel
OK
4


- Excel removes the worksheet.

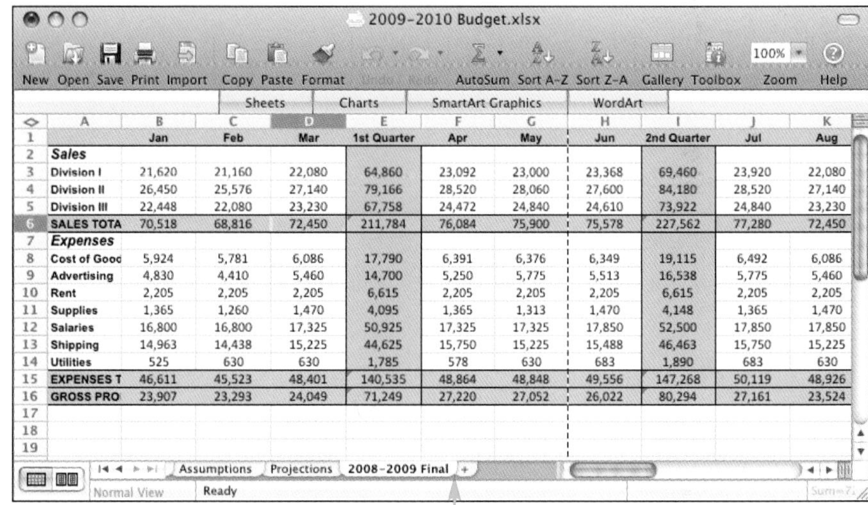


| | A | B | C | D | E | F | G | H | I | J | K |
|---|---|---|---|---|---|---|---|---|---|---|---|
| 1 | | Jan | Feb | Mar | 1st Quarter | Apr | May | Jun | 2nd Quarter | Jul | Aug |
| 2 | Sales | | | | | | | | | | |
| 3 | Division I | 21,620 | 21,160 | 22,080 | 64,860 | 23,092 | 23,000 | 23,368 | 69,460 | 23,920 | 22,080 |
| 4 | Division II | 26,450 | 25,576 | 27,140 | 79,166 | 28,520 | 28,060 | 27,600 | 84,180 | 28,520 | 27,140 |
| 5 | Division III | 22,448 | 22,080 | 23,230 | 67,758 | 24,472 | 24,840 | 24,610 | 73,922 | 24,840 | 23,230 |
| 6 | SALES TOTA | 70,518 | 68,816 | 72,450 | 211,784 | 76,084 | 75,900 | 75,578 | 227,562 | 77,280 | 72,450 |
| 7 | Expenses | | | | | | | | | | |
| 8 | Cost of Good | 5,924 | 5,781 | 6,086 | 17,790 | 6,391 | 6,376 | 6,349 | 19,115 | 6,492 | 6,086 |
| 9 | Advertising | 4,830 | 4,410 | 5,460 | 14,700 | 5,250 | 5,775 | 5,513 | 16,538 | 5,775 | 5,460 |
| 10 | Rent | 2,205 | 2,205 | 2,205 | 6,615 | 2,205 | 2,205 | 2,205 | 6,615 | 2,205 | 2,205 |
| 11 | Supplies | 1,365 | 1,260 | 1,470 | 4,095 | 1,365 | 1,313 | 1,470 | 4,148 | 1,365 | 1,470 |
| 12 | Salaries | 16,800 | 16,800 | 17,325 | 50,925 | 17,325 | 17,325 | 17,850 | 52,500 | 17,850 | 17,850 |
| 13 | Shipping | 14,963 | 14,438 | 15,225 | 44,625 | 15,750 | 15,225 | 15,488 | 46,463 | 15,750 | 15,225 |
| 14 | Utilities | 525 | 630 | 630 | 1,785 | 578 | 630 | 683 | 1,890 | 683 | 630 |
| 15 | EXPENSES T | 46,611 | 45,523 | 48,401 | 140,535 | 48,864 | 48,848 | 49,556 | 147,268 | 50,119 | 48,926 |
| 16 | GROSS PRO | 23,907 | 23,293 | 24,049 | 71,249 | 27,220 | 27,052 | 26,022 | 80,294 | 27,161 | 23,524 |
| 17 | | | | | | | | | | | |
| 18 | | | | | | | | | | | |
| 19 | | | | | | | | | | | |

**I have several worksheets I need to delete. Do I have to delete them individually?**

No. You can select all the sheets you want to remove and then run the deletion. To select multiple worksheets, click the tab of one of the worksheets, hold down ⌘, and then click the tabs of the other worksheets. After you select your worksheets, follow Steps **3** to **5** to delete all the worksheets at once.

**Is it possible to temporarily remove a worksheet from a workbook?**

Yes. You can hide the worksheet so that it no longer appears in the workbook. This is useful if you have a worksheet that contains sensitive data, but you need to show the workbook to other people. To hide a worksheet, click its tab, click **Format**, click **Sheet**, and then click **Hide**. To display the worksheet again, click **Format**, click **Sheet**, and then click **Unhide** to display the Unhide dialog. Click the worksheet in the Unhide sheet list, and then click **OK**.

# Insert a Row or Column

You can insert a row or column into your existing worksheet data to accommodate more information. This is particularly useful if the information you need to add fits naturally within the existing data, rather than at the end.

## Insert a Row or Column

### INSERT A ROW

1. Click in any cell in the row above which you want to insert the new row.
2. Click **Insert**.
3. Click **Rows**.

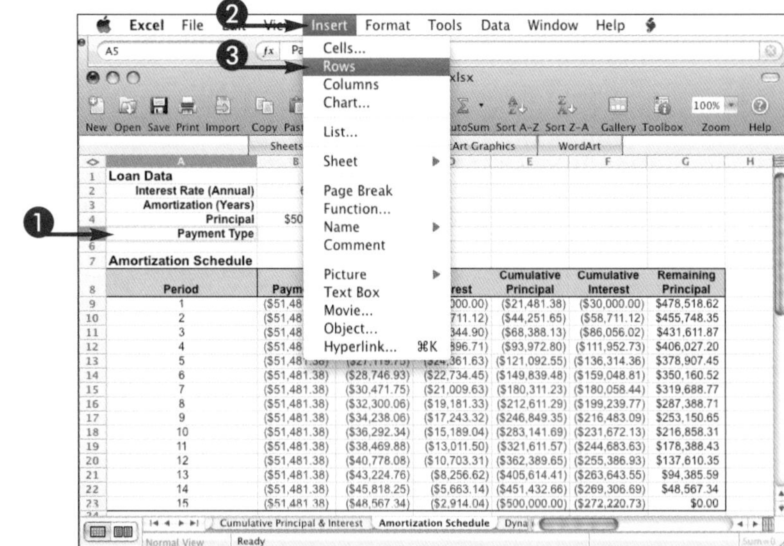


- Excel inserts the new row.
- The rows below the new row are shifted down.

4. Click the **Format** smart tag (▯).
5. Select a formatting option for the new row (○ changes to ◉).

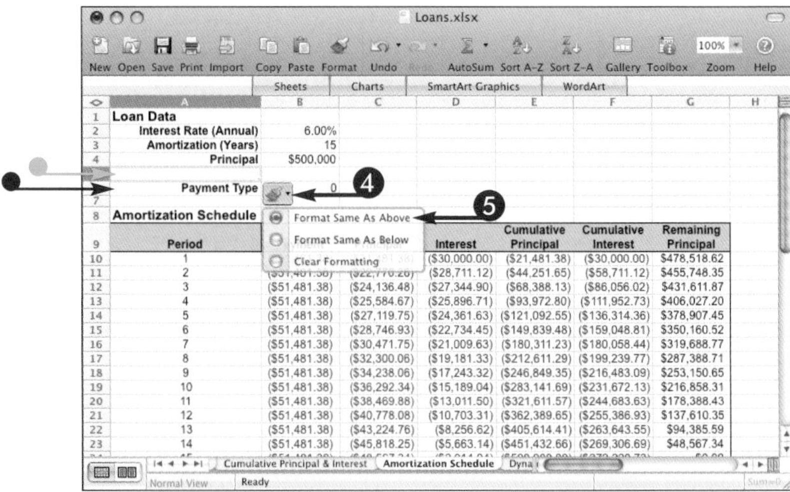

## INSERT A COLUMN

1. Click any cell in the row to the left of which you want to insert the new column.
2. Click **Insert**.
3. Click **Columns**.

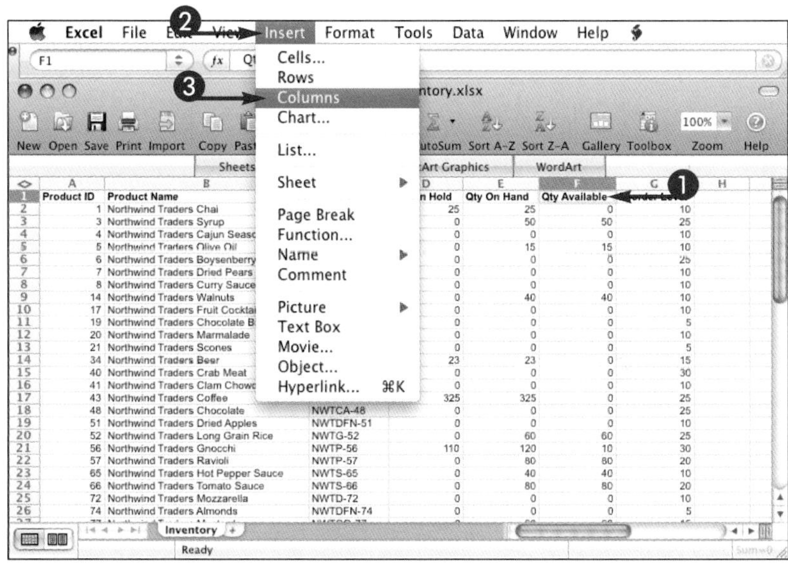

- Excel inserts the new column.
- The columns to the right of the new column are shifted to the right.

4. Click the **Format** smart tag.
5. Select a formatting option for the new row (○ changes to ◉).

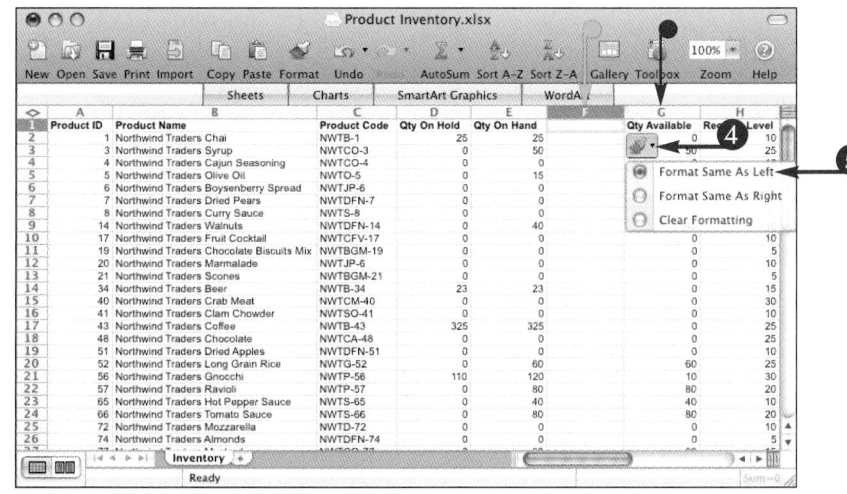

### Can I insert more than one row or column at a time?

Yes. You can insert as many new rows or columns as you need. First, select the same number of rows or columns that you want to insert. (See Chapter 11 to learn how to select rows and columns.) For example, if you want to insert four rows, select four existing rows. Follow Steps **2** and **3** in the section "Insert a Row or Column" to insert rows or Steps **2** and **3** in the section "Insert a Column" to insert columns.

# Delete Worksheet Data

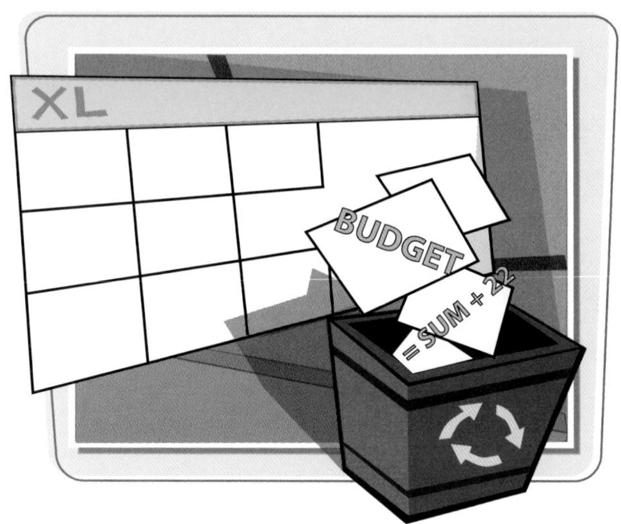


If your worksheet contains data that you no longer need, you can delete that data. You can either delete just the data within one or more cells, or you can delete the cells themselves. If you delete the cells, Excel shifts the remaining worksheet data to replace the cells.

**When you delete cells, you can delete a single cell, a collection of cells, or entire rows or columns.**

## Delete Worksheet Data

### DELETE CELL DATA

1. Select the cell or cells that contain the data you want to delete.

***Note:*** *See Chapter 11 to learn how to select cells.*

2. Press Del.

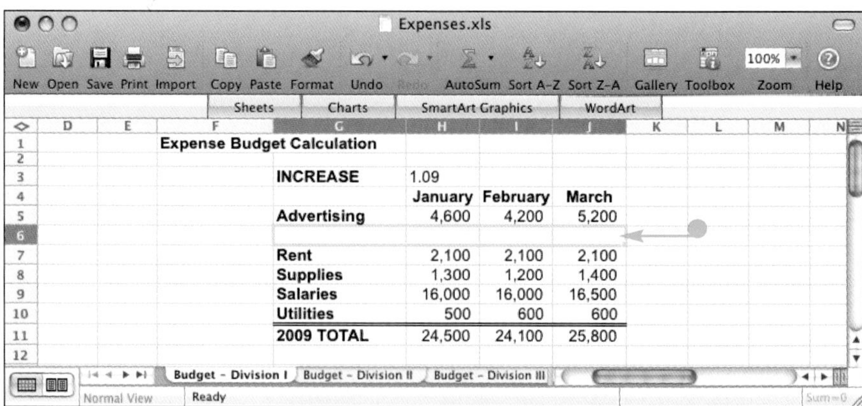


- Excel removes the cell data.

### DELETE CELLS

1. Select the cell or cells that contain the data you want to delete.

***Note:** See Chapter 11 to learn how to select cells.*

2. Click **Edit**.
3. Click **Delete**.

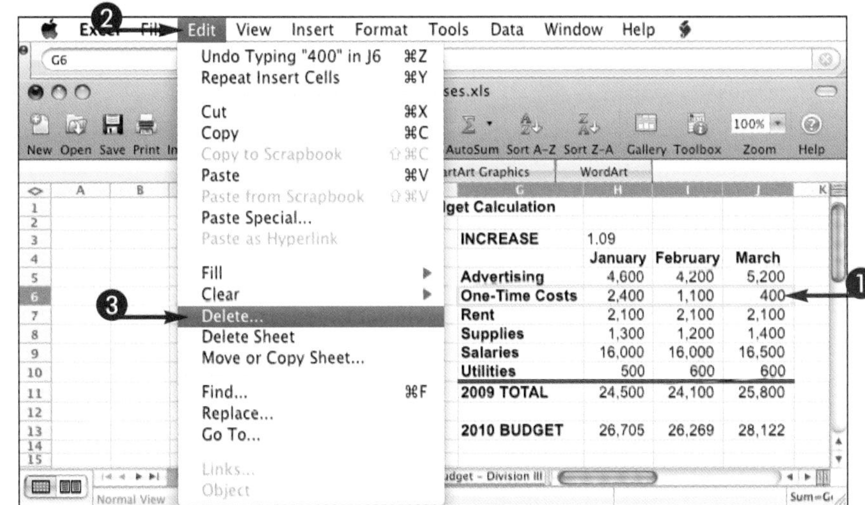

The Delete dialog appears.

4. Select the deletion option you want to use (○ changes to ◉).
5. Click **OK**.

- Excel deletes the selected cells.
- Excel shifts the remaining worksheet data to replace the cells.

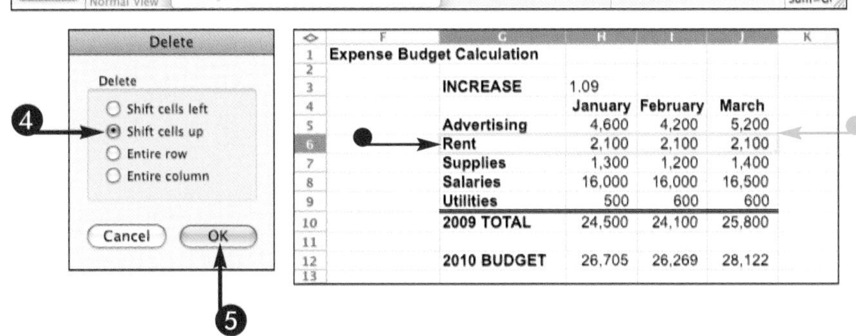

**When I delete cell data, Excel keeps the cell formatting intact. Is it possible to delete the data and the formatting?**

Yes. Excel offers a command that deletes everything from a cell. First, select the cell or cells with the data and formatting that you want to delete. Click **Edit**, click **Clear**, and then click **All**. Excel removes both the data and the formatting from the selected cells.

**Is it possible to delete just a cell's formatting?**

Yes. Excel offers a command that deletes just the cell formatting while leaving the cell data intact. Select the cell or cells with the formatting that you want to delete. Click **Edit**, click **Clear**, and then click **Formats**. Excel removes just the formatting from the selected cells.

CHAPTER

11

# Working with Excel Ranges

In Excel, a *range* is a collection of two or more cells that you work with as a group rather than separately. This enables you to fill the range with values, move or copy the range, sort the range data, and filter the range to show only certain values. You learn these range techniques in this chapter, and in later chapters you learn techniques such as formatting a range, applying a formula to a range, and building a chart from a range.

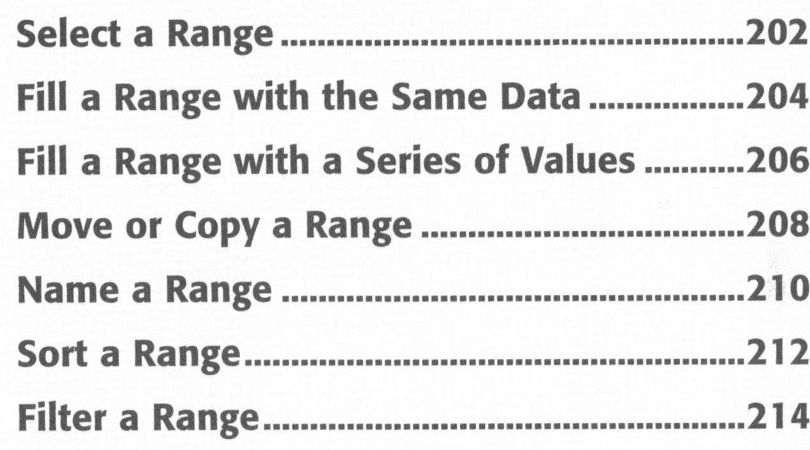

# Select a Range

To work with a range in Excel, you must select the cells that you want to include in the range. After you select the range, you can fill it with data, move it to another part of the worksheet, format the cells, and so on.

**You can select a range as a rectangular group of cells, as a collection of individual cells, or as an entire row or column.**

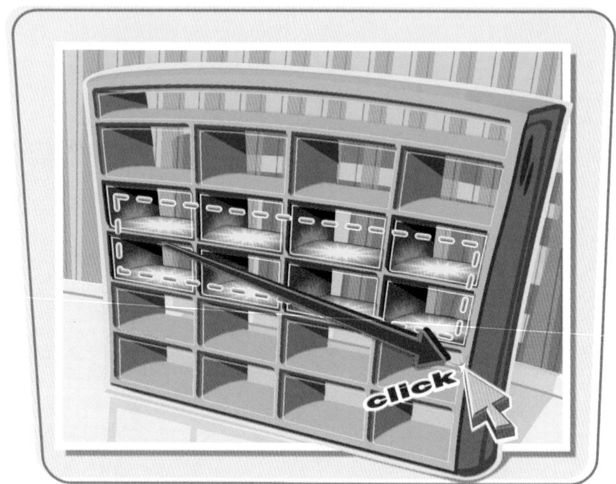


## Select a Range

### SELECT A RECTANGULAR RANGE

1. Position ✣ over the first cell you want to include in the range.
2. Click and drag ✣ over the cells that you want to include in the range.
   - Excel selects the cells.
3. Release the mouse button.

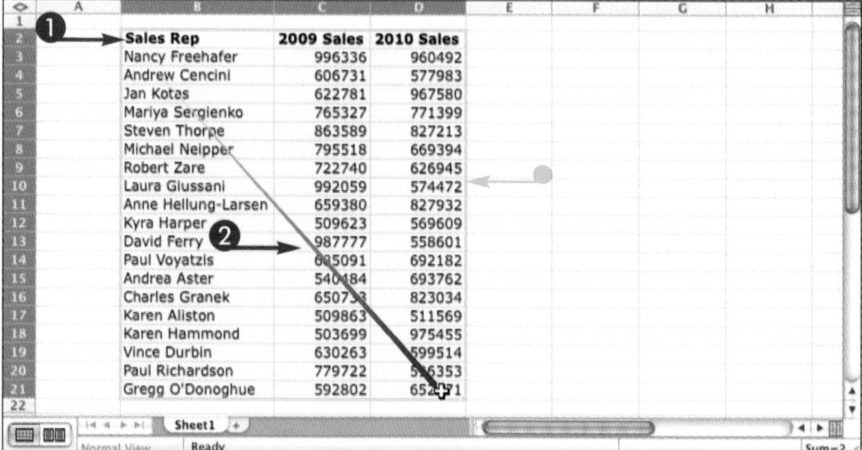

| | A | B | C | D |
|---|---|---|---|---|
| 1 | | | | |
| 2 | | Sales Rep | 2009 Sales | 2010 Sales |
| 3 | | Nancy Freehafer | 996336 | 960492 |
| 4 | | Andrew Cencini | 606731 | 577983 |
| 5 | | Jan Kotas | 622781 | 967580 |
| 6 | | Mariya Sergienko | 765327 | 771399 |
| 7 | | Steven Thorpe | 863589 | 827213 |
| 8 | | Michael Neipper | 795518 | 669394 |
| 9 | | Robert Zare | 722740 | 626945 |
| 10 | | Laura Giussani | 992059 | 574472 |
| 11 | | Anne Hellung-Larsen | 659380 | 827932 |
| 12 | | Kyra Harper | 509623 | 569609 |
| 13 | | David Ferry | 987777 | 558601 |
| 14 | | Paul Voyatzis | 685091 | 692182 |
| 15 | | Andrea Aster | 540484 | 693762 |
| 16 | | Charles Granek | 650733 | 823034 |
| 17 | | Karen Aliston | 509863 | 511569 |
| 18 | | Karen Hammond | 503699 | 975455 |
| 19 | | Vince Durbin | 630263 | 599514 |
| 20 | | Paul Richardson | 779722 | 596353 |
| 21 | | Gregg O'Donoghue | 592802 | 652171 |
| 22 | | | | |



### SELECT A RANGE OF INDIVIDUAL CELLS

1. Click in the first cell that you want to include in the range.
2. Hold down ⌘ and click in each of the other cells that you want to include in the range.
   - Each time you click in a cell, Excel adds it to the range.
3. Release ⌘.

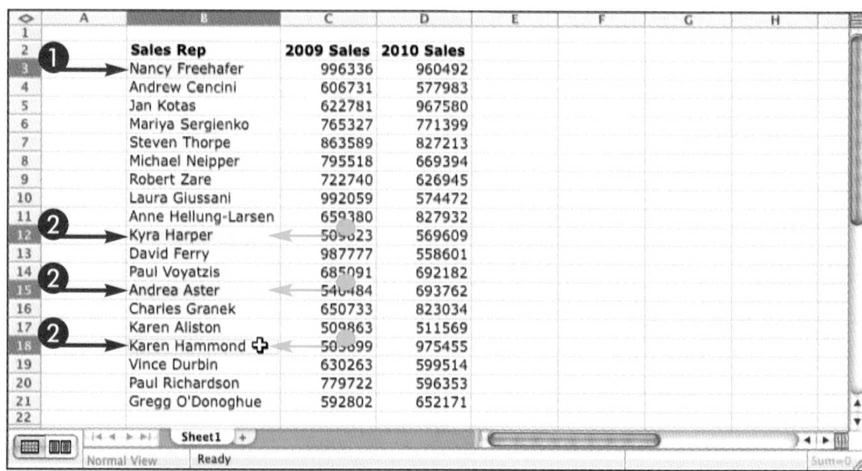

| | A | B | C | D |
|---|---|---|---|---|
| 1 | | | | |
| 2 | | Sales Rep | 2009 Sales | 2010 Sales |
| 3 | | Nancy Freehafer | 996336 | 960492 |
| 4 | | Andrew Cencini | 606731 | 577983 |
| 5 | | Jan Kotas | 622781 | 967580 |
| 6 | | Mariya Sergienko | 765327 | 771399 |
| 7 | | Steven Thorpe | 863589 | 827213 |
| 8 | | Michael Neipper | 795518 | 669394 |
| 9 | | Robert Zare | 722740 | 626945 |
| 10 | | Laura Giussani | 992059 | 574472 |
| 11 | | Anne Hellung-Larsen | 659380 | 827932 |
| 12 | | Kyra Harper | 509623 | 569609 |
| 13 | | David Ferry | 987777 | 558601 |
| 14 | | Paul Voyatzis | 685091 | 692182 |
| 15 | | Andrea Aster | 540484 | 693762 |
| 16 | | Charles Granek | 650733 | 823034 |
| 17 | | Karen Aliston | 509863 | 511569 |
| 18 | | Karen Hammond | 503699 | 975455 |
| 19 | | Vince Durbin | 630263 | 599514 |
| 20 | | Paul Richardson | 779722 | 596353 |
| 21 | | Gregg O'Donoghue | 592802 | 652171 |
| 22 | | | | |

### SELECT AN ENTIRE ROW

1. Position ↖ over the header of the row you want to select.

   ↖ changes to ➡.

2. Click the row header.

- Excel selects the entire row.

  To select multiple rows, click and drag across the row headers or hold down ⌘ and click each row header.

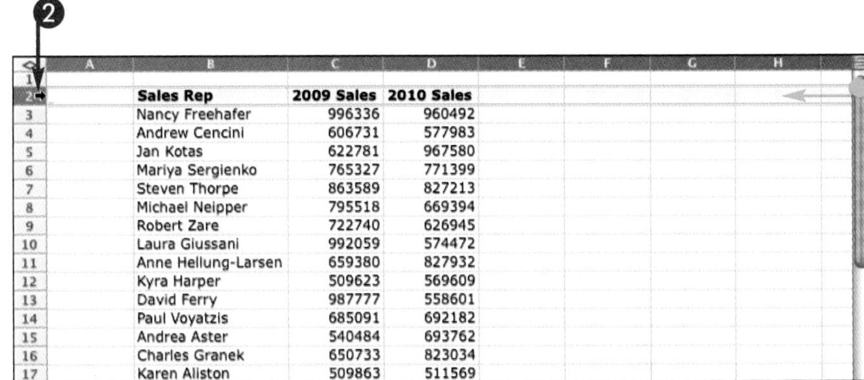

| | A | B | C | D | E | F | G | H |
|---|---|---|---|---|---|---|---|---|
| 1 | | | | | | | | |
| 2 | | Sales Rep | 2009 Sales | 2010 Sales | | | | |
| 3 | | Nancy Freehafer | 996336 | 960492 | | | | |
| 4 | | Andrew Cencini | 606731 | 577983 | | | | |
| 5 | | Jan Kotas | 622781 | 967580 | | | | |
| 6 | | Mariya Sergienko | 765327 | 771399 | | | | |
| 7 | | Steven Thorpe | 863589 | 827213 | | | | |
| 8 | | Michael Neipper | 795518 | 669394 | | | | |
| 9 | | Robert Zare | 722740 | 626945 | | | | |
| 10 | | Laura Giussani | 992059 | 574472 | | | | |
| 11 | | Anne Hellung-Larsen | 659380 | 827932 | | | | |
| 12 | | Kyra Harper | 509623 | 569609 | | | | |
| 13 | | David Ferry | 987777 | 558601 | | | | |
| 14 | | Paul Voyatzis | 685091 | 692182 | | | | |
| 15 | | Andrea Aster | 540484 | 693762 | | | | |
| 16 | | Charles Granek | 650733 | 823034 | | | | |
| 17 | | Karen Aliston | 509863 | 511569 | | | | |

### SELECT AN ENTIRE COLUMN

1. Position ↖ over the header or the column you want to select.

   ↖ changes to ⬇.

2. Click the column header.

- Excel selects the entire column.

  To select multiple columns, click and drag across the column headers, or hold down ⌘ and click each column header.

| | A | B | C | D | E | F | G | H |
|---|---|---|---|---|---|---|---|---|
| 1 | | | | | | | | |
| 2 | | Sales Rep | 2009 Sales | 2010 Sales | | | | |
| 3 | | Nancy Freehafer | 996336 | 960492 | | | | |
| 4 | | Andrew Cencini | 606731 | 577983 | | | | |
| 5 | | Jan Kotas | 622781 | 967580 | | | | |
| 6 | | Mariya Sergienko | 765327 | 771399 | | | | |
| 7 | | Steven Thorpe | 863589 | 827213 | | | | |
| 8 | | Michael Neipper | 795518 | 669394 | | | | |
| 9 | | Robert Zare | 722740 | 626945 | | | | |
| 10 | | Laura Giussani | 992059 | 574472 | | | | |
| 11 | | Anne Hellung-Larsen | 659380 | 827932 | | | | |
| 12 | | Kyra Harper | 509623 | 569609 | | | | |
| 13 | | David Ferry | 987777 | 558601 | | | | |
| 14 | | Paul Voyatzis | 685091 | 692182 | | | | |
| 15 | | Andrea Aster | 540484 | 693762 | | | | |
| 16 | | Charles Granek | 650733 | 823034 | | | | |
| 17 | | Karen Aliston | 509863 | 511569 | | | | |
| 18 | | Karen Hammond | 503699 | 975455 | | | | |
| 19 | | Vince Durbin | 630263 | 599514 | | | | |
| 20 | | Paul Richardson | 779722 | 596353 | | | | |
| 21 | | Gregg O'Donoghue | 59[illegible]02 | 652171 | | | | |
| 22 | | | | | | | | |

Sheet1

Normal View Ready

**Are there keyboard techniques I can use to select a range?**

Yes. To select a rectangular range, navigate to the first cell that you want to include in the range, hold down Shift, and then press ← or ↓ to extend the selection. To select an entire row, navigate to any cell in the row and then press Shift+Spacebar. To select an entire column, navigate to any cell in the column and then press Ctrl+Spacebar.

**Is there an easy way to select every cell in the worksheet?**

Yes. Excel offers two methods you can use. From the keyboard, press ⌘+A. Click the **Select All** button (◇) in the upper-left corner of the worksheet. Alternatively, click **Select All** to select every cell.

| ◇ | A | B |
|---|---|---|
| 1 | | |
| 2 | | **Sales Rep** |
| 3 | | Nancy Freehafer |
| 4 | | Andrew Cencini |

# Fill a Range with the Same Data

If you need to fill a range with the same data, you can save time by getting Excel to fill the range for you. Excel's AutoFill feature makes it easy to fill a vertical or horizontal range with the same value, but you can also fill any selected range.

**See the section "Select a Range" to learn how to select a range of cells.**

## Fill a Range with the Same Data

### FILL A VERTICAL OR HORIZONTAL RANGE

1. Click in the first cell in the range and type the text, number, or other data.
2. Position ✣ over the bottom-right corner of the cell.

   ✣ changes to +.

3. Click and drag + down to fill a vertical range or across to fill a horizontal range.

   + changes to ⬚.

4. Release the mouse button.

- Excel fills the range with the initial cell value.

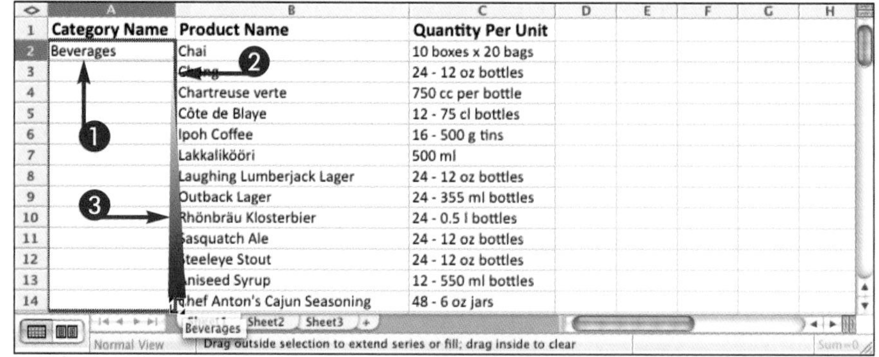

Category Name
Product Name
Quantity Per Unit
Beverages
Chai
Chang
Chartreuse verte
Côte de Blaye
Ipoh Coffee
Lakkaliköôri
Laughing Lumberjack Lager
Outback Lager
Rhönbräu Klosterbier
Sasquatch Ale
Steeleye Stout
Aniseed Syrup
Chef Anton's Cajun Seasoning
10 boxes x 20 bags
24 - 12 oz bottles
750 cc per bottle
12 - 75 cl bottles
16 - 500 g tins
500 ml
24 - 12 oz bottles
24 - 355 ml bottles
24 - 0.5 l bottles
24 - 12 oz bottles
24 - 12 oz bottles
12 - 550 ml bottles
48 - 6 oz jars
Sheet1
Sheet2
Sheet3
Normal View
Drag outside selection to extend series or fill; drag inside to clear

Category Name
Product Name
Quantity Per Unit
Beverages
Chai
Chang
Chartreuse verte
Côte de Blaye
Ipoh Coffee
Lakkaliköôri
Laughing Lumberjack Lager
Outback Lager
Rhönbräu Klosterbier
Sasquatch Ale
Aniseed Syrup
10 boxes x 20 bags
24 - 12 oz bottles
750 cc per bottle
12 - 75 cl bottles
16 - 500 g tins
500 ml
24 - 12 oz bottles
24 - 355 ml bottles
24 - 0.5 l bottles
24 - 12 oz bottles
24 - 12 oz bottles
12 - 550 ml bottles
48 - 6 oz jars
Sheet1
Sheet2
Sheet3
Normal View
Ready

## FILL A SELECTED RANGE

1. Select the range you want to fill.
2. Type the text, number, or other data.
3. Press Ctrl + Return.

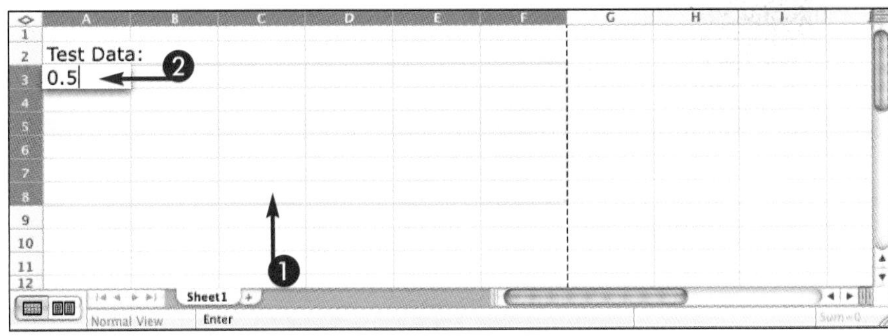


- Excel fills the range with the value you typed.

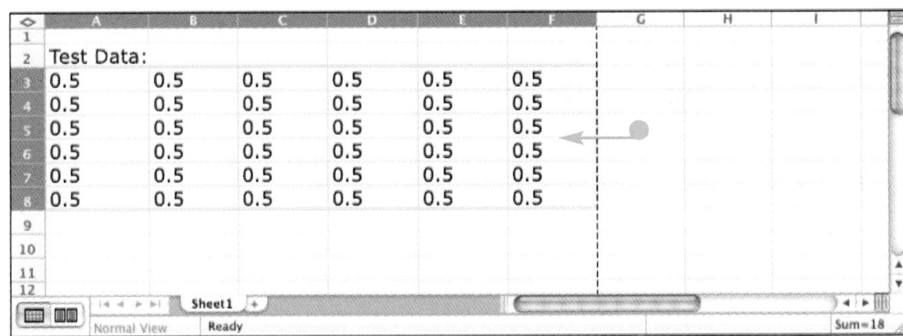


## TIP

**How do I fill a vertical or horizontal range without also copying the formatting of the original cell?**

Follow these steps:

1. Perform Steps **1** to **4** to fill the data.
   - Excel displays the AutoFill Options smart tag.
2. Click the AutoFill Options ▾.
3. Click **Fill Without Formatting**.

Excel removes the original cell's formatting from the copied cells.

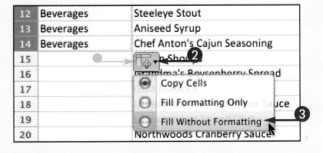

# Fill a Range with a Series of Values

If you need to fill a range with a series of values, you can save time by using Excel's AutoFill feature to create the series for you. AutoFill can fill a series of numeric values such as 5, 10, 15, 20, and so on; a series of date values such as January 1, 2010; January 2, 2010; and so on; or a series of alphanumeric values such as Chapter 1, Chapter 2, Chapter 3, and so on.

**You can also create your own series with a custom step value, which determines the numeric difference between each item in the series.**

## Fill a Range with a Series of Values

### AUTOFILL A SERIES OF NUMERIC, DATE, OR ALPHANUMERIC VALUES

1. Click the first cell and type the first value in the series.
2. Click in an adjacent cell and type the second value in the series.
3. Select the two cells.
4. Position ✥ over the bottom-right corner of the second cell.

   ✥ changes to +.

5. Click and drag + down to fill a vertical range or across to fill a horizontal range.

   + changes to ⌜⌟.

6. Release the mouse button.

- Excel fills the range with a series that continues the pattern of the initial two cell values.

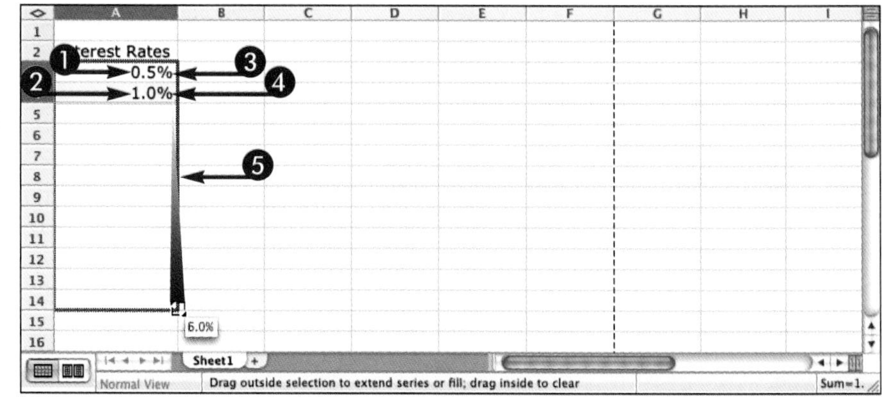


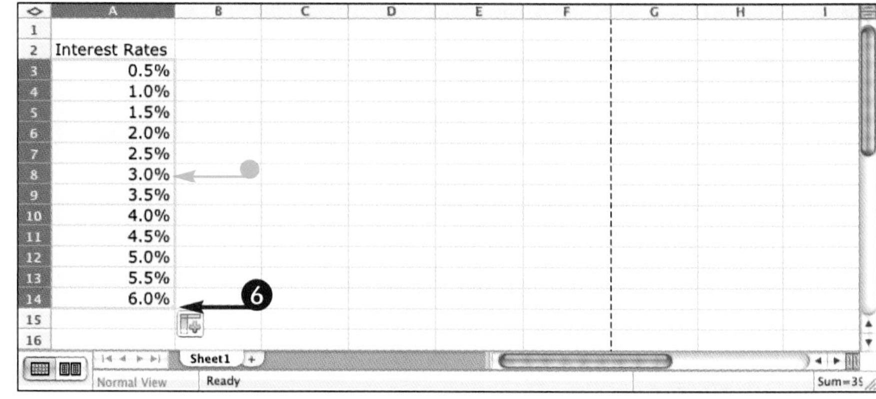

## FILL A CUSTOM SERIES OF VALUES

1. Click the first cell and type the first value in the series.
2. Select the range you want to fill, including the initial value.
3. Click **Edit**.
4. Click **Fill**.
5. Click **Series**.

   The Series dialog appears.

6. In the Type group, select the type of series you want to fill (○ changes to ◉).
7. If you selected **Date** in Step **6**, select an option in the **Date unit** group (○ changes to ◉).
8. In the Step value text box, type the value you want to use.
9. Click **OK**.

- Excel fills the range with the series you created.

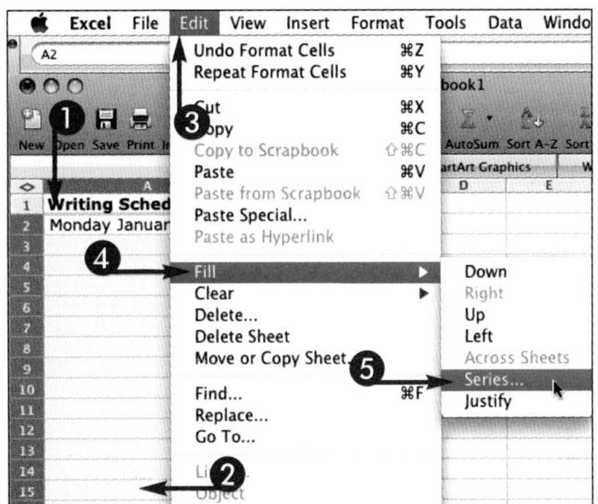


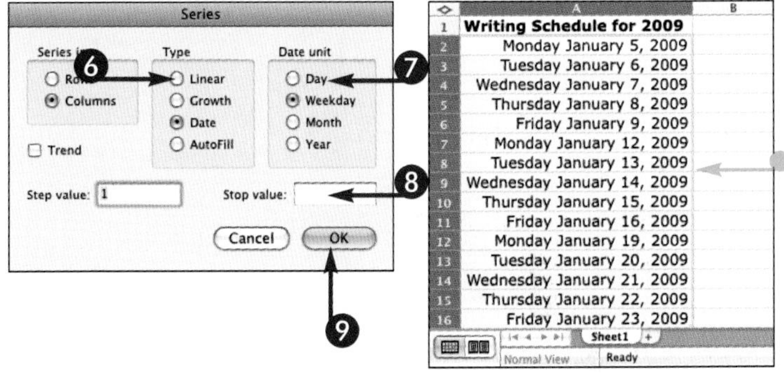

### Can I create my own AutoFill series?

Yes. You can create a *custom list*, which is a series of text values. When you add the first value in your custom list, you can then use AutoFill to fill a range with the rest of the series. Follow these steps to create a custom list:

1. Click **Excel**.
2. Click **Preferences**.
3. Click **Custom Lists**.
4. Click **NEW LIST**.
5. In the List entries box, type each item in your list, and press Return after each item.
6. Click **Add**.
7. Click **OK**.

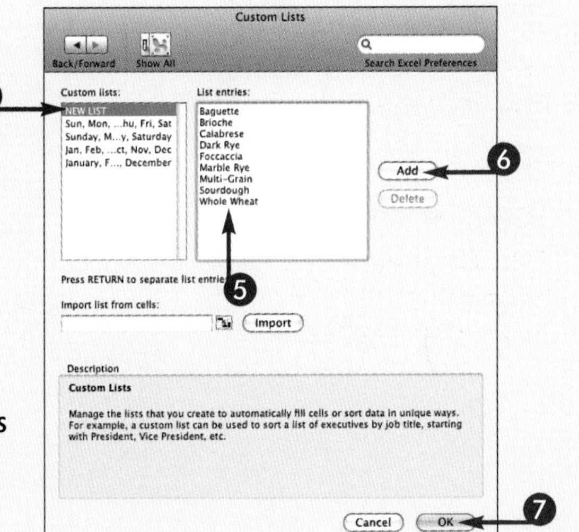

# Move or Copy a Range

You can restructure or reorganize a worksheet by moving an existing range to a different part of the worksheet.

**You can also make a copy of a range, which is a useful technique if you require either a duplicate of the range elsewhere, or if you require a range that is similar to an existing range.**

## Move or Copy a Range

### MOVE A RANGE

1. Select the range you want to move.
2. Position over any outside border of the range.

   changes to .
3. Click and drag the range to the new location.

- Excel displays an outline of the range.
- Excel displays the address of the new location.

4. Release the mouse button.

- Excel moves the range to the new location.

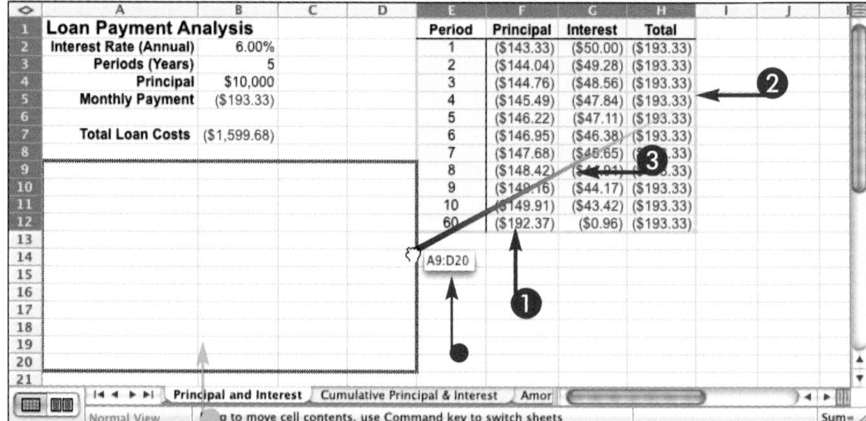


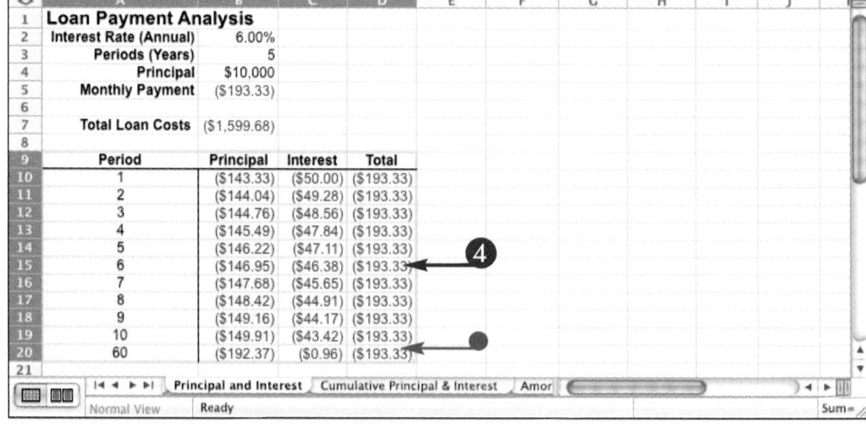

| | A | B | C | D |
|---|---|---|---|---|
| 1 | Loan Payment Analysis | | | |
| 2 | Interest Rate (Annual) | 6.00% | | |
| 3 | Periods (Years) | 5 | | |
| 4 | Principal | $10,000 | | |
| 5 | Monthly Payment | ($193.33) | | |
| 6 | | | | |
| 7 | Total Loan Costs | ($1,599.68) | | |
| 8 | | | | |
| 9 | Period | Principal | Interest | Total |
| 10 | 1 | ($143.33) | ($50.00) | ($193.33) |
| 11 | 2 | ($144.04) | ($49.28) | ($193.33) |
| 12 | 3 | ($144.76) | ($48.56) | ($193.33) |
| 13 | 4 | ($145.49) | ($47.84) | ($193.33) |
| 14 | 5 | ($146.22) | ($47.11) | ($193.33) |
| 15 | 6 | ($146.95) | ($46.38) | ($193.33) |
| 16 | 7 | ($147.68) | ($45.65) | ($193.33) |
| 17 | 8 | ($148.42) | ($44.91) | ($193.33) |
| 18 | 9 | ($149.16) | ($44.17) | ($193.33) |
| 19 | 10 | ($149.91) | ($43.42) | ($193.33) |
| 20 | 60 | ($192.37) | ($0.96) | ($193.33) |

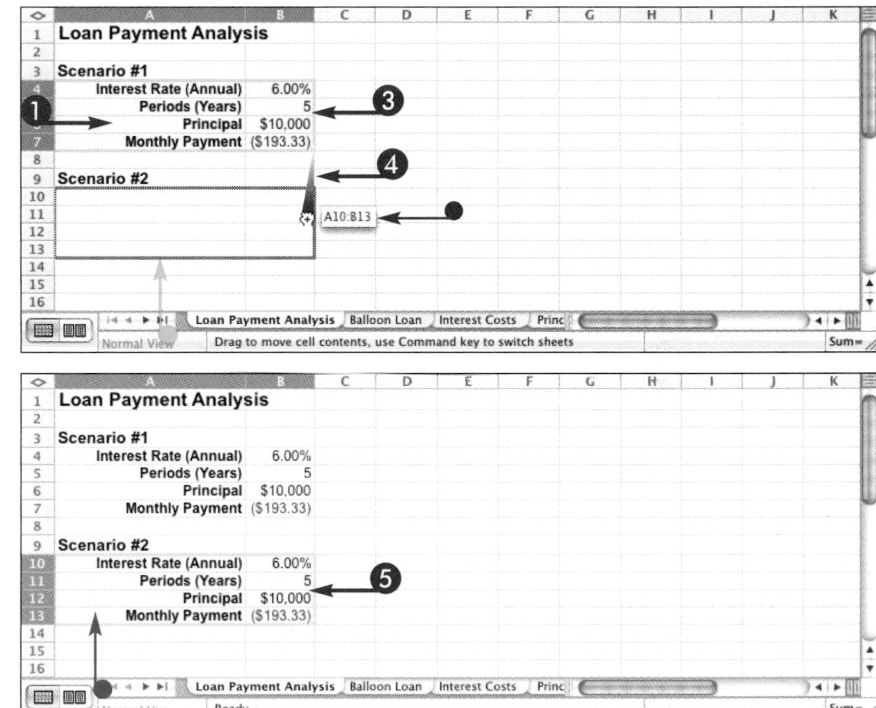


## COPY A RANGE

1. Select the range you want to copy.
2. Press and hold Option.
3. Position ✥ over any outside border of the range.

   ✥ changes to ☝.

4. Click and drag the range to the location where you want the copy to appear.

- Excel displays an outline of the range.
- Excel displays the address of the new location.

5. Release the mouse button.
6. Release Option.

- Excel creates a copy of the range in the new location.

### Can I move or copy a range to another worksheet?

Yes. Click and drag the range as described in this section. Remember to hold down Option if you are copying the range. Press and hold ⌘ and then drag the mouse pointer over the tab of the sheet you want to use as the destination. Excel displays the worksheet. Release ⌘ and then drop the range on the worksheet.

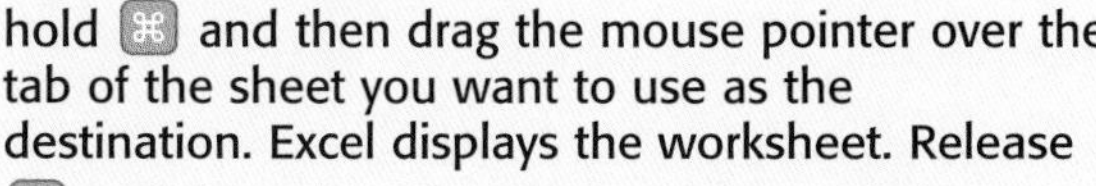

### Can I move or copy a range to another workbook?

Yes. If you can see the other workbook on-screen, click and drag the range as described in this section, and then drop it on the other workbook. Remember to hold down Option if you are copying the range. Otherwise, select the range, click **Edit**, click **Cut** to move the range or **Copy** to copy it, switch to the other workbook, select the cell where you want the range to appear, click **Edit**, and then click **Paste**.

# Name a Range

You can make it easier to work with a range by assigning a name to the range. This is most useful when you build formulas, as described in Chapter 13. A formula that uses range names such as Sales and Expenses is much easier to understand than one that uses range addresses such as A2:A8 and B10:C15.

**You can create range names by hand, or you can get Excel to create the names for you automatically based on the existing text labels in a worksheet.**

## Name a Range

### ASSIGN A RANGE NAME MANUALLY

1. Select the range you want to name.
2. Click inside the **Name** text box.
3. Type the name you want to use.

*Note: The first character of the name must be a letter or an underscore (_). The name cannot include spaces or cell references, and it cannot be any longer than 255 characters.*

4. Press Return.

   Excel assigns the name to the range.

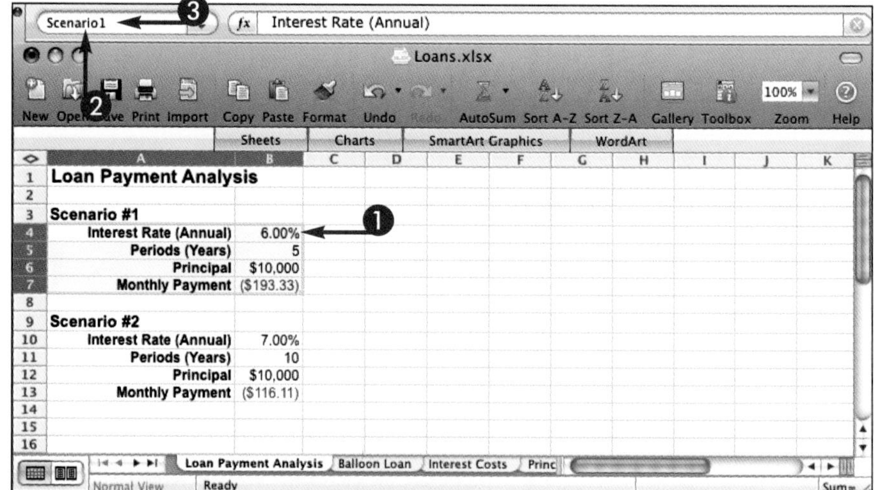


### ASSIGN RANGE NAMES AUTOMATICALLY

1. Select the range you want to name.

- Be sure to include the text labels you want to use for the range names.

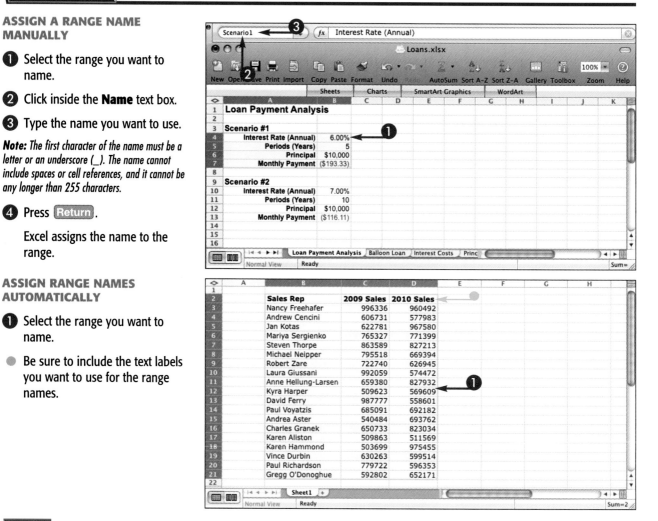

| Sales Rep | 2009 Sales | 2010 Sales |
|---|---|---|
| Nancy Freehafer | 996336 | 960492 |
| Andrew Cencini | 606731 | 577983 |
| Jan Kotas | 622781 | 967580 |
| Mariya Sergienko | 765327 | 771399 |
| Steven Thorpe | 863589 | 827213 |
| Michael Neipper | 795518 | 669394 |
| Robert Zare | 722740 | 626945 |
| Laura Giussani | 992059 | 574472 |
| Anne Hellung-Larsen | 659380 | 827932 |
| Kyra Harper | 509623 | 569609 |
| David Ferry | 987777 | 558601 |
| Paul Voyatzis | 685091 | 692182 |
| Andrea Aster | 540484 | 693762 |
| Charles Granek | 650733 | 823034 |
| Karen Aliston | 509863 | 511569 |
| Karen Hammond | 503699 | 975455 |
| Vince Durbin | 630263 | 599514 |
| Paul Richardson | 779722 | 596353 |
| Gregg O'Donoghue | 592802 | 652171 |

2. Click **Insert**.
3. Click **Name**.
4. Click **Create**.

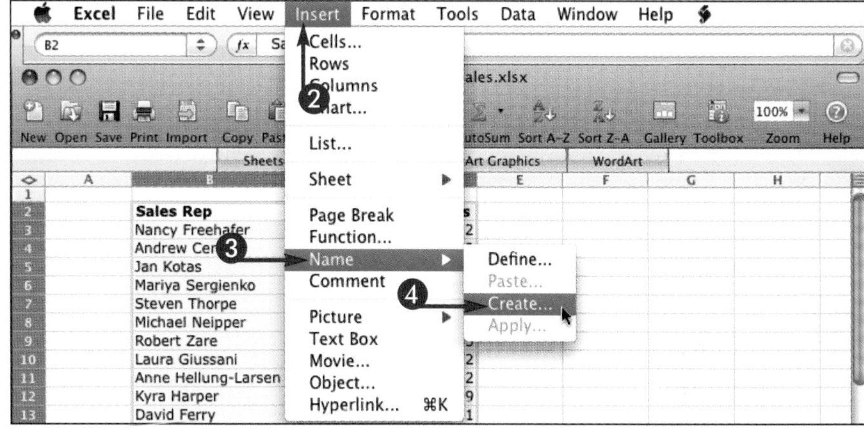


The Create Names dialog appears.

5. Select the option that corresponds to where the text labels are located in the selected range (☐ changes to ☑).

   If Excel has activated a check box that does not apply to your data, click it (☑ changes to ☐).

6. Click **OK**.

   Excel assigns the text labels as range names.

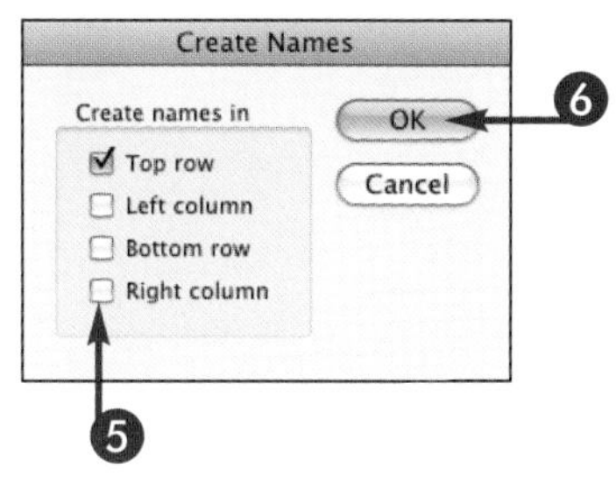

### How do I modify a range name?

Click **Insert**, click **Name**, and then click **Define** to open the Define Name dialog. Click the name you want to work in the list box. To modify the name, edit the name in the Names in workbook text box, and then click **Add**. Click the old range name, and then click **Delete**. Click **OK**.

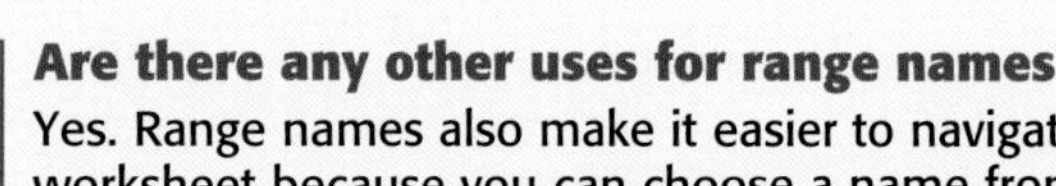

### Are there any other uses for range names?

Yes. Range names also make it easier to navigate a worksheet because you can choose a name from a list and Excel automatically selects the associated range. In the Formula bar's **Name** box, click ⬍ (B) to see a list of your assigned range names. Click the name you want to use (C), and Excel selects the associated range.

# Sort a Range

You can make a range easier to read and easier to analyze by sorting the data based on the values in one or more columns.

**You can sort the data in either ascending or descending order. An ascending sort arranges the values alphabetically from A to Z, or numerically from 0 to 9; a descending sort arranges the values alphabetically from Z to A, or numerically from 9 to 0.**

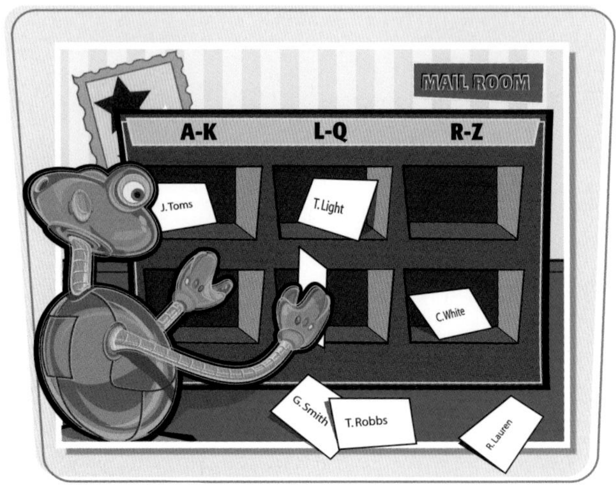


## Sort a Range

1. Click in any cell in the column that you want to use for the main sort order.

| | A | B | C | D | E | F | G |
|---|---|---|---|---|---|---|---|
| 1 | Customer ID | Company Name | Address | City | Region | Postal Code | Country |
| 2 | ALFKI | Alfreds Futterkiste | Obere Str. 57 | Berlin | | 12209 | Germany |
| 3 | ANATR | Ana Trujillo Emparedados y helados | Avda. de la Constitución 2222 | México D.F. | | 05021 | Mexi |
| 4 | ANTON | Antonio Moreno Taquería | Mataderos 2312 | México D.F. | | 05023 | Mexi |
| 5 | AROUT | Around the Horn | 120 Hanover Sq. | London | | WA1 1DP | UK |
| 6 | BERGS | Berglunds snabbköp | Berguvsvägen 8 | Luleå | | S-958 22 | Swed |
| 7 | BLAUS | Blauer See Delikatessen | Forsterstr. 57 | Mannheim | | 68306 | Germ |
| 8 | BLONP | Blondel père et fils | 24, place Kléber | Strasbourg | | 67000 | France |
| 9 | BOLID | Bólido Comidas preparadas | C/ Araquil, 67 | Madrid | | 28023 | Spain |
| 10 | BONAP | Bon app' | 12, rue des Bouchers | Marseille | | 13008 | France |
| 11 | BOTTM | Bottom-Dollar Markets | 23 Tsawassen Blvd. | Tsawassen | BC | T2F 8M4 | Canada |
| 12 | BSBEV | B's Beverages | Fauntleroy Circus | London | | EC2 5NT | UK |
| 13 | CACTU | Cactus Comidas para llevar | Cerrito 333 | Buenos Aires | | 1010 | Argentina |
| 14 | CENTC | Centro comercial Moctezuma | Sierras de Granada 9993 | México D.F. | | 05022 | Mexico |
| 15 | CHOPS | Chop-suey Chinese | Hauptstr. 29 | Bern | | 3012 | Switzerland |
| 16 | COMMI | Comércio Mineiro | Av. dos Lusiadas, 23 | São Paulo | SP | 05432-043 | Brazil |
| 17 | CONSH | Consolidated Holdings | Berkeley Gardens 12 Brewery | London | | WX1 6LT | UK |
| 18 | DRACD | Drachenblut Delikatessen | Walserweg 21 | Aachen | | 52066 | Germany |
| 19 | DUMON | Du monde entier | 67, rue des Cinquante Otages | Nantes | | 44000 | France |
| 20 | EASTC | Eastern Connection | 35 King George | London | | WX3 6FW | UK |
| 21 | ERNSH | Ernst Handel | Kirchgasse 6 | Graz | | 8010 | Austria |
| 22 | FAMIA | Familia Arquibaldo | Rua Orós, 92 | São Paulo | SP | 05442-030 | Brazil |
| 23 | FISSA | FISSA Fabrica Inter. Salchichas S.A. | C/ Moralzarzal, 86 | Madrid | | 28034 | Spain |
| 24 | FOLIG | Folies gourmandes | 184, chaussée de Tournai | Lille | | 59000 | France |
| 25 | FOLKO | Folk och fä HB | Åkergatan 24 | Bräcke | | S-844 67 | Sweden |



2. Click **Data**.
3. Click **Sort**.

   The Sort dialog appears.

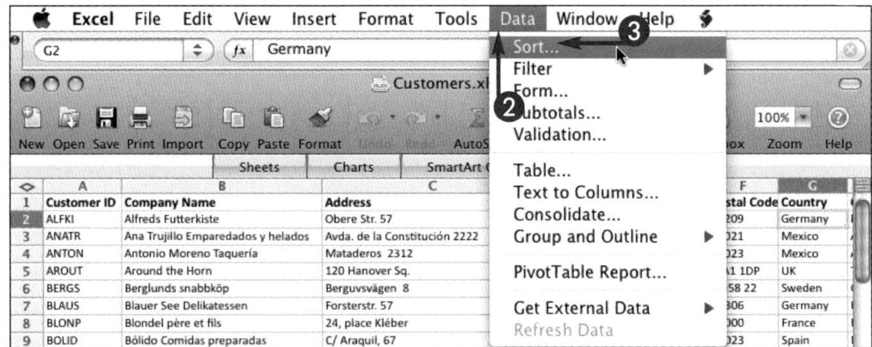

- The column you chose in Step **1** appears here.

4. To sort on a second column, click ⬍ and then click the column.
5. To sort on a third column, click ⬍ and then click the column.
6. For each field, select a sort order (○ changes to ◉).
7. If your data does not have headers, select the **No header row** option (○ changes to ◉).
8. Click **OK**.

- Excel sorts the range.

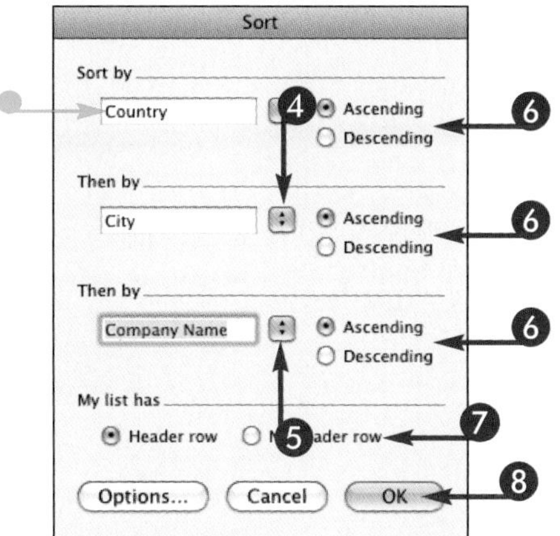


| | A | B | C | D | E | F | G |
|---|---|---|---|---|---|---|---|
| 1 | Customer ID | Company Name | Address | City | Region | Postal Code | Country |
| 2 | CACTU | Cactus Comidas para llevar | Cerrito 333 | Buenos Aires | | 1010 | Argentina |
| 3 | OCEAN | Océano Atlántico Ltda. | Ing. Gustavo Moncada 8585 Piso 20-A | Buenos Aires | | 1010 | Argentina |
| 4 | RANCH | Rancho grande | Av. del Libertador 900 | Buenos Aires | | 1010 | Argentina |
| 5 | ERNSH | Ernst Handel | Kirchgasse 6 | Graz | | 8010 | Austria |
| 6 | PICCO | Piccolo und mehr | Geislweg 14 | Salzburg | | 5020 | Austria |
| 7 | MAISD | Maison Dewey | Rue Joseph-Bens 532 | Bruxelles | | B-1180 | Belgium |
| 8 | SUPRD | Suprêmes délices | Boulevard Tirou, 255 | Charleroi | | B-6000 | Belgium |
| 9 | GOURL | Gourmet Lanchonetes | Av. Brasil, 442 | Campinas | SP | 04876-786 | Brazil |
| 10 | WELLI | Wellington Importadora | Rua do Mercado, 12 | Resende | SP | 08737-363 | Brazil |
| 11 | HANAR | Hanari Carnes | Rua do Paço, 67 | Rio de Janeiro | RJ | 05454-876 | Brazil |
| 12 | QUEDE | Que Delicia | Rua da Panificadora, 12 | Rio de Janeiro | RJ | 02389-673 | Brazil |
| 13 | RICAR | Ricardo Adocicados | Av. Copacabana, 267 | Rio de Janeiro | RJ | 02389-890 | Brazil |
| 14 | COMMI | Comércio Mineiro | Av. dos Lusíadas, 23 | São Paulo | SP | 05432-043 | Brazil |
| 15 | FAMIA | Familia Arquibaldo | Rua Orós, 92 | São Paulo | SP | 05442-030 | Brazil |
| 16 | QUEEN | Queen Cozinha | Alameda dos Canàrios, 891 | São Paulo | SP | 05487-020 | Brazil |
| 17 | TRADH | Tradição Hipermercados | Av. Inês de Castro, 414 | São Paulo | SP | 05634-030 | Brazil |
| 18 | MEREP | Mère Paillarde | 43 rue St. Laurent | Montréal | Québec | H1J 1C3 | Canada |
| 19 | BOTTM | Bottom-Dollar Markets | 23 Tsawassen Blvd. | Tsawassen | BC | T2F 8M4 | Canada |
| 20 | LAUGB | Laughing Bacchus Wine Cellars | 1900 Oak St. | Vancouver | BC | V3F 2K1 | Canada |
| 21 | VAFFE | Vaffeljernet | Smagsløget 45 | Århus | | 8200 | Denmark |
| 22 | SIMOB | Simons bistro | Vinbæltet 34 | København | | 1734 | Denmark |
| 23 | WILMK | Wilman Kala | Keskuskatu 45 | Helsinki | | 21240 | Finland |
| 24 | WARTH | Wartian Herkku | Torikatu 38 | Oulu | | 90110 | Finland |
| 25 | FOLIG | Folies gourmandes | 184, chaussée de Tournai | Lille | | 59000 | France |

Sheet1 Sheet2 Sheet3
Normal View Ready

### Is there a faster way to sort a range?

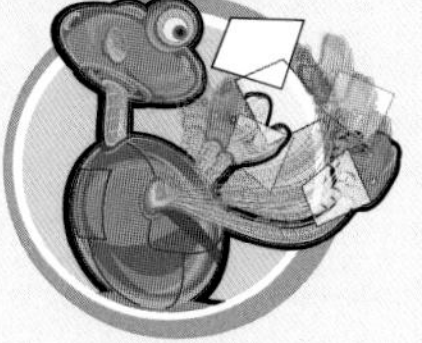

Yes, as long as you only need to sort your range on a single column. First, click in any cell inside the column you want to use for the sort. Then click one of the following buttons on the Standard toolbar:

| | |
|---|---|
| A↓Z | Click for an ascending sort. |
| Z↓A | Click for a descending sort. |

### How do I sort a range using the values in a row instead of a column?

Excel normally sorts a range from top to bottom based on the values in one or more columns. However, you can tell Excel to sort the range from left to right based on the values in one or more rows. Follow Steps **1** to **3** to display the Sort dialog. Click **Options** to display the Sort Options dialog, select the **Sort left to right** option (○ changes to ◉), and then click **OK**.

# Filter a Range

You can make a range of data easier to read and simpler to navigate by displaying only those items that match a particular value in a column. This is called *filtering* the range, and Excel's AutoFilter feature lets you do this with just a few mouse clicks.

## Filter a Range

1. Click in any cell within the data you want to filter.

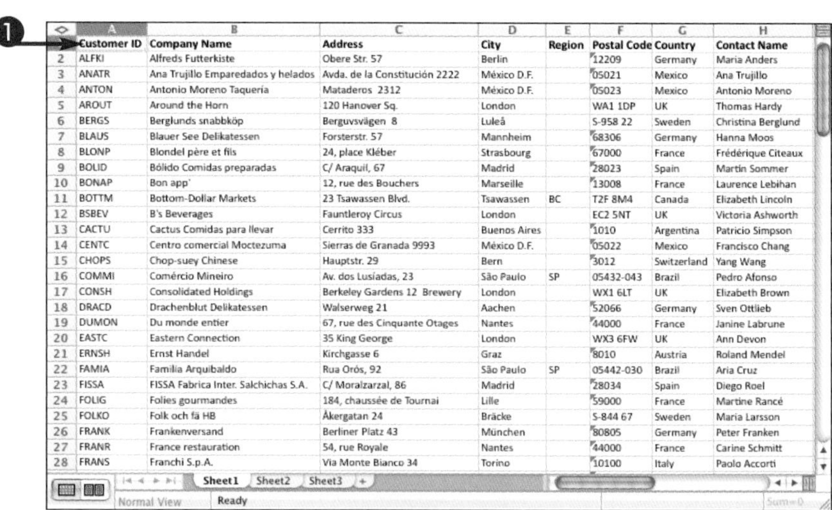


2. Click **Data**.
3. Click **Filter**.
4. Click **AutoFilter**.

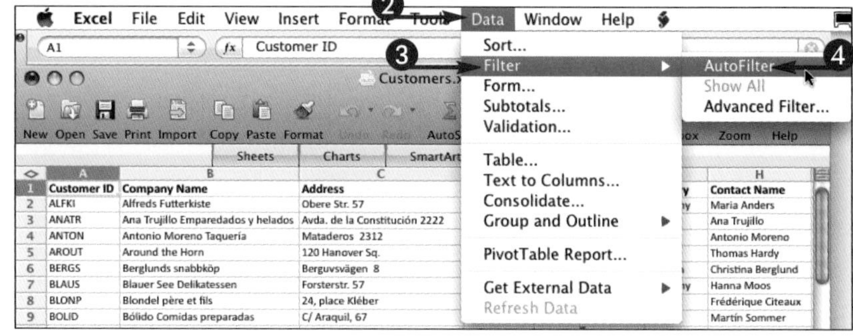

- Excel adds pop-up buttons (⇕) to the column headers.

5. Click ⇕ for the field you want to use for the filter.

- Excel displays a list of the unique values in the field.

6. Click the value that you want to use to filter the range.

| | Customer | Company Name | Address | City | Regio | Postal Co |
|---|---|---|---|---|---|---|
| 2 | ALFKI | Alfreds Futterkiste | Obere Str. 57 | Berlin | | 12209 |
| 3 | ANATR | Ana Trujillo Emparedados y helados | Avda. de la Constitución 2222 | México D.F. | | 05021 |
| 4 | ANTON | Antonio Moreno Taquería | Mataderos 2312 | México D.F. | | 05023 |
| 5 | AROUT | Around the Horn | 120 Hanover Sq. | London | | WA1 1DP |
| 6 | BERGS | Berglunds snabbköp | Berguvsvägen 8 | Luleå | | S-958 22 |
| 7 | BLAUS | Blauer See Delikatessen | Forsterstr. 57 | Mannheim | | 68306 |
| 8 | BLONP | Blondel père et fils | 24, place Kléber | Strasbourg | | 67000 |
| 9 | BOLID | Bólido Comidas preparadas | C/ Araquil, 67 | Madrid | | 28023 |
| 10 | BONAP | Bon app' | 12, rue des Bouchers | Marseille | | 13008 |
| 11 | BOTTM | Bottom-Dollar Markets | 23 Tsawassen Blvd. | Tsawassen | BC | T2F 8M4 |
| 12 | BSBEV | B's Beverages | Fauntleroy Circus | London | | EC2 5NT |
| 13 | CACTU | Cactus Comidas para llevar | Cerrito 333 | Buenos Aires | | 1010 |
| 14 | CENTC | Centro comercial Moctezuma | Sierras de Granada 9993 | México D.F. | | 05022 |
| 15 | CHOPS | Chop-suey Chinese | Hauptstr. 29 | Bern | | 3012 |
| 16 | COMMI | Comércio Mineiro | Av. dos Lusíadas, 23 | São Paulo | SP | 05432-043 |
| 17 | CONSH | Consolidated Holdings | Berkeley Gardens 12 Brewery | London | | WX1 6LT |
| 18 | DRACD | Drachenblut Delikatessen | Walserweg 21 | Aachen | | 52066 |
| 19 | DUMON | Du monde entier | 67, rue des Cinquante Otages | Nantes | | 44000 |
| 20 | EASTC | Eastern Connection | 35 King George | London | | WX3 6FW |
| 21 | ERNSH | Ernst Handel | Kirchgasse 6 | Graz | | 8010 |
| 22 | FAMIA | Familia Arquibaldo | Rua Orós, 92 | São Paulo | SP | 05442-030 |
| 23 | FISSA | FISSA Fabrica Inter. Salchichas S.A. | C/ Moralzarzal, 86 | Madrid | | 28034 |
| 24 | FOLIG | Folies gourmandes | 184, chaussée de Tournai | Lille | | 59000 |
| 25 | FOLKO | Folk och fä HB | Åkergatan 24 | Bräcke | | S-844 67 |
| 26 | FRANK | Frankenversand | Berliner Platz 43 | München | | 80805 |
| 27 | FRANR | France restauration | 54, rue Royale | Nantes | | 44000 |
| 28 | FRANS | Franchi S.p.A. | Via Monte Bianco 34 | Torino | | 10100 |

Country ⇕
Sort Ascending
Sort Descending
✓ (Show All)
(Show Top 10...)
(Custom Filter...)
Argentina
Austria
Belgium
Brazil
Canada
Denmark
Finland
France
Germany
Ireland
Italy
Mexico
Norway
Poland
Portugal
Spain
Sweden
Switzerland
UK
USA
Venezuela

Sheet1 Sheet2 Sheet3
Normal View Ready

- Excel filters the range.

To remove the filter, click ⇕ in the field you used for the filter, and then click **Show All**.

To remove each ⇕ from the field headers, follow Steps **2** to **4** to turn off AutoFilter.

| | Customer | Company Name | Address | City | Regio | Postal Co | Country | Contact Name |
|---|---|---|---|---|---|---|---|---|
| 33 | GREAL | Great Lakes Food Market | 2732 Baker Blvd. | Eugene | OR | 97403 | USA | Howard Snyder |
| 37 | HUNGC | Hungry Coyote Import Store | City Center Plaza 516 Main St. | Elgin | OR | 97827 | USA | Yoshi Latimer |
| 44 | LAZYK | Lazy K Kountry Store | 12 Orchestra Terrace | Walla Walla | WA | 99362 | USA | John Steel |
| 46 | LETSS | Let's Stop N Shop | 87 Polk St. Suite 5 | San Francisco | CA | 94117 | USA | Jaime Yorres |
| 49 | LONEP | Lonesome Pine Restaurant | 89 Chiaroscuro Rd. | Portland | OR | 97219 | USA | Fran Wilson |
| 56 | OLDWO | Old World Delicatessen | 2743 Bering St. | Anchorage | AK | 99508 | USA | Rene Phillips |
| 66 | RATTC | Rattlesnake Canyon Grocery | 2817 Milton Dr. | Albuquerque | NM | 87110 | USA | Paula Wilson |
| 72 | SAVEA | Save-a-lot Markets | 187 Suffolk Ln. | Boise | ID | 83720 | USA | Jose Pavarotti |
| 76 | SPLIR | Split Rail Beer & Ale | P.O. Box 555 | Lander | WY | 82520 | USA | Art Braunschweiger |
| 78 | THEBI | The Big Cheese | 89 Jefferson Way Suite 2 | Portland | OR | 97201 | USA | Liz Nixon |
| 79 | THECR | The Cracker Box | 55 Grizzly Peak Rd. | Butte | MT | 59801 | USA | Liu Wong |
| 83 | TRAIH | Trail's Head Gourmet Provisioners | 722 DaVinci Blvd. | Kirkland | WA | 98034 | USA | Helvetius Nagy |
| 90 | WHITC | White Clover Markets | 305 - 14th Ave. S. Suite 3B | Seattle | WA | 98128 | USA | Karl Jablonski |
| 93 | | | | | | | | |
| 94 | | | | | | | | |

### Can I filter my range to show just the top values in a column?

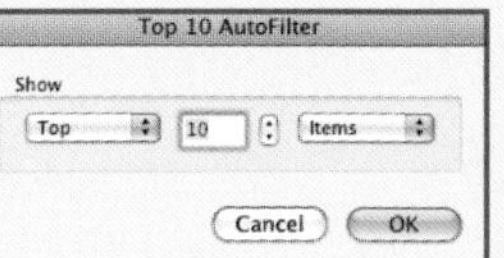


Yes. Excel includes a feature called Top 10 AutoFilter that enables you to filter the range to show just the top items based on the numeric values in a particular column. Click ⇕ in the field you want to use for the filter, and then click **Show Top 10** to display the Top 10 AutoFilter dialog. Click the left ⇕ and then click either **Top** or **Bottom**, type the number of items you want to return, click the right ⇕, and click either **Items** or **Percent**. Click **OK**.

### Can I customize the filter?

Yes. You can create a custom AutoFilter where you choose an operator such as begins with or contains, and then specify your filter criteria. Click ⇕ in the field you want to use for the filter, and then click **Custom Filter** to display the Custom AutoFilter dialog. Click ⇕ and then click the operator you want to use. Use the text box to type the criteria for the filter. Click **OK**.

CHAPTER

12

# Formatting Excel Data

Although you can build a useful spreadsheet model without resorting to formatting, your worksheets are easier to read and more organized when you apply formatting. Besides standard formatting such as fonts and alignment discussed in Chapter 3, Excel also enables you to change the number format, add conditional formatting, modify the row height and column width, and more.

# Apply a Number Format

You can make your worksheet easier to read by applying a number format to your data. For example, if your worksheet includes monetary data, you can apply the Currency format to display the data with dollar signs and two decimal places.

**Excel offers ten number formats, most of which apply to numeric data. However, you can also apply the Date format to date data, the Time format to time data, and the Text format to text data.**

## Apply a Number Format

❶ Select the range you want to format.

***Note:*** *For information on how to select a range,* *see Chapter 11.*

Sales Reps Sales.xlsx

| Sales Rep | 2009 Sales | 2010 Sales |
|---|---|---|
| Nancy Freehafer | 996336 | 960492 |
| Andrew Cencini | 606731 | 577983 |
| Jan Kotas | 622781 | 967580 |
| Mariya Sergienko | 765327 | 771399 |
| Steven Thorpe | 863589 | 827213 |
| Michael Neipper | 795518 | 669394 |
| Robert Zare | 722740 | 626945 |
| Laura Giussani | 992059 | 574472 |
| Anne Hellung-Larsen | 659380 | 827932 |
| Kyra Harper | 509623 | 569609 |
| David Ferry | 987777 | 558601 |
| Paul Voyatzis | 685091 | 692182 |
| Andrea Aster | 540484 | 693762 |
| Charles Granek | 650733 | 823034 |
| Karen Aliston | 509863 | 511569 |
| Karen Hammond | 503699 | 975455 |
| Vince Durbin | 630263 | 599514 |
| Paul Richardson | 779722 | 596353 |
| Gregg O'Donoghue | 592802 | 652171 |

❷ Display the Formatting Palette.

***Note:*** *To learn how to display the Formatting Palette,* *see Chapter 3.*

❸ Click the **Number** panel.

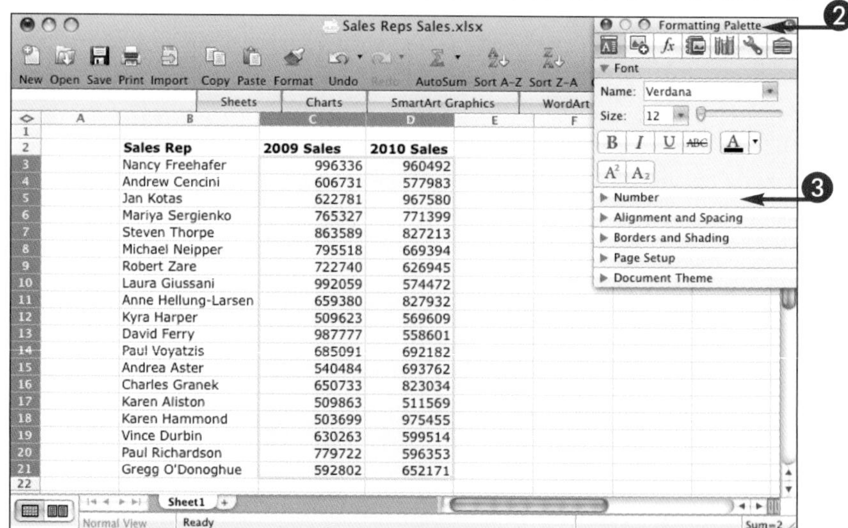

4 Click the **Format** ▾ and then click the number format you want to use.

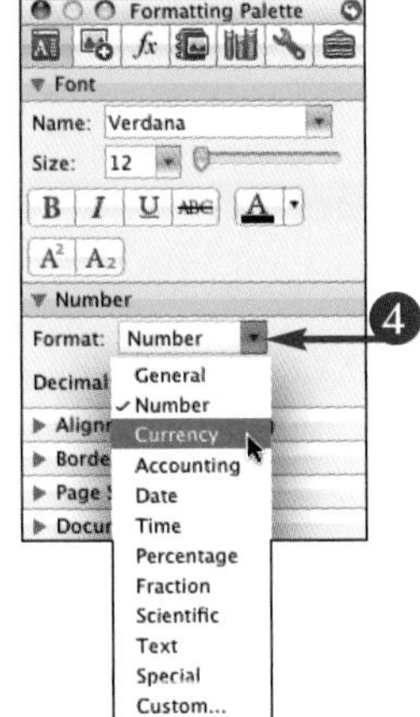


- Excel applies the number format to the selected range.
- To increase the number of decimal places, click the **Increase Decimal** button (⇐.0 .00).
- To decrease the number of decimal places, click the **Decrease Decimal** button (.00 ⇒.0).

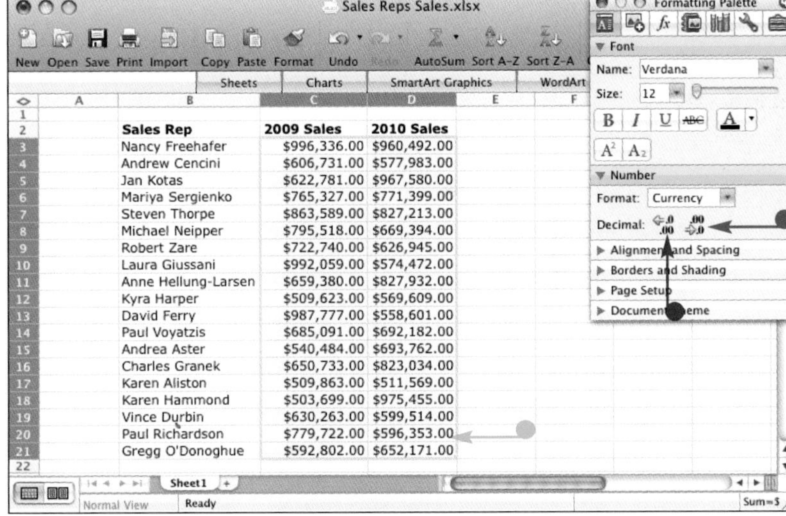


## TIP

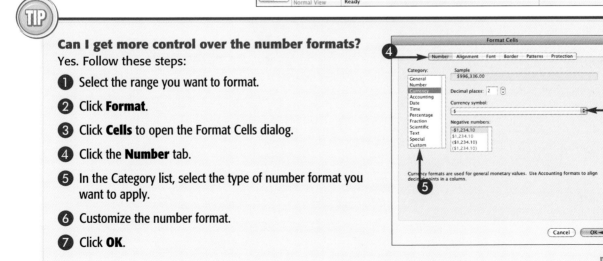

**Can I get more control over the number formats?**

Yes. Follow these steps:

1 Select the range you want to format.

2 Click **Format**.

3 Click **Cells** to open the Format Cells dialog.

4 Click the **Number** tab.

5 In the Category list, select the type of number format you want to apply.

6 Customize the number format.

7 Click **OK**.

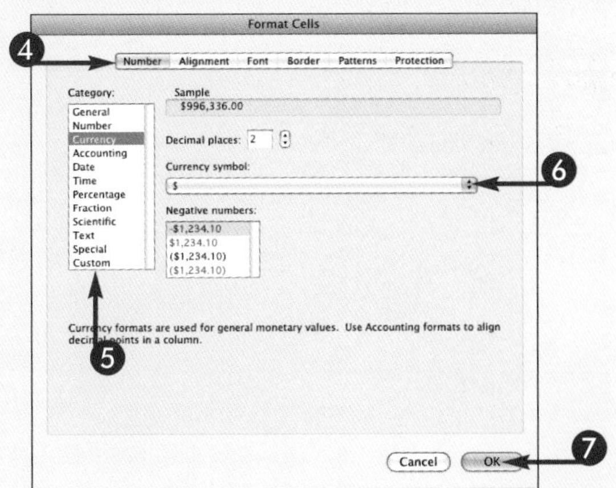

# Apply an AutoFormat to a Range

You can save time when formatting your Excel worksheets by using the AutoFormat feature. This feature offers a number of predefined formatting options that you can apply to a range all at once. The formatting options include the number format, font, cell alignment, borders, patterns, row height, and column width.

**The AutoFormats are designed for data in a tabular format, particularly where you have headings in the top row and left column, numeric data in the rest of the cells, and a bottom row that shows the totals for each column.**

## Apply an AutoFormat to a Range

❶ Select the range you want to format.

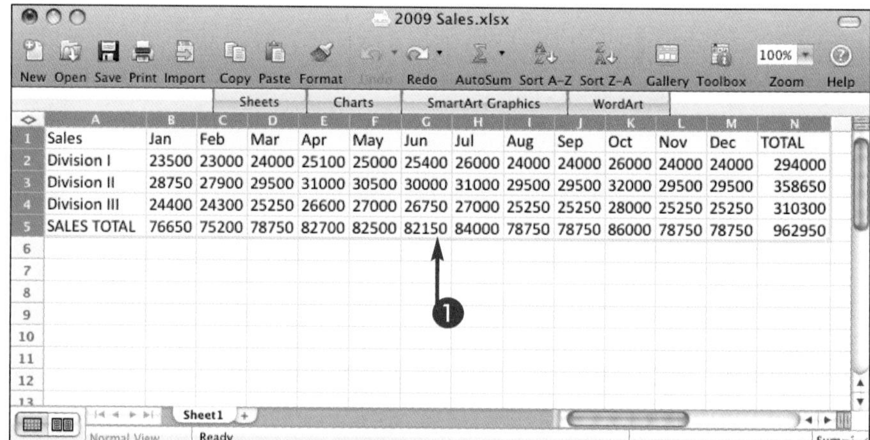

2009 Sales.xlsx
New Open Save Print Import Copy Paste Format Undo Redo AutoSum Sort A-Z Sort Z-A Gallery Toolbox Zoom Help
100%
Sheets Charts SmartArt Graphics WordArt
Sales Jan Feb Mar Apr May Jun Jul Aug Sep Oct Nov Dec TOTAL
Division I 23500 23000 24000 25100 25000 25400 26000 24000 24000 26000 24000 24000 294000
Division II 28750 27900 29500 31000 30500 30000 31000 29500 29500 32000 29500 29500 358650
Division III 24400 24300 25250 26600 27000 26750 27000 25250 25250 28000 25250 25250 310300
SALES TOTAL 76650 75200 78750 82700 82500 82150 84000 78750 78750 86000 78750 78750 962950
1
Sheet1
Normal View Ready


❷ Click **Format**.

❸ Click **AutoFormat**.

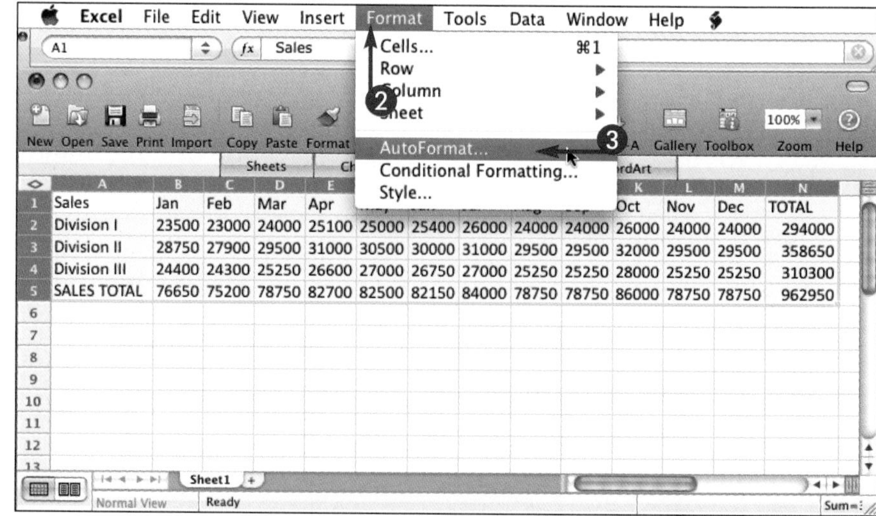

The AutoFormat dialog appears.

4. In the Table format list, click the AutoFormat you want to use.

- The Sample area shows you what the AutoFormat looks like

5. Click **OK**.

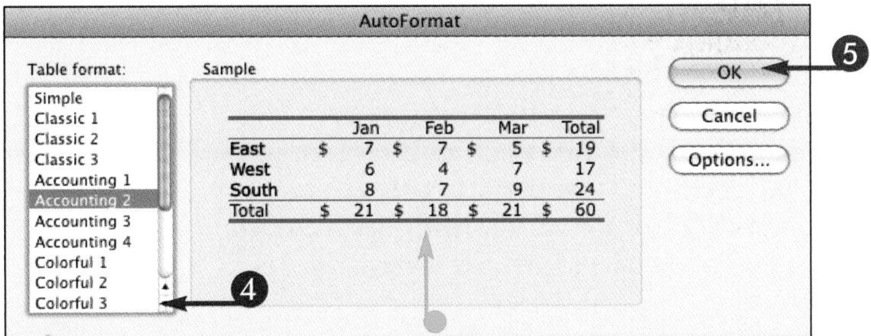


- Excel applies the AutoFormat to the selected range.

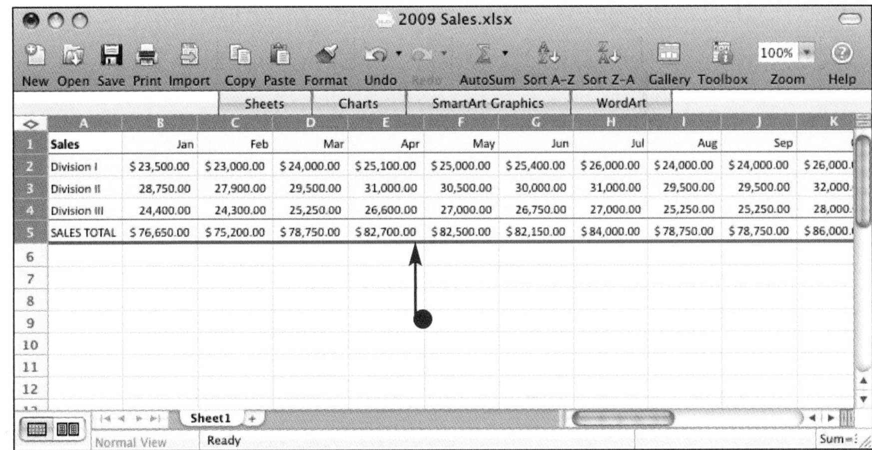

**Is there a way to apply an AutoFormat without using some of its formatting?**

Yes. Excel enables you to control all six formats that are part of each AutoFormat: Number, Font, Alignment, Border, Patterns, and Width/Height. Follow Steps **1** to **4** to choose the AutoFormat you want to apply. Click **Options** to expand the dialog and display the **Formats to apply** group. Deselect the option for each format you do not want to apply (☑ changes to ☐), and then click **OK**.

AutoFormat
✔ Number
✔ Font
Alignment
✔ Border
Patterns
✔ Width/Height

**How do I remove an AutoFormat?**

If you do not like or no longer need the AutoFormat you applied to the cells, you can revert to a plain, unformatted state. Select the range and then follow Steps **2** and **3** to display the AutoFormat dialog. In the Table format list, click **None**, and then click **OK**. Excel removes the AutoFormat from the selected range.

# Apply a Conditional Format to a Range

You can make a worksheet easier to analyze by applying a conditional format to a range. A conditional format is formatting that Excel applies only to cells that meet the condition you specify. For example, you can tell Excel to only apply the formatting if a cell's value is greater than some specified amount.

**When you set up your conditional format, you can specify the font, border, and background pattern, which helps to ensure that the cells that meet your criteria stand out from the other cells in the range.**

## Apply a Conditional Format to a Range

1. Select the range you want to work with.
2. Click **Format**.
3. Click **Conditional Formatting**.

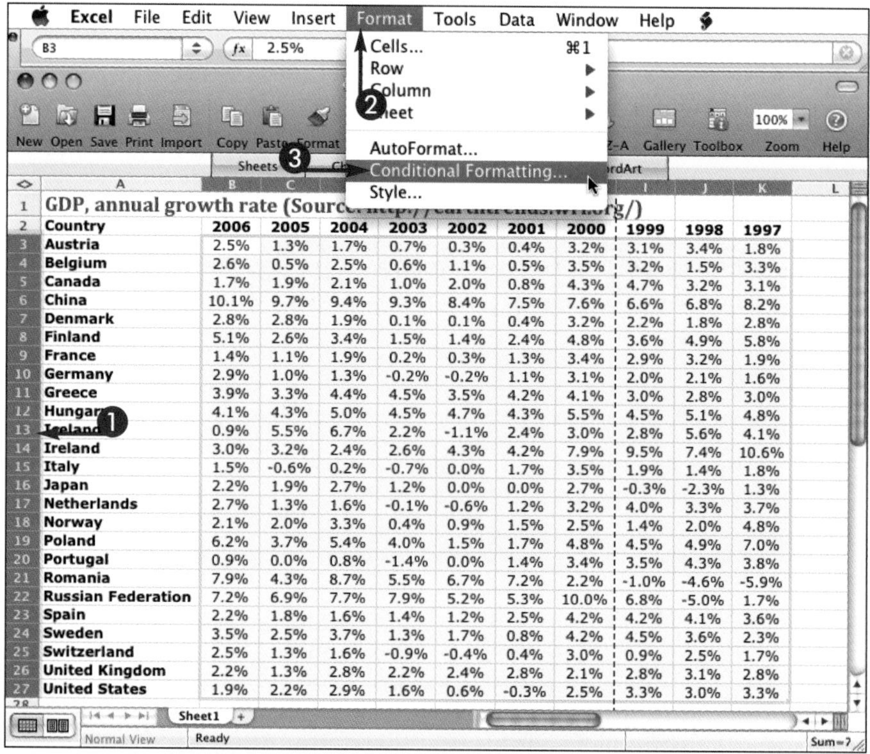


| Country | 2006 | 2005 | 2004 | 2003 | 2002 | 2001 | 2000 | 1999 | 1998 | 1997 |
|---|---|---|---|---|---|---|---|---|---|---|
| Austria | 2.5% | 1.3% | 1.7% | 0.7% | 0.3% | 0.4% | 3.2% | 3.1% | 3.4% | 1.8% |
| Belgium | 2.6% | 0.5% | 2.5% | 0.6% | 1.1% | 0.5% | 3.5% | 3.2% | 1.5% | 3.3% |
| Canada | 1.7% | 1.9% | 2.1% | 1.0% | 2.0% | 0.8% | 4.3% | 4.7% | 3.2% | 3.1% |
| China | 10.1% | 9.7% | 9.4% | 9.3% | 8.4% | 7.5% | 7.6% | 6.6% | 6.8% | 8.2% |
| Denmark | 2.8% | 2.8% | 1.9% | 0.1% | 0.1% | 0.4% | 3.2% | 2.2% | 1.8% | 2.8% |
| Finland | 5.1% | 2.6% | 3.4% | 1.5% | 1.4% | 2.4% | 4.8% | 3.6% | 4.9% | 5.8% |
| France | 1.4% | 1.1% | 1.9% | 0.2% | 0.3% | 1.3% | 3.4% | 2.9% | 3.2% | 1.9% |
| Germany | 2.9% | 1.0% | 1.3% | -0.2% | -0.2% | 1.1% | 3.1% | 2.0% | 2.1% | 1.6% |
| Greece | 3.9% | 3.3% | 4.4% | 4.5% | 3.5% | 4.2% | 4.1% | 3.0% | 2.8% | 3.0% |
| Hungary | 4.1% | 4.3% | 5.0% | 4.5% | 4.7% | 4.3% | 5.5% | 4.5% | 5.1% | 4.8% |
| Iceland | 0.9% | 5.5% | 6.7% | 2.2% | -1.1% | 2.4% | 3.0% | 2.8% | 5.6% | 4.1% |
| Ireland | 3.0% | 3.2% | 2.4% | 2.6% | 4.3% | 4.2% | 7.9% | 9.5% | 7.4% | 10.6% |
| Italy | 1.5% | -0.6% | 0.2% | -0.7% | 0.0% | 1.7% | 3.5% | 1.9% | 1.4% | 1.8% |
| Japan | 2.2% | 1.9% | 2.7% | 1.2% | 0.0% | 0.0% | 2.7% | -0.3% | -2.3% | 1.3% |
| Netherlands | 2.7% | 1.3% | 1.6% | -0.1% | -0.6% | 1.2% | 3.2% | 4.0% | 3.3% | 3.7% |
| Norway | 2.1% | 2.0% | 3.3% | 0.4% | 0.9% | 1.5% | 2.5% | 1.4% | 2.0% | 4.8% |
| Poland | 6.2% | 3.7% | 5.4% | 4.0% | 1.5% | 1.7% | 4.8% | 4.5% | 4.9% | 7.0% |
| Portugal | 0.9% | 0.0% | 0.8% | -1.4% | 0.0% | 1.4% | 3.4% | 3.5% | 4.3% | 3.8% |
| Romania | 7.9% | 4.3% | 8.7% | 5.5% | 6.7% | 7.2% | 2.2% | -1.0% | -4.6% | -5.9% |
| Russian Federation | 7.2% | 6.9% | 7.7% | 7.9% | 5.2% | 5.3% | 10.0% | 6.8% | -5.0% | 1.7% |
| Spain | 2.2% | 1.8% | 1.6% | 1.4% | 1.2% | 2.5% | 4.2% | 4.2% | 4.1% | 3.6% |
| Sweden | 3.5% | 2.5% | 3.7% | 1.3% | 1.7% | 0.8% | 4.2% | 4.5% | 3.6% | 2.3% |
| Switzerland | 2.5% | 1.3% | 1.6% | -0.9% | -0.4% | 0.4% | 3.0% | 0.9% | 2.5% | 1.7% |
| United Kingdom | 2.2% | 1.3% | 2.8% | 2.2% | 2.4% | 2.8% | 2.1% | 2.8% | 3.1% | 2.8% |
| United States | 1.9% | 2.2% | 2.9% | 1.6% | 0.6% | -0.3% | 2.5% | 3.3% | 3.0% | 3.3% |

The Conditional Formatting dialog appears.

4. Click this ⬍ and then click the operator you want to use for your condition.
5. Type the value you want to use for your condition.

- You can also click here and then click in a worksheet cell.

Depending on the operator, you may need to specify two values.

6. Click **Format**.

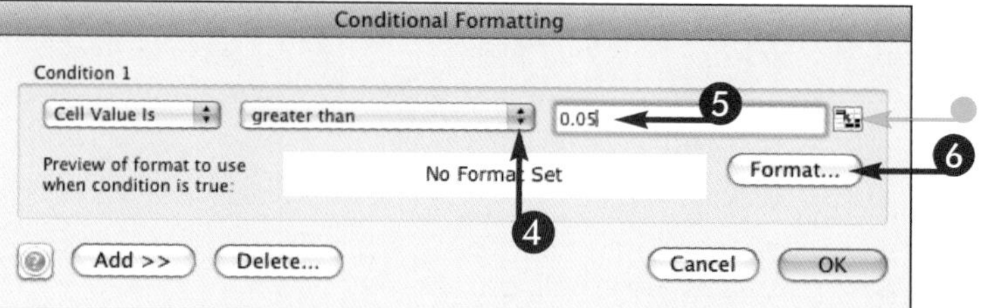

The Format Cells dialog appears.

7. Click the **Font** tab and then click the font you want to apply to cells that meet the condition.
8. Click the **Border** tab to set the border format.
9. Click the **Patterns** tab to set the background color or pattern.
10. Click **OK**.

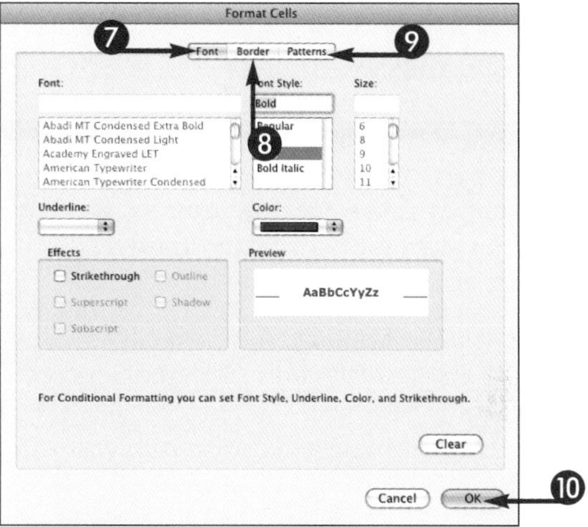

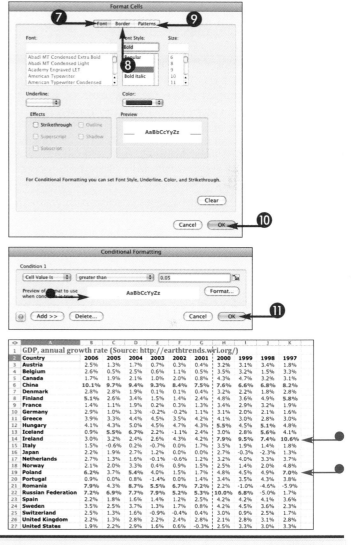

- A preview of the formatting appears here.

11. Click **OK**.

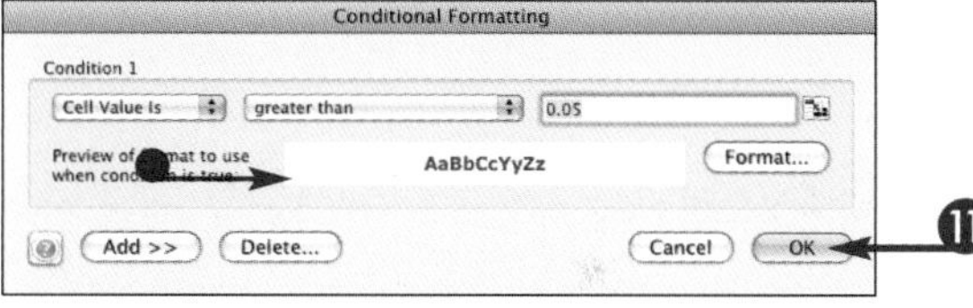


- Excel applies the formatting to cells that meet your condition.

| | A | B | C | D | E | F | G | H | I | J | K |
|---|---|---|---|---|---|---|---|---|---|---|---|
| 1 | GDP, annual growth rate (Source: http://earthtrends.wri.org/) | | | | | | | | | | |
| 2 | **Country** | **2006** | **2005** | **2004** | **2003** | **2002** | **2001** | **2000** | **1999** | **1998** | **1997** |
| 3 | **Austria** | 2.5% | 1.3% | 1.7% | 0.7% | 0.3% | 0.4% | 3.2% | 3.1% | 3.4% | 1.8% |
| 4 | **Belgium** | 2.6% | 0.5% | 2.5% | 0.6% | 1.1% | 0.5% | 3.5% | 3.2% | 1.5% | 3.3% |
| 5 | **Canada** | 1.7% | 1.9% | 2.1% | 1.0% | 2.0% | 0.8% | 4.3% | 4.7% | 3.2% | 3.1% |
| 6 | **China** | **10.1%** | **9.7%** | **9.4%** | **9.3%** | **8.4%** | **7.5%** | **7.6%** | **6.6%** | **6.8%** | **8.2%** |
| 7 | **Denmark** | 2.8% | 2.8% | 1.9% | 0.1% | 0.1% | 0.4% | 3.2% | 2.2% | 1.8% | 2.8% |
| 8 | **Finland** | **5.1%** | 2.6% | 3.4% | 1.5% | 1.4% | 2.4% | 4.8% | 3.6% | 4.9% | **5.8%** |
| 9 | **France** | 1.4% | 1.1% | 1.9% | 0.2% | 0.3% | 1.3% | 3.4% | 2.9% | 3.2% | 1.9% |
| 10 | **Germany** | 2.9% | 1.0% | 1.3% | -0.2% | -0.2% | 1.1% | 3.1% | 2.0% | 2.1% | 1.6% |
| 11 | **Greece** | 3.9% | 3.3% | 4.4% | 4.5% | 3.5% | 4.2% | 4.1% | 3.0% | 2.8% | 3.0% |
| 12 | **Hungary** | 4.1% | 4.3% | 5.0% | 4.5% | 4.7% | 4.3% | **5.5%** | 4.5% | **5.1%** | 4.8% |
| 13 | **Iceland** | 0.9% | **5.5%** | **6.7%** | 2.2% | -1.1% | 2.4% | 3.0% | 2.8% | **5.6%** | 4.1% |
| 14 | **Ireland** | 3.0% | 3.2% | 2.4% | 2.6% | 4.3% | 4.2% | **7.9%** | **9.5%** | **7.4%** | **10.6%** |
| 15 | **Italy** | 1.5% | -0.6% | 0.2% | -0.7% | 0.0% | 1.7% | 3.5% | 1.9% | 1.4% | 1.8% |
| 16 | **Japan** | 2.2% | 1.9% | 2.7% | 1.2% | 0.0% | 0.0% | 2.7% | -0.3% | -2.3% | 1.3% |
| 17 | **Netherlands** | 2.7% | 1.3% | 1.6% | -0.1% | -0.6% | 1.2% | 3.2% | 4.0% | 3.3% | 3.7% |
| 18 | **Norway** | 2.1% | 2.0% | 3.3% | 0.4% | 0.9% | 1.5% | 2.5% | 1.4% | 2.0% | 4.8% |
| 19 | **Poland** | **6.2%** | 3.7% | **5.4%** | 4.0% | 1.5% | 1.7% | 4.8% | 4.5% | 4.9% | **7.0%** |
| 20 | **Portugal** | 0.9% | 0.0% | 0.8% | -1.4% | 0.0% | 1.4% | 3.4% | 3.5% | 4.3% | 3.8% |
| 21 | **Romania** | **7.9%** | 4.3% | **8.7%** | **5.5%** | **6.7%** | **7.2%** | 2.2% | -1.0% | -4.6% | -5.9% |
| 22 | **Russian Federation** | **7.2%** | **6.9%** | **7.7%** | **7.9%** | **5.2%** | **5.3%** | **10.0%** | **6.8%** | -5.0% | 1.7% |
| 23 | **Spain** | 2.2% | 1.8% | 1.6% | 1.4% | 1.2% | 2.5% | 4.2% | 4.2% | 4.1% | 3.6% |
| 24 | **Sweden** | 3.5% | 2.5% | 3.7% | 1.3% | 1.7% | 0.8% | 4.2% | 4.5% | 3.6% | 2.3% |
| 25 | **Switzerland** | 2.5% | 1.3% | 1.6% | -0.9% | -0.4% | 0.4% | 3.0% | 0.9% | 2.5% | 1.7% |
| 26 | **United Kingdom** | 2.2% | 1.3% | 2.8% | 2.2% | 2.4% | 2.8% | 2.1% | 2.8% | 3.1% | 2.8% |
| 27 | **United States** | 1.9% | 2.2% | 2.9% | 1.6% | 0.6% | -0.3% | 2.5% | 3.3% | 3.0% | 3.3% |

### Can I set up more than one condition for a single range?

Yes. Excel enables you to specify up to three conditional formats. For example, you could set up one condition for cells that are greater than some value, and a separate condition for cells that are less than some other value. You can apply unique formats to each condition. After you set up the initial condition, click **Add** to add a second condition. Follow Steps **4** to **10** to configure the new condition.

### How do I remove a conditional format from a range?

If you no longer require a conditional format, you can delete it. Follow Steps **1** to **3** to select the range and display the Conditional Formatting dialog, and then click **Delete**. Excel displays the Delete Conditional Format dialog. Select the check box beside each conditional format you want to remove (☐ changes to ☑), and then click **OK**.

# Change the Column Width

If you have a large number or a long line of text in a cell, Excel may display only part of the cell value. To avoid this, you can increase the width of the column. Similarly, if a column only contains a few characters in each cell, you can decrease the width to fit more columns on the screen.

## Change the Column Width

1. Click in any cell in the column you want to resize.

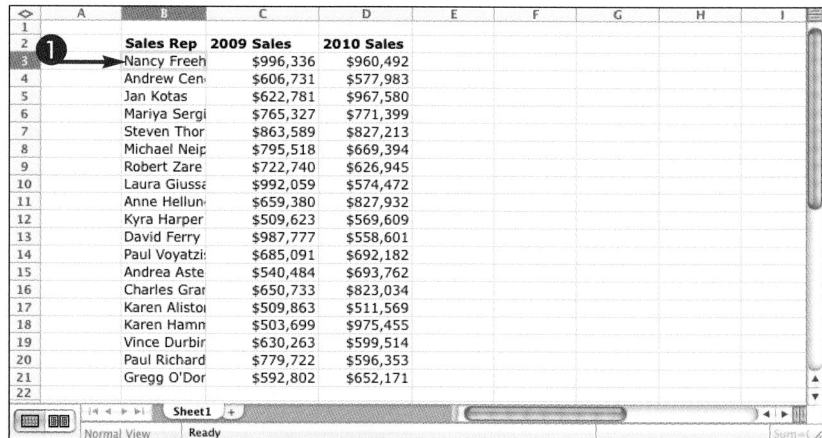



| | A | B | C | D |
|---|---|---|---|---|
| 1 | | | | |
| 2 | | Sales Rep | 2009 Sales | 2010 Sales |
| 3 | | Nancy Freeh | $996,336 | $960,492 |
| 4 | | Andrew Cen | $606,731 | $577,983 |
| 5 | | Jan Kotas | $622,781 | $967,580 |
| 6 | | Mariya Sergi | $765,327 | $771,399 |
| 7 | | Steven Thor | $863,589 | $827,213 |
| 8 | | Michael Neip | $795,518 | $669,394 |
| 9 | | Robert Zare | $722,740 | $626,945 |
| 10 | | Laura Giussa | $992,059 | $574,472 |
| 11 | | Anne Hellun | $659,380 | $827,932 |
| 12 | | Kyra Harper | $509,623 | $569,609 |
| 13 | | David Ferry | $987,777 | $558,601 |
| 14 | | Paul Voyatzi | $685,091 | $692,182 |
| 15 | | Andrea Aste | $540,484 | $693,762 |
| 16 | | Charles Grar | $650,733 | $823,034 |
| 17 | | Karen Alistoi | $509,863 | $511,569 |
| 18 | | Karen Hamn | $503,699 | $975,455 |
| 19 | | Vince Durbir | $630,263 | $599,514 |
| 20 | | Paul Richard | $779,722 | $596,353 |
| 21 | | Gregg O'Dor | $592,802 | $652,171 |
| 22 | | | | |

2. Click **Format**.
3. Click **Column**.
4. Click **Width**.

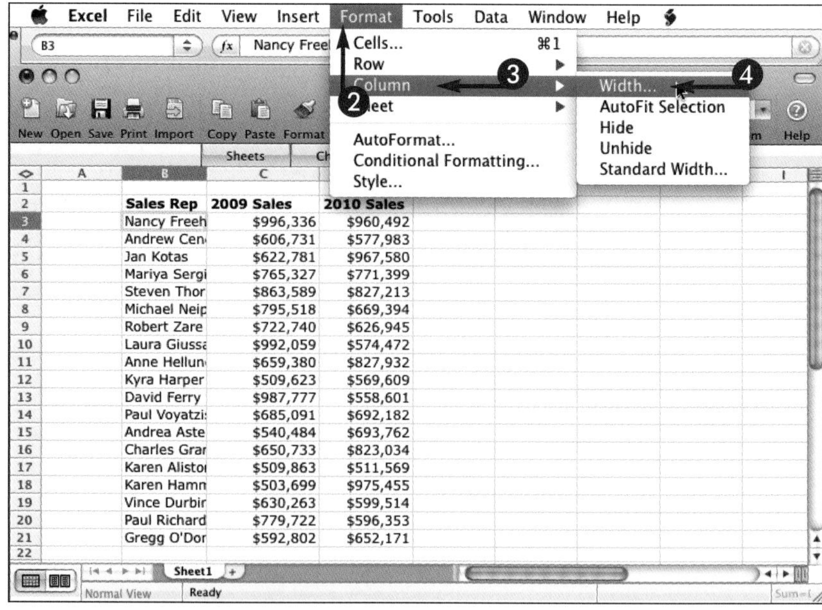



| | A | B | C | D |
|---|---|---|---|---|
| 1 | | | | |
| 2 | | Sales Rep | 2009 Sales | 2010 Sales |
| 3 | | Nancy Freeh | $996,336 | $960,492 |
| 4 | | Andrew Cen | $606,731 | $577,983 |
| 5 | | Jan Kotas | $622,781 | $967,580 |
| 6 | | Mariya Sergi | $765,327 | $771,399 |
| 7 | | Steven Thor | $863,589 | $827,213 |
| 8 | | Michael Neip | $795,518 | $669,394 |
| 9 | | Robert Zare | $722,740 | $626,945 |
| 10 | | Laura Giussa | $992,059 | $574,472 |
| 11 | | Anne Hellun | $659,380 | $827,932 |
| 12 | | Kyra Harper | $509,623 | $569,609 |
| 13 | | David Ferry | $987,777 | $558,601 |
| 14 | | Paul Voyatzi | $685,091 | $692,182 |
| 15 | | Andrea Aste | $540,484 | $693,762 |
| 16 | | Charles Grar | $650,733 | $823,034 |
| 17 | | Karen Alistoi | $509,863 | $511,569 |
| 18 | | Karen Hamn | $503,699 | $975,455 |
| 19 | | Vince Durbir | $630,263 | $599,514 |
| 20 | | Paul Richard | $779,722 | $596,353 |
| 21 | | Gregg O'Dor | $592,802 | $652,171 |
| 22 | | | | |

The Column Width dialog appears.

5. In the Column width text box, type the width you want to use.

6. Click **OK**.

- Excel adjusts the column width.

- You can also move ↖ over the right edge of the column heading (↖ changes to ↔) and then click and drag the edge to set the width.

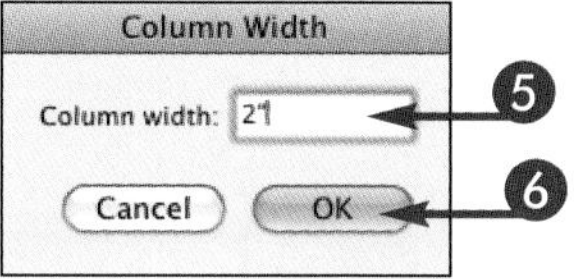


| | A | B | C | D |
|---|---|---|---|---|
| 1 | | | | |
| 2 | | **Sales Rep** | **2009 Sales** | **2010 Sales** |
| 3 | | Nancy Freehafer | $996,336 | $960,492 |
| 4 | | Andrew Cencini | $606,731 | $577,983 |
| 5 | | Jan Kotas | $622,781 | $967,580 |
| 6 | | Mariya Sergienko | $765,327 | $771,399 |
| 7 | | Steven Thorpe | $863,589 | $827,213 |
| 8 | | Michael Neipper | $795,518 | $669,394 |
| 9 | | Robert Zare | $722,740 | $626,945 |
| 10 | | Laura Giussani | $992,059 | $574,472 |
| 11 | | Anne Hellung-Larsen | $659,380 | $827,932 |
| 12 | | Kyra Harper | $509,623 | $569,609 |
| 13 | | David Ferry | $987,777 | $558,601 |
| 14 | | Paul Voyatzis | $685,091 | $692,182 |
| 15 | | Andrea Aster | $540,484 | $693,762 |
| 16 | | Charles Granek | $650,733 | $823,034 |
| 17 | | Karen Aliston | $509,863 | $511,569 |
| 18 | | Karen Hammond | $503,699 | $975,455 |
| 19 | | Vince Durbin | $630,263 | $599,514 |
| 20 | | Paul Richardson | $779,722 | $596,353 |
| 21 | | Gregg O'Donoghue | $592,802 | $652,171 |
| 22 | | | | |

Sheet1 | Normal View | Ready

## TIPS

**Is there an easier way to adjust the column width to fit the contents of a column?**

AUTOFIT

Yes. You can use Excel's AutoFit feature, which automatically adjusts the column width to fit the widest item in a column. Click the widest item in the column, click **Format**, click **Column**, and then click **AutoFit Selection**. Alternatively, move ↖ over the right edge of the column heading (↖ changes to ↔) and then double-click.

**Is there a way to change all the column widths at once?**

Yes. Click ◇ (or press ⌘ + A) to select the entire worksheet, then follow the steps in this section to set the width you prefer. If you have already adjusted some column widths and you want to change all the other widths, click **Format**, click **Column**, and then click **Standard Width** to open the Standard Width dialog. Type the new standard column width, and then click **OK**.

Standard Width
Standard column width: 1.04"
Cancel OK

# Change the Row Height

You can make your worksheet more visually appealing by increasing the row heights to create more space. This is particularly useful in worksheets that are crowded with text.

**If you want to change the row height to display multiline text within a cell, you must also turn on text wrapping within the cell. See the section "Wrap Text within a Cell" later in this chapter.**

## Change the Row Height

1. Select a range that includes at least one cell in every row you want to resize.

| | A | B | C | D | E | F | G | H | I | J | K |
|---|---|---|---|---|---|---|---|---|---|---|---|
| 1 | GDP, annual growth rate (Source: http://earthtrends.wri.org/) | | | | | | | | | | |
| 2 | **Country** | **2006** | **2005** | **2004** | **2003** | **2002** | **2001** | **2000** | **1999** | **1998** | **1997** |
| 3 | **Austria** | 2.5% | 1.3% | 1.7% | 0.7% | 0.3% | 0.4% | 3.2% | 3.1% | 3.4% | 1.8% |
| 4 | **Belgium** | 2.6% | 0.5% | 2.5% | 0.6% | 1.1% | 0.5% | 3.5% | 3.2% | 1.5% | 3.3% |
| 5 | **Canada** | 1.7% | 1.9% | 2.1% | 1.0% | 2.0% | 0.8% | 4.3% | 4.7% | 3.2% | 3.1% |
| 6 | **China** | 10.1% | 9.7% | 9.4% | 9.3% | 8.4% | 7.5% | 7.6% | 6.6% | 6.8% | 8.2% |
| 7 | **Denmark** | 2.8% | 2.8% | 1.9% | 0.1% | 0.1% | 0.4% | 3.2% | 2.2% | 1.8% | 2.8% |
| 8 | **Finland** | 5.1% | 2.6% | 3.4% | 1.5% | 1.4% | 2.4% | 4.8% | 3.6% | 4.9% | 5.8% |
| 9 | **France** | 1.4% | 1.1% | 1.9% | 0.2% | 0.3% | 1.3% | 3.4% | 2.9% | 3.2% | 1.9% |
| 10 | **Germany** | 2.9% | 1.0% | 1.3% | -0.2% | -0.2% | 1.1% | 3.1% | 2.0% | 2.1% | 1.6% |
| 11 | **Greece** | 3.9% | 3.3% | 4.4% | 4.5% | 3.5% | 4.2% | 4.1% | 3.0% | 2.8% | 3.0% |
| 12 | **Hungary** | 4.1% | 4.3% | 5.0% | 4.5% | 4.7% | 4.3% | 5.5% | 4.5% | 5.1% | 4.8% |
| 13 | **Iceland** | 0.9% | 5.5% | 6.7% | 2.2% | -1.1% | 2.4% | 3.0% | 2.8% | 5.6% | 4.1% |
| 14 | **Ireland** | 3.0% | 3.2% | 2.4% | 2.6% | 4.3% | 4.2% | 7.9% | 9.5% | 7.4% | 10.6% |
| 15 | **Italy** | 1.5% | -0.6% | 0.2% | -0.7% | 0.0% | 1.7% | 3.5% | 1.9% | 1.4% | 1.8% |
| 16 | **Japan** | 2.2% | 1.9% | 2.7% | 1.2% | 0.0% | 0.0% | 2.7% | -0.3% | -2.3% | 1.3% |
| 17 | **Netherlands** | 2.7% | 1.3% | 1.6% | -0.1% | -0.6% | 1.2% | 3.2% | 4.0% | 3.3% | 3.7% |
| 18 | **Norway** | 2.1% | 2.0% | 3.3% | 0.4% | 0.9% | 1.5% | 2.5% | 1.4% | 2.0% | 4.8% |
| 19 | **Poland** | 6.2% | 3.7% | 5.4% | 4.0% | 1.5% | 1.7% | 4.8% | 4.5% | 4.9% | 7.0% |
| 20 | **Portugal** | 0.9% | 0.0% | 0.8% | -1.4% | 0.0% | 1.4% | 3.4% | 3.5% | 4.3% | 3.8% |
| 21 | **Romania** | 7.9% | 4.3% | 8.7% | 5.5% | 6.7% | 7.2% | 2.2% | -1.0% | -4.6% | -5.9% |
| 22 | **Russian Federation** | 7.2% | 6.9% | 7.7% | 7.9% | 5.2% | 5.3% | 10.0% | 6.8% | -5.0% | 1.7% |
| 23 | **Spain** | 2.2% | 1.8% | 1.6% | 1.4% | 1.2% | 2.5% | 4.2% | 4.2% | 4.1% | 3.6% |
| 24 | **Sweden** | 3.5% | 2.5% | 3.7% | 1.3% | 1.7% | 0.8% | 4.2% | 4.5% | 3.6% | 2.3% |
| 25 | **Switzerland** | 2.5% | 1.3% | 1.6% | -0.9% | -0.4% | 0.4% | 3.0% | 0.9% | 2.5% | 1.7% |
| 26 | **United Kingdom** | 2.2% | 1.3% | 2.8% | 2.2% | 2.4% | 2.8% | 2.1% | 2.8% | 3.1% | 2.8% |
| 27 | **United States** | 1.9% | 2.2% | 2.9% | 1.6% | 0.6% | -0.3% | 2.5% | 3.3% | 3.0% | 3.3% |

Sheet1

Normal View Ready Sum=2

2. Click **Format**.
3. Click **Row**.
4. Click **Height**.

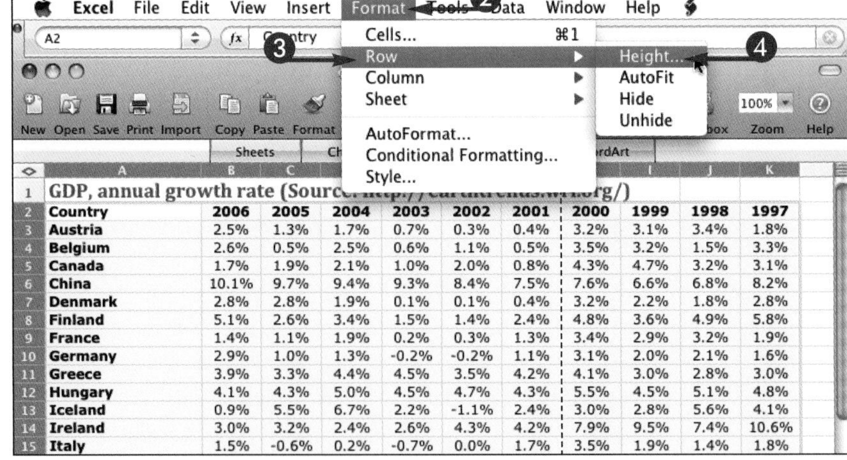

The Row Height dialog appears.

5 In the Row height text box, type the height you want to use.

6 Click **OK**.

- Excel adjusts the row heights.
- You can also move ↖ over the bottom edge of a row heading (↖ changes to ‡) and then click and drag the edge to set the height.

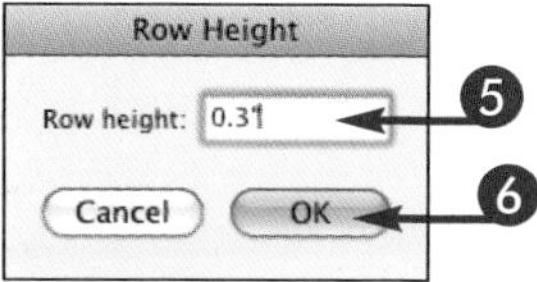


| | A | B | C | D | E | F | G | H | I | J | K |
|---|---|---|---|---|---|---|---|---|---|---|---|
| 1 | GDP, annual growth rate (Source: http://earthtrends.wri.org/) | | | | | | | | | | |
| 2 | Country | 2006 | 2005 | 2004 | 2003 | 2002 | 2001 | 2000 | 1999 | 1998 | 1997 |
| 3 | Austria | 2.5% | 1.3% | 1.7% | 0.7% | 0.3% | 0.4% | 3.2% | 3.1% | 3.4% | 1.8% |
| 4 | Belgium | 2.6% | 0.5% | 2.5% | 0.6% | 1.1% | 0.5% | 3.5% | 3.2% | 1.5% | 3.3% |
| 5 | Canada | 1.7% | 1.9% | 2.1% | 1.0% | 2.0% | 0.8% | 4.3% | 4.7% | 3.2% | 3.1% |
| 6 | China | 10.1% | 9.7% | 9.4% | 9.3% | 8.4% | 7.5% | 7.6% | 6.6% | 6.8% | 8.2% |
| 7 | Denmark | 2.8% | 2.8% | 1.9% | 0.1% | 0.1% | 0.4% | 3.2% | 2.2% | 1.8% | 2.8% |
| 8 | Finland | 5.1% | 2.6% | 3.4% | 1.5% | 1.4% | 2.4% | 4.8% | 3.6% | 4.9% | 5.8% |
| 9 | France | 1.4% | 1.1% | 1.9% | 0.2% | 0.3% | 1.3% | 3.4% | 2.9% | 3.2% | 1.9% |
| 10 | Germany | 2.9% | 1.0% | 1.3% | -0.2% | -0.2% | 1.1% | 3.1% | 2.0% | 2.1% | 1.6% |
| 11 | Greece | 3.9% | 3.3% | 4.4% | 4.5% | 3.5% | 4.2% | 4.1% | 3.0% | 2.8% | 3.0% |
| 12 | Hungary | 4.1% | 4.3% | 5.0% | 4.5% | 4.7% | 4.3% | 5.5% | 4.5% | 5.1% | 4.8% |
| 13 | Iceland | 0.9% | 5.5% | 6.7% | 2.2% | -1.1% | 2.4% | 3.0% | 2.8% | 5.6% | 4.1% |
| 14 | Ireland | 3.0% | 3.2% | 2.4% | 2.6% | 4.3% | 4.2% | 7.9% | 9.5% | 7.4% | 10.6% |
| 15 | Italy | 1.5% | -0.6% | 0.2% | -0.7% | 0.0% | 1.7% | 3.5% | 1.9% | 1.4% | 1.8% |
| 16 | Japan | 2.2% | 1.9% | 2.7% | 1.2% | 0.0% | 0.0% | 2.7% | -0.3% | -2.3% | 1.3% |
| 17 | Netherlands | 2.7% | 1.3% | 1.6% | -0.1% | -0.6% | 1.2% | 3.2% | 4.0% | 3.3% | 3.7% |

**Is there an easier way to adjust the row height to fit the contents of a row?**

Yes. You can use Excel's AutoFit feature, which automatically adjusts the row height to fit the tallest item in a row. Click in any cell in the row, click **Format**, click **Row**, and then click **AutoFit**.

Alternatively, move ↖ over the bottom edge of the row heading (↖ changes to ‡) and then double-click.

**Is there a way to change all the row heights at once?**

Yes. Click ◇ (or press ⌘+A) to select the entire worksheet. You can then either follow the steps in this section to set the height by hand, or you can move ↖ over the bottom edge of any row heading (↖ changes to ‡) and then click and drag the edge to set the height of all the rows.

Height: 25.00 (0.35 inches)

# Hide a Row or Column

If you do not need to see or work with a row or column temporarily, you can make your worksheet easier to read and to navigate by hiding the row or column.

**Hiding a row or column is also useful if you are showing someone a worksheet that contains private or sensitive data that you do not want the person to see.**

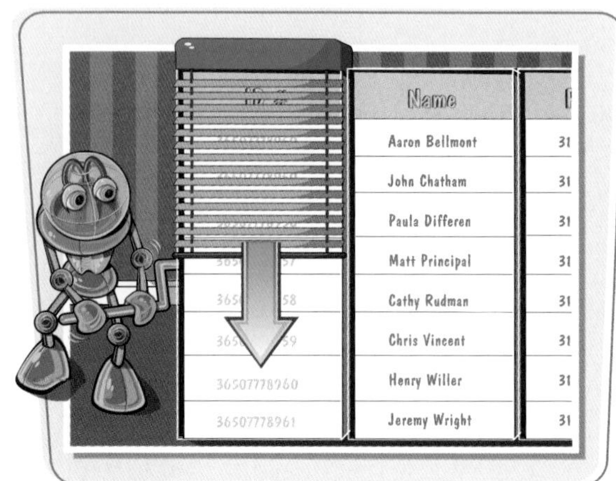


## Hide a Row or Column

### HIDE A ROW

1. Click in any cell in the row you want to hide.
2. Click **Format**.
3. Click **Row**.
4. Click **Hide**.

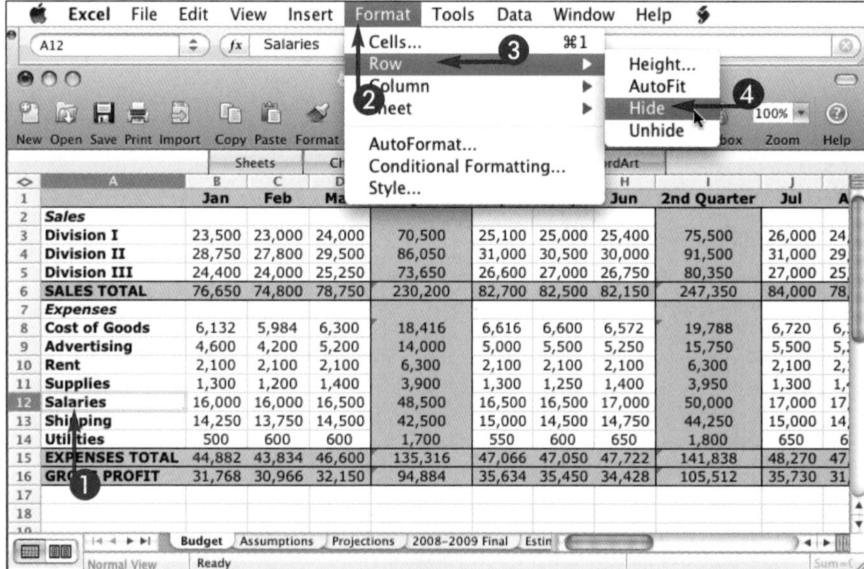


- Excel removes the row from the worksheet display.
- Excel displays the surrounding row numbers in blue to indicate that a hidden row lies between them.

Another way to hide a row is to move ↖ over the bottom edge of the row heading (↖ changes to ‡) and then click and drag the edge up until the height displays 0.

| | A | B | C | D | E | F | G | H | I | J |
|---|---|---|---|---|---|---|---|---|---|---|
| 1 | | Jan | Feb | Mar | 1st Quarter | Apr | May | Jun | 2nd Quarter | Jul |
| 2 | *Sales* | | | | | | | | | |
| 3 | Division I | 23,500 | 23,000 | 24,000 | 70,500 | 25,100 | 25,000 | 25,400 | 75,500 | 26,000 |
| 4 | Division II | 28,750 | 27,800 | 29,500 | 86,050 | 31,000 | 30,500 | 30,000 | 91,500 | 31,000 |
| 5 | Division III | 24,400 | 24,000 | 25,250 | 73,650 | 26,600 | 27,000 | 26,750 | 80,350 | 27,000 |
| 6 | SALES TOTAL | 76,650 | 74,800 | 78,750 | 230,200 | 82,700 | 82,500 | 82,150 | 247,350 | 84,000 |
| 7 | *Expenses* | | | | | | | | | |
| 8 | Cost of Goods | 6,132 | 5,984 | 6,300 | 18,416 | 6,616 | 6,600 | 6,572 | 19,788 | 6,720 |
| 9 | Advertising | 4,600 | 4,200 | 5,200 | 14,000 | 5,000 | 5,500 | 5,250 | 15,750 | 5,500 |
| 10 | Rent | 2,100 | 2,100 | 2,100 | 6,300 | 2,100 | 2,100 | 2,100 | 6,300 | 2,100 |
| 11 | Supplies | 1,300 | 1,200 | 1,400 | 3,900 | 1,300 | 1,250 | 1,400 | 3,950 | 1,300 |
| 13 | Shipping | 14,250 | 13,750 | 14,500 | 42,500 | 15,000 | 14,500 | 14,750 | 44,250 | 15,000 |
| 14 | Utilities | 500 | 600 | 600 | 1,700 | 550 | 600 | 650 | 1,800 | 650 |
| 15 | EXPENSES TOTAL | 44,882 | 43,834 | 46,600 | 135,316 | 47,066 | 47,050 | 47,722 | 141,838 | 48,270 |
| 16 | GROSS PROFIT | 31,768 | 30,966 | 32,150 | 94,884 | 35,634 | 35,450 | 34,428 | 105,512 | 35,730 |

Budget | Assumptions | Projections | 2008-2009 Final | Estin

Normal View | Ready

## HIDE A COLUMN

1. Click in any cell in the column you want to hide.
2. Click **Format**.
3. Click **Column**.
4. Click **Hide**.

- Excel removes the column from the worksheet display.
- Excel displays the surrounding column letters in blue to indicate that a hidden column lies between them.

Another way to hide a column is to move ↖ over the right edge of the column heading (↖ changes to ↔) and then click and drag the edge left until the width displays 0.

### How do I display a hidden row or column?

To display a hidden row, select the row above and the row below the hidden row, click **Format**, click **Row**, and then click **Unhide**. Alternatively, move ↖ between the headings of the selected rows (↖ changes to ↕) and then double-click. To unhide row 1, right-click the top edge of the row 2 header and then click **Unhide**.

To display a hidden column, select the column to the left and the column to the right of the hidden row, click **Format**, click **Column**, and then click **Unhide**. Alternatively, move ↖ between the headings of the selected rows (↖ changes to ↔) and then double-click. To unhide column A, right-click the left edge of the column B header and then click **Unhide**.

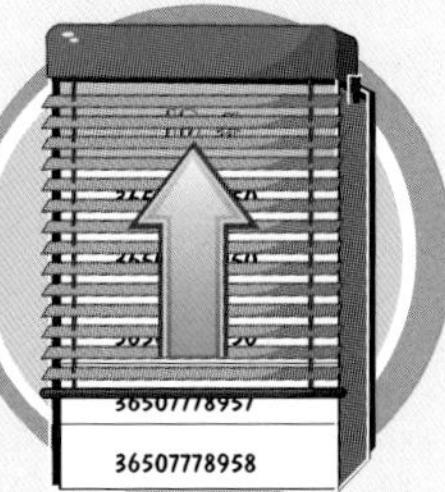

# Freeze Rows or Columns

You can keep your column labels in view as you scroll the worksheet by freezing the row or rows that contain the labels. This makes it easier to review and add data to the worksheet because you can always see the column labels.

**If your worksheet also includes row labels, you can keep those labels in view as you horizontally scroll the worksheet by freezing the column or columns that contain the labels.**

## Freeze Rows or Columns

### FREEZE ROWS

1. Scroll the worksheet so that the row or rows that you want to freeze are visible.
2. Position ↖ over the horizontal split bar (▤).

   ↖ changes to ⇕.
3. Click and drag ▤ and drop it below the row you want to freeze.

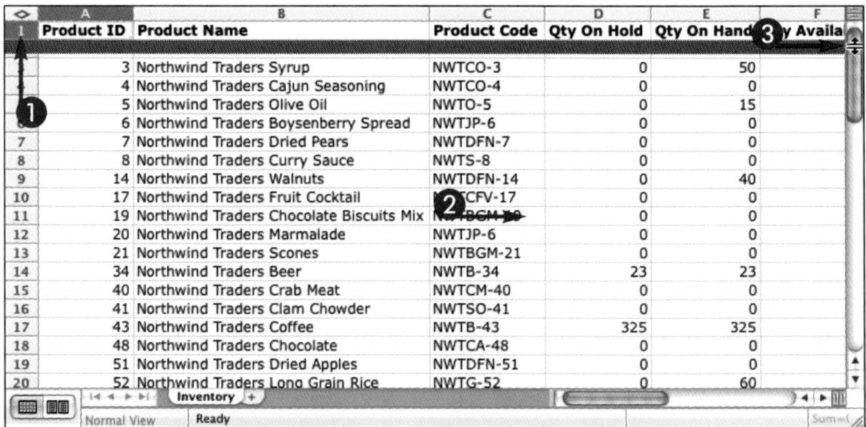


- Excel splits the worksheet into two horizontal panes.

4. Click **Window**.
5. Click **Freeze Panes**.

   Excel freezes the panes.

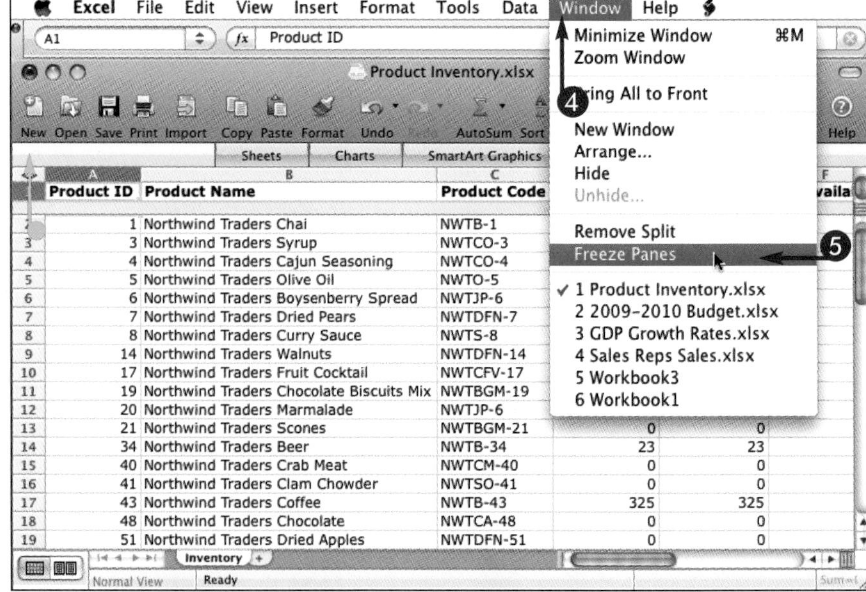

## FREEZE COLUMNS

1. Scroll the worksheet so that the column or columns that you want to freeze are visible.
2. Position ↖ over the vertical split bar (▥).

   ↖ changes to ⇹.

3. Click and drag ▥ and drop it on the right edge of the column you want to freeze.

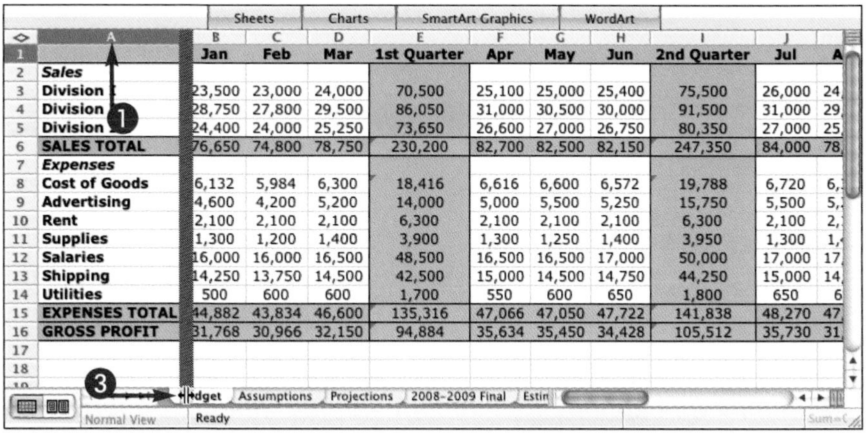


- Excel splits the worksheet into vertical two panes.

4. Click **Window**.
5. Click **Freeze Panes**.

   Excel freezes the panes.

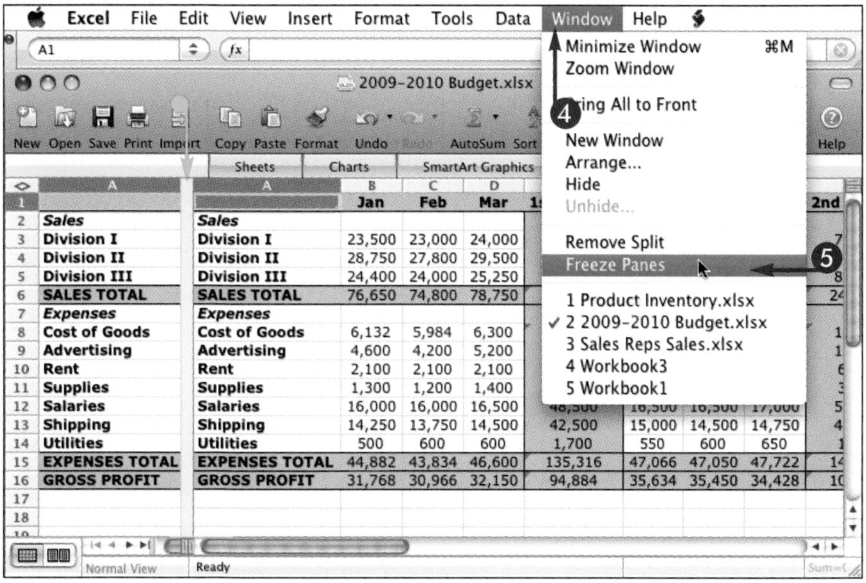


## TIPS

### Can I adjust the position of a frozen row or column?

Yes. Begin by unfreezing the panes: click **Window** and then click **Unfreeze Panes**. Excel unfreezes the panes and displays the split bar. Click and drag the split bar to the new location. Click **Window** and then click **Freeze Panes**.

### How do I unfreeze a row or column?

If you no longer require a row or column to be frozen, you can unfreeze it by clicking **Window** and then clicking **Unfreeze Panes**. If you no longer want your worksheet split into two panes, click **Window** and then click **Remove Split**.

# Merge Two or More Cells

You can create a single large cell by merging two or more cells. For example, it is common to merge some of the top row of cells to use as a worksheet title.

**Another common reason for merging cells is to create a label that applies to multiple columns of data.**

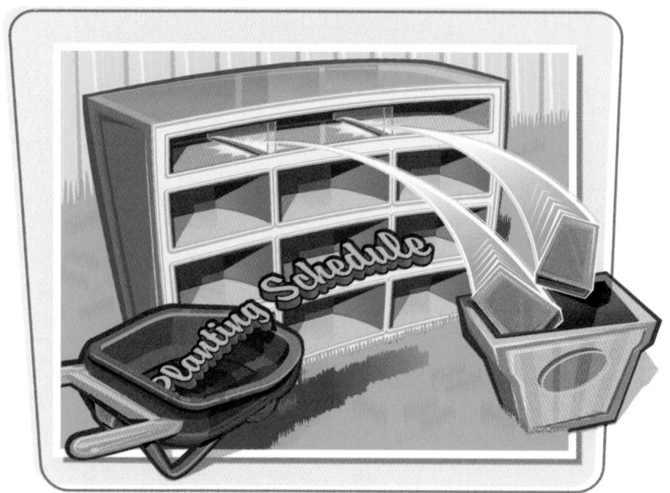


## Merge Two or More Cells

1. Select the cells that you want to merge.

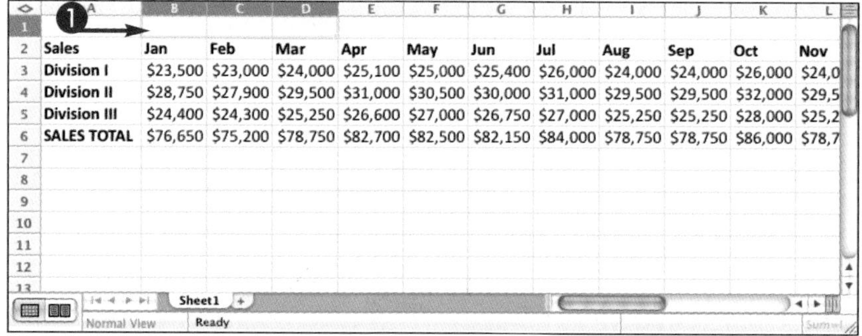

2. Display the Formatting Palette.

*Note: See Chapter 3 to learn how to display and hide the Formatting Palette.*

3. Click the **Alignment and Spacing** panel.

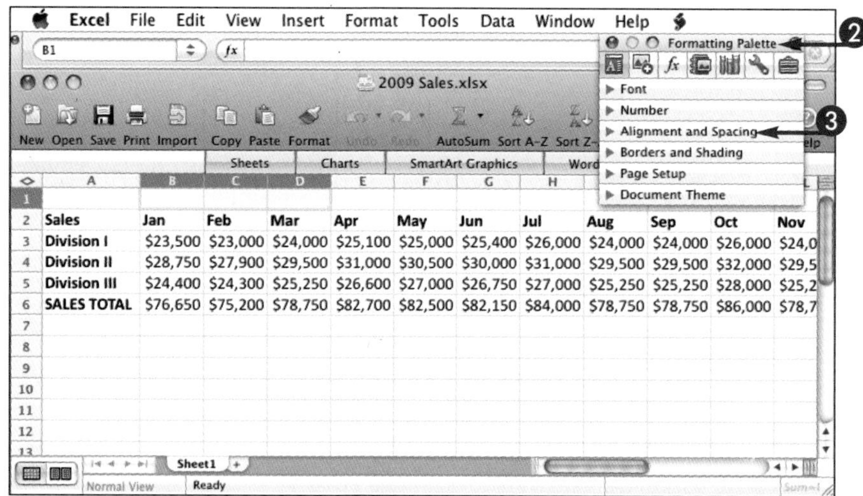

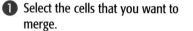

4 Select the **Merge cells** option (☐ changes to ☑).

● Excel merges the selected cells.

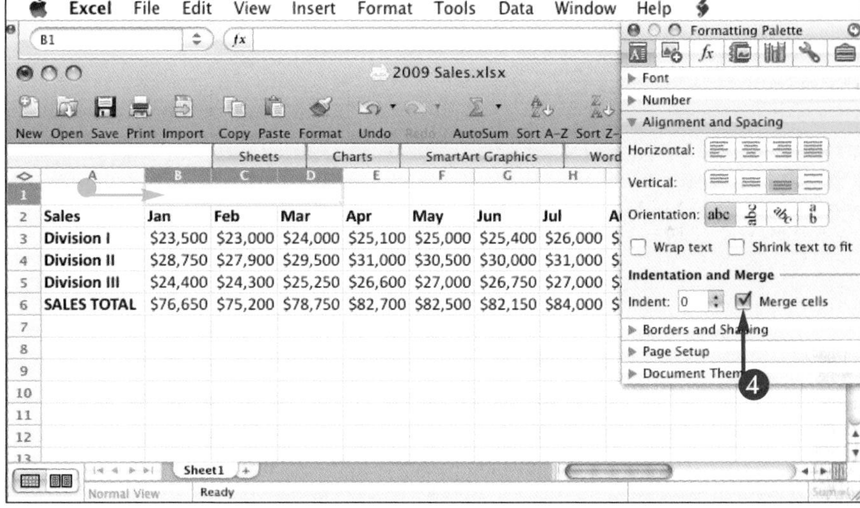

5 Type your text in the merged cell.

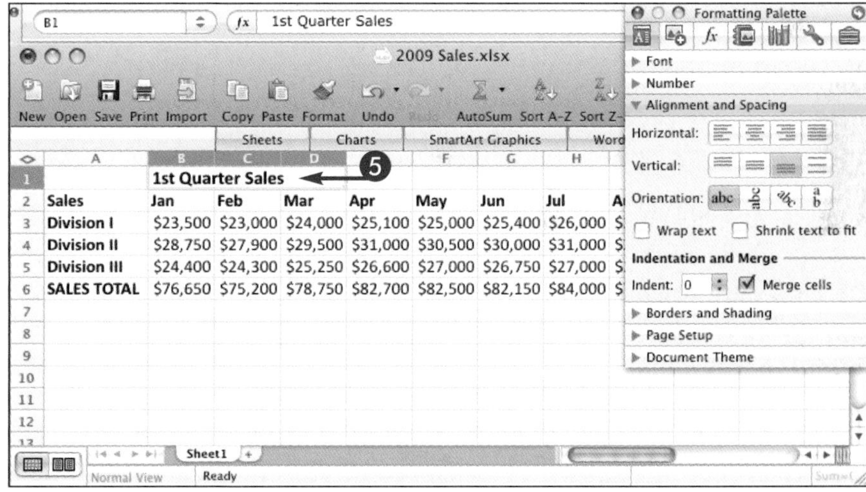

### How do I center text across multiple columns?

This is a useful technique for your worksheet titles or headings. You can center a title across the entire worksheet, or you can center a heading across the columns that it refers to. Follow Steps **1** to **5** to create the merged cell and type your title or heading. In the Formatting Palette's Alignment and Spacing panel, click ☰ to center the text within the merged cell.

# Wrap Text within a Cell

If you type more text in a cell than can fit horizontally, Excel either displays the text over the next cell if it is empty or displays only part of the text if the next cell contains data. To prevent Excel from showing only truncated cell data, you can format the cell to wrap text within the cell.

## Wrap Text within a Cell

1. Select the cell that you want to format.

| | A | B | C | D | E | F | G | H | I | J | K |
|---|---|---|---|---|---|---|---|---|---|---|---|
| 1 | | Gross Domestic Product (annual growth rate) | | | | | | | | | |
| 2 | Country | 2006 | 2005 | 2004 | 2003 | 2002 | 2001 | 2000 | 1999 | 1998 | 1997 |
| 3 | Austria | 2.5% | 1.3% | 1.7% | 0.7% | 0.3% | 0.4% | 3.2% | 3.1% | 3.4% | 1.8% |
| 4 | Belgium | 2.6% | 0.5% | 2.5% | 0.6% | 1.1% | 0.5% | 3.5% | 3.2% | 1.5% | 3.3% |
| 5 | Canada | 1.7% | 1.9% | 2.1% | 1.0% | 2.0% | 0.8% | 4.3% | 4.7% | 3.2% | 3.1% |
| 6 | China | 10.1% | 9.7% | 9.4% | 9.3% | 8.4% | 7.5% | 7.6% | 6.6% | 6.8% | 8.2% |
| 7 | Denmark | 2.8% | 2.8% | 1.9% | 0.1% | 0.1% | 0.4% | 3.2% | 2.2% | 1.8% | 2.8% |
| 8 | Finland | 5.1% | 2.6% | 3.4% | 1.5% | 1.4% | 2.4% | 4.8% | 3.6% | 4.9% | 5.8% |
| 9 | France | 1.4% | 1.1% | 1.9% | 0.2% | 0.3% | 1.3% | 3.4% | 2.9% | 3.2% | 1.9% |
| 10 | Germany | 2.9% | 1.0% | 1.3% | -0.2% | -0.2% | 1.1% | 3.1% | 2.0% | 2.1% | 1.6% |
| 11 | Greece | 3.9% | 3.3% | 4.4% | 4.5% | 3.5% | 4.2% | 4.1% | 3.0% | 2.8% | 3.0% |
| 12 | Hungary | 4.1% | 4.3% | 5.0% | 4.5% | 4.7% | 4.3% | 5.5% | 4.5% | 5.1% | 4.8% |
| 13 | Iceland | 0.9% | 5.5% | 6.7% | 2.2% | -1.1% | 2.4% | 3.0% | 2.8% | 5.6% | 4.1% |
| 14 | Ireland | 3.0% | 3.2% | 2.4% | 2.6% | 4.3% | 4.2% | 7.9% | 9.5% | 7.4% | 10.6% |
| 15 | Italy | 1.5% | -0.6% | 0.2% | -0.7% | 0.0% | 1.7% | 3.5% | 1.9% | 1.4% | 1.8% |

2. Display the Formatting Palette.

***Note:*** *See Chapter 3 to learn how to display and hide the Formatting Palette.*

3. Click the **Alignment and Spacing** panel.

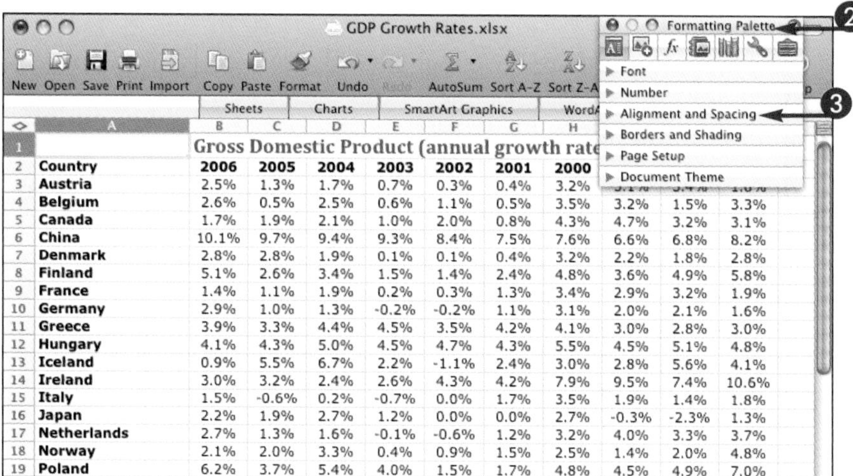


| | A | B | C | D | E | F | G | H | I | J | K |
|---|---|---|---|---|---|---|---|---|---|---|---|
| 1 | | Gross Domestic Product (annual growth rate | | | | | | | | | |
| 2 | Country | 2006 | 2005 | 2004 | 2003 | 2002 | 2001 | 2000 | | | |
| 3 | Austria | 2.5% | 1.3% | 1.7% | 0.7% | 0.3% | 0.4% | 3.2% | | | |
| 4 | Belgium | 2.6% | 0.5% | 2.5% | 0.6% | 1.1% | 0.5% | 3.5% | 3.2% | 1.5% | 3.3% |
| 5 | Canada | 1.7% | 1.9% | 2.1% | 1.0% | 2.0% | 0.8% | 4.3% | 4.7% | 3.2% | 3.1% |
| 6 | China | 10.1% | 9.7% | 9.4% | 9.3% | 8.4% | 7.5% | 7.6% | 6.6% | 6.8% | 8.2% |
| 7 | Denmark | 2.8% | 2.8% | 1.9% | 0.1% | 0.1% | 0.4% | 3.2% | 2.2% | 1.8% | 2.8% |
| 8 | Finland | 5.1% | 2.6% | 3.4% | 1.5% | 1.4% | 2.4% | 4.8% | 3.6% | 4.9% | 5.8% |
| 9 | France | 1.4% | 1.1% | 1.9% | 0.2% | 0.3% | 1.3% | 3.4% | 2.9% | 3.2% | 1.9% |
| 10 | Germany | 2.9% | 1.0% | 1.3% | -0.2% | -0.2% | 1.1% | 3.1% | 2.0% | 2.1% | 1.6% |
| 11 | Greece | 3.9% | 3.3% | 4.4% | 4.5% | 3.5% | 4.2% | 4.1% | 3.0% | 2.8% | 3.0% |
| 12 | Hungary | 4.1% | 4.3% | 5.0% | 4.5% | 4.7% | 4.3% | 5.5% | 4.5% | 5.1% | 4.8% |
| 13 | Iceland | 0.9% | 5.5% | 6.7% | 2.2% | -1.1% | 2.4% | 3.0% | 2.8% | 5.6% | 4.1% |
| 14 | Ireland | 3.0% | 3.2% | 2.4% | 2.6% | 4.3% | 4.2% | 7.9% | 9.5% | 7.4% | 10.6% |
| 15 | Italy | 1.5% | -0.6% | 0.2% | -0.7% | 0.0% | 1.7% | 3.5% | 1.9% | 1.4% | 1.8% |
| 16 | Japan | 2.2% | 1.9% | 2.7% | 1.2% | 0.0% | 0.0% | 2.7% | -0.3% | -2.3% | 1.3% |
| 17 | Netherlands | 2.7% | 1.3% | 1.6% | -0.1% | -0.6% | 1.2% | 3.2% | 4.0% | 3.3% | 3.7% |
| 18 | Norway | 2.1% | 2.0% | 3.3% | 0.4% | 0.9% | 1.5% | 2.5% | 1.4% | 2.0% | 4.8% |
| 19 | Poland | 6.2% | 3.7% | 5.4% | 4.0% | 1.5% | 1.7% | 4.8% | 4.5% | 4.9% | 7.0% |

4 Select the **Wrap text** option (☐ changes to ☑).

Excel turns on text wrapping for the selected cell.

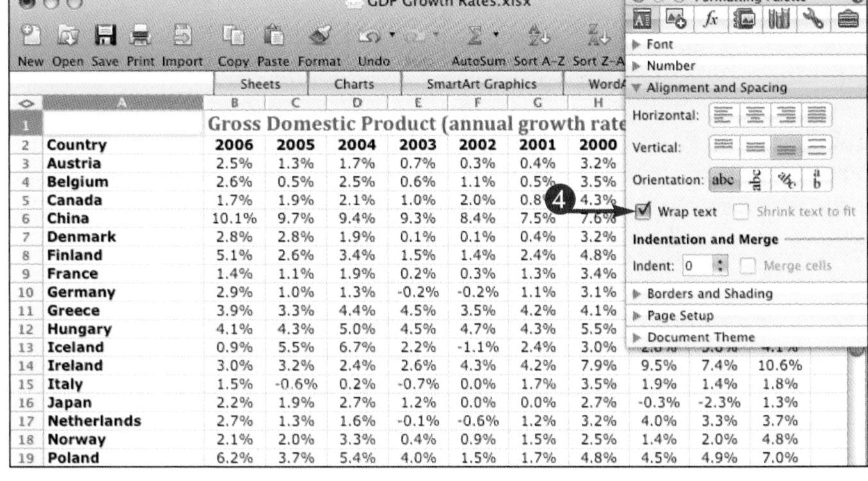


5 Type your text in the cell.

- If you type more text than can fit horizontally, Excel wraps the text onto multiple lines and increases the row height to compensate.

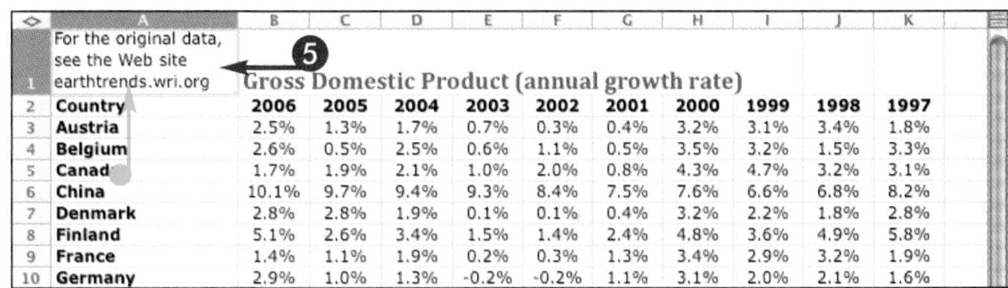

**My text is only slightly bigger than the cell. Is there a way to view the entire text without turning on text wrapping?**

Yes. There are several things you can try. For example, you can widen the column until you see all your text; see the section "Change the Column Width" earlier in this chapter. Alternatively, you can try reducing the cell font size. You can choose a smaller value in the Size list of the Formatting Palette's Font panel, but an easier way to do this is to select the **Shrink text to fit** (☐ changes to ☑) option in the Alignment and Spacing panel.

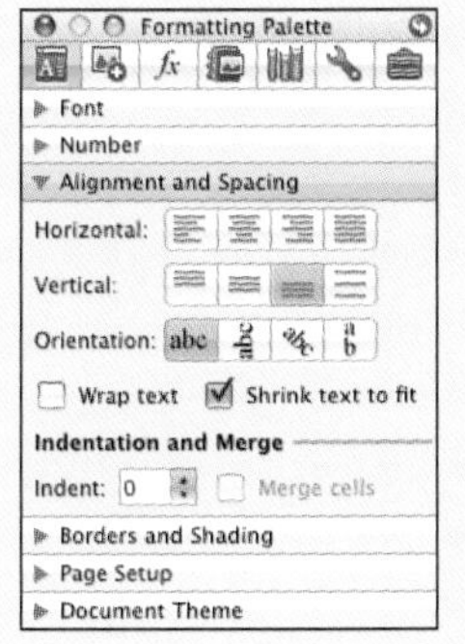

# Add Borders and Shading to a Range

You can make a range stand out from the rest of your worksheet data by adding a border around the range. You can also use borders to make a range easier to read. For example, if your range has totals on the bottom row, you can add a double border above the totals.

**To make a range stand out even more and to add visual appeal to your worksheet, you can add shading to the range. Shading applies a color or pattern to the background of the range.**

## Add Borders and Shading to a Range

1. Select the range that you want to format.
2. Display the Formatting Palette.

*Note: See Chapter 3 to learn how to display and hide the Formatting Palette.*

3. Click the **Borders and Shading** panel.
4. Click the **Type** and then click the type of border you want to use.

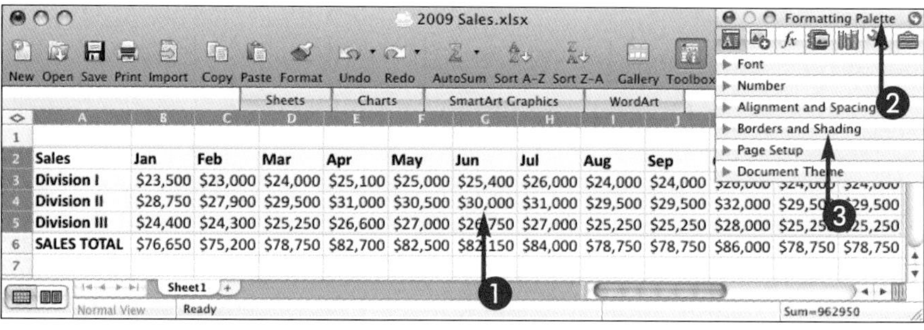

- Excel applies the border to the range.

5. Click the **Style** and then click a border style.

6. Click the **Color** and then click a border color.

7. In the Shading section, click the **Color** and then click a background color.

- If you want a pattern instead of a solid color, click **Pattern** and then click the pattern you want to use.

- Excel applies the color or pattern to the range background.

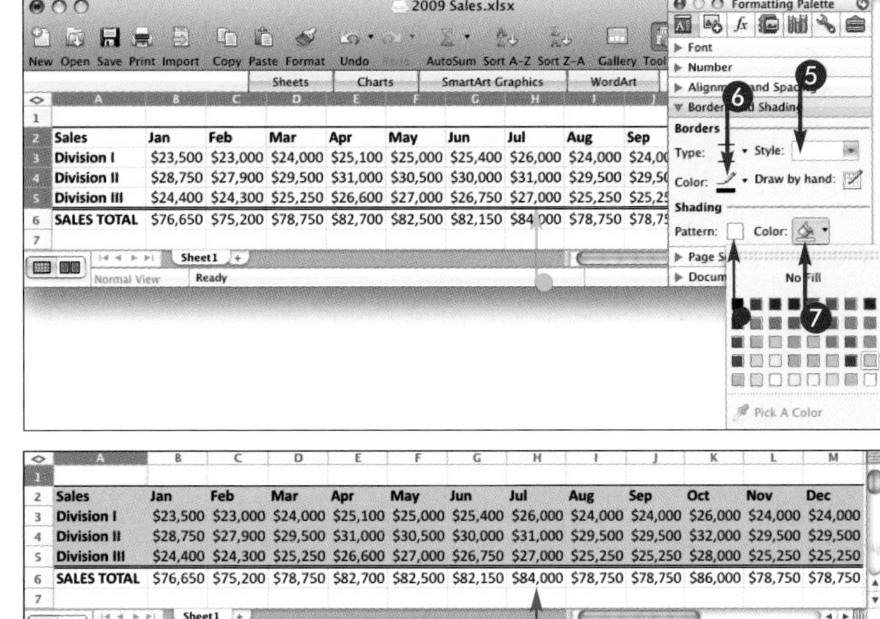

**How do I get my borders to stand out from the worksheet gridlines?**

One way to make your borders stand out is to click the **Style** and then click a thicker border style. You can also click the **Color** and then click a color that is not a shade of gray. However, perhaps the most effective method is to turn off the worksheet gridlines. Click **Excel**, click **Preferences**, and then click **View**. In the View preferences, deselect the **Show gridlines** check box (☑ changes to ☐), and then click **OK**.

**None of the border types is quite right for my worksheet. Can I create a custom border?**

Yes. You can draw the border by hand. In the Borders and Shading panel, click **Draw by hand** to display the Border Drawing toolbar. Use the toolbar's **Border Style** and **Border Color** lists to configure your border. Click a cell edge to add a border to that edge; click and drag a range to add a border around that range.

CHAPTER 13

# Manipulating Formulas and Functions

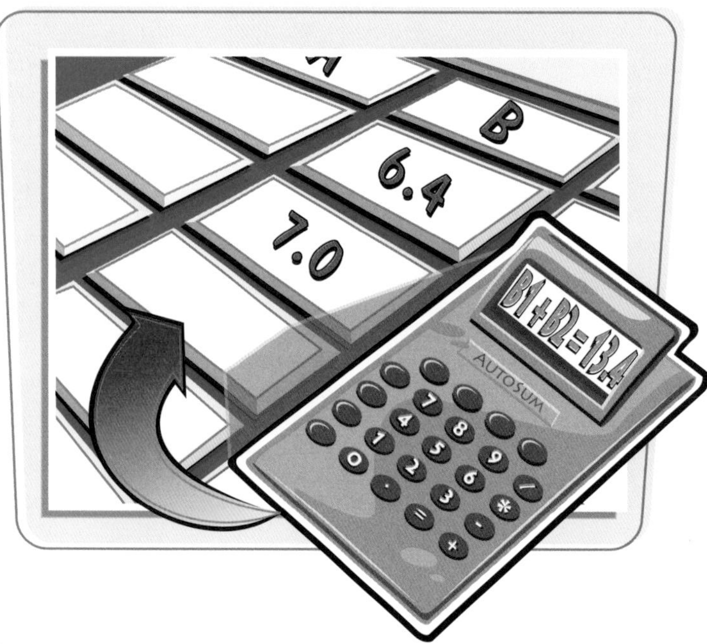


Although you can use Excel just to store data, you utilize the true power of the program when you add formulas and functions to your worksheets. Formulas and functions enable you to make fast and powerful calculations based on your worksheet data.

# Understanding Excel Formulas

**To get the most out of Excel, you need to understand formulas so that you can perform calculations on your worksheet data. You need to know the components of a formula, you need to understand arithmetic and comparison formulas, and you need to understand the importance of precedence when building a formula.**

## FORMULAS

A *formula* is a set of symbols and values that perform some kind of calculation and produce a result. All Excel formulas have the same general structure: an equal sign (=) followed by one or more operands and operators. The equal sign tells Excel to interpret everything that follows in the cell as a formula. For example, if you type =5+8 into a cell, Excel interprets the 5+8 text as a formula, and displays the result in the cell (13).

## OPERANDS

Every Excel formula includes one or more *operands*, which are the data that Excel uses in the calculation. The simplest type of operand is a constant value, which is usually a number. However, most Excel formulas include references to worksheet data, which can be a cell address (such as B1), a range address (such as B1: B5), or a range name. Finally, you can also use any of Excel's built-in functions as an operand.

## OPERATORS

In an Excel formula that contains two or more operands, each operand is separated by an *operator*, which is a symbol that combines the operands in some way, usually mathematically. Example operators include the plus sign (+) and the multiplication sign (*). For example, the formula =B1+B2 adds the values in cells B1 and B2.

## ARITHMETIC FORMULAS

An arithmetic formula combines numeric operands – numeric constants, functions that return numeric results, and fields or items that contain numeric values – with mathematical operators to perform a calculation. Because Excel worksheets primarily deal with numeric data, arithmetic formulas are by far the most common formulas used in worksheet calculations.

The following table lists the seven arithmetic operators that you can use to construct arithmetic formulas:

| *Operator* | *Name* | *Example* | *Result* |
|---|---|---|---|
| + | Addition | =10 + 5 | 15 |
| – | Subtraction | =10 – 5 | 5 |
| – | Negation | =–10 | –10 |
| * | Multiplication | =10 * 5 | 50 |
| / | Division | =10 / 5 | 2 |
| % | Percentage | =10% | 0.1 |
| ^ | Exponentiation | =10 ^ 5 | 100000 |

### COMPARISON FORMULAS

A comparison formula combines numeric operands — numeric constants, functions that return numeric results, and fields or items that contain numeric values — with special operators to compare one operand with another. A comparison formula always returns a logical result. This means that if the comparison is true, then the formula returns the value 1, which is equivalent to the logical value TRUE; if the comparison is false, instead, then the formula returns the value 0, which is equivalent to the logical value FALSE.

The following table lists the six operators that you can use to construct comparison formulas:

| ***Operator*** | ***Name*** | ***Example*** | ***Result*** |
|---|---|---|---|
| = | Equal to | =10 = 5 | 0 |
| < | Less than | =10 < 5 | 0 |
| <= | Less than or equal to | =10 <= 5 | 0 |
| > | Greater than | =10 > 5 | 1 |
| >= | Greater than or equal to | =10 >= 5 | 1 |
| <> | Not equal to | =10 <> 5 | 1 |

### OPERATOR PRECEDENCE

Most of your formulas include multiple operands and operators. In many cases, the order in which Excel performs the calculations is crucial. For example, consider the formula =3 + 5 ^ 2. If you calculate from left to right, the answer you get is 64 (3 + 5 equals 8, and 8 ^ 2 equals 64). However, if you perform the exponentiation first and then the addition, the result is 28 (5 ^ 2 equals 25, and 3 + 25 equals 28). Therefore, a single formula can produce multiple answers, depending on the order in which you perform the calculations.

To control this problem, Excel evaluates a formula according to a predefined order of precedence, which is determined by the formula operators, as shown in the following table:

| ***Operator*** | ***Operation*** | ***Precedence*** |
|---|---|---|
| () | Parentheses | 1st |
| – | Negation | 2nd |
| % | Percentage | 3rd |
| ^ | Exponentiation | 4th |
| * and / | Multiplication and division | 5th |
| + and – | Addition and subtraction | 6th |
| = < <= > >= <> | Comparison | 7th |

# Build a Formula

You can add a formula to a worksheet cell using a technique similar to adding data to a cell. To ensure that Excel treats the text as a formula, be sure to begin with an equal sign (=) and then type your operands and operators.

**When you add a formula to a cell, Excel displays the formula result in the cell, not the formula itself. For example, if you add the formula =C3+C4 to a cell, that cell displays the sum of the values in cells C3 and C4. To see the formula, click the cell and examine the Formula bar.**

## Build a Formula

1. Click in the cell in which you want to build the formula.
2. Type =.
   - Your typing also appears in the Formula bar.

***Note:** You can also type the formula into the Formula bar.*

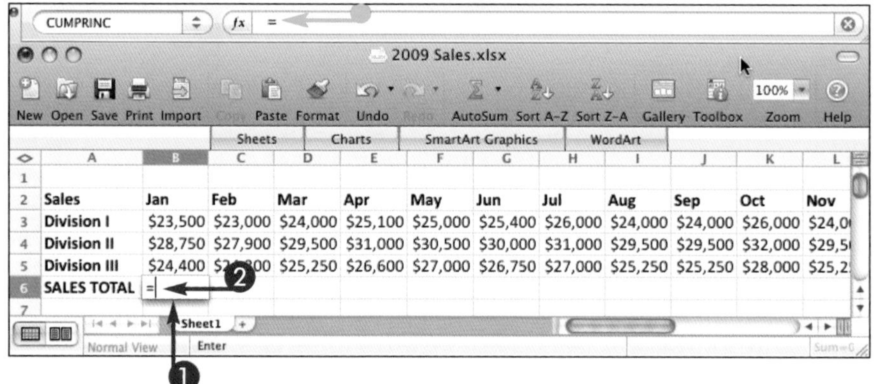


3. Type or click an operand. For example, to reference a cell in your formula, click in the cell.
   - Excel inserts the address of the clicked cell into the formula.

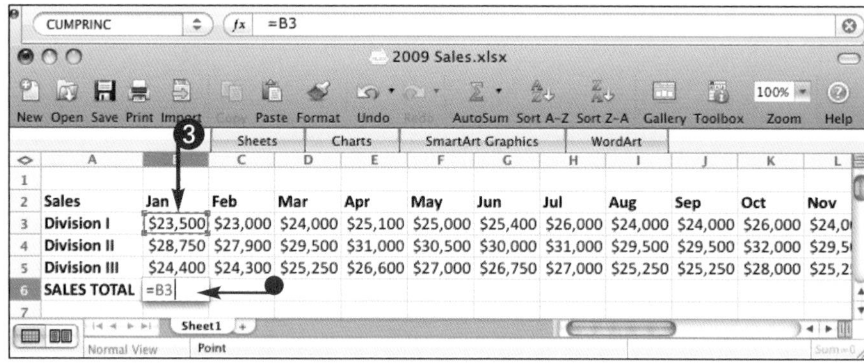

4 Type an operator.

5 Repeat Steps **3** and **4** to add other operands and operators to your formula.

6 Press Return.

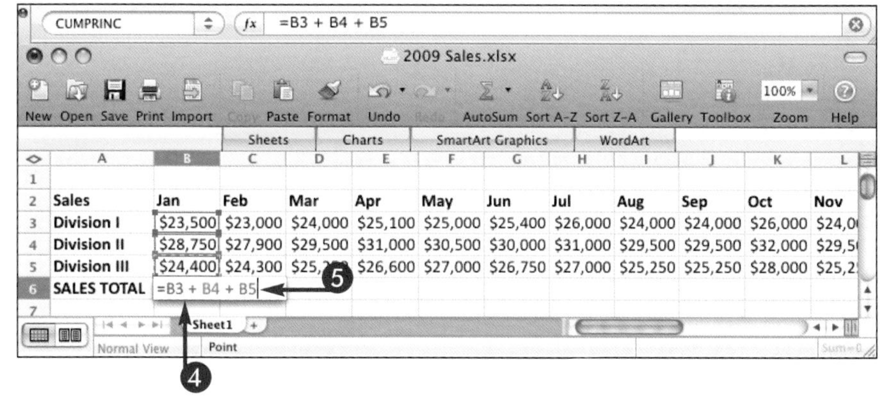


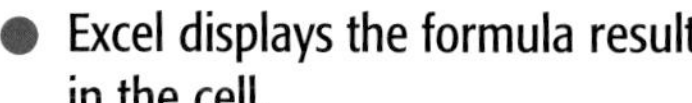

- Excel displays the formula result in the cell.

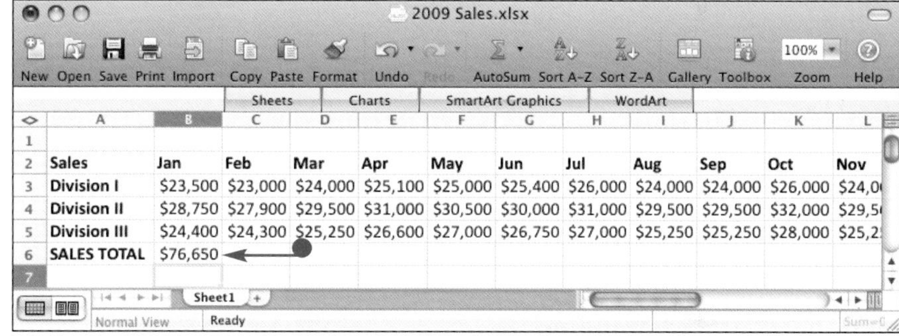


## TIPS

### If Excel only displays the result of the formula, how do I make changes to the formula?

Excel displays the formula result in the cell, but it still keeps tracks of the original formula. To display the formula again, you have two choices: click in the cell and then edit the formula using the Formula bar, or double-click in the cell to display the original formula in the cell and then edit the formula. In both cases, press Return when you finish editing the formula.

### I have a lot of formulas in my worksheet. Is there an easy way to view all of my formulas?

Yes. You can configure the worksheet to show the formulas instead of their results. Click **Excel**, click **Preferences**, and then click **View** to open the View preferences. Select the **Show formulas** option (☐ changes to ☑), and then click **OK**. An even easier way to toggle between formulas and results is to press Ctrl + '.

# Understanding Excel Functions

**To build powerful and useful formulas, you often need to include one or more Excel functions as operands. You need to understand the advantages of using functions, you need to know the basic structure of every function, and you need to review Excel's function types.**

## FUNCTIONS

A *function* is a predefined formula that performs a specific task. For example, the SUM function calculates the total of a list of numbers, and the PMT (payment) function calculates a loan or mortgage payment. You can use functions on their own, preceded by =, or as part of a larger formula.

## FUNCTION ADVANTAGES

Functions are designed to take you beyond the basic arithmetic and comparison formulas by offering two main advantages. First, functions make simple but cumbersome formulas easier to use. For example, calculating a loan payment requires a complex formula, but Excel's PMT function makes this easy. Second, functions enable you to include complex mathematical expressions in your worksheets that otherwise are difficult or impossible to construct using simple arithmetic operators.

## FUNCTION STRUCTURE

Every worksheet function has the same basic structure: NAME(Argument1, Argument2, ...). The NAME part identifies the function. In worksheet formulas and custom PivotTable formulas, the function name always appears in uppercase letters: PMT, SUM, AVERAGE, and so on. The items that appear within the parentheses are the functions' *arguments*. The arguments are the inputs that functions use to perform calculations. For example, the function SUM(A1,B2,B3) adds the values in cells A1, B2, and C3.

## MATHEMATICAL FUNCTIONS

The following table lists some common mathematical functions.

| *Function* | *Description* |
|---|---|
| MOD(number,divisor) | Returns the remainder of number after dividing by divisor |
| PI() | Returns the value Pi |
| PRODUCT(number1,number2,...) | Multiplies the specified numbers |
| RAND() | Returns a random number between 0 and 1 |
| RANDBETWEEN(number1,number2) | Returns a random number between the two numbers |
| ROUND(number,digits) | Rounds number to a specified number of digits |
| SQRT(number) | Returns the positive square root of number |
| SUM(number1,number2,...) | Adds the arguments |

## STATISTICAL FUNCTIONS

The following table lists some common statistical functions.

| ***Function*** | ***Description*** |
|---|---|
| AVERAGE(number1,number2,...) | Returns the average of the arguments |
| COUNT(number1,number2,...) | Counts the numbers in the argument list |
| MAX(number1,number2,...) | Returns the maximum value of the arguments |
| MEDIAN(number1,number2,...) | Returns the median value of the arguments |
| MIN(number1,number2,...) | Returns the minimum value of the arguments |
| MODE(number1,number2,...) | Returns the most common value of the arguments |
| STDEV(number1,number2,...) | Returns the standard deviation based on a sample |
| STDEVP(number1,number2,...) | Returns the standard deviation based on an entire population |

## FINANCIAL FUNCTIONS

Most of Excel's financial functions use the following arguments.

| ***Argument*** | ***Description*** |
|---|---|
| rate | The fixed rate of interest over the term of the loan or investment |
| nper | The number of payments or deposit periods over the term of the loan or investment |
| pmt | The periodic payment or deposit |
| pv | The present value of the loan (the principal) or the initial deposit in an investment |
| fv | The future value of the loan or investment |
| type | The type of payment or deposit: 0 (the default) for end-of-period payments or deposits; 1 for beginning-of-period payments or deposits |

The following table lists some common financial functions.

| ***Function*** | ***Description*** |
|---|---|
| FV(rate,nper,pmt,pv,type) | Returns the future value of an investment or loan |
| IPMT(rate,per,nper,pv,fv,type) | Returns the interest payment for a specified period of a loan |
| NPER(rate,pmt,pv,fv,type) | Returns the number of periods for an investment or loan |
| PMT(rate,nper,pv,fv,type) | Returns the periodic payment for a loan or investment |
| PPMT(rate,per,nper,pv,fv,type) | Returns the principal payment for a specified period of a loan |
| PV(rate,nper,pmt,fv,type) | Returns the present value of an investment |
| RATE(nper,pmt,pv,fv,type,guess) | Returns the periodic interest rate for a loan or investment |

# Build an AutoSum Formula

You can reduce the time it takes to build a worksheet as well as reduce the possibility of errors by using Excel's AutoSum feature. This tool adds a SUM function formula to a cell and automatically adds the function arguments based on the structure of the worksheet data.

## Build an AutoSum Formula

1. Click in the cell where you want the sum to appear.

*Note: For AutoSum to work, the cell you select should be below or to the right of the range you want to sum.*

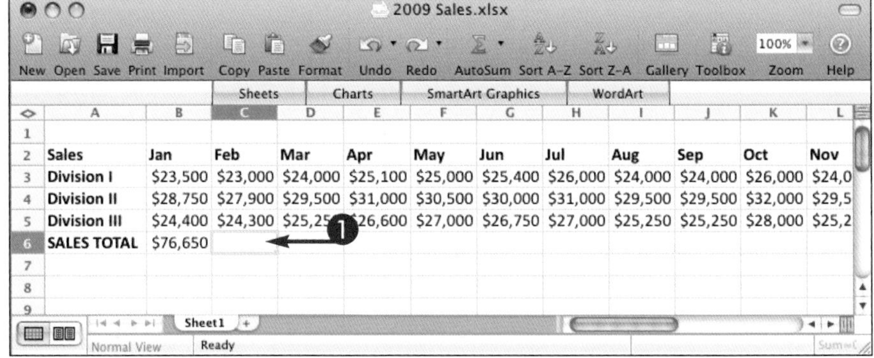


2. Click the **AutoSum** button ().

- If you want to use a function other than SUM, click the **AutoSum** and then click the operation you want to use: Average, Count Numbers, Max, or Min.

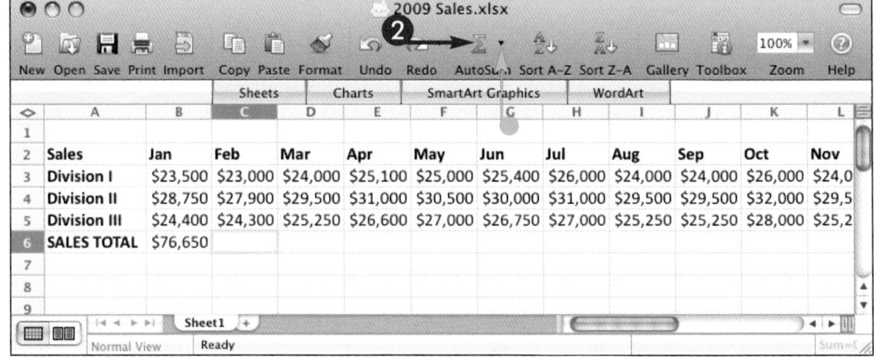

- Excel adds a SUM function formula to the cell.
- Excel guesses that the range above (or to the left) of the cell is the one you want to add.

  If Excel guessed wrong, select the correct range.

3 Press Return.

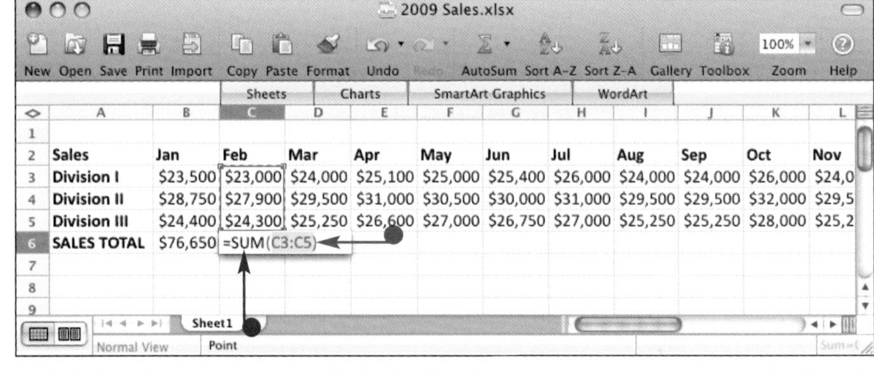


- Excel displays the sum.

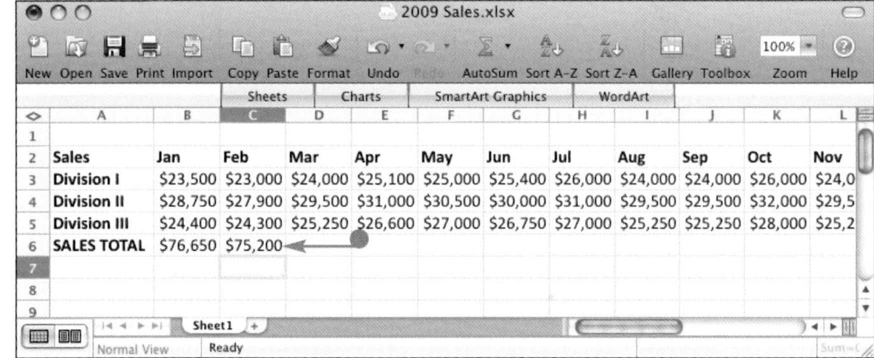

**Is there a way to see the sum of a range without adding an AutoSum formula?**

Yes. You can use Excel's status bar to do this. When you select any range, Excel adds the range's numeric values and displays the result on the right side of the status bar — for example, Sum=257. If you want to see a different calculation, click the result in the status bar and then click the operation you want to use: Average, Count, Count Nums (count the numeric values in the range), Max, or Min.

**Is there a faster way to add an AutoSum formula?**

Yes. If you know the range you want to sum, and that range is either a vertical column with a blank cell below it or a horizontal row with a blank cell to its right, select the range and then click the AutoSum button. Excel populates the blank cell with an AutoSum formula that totals the selected range.

# Add a Function to a Formula

To get the benefit of an Excel function, you need to use it within a formula. You can use a function as the only operand in the formula, or you can include the function as part of a larger formula.

**To make it easy to choose the function you need and to add the appropriate arguments, Excel offers the Formula Builder palette.**

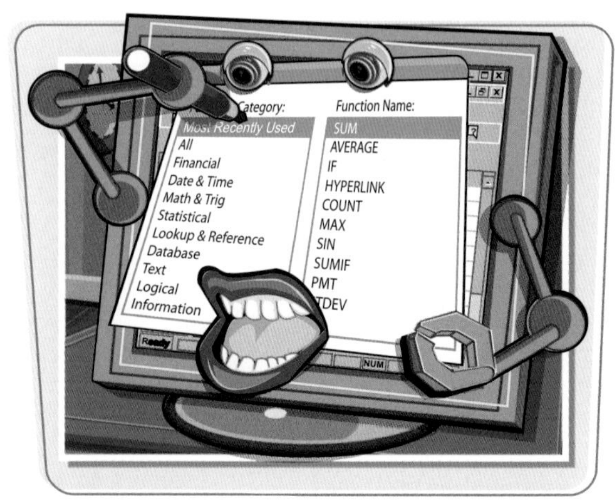


## Add a Function to a Formula

1. Click in the cell in which you want to build the formula.
2. Type **=**.
3. Type any operands and operators you need before adding the function.
4. Click the **Formula Builder** button (fx).

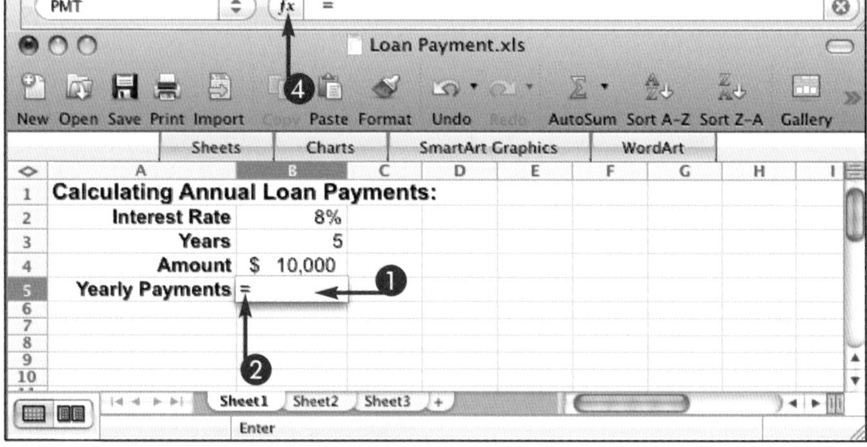


The Formula Builder appears.

- Excel's functions are listed here by category.

5. Locate the function you want to add and then double-click the function.

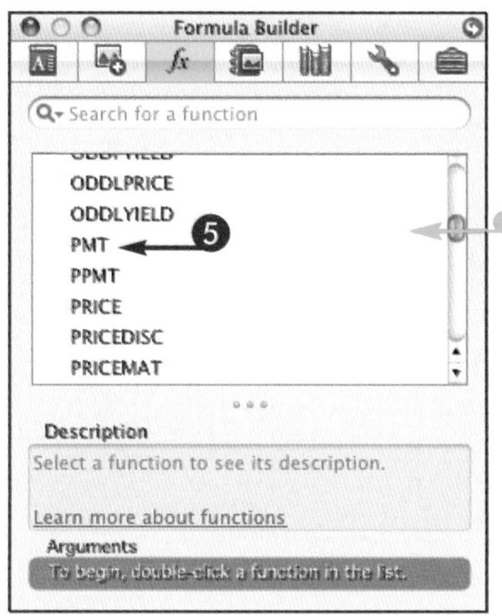

- The Formula Builder displays the function arguments.

6 Click inside an argument box.

7 Click the cell that contains the argument value.

   You can also type the argument value.

8 Repeat Steps **6** and **7** to fill as many arguments as you need.

- The function result appears here.

9 Type any operands and operators you need to complete your formula.

10 Press Return.

- Excel displays the formula result.

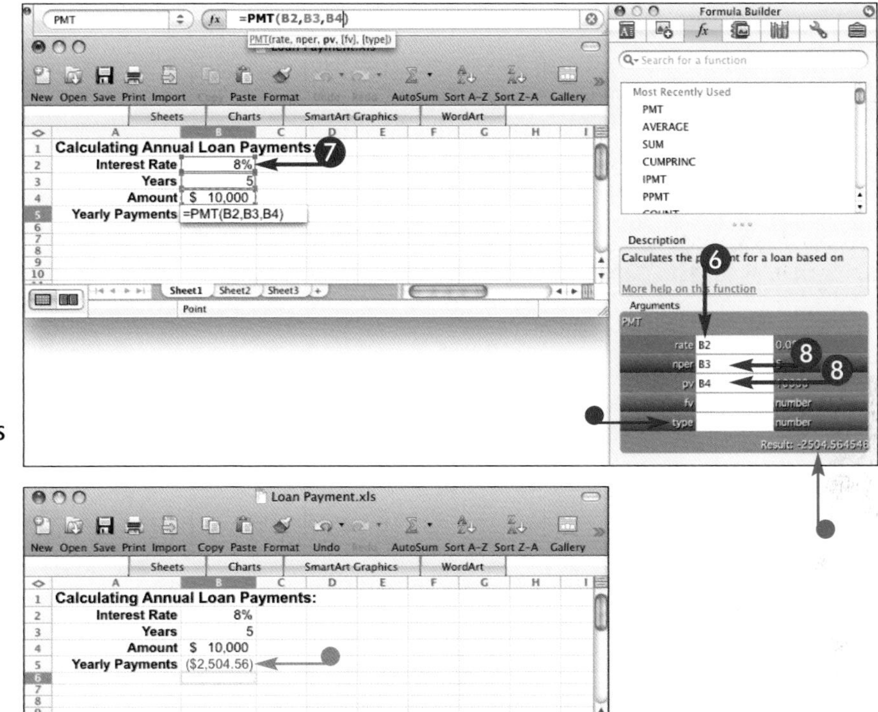


## TIPS

### Do I have to specify a value for every function argument?

Not necessarily. Some function arguments are required to obtain a result, but some are optional. In the PMT function, for example, the rate, nper, and pv arguments are required, but the fv and type arguments are optional. When the Formula Builder displays a result for the function, then you know you have entered all of the required arguments.

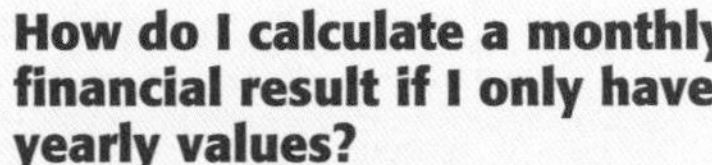

### How do I calculate a monthly financial result if I only have yearly values?

This is a common problem. For example, if your loan payment worksheet contains an annual interest rate and a loan term in years, how do you calculate the monthly payment using the PMT function? You need to convert the rate and term to monthly values. That is, you divide the annual interest rate by 12, and you multiply the term by 12. For example, if the annual rate is in cell B2, the term in years is in B3, and the loan amount is in B4, the function PMT(B2/12, B3*12, B4) calculates the monthly payment.

# Add a Range Name to a Formula

You can make your formulas easier to build, more accurate, and easier to read by using range names as operands. For example, the formula =SUM(B2:B10) is difficult to decipher on its own, but the formula =SUM(Expenses) is immediately obvious.

**See Chapter 11 to learn how to define names for ranges in Excel.**

## Add a Range Name to a Formula

1. Click in the cell in which you want to build the formula, type **=**, and then type any operands and operators you need before adding the range name.
2. Click **Insert**.
3. Click **Name**.
4. Click **Paste**.

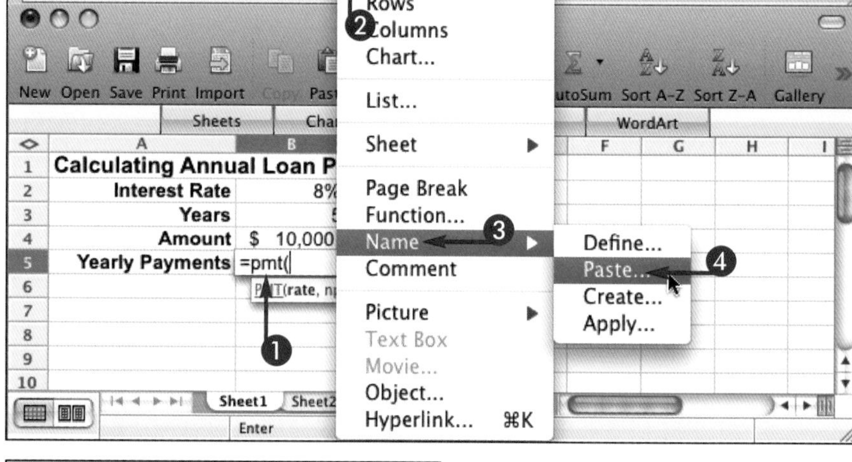

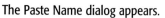

The Paste Name dialog appears.

5. In the Paste name list, click the range name you want to use.
6. Click **OK**.

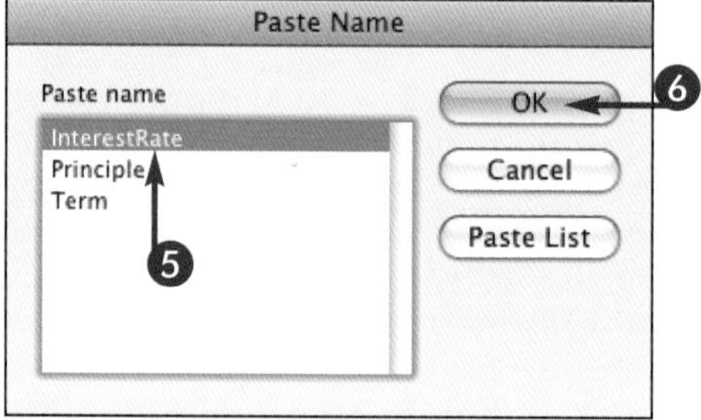

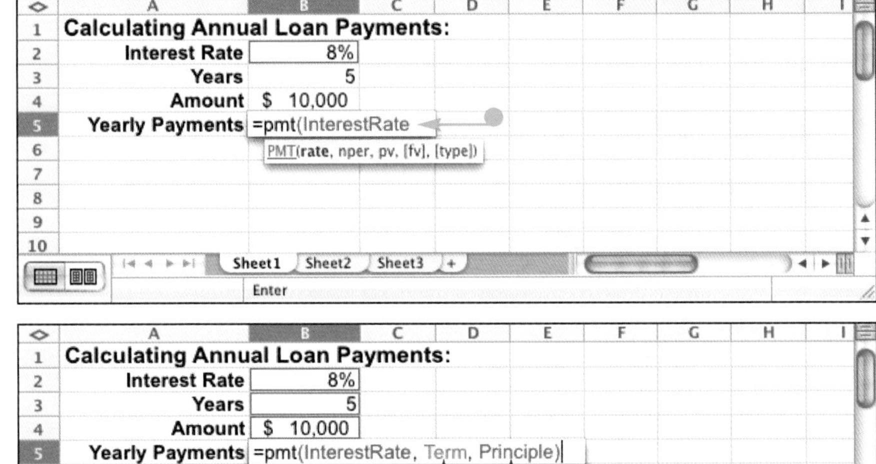


- Excel inserts the range name into the formula.

7. Type any operands and operators you need to complete your formula.

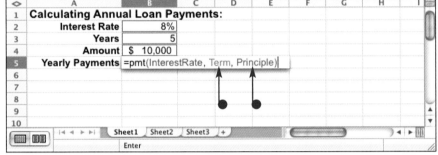

- If you need to insert other range names into your formula, repeat Steps **2** to **6** for each name.

8. Press Return.

Excel calculates the formula result.

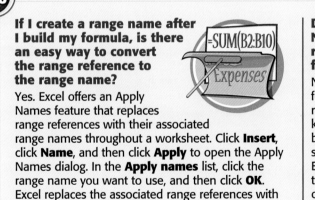

**If I create a range name after I build my formula, is there an easy way to convert the range reference to the range name?**

Yes. Excel offers an Apply Names feature that replaces range references with their associated range names throughout a worksheet. Click **Insert**, click **Name**, and then click **Apply** to open the Apply Names dialog. In the **Apply names** list, click the range name you want to use, and then click **OK**. Excel replaces the associated range references with the range name in each formula in the current worksheet.

**Do I have to use the Paste Names dialog to insert range names into my formulas?**

No. As you build your formula, you can type the range name by hand, if you know it. Alternatively, as you build your formula, click the cell or select the range that has the defined name, and Excel adds the name to your formula instead of the range address. If you want to work from a list of the defined range names, click an empty area of the worksheet, click **Insert**, click **Name**, click **Paste**, and then click **Paste List**.

# Reference another Worksheet Range in a Formula

You can add flexibility to your formulas by adding references to ranges that reside in other worksheets. This enables you to take advantage of work you have done in other worksheets, so you do not have to waste time repeating your work on the current worksheet.

## Reference another Worksheet Range in a Formula

1. Click in the cell in which you want to build the formula, type **=**, and then type any operands and operators you need before adding the range reference.

| | A | M | N | O | P | Q | R | S | T | U |
|---|---|---|---|---|---|---|---|---|---|---|
| 1 | | 3rd Quarter | Oct | Nov | Dec | 4th Quarter | TOTAL | | | |
| 2 | *Sales* | | | | | | | | | |
| 3 | Division I | 74,000 | 26,000 | 24,000 | 24,000 | 74,000 | 294,000 | | | |
| 4 | Division II | 90,000 | 32,000 | 29,500 | 29,500 | 91,000 | 358,550 | | | |
| 5 | Division III | 77,500 | 28,000 | 25,250 | 25,250 | 78,500 | 310,000 | | | |
| 6 | SALES TOTAL | 241,500 | 86,000 | 78,750 | 78,750 | 243,500 | 962,550 | | | |
| 7 | *Expenses* | | | | | | | | | |
| 8 | Cost of Goods | 19,320 | 6,880 | 6,300 | 6,300 | 19,480 | 77,004 | | | |
| 9 | Advertising | 15,900 | 4,500 | 5,200 | 5,200 | 14,900 | 60,550 | | | |
| 10 | Rent | 6,300 | 2,100 | 2,100 | 2,100 | 6,300 | 25,200 | | | |
| 11 | Supplies | 4,100 | 1,250 | 1,350 | 1,400 | 4,000 | 15,950 | | | |
| 12 | Salaries | 51,000 | 17,000 | 17,500 | 17,500 | 52,000 | 201,500 | | | |
| 13 | Shipping | 44,000 | 15,750 | 15,250 | 14,500 | 45,500 | 176,250 | | | |
| 14 | Utilities | 1,850 | 650 | 600 | 600 | 1,850 | 7,200 | | | |
| 15 | EXPENSES TOTAL | 142,470 | 48,130 | 48,300 | 47,600 | 144,030 | 563,654 | | | |
| 16 | GROSS PROFIT | 99,030 | 37,870 | 30,450 | 31,150 | 99,470 | 398,896 | | | |
| 17 | | | Difference from Last Year's Profit: | | | | =R16 - | | | |
| 18 | | | | | | | | | | |

Budget | Assumptions | Projections | 2008-2009 Final | Estin

Normal View | Enter | Sum=0

2. Press Ctrl + Page down until the worksheet you want to use appears.

| | A | B | C | D | E | F | G | H | I |
|---|---|---|---|---|---|---|---|---|---|
| 1 | | Jan | Feb | Mar | 1st Quarter | Apr | May | Jun | 2nd Quarter |
| 2 | *Sales* | | | | | | | | |
| 3 | Division I | 21,620 | 21,160 | 22,080 | 64,860 | 23,092 | 23,000 | 23,368 | 69,460 |
| 4 | Division II | 26,450 | 25,576 | 27,140 | 79,166 | 28,520 | 28,060 | 27,600 | 84,180 |
| 5 | Division III | 22,448 | 22,080 | 23,230 | 67,758 | 24,472 | 24,840 | 24,610 | 73,922 |
| 6 | SALES TOTAL | 70,518 | 68,816 | 72,450 | 211,784 | 76,084 | 75,900 | 75,578 | 227,562 |
| 7 | *Expenses* | | | | | | | | |
| 8 | Cost of Goods | 5,924 | 5,781 | 6,086 | 17,790 | 6,391 | 6,376 | 6,349 | 19,115 |
| 9 | Advertising | 4,830 | 4,410 | 5,460 | 14,700 | 5,250 | 5,775 | 5,513 | 16,538 |
| 10 | Rent | 2,205 | 2,205 | 2,205 | 6,615 | 2,205 | 2,205 | 2,205 | 6,615 |
| 11 | Supplies | 1,365 | 1,260 | 1,470 | 4,095 | 1,365 | 1,313 | 1,470 | 4,148 |
| 12 | Salaries | 16,800 | 16,800 | 17,325 | 50,925 | 17,325 | 17,325 | 17,850 | 52,500 |
| 13 | Shipping | 14,963 | 14,438 | 15,225 | 44,625 | 15,750 | 15,225 | 15,488 | 46,463 |
| 14 | Utilities | 525 | 630 | 630 | 1,785 | 578 | 630 | 683 | 1,890 |
| 15 | EXPENSES TOTAL | 46,611 | 45,523 | 48,401 | 140,535 | 48,864 | 48,848 | 49,556 | 147,268 |
| 16 | GROSS PROFIT | 23,907 | 23,293 | 24,049 | 71,249 | 27,220 | 27,052 | 26,022 | 80,294 |
| 17 | | | | | | | | | |
| 18 | | | | | | | | | |

Budget | Assumptions | Projections | 2008-2009 Final

Normal View | Point | Sum=0

3. Select the range you want to use.
4. Press Ctrl + Page up until you return to the original worksheet.

| | A | M | N | O | P | Q | R | S | T |
|---|---|---|---|---|---|---|---|---|---|
| 1 | | 3rd Quarter | Oct | Nov | Dec | 4th Quarter | TOTAL | | |
| 2 | *Sales* | | | | | | | | |
| 3 | Division I | 68,080 | 23,920 | 22,080 | 22,080 | 68,080 | 270,480 | | |
| 4 | Division II | 82,800 | 29,440 | 27,140 | 27,140 | 83,720 | 329,866 | | |
| 5 | Division III | 71,300 | 25,760 | 23,230 | 23,230 | 72,220 | 285,200 | | |
| 6 | SALES TOTAL | 222,180 | 79,120 | 72,450 | 72,450 | 224,020 | 885,546 | | |
| 7 | *Expenses* | | | | | | | | |
| 8 | Cost of Goods | 18,663 | 6,646 | 6,086 | 6,086 | 18,818 | 74,386 | | |
| 9 | Advertising | 16,695 | 4,725 | 5,460 | 5,460 | 15,645 | 63,578 | | |
| 10 | Rent | 6,615 | 2,205 | 2,205 | 2,205 | 6,615 | 26,460 | | |
| 11 | Supplies | 4,305 | 1,313 | 1,418 | 1,470 | 4,200 | 16,748 | | |
| 12 | Salaries | 53,550 | 17,850 | 18,375 | 18,375 | 54,600 | 211,575 | | |
| 13 | Shipping | 46,200 | 16,538 | 16,013 | 15,225 | 47,775 | 185,063 | | |
| 14 | Utilities | 1,943 | 683 | 630 | 630 | 1,943 | 7,560 | | |
| 15 | EXPENSES TOTAL | 147,971 | 49,959 | 50,186 | 49,451 | 149,595 | 585,368 | | |
| 16 | GROSS PROFIT | 74,209 | 29,161 | 22,264 | 22,999 | 74,425 | 300,178 | | |
| 17 | | | | | | | | | |
| 18 | | | | | | | | | |

Budget | Assumptions | Projections | 2008-2009 Final | Estin

Normal View | Point

- A reference to the range on the other worksheet appears in your formula.

5. Type any operands and operators you need to complete your formula.
6. Press Return.

Excel calculates the formula result.

| | A | M | N | O | P | Q | R | S | T | U |
|---|---|---|---|---|---|---|---|---|---|---|
| 1 | | 3rd Quarter | Oct | Nov | Dec | 4th Quarter | TOTAL | | | |
| 2 | *Sales* | | | | | | | | | |
| 3 | Division I | 74,000 | 26,000 | 24,000 | 24,000 | 74,000 | 294,000 | | | |
| 4 | Division II | 90,000 | 32,000 | 29,500 | 29,500 | 91,000 | 358,550 | | | |
| 5 | Division III | 77,500 | 28,000 | 25,250 | 25,250 | 78,500 | 310,000 | | | |
| 6 | SALES TOTAL | 241,500 | 86,000 | 78,750 | 78,750 | 243,500 | 962,550 | | | |
| 7 | *Expenses* | | | | | | | | | |
| 8 | Cost of Goods | 19,320 | 6,880 | 6,300 | 6,300 | 19,480 | 77,004 | | | |
| 9 | Advertising | 15,900 | 4,500 | 5,200 | 5,200 | 14,900 | 60,550 | | | |
| 10 | Rent | 6,300 | 2,100 | 2,100 | 2,100 | 6,300 | 25,200 | | | |
| 11 | Supplies | 4,100 | 1,250 | 1,350 | 1,400 | 4,000 | 15,950 | | | |
| 12 | Salaries | 51,000 | 17,000 | 17,500 | 17,500 | 52,000 | 201,500 | | | |
| 13 | Shipping | 44,000 | 15,750 | 15,250 | 14,500 | 45,500 | 176,250 | | | |
| 14 | Utilities | 1,850 | 650 | 600 | 600 | 1,850 | 7,200 | | | |
| 15 | EXPENSES TOTAL | 142,470 | 48,130 | 48,300 | 47,600 | 144,030 | 563,654 | | | |
| 16 | GROSS PROFIT | 99,030 | 37,870 | 30,450 | 31,150 | 99,470 | 398,896 | | | |
| 17 | | | | | | Difference from Last Year's Profit: | =R16 - '2008-2009 Final'!R16 | | | |
| 18 | | | | | | | | | | |

Budget | Assumptions | Projections | 2008-2009 Final | Estin

Normal View | Point

### Can I reference a range in another worksheet by hand?

Yes. Rather than selecting the other worksheet range with your mouse, you can type the range reference directly into your formula. Type the worksheet name, surrounded by single quotation marks (') if the name contains a space; type an exclamation mark (!); then type the cell or range address. Here is an example: 'Expenses 2009'!B2:B10.

### Can I reference a range in another workbook in my formula?

Yes. First make sure the workbook you want to reference is open. When you reach the point in your formula where you want to add the reference, click **Window** and then click the other workbook to switch to it. Click the worksheet that has the range you want to reference, and then select the range. Click **Window** and then click the original workbook to switch back to it. Excel adds the other workbook range reference to your formula.

# Move or Copy a Formula

You can restructure or reorganize a worksheet by moving an existing formula to a different part of the worksheet. When you move a formula, Excel preserves the formula's range references.

**Excel also enables you to make a copy of a formula, which is a useful technique if you require a duplicate of the formula elsewhere or if you require a formula that is similar to an existing formula. When you copy a formula, Excel adjusts the range references to the new location.**

## Move or Copy a Formula

### MOVE A FORMULA

1. Select the cell that contains the formula you want to move.
2. Position ✥ over any outside border of the cell.

   ✥ changes to ✋.
3. Click and drag the cell to the new location.

- Excel displays an outline of the cell.
- Excel displays the address of the new location.

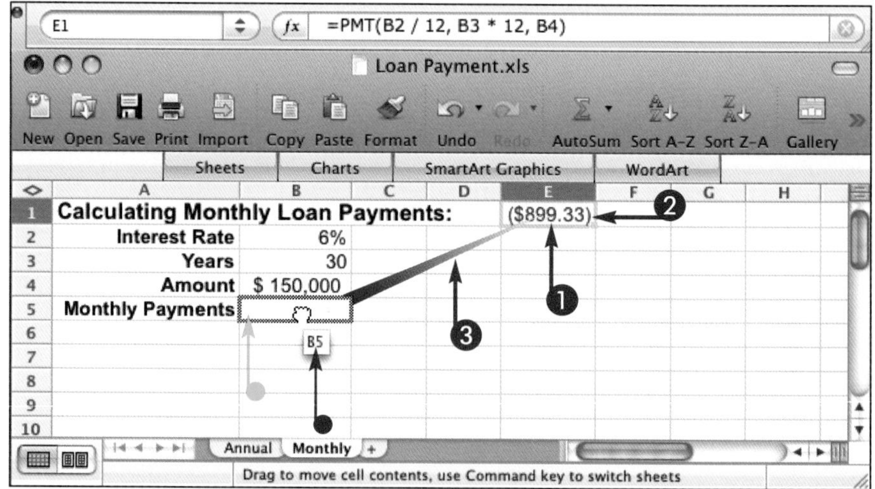


4. Release the mouse button.

- Excel moves the formula to the new location.

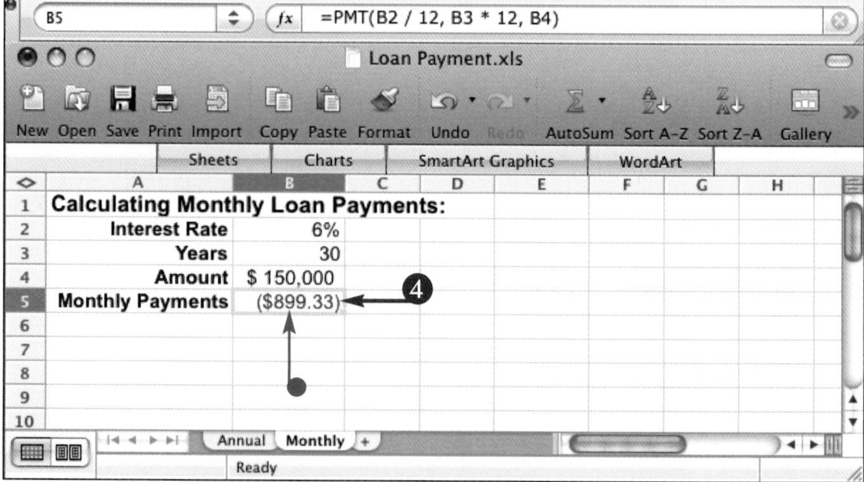

## COPY A FORMULA

1. Select the cell that contains the formula you want to copy.
2. Press and hold Option.
3. Position ✥ over any outside border of the cell.

   ✥ changes to ☝.
4. Click and drag the cell to the location where you want the copy to appear.

- Excel displays an outline of the cell.
- Excel displays the address of the new location.

5. Release the mouse button.
6. Release Option.

- Excel creates a copy of the formula in the new location.
- Excel adjusts the range references.

***Note:*** *You can make multiple copies by dragging the bottom-right corner of the cell. Excel fills the adjacent cells with copies of the formula. See the section "Switch to Absolute Cell References" for an example.*

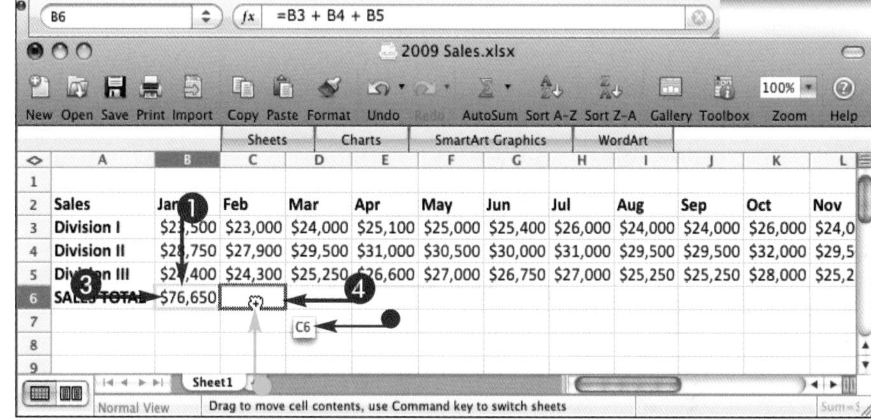


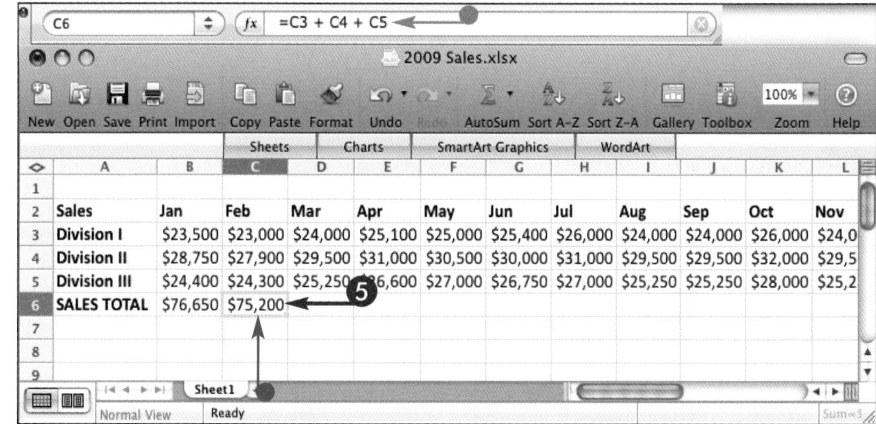

### Why does Excel adjust the range references when I copy a formula?

When you make a copy of a formula, Excel assumes that you want that copy to reference different ranges than in the original formula. In particular, Excel assumes that the ranges you want to use in the new formula are positioned relative to the ranges used in the original formula, and that the relative difference is equal to the number of rows and columns you dragged the cell to create the copy.

For example, suppose your original formula references cell A1, and you make a copy of the formula in the cell one column to the right. In that case, Excel also adjusts the cell reference one column to the right, so it becomes B1 in the new formula. To learn how to control this behavior, see the section "Switch to Absolute Cell References."

# Switch to Absolute Cell References

You can make some formulas easier to copy by switching to absolute cell references. When you use a regular cell address — called a *relative cell reference* — such as A1 in a formula, Excel adjusts that reference when you copy the formula to another location. To prevent that reference from changing, you must change it to the *absolute cell reference* format: $A$1.

**See the tip on the following page to learn more about the difference between relative and absolute cell references.**

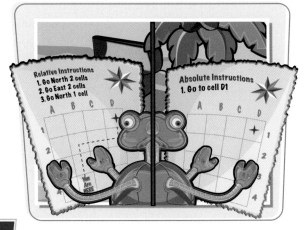

## Switch Between Relative and Absolute Cell References

1. Double-click the cell that contains the formula you want to edit.
2. Select the cell reference you want to change.
3. Press ⌘ + T.

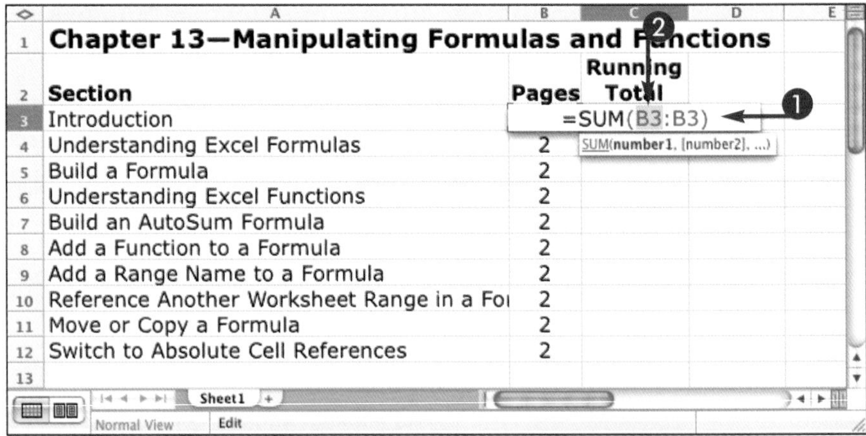


- Excel switches the address to an absolute cell reference.

4. Repeat Steps **2** and **3** to switch any other cell addresses that you require in the absolute reference format.
5. Press Return.

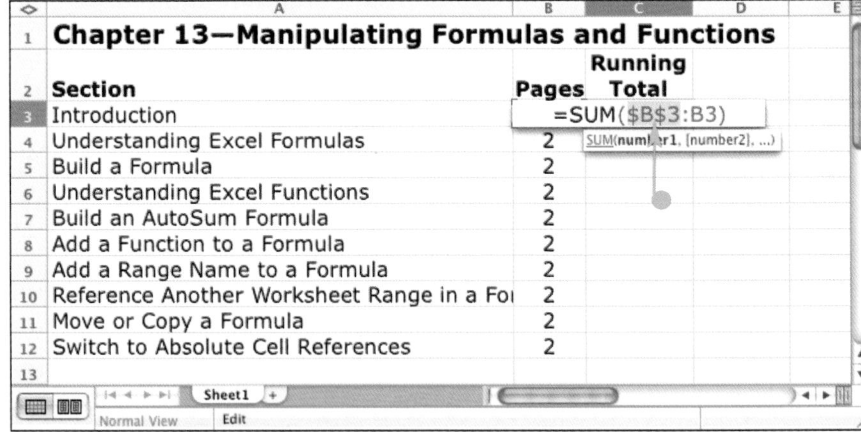

Excel adjusts the formula.

6 Copy the formula.

***Note:*** *See the section "Move or Copy a Formula" to learn how to copy a formula.*

| | A | B | C | D | E |
|---|---|---|---|---|---|
| 1 | **Chapter 13—Manipulating Formulas and Functions** | | | | |
| 2 | **Section** | **Pages** | **Running Total** | | |
| 3 | Introduction | 2 | 2 | | |
| 4 | Understanding Excel Formulas | 2 | | | |
| 5 | Build a Formula | 2 | | | |
| 6 | Understanding Excel Functions | 2 | | | |
| 7 | Build an AutoSum Formula | 2 | | | |
| 8 | Add a Function to a Formula | 2 | | | |
| 9 | Add a Range Name to a Formula | 2 | | | |
| 10 | Reference Another Worksheet Range in a Fo | 2 | | | |
| 11 | Move or Copy a Formula | 2 | | | |
| 12 | Switch to Absolute Cell References | 2 | | | |
| 13 | | | | | |

Sheet1

Normal View — Drag outside selection to extend series or fill; drag inside to clear

6

- Excel preserves the absolute cell references in the copied formulas.

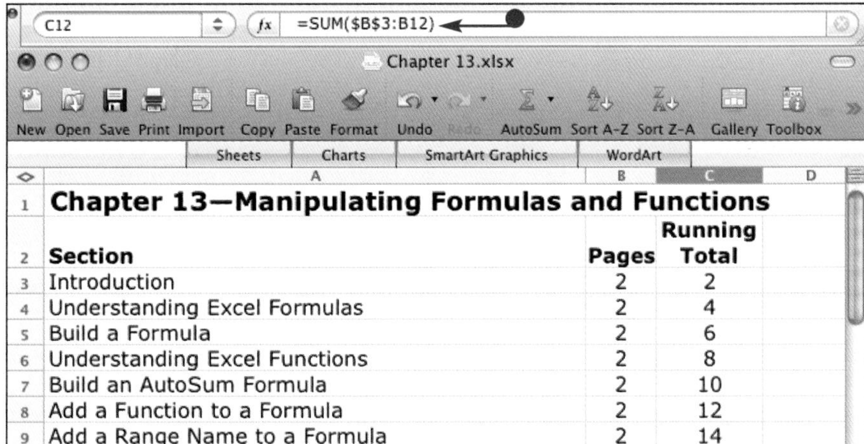


| | A | B | C | D |
|---|---|---|---|---|
| 1 | **Chapter 13—Manipulating Formulas and Functions** | | | |
| 2 | **Section** | **Pages** | **Running Total** | |
| 3 | Introduction | 2 | 2 | |
| 4 | Understanding Excel Formulas | 2 | 4 | |
| 5 | Build a Formula | 2 | 6 | |
| 6 | Understanding Excel Functions | 2 | 8 | |
| 7 | Build an AutoSum Formula | 2 | 10 | |
| 8 | Add a Function to a Formula | 2 | 12 | |
| 9 | Add a Range Name to a Formula | 2 | 14 | |

## TIPS

### What is the difference between absolute cell references and relative cell references?

When you use a cell reference in a formula, Excel treats that reference as being relative to the formula's cell. For example, if the formula is in B5 and it references cell A1, Excel effectively treats A1 as the cell four rows up and one column to the left. If you copy the formula to cell D10, then the cell four rows up and one column to the left now refers to cell C6, so in the copied formula Excel changes A1 to C6. If the original formula instead refers to $A$1, then the copied formula in cell D10 also refers to $A$1.

### How do I return a cell address back to a relative cell reference?

The ⌘+T keyboard technique actually runs the address through four different reference formats. Press ⌘+T once to switch to the absolute cell reference format, such as $A$1. Press ⌘+T again to switch to a mixed reference format that uses a relative column and absolute row (A$1). Press ⌘+T a third time to switch to a mixed reference format that uses an absolute column and relative row ($A1). Finally, press ⌘+T a fourth time to return to the relative cell reference (A1).

CHAPTER

14

# Visualizing Data with Excel Charts

You can take a worksheet full of numbers and display them as a chart. Visualizing your data in this way makes the data easier to understand and easier to analyze. To help you see your data exactly the way you want, Excel offers a wide variety of chart types, and a large number of chart options.

# Create a Chart

You can create a chart from your Excel worksheet data with just a few mouse clicks. Excel offers more than 70 chart types, so there should always be a type that best visualizes your data.

**Regardless of the chart type you choose originally, you can change to a different chart type at any time. See the section "Select a Different Chart Type."**

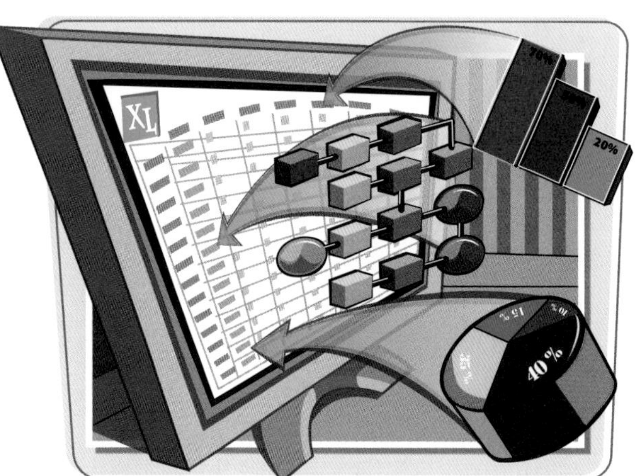

## Create a Chart

1. Select the data that you want to visualize in a chart.
   - If your data includes headings, be sure to include those headings in the selection.
2. Click **Charts**.

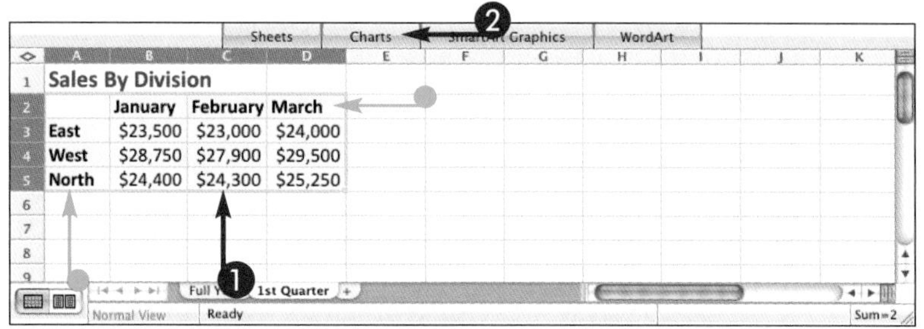


The Charts gallery appears.

3. Click a chart type category.
4. Click and to review the chart types.
   - Move over the chart type.
   - The name of the chart type appears here.

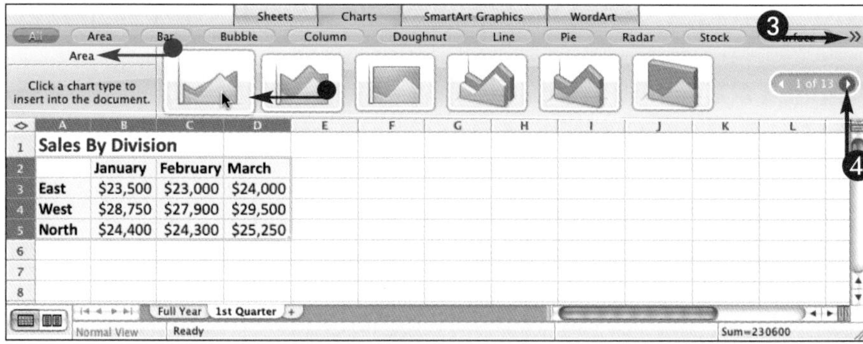

5 Click the chart type you want to use.

- Excel inserts the chart.

The tasks in the rest of this chapter show you how to configure, format, and move the chart.

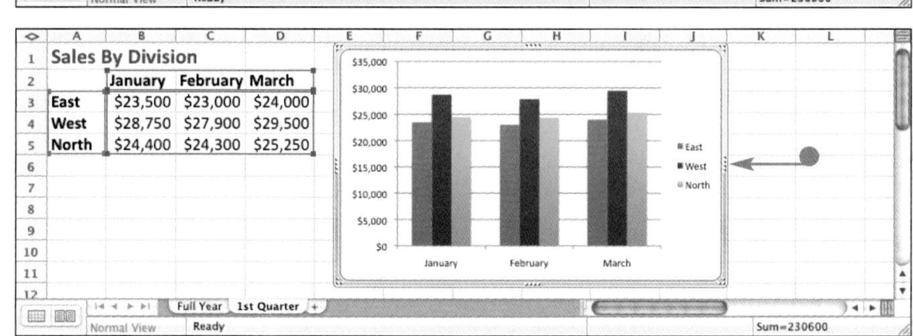


## TIP

**Is there a way to create a chart on a separate sheet?**

Yes. You can use a special workbook sheet called a *chart sheet*. If you have not yet created your chart, select the worksheet data, click **Insert**, click **Sheet**, and then click **Chart Sheet**. Excel creates a new chart sheet and inserts the chart. If you have already created your chart, you can move it to a separate chart sheet. See the tip in the section "Move or Resize a Chart."

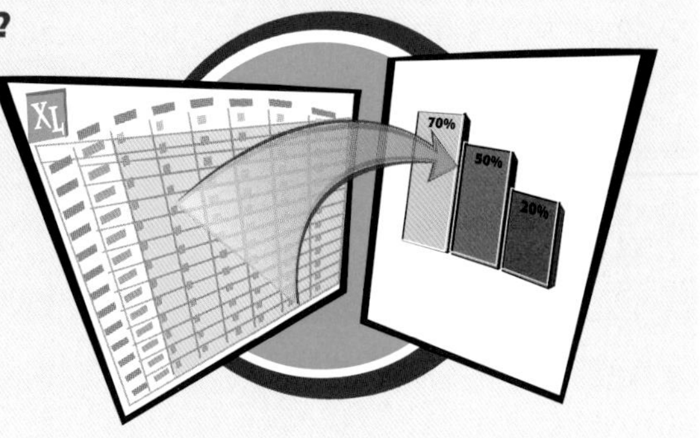

# Add Chart Titles

You can make your chart easier to understand by adding chart titles. You can add an overall chart title, which appears at the top of the chart, and you can add titles to the horizontal and vertical axes.

## Add Chart Titles

1. Click the chart.
2. Display the Formatting Palette.

***Note:*** *See Chapter 3 to learn how to display and hide the Formatting Palette.*

3. Click the **Chart Options** panel.
4. Click the **Titles** ▾ and then click **Chart Title**.
5. Type the title.

- Excel adds the title to the chart.

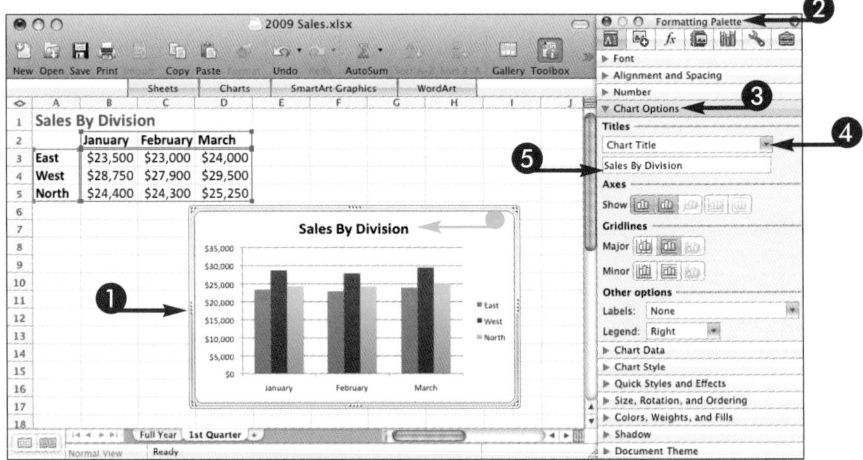


6. Click the **Titles** ▾ and then click **Vertical (Value) Axis**.
7. Type the title.

- Excel adds the title to the chart.

8. Click the **Titles** ▾ and then click **Horizontal (Category) Axis**.
9. Type the title.

- Excel adds the title to the chart.

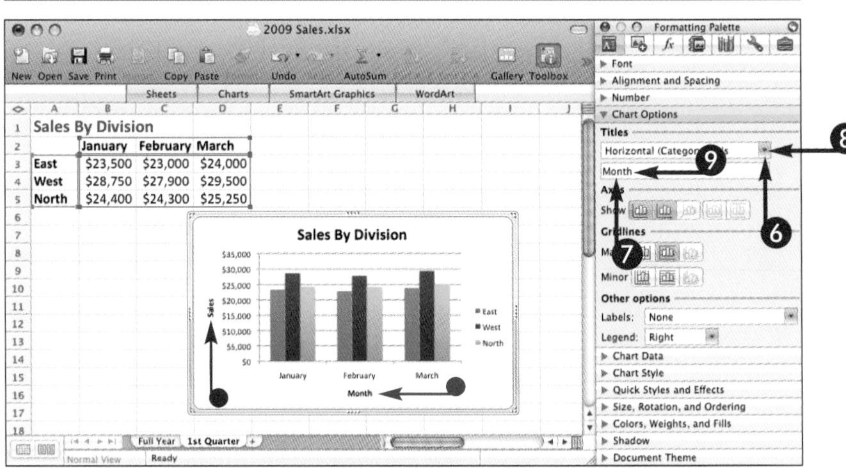

# Add Chart Labels

**You can make your chart easier to read by adding chart labels. In most cases, you add to each data marker a label that shows the value of that data point. Alternatively, you can add to each data marker a label that shows the category (horizontal axis value) associated with that data point.**

## Add Chart Labels

1. Click the chart.
2. Display the Formatting Palette.

***Note:*** *See Chapter 3 to learn how to display and hide the Formatting Palette.*

3. Click the **Chart Options** panel.
4. Click the **Labels** ▾ and then click **Value**.

   If you prefer to see the horizontal axis value associated with each data point, click **Category Name**.

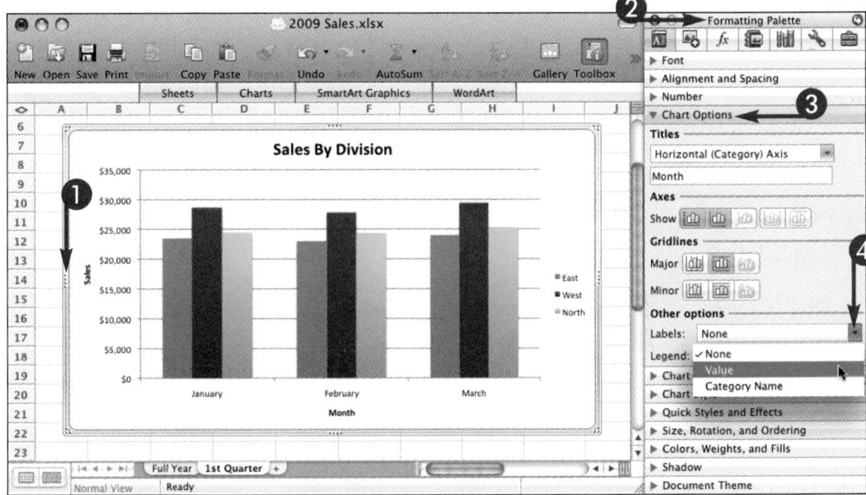


- Excel adds the labels to the chart.

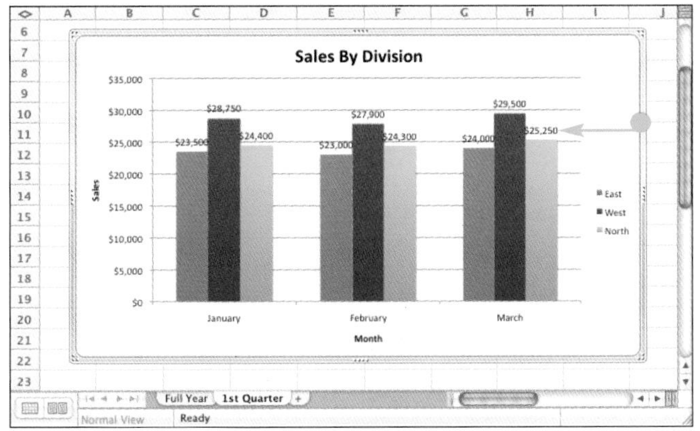

# Position the Chart Legend

You can change the position of the chart *legend*, which identifies the colors associated with each data series in the chart. For example, you might find the legend easier to read if it appears to the left of the chart. Alternatively, if you want more horizontal room to display your chart, you can move the legend above or below the chart.

## Position the Chart Legend

1. Click the chart.
2. Display the Formatting Palette.

***Note:*** *See Chapter 3 to learn how to display and hide the Formatting Palette.*

3. Click the **Chart Options** panel.
4. Click the **Legend** ▾ and then click the position you want to use.

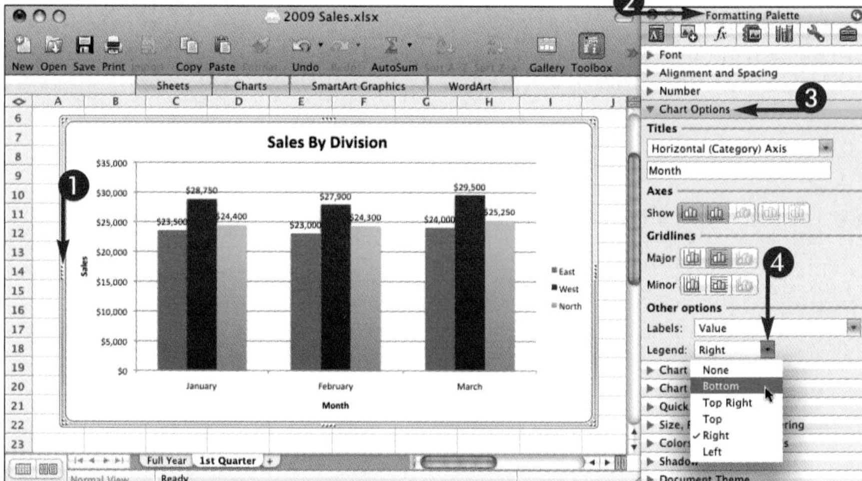


● Excel moves the legend.

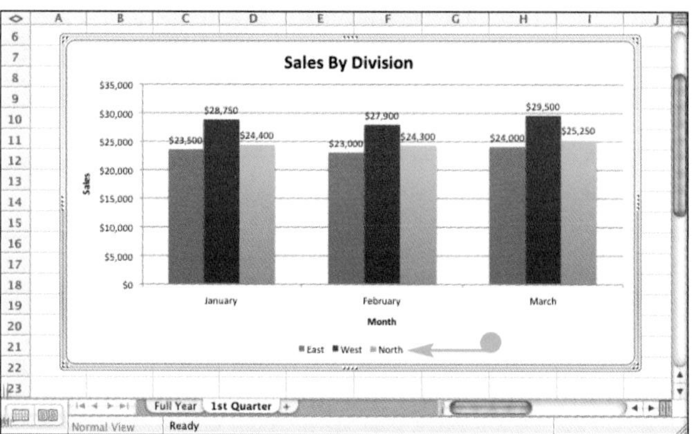

# Display Chart Gridlines

You can make your chart easier to read and easier to analyze by adding gridlines. Horizontal gridlines extend from the vertical (value) axis, and are useful with area, bubble, and column charts. Vertical gridlines extend from the horizontal (category) axis and are useful with bar and line charts.

## Display Chart Gridlines

1. Click the chart.
2. Display the Formatting Palette.

*Note:* *See Chapter 3 to learn how to display and hide the Formatting Palette.*

3. Click the **Chart Options** panel.
4. To view horizontal gridlines, click the **Horizontal Gridlines for Major Units** button.
5. To view vertical gridlines, click the **Vertical Gridlines for Major Units** button.

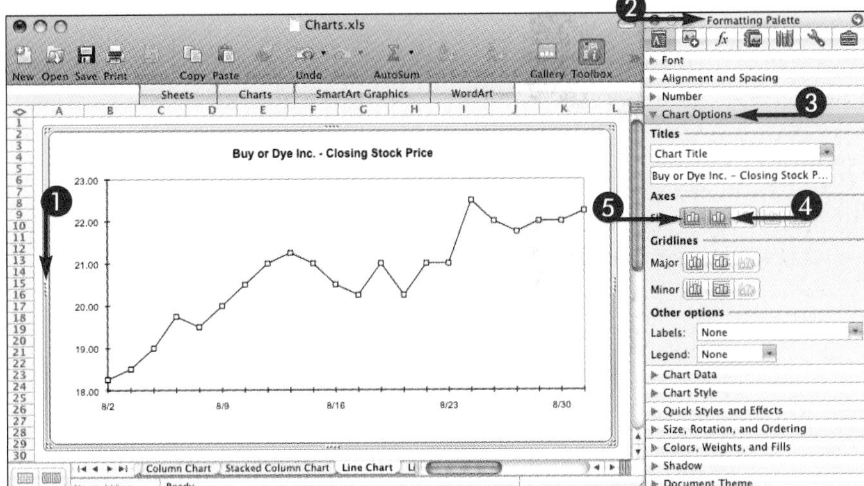


- Excel displays the gridlines.
- For greater horizontal accuracy, you can click the **Horizontal Gridlines for Minor Units** button.
- For greater vertical accuracy, you can click the **Vertical Gridlines for Minor Units** button.

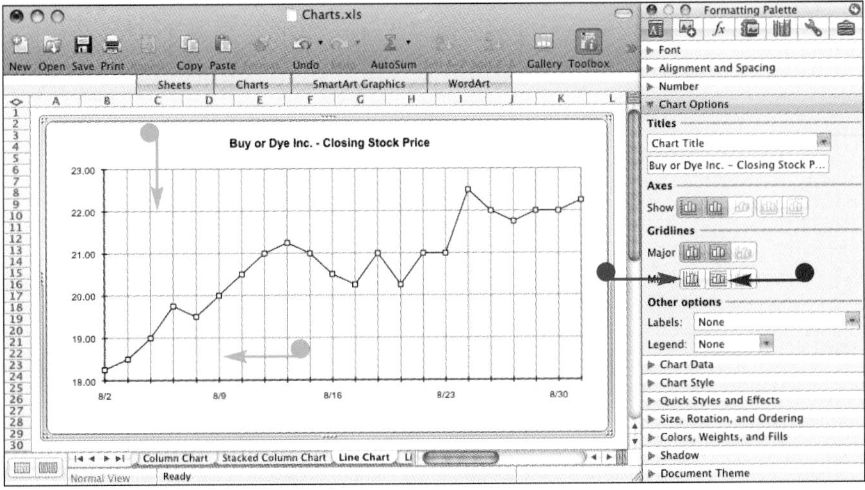

# Format Chart Objects

You can customize the look of your chart by formatting the various chart objects. These objects include the axes, titles, labels, legend, gridlines, data series, plot area (the area where the chart data appears), and the chart area (the overall background of the chart).

**You can format chart objects using either the Format dialog or the Formatting Palette.**

## Format Chart Objects

### FORMAT CHART OBJECTS USING THE FORMAT DIALOG

1. Click the chart object you want to format.
2. Click **Format**.
3. Click the name of the chart object.

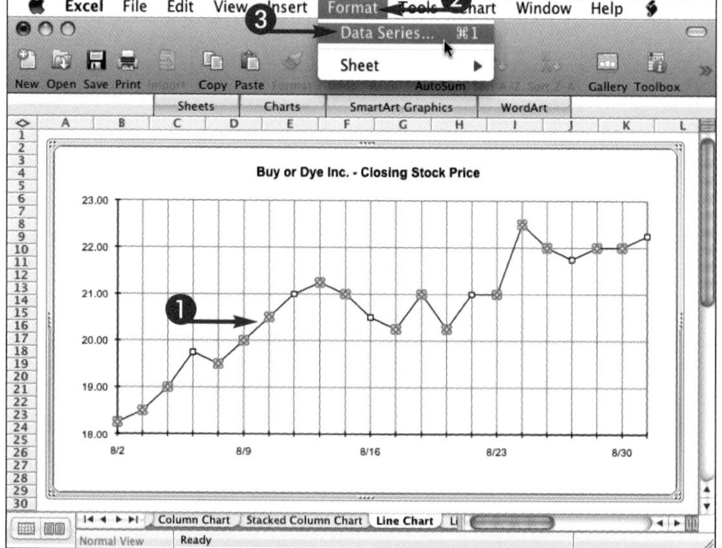


The Format dialog for the object you selected appears.

4. Click a panel.
5. Click a tab.
6. Change the formatting options.
7. Repeat Steps **4** to **6** to set other formatting options.
8. Click **OK**.

Excel applies the formatting.

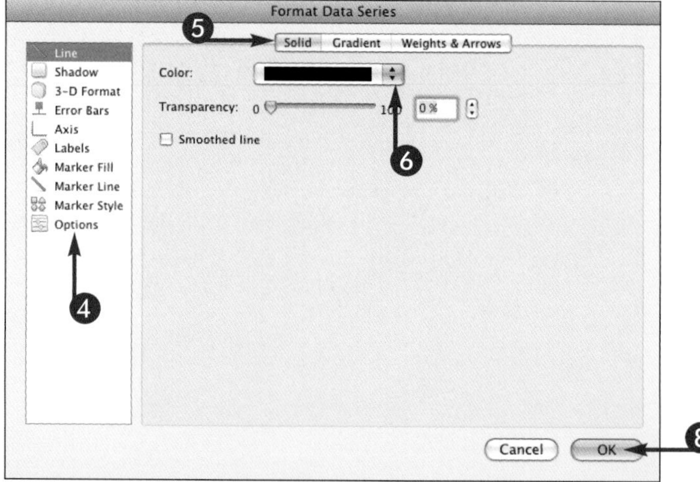

## FORMAT CHART OBJECTS USING THE FORMATTING PALETTE

1. Display the Formatting Palette.

*Note: See Chapter 3 to learn how to display and hide the Formatting Palette.*

2. Click the chart object you want to format.

- The number of Formatting Palette panels changes depending on the object you select.

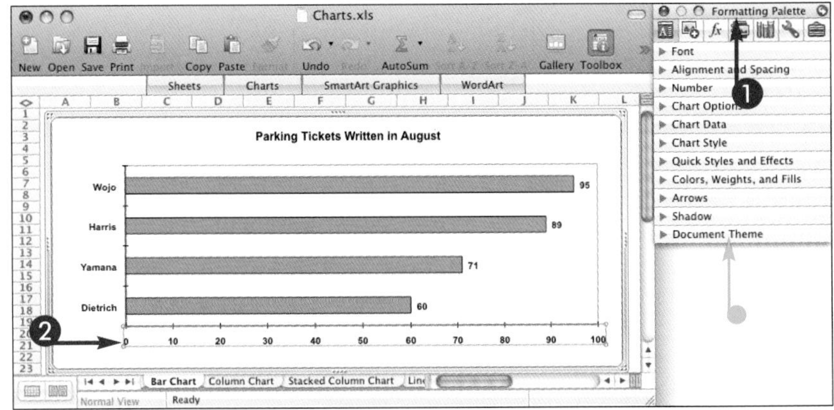


3. Click a panel.
4. Change the formatting options.
5. Repeat Steps **2** to **4** to set other formatting options.

Excel applies the formatting.

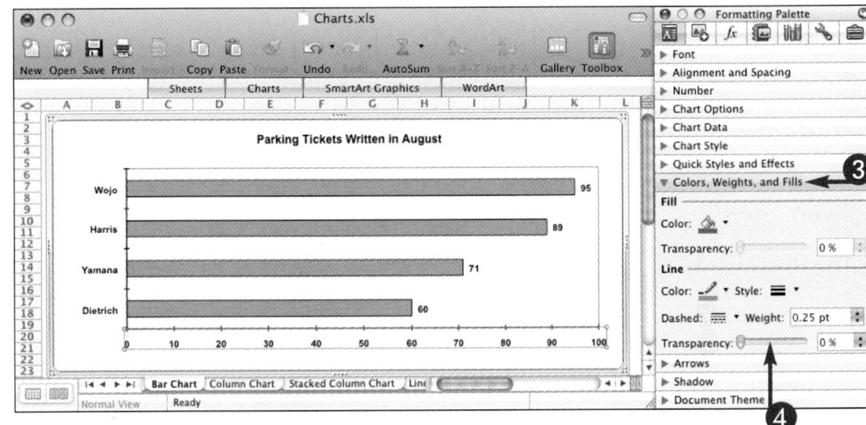

### Are there any formatting shortcuts I can use?

Yes. Excel offers several methods you can use to quickly open the Format dialog. If you are using your mouse, position the mouse pointer over the object you want to format, and then double-click. From the keyboard, first click the chart object you want to format and then press ⌘+1. You can also right-click or Ctrl+click the chart object and then click **Format** *Object* (where *Object* is the name of the object).

### How do I know where to click to select a chart object?

The easiest way to be sure you are clicking the correct object is to position the mouse pointer over the object. If the pointer is positioned correctly, a yellow banner appears and the banner text displays the name of the chart object. If the banner does not appear, or if the banner displays a chart object name other than the one you want to format, move the pointer until the correct banner appears.

# Apply a Chart Style

You can quickly and easily change the look of your chart by applying one of Excel's predefined chart styles. There are dozens of styles to choose from, and each style applies a variety of formatting options, including colors, fonts, and 3-D effects.

## Apply a Chart Style

1. Click the chart.
2. Display the Formatting Palette.

***Note:*** *See Chapter 3 to learn how to display and hide the Formatting Palette.*

3. Click the **Chart Style** panel.
4. Click ▼ and ▲ to scroll through the available styles.
5. Click the chart style you want to use.

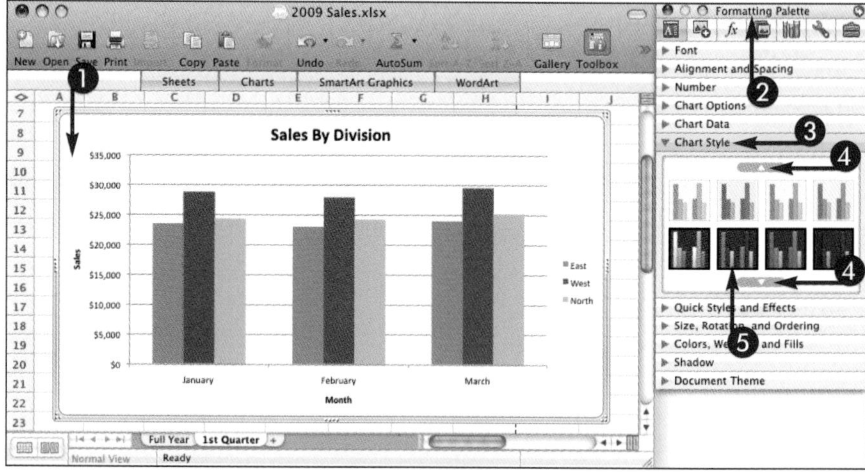


- Excel applies the style to the chart.

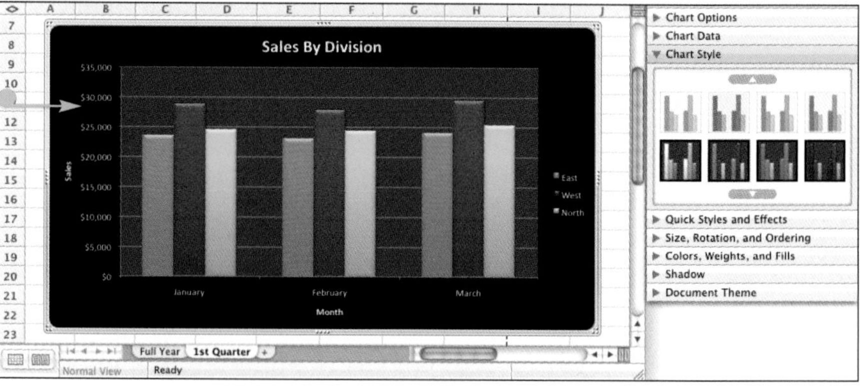

# Select a Different Chart Type



If you feel that the current chart type is not showing your data in the best way, you can change the chart type with just a few mouse clicks. For example, you might want to change a bar chart to a pie chart or a line chart to a stock chart.

## Select a Different Chart Type

1. Click the chart.
2. Click **Charts**.

   The Charts gallery appears.
3. Click a chart type category.
4. Click ▶ and ◀ to review the chart types.
5. Click the chart type you want to use.

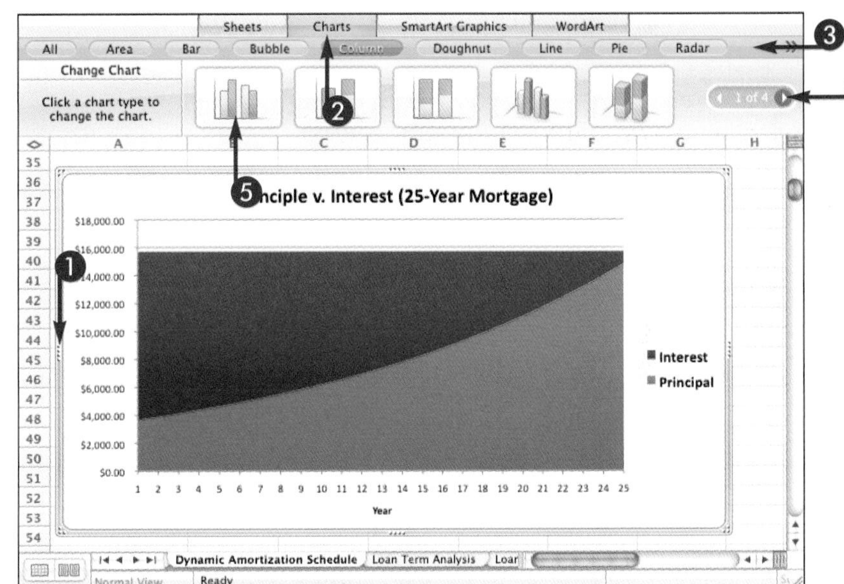


- Excel applies the new type to the chart.

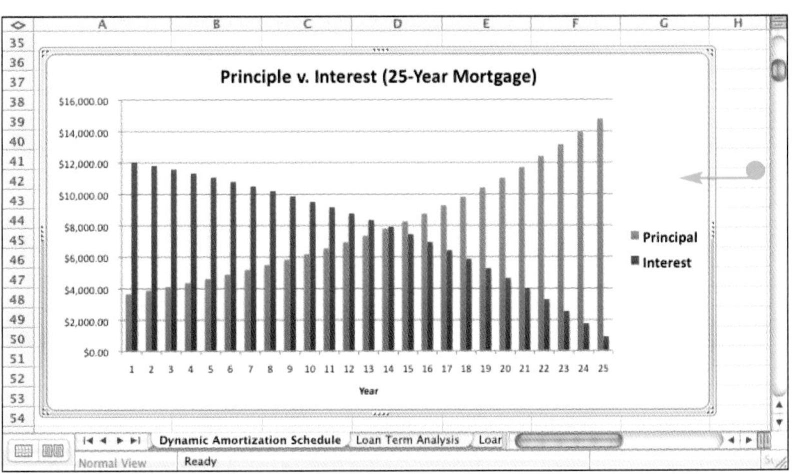

# Move or Resize a Chart

You can move a chart to another part of the worksheet. This is useful if the chart is blocking the worksheet data or if you want the chart to appear in a particular part of the worksheet.

**You can also resize a chart. For example, if you find that the chart is difficult to read, making the chart bigger often solves the problem. Similarly, if the chart takes too much room on the worksheet, you can make it smaller.**

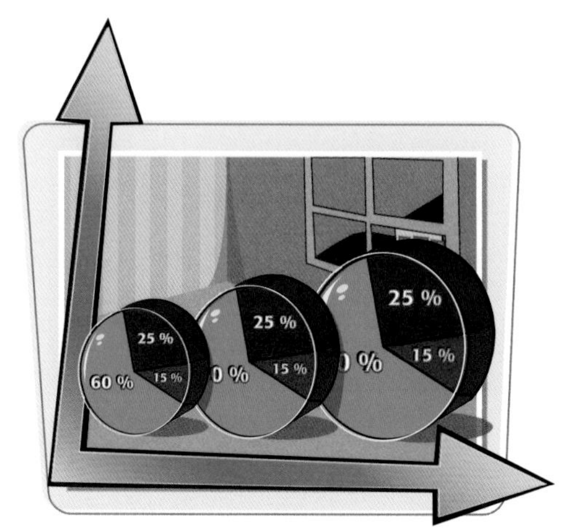


## Move or Resize a Chart

### MOVE A CHART

1. Click the chart.
   - Excel displays a border around the chart.
2. Move ↖ over the chart border.

   ↖ changes to ✥.

***Note:** Do not position the mouse pointer over a corner or over the middle of any side of the border.*

3. Click and drag the chart border to the location you want.
   - Excel displays a gray outline of the new chart position.

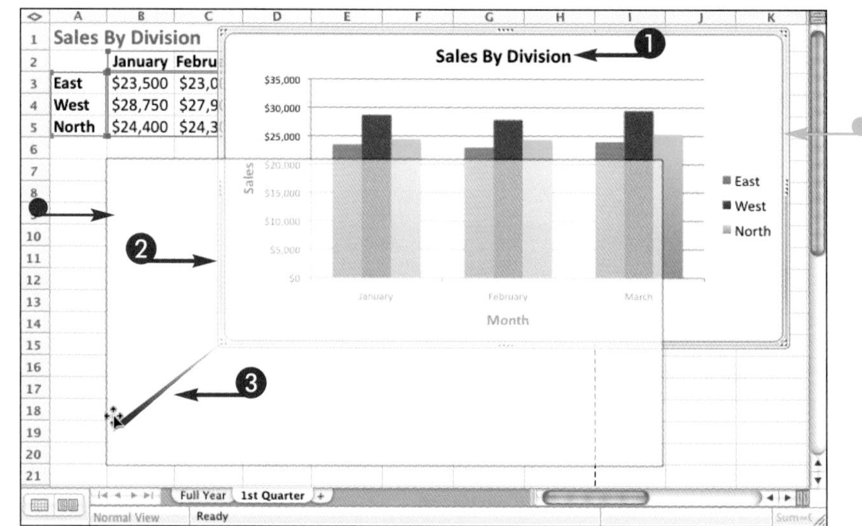


4. Release the mouse button.
   - Excel moves the chart.

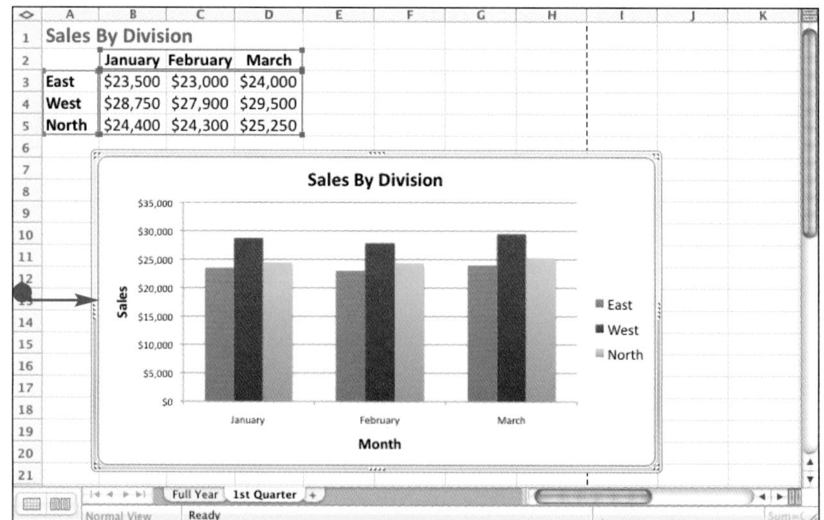

## RESIZE A CHART

1. Click the chart.
   - Excel displays a border around the chart.
   - The border includes sizing handles on the corners and sides.
2. Move ↖ over a sizing handle.

   ↖ changes to ↔.
3. Click and drag the handle.
   - Excel displays a gray outline of the new chart size.

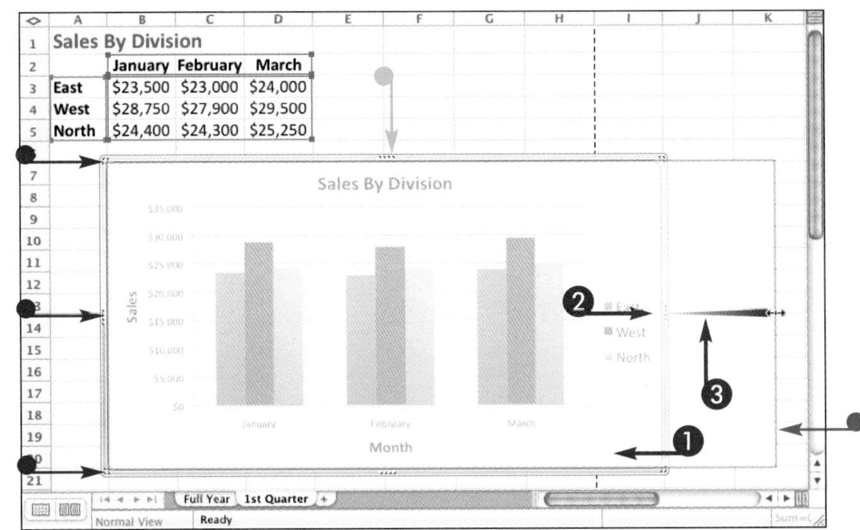

4. Release the mouse button.
   - Excel resizes the chart.

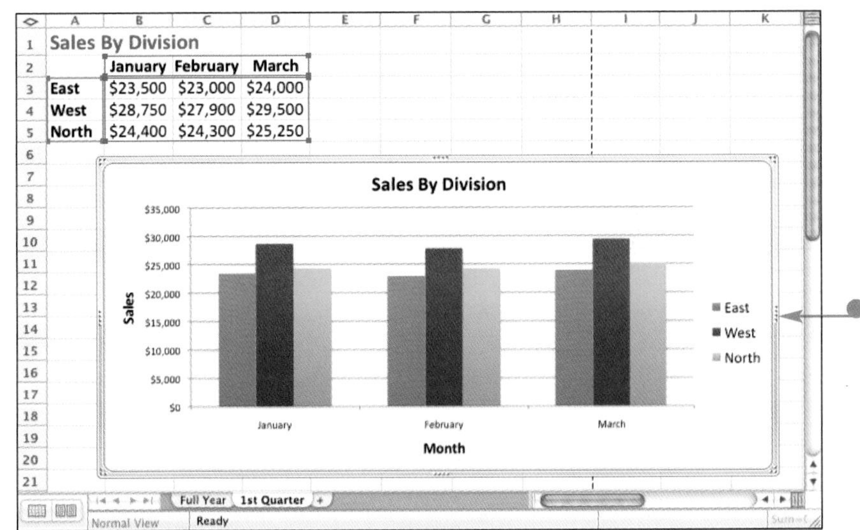

**TIPS**

### Can I move a chart to a separate sheet?

Yes. In the section "Create a Chart" you learned how to create a new chart in a separate sheet. If your chart already exists on a worksheet, you can move it to a new sheet. Click the chart, click **Chart**, and then click **Move Chart** to open the Move Chart dialog. Select the **New sheet** option (○ changes to ◉). In the New sheet text box, type a name for the new sheet, and then click **OK**.

### How do I delete a chart?

This depends on whether your chart exists as an object in a worksheet or in its own sheet. If the chart is on a worksheet, click the chart and then press Del. If the chart exists on a separate sheet, right-click or Ctrl+click the sheet tab and then click **Delete**.

CHAPTER

15

# Building a PowerPoint Presentation

You use PowerPoint to create presentations that you display as slide shows to an audience. Presentations are common in business for detailing budgets, products, and marketing campaigns, but you can also build presentations for teaching a subject, displaying vacation photos, and giving a lecture on just about any topic. You build a presentation by inserting slides and then adding slide data such as text, images, bulleted lists, numbered lists, and more.

# Add Presentation Titles

When you create a new, blank presentation, PowerPoint creates the new file with a title slide added automatically. To complete this slide, you add your presentation title and subtitle.

**A title slide includes two text placeholders: one for the title and the other for the subtitle.**

## Add Presentation Titles

1. Click inside the title text box.
2. Type your presentation title.
3. Click outside the title text box.

   PowerPoint sets the title text.

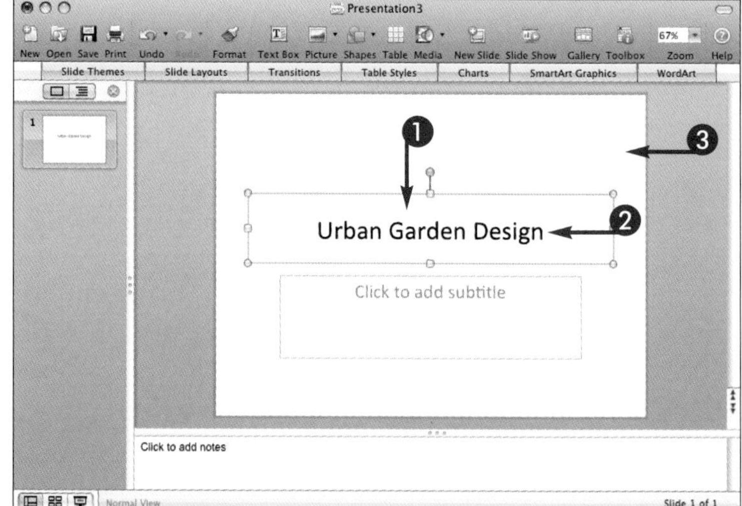


4. Click inside the subtitle text box.
5. Type your presentation subtitle.
6. Click outside the subtitle text box.

   PowerPoint sets the subtitle text.

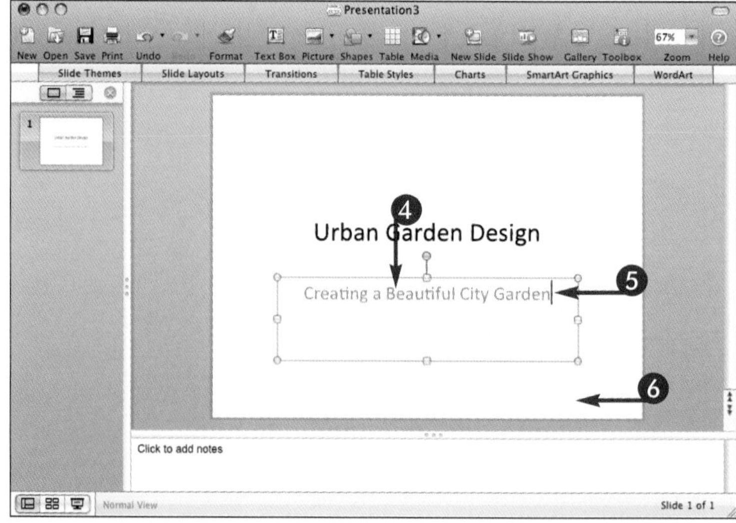

Most presentations consist of multiple slides, so you need to know how to add slides to your presentation.

**Each slide should focus on a single overall topic, so always begin a new slide when you switch topics.**

## Insert a Slide

1. Click **Insert**.
2. Click **New Slide**.

- You can also click the **New Slide** button (▣) in the toolbar.

  You can also press Shift + ⌘ + N.

- PowerPoint inserts and displays the new slide.
- PowerPoint adds the new slide to the Slides pane.

***Note:*** *If the new slide does not have the layout you want, you can change it. See the section "Change the Slide Layout."*

To delete a slide you no longer need, click the slide in the Slides tab, click **Edit**, and then click **Delete Slide**.

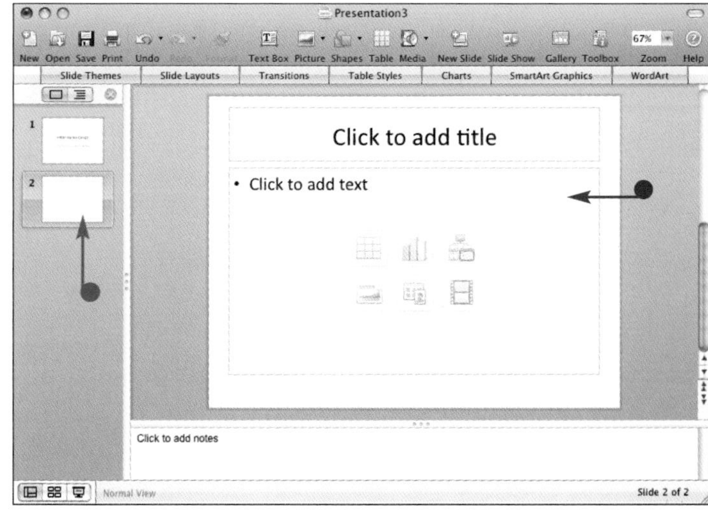

# Add Text to a Slide

Most slides consist of text, usually a slide title followed by two or more bullet points. When you insert a new slide into your presentation, you fill in the title and then usually add the bullet text.

**By default, a new slide contains two text placeholders: one for the slide title and the other for the main slide text. All slides also have a notes section that you can use for notes to yourself.**

## Add Slide Text

1. Click inside the slide title placeholder.
2. Type your slide title.
3. Click outside the title text box.

   PowerPoint sets the slide's title text.

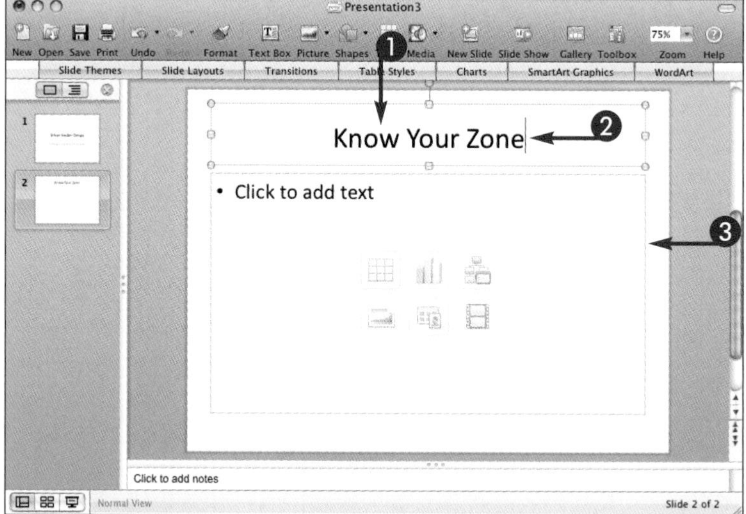


4. Click inside the content placeholder.
5. Type your bullet text and press Return.

- PowerPoint adds the next bullet point.

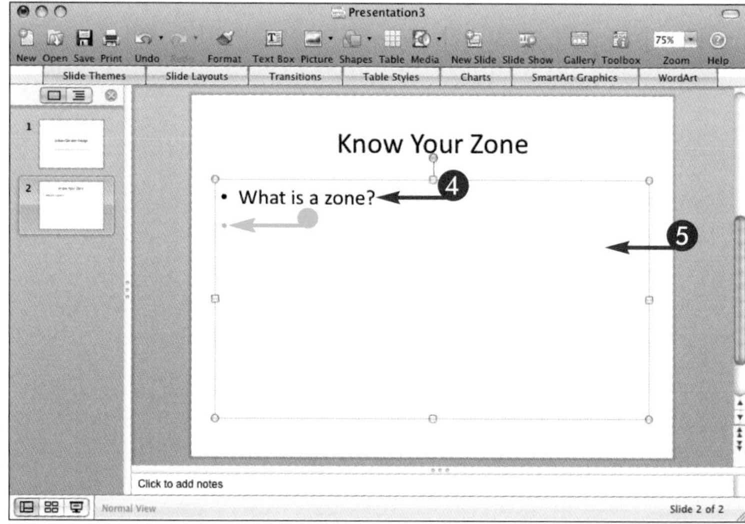

6 Repeat Step **5** to add all the bullet text you want to display on the slide.

When you finish typing your final bullet for the slide, do not press Return.

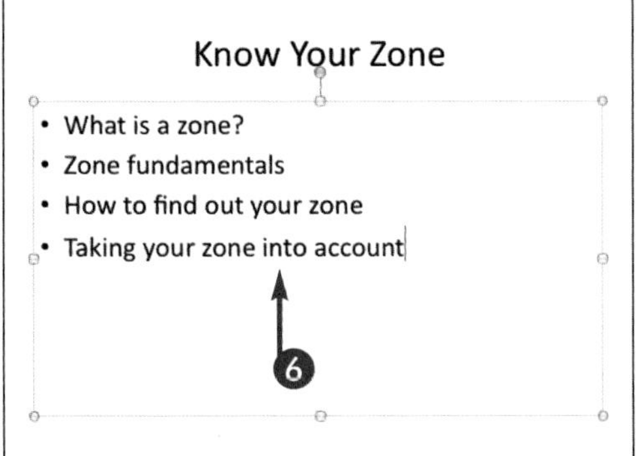


7 If you want to add notes to yourself for this slide, click inside the Notes section and type your note.

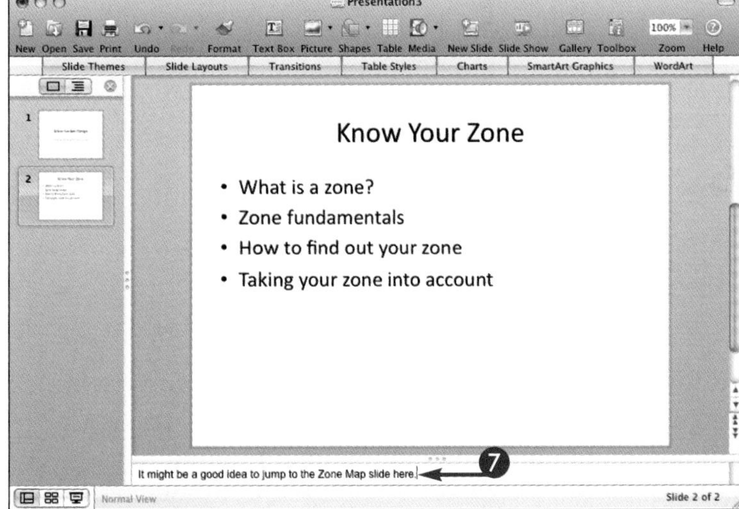

### How do I create sub-bullets?

PowerPoint recognizes a bulleted list hierarchy that is controlled by manipulating the *list levels*, where the main bullets are at level 1, sub-bullets are at level 2, and so on. To increase a bullet's list level, position the cursor at the beginning of the bullet text and then press Tab. To decrease the list level, press Shift + Tab. Alternatively, open the Formatting Palette, click the **Bullets and Numbering** panel, and then click either **Increase List Level** (icon) or **Decrease List Level** (icon).

### Can I create a numbered list instead?

Yes. Although most of the nontitle text in a PowerPoint presentation consists of bulleted lists, you may require a numbered list to detail a series of steps, for example. Open the Formatting Palette (see Chapter 3), click the **Bullets and Numbering** panel, and then click **Numbering** (icon). If you do not want a list at all, click **Bullets** (icon), instead.

# Add a Table to a Slide

If you want a slide to display data that consists of a list of items, each with several details, such as a product list or employee roster, you can display that data in an organized fashion using a table. A PowerPoint table uses the same row-and-column format that you may be familiar with from Word tables (see Chapter 8) or Excel worksheets (see Chapter 10).

## Add a Table to a Slide

1. In the content placeholder, click the **Insert Table** icon (▦).

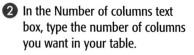

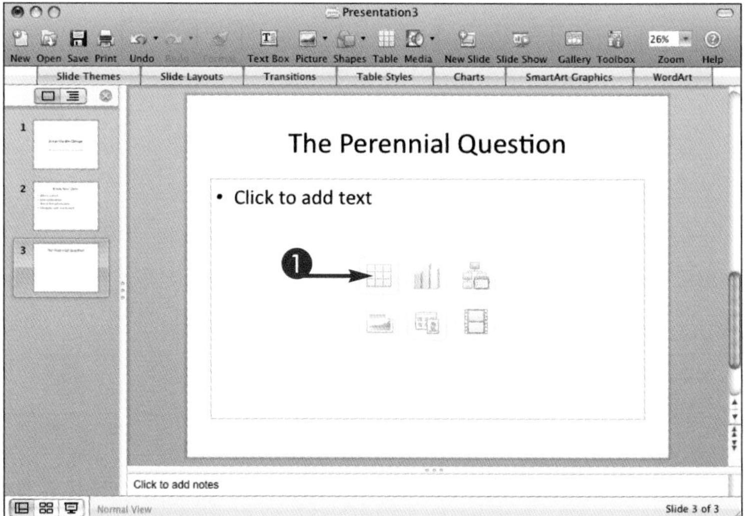


The Insert Table dialog appears.

2. In the Number of columns text box, type the number of columns you want in your table.
3. In the Number of rows text box, type the number of rows you want in your table.
4. Click **OK**.

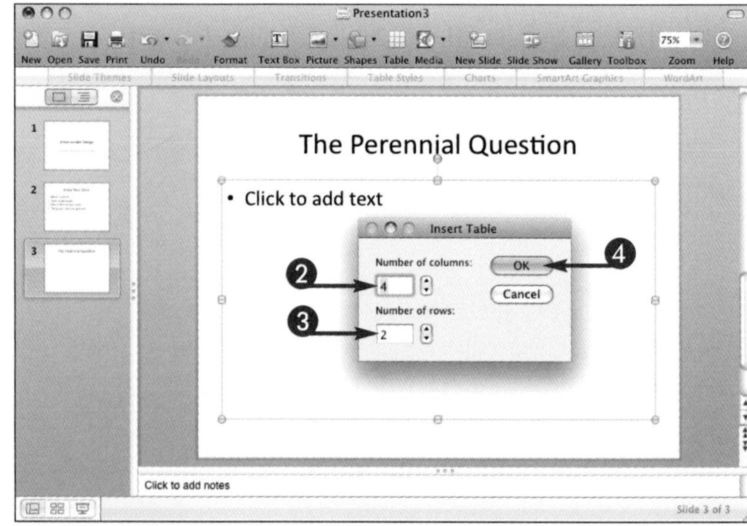

- PowerPoint inserts the table.
- PowerPoint displays the Table Styles gallery.

5. Click a table style category.
6. Click ▶ and ◀ to review the table styles.
7. Click the table style you want to use.

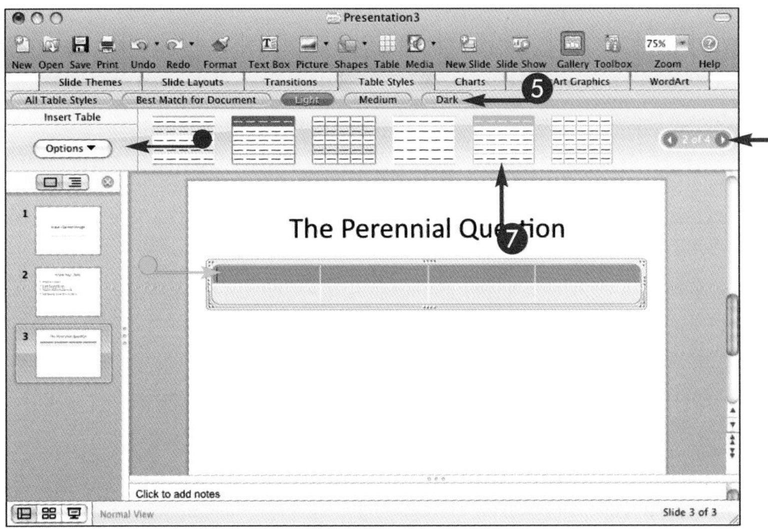


- PowerPoint applies the table style.

8. Type your table heading in the cells in the top row.
9. Type your table data in the cells in the subsequent rows.

- To add a new row, move the cursor to the end of the text in the last cell in the last row, and then press Tab.

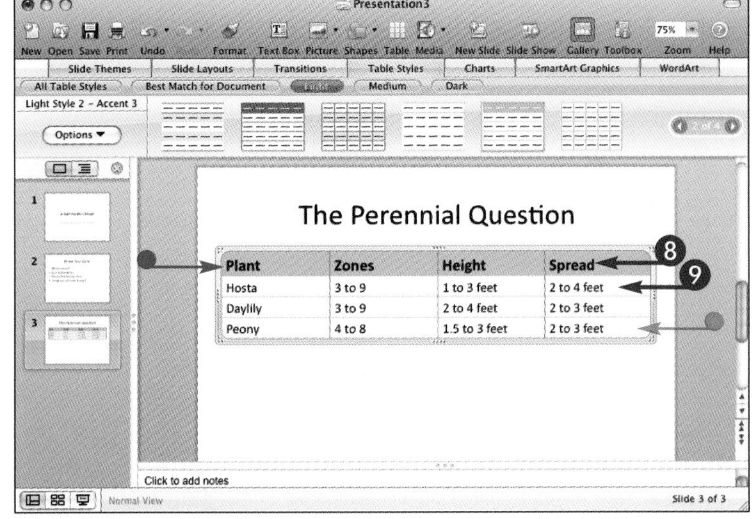

### How do I insert new rows and columns into my table?

To insert a column at the end of the table, click the table, display the Formatting Palette (see Chapter 3), click the **Table** panel, and then increase the **Columns** value by 1. To insert data within the table, right-click or Ctrl+click the table, click **Insert**, and then click one of the commands. For example, to insert a row above an existing row, right-click the existing row, click **Insert**, and then click **Insert Rows Above**.

### How do I delete a row or column?

To delete the last row or column, click the table, display the Formatting Palette (see Chapter 3), click the **Table** panel, and then decrease the **Rows** or **Columns** value by 1. To delete any other row or column, right-click or Ctrl+click the row or column, click **Delete**, and then click either **Delete Rows** or **Delete Columns**.

# Add a Chart to a Slide

Rather than displaying a slide full of numeric data, you can take those numbers and display them as a chart. Visualizing your data in this way makes the data easier to understand and easier to analyze.

**PowerPoint uses Excel to create the chart, so you must have Excel installed on your Mac to use this feature.**

## Add a Chart to a Slide

1. In the content placeholder, click the **Insert Chart** icon ( ).

- PowerPoint displays the Charts gallery.

2. Click a chart type category.
3. Click ▶ and ◀ to review the chart types.
4. Click the chart type you want to use.

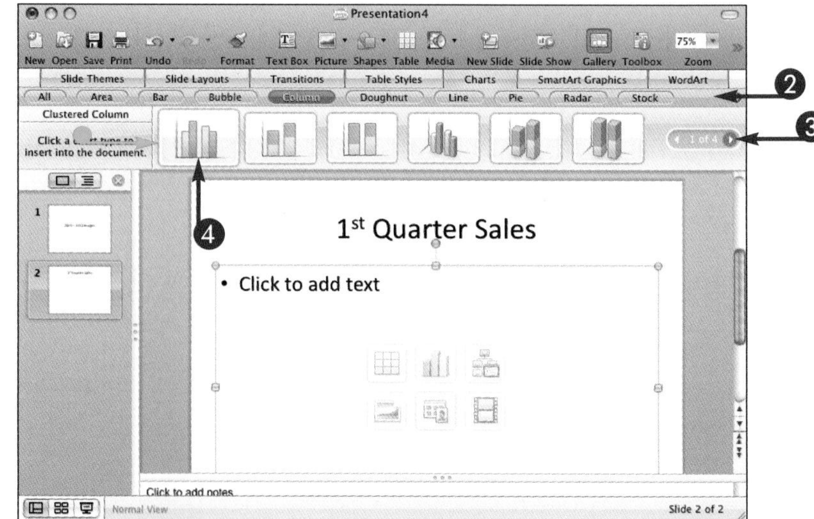

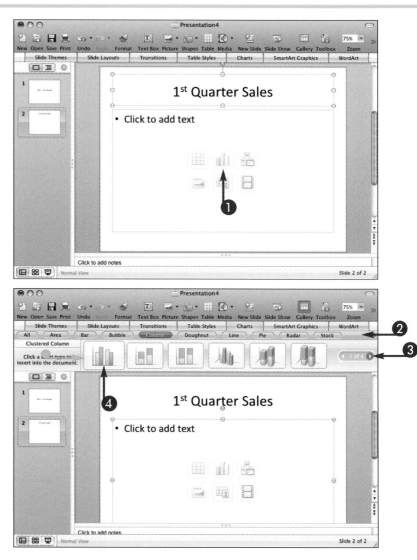

Excel launches and an Excel worksheet window appears.

- Excel displays some sample data.

5. Replace the existing data with the data you want to use as the basis for your PowerPoint chart.
6. Click **Excel**.
7. Click **Quit Excel**.

   You can also press ⌘ + Q.

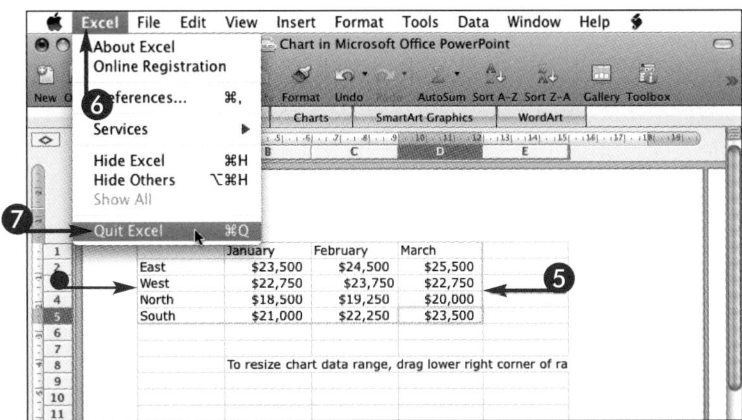


- PowerPoint displays the updated chart.

***Note:** To configure and format the chart, click the chart, display the Formatting Palette (see Chapter 3), and use the panels to modify the chart style, chart options, and so on. See Chapter 14 to learn about modifying charts.*

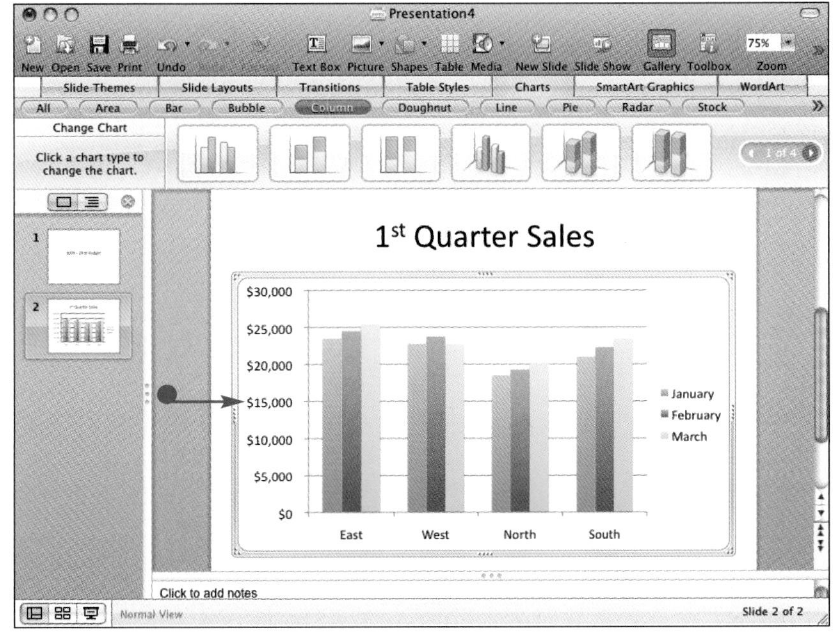


## TIPS

### How do I make changes to the chart's underlying data?

PowerPoint gives you a couple of ways to do this. One method is to right-click or Ctrl+click any data series in the chart, and then click **Edit Data**. Alternatively, click the chart, display the Formatting Palette (see Chapter 3), click the **Chart Data** panel, and then click **Edit in Excel**. Either way, Excel opens and displays the data. Follow Steps **5** to **7** to edit the data and quit Excel.

### Can I use an existing Excel chart instead of creating a new chart from scratch?

Yes. Open Excel, open the workbook that contains the chart, click the chart, click **Edit**, and then click **Copy**. Return to PowerPoint, click **Edit**, and then click **Paste Special** to display the Paste Special dialog. Click **Microsoft Excel Chart Object**, and then click **OK**. Double-click the chart. If PowerPoint asks to convert the chart, click **Convert**.

# Add Data to the Slide Footer

In a large presentation, you can easily lose track of what slide number you are working with or viewing. Similarly, if you work with many presentations, you can easily get confused as to which presentation you are currently working on. To help overcome these and other organizational handicaps, you can add data to the slide footer.

**You can add three types of data to the slide footer: the date and time, the slide number, and a custom text message.**

## Add Data to the Slide Footer

1. Click **View**.
2. Click **Header and Footer**.

   The Header and Footer dialog appears.

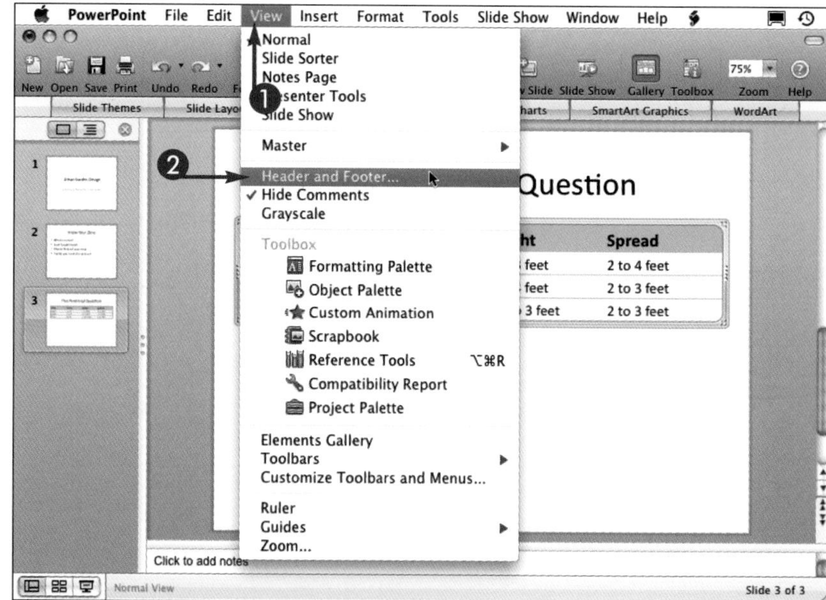


3. Click the **Slide** tab.
4. Select the **Date and time** option (☐ changes to ☑).

- If you want PowerPoint to update the date and time each time you open the file, select **Update automatically** (○ changes to ◉) and then click the ⬍ to set the format.
- If you want the same date to always appear, select **Fixed** (○ changes to ◉) and then type the date in the text box.

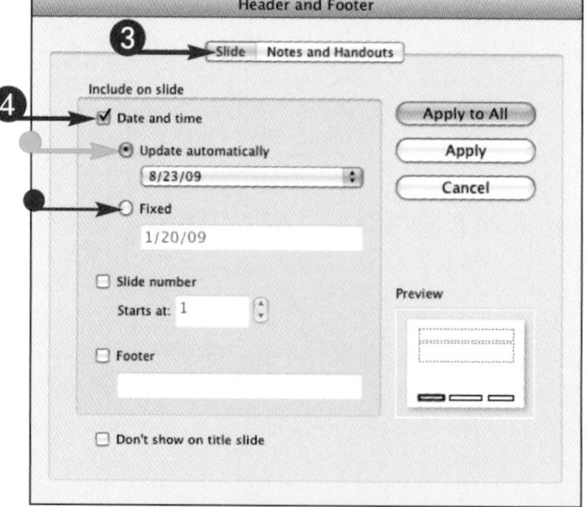

5 Select the **Slide number** option (☐ changes to ☑).

6 In the Starts at text box, specify the first slide number.

7 Select the **Footer** option (☐ changes to ☑).

8 Click here and type the text you want to appear.

9 Click **Apply to All**.

- If you only want the footer to appear on the current slide, click **Apply**.

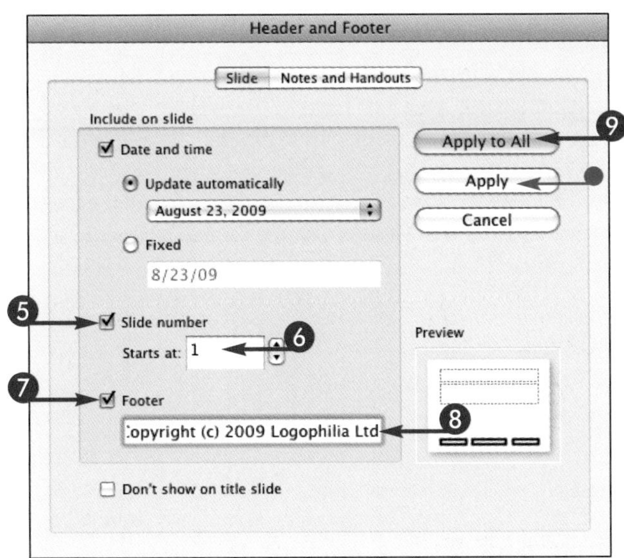


- PowerPoint adds the footer.

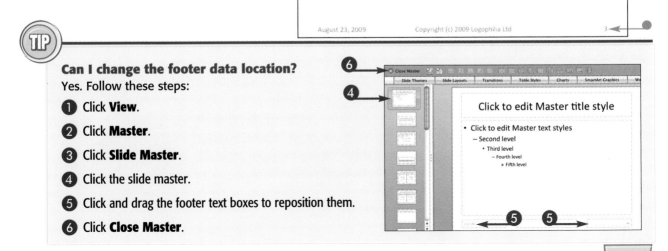

The Perennial Question

| Plant | Zones | Height | Spread |
| --- | --- | --- | --- |
| Hosta | 3 to 9 | 1 to 3 feet | 2 to 4 feet |
| Daylily | 3 to 9 | 2 to 4 feet | 2 to 3 feet |
| Peony | 4 to 8 | 1.5 to 3 feet | 2 to 3 feet |

August 23, 2009 Copyright (c) 2009 Logophilia Ltd 3

TIP

**Can I change the footer data location?**

Yes. Follow these steps:

1 Click **View**.

2 Click **Master**.

3 Click **Slide Master**.

4 Click the slide master.

5 Click and drag the footer text boxes to reposition them.

6 Click **Close Master**.

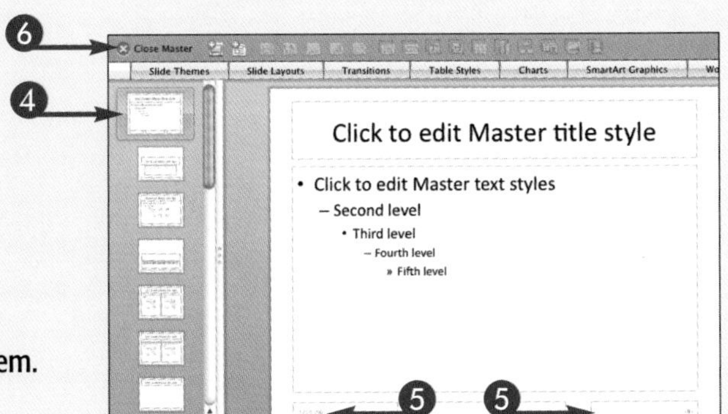

# Move a Slide Object

You can move a slide object to another part of the slide. This is useful if the object is blocking other data on the slide or if you want the object to appear in a particular part of the slide.

## Move a Slide Object

❶ Click the object.

- Excel displays a border around the object.

❷ Move ↖ over the object.

↖ changes to ✥.

***Note:** Do not position the mouse pointer over a corner or over the middle of any side of the border.*

❸ Click and drag the object to the location you want.

- Excel displays a dimmed version of the object as you drag.

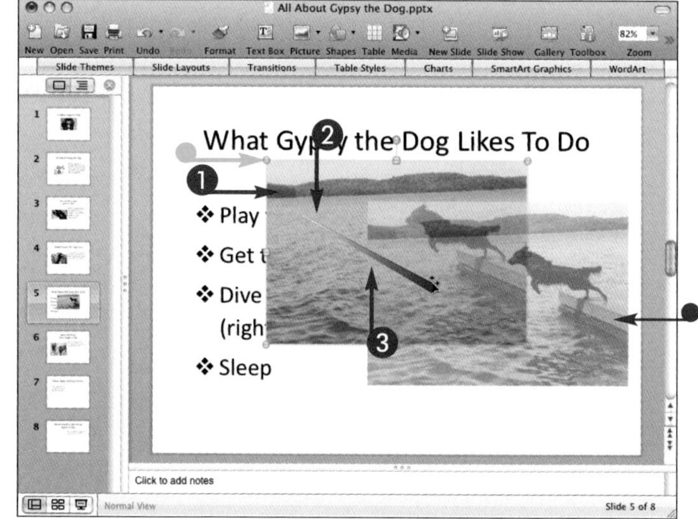


❹ Release the mouse button.

- Excel moves the object.

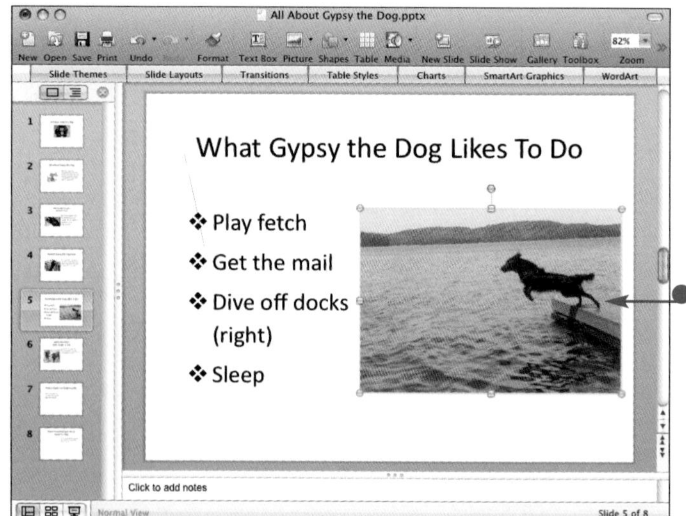

# Resize a Slide Object



**You can resize a slide object. For example, if you find that the object is difficult to see or read, making the object bigger often solves the problem. Similarly, if the object takes too much room on the slide, you can make it smaller.**

## Resize a Slide Object

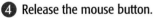

1. Click the object.
   - Excel displays a border around the object.
   - The border includes sizing handles on the corners and sides.
2. Move ↖ over a sizing handle.

   ↖ changes to ↔.
3. Click and drag the handle.
   - Excel displays a dimmed version of the new object size.

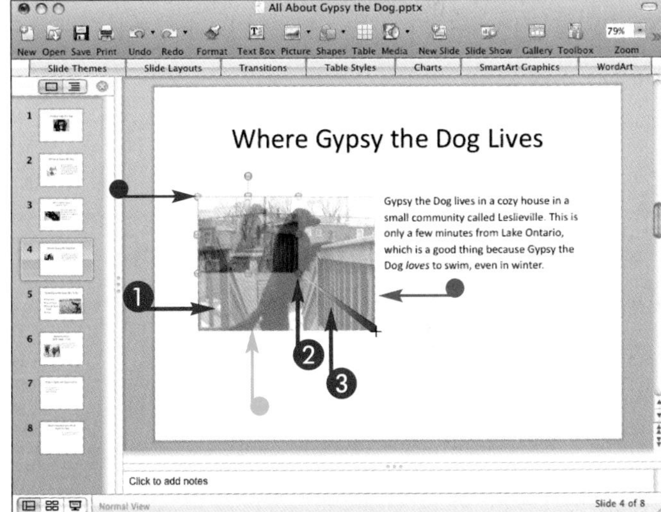


To keep the object's original proportions, hold down ⌘ while you drag.

4. Release the mouse button.
   - Excel resizes the object.

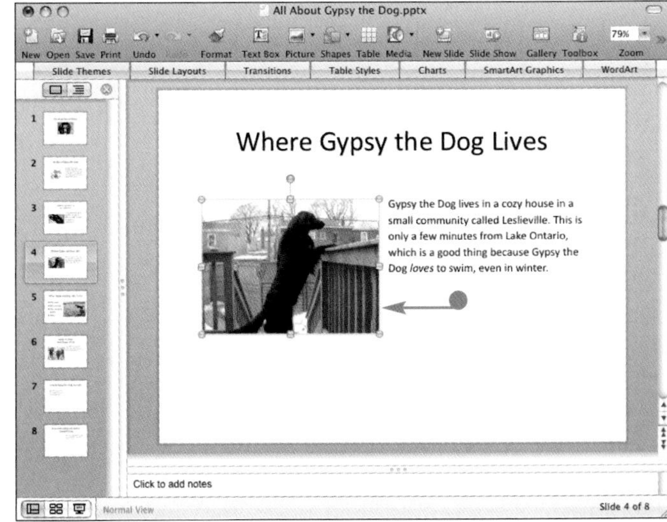

# Select Slides

Before you can perform certain slide tasks such as rearranging the slides within your presentation and changing the layout or theme of one or more slides, you must first select the slides you want to work with.

**You can select slides either in Normal view or in Slide Sorter view.**

## Select Slides

### SELECT SLIDES IN NORMAL VIEW

1. Click the **Normal view** icon (▤).
2. Click a slide in the Slides pane.
   - PowerPoint highlights the slide.

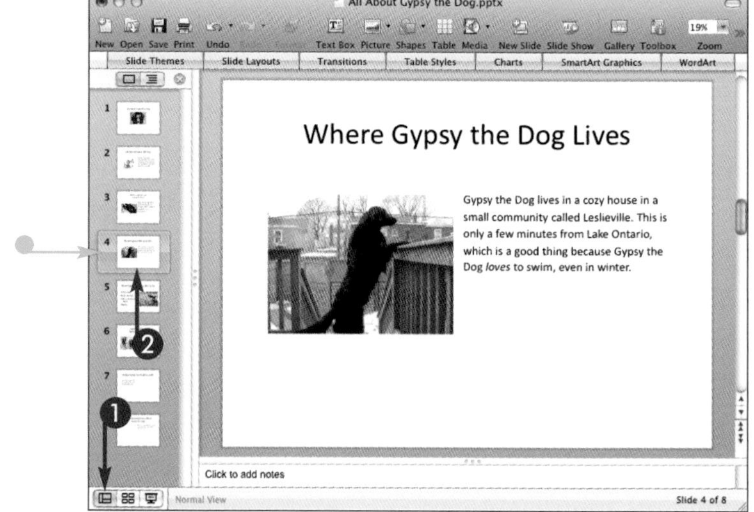


3. Hold down ⌘.
4. Click each of the other slides you want to select.
5. Release ⌘.

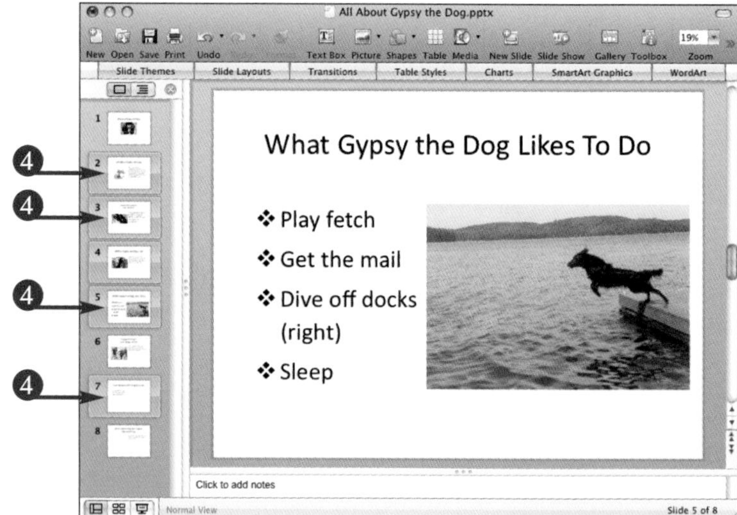

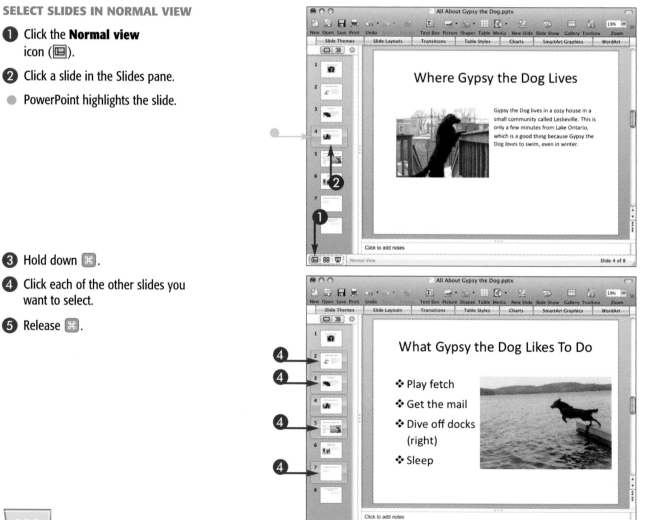

## SELECT SLIDES IN SLIDE SORTER VIEW

1. Click the **Slide Sorter view** icon (⊞).
2. Click a slide.

- PowerPoint highlights the slide.

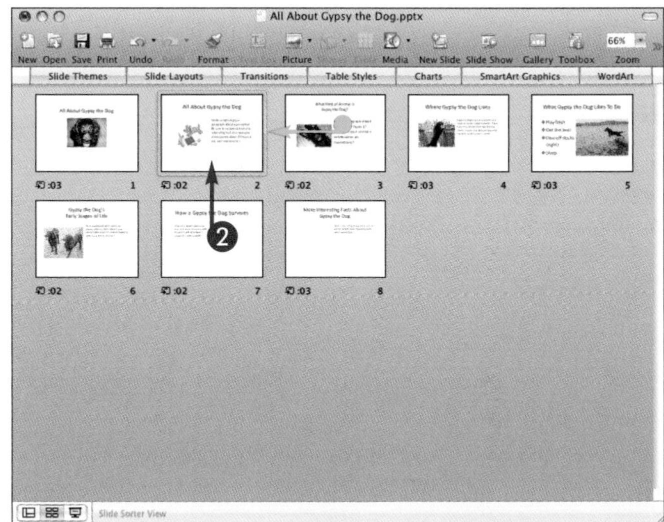

3. Hold down ⌘.
4. Click each of the other slides you want to select.
5. Release ⌘.

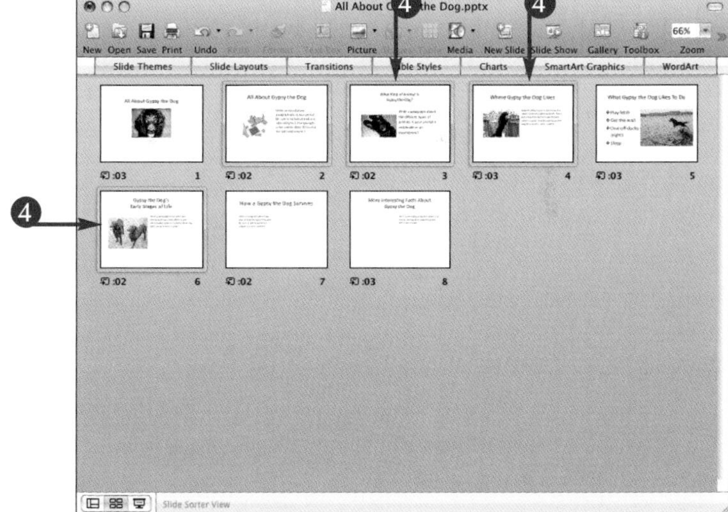

**Is there a quick way to select every slide in the presentation?**

Yes. PowerPoint offers several ways to do this:

- Click any slide either in the Normal view's Slides pane or in the Slide Sorter view, click **Edit**, and then click **Select All**.
- Click any slide either in the Normal view's Slides pane or in the Slide Sorter view, and then press ⌘+A.
- Click the first slide either in the Normal view's Slides pane or in the Slide Sorter view, hold down Shift, and then click the last slide.

# Rearrange Slides

You can rearrange the slides within the presentation if your slides are not in the order that you prefer. For example, you can reorganize your presentation to position more important information closer to the beginning.

**You can rearrange slides either in Normal view or in Slide Sorter view.**

## Rearrange Slides

### REARRANGE SLIDES IN NORMAL VIEW

1. Click the **Normal view** icon (▣).
2. Click the slide you want to move.
3. Drag the slide up or down within the Slides pane.
   - A line shows the new position of the slide.

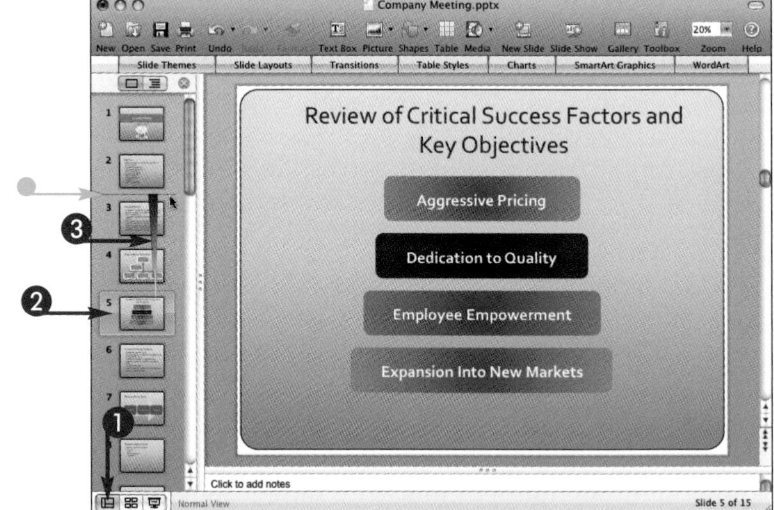


4. Release the mouse button.
   - PowerPoint moves the slide to the new position.

## REARRANGE SLIDES IN SLIDE SORTER VIEW

1. Click the **Slide Sorter view** icon (▦).
2. Click the slide you want to move.
3. Drag the slide to the new position.

- A line shows the new position of the slide.

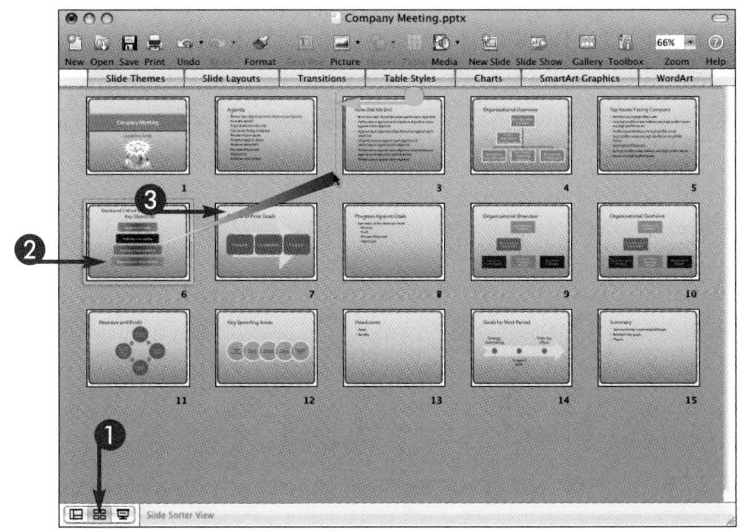


4. Release the mouse button.

- PowerPoint moves the slide to the new position.

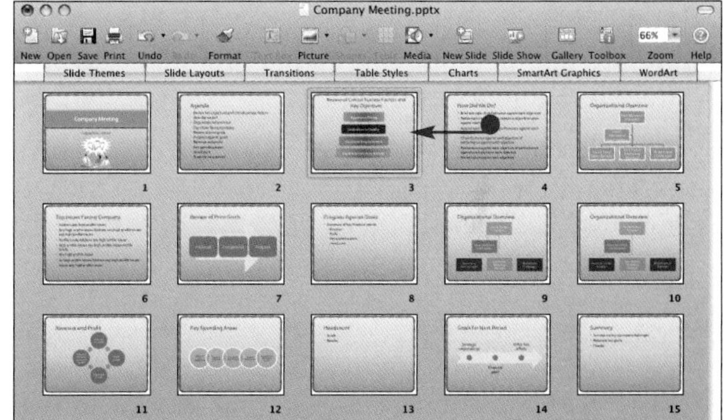

### Can I save time by rearranging multiple slides at once?

Yes. You can rearrange as many slides as you want. First, select the slides you want to move (see the section "Select Slides" earlier in this chapter). Then click and drag any one of the selected slides, and drop them in the new position. PowerPoint maintains the same order for the selected slides in the new position. For example, if you move slides 5 and 7 to the second position, those slides become numbers 2 and 3.

### Is there a way to skip a slide in my presentation without deleting the slide?

Yes. PowerPoint enables you to hide the slide. This means that the slide still appears in your presentation file, so you can still add data to and format the slide. However, when you present your slide show, that slide does not appear. Click the slide you want to hide (you can do this in either Normal view or Slide Sorter view), click **Slide Show**, and then click **Hide Slide**.

# Change the Slide Layout

You can customize the slide content by changing the layout. Each PowerPoint slide contains one or more *placeholders*, and you fill in each placeholder with text or content such as a table, chart, or picture. Each slide uses some combination of title, text, and content placeholders, and the arrangement of these placeholders on a slide is called the *slide layout.*

## Change the Slide Layout

1. Click the slide you want to work with.
2. Click **Slide Layouts**.

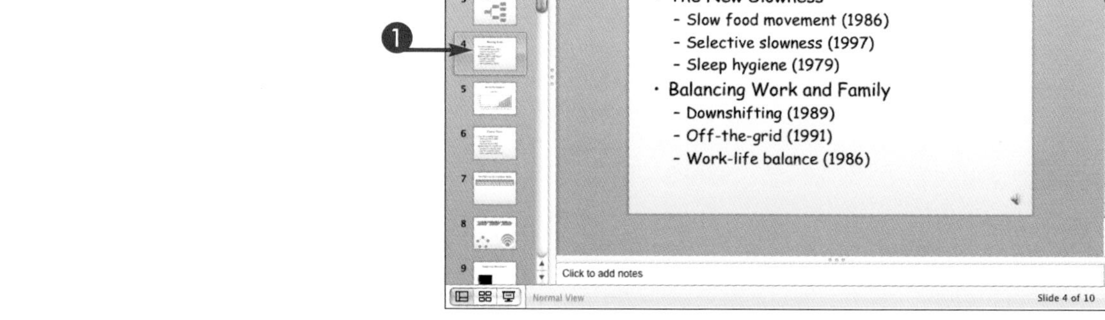


The Slide Layouts gallery appears.

3. Click ▶ and ◀ to review the slide layouts.

- Move ↖ over the slide layout.
- The name of the slide layout appears here.

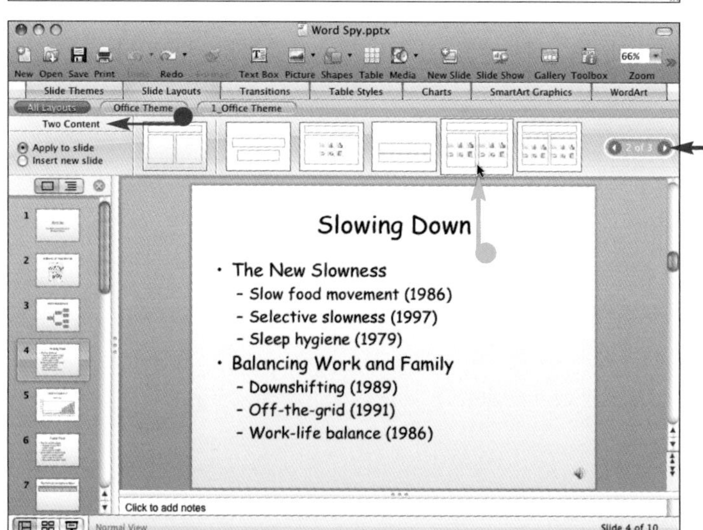

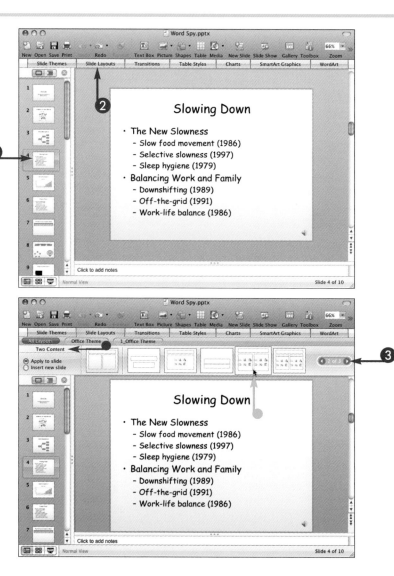

4 Select **Apply to slide** (○ changes to ◉).

5 Click the slide layout you want to use.

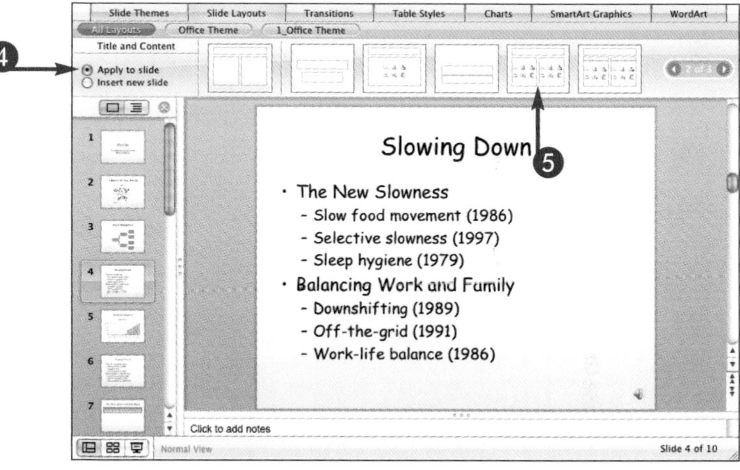


● Excel changes the slide layout.

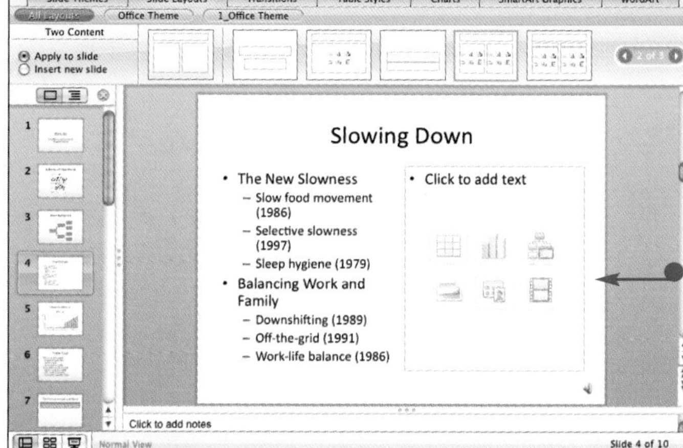

**What slide layouts are available?**

Here are the most common layouts you will use:

- Title Slide. Two text boxes: one for the overall presentation title and one for the subtitle
- Title and Content. A title placeholder and a content placeholder
- Two Content. A title placeholder and two content placeholders placed side by side
- Comparison. A title placeholder, two content placeholders placed side by side, and two text placeholders above each content placeholder
- Title Only. A title placeholder only
- Blank. No placeholders
- Content with Caption. A content placeholder with two text placeholders to the left of it: one for the content title and another for the content description
- Picture with Caption. A picture placeholder with two text placeholders beneath it: one for the picture title and another for the picture description

CHAPTER 16

# Formatting PowerPoint Slides

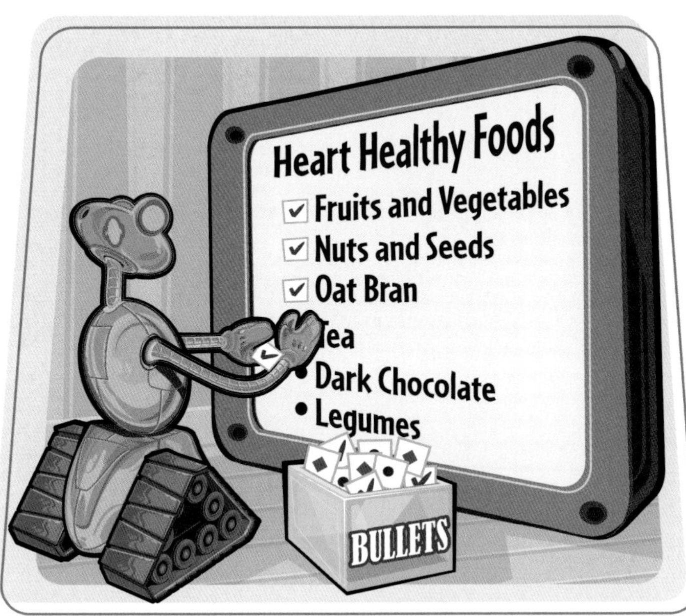


You can make your PowerPoint presentation more visually appealing and more interesting by applying formatting to the slides. You can apply text effects, modify the spacing, change the background, apply themes, and even create custom formats.

# Apply a Quick Style

You can enhance a slide's visual appeal with just a few mouse clicks by applying a Quick Style. Each Quick Style is a predefined collection of formatting that applies shadows, reflections, borders, backgrounds, and 3-D effects.

## Apply a Quick Style

1. Select the text that you want to format.

   Click a text box to format all of its text, or click and drag over the text.

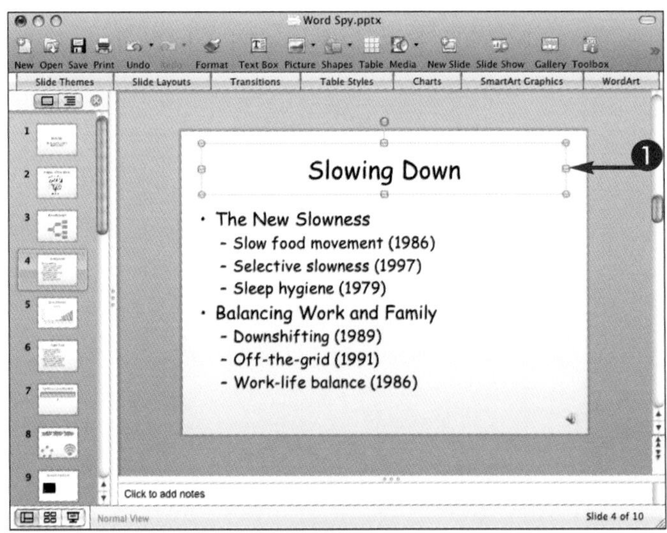


2. Display the Formatting Palette.

***Note:*** *See Chapter 3 to learn how to display and hide the Formatting Palette.*

3. Click the **Quick Styles and Effects** panel.

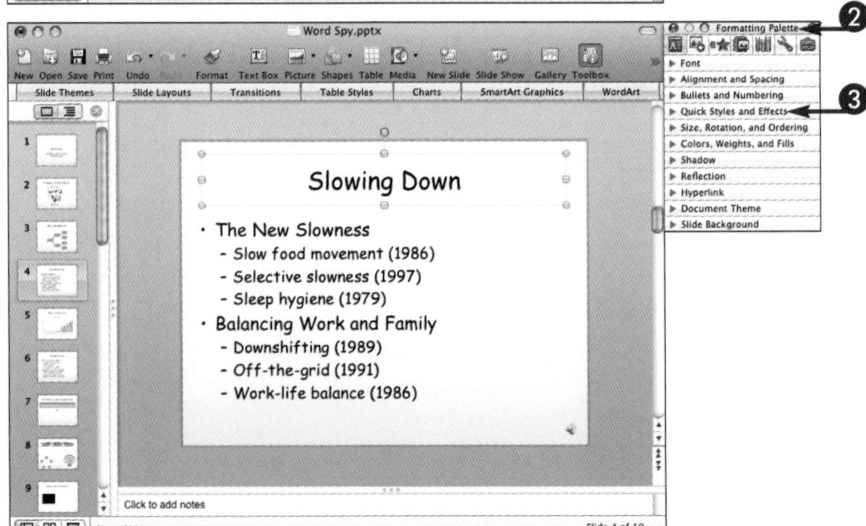

4 Click the **Quick Styles** button ( ).

5 Click [▼] and [▲] to scroll through the available Quick Styles.

6 Click the Quick Style you want to apply.

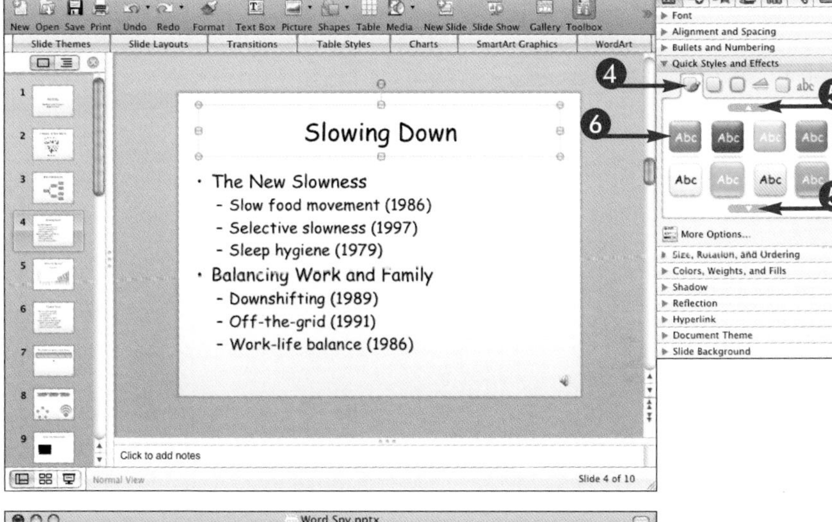


- PowerPoint applies the Quick Style to the text.

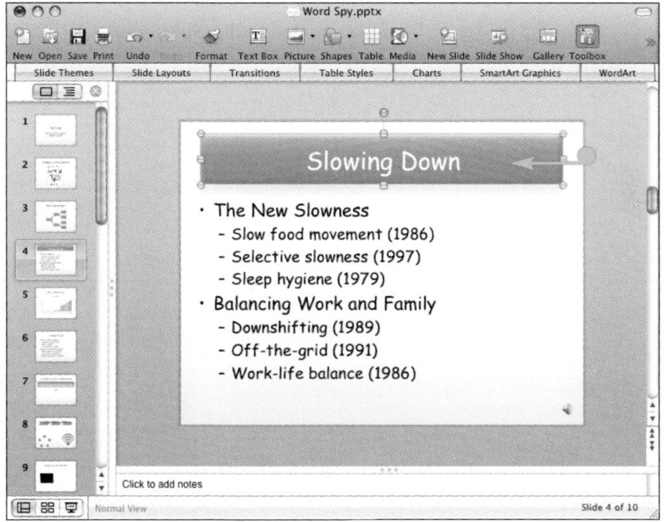


TIP

**Can I apply the Quick Style effects individually?**

Yes. Use the following buttons:

- Click this button and then click a shadow effect.
- Click this button and then click a glow effect.
- Click this button and then click a reflection effect.
- Click this button and then click a 3-D effect.
- abc Click this button and then click a text transform effect.

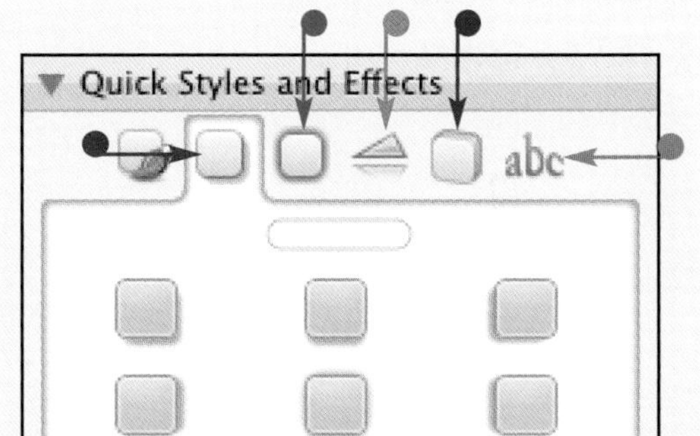

# Set Line and Paragraph Spacing

You can improve the look of your PowerPoint slides by adjusting the line and paragraph spacing. For example, you can produce more white space by increasing the spacing, which makes the slide easier to read, especially from a distance.

**The line spacing determines the amount of space between each line in a paragraph. For example, double spacing leaves twice as much space between the lines as the standard single spacing. Paragraph spacing determines the amount of space, measured in points, before and after a paragraph.**

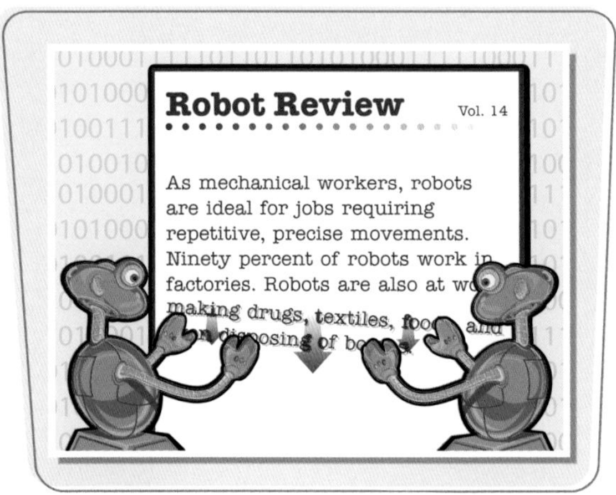


## Set Line and Paragraph Spacing

1. Select the text you want to format.
2. Click **Format**.
3. Click **Paragraph**.

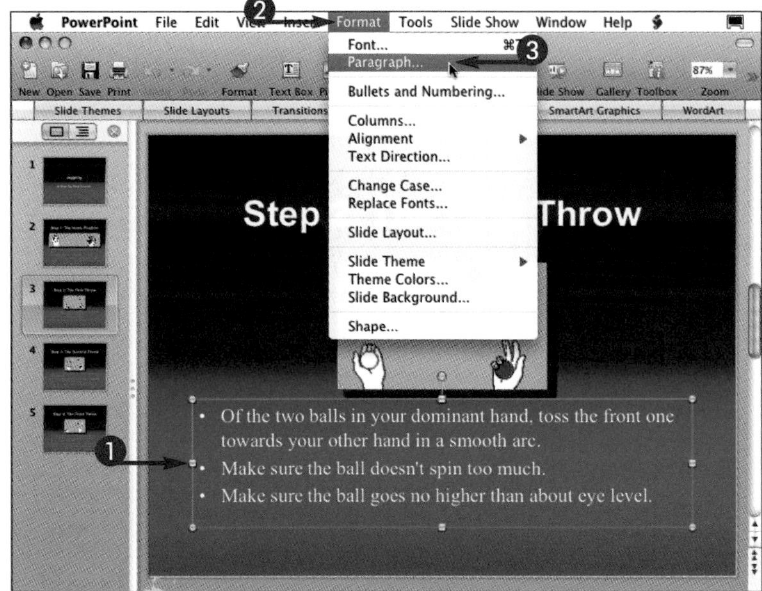


The Format Text dialog appears.

4. Click **Paragraph**.
5. In the Before text box, type the number of points of space you want before each paragraph.
6. In the After text box, type the number of points of space you want after each paragraph.

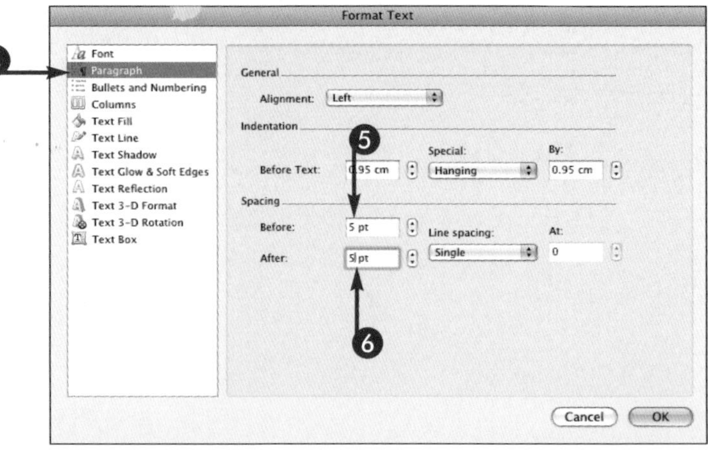

7 Click the **Line spacing** and then click the line spacing you want.

8 Click **OK**.

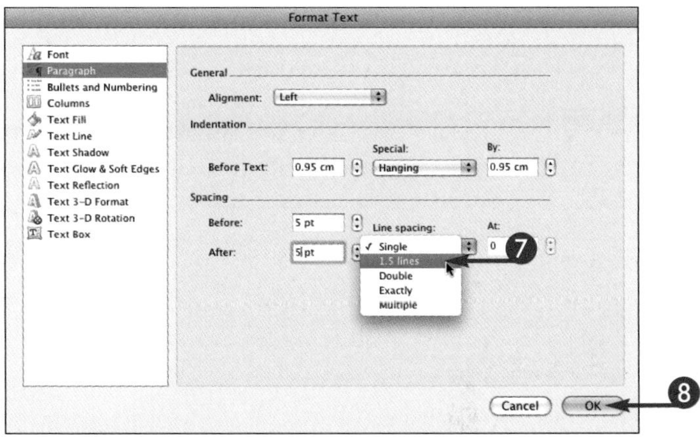


- Word applies the spacing to the selected paragraphs.

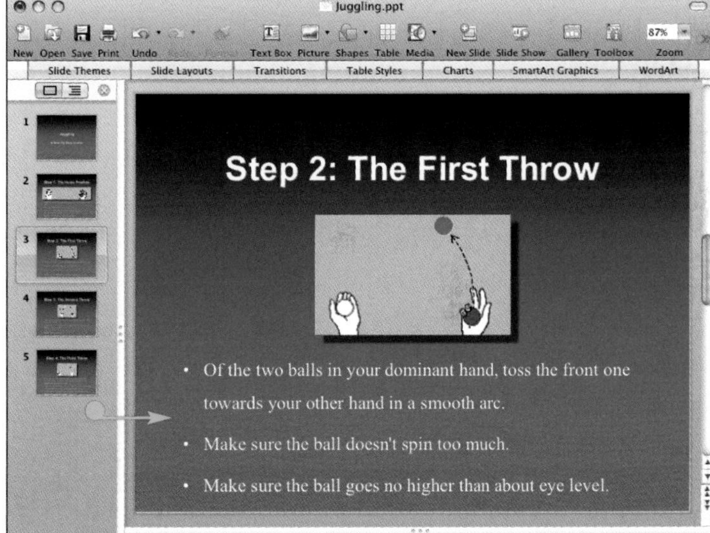


## TIPS

### Is there an easier way to change the paragraph spacing?

Yes. Select the text you want to format, display the Formatting Palette (see Chapter 3), and then click the **Alignment and Spacing** panel. Click **Increase Paragraph Spacing** ( ) to increase the spacing after each paragraph by 6 points. Click **Decrease Paragraph Spacing** ( ) to decrease the spacing after each paragraph by 6 points.

### Can I adjust the spacing between characters?

Yes. You can increase the spacing to open up the text, which often makes a document easier to read. Similarly, you can decrease the spacing as a special effect or to squeeze more text onto a line. Click **Format**, click **Font** (or press ⌘+D), and then click the **Character Spacing** tab. Type a percentage value in the Scale text box. Alternatively, click the **Spacing** , click either **Expanded** or **Condensed**, and then type a value in the By text box. Click **OK**.

# Change the Bullet Style

You can add visual interest to your slides by using a custom bullet style. PowerPoint applies different bullet styles to bulleted list items that are on different list levels: a dot for level 1, a dash for level 2, and so on. You can change any default style to one of the predefined styles, such as a diamond or a check mark.

**You can also change the color of your bullets to match or complement your slide colors.**

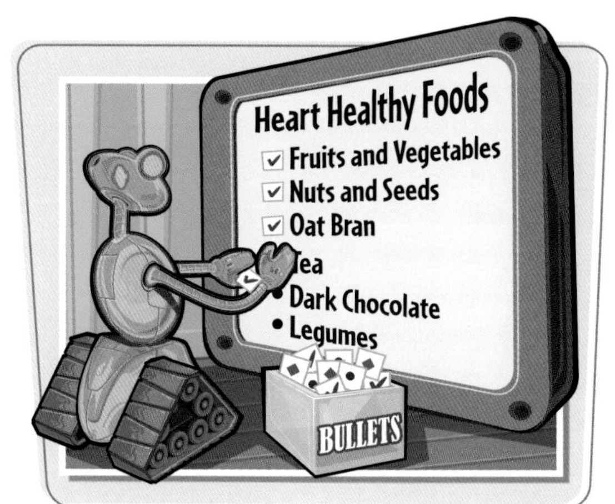


## Change the Bullet Style

1. Select the text you want to format.
2. Click **Format**.
3. Click **Bullets and Numbering**.

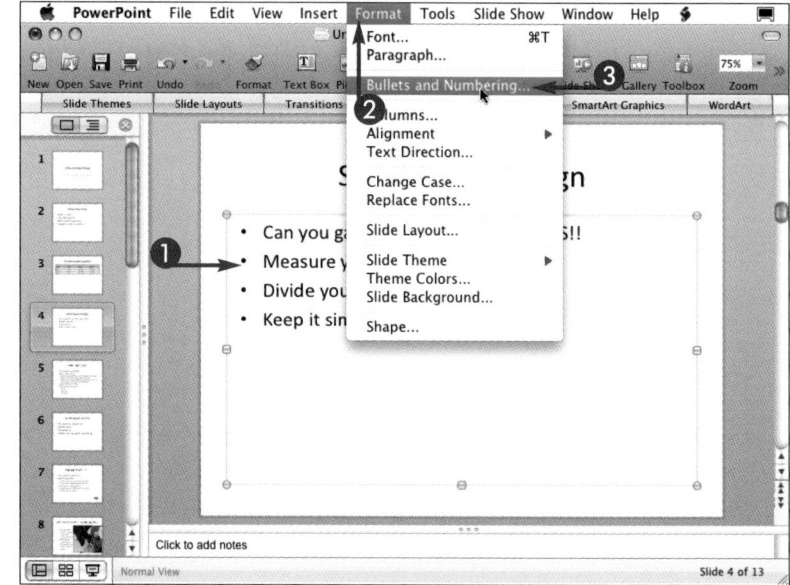


The Format Text dialog appears.

4. Click **Bullets and Numbering**.
5. Click the **Bullets** tab.
6. Click the bullet style you want to use.

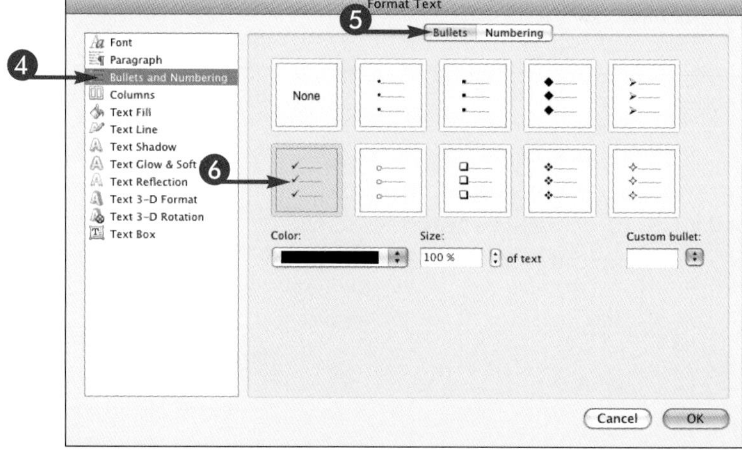

7 Click the **Color** ⬍ and then click the bullet color you want to use.

8 Click **OK**.

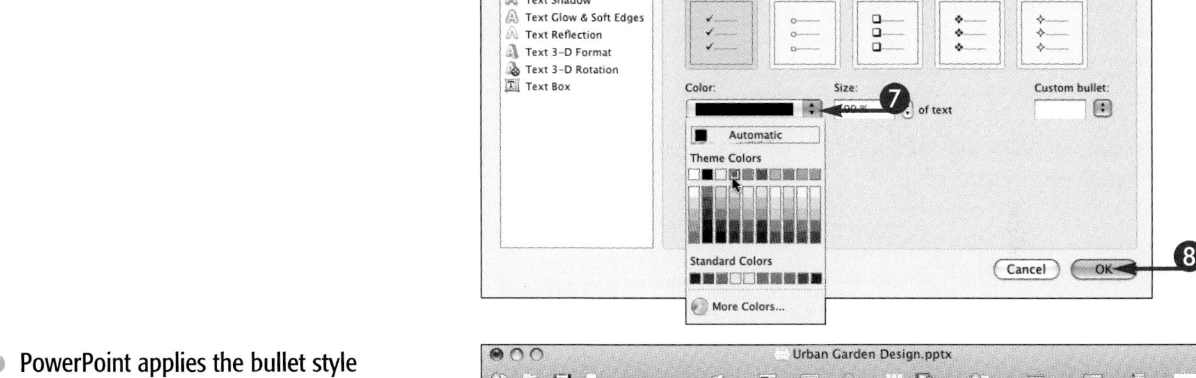

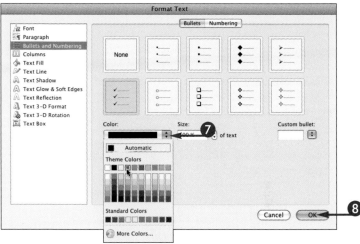

- PowerPoint applies the bullet style to the selected text.

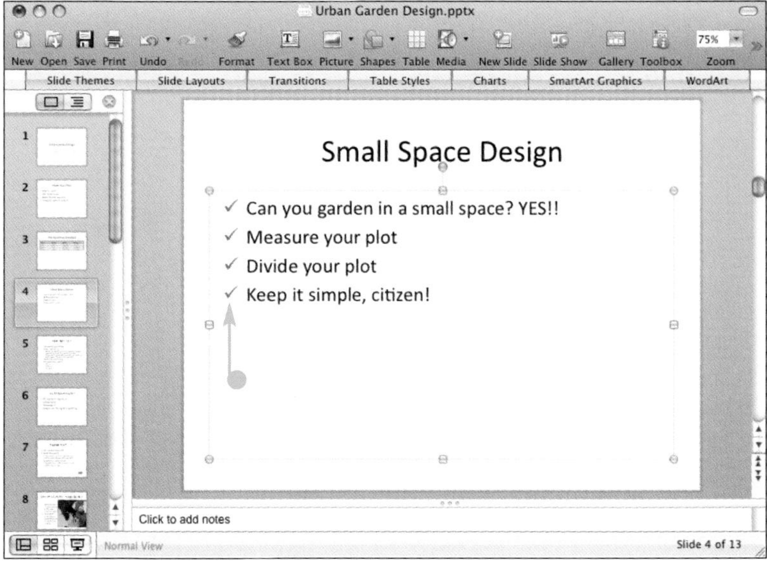


## TIPS

### Some of the predefined bullets are quite large. Can I fix that?

Yes. PowerPoint displays each bullet as a percentage of the bullet text. To reduce the size of these bullet styles, follow Steps **1** to **6** to select the bullet style and then type a relative size for the bullet (such as 75 percent or 50 percent) in the Size text box.

### Can I use a custom character or picture as a bullet?

Yes. PowerPoint has 11 custom characters you can use, including the ⌘ symbol. Follow Steps **1** to **6** to display the Bullets pane and then click the **Custom bullet** ⬍. Click one of the custom characters displayed in the pull-down menu. Alternatively, click **Character** to select a symbol of your own, or click **Picture** to select an image.

# Change the Slide Background

You can often improve the look of your PowerPoint slides by changing the slide background. The default presentation theme creates slides with a white background, which is usually a good choice because it makes the slide text easy to read. However, PowerPoint gives you a choice of predefined background colors and effects.

**PowerPoint automatically adjusts the text color if you choose a darker or lighter background color.**

## Change the Slide Background

1. Open the presentation that you want to format.

***Note:*** *To open an Office document, see Chapter 2.*

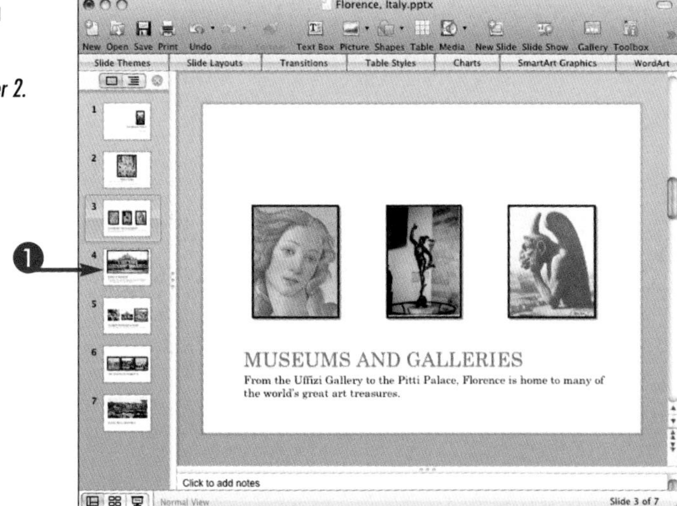

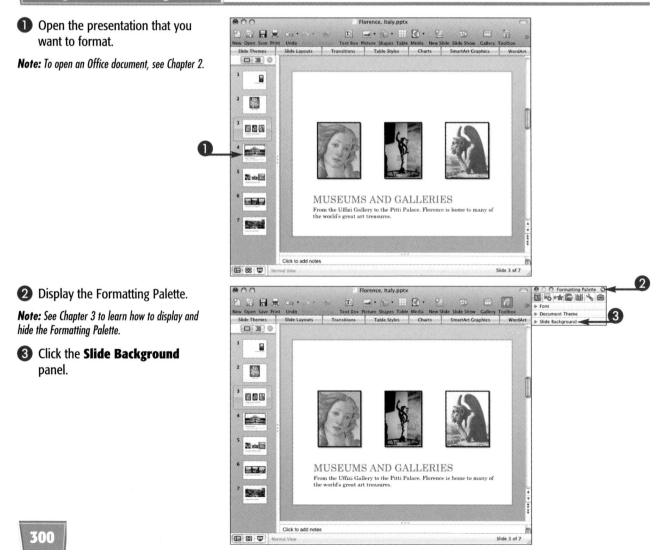

2. Display the Formatting Palette.

***Note:*** *See Chapter 3 to learn how to display and hide the Formatting Palette.*

3. Click the **Slide Background** panel.

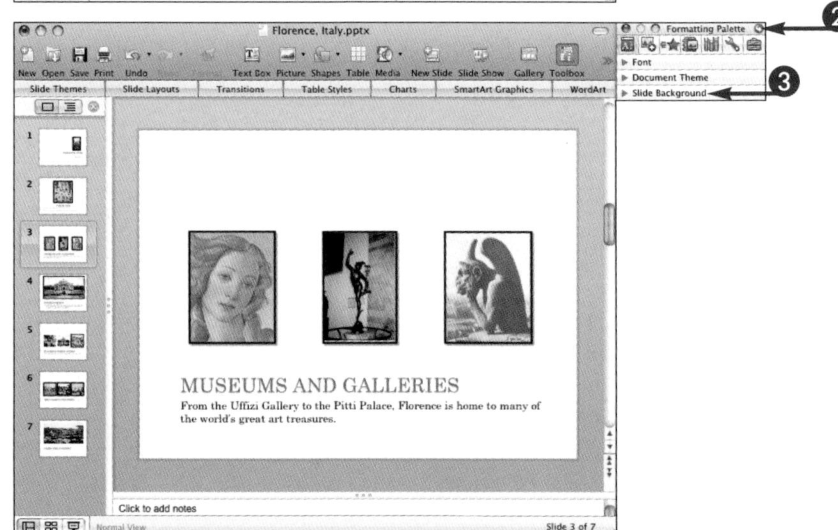

4 Click the background you want to use.

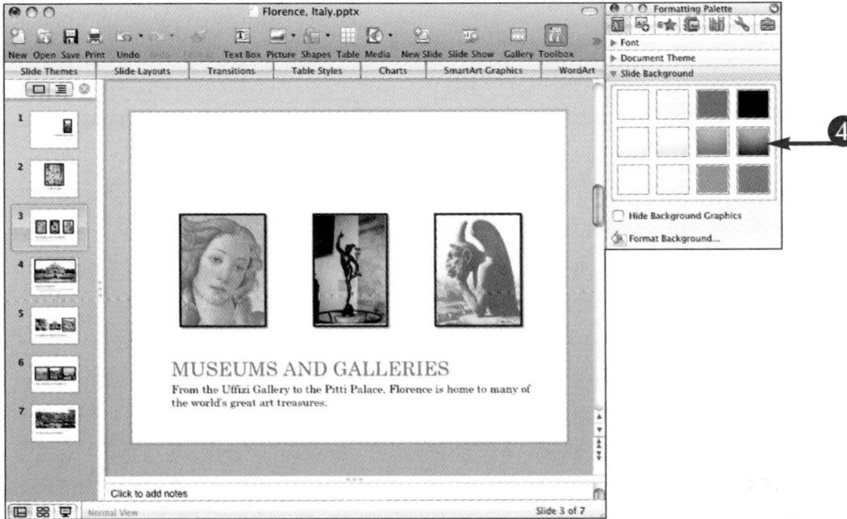


- PowerPoint applies the background to all the slides in your presentation.

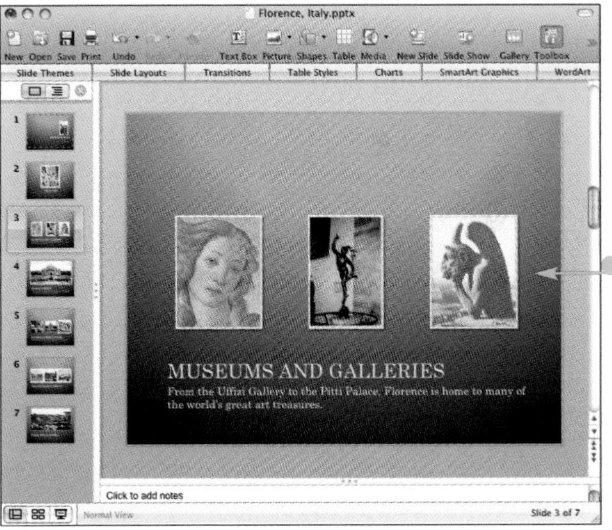

**PowerPoint applies the background to all my slides. Can I apply a background to a single slide?**

Yes. The Format Background dialog enables you to apply a custom background to one or more selected slides. Select the slides you want to format and then click **Format Background** in the Slide Background panel. Use the Format Background dialog to define your custom background and then click **Apply**.

**Can I apply a picture as a background?**

Yes, although you need to be careful that the picture you use does not make your slide text difficult to read. Select the slides you want to format and then click **Format Background** in the Slide Background panel. In the Format Background dialog, click the **Picture** tab, click **Choose a Picture**, click the image file you want to use, and then click **Insert**. Click **Apply** to format just the selected slides, or click **Apply to All** to format all the slides.

# Apply a Slide Theme

You can apply a slide theme to improve almost every aspect of the design of your PowerPoint presentation. A *slide theme* is a predefined collection of slide layouts, colors, fonts, backgrounds, and graphics that you can apply to your entire presentation with just a few mouse clicks.

**PowerPoint includes 50 eye-catching slide themes, so you should be able to find something appropriate for your presentation. You can also create your own theme. See the section "Create a Custom Theme."**

## Apply a Slide Theme

1. Open the presentation you want to work with.

*Note: To open an Office document, see Chapter 2.*

2. Click **Slide Themes**.

The Slide Themes gallery appears.

3. Click **Built-in Themes**.
4. Click ▶ and ◀ to review the slide themes.

- Move the mouse pointer over the slide theme.
- The name of the slide theme appears here.

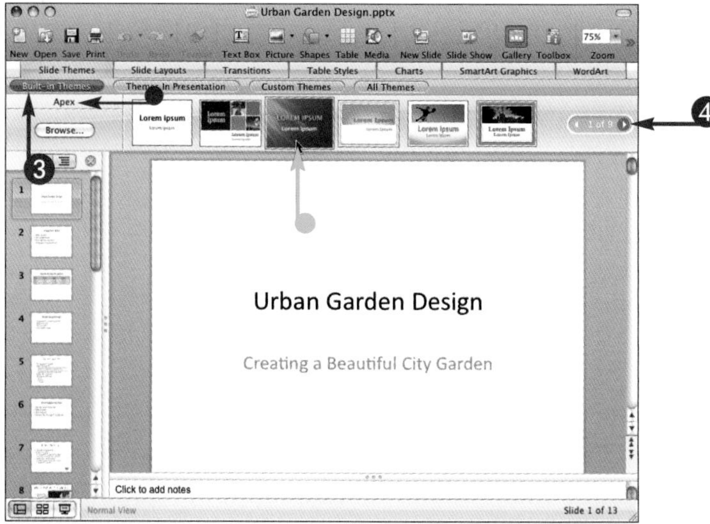

5 Click the slide theme you want to use.

- Excel applies the theme to the slides.

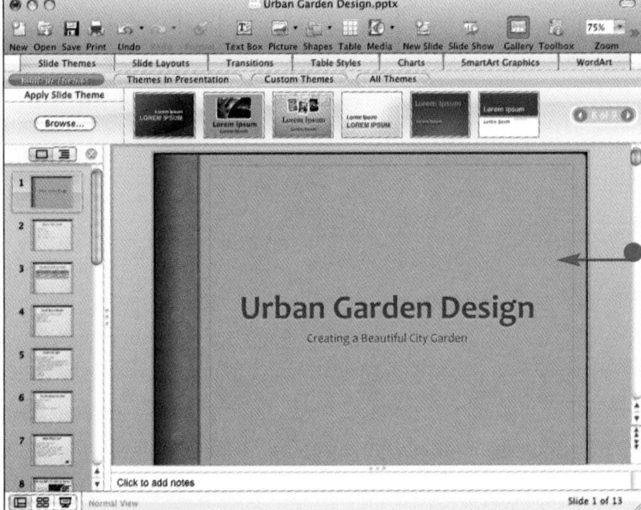


TIP

**Someone sent me a theme file. How do I apply it to my presentation?**

First, be sure to save the theme file to your Mac's hard drive. Ideally, you should save it to the My Themes folder. Open your home folder and then open Library:Application Support:Microsoft:Office:User Templates:My Themes.

Return to PowerPoint, open the presentation you want to work with, and then click **Slide Themes**. Click **Custom Themes**, which displays thumbnails for each theme file in the My Themes folder. Click the theme you saved.

If you saved the theme file in some other folder, click **Browse** to open the Choose Themed Document or Slide Template dialog. Locate and click the theme file you want to use, and then click **Apply**.

# Create a Custom Theme

If you go to the trouble of choosing a slide theme and then customizing that scheme with effects and with predefined or custom colors and fonts, you probably do not want to go through the entire process the next time you want the same theme for a presentation. Fortunately, you do not have to because PowerPoint enables you to save all of your theme details as a custom theme.

## Create a Custom Theme

1. Start a new presentation or open a presentation that you want to format.
2. Apply a slide theme if you want to use that theme as a starting point.

**Note:** *See the section "Apply a Slide Theme."*

3. Display the Formatting Palette.

**Note:** *See Chapter 3 to learn how to display and hide the Formatting Palette.*

4. Click the **Document Theme** panel.

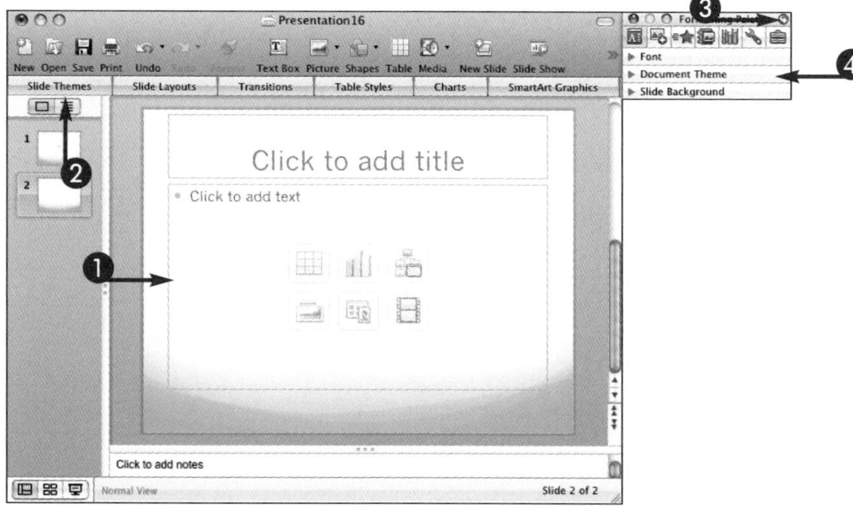


5. Click the **Colors** ▾ and then click the theme colors you want to use.
6. Click the **Fonts** ▾ and then click the fonts you want to use.

**Note:** *Each theme includes a pair of fonts. The first font applies to the slide titles, and the second font applies to the slide.*

7. Apply any other formatting you want to include in your custom theme.
8. Click **Save Theme**.

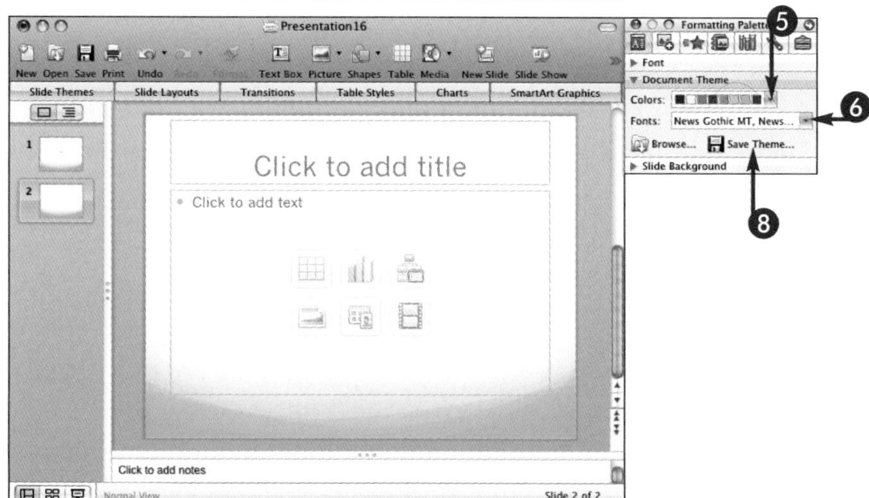

A Save as dialog appears.

9 In the Save As text box, type a name for the theme.

10 Click **Save**.

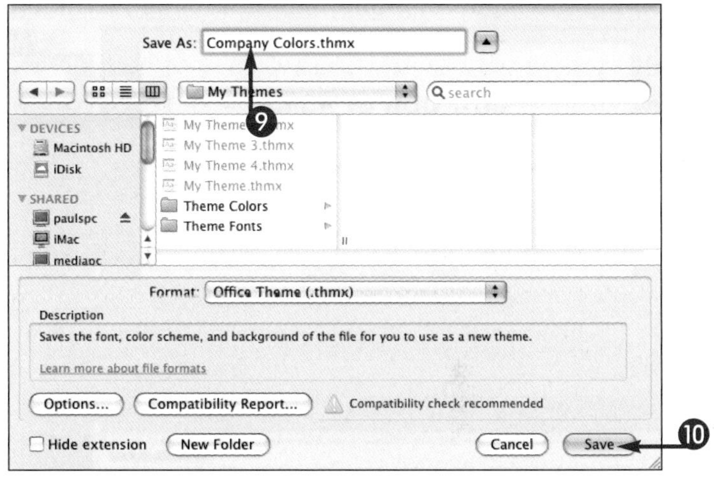


PowerPoint saves your formatting as an Office Theme file.

- A thumbnail for the custom theme appears in the **Custom Themes** section of the Slide Themes gallery. Click this thumbnail to apply your custom theme to another presentation.

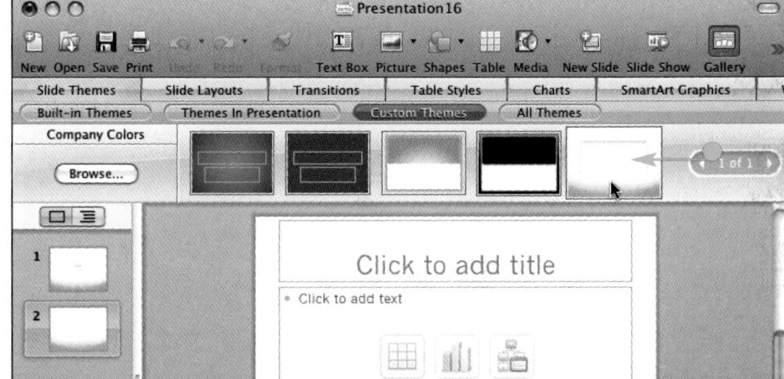

**Can I create a custom color scheme?**

Yes. Follow these steps:

1 Click **Format**.

2 Click **Theme Colors**.

3 In the Create Theme Colors dialog, select a theme color.

4 Click **Change Color**.

5 In the Color Picker choose the color you want to use.

6 Click **OK**.

7 Repeat Steps **3** to **6** to customize the other theme colors.

8 In the Name text box, type a name for your scheme.

9 Click **Apply to All**.

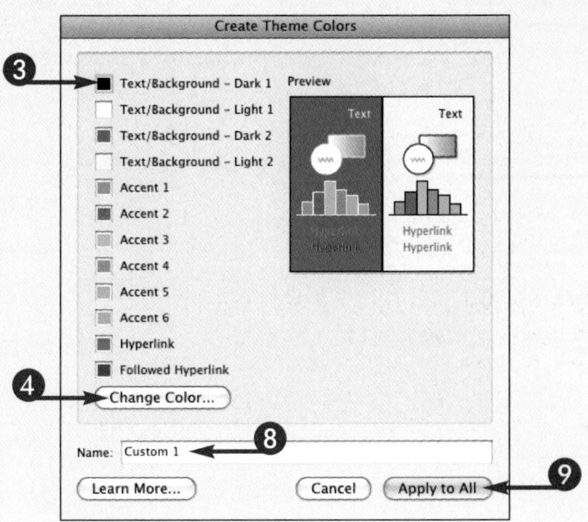

# Replace a Font

You can keep your presentation design consistent by replacing fonts that do not fit with your design. Fonts can become inconsistent if, for example, you insert slides from another presentation that uses a different font or you collaborate on a presentation and the other person uses a different typeface.

## Replace a Font

1. Open the presentation that contains the font you want to replace.
2. Click **Format**.
3. Click **Replace Fonts**.

The Replace Font dialog appears.

4. Click the **Replace** and then click the font that you want to replace.

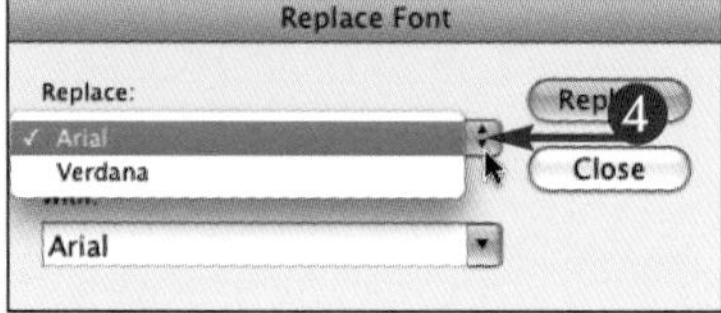

5 Click the **With** ▾ and then click the font that you want as a replacement.

6 Click **Replace**.

PowerPoint replaces the font throughout the presentation.

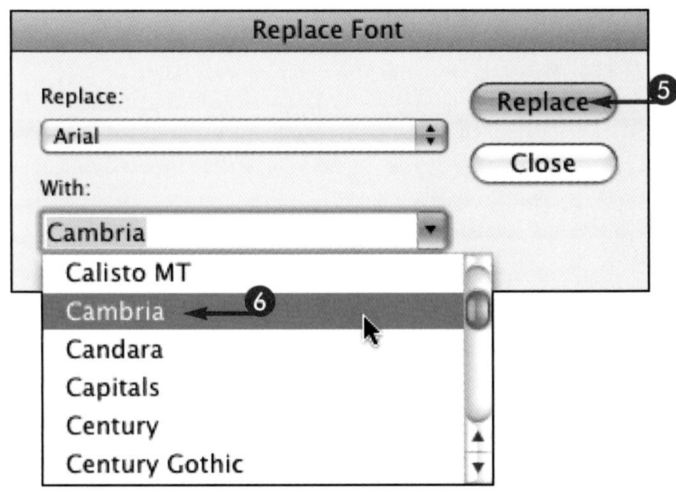


7 Repeat Steps **4** to **6** to replace any other fonts in the presentation.

8 Click **Close**.

TIP

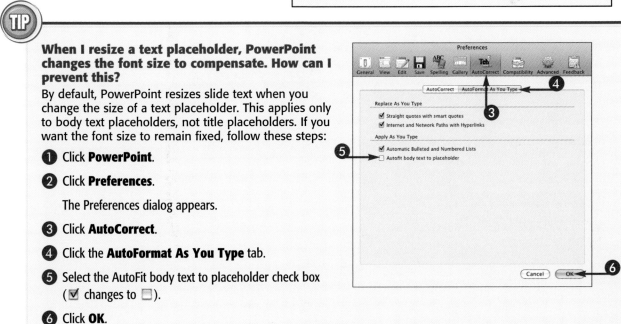

**When I resize a text placeholder, PowerPoint changes the font size to compensate. How can I prevent this?**

By default, PowerPoint resizes slide text when you change the size of a text placeholder. This applies only to body text placeholders, not title placeholders. If you want the font size to remain fixed, follow these steps:

1 Click **PowerPoint**.

2 Click **Preferences**.

The Preferences dialog appears.

3 Click **AutoCorrect**.

4 Click the **AutoFormat As You Type** tab.

5 Select the AutoFit body text to placeholder check box (☑ changes to ☐).

6 Click **OK**.

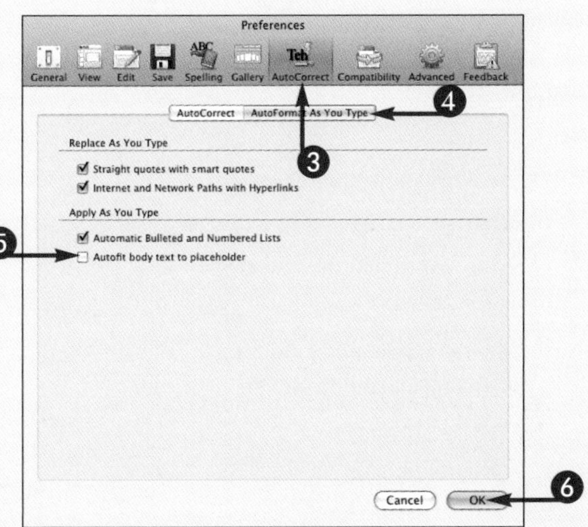

# Create a Custom Format Using the Slide Master

You can modify a PowerPoint presentation's slide master to create a custom presentation template. The slide master acts as a kind of design center for your presentation. The slide master's fonts, bullet styles, and other formatting are used on each slide in your presentation.

**Also, any object you add to the slide master — such as clip art or a company logo — appears in the same position on each slide. You can also work with *layout masters*, which control the look of each type of slide layout.**

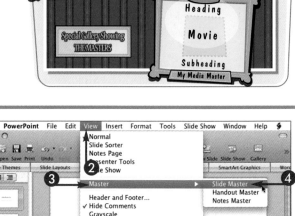

## Create a Custom Format Using the Slide Master

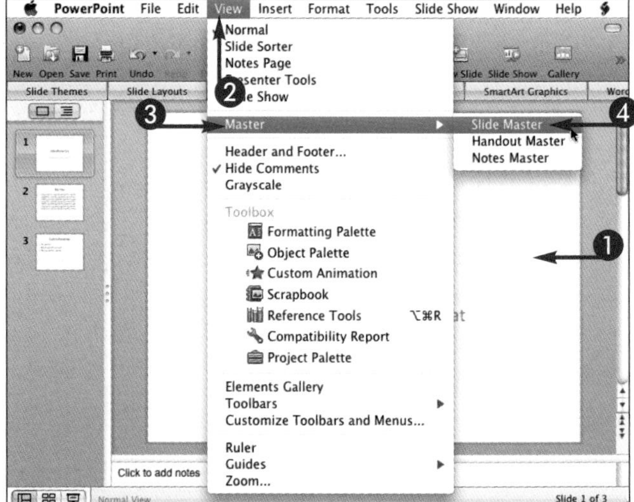


1. Open the presentation you want to format.
2. Click **View**.
3. Click **Master**.
4. Click **Slide Master**.

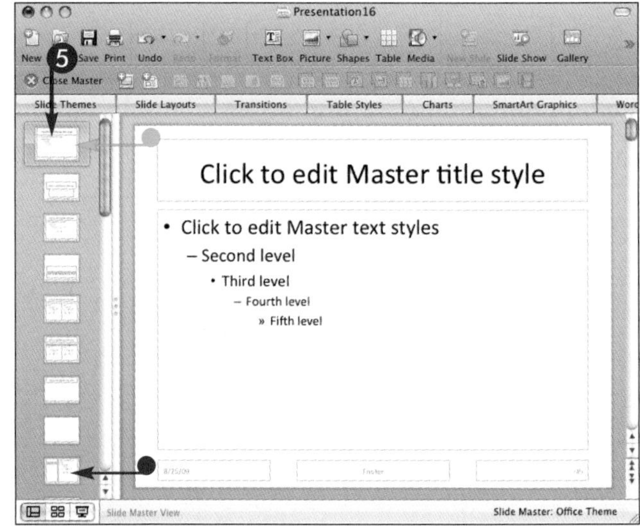


The presentation's slide master appears.

5. Click the layout master you want to customize.

- Click the theme's slide master to apply the formatting to all the layouts.
- Click a layout master to apply the formatting to just that layout.

6 Click the placeholder you want to format.

If you want to format specific text, select the text.

7 Make your changes to the placeholder or text, such as altering the font, changing the spacing, or moving or resizing the placeholder.

8 Make your changes to other slide formatting, such as the background

9 Repeat Steps **6** and **8** to format the other placeholders or text.

10 To add an object to a master, click **Insert**, click the object type (such as Picture), and then add the object.

11 Repeat Steps **5** to **10** to customize other layout masters.

12 Click **Close Master**.

PowerPoint closes the slide master and returns you to your presentation.

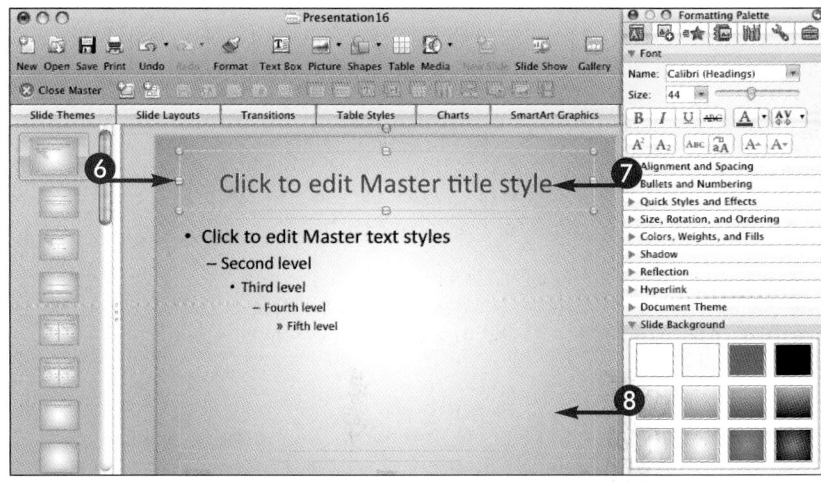


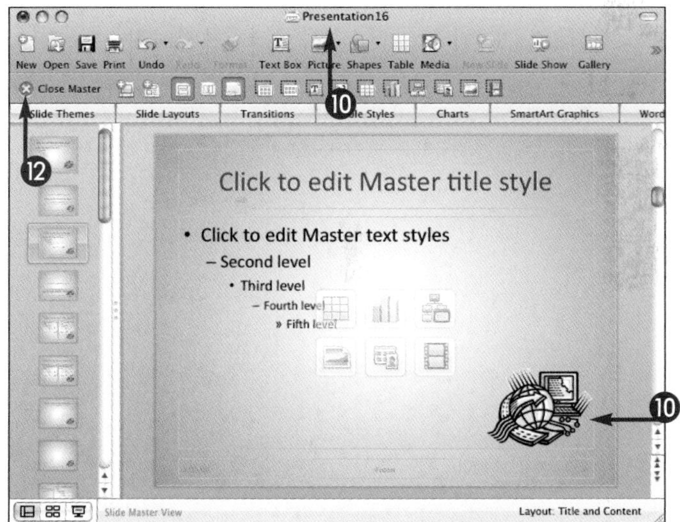

### Can I add a custom layout to the slide master?

Yes. In the Slide Master view, click **Insert** and then click **New Layout** to create a new layout with just a Title placeholder. You can also click . Click the buttons in the Master toolbar to add placeholders to the layout. For example, click the **Content** button () to create a Content placeholder, or click the **Text** button () to create a Text placeholder. Click and drag inside the layout to create the placeholder. You can also move and resize the placeholder as needed.

### Can I use my custom format in another presentation?

Yes. With the custom presentation open, click **File** and then click **Save As** to open a Save as dialog. In the Save As text box, type a name for the file, click the **Format** , click **PowerPoint Template**, and then click **Save**. To use the template for a new presentation, click **File**, click **Project Gallery**, click **New**, and then click **My Templates**. Click the icon for your custom template, and then click **Open**.

CHAPTER

17

# Setting Up and Running a Slide Show

When you are ready to show other people your presentation, it is time to work on the slide show that you are presenting. This involves adding slide transitions, animation effects, action buttons, timings, and narration. When these tasks are done, you are ready to run the slide show.

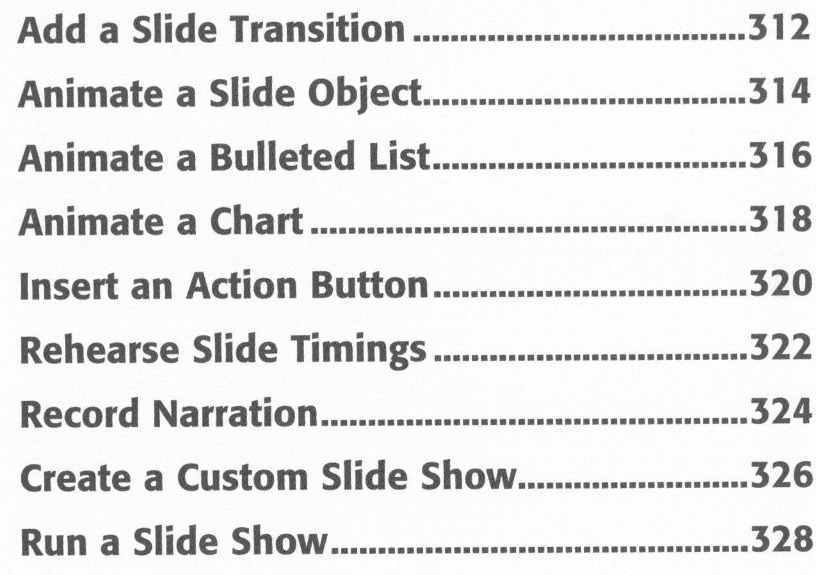

# Add a Slide Transition

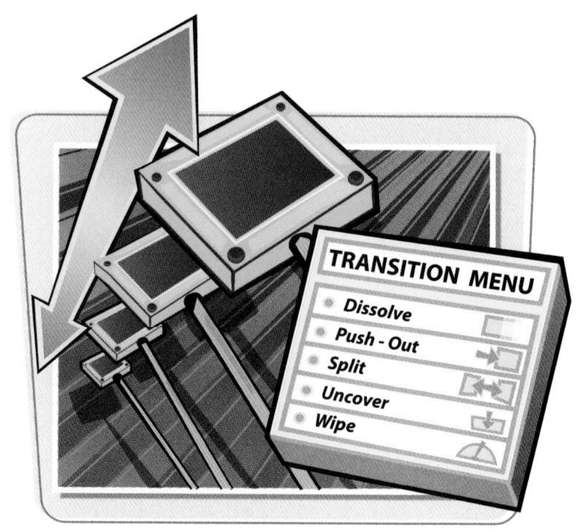


You can enhance your slide show with *slide transitions*, which are special effects that display the next slide in the presentation. For example, in a *fade* transition, the next slide gradually materializes, while in a *blinds* transition the next slide appears with an effect similar to opening Venetian blinds.

**PowerPoint has nearly 60 slide transitions, and for each one you can control the transition speed, the sound effect that goes with the transition, and the trigger for the transition, such as a mouse click or a time interval.**

## Add a Slide Transition

1. Open the presentation you want to work with.
2. Click **Transitions**.

   The Transitions gallery appears.
3. Click the slide you want to animate with a transition.
4. Click a transition category.

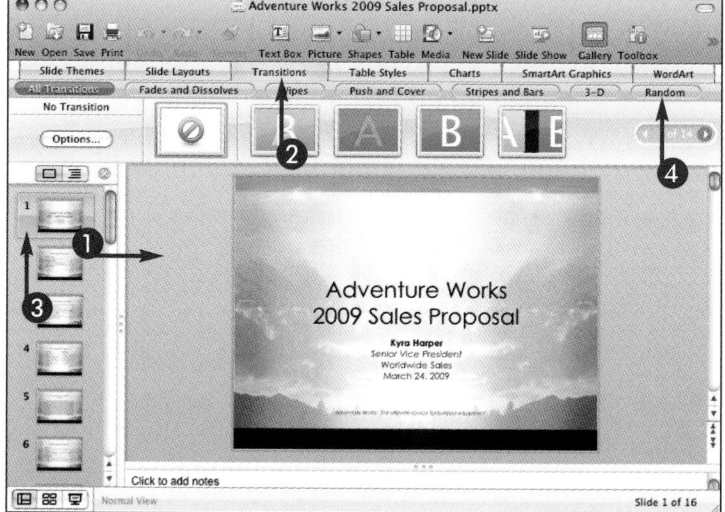


5. Click and to review the transitions.

- Move over the transition.
- The name of the transition appears here.

6. Click the transition you want to use.

   PowerPoint previews the transition.
7. Click **Options**.

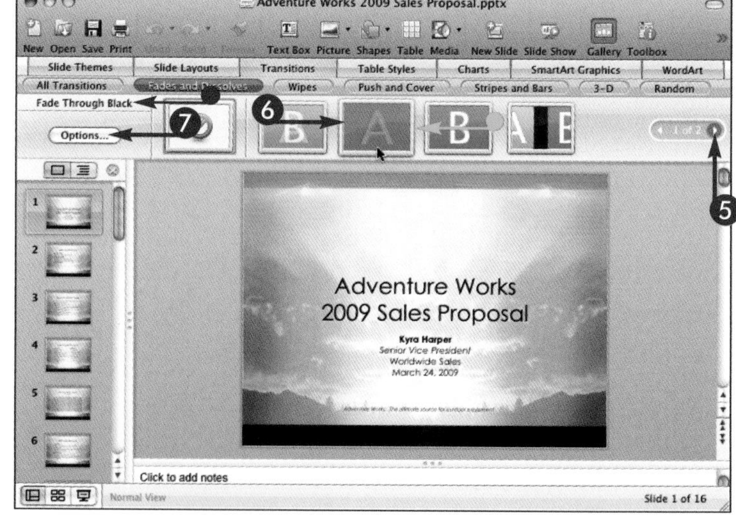

The Transition Options dialog appears.

8 Select the transition speed you want to use (○ changes to ◉).

9 Click the **Sound** ⬍ and then click the sound effect you want to play along with the transition.

10 To advance the slide when you click your mouse, select the **On mouse click** option (☐ changes to ☑).

- To advance the slide after a time interval, select the **Automatically after** option (☐ changes to ☑) and type a time in the **seconds** text box.

11 Click **Apply**.

- If you want to apply the transition to every slide, click **Apply to All**.

12 Repeat Steps **3** to **11** to add transitions to your other slides.

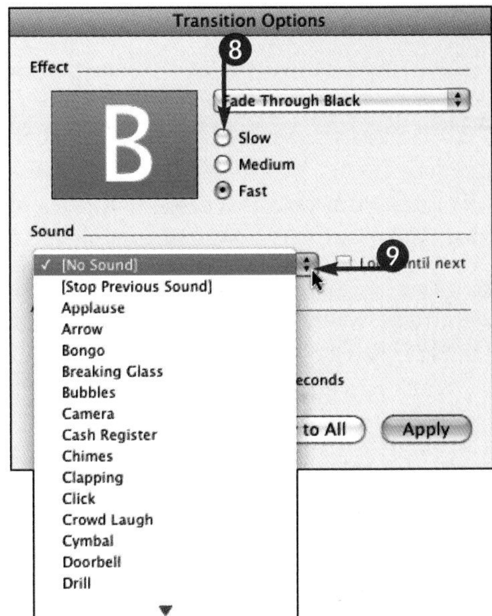


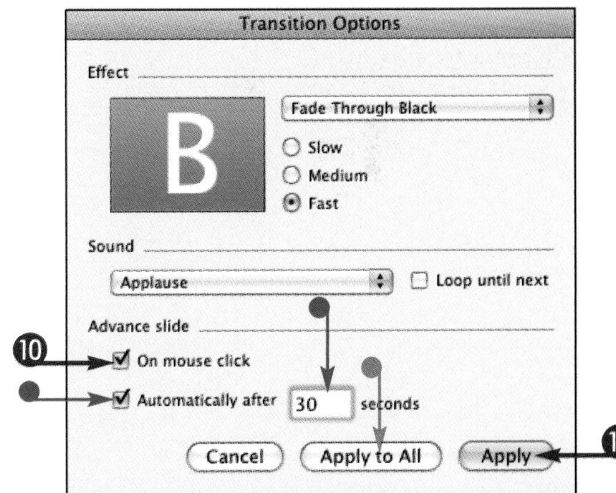

### Are there any guidelines I should follow when I use transitions?

Yes. First, remember that using some sort of effect to transition from one slide to the next is a good idea because it adds visual interest, gives the audience a short breather, and helps you control the pacing of your presentation. However, transitions can also be distracting. Simple transitions such as fades, wipes, and dissolves add interest but do not get in the way. Similarly, avoid using many different types of transitions in a single presentation. Finally, use the Fast setting to ensure that the transition from one slide to another never takes more than a few seconds.

### How do I turn off a transition for a slide?

First, select the slide you want to work with. If you want to remove the transitions from all your slides, select every slide. Click **Transitions** to open the Transitions gallery, click any category, and then click the **No Transition** button (⊘). PowerPoint removes the transition.

# Animate a Slide Object

You can add dynamism and visual appeal to your slide show by animating a slide object. An *animation* is a visual effect applied to a specific slide element. In this section, you learn how to animate slide objects such as title placeholders, as well as content such as pictures, clip art, and tables.

**You can add an *entrance effect*, which brings the object into the slide; an *exit effect*, which removes the object from the slide; or an *emphasis effect*, which emphasizes the object in some way.**

## Animate a Slide Object

1. Click **Toolbox** ( ).
2. Click **Custom Animation** ( ).
3. Click the slide object you want to animate.
4. Click the **Add Entrance Effect** button ( ).
   - For an emphasis effect, click the **Add Emphasis Effect** button ( ).
   - For an exit effect, click the **Add Exit Effect** button ( ).
5. Click **More Effects**.
   - You can also click one of the standard effects listed here and then skip to Step **8**.

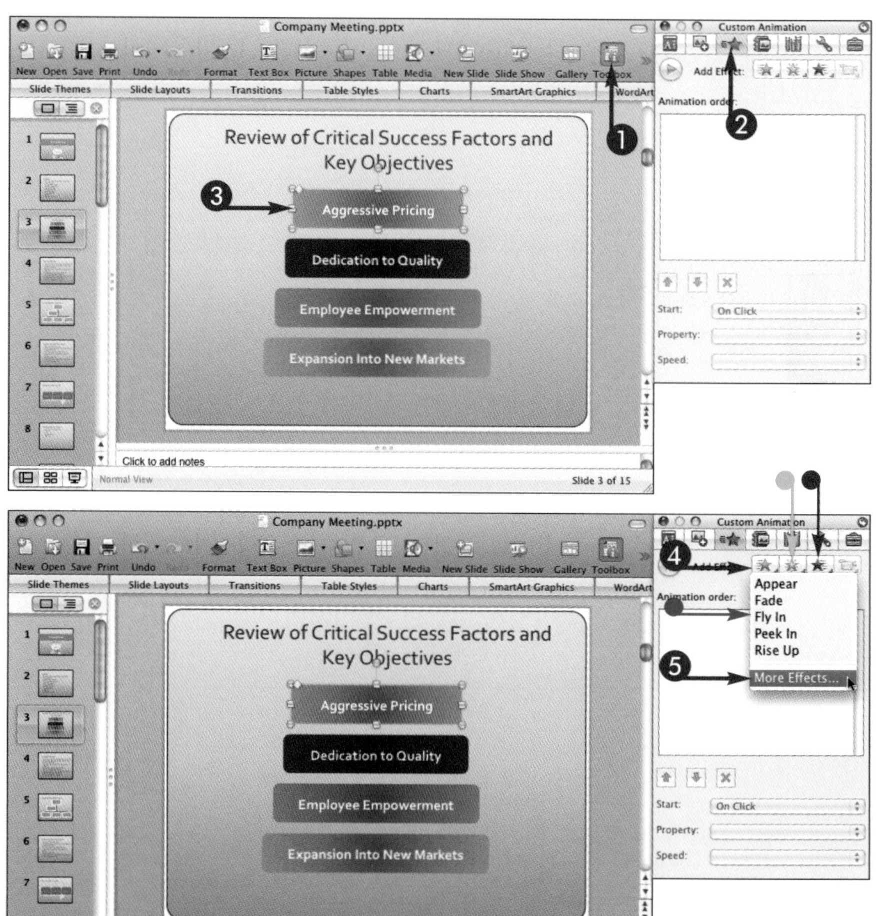

The Animation Effects dialog appears.

6. Click the animation effect you want to use.

PowerPoint previews the effect.

- If you do not want to see the animation previews, deselect the **Show preview** option (☑ changes to ☐).

7. Click **OK**.

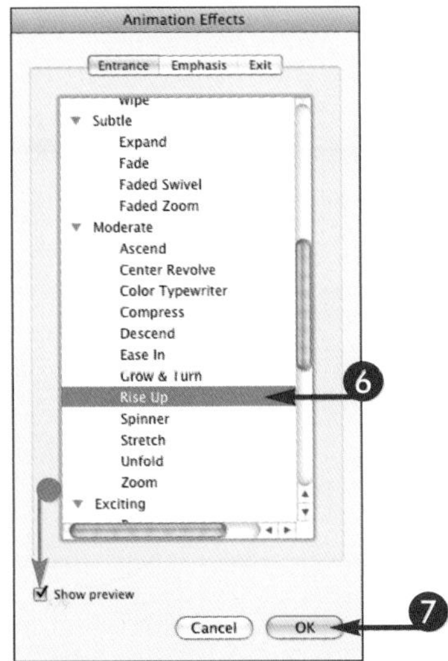


- PowerPoint adds the effect to the **Animation order** list.

8. Click the **Speed** button and then click the duration of the animation.

- You can click the **Play** button at any time to see the animation.

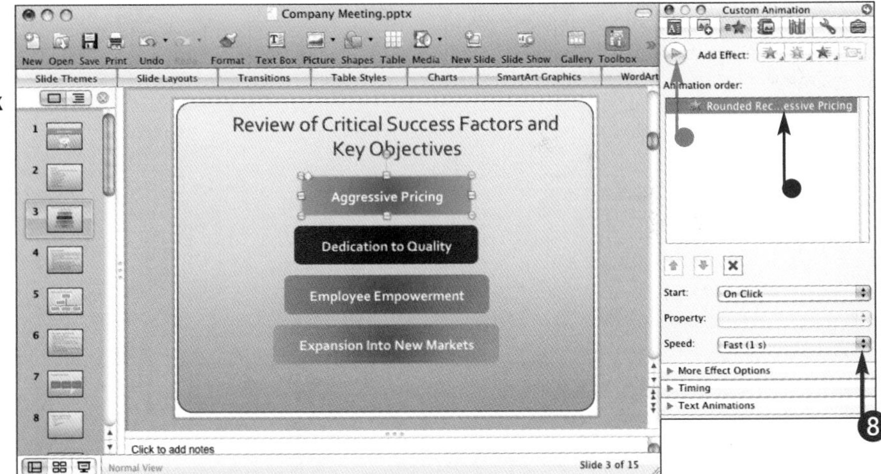

### How do I change an effect?

First, display the slide that contains the effect you want to change. Follow Steps **1** and **2** to display the Custom Animation palette, and in the Animation order list, double-click the animation effect you want to edit. In the Animation Effects dialog, click the new animation you want to use and then click **Replace**. To change the order in which the animation runs, click the animation and then click the **Move Up** button or the **Move Down** button.

### How do I remove an effect from an object?

First, display the slide that contains the effect you want to remove. Follow Steps **1** and **2** to display the Custom Animation palette. In the Animation order list, click the animation effect you want to remove. Click the **Delete** button to remove the effect.

# Animate a Bulleted List

You can add dynamic tension to your presentation and gain more control over the slide show by animating a bulleted list so that each item in the list appears one at a time each time you click the mouse.

**If you want your bulleted list to appear all at once, see the section "Animate a Slide Object."**

## Animate a Bulleted List

1. Click **Toolbox** ( ).
2. Click the **Custom Animation** button ( ).
3. Click the placeholder for the bulleted list you want to animate.

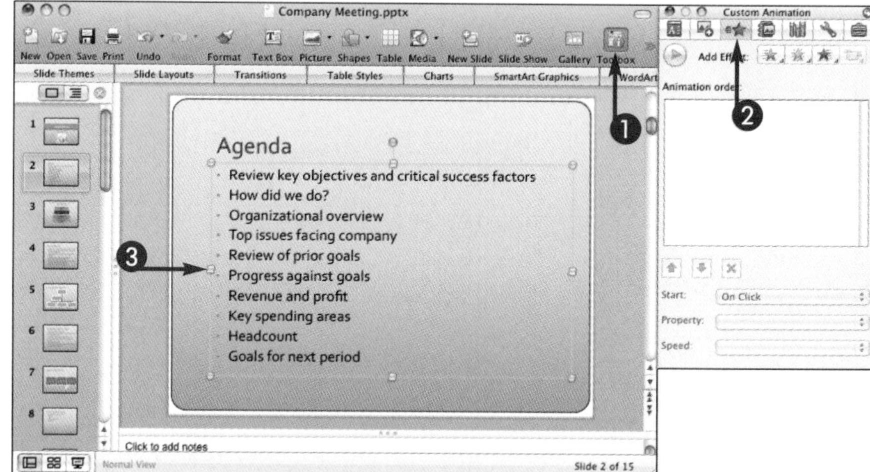


4. Click ( ).
5. Click **More Effects**.

- You can also click one of the standard effects listed here and then skip to Step **8**.

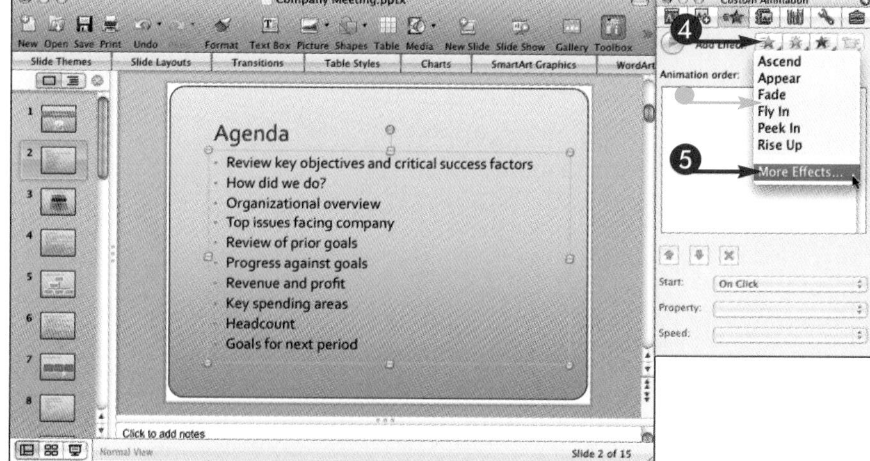

The Animation Effects dialog appears.

6 Click the animation effect you want to use.

PowerPoint previews the effect.

- If you do not want to see the animation previews, deselect the **Show preview** option (☑ changes to ☐).

7 Click **OK**.

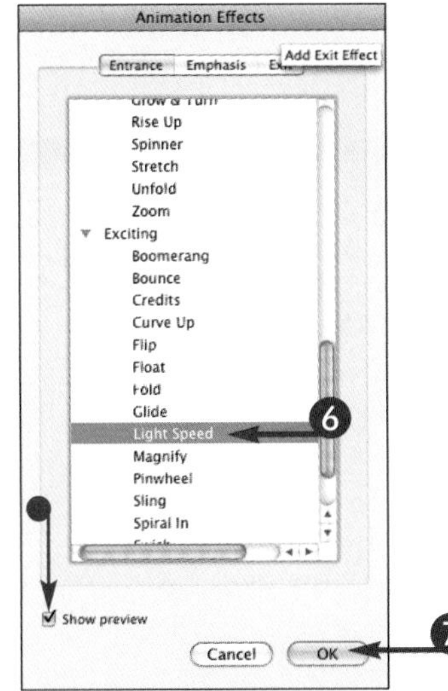


- PowerPoint adds the effect to the **Animation order** list.

8 Click the **Speed** ⬍ and then click the duration of the animation.

9 Click the **Text Animations** panel.

10 Click the **Group text** ⬍ and then click **1st level**.

If you want the second-level bullet items to appear separately with each mouse click, click **2nd level** instead.

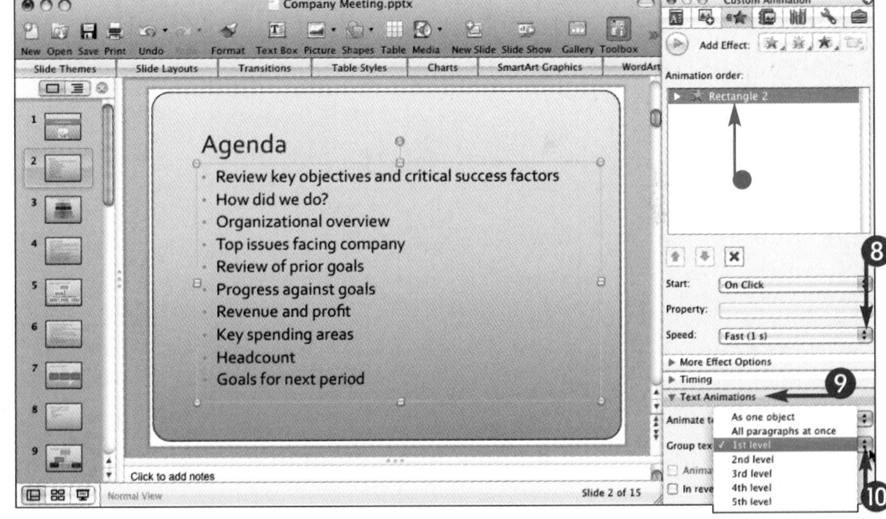

## How can I apply different animations to bulleted list items?

1 Display the slide that contains the bulleted list.

2 Follow Steps **1** and **2** to display the Custom Animation palette.

3 Click ▶ beside the effect you applied to the bulleted list (▶ changes to ▼).

4 Double-click the animation effect you want to edit.

5 Click the new animation you want to use.

6 Click **Replace** and then repeat Steps **4** to **6** as needed.

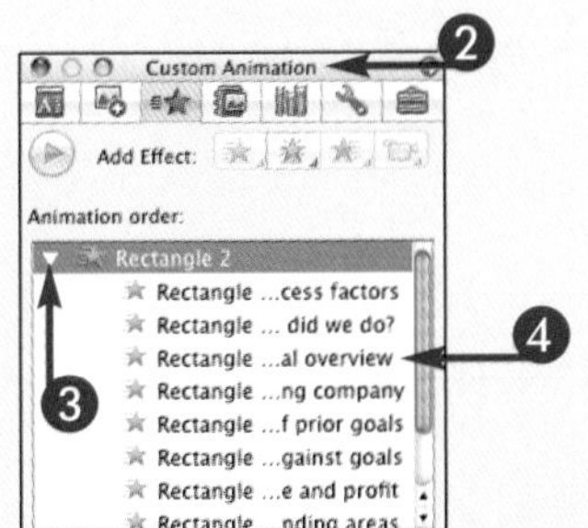

# Animate a Chart

If your slide show includes a chart, you can animate the components of the chart, such as the data series or the categories. This enables you to fully control when and how the various components of the chart appear during the slide show.

**If you want your chart to appear all at once, see the section "Animate a Slide Object."**

## Animate a Chart

1. Click **Toolbox** ( ).
2. Click the **Custom Animation** button ( ).
3. Click the placeholder for the chart you want to animate.

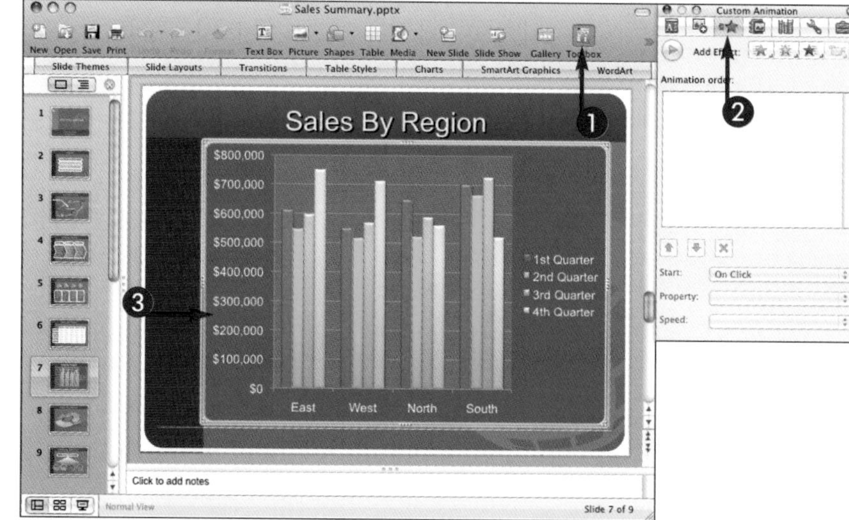


4. Click ( ).
5. Click **More Effects**.

- You can also click one of the standard effects listed here and then skip to Step **8**.

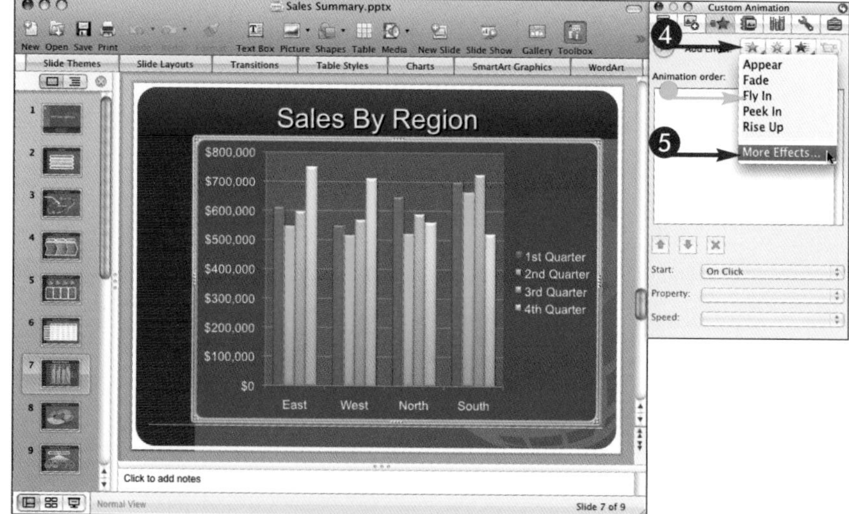

The Animation Effects dialog appears.

6. Click the animation effect you want to use.

   PowerPoint previews the effect.

- If you do not want to see the animation previews, deselect the **Show preview** option (☑ changes to ☐).

7. Click **OK**.

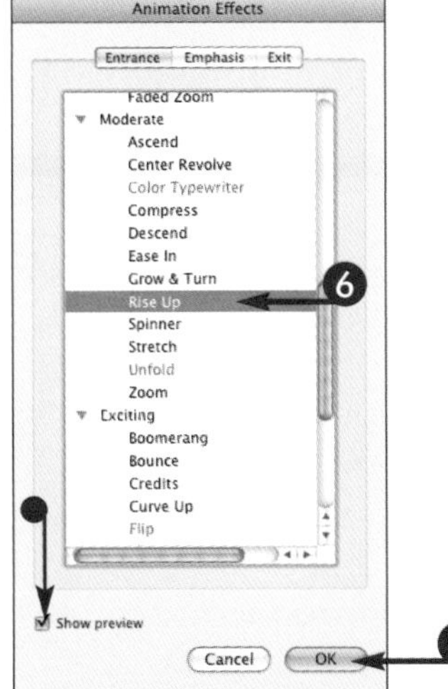


- PowerPoint adds the effect to the **Animation order** list.

8. Click the **Speed** ⬍ and then click the duration of the animation.

9. Click the **Chart Animations** panel.

10. Click the **Group graphic** ⬍ and then click the type of animation you want to use.

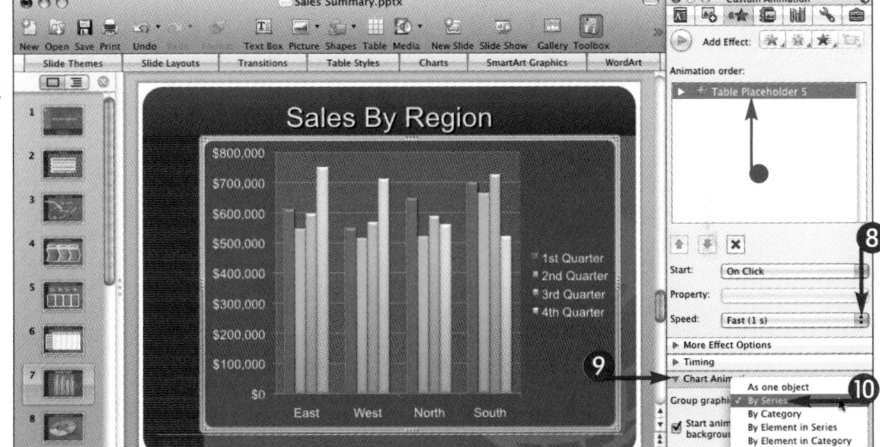

**What is the difference between the various options in the Group graphic pull-down menu?**

- **As one object**. This option applies the effect to the entire chart.
- **By Series**. This option applies the effect to each data series, one series at a time. For example, if you have a column chart that shows quarterly sales figures by region, you could display the columns one quarter at a time.
- **By Category**. This option applies the effect to each data category, one category at a time. For example, if you have a column chart that shows quarterly sales figures by region, you could display the columns one region at a time.
- **By Element in Series**. This option applies the effect to each data marker in each series, one marker at a time. For example, if you have a column chart that shows quarterly sales figures by region, you could display the columns for each region one quarter at a time.
- **By Element in Category**. This option applies the effect to each data marker in each category, one marker at a time.

# Insert an Action Button

Although most of your presentations will proceed from one slide to the next, you may sometimes need to skip forward or backward several slides. For example, you may need to return to a previously viewed slide for further discussion or clarification, or you may need to jump ahead to a slide later in the presentation if you realize that the next few slides are not relevant or useful to your audience. You can perform these jumps by adding action buttons.

## Insert an Action Button

1. Click the slide you want to work with.
2. Click **Slide Show**.
3. Click **Action Buttons**.
4. Click **Custom**.

- If you know the type of action you want the button to perform, you can click one of these predefined actions.

  ↖ changes to +.

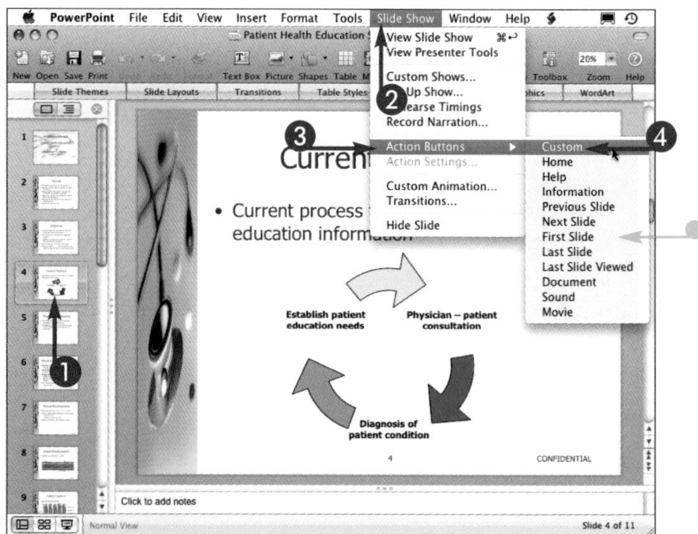


5. Click and drag + to draw the button where you want it to appear on the slide.
6. Release the mouse button.

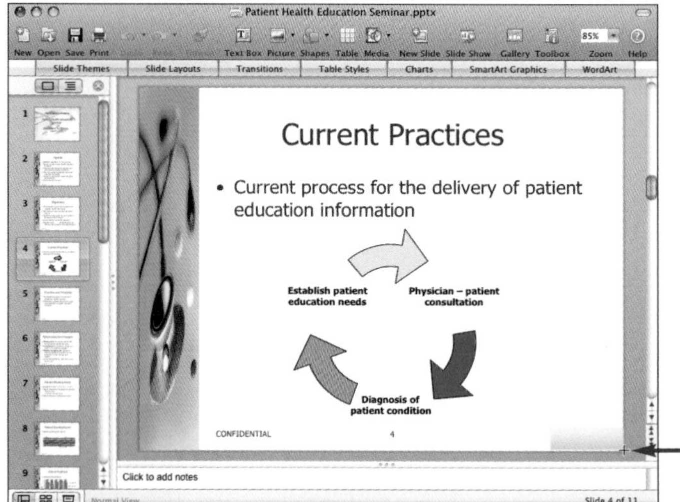

The Action Settings dialog appears.

7. Select the **Hyperlink to** option (○ changes to ◉).

8. Click the **Hyperlink to** ⬍, and then click the action you want PowerPoint to perform when you click the object.

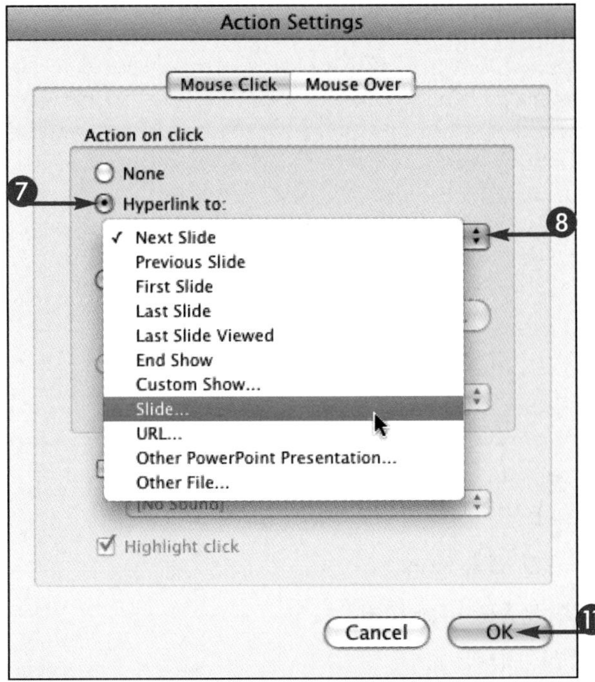


If you click **Slide** in Step **8**, the Hyperlink to Slide dialog appears.

9. In the Slide Title list, click the slide to which you want to jump when you click the action button.

10. Click **OK**.

11. Click **OK** in the Action Settings dialog.

PowerPoint inserts the action button on the slide.

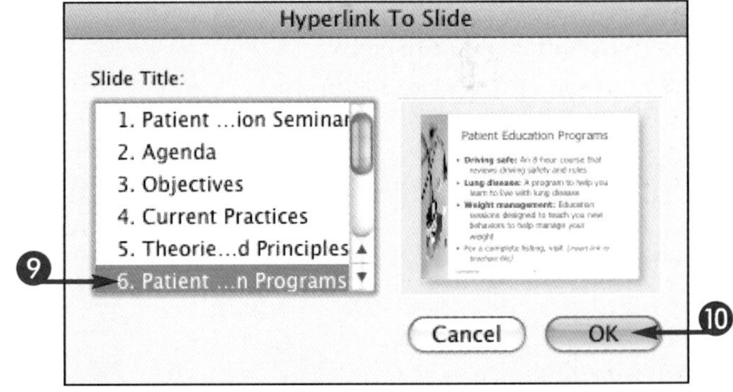

**Is there an easy way to insert an action button on every slide?**

Yes. You can do this using the presentation's slide master. Click **View**, click **Master**, and then click **Slide Master** to open the slide master. Click the Slide Master layout at the top of the Slides pane and then follow Steps **2** to **11** to insert the action button. Click **Close Master**.

**Can I assign an action to a picture, shape, or clip art?**

Yes. Click the object you want to work with, click **Slide Show** and then click **Action Settings** to open the Action Settings dialog. Select the **Hyperlink to** option (○ changes to ◉), click the **Hyperlink to** ⬍, and then click the action you want PowerPoint to perform when you click the object.

# Rehearse Slide Timings

You can use the Rehearse Timings feature to rehearse your presentation. While you do this, PowerPoint keeps track of the amount of time you spend on each slide. If you have only so much time to present the slide show, Rehearse Timings lets you know if your overall presentation runs too long or too short.

**You can also examine the time you spend on each slide to look for slide presentations that are either too short or too long.**

## Rehearse Slide Timings

1. Open the presentation you want to rehearse.
2. Click **Slide Show**.
3. Click **Rehearse Timings**.

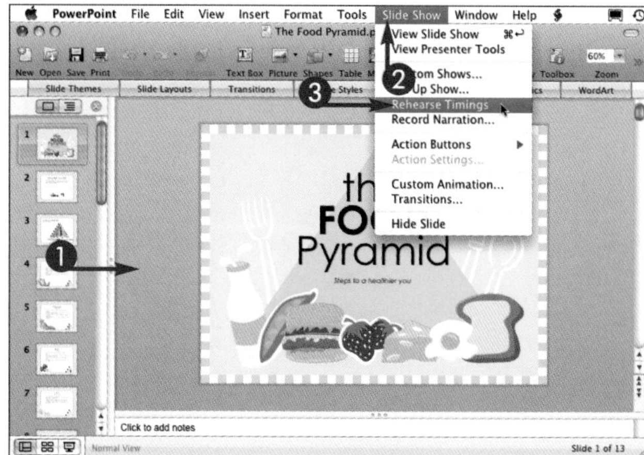


- PowerPoint starts the slide show and displays the timing for the current slide.

4. Present the slide exactly as you would during an actual presentation.
5. Move on to the next slide.

***Note:** See the section "Run a Slide Show" later in this chapter.*

PowerPoint resets the slide timing value to 0:00:00.

6. Repeat Steps **4** and **5** to run through the entire presentation.

PowerPoint displays the total presentation time and asks whether you want to save the slide timings.

7. To save the timings, click **Yes**.

- If you do not want to save the timings, click **No**.

If you decide to save the timings, PowerPoint asks if you want to review the timings in Slide Sorter view.

8. Click **Yes**.

PowerPoint opens the Slide Sorter view.

- PowerPoint displays the timing of each slide.

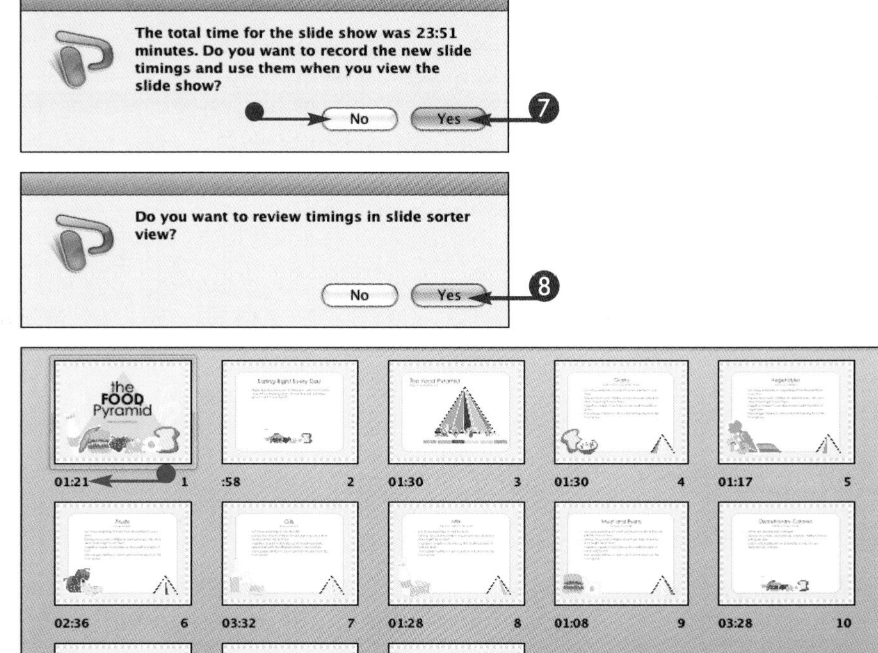

**Can I use the timings to run my slide show automatically?**

Yes. This is useful if you want to show a presentation at a trade show, fair, or other public event, but you cannot have a person presenting the slide show, or if you want to send a presentation to a customer or prospect and you cannot be there to go through the slide show yourself. Follow these steps:

1. Rehearse the slide show timings and save the timings when you finish.
2. Click **Slide Show**.
3. Click **Set Up Show**.

   The Set Up Show dialog appears.

4. Select the **Browsed at a kiosk (full screen)** option (○ changes to ◉).
5. Select the **Using timings, if present** option (○ changes to ◉).
6. Click **OK**.

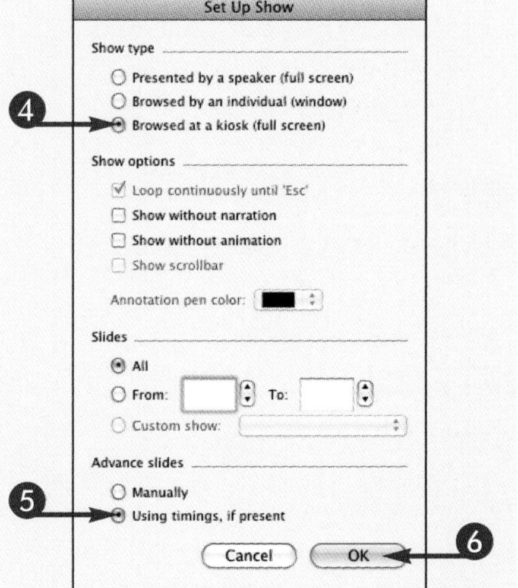

# Record Narration

You can record narration if you require a recorded voice for some or all of a presentation. For example, you might have a slide that consists of a recorded greeting from the CEO or someone else at your company. Similarly, you might require another person to present some material, but if that person cannot be at your presentation, you need to record his or her material.

**You can also record narration for an entire presentation. For example, you might be setting up an automatic presentation and require recorded narration for the whole show. If your Mac does not have a built-in microphone, you will need to attach a microphone for this task.**

## Record Narration

### RECORD NARRATION FOR A SLIDE

1. Click the slide you want to work with.
2. Click **Insert**.
3. Click **Sound and Music**.
4. Click **Record Sound**.

The Record Sound dialog appears.

5. Type a name for the recording.
6. Click the **Sound input device** and then click the device you want to use for recording.
7. Click **Record**.
8. Record your narration.
9. Click **Stop**.
10. Click **Save**.

PowerPoint adds a sound icon to the slide.

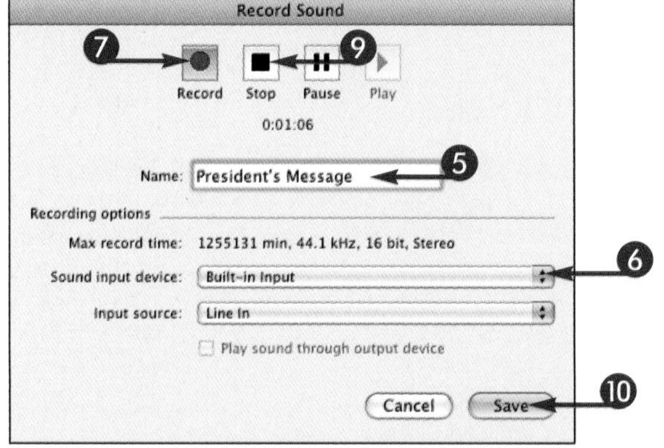

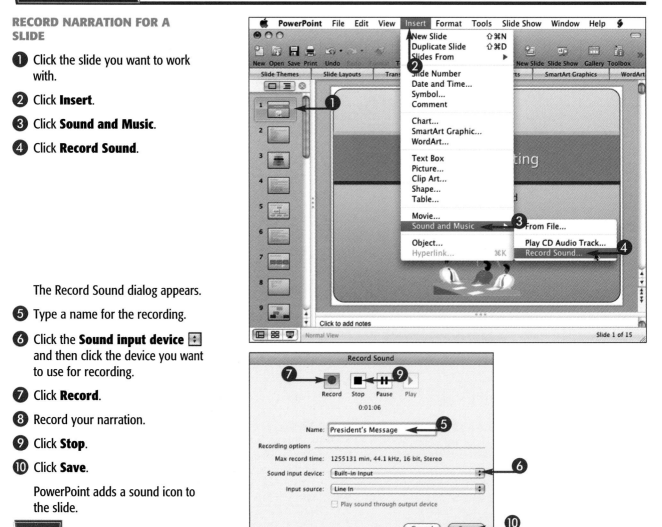

## RECORD NARRATION FOR A PRESENTATION

1. Open the presentation you want to work with.
2. Click **Slide Show**.
3. Click **Record Narration**.

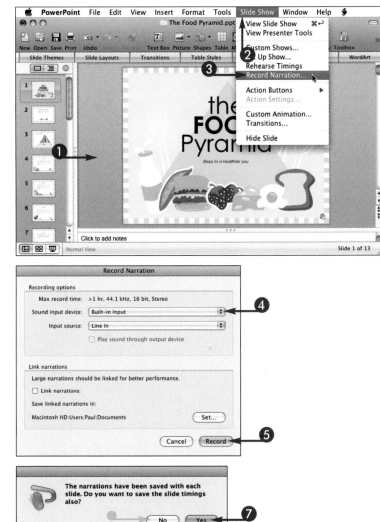

The Record Narration dialog appears.

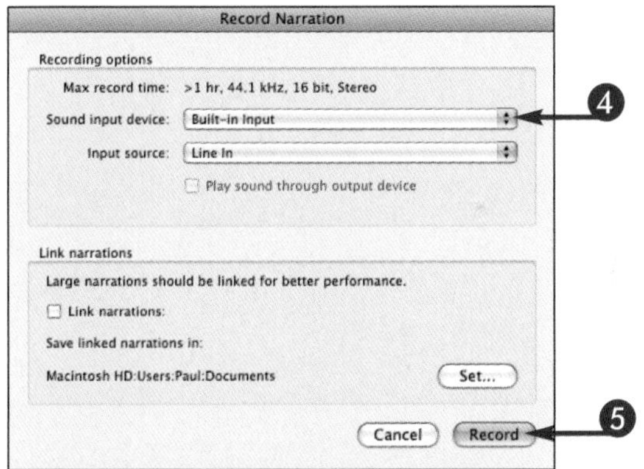


4. Click the **Sound input device** and then click the device you want to use for recording.
5. Click **Record**.
6. Record your narration.

When you finish, PowerPoint asks whether you want to save the slide timings.

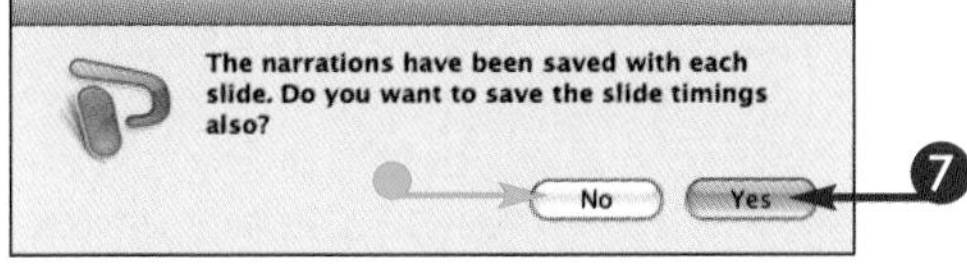


7. To save the timings, click **Yes**.

- If you do not want to save the timings, click **No**.

### Can I control when a slideís narration is played?

Yes. By default, PowerPoint plays the slide narration when you click the sound icon. However, you can configure the recording to play automatically when you display the slide. Click the sound icon, display the Formatting Palette (see Chapter 3), and click the **Sound** panel. Click the **Play** and then click **Automatically**.

### What does the Link narrations option do?

If you are recording a long narration or are using a very high sound quality, you probably do not want PowerPoint to embed the sound file in the presentation because doing so slows down the entire presentation. To create the narration as separate sound files, in the Record Narration dialog select the **Link narrations** option (☐ changes to ☑). The narration files are given the same name as your presentation, followed by a three-digit code, one for each narrated slide in the presentation.

# Create a Custom Slide Show

You can create a custom version of a slide show that excludes certain slides or displays the slides in a different order. For example, you can create both a short version and a long version of a presentation. Similarly, you might want to omit certain slides depending on whether you are presenting to managers, salespeople, or engineers.

**Custom slide shows enable you to have internal and external versions of the presentation. That is, you might have one version for people who work at your company and a different version for people from outside the company.**

## Create a Custom Slide Show

1. Open the presentation you want to work with.
2. Click **Slide Show**.
3. Click **Custom Shows**.

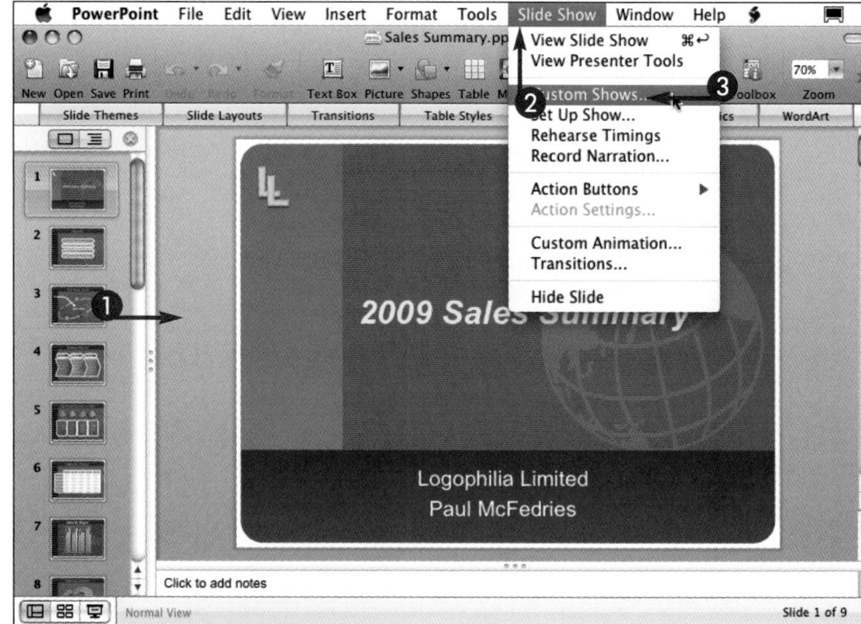


The Custom Shows dialog appears.

4. Click **New**.

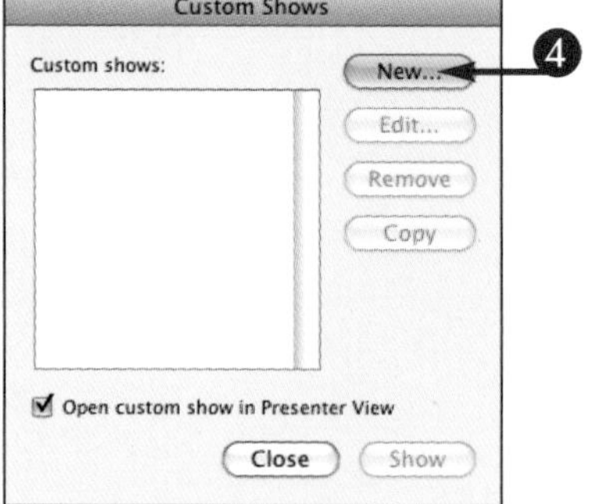

The Define Custom Show dialog appears.

5. In the Slide show name text box, type a name for your custom show.
6. Click a slide in the Slides in presentation list.
7. Click **Add**.
   - PowerPoint adds the slide to the Slides in custom show list.
8. Click a slide and then click **Move Up** (⇧) and **Move Down** (⇩) to order the slides.
9. Click **OK**.
   - The custom show appears in the Custom shows list.
10. Click **Close**.
   - To run a custom slide show, follow Steps **1** to **3**, click the show, and then click **Show**.

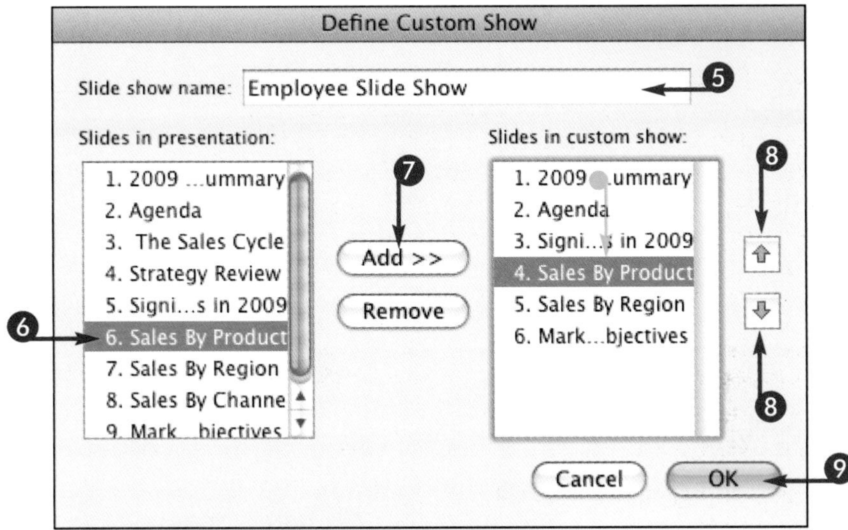


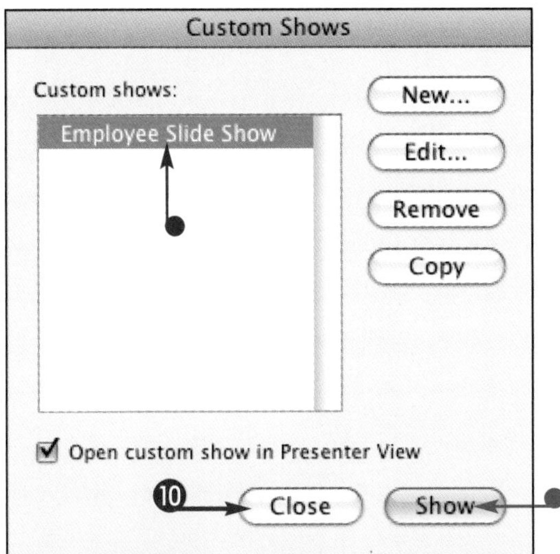

## TIPS

### How do I create a custom show that includes all the slides, but in a different order?

Follow Steps **1** to **5** to create and name your custom slide show. There are two ways to create your custom order. One method is to follow Steps **6** and **7** in the order that you want the slides to appear. Alternatively, in the Slides in presentation list, click the first slide, hold down Shift, and then click the last slide. Click **Add** to add all the slides to the Slides in custom show list and then use ⇧ and ⇩ to order the slides.

### How do I edit a custom slide show?

Follow Steps **1** to **3** to open the Custom Shows dialog. In the Custom shows list, click the custom slide show you want to change and then click **Edit**. Follow Steps **6** to **8** to add more slides and change the slide order. To delete a slide from the show, click the slide in the Slides in custom show list, and then click **Remove**. Click **OK** when you finish.

# Run a Slide Show

After you build your presentation and add your transitions, animations, action buttons, and narration, you are ready to present the slide show. PowerPoint uses a special full-screen Slide Show view that displays each slide. You can display a menu of navigation tools on-screen to control the slide show.

## Run a Slide Show

1. Open the presentation you want to run.
2. Click **Slide Show**.
3. Click **View Slide Show**.

   You can also press ⌘ + Return or click [icon] in the Standard toolbar.

- If you want to start the slide show from a specific slide, right-click or Ctrl+click that slide and then click **View Slide Show**.

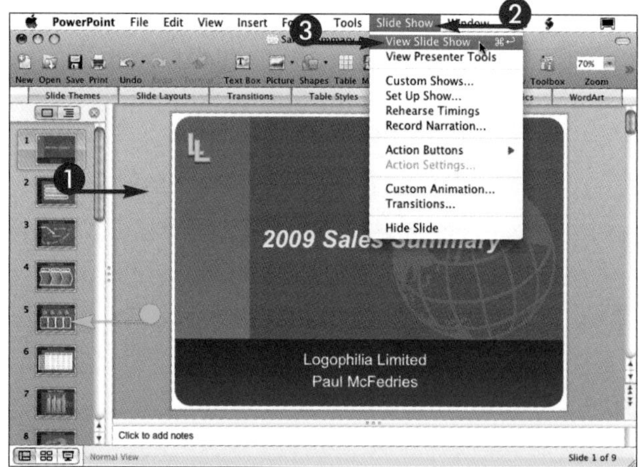


PowerPoint switches to Slide Show view and displays the first slide full screen.

4. Click the mouse to advance to the next slide.
5. To display the slide show controls, move the pointer.

- The menu button appears.

6. Click the button.

   You can also right-click or Ctrl+click the slide.

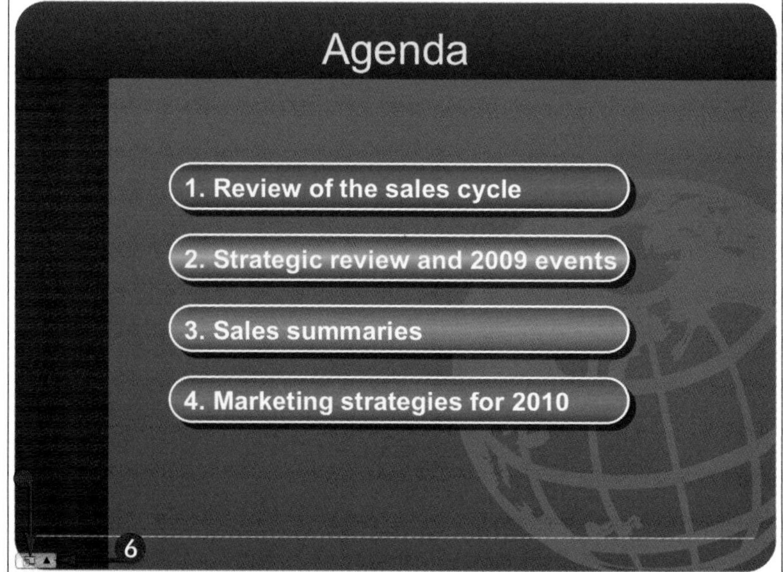

The navigation menu appears.

- You can click **Next** to advance to the next slide.
- You can click **Previous** to return to the previous slide.
- You can click **Go to Slide** and then click a slide to jump to any slide.
- To annotate a slide, click **Pointer Options**, click **Pen**, and then use the mouse pointer to mark up the slide.

  When you click the last slide, PowerPoint automatically ends the show.
- You can end the show at any time by clicking **End Show** in the menu.

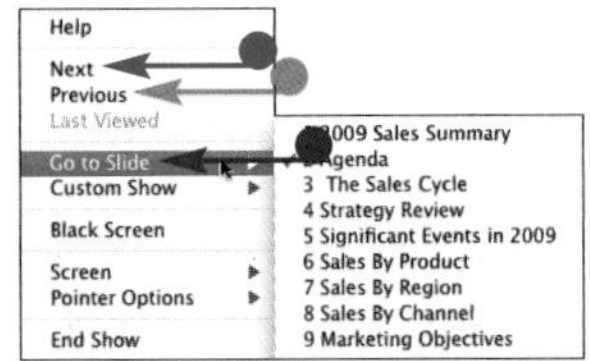


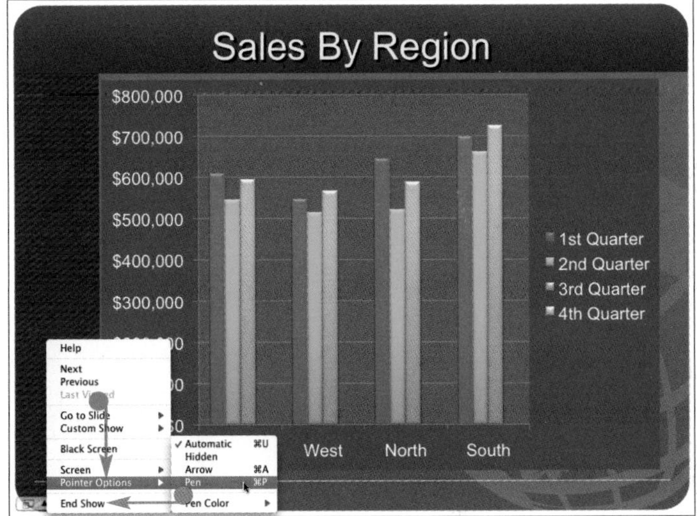

### What keyboard techniques can I use to control a slide show?

| *Press* | *To* |
|---|---|
| N | Advance to the next slide or animation. |
| P | Return to the previous slide or animation. |
| S | Pause or resume an automatic slide show. |
| B | Toggle black screen on and off. |
| W | Toggle white screen on and off. |
| A | Toggle the mouse pointer and slide show navigation tools on and off. |
| ⌘+A | Change to an arrow. |
| ⌘+P | Change to a pen. |
| Esc | End the slide show. You can also press -. |

CHAPTER 18

# Sending and Receiving E-Mail

You can use Office 2008 for Mac's Entourage program to send e-mail to and read e-mail from friends, family, colleagues, and even total strangers almost anywhere in the world. This chapter shows you how to perform these and many more e-mail tasks.

# Send an E-Mail Message

If you know the e-mail address of a person or organization, you can send an e-mail message to that address. In most cases, the message is delivered within a few minutes.

**If you do not know any e-mail addresses, or, if at first, you prefer to just practice sending messages, you can send messages to your own e-mail address.**

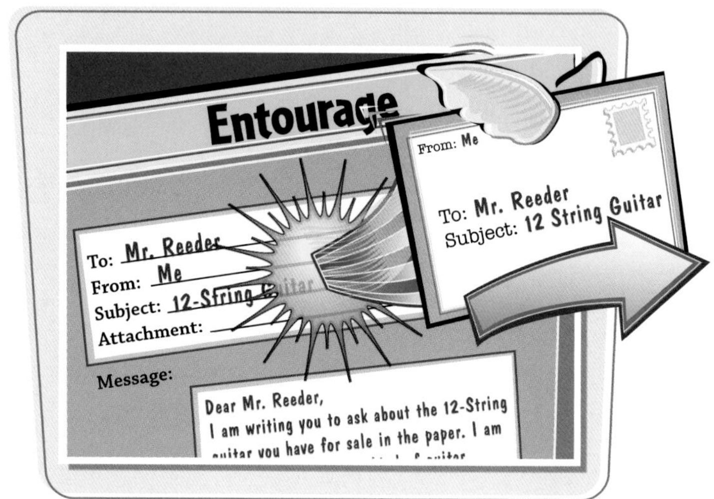


## Send an E-Mail Message

1. In Entourage, click the **Mail** button (✉).
2. Click the **New Mail Message** button (✉).

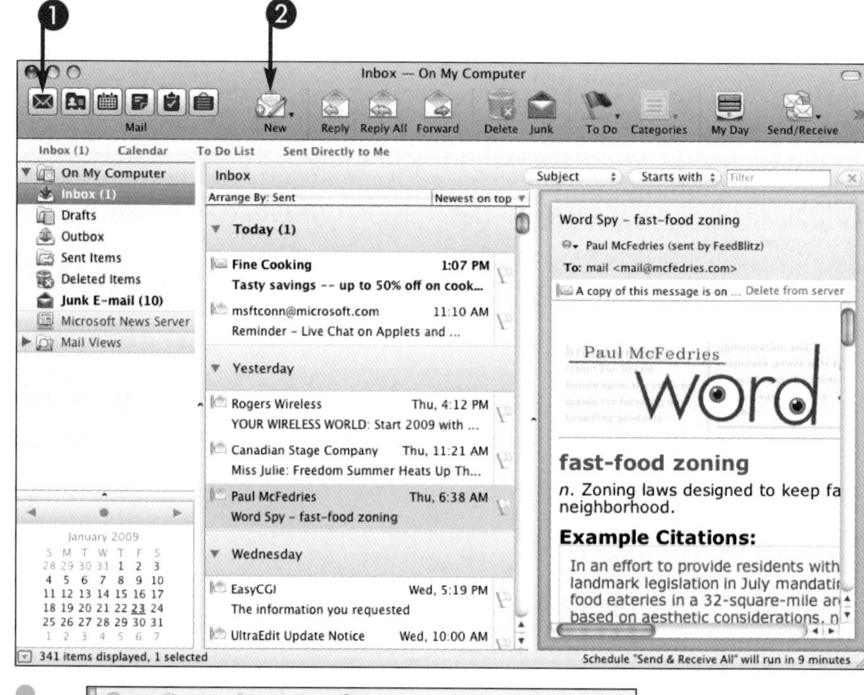


The address dialog appears.

3. In the To text box, type the e-mail address of the person to whom you are sending the message.
4. To send a copy of the message to another person, type that person's e-mail address in the Cc text box.

- You can click the **Add** button (⊕) to specify multiple To or Cc addresses.

5. Press Return.

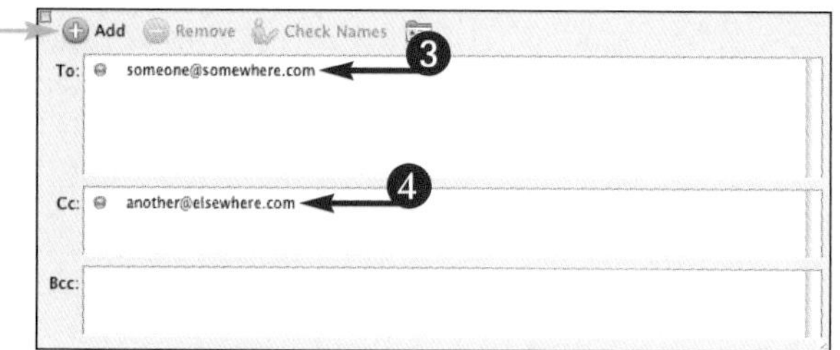

6. Type a title or short description for the message in the Subject text box.
7. Type the message.
8. Use these buttons and the commands in the Format menu to format the message text.

***Note:** Many people use e-mail programs that cannot process text formatting. Unless you are sure your recipient's program supports formatting, it is best to send plain text messages. See the section "Change the Message Format" later in this chapter.*

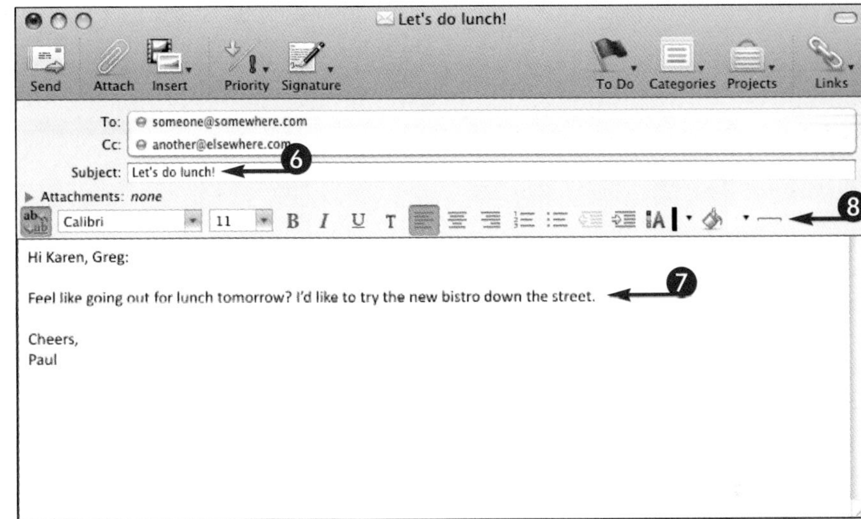

9. Click **Send** ( ).

   Entourage sends your message.

***Note:** Entourage stores a copy of your message in the Sent Items folder.*

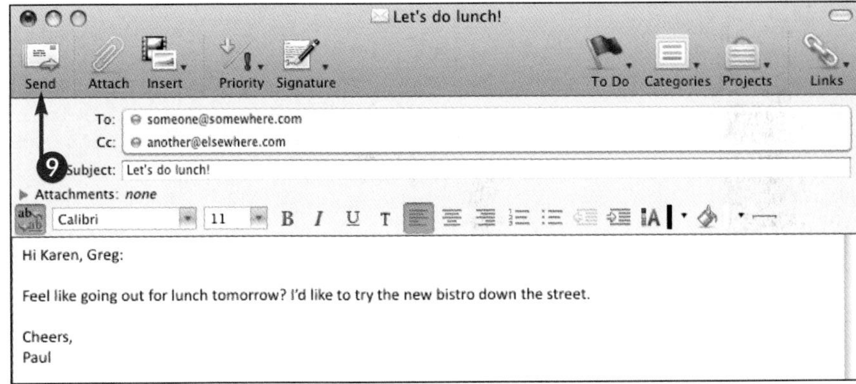

### How do I add an e-mail account to Entourage?

Click **Entourage** and then click **Account Settings** to open the Accounts dialog. Click **New** and then click **Mail** to run the Account Setup Assistant. To set up your account automatically, type your e-mail address and press Return. If that does not work, click **Configure Account Manually**, specify your account type (usually POP), click **OK**, and then type account settings such as your e-mail address and your account provider's e-mail server names.

### I have a large number of messages to compose. Do I have to be online to do this?

No. It is possible to compose all the messages while you are offline. Click **Entourage** and then click the **Work Offline** command if you do not see a check mark beside it. Compose and send each of your messages. Each time you click **Send**, Entourage stores the message temporarily in the Outbox folder. When you finish, connect to the Internet, click **Entourage**, and then Click **Work Offline**. Click **Tools**, click **Send & receive**, and then click **Send All**, or press Shift + ⌘ + K.

# Select a Contact Address

You can select the address to which you want to send an e-mail message directly from the Entourage Address Book instead of typing the address if you have e-mail addresses and names in your Address Book.

**See Chapter 20 to learn how to add contacts to your Entourage Address Book.**

## Select a Contact Address

1. Start a new mail message.

***Note:*** *See the section "Send an E-Mail Message."*

The address dialog appears.

2. Click the **Address Book** button (📇).

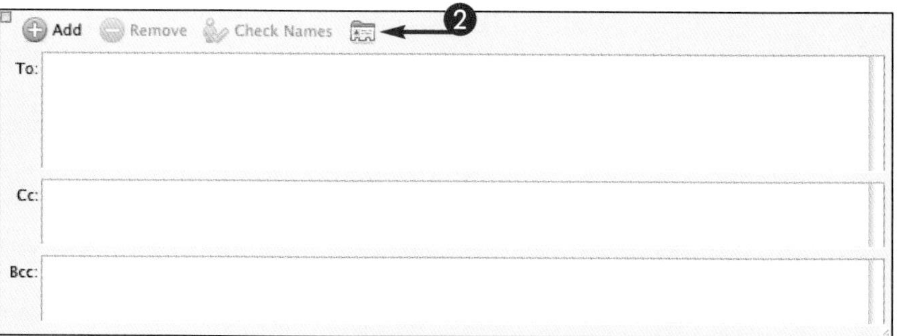


- Entourage displays the names and e-mail addresses of your Address Book contacts.

3. Click in the **To** box.
4. Double-click the person to whom you want to send the message.

***Note:*** *You can also click and drag a contact and drop it on the To, Cc, or Bcc box.*

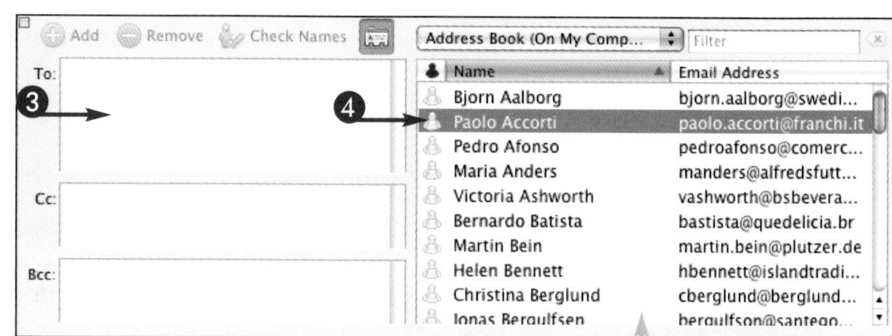

- The person's name and address appear in the To box.

5 Repeat Step **4** to add other recipients to the To box.

6 Click in the **Cc** box.

7 Double-click the person to whom you want to send a copy of the message.

- The person's name and address appear in the Cc box.

8 Repeat Step **7** to add other recipients to the Cc box.

9 Press .

- Entourage adds the recipients to the To and Cc lines of the new message.

10 Complete and send your message.

***Note:*** *See the Section "Send an E-Mail Message" for the specifics of creating and sending a message.*

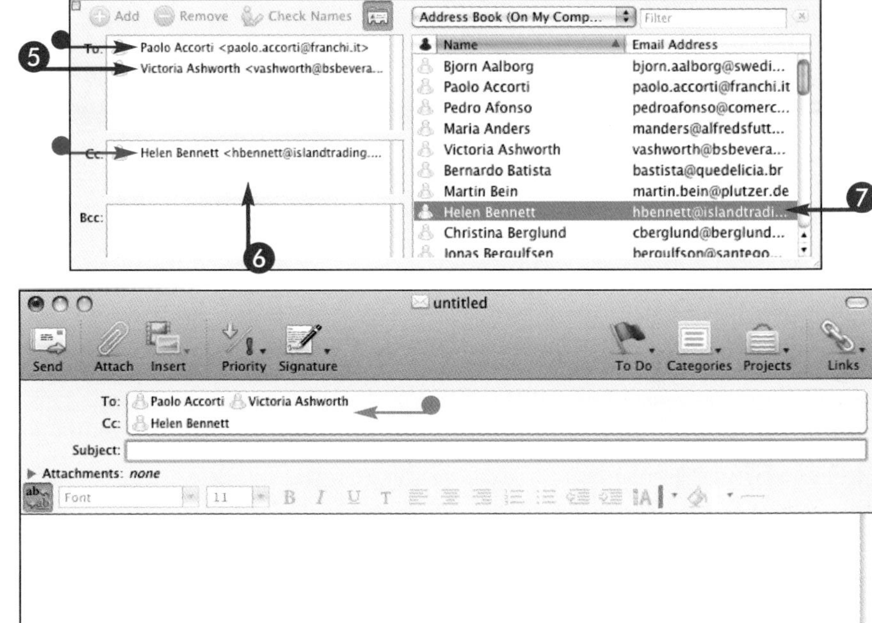


## TIPS

### In the address window, what does the Bcc button do?

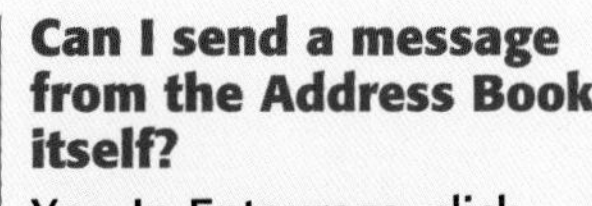


You click **Bcc** and then double-click a contact to add that person to the message's Bcc field. Bcc stands for *blind courtesy copy* and it means that any addresses in the Bcc field are not displayed to the other message recipients. Note, however, that you only see the Bcc field in the message if you have added at least one Bcc recipient.

### Can I send a message from the Address Book itself?

Yes. In Entourage, click the **Address Book** button (icon) to open the Address Book window. Click the contact you want to work with, click **Contact**, and then click **New Message To**. Alternatively, click the contact and then either press ⌘+R or click the **E-mail** button (icon) in the toolbar. Entourage starts a new message and automatically addresses it to the contact.

# Add a File Attachment

You can attach a memo, an image, or another document that you want to send to another person to an e-mail message. The other person can then open the document after he or she receives your message.

## Add a File Attachment

### ADD AN ATTACHMENT

1. Start a new mail message and add the recipients.

***Note:*** *See the section "Send an E-Mail Message" earlier in this chapter.*

2. Click **Message**.
3. Click **Add Attachments**.

- You can also click **Attach** ( ).

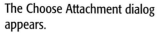

You can also press ⌘ + E.

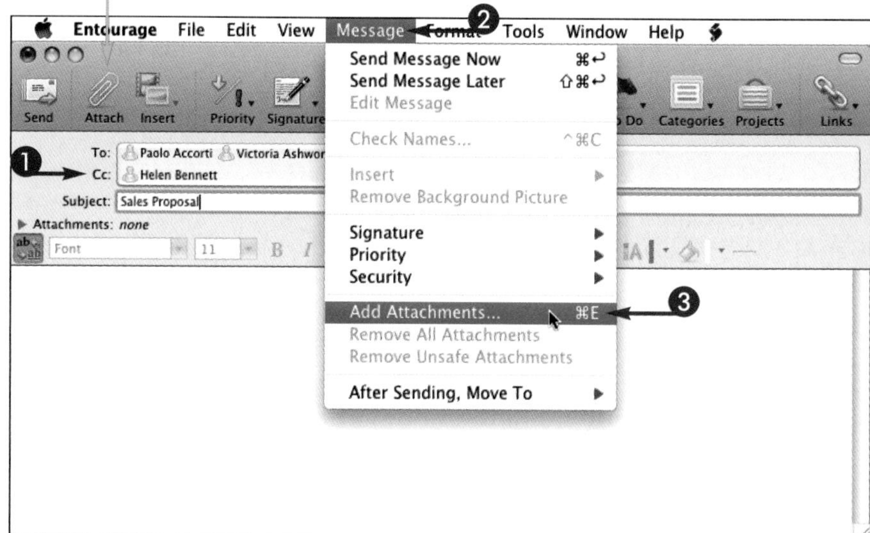


The Choose Attachment dialog appears.

4. Click the file you want to attach.

***Note:*** *To attach multiple files, hold down ⌘ and click each file.*

5. Click **Open**.

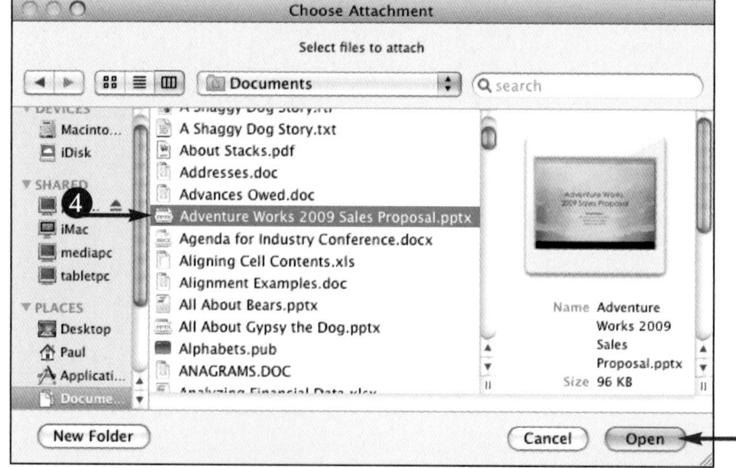

- Entourage attaches the file to the message.

6 Repeat Steps **2** to **5** to attach additional files to the message.

7 Complete and send your message.

***Note:** See the Section "Send an E-Mail Message" for the specifics of creating and sending a message.*

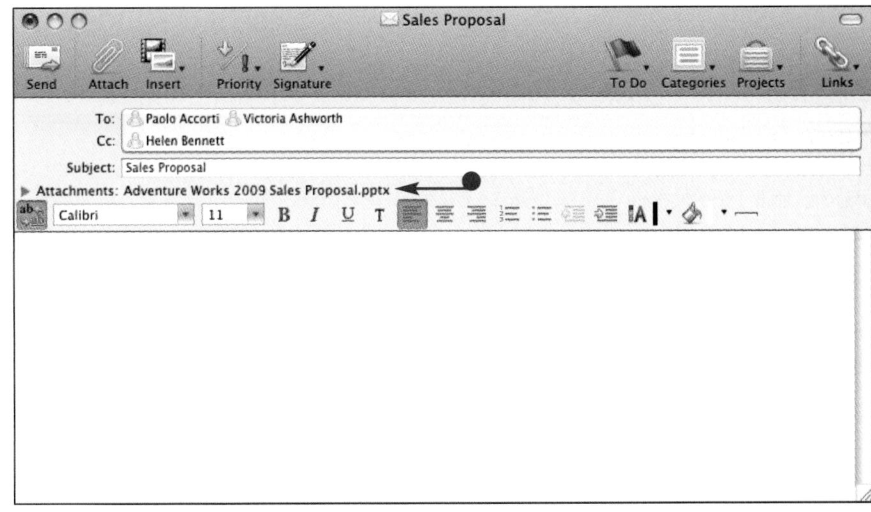


## REMOVE AN ATTACHMENT

1 Click ▶ next to Attachments (▶ changes to ▼).

2 Click the file.

3 Click **Remove**.

Entourage removes the file from the list of attachments.

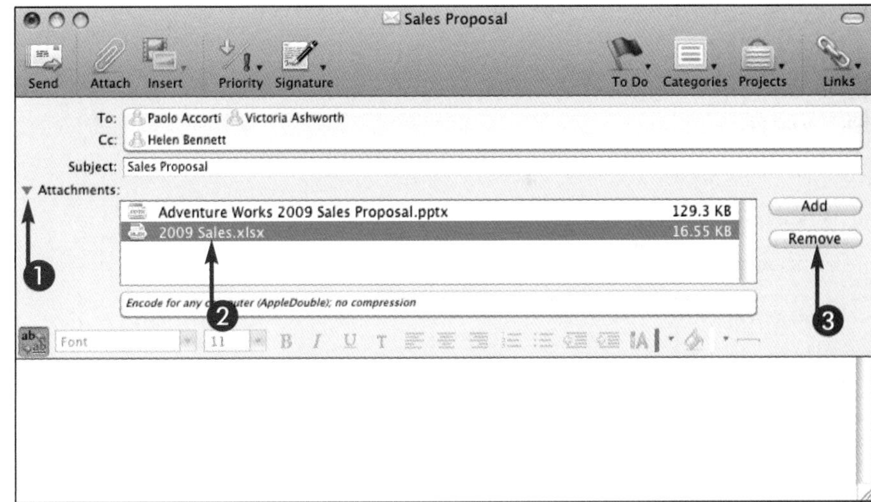

### Are there any restrictions related to sending file attachments?

Many e-mail programs and e-mail servers block certain types of files that could potentially contain a computer virus or other form or malware. Such files include scripts, batch files, and program files. When you add such a file, Entourage displays **Attachments potentially unsafe** in the message window. Since the files probably will not get delivered, you can click **Remove them** to remove the unsafe files.

There is no practical limit to the number of files you can attach to the message. However, you should be careful with the total size of the files you send. If you or the recipient have a slow Internet connection, sending or receiving the message can take an extremely long time. Also, many Internet service providers (ISPs) place a limit on the size of a message's attachments, which is usually between 2 and 5MB. In general, use e-mail to send only a few small files at a time.

# Create a Signature

In an e-mail message, a *signature* is a small amount of text that appears at the bottom of the message. Rather than typing this information manually, you can create the signature once and then have Entourage insert the signature into any message you create.

**Signatures usually contain personal contact information, such as your phone numbers, business address, and e-mail and Web site addresses. Some people supplement their signatures with wise or witty quotations.**

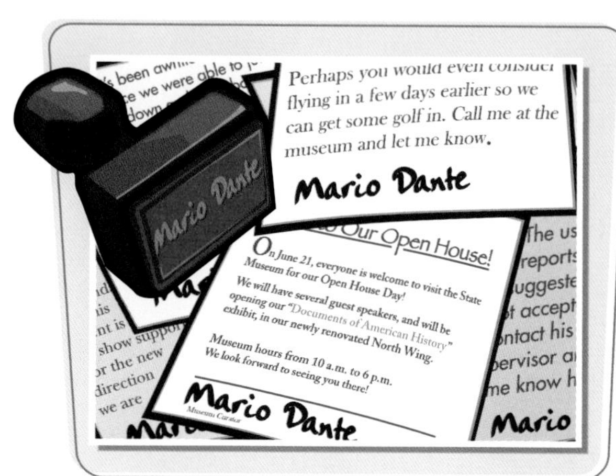

## Create a Signature

1. Click **Tools**.
2. Click **Signatures**.

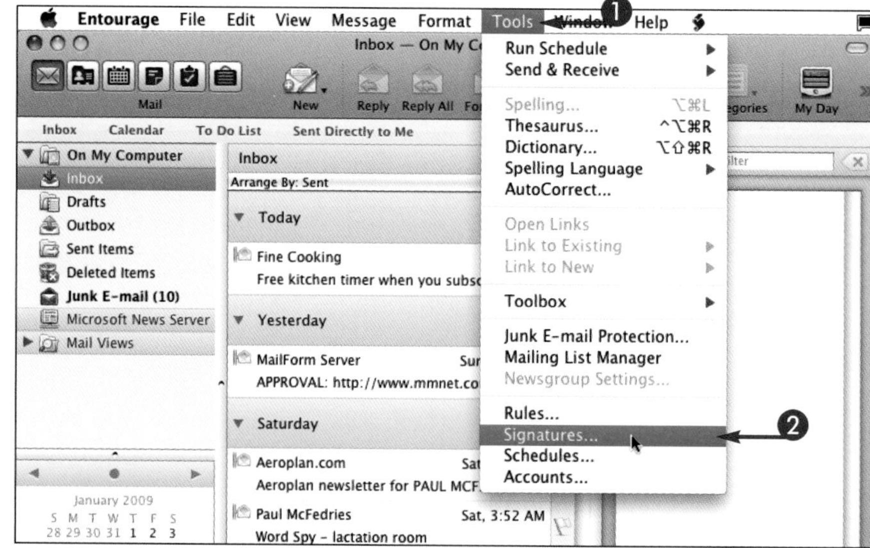

The Signatures dialog appears.

3. Click the **New** button (⊕).

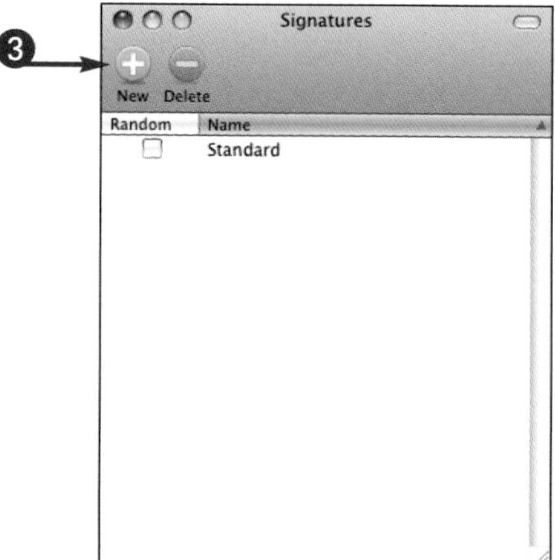

A signature dialog appears.

4 In the Name text box, type a name for the signature.

5 Type the signature text.

6 Use these buttons and the commands in the Format menu to format the signature text.

7 Press ⌘+S.

Entourage saves the signature.

8 Click the **Close** button.

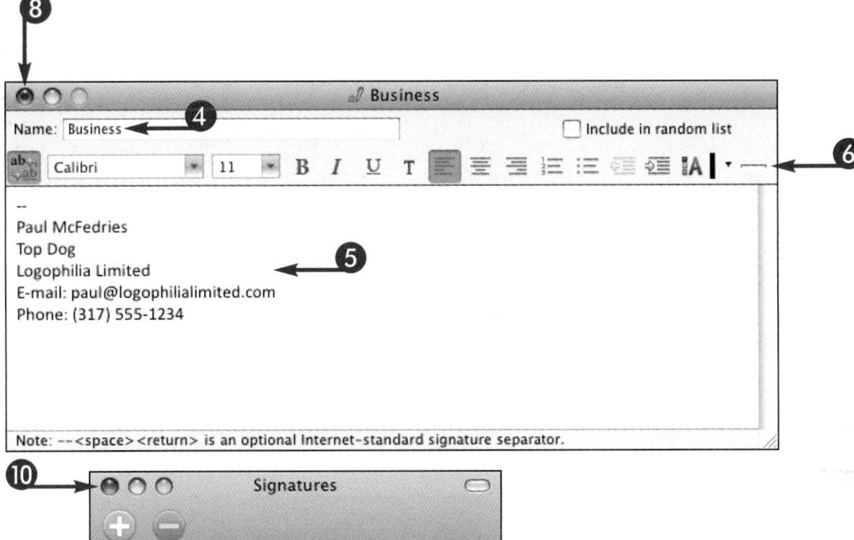


- Entourage adds the signature to the Signatures dialog.

9 Repeat Steps **3** to **7** to add more signatures, if necessary.

***Note:*** *It is common to have different signatures for different types of messages. For example, many people use one signature for business messages and another for personal messages.*

10 Click .

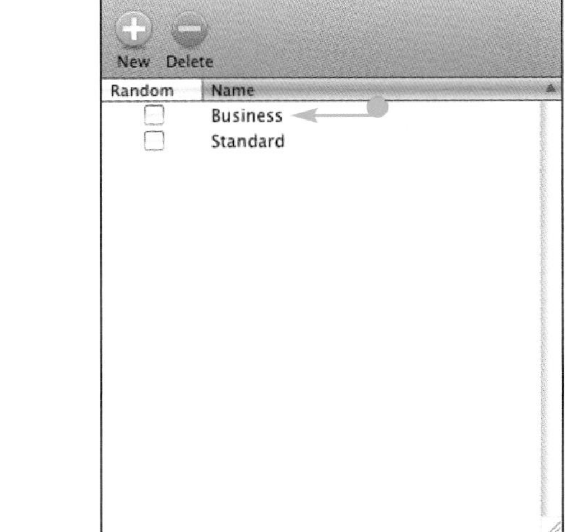


TIPS

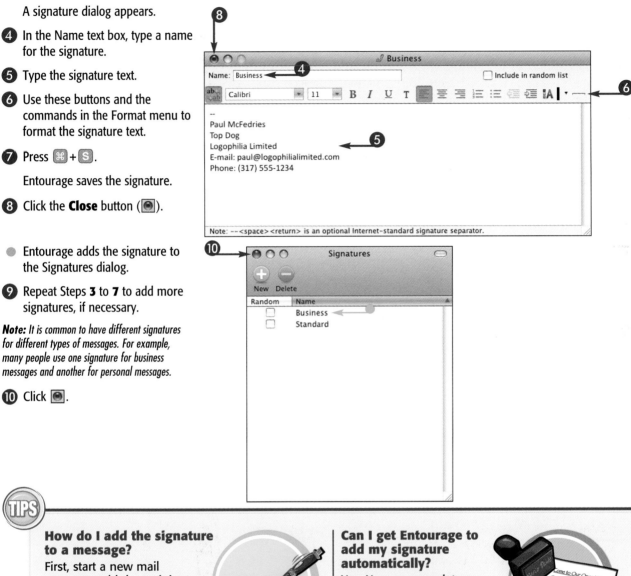

### How do I add the signature to a message?

First, start a new mail message, add the recipients, the subject line, and your message text. Position the insertion point cursor below your message text. Click **Message** and then click **Signature** (or click the **Signature** button in the toolbar) to see a menu of your signatures. Click the signature you want to use. Entourage adds the signature to the message.

### Can I get Entourage to add my signature automatically?

Yes. You can associate a signature with an e-mail account. Click **Entourage** and then click **Account Settings** to open the Accounts dialog. Click the **Mail** tab and then double-click the e-mail account you want to work with. In the Edit Account dialog, click the **Options** tab.

Click the **Default signature** , click the signature you want to associate with the account, and then click **OK**.

# Set the Message Priority

You can alert that recipient of your e-mail message that it requires a quick response or contains important material by giving the message a higher priority level than normal. The recipient usually sees the message with a red exclamation mark to indicate the higher priority.

**Similarly, if your message requires no response or can be answered at a later date, you can give the message a lower priority level than normal. The recipient usually sees the message with a blue downward-pointing arrow to indicate the lower priority.**

## Set the Message Priority

1. Start a new mail message and add the recipients.

*Note:* *See the section "Send an E-mail Message" earlier in this chapter.*

2. Click **Message**.
3. Click **Priority**.
4. Click the priority level you want to use.

- You can also click the **Priority** (icon) button in the toolbar and then click the priority level you want.

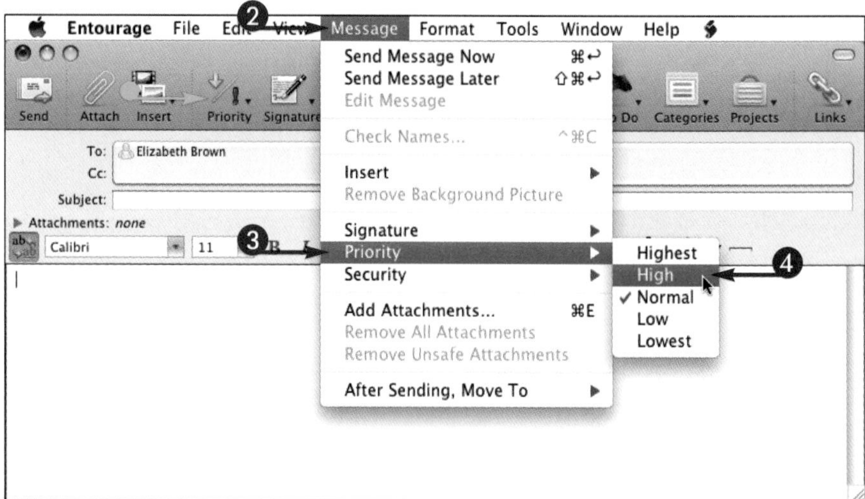


- If you choose Highest, High, Low, or Lowest, Entourage displays the priority level.

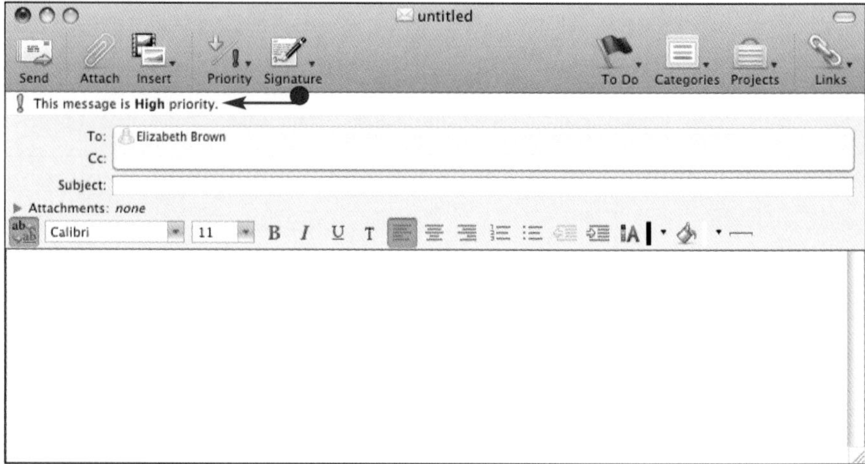

# Change the Message Format



You can control the format that Entourage uses for your e-mail messages. By default, Entourage uses the HTML (Hypertext Markup Language) format, which enables you to format your messages with fonts, text effects, colors, bulleted lists, backgrounds, and more.

**If you have a recipient who uses a mail program that does not support HTML formatting, your formatted message may appear garbled, so you should turn off HTML and use plain text.**

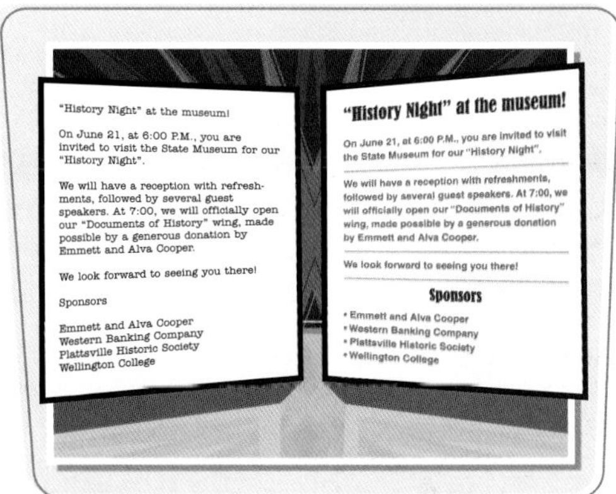


## Change the Message Format

1. Start a new mail message and add the recipients.

*Note:* *See the section "Send an E-mail Message" earlier in this chapter.*

2. Click **Format**.
3. Click **HTML**.

- You can also click the **Use HTML** button (abab).

  You can also toggle your message between HTML and plain text by pressing Shift + ⌘ + T.

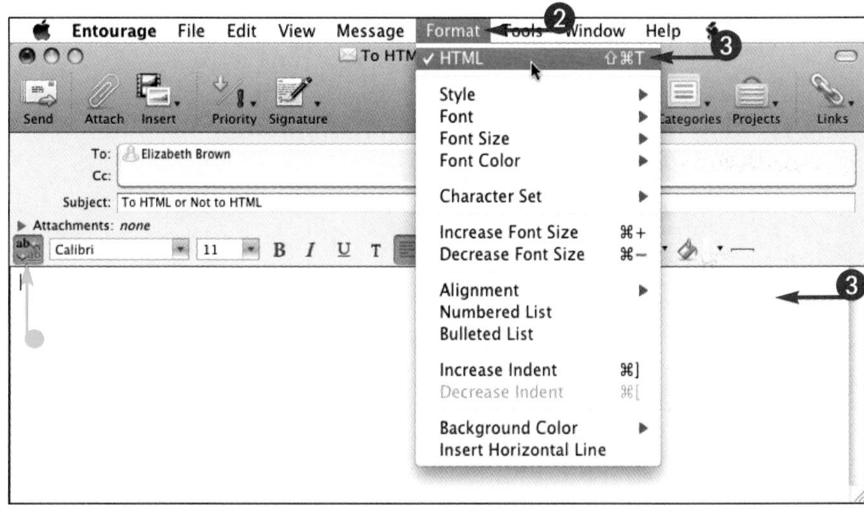


- If you turn off HTML, Entourage disables the formatting buttons.

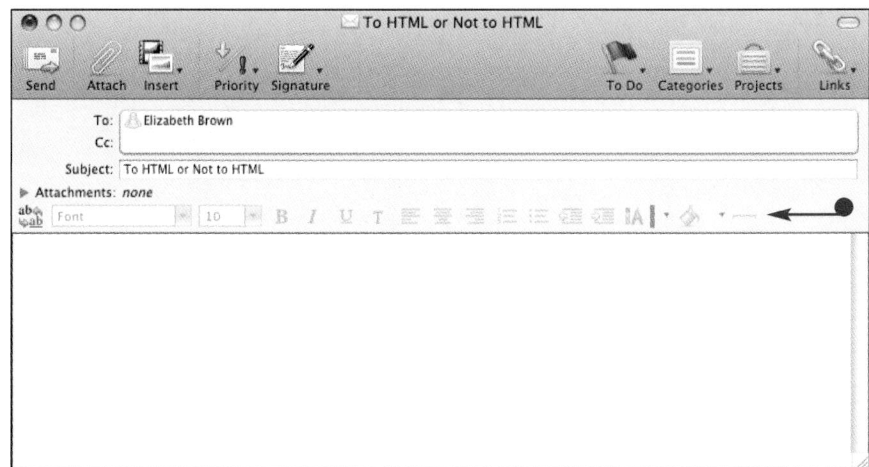

# Receive and Read E-Mail Messages

A message sent to you by another person is stored on your ISP's e-mail server computer. You must connect to the ISP's computer to retrieve and read the message. As you see in this task, Entourage does most of the work for you automatically.

**Entourage checks for new messages when you start the program automatically, and then checks for more messages every 10 minutes while you are online.**

## Receive and Read E-Mail Messages

### RECEIVE E-MAIL MESSAGES

❶ Click **Tools**.

❷ Click **Send & Receive**.

❸ Click **Send & Receive All**.

You can also press ⌘ + K.

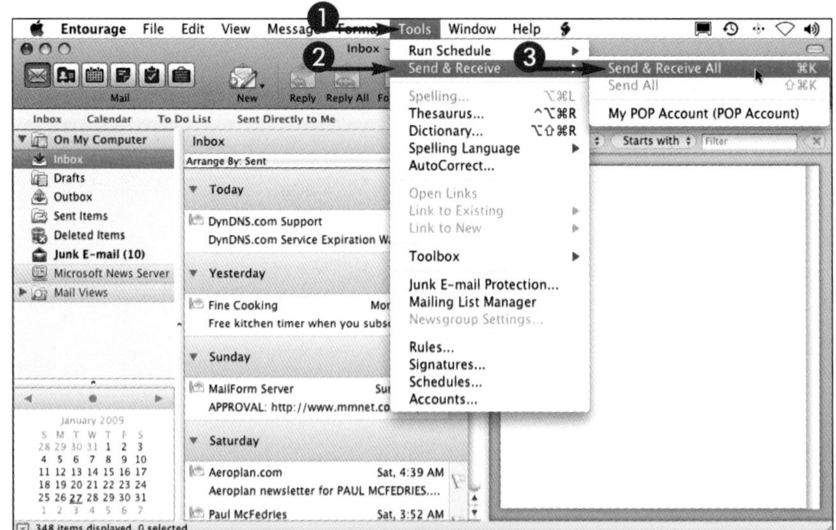


- If you have new messages, they appear in your Inbox folder in bold type.
- This symbol (📎) means that the message came with a file attached.
- This symbol (!) means the message was sent as high priority.
- This symbol (↓) means the message was sent as low priority.
- You can also receive e-mail messages by clicking the **Send/Receive** button (✉).

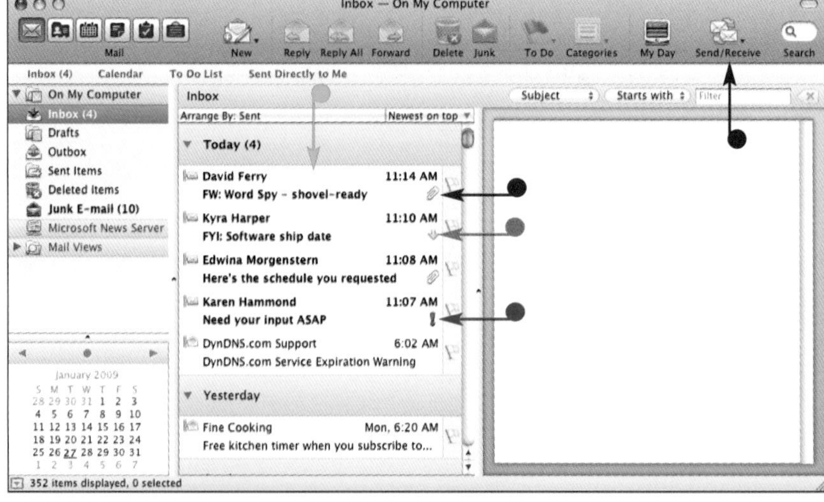

## READ A MESSAGE

❶ Click the message.

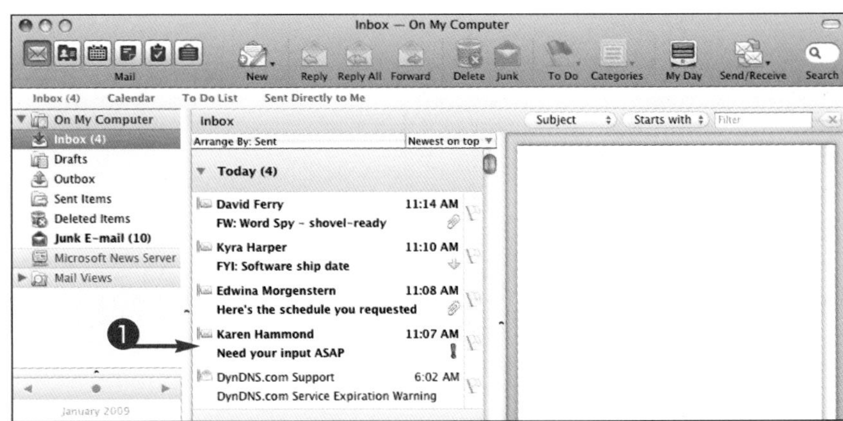


❷ Read the message text in the preview pane.

***Note:*** *If you want to open the message in its own window, double-click the message.*

**TIP**

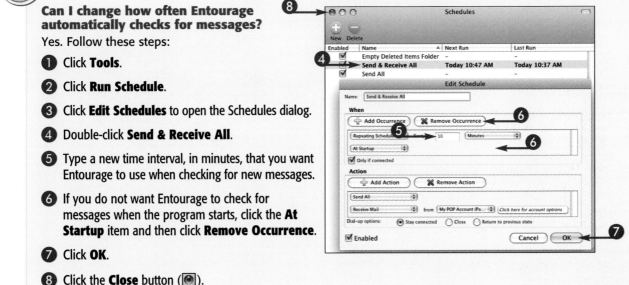

### Can I change how often Entourage automatically checks for messages?

Yes. Follow these steps:

❶ Click **Tools**.

❷ Click **Run Schedule**.

❸ Click **Edit Schedules** to open the Schedules dialog.

❹ Double-click **Send & Receive All**.

❺ Type a new time interval, in minutes, that you want Entourage to use when checking for new messages.

❻ If you do not want Entourage to check for messages when the program starts, click the **At Startup** item and then click **Remove Occurrence**.

❼ Click **OK**.

❽ Click the **Close** button (◉).

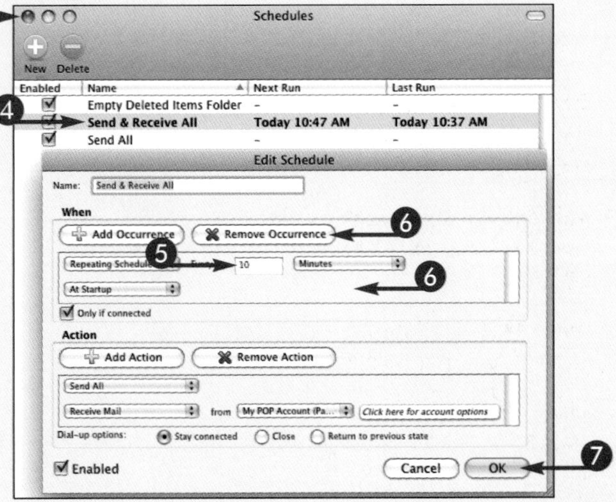

# Reply to a Message

When a message you receive requires some kind of response — whether it is answering a question, supplying information, or providing comments or criticisms — you can reply to any message you receive.

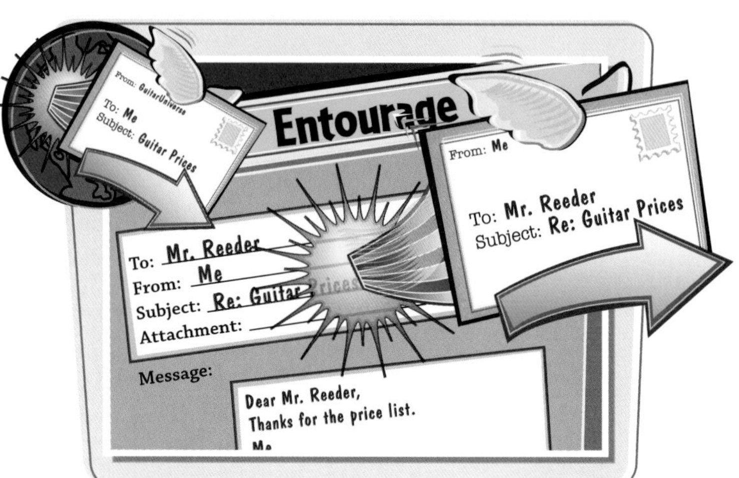


## Reply to a Message

1. Click the message to which you want to reply.
2. Click **Reply** to respond only to the first address displayed on the From line.

- You can click **Reply All** to respond to the sender and all the addresses in the To and Cc lines.

You can also press ⌘ + R to reply, or Shift + ⌘ + R to reply to all.

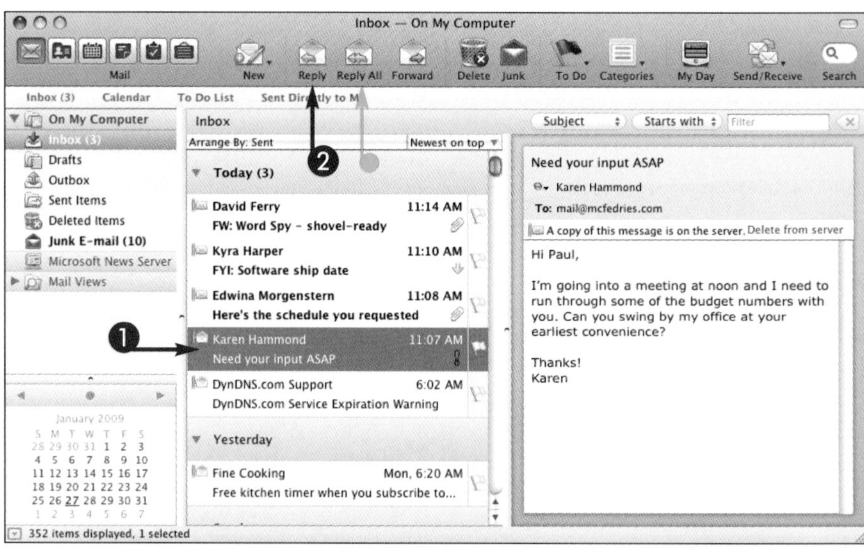


A message window appears.

- Entourage automatically inserts the recipient addresses.
- Entourage also inserts the subject line, preceded by Re:.
- Entourage includes the original message text at the bottom of the reply.

3. Edit the original message to include only the text that is relevant to your reply.

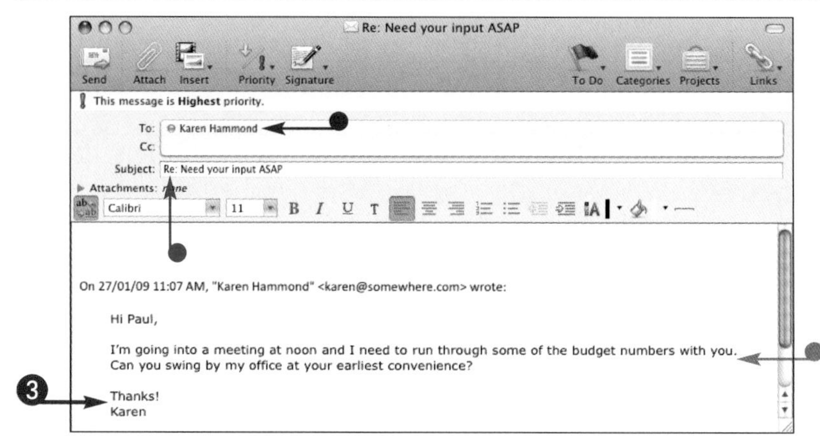

4 Click the area above the original message text and type your reply.

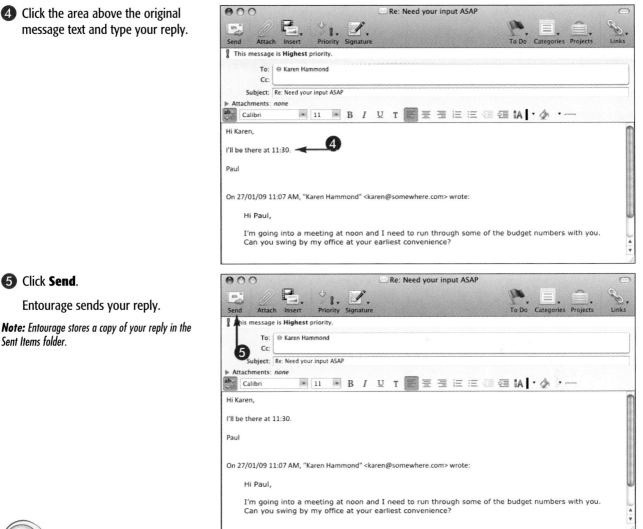

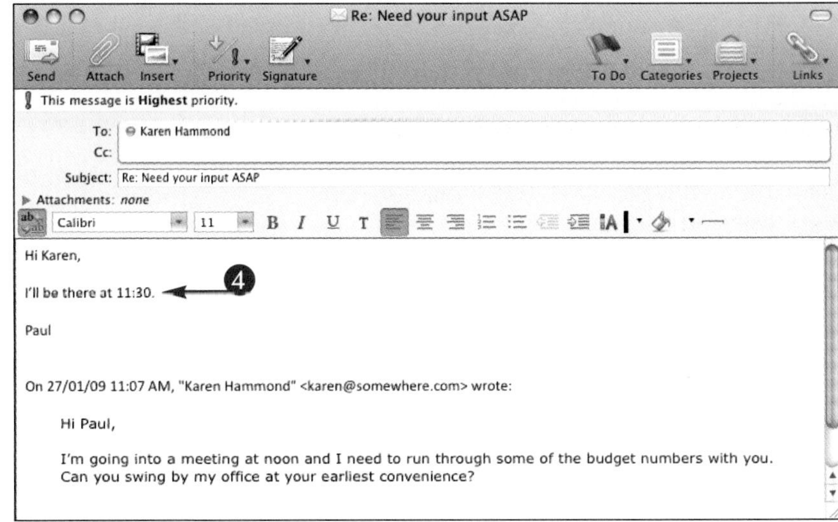


5 Click **Send**.

Entourage sends your reply.

***Note:** Entourage stores a copy of your reply in the Sent Items folder.*

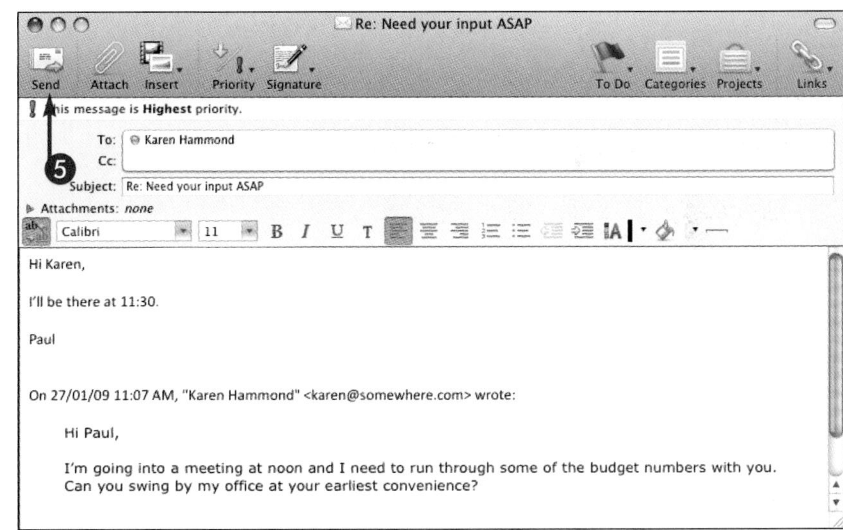

### How much of the original message should I quote in my reply?

If the original message is fairly short, you usually do not need to edit the text. However, if the original message is long, and your response deals only with part of that message, you will save the recipient time by deleting everything except the relevant portion of the text.

If you do not want Entourage to include the original text at all, click **Entourage**, click **Preferences**, click **Reply & Forward**, and then deselect the **Include entire message in reply** option (☑ changes to ☐). Click **OK** to put the new setting into effect.

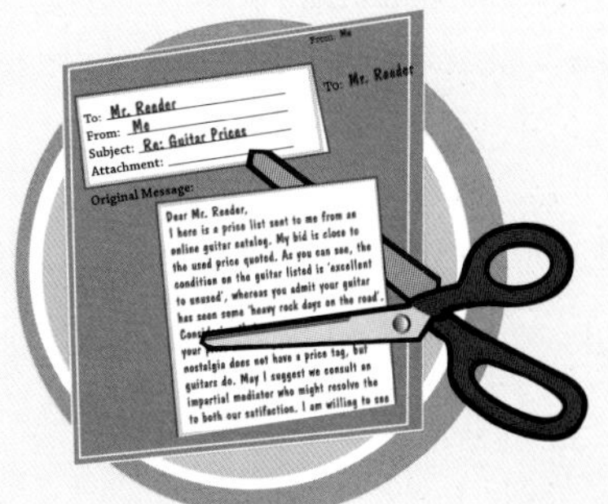

# Forward a Message

If a message has information that is relevant to or concerns another person, you can forward a copy of that message to the other recipient. You can also include your own comments in the forwarded message.

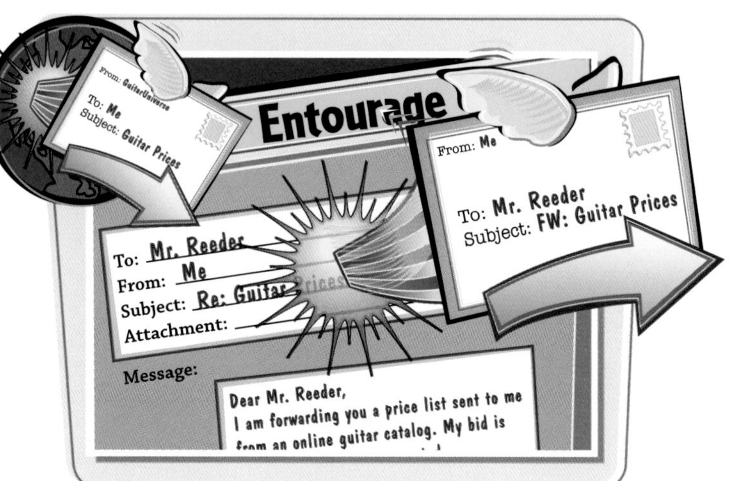


## Forward a Message

1. Click the message that you want to forward.
2. Click **Forward**.

   You can also press ⌘ + J.

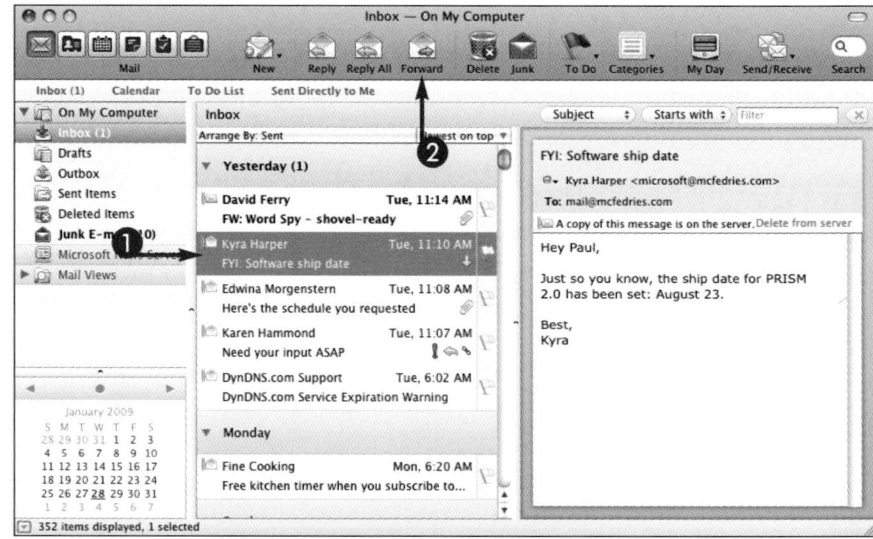

An addressing dialog appears.

3. Click the **To** field and then either type the recipient's address or click [icon] and then double-click the recipient in your Address Book list.
4. Press Return.

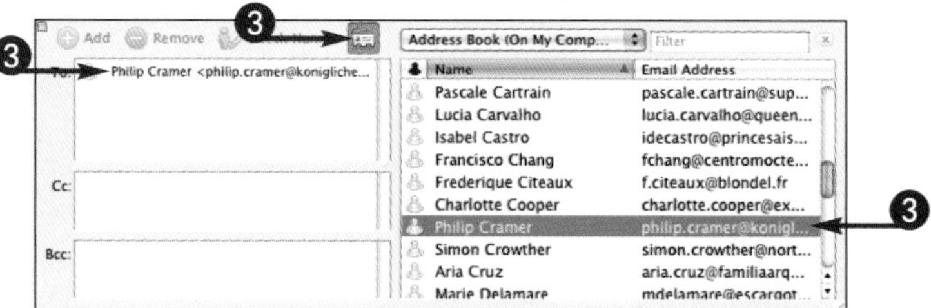

A message window appears.

- Entourage inserts the subject line, preceded by FW:.
- The original message's addresses (To and From), date, subject, and text are included in the forward.

5 Edit the original message to include only the text that is relevant to your forward.

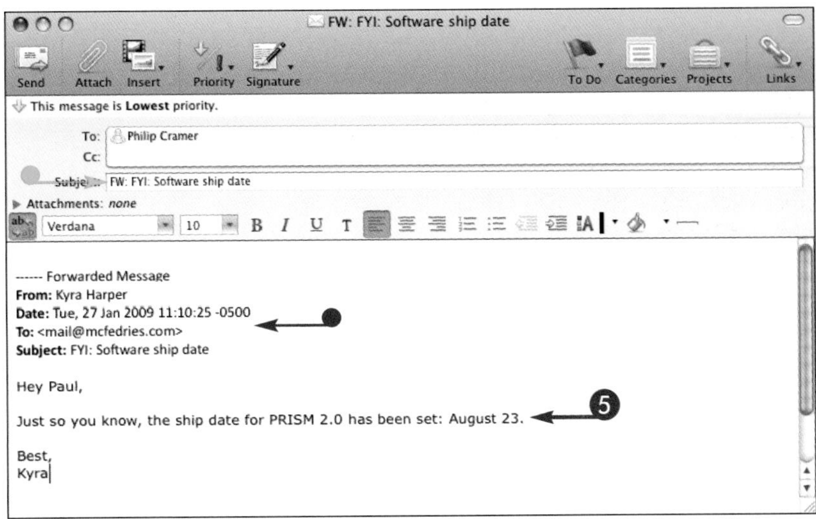

6 Click the area above the original message text and type your comments.

7 Click **Send**.

Entourage forwards the message with your comments.

***Note:** Entourage stores a copy of your forwarded message in the Sent Items folder.*

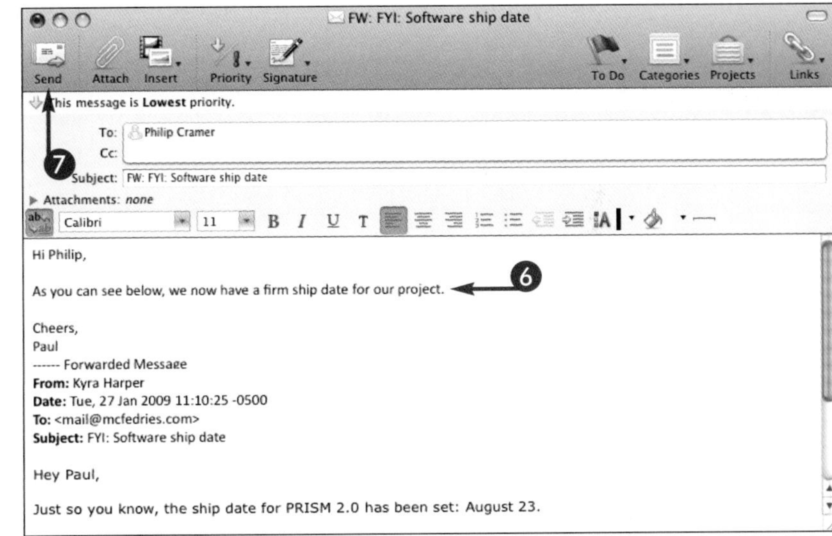

**How do I forward someone a copy of the actual message instead of just a copy of the message text?**

You can send the original message as an attachment. When the recipient opens the attachment, he or she sees an exact copy of the original message. Click the message, click **Message**, and then click **Forward as Attachment** (or press Ctrl + ⌘ + J). Entourage creates a new message and includes the original message as an attachment.

**Is there a way to forward a message to someone, but make it appear as though the message come directly from the original sender?**

Yes. You can redirect the original message to your recipient. Click the message, click **Message**, and then click **Redirect** (or press Option + ⌘ + J). Entourage creates a new message and includes the original message's subject line and text.

# Open and Save an Attachment

If you receive a message that has a file attached, you can open the attachment to view the contents of the file. You can also save the attachment as a file on your computer.

**Be careful when dealing with attached files. Computer viruses are often transmitted by e-mail attachments.**

## Open and Save an Attachment

### OPEN AN ATTACHMENT

1. Click the message that has the attachment, as indicated by the Attachment symbol (📎).
   - A list of the message attachments appears in the preview pane's Attachments list.
2. Click the attachment you want to open.
3. Click **Open**.

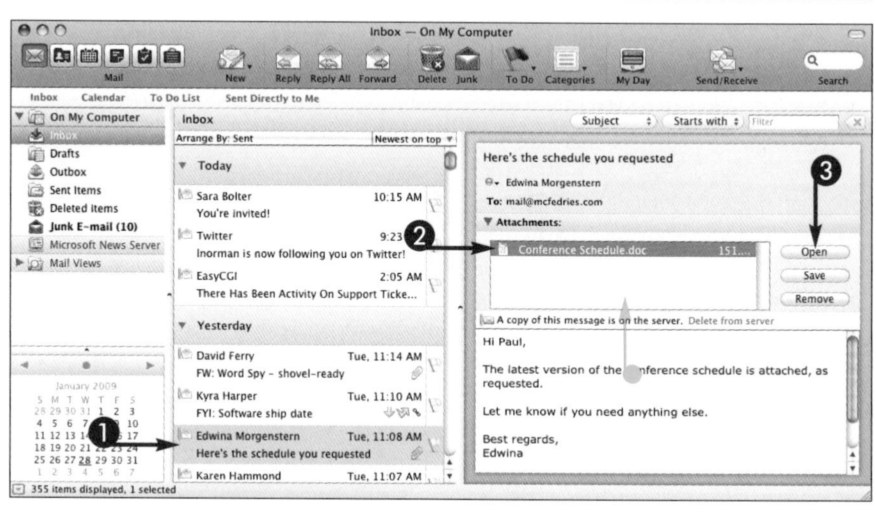


Entourage asks you to confirm that you want to open the file.

4. Click **Open**.

The file opens in the appropriate program.

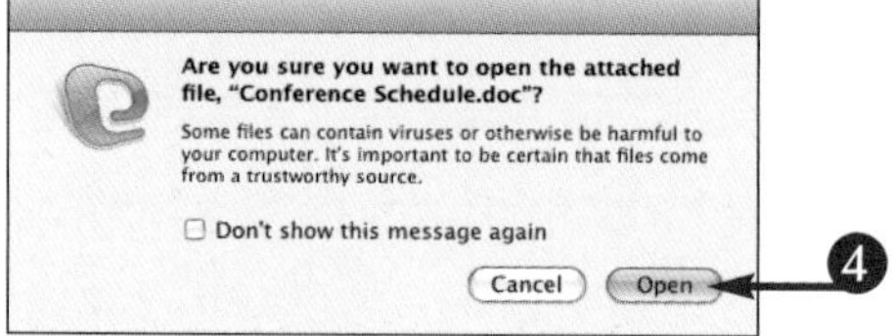

Are you sure you want to open the attached file, "Conference Schedule.doc"?
Some files can contain viruses or otherwise be harmful to your computer. It's important to be certain that files come from a trustworthy source.
Don't show this message again
Cancel
Open


***Note:** Instead of opening the file, Mac OS X may display a dialog box telling you that the file does not have a program associated with it. This means you need to install the appropriate program for the type of file. If you are not sure, ask the person who sent you the file what program you need.*

## SAVE AN ATTACHMENT

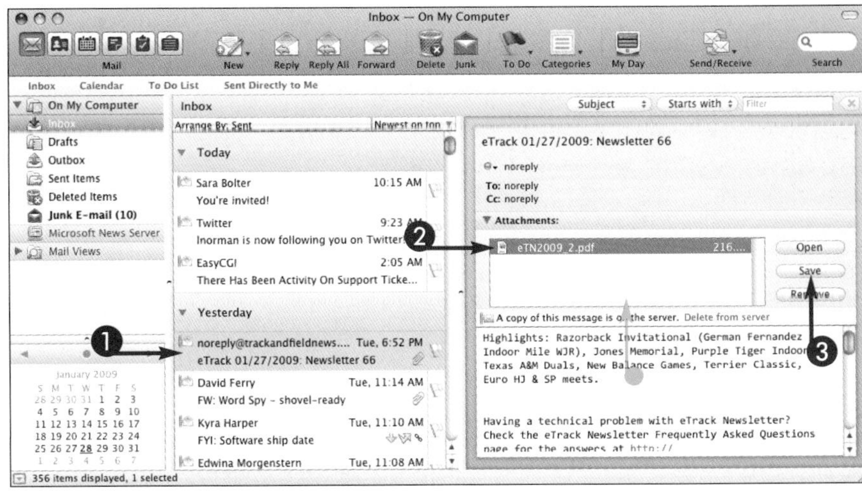


1. Click the message that has the attachment, as indicated by the Attachment symbol (📎).

- A list of the message attachments appears in the preview pane's Attachments list.

2. Click the attachment you want to save.

3. Click **Save**.

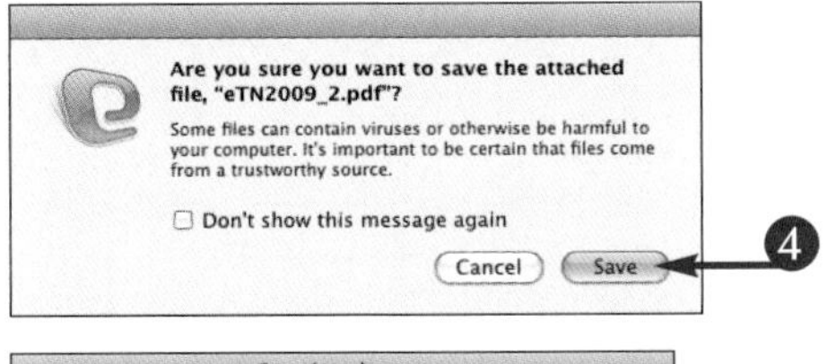


Entourage asks you to confirm that you want to save the file.

4. Click **Save**.

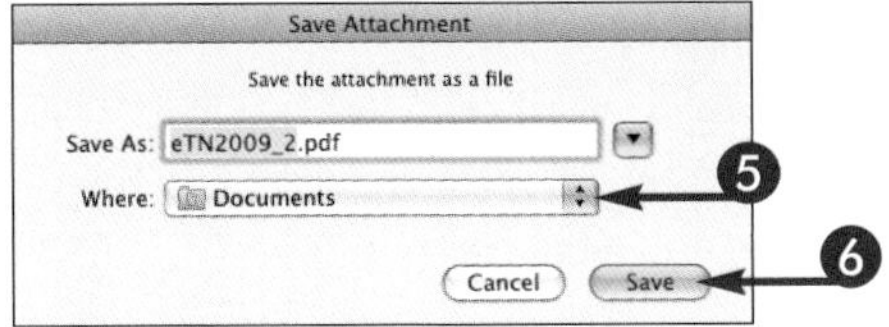


The Save Attachment dialog appears.

5. Click the **Where** ⇕ and then click the folder where you want to save the file.

6. Click **Save**.

### What should I do if I suspect an attachment contains a virus or other malware?

In most cases, Entourage detects unsafe files, and when you display a message with such a file, you should see a message saying "Entourage has blocked the following potentially unsafe attachments." Click **Remove them** to delete the attachment(s).

If you believe that an attached file may be unsafe, but Entourage has not blocked the file, you should delete the message. However, before you do that it is a good idea to delete the attached file from the message. Click the message, click the attachment in the preview pane, and then click **Remove**. When Entourage asks you to confirm, click **Delete**.

# Create a Folder for Saving Messages

You can create new folders and move messages from the Inbox to the new folders to keep the Inbox uncluttered. After you use Entourage for a while, you may find that you have many messages in your Inbox folder.

**You should use each folder you create to save related messages. For example, you could create separate folders for people you correspond with regularly, projects you are working on, different work departments, and so on.**

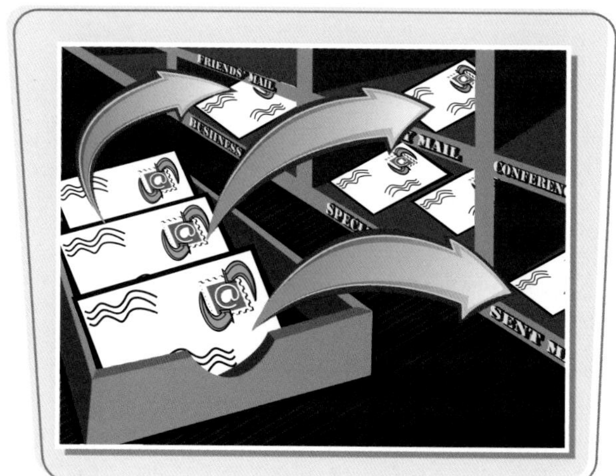

## Create a Folder for Saving Messages

### CREATE A FOLDER

1. Click **File**.
2. Click **New**.
3. Click **Folder**.

   You can also press Shift + ⌘ + N.

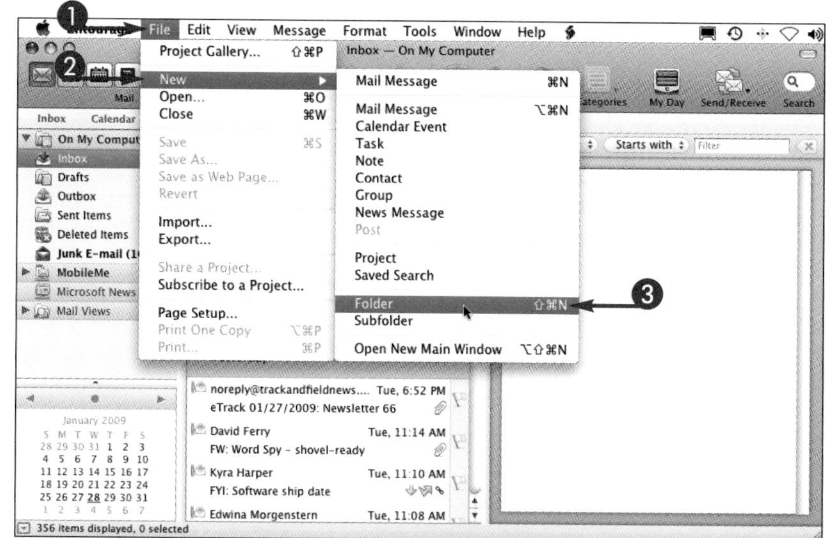

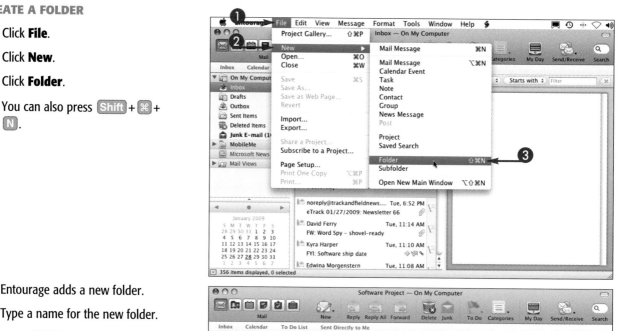

- Entourage adds a new folder.

4. Type a name for the new folder.
5. Press Return.

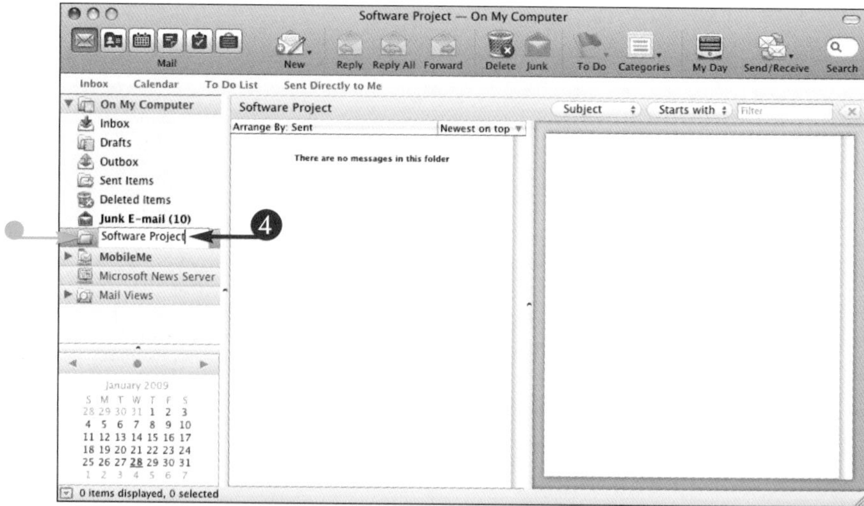

## MOVE A MESSAGE TO ANOTHER FOLDER

1. Click the folder that contains the message you want to move.
2. Position the mouse over the message you want to move.
3. Click and drag the message and drop it on the folder to which you want to move the message.

***Note:*** *To move multiple messages, hold down ⌘, click each message, and then drag any selected message to the destination folder.*

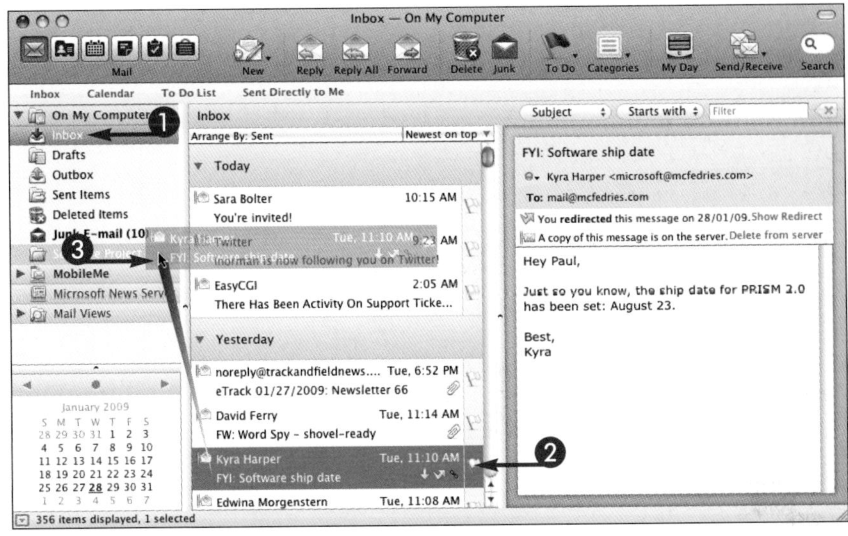

Entourage moves the message.

- You can click the destination folder to confirm the message has been moved.

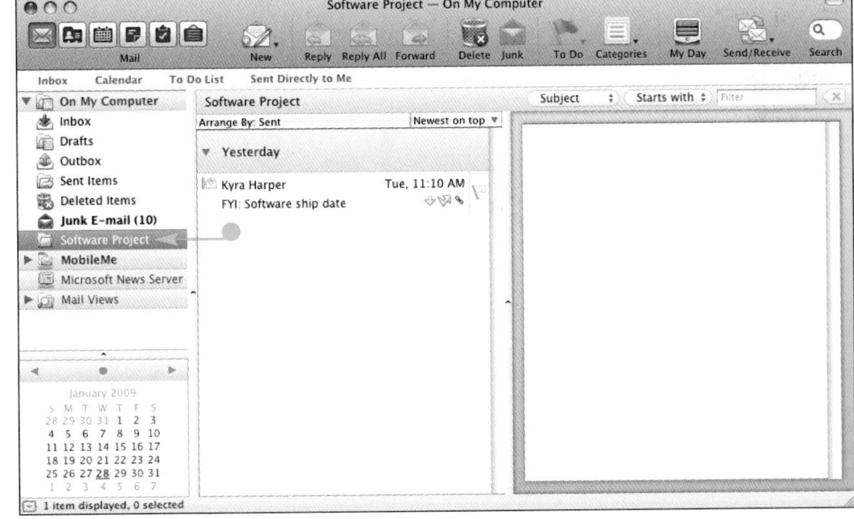

## TIPS

### How do I rename a folder?

Double-click the folder. A text box opens that displays the current folder name. In the text box, type the new name and then press Return. Note that Entourage only allows you to rename folders that you created yourself.

### How do I delete a folder?

Click the folder, click **Edit**, and then click **Delete Folder** (or press ⌘ + Del). Note that Entourage only allows you to delete folders that you created yourself. Also remember that when you delete a folder, you also delete any messages stored in that folder.

# Set the Junk E-Mail Protection Level

You can control junk e-mail by setting the protection level. Junk e-mail, or *spam*, is unsolicited, commercial e-mail messages that advertise anything from baldness cures to cheap printer cartridges. Most people receive at least a few junk e-mails a day, while some people receive hundreds of them. No matter how many you receive, reducing junk e-mail saves time and reduces e-mail frustration.

**Some junk messages are more than just annoying. For example, many spams advertise deals that are simply fraudulent, and others feature such unsavory practices as linking to adult-oriented sites and sites that install spyware.**

## Set the Junk E-Mail Protection Level

1. Click **Tools**.
2. Click **Junk E-mail Protection**.

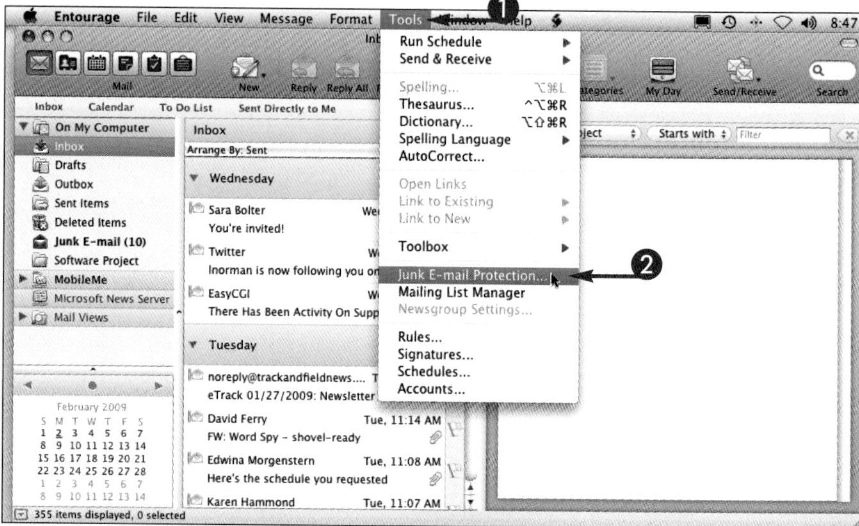

The Junk E-mail Protection dialog appears.

3. Click the **Level** tab.
4. Select the junk e-mail protection level option you want to use (○ changes to ◉).

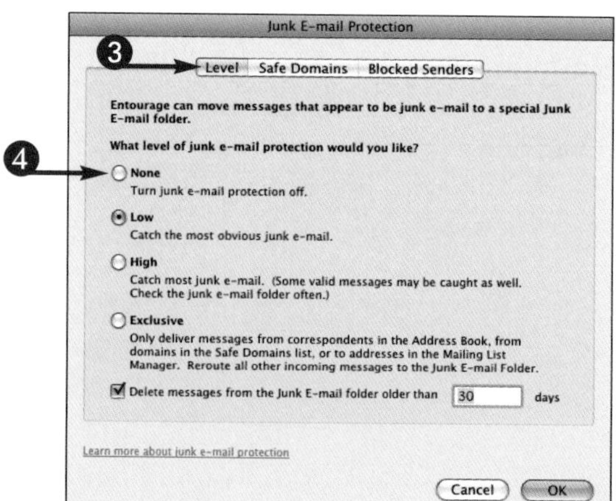

- Click **Low** to move messages with obvious spam content to the Junk E-mail folder.

  This level catches most spam and has only a small risk of false positives.

- Click **High** to handle spam aggressively.

  Use this level if you get a few dozen messages or more daily. This level usually creates false positives.

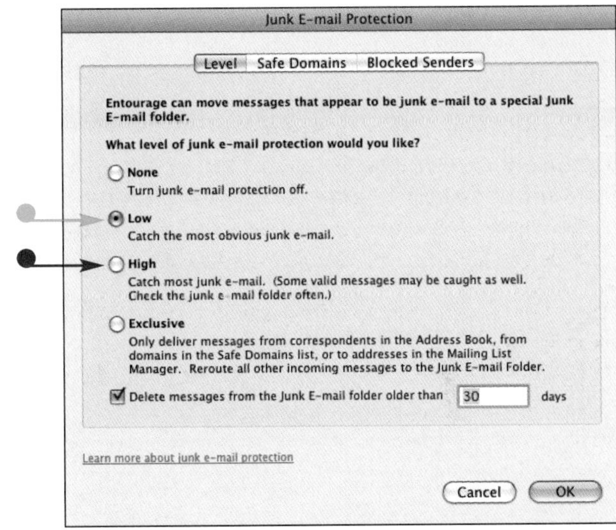

Junk E-mail Protection
Level Safe Domains Blocked Senders
Entourage can move messages that appear to be junk e-mail to a special Junk E-mail folder.
What level of junk e-mail protection would you like?
None
Turn junk e-mail protection off.
Low
Catch the most obvious junk e-mail.
High
Catch most junk e-mail. (Some valid messages may be caught as well. Check the junk e-mail folder often.)
Exclusive
Only deliver messages from correspondents in the Address Book, from domains in the Safe Domains list, or to addresses in the Mailing List Manager. Reroute all other incoming messages to the Junk E-mail Folder.
Delete messages from the Junk E-mail folder older than 30 days
Learn more about junk e-mail protection
Cancel
OK


- Click **Exclusive** to treat all incoming messages, except for messages that come from people in your Address Book or domains you add to the Safe Domains list, as spam.

  Use this level if you receive 100 or more spam messages each day and if most of your nonspam e-mail comes from people you know or from mailing lists you subscribe to.

5. Click **OK**.

   Entourage sets the junk e-mail protection level.

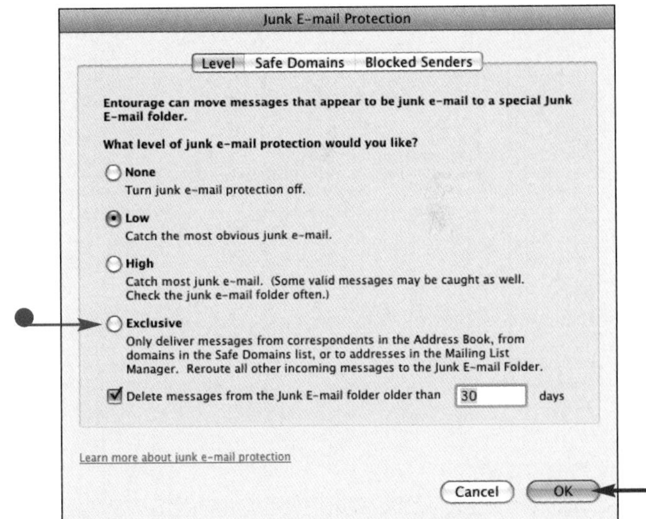

Junk E-mail Protection
Level Safe Domains Blocked Senders
Entourage can move messages that appear to be junk e-mail to a special Junk E-mail folder.
What level of junk e-mail protection would you like?
None
Turn junk e-mail protection off.
Low
Catch the most obvious junk e-mail.
High
Catch most junk e-mail. (Some valid messages may be caught as well. Check the junk e-mail folder often.)
Exclusive
Only deliver messages from correspondents in the Address Book, from domains in the Safe Domains list, or to addresses in the Mailing List Manager. Reroute all other incoming messages to the Junk E-mail Folder.
Delete messages from the Junk E-mail folder older than 30 days
Learn more about junk e-mail protection
Cancel
OK
5


TIPS

### What is a false positive?

This is a legitimate message that Entourage flags as junk and moves to the Junk E-mail folder. The stronger the protection level, the more likely it is that false positives will occur, so the more time you must spend checking the Junk E-mail folder.

### How do I specify safe domains?

In the Junk E-mail Protection dialog, click the **Safe Domains** tab, type the domains you consider safe, separated by commas, and then click **OK**.

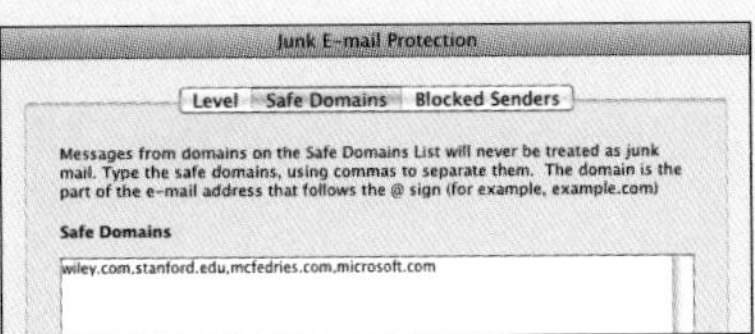

Junk E-mail Protection
Level Safe Domains Blocked Senders
Messages from domains on the Safe Domains List will never be treated as junk mail. Type the safe domains, using commas to separate them. The domain is the part of the e-mail address that follows the @ sign (for example, example.com)
Safe Domains
wiley.com,stanford.edu,mcfedries.com,microsoft.com

# Block a Person Who Sends You Junk Mail

You can reduce the amount of junk e-mail you have to deal with by blocking those people who send you such messages. Entourage automatically moves existing and future messages from that person to the Junk E-mail folder.

You can block a person using a message he or she has sent, or by adding the sender's address to the Blocked Senders list.

## Block a Person Who Sends You Junk Mail

### USE A MESSAGE TO BLOCK A PERSON WHO SENDS YOU JUNK MAIL

1. Click a message from the person you want to block.

2. Click **Message**.
3. Click **Block Sender**.

   Entourage moves the message to the Junk E-mail folder and blocks future messages from the sender's address.

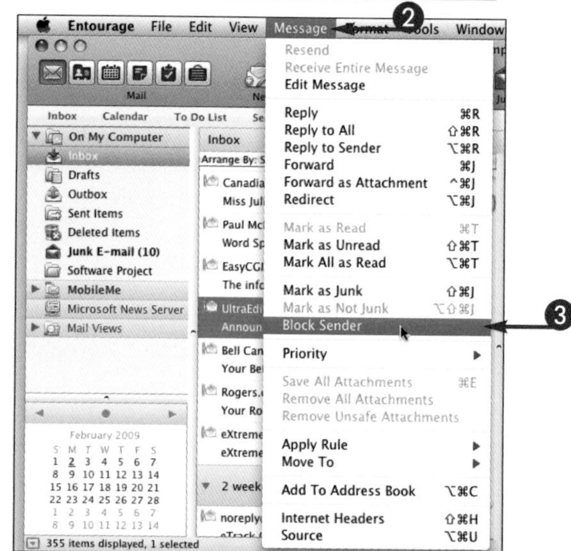

## ADD A PERSON'S ADDRESS TO THE BLOCKED SENDERS LIST

1. Click **Tools**.
2. Click **Junk E-mail Protection**.

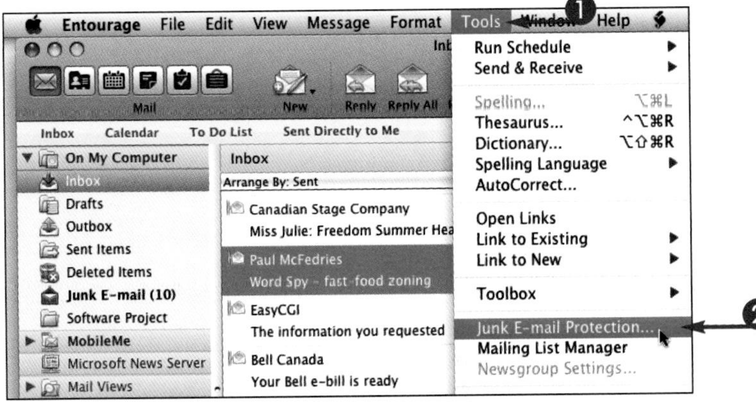


The Junk E-mail Protection dialog appears.

3. Click the **Blocked Senders** tab.
4. Type the person's address in the Blocked Senders list.

***Note:** If you want to add multiple addresses to the Blocked Senders list, separate each address with a comma.*

5. Click **OK**.

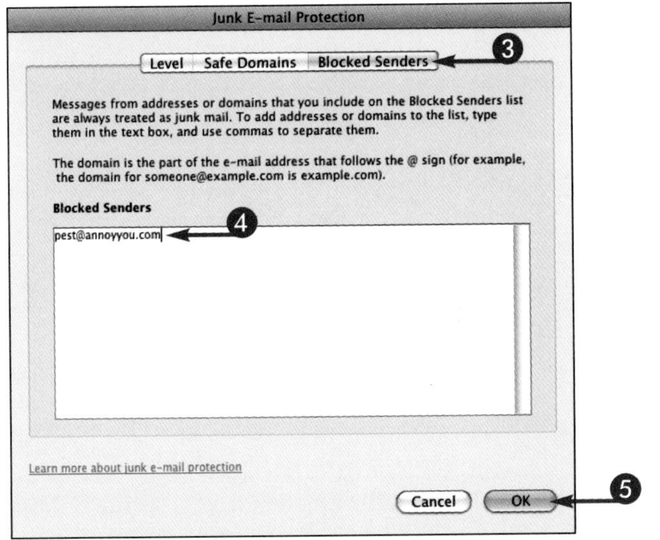

### How do I handle a legitimate message that Entourage flags as junk?

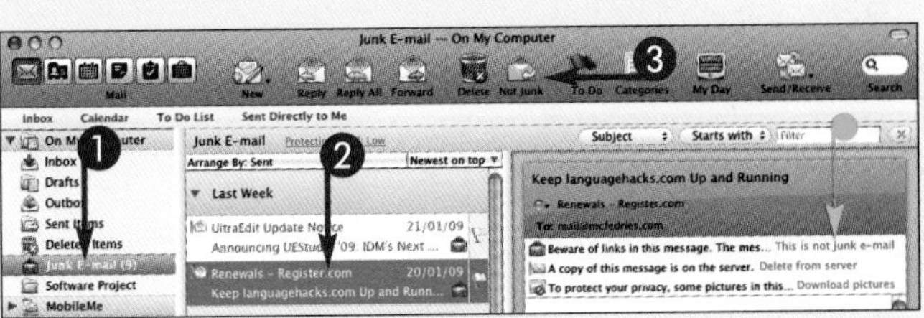


1. Click Junk E-mail.
2. Click the message.
3. Click Not Junk.

- If the Preview Pane is visible, you can also click the This is not junk e-mail link.

4. Select the Just classify this message as "not junk" option (○ changes to ◉).
5. Click OK.

Entourage moves the message to your Inbox folder.

# Create Rules to Filter Incoming Messages

You can make your e-mail chores faster and more efficient if you create *rules* that handle incoming messages automatically. For example, you can create a rule that moves all incoming messages with a certain subject line to a folder.

**A rule combines message criterion and an action. The criterion specifies the type of information you want to identify, such as the address of the sender or words in the subject line. The action is what happens to a message that satisfies the condition, such as moving the message to another folder or sending a reply.**

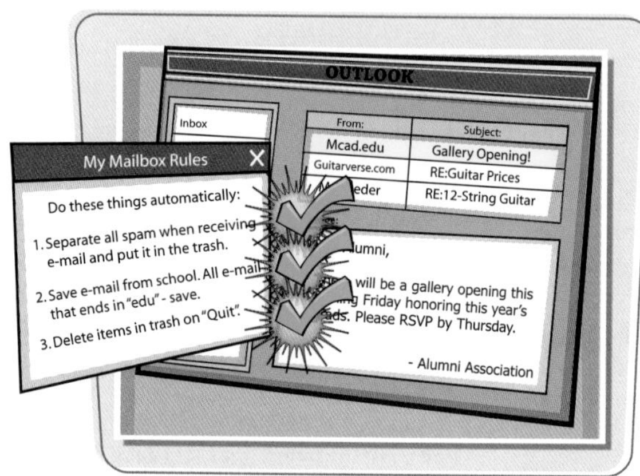


## Create Rules to Filter Incoming Messages

1. Click **Tools**.
2. Click **Rules**.

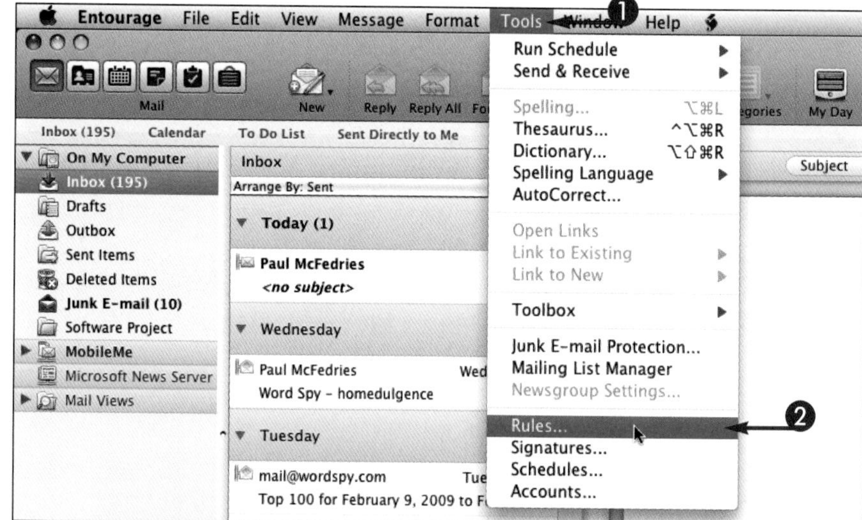


The Rules dialog appears.

3. Click the type of mail account you want to work with.
4. Click **New**.

The Edit Rule dialog appears.

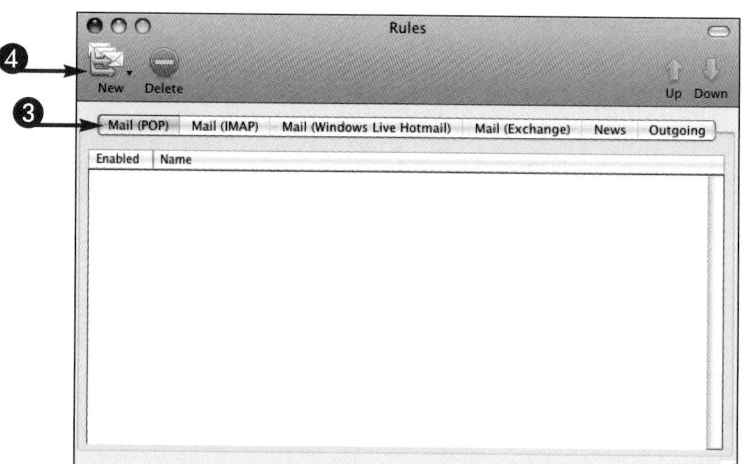

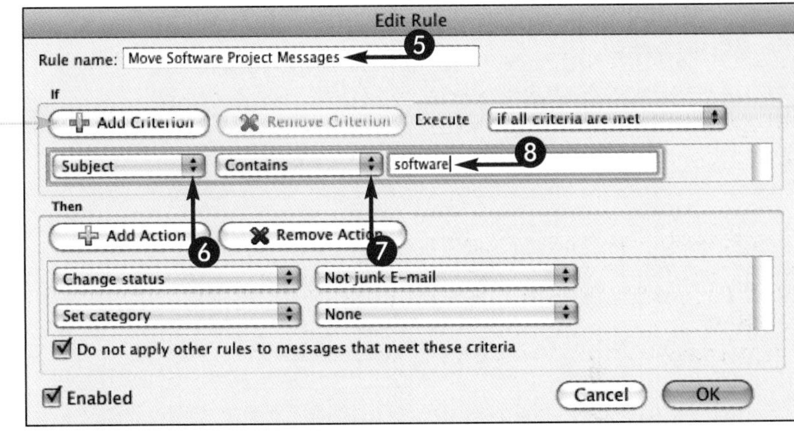


5 Type a rule name.

6 Click the **All messages** and then click the type of data you want to identify.

7 If the criterion requires a value, click the **Contains** and click an operator.

8 If the criterion requires a value, type the text, address, or other required information.

- If you want to use multiple criteria, click **Add Criterion** and then repeat Steps **6** to **8** to add other data to the rule.

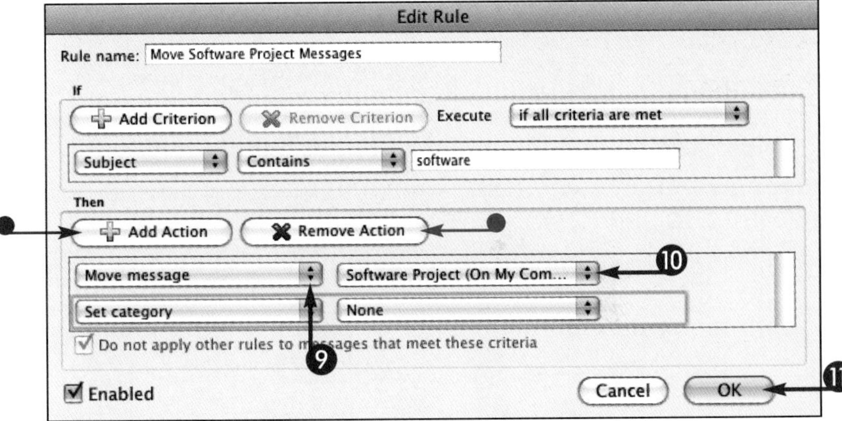


9 Click the **Change status** and then click the action you want to use.

10 If the action requires a value, type the text or select the value from the pop-up menu.

- If you want to run multiple actions, click **Add Action** and then repeat Steps **8** and **9**.

- To remove an action, click the action and then click **Remove Action**.

11 Click **OK**.

Entourage adds the rule to the Rules dialog.

### How do I make changes to a rule?

Follow Steps **1** to **3** from this task to open the Rules dialog and select an account type. Double-click the rule you want to change. Use the Edit Rule dialog that appears to make your changes to the rule. If you want to delete a criterion, click an empty area within the criterion and then click **Remove Criterion**. When you are done, click **OK**.

### Can I prevent a rule from running?

Yes. Follow Steps **1** to **3** from this task to open the Rules dialog and select an account type. If you only want to temporarily disable a rule, deselect the rule's **Enabled** check box (☑ changes to ☐). To remove the rule completely, click the rule and then click **Delete**. When Entourage asks you to confirm, click **Delete**.

CHAPTER 19

# Working with Appointments and Tasks

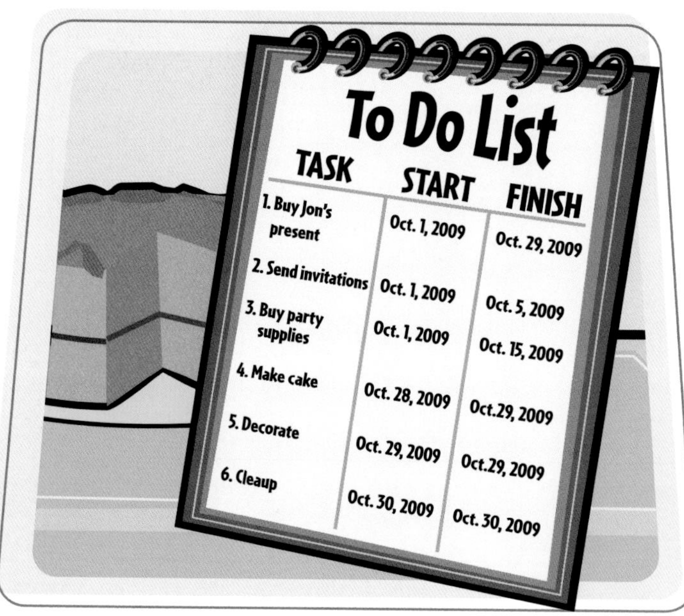


If you find that your life just keeps getting busier, Microsoft Entourage can help you keep track of your ever increasing load of appointments and tasks. Entourage comes with two components — called Calendar and Tasks — that can help you manage your busy schedule. You use Calendar to enter and track appointments and all-day events, and you use Tasks to organize your to-do list.

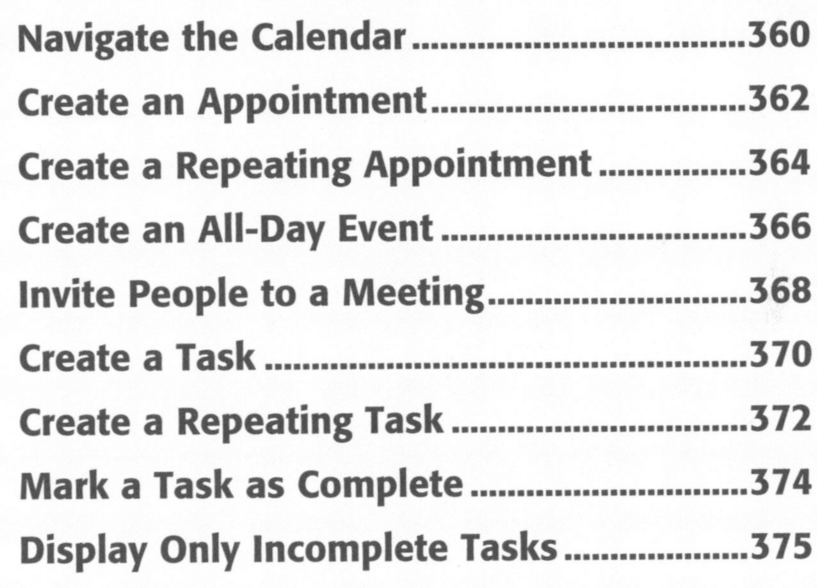

# Navigate the Calendar

Calendar makes scheduling easy. However, before you create an appointment or event, you must first select the date on which the appointment or event occurs.

## Navigate the Calendar

### NAVIGATE USING THE MINI CALENDAR

1. In Entourage, click the **Calendar** button (📅).

   You can also switch to Calendar by pressing ⌘+3.

2. Click **Day**.
3. In the Mini Calendar, click the **Next Month** button (▶) until the month of your appointment appears.

- If you go too far, click the **Previous Month** button (◀) to move back to the month you want.
- If you want to return to the current month, click the **Current Month** button (●).

4. Click the date.

- The date appears in the Calendar.
- If you want to return to today's date, click **Today** or press ⌘+T.

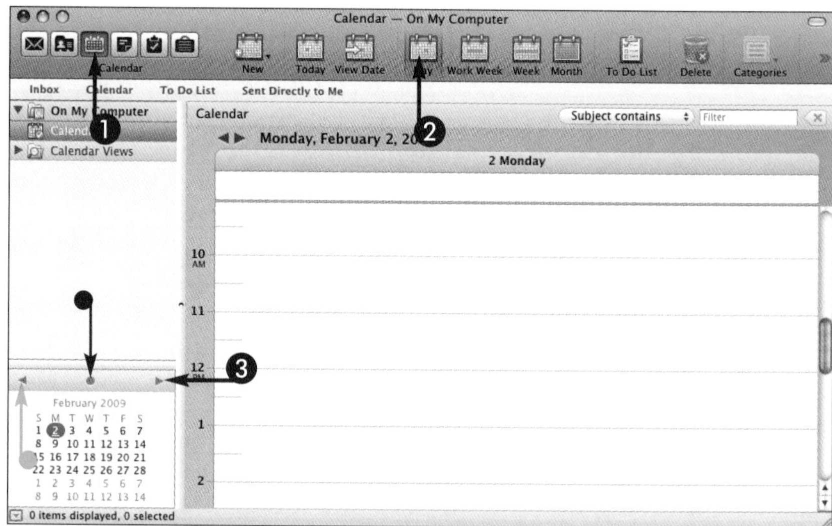


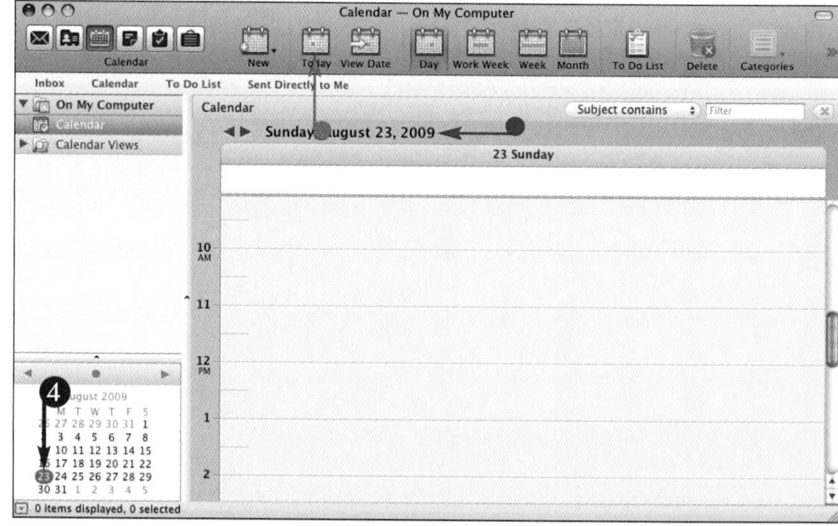

## NAVIGATE TO A SPECIFIC DATE

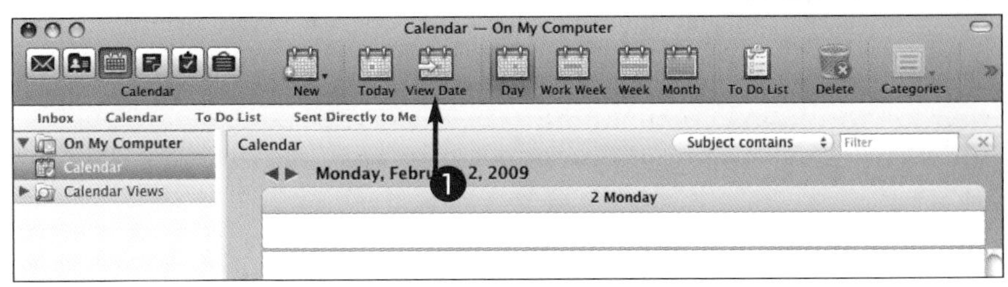


1. Click **View Date**.

   You can also select the View Date command by pressing Shift + ⌘ + T.

   The View Date dialog appears.

2. In the Date text box, type the date you want using the format mm/dd/yyyy.

- You can also click here to display a Date Navigator that you can use to click the date you want.

3. Click **OK**.

   Entourage displays the date in the Calendar.

**TIP**

**Can I see more than one day at a time in the Calendar?**

Yes. Use the following toolbar buttons and keyboard shortcuts:

- **Work Week.** Click this button to show the work week (Monday through Friday) that includes the date that is currently selected in the Mini Calendar. (You can also press Option + ⌘ + 2.)
- **Week.** Click this button to show the full week that includes the date that is currently selected in the Mini Calendar. (You can also press Option + ⌘ + 3.)
- **Month.** Click this button to show the month that includes the date that is currently selected in the Mini Calendar. (You can also press Option + ⌘ + 4.)

# Create an Appointment

You can help organize your life by using Calendar to record your appointments on the date and time they occur. For each appointment, you specify details such as the location, start and end times, and notes related to the event.

**You can also specify a time interval before the appointment when Calendar displays a dialog to remind you of the appointment.**

## Create an Appointment

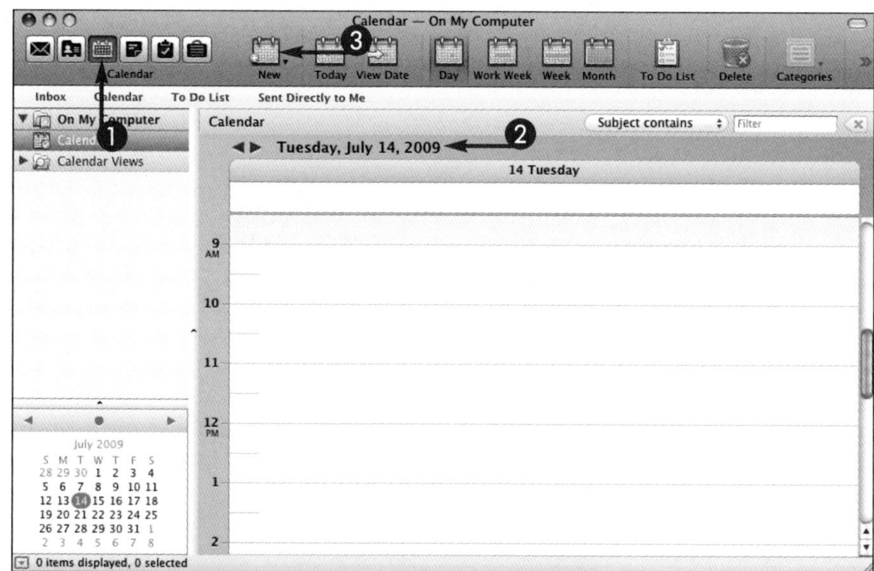


1. In Entourage, click the **Calendar** button (▦).
2. Navigate to the date when the appointment occurs.
3. Click **New**.

   When you are in the Calendar window, you can also press ⌘ + N to start a new appointment.

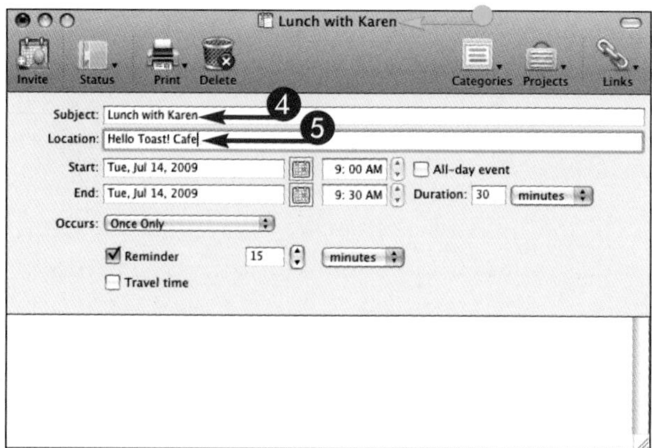


Calendar displays the New Event window.

4. In the Subject text box, type a name for the appointment.

- The window name changes to the name of the appointment.

5. In the Location text box, type the appointment location.

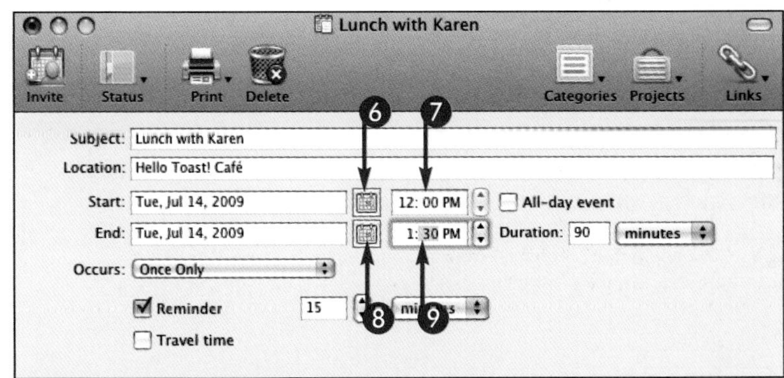


6. If the start date is incorrect, use the Start date navigator to click the correct date.
7. If the start time is incorrect, use the Start time spin box to click the correct time.
8. If the end date is incorrect, use the End date navigator to click the correct date.
9. If the end time is incorrect, use the End time spin box to click the correct time.
10. Click the **Reminder** ⬍ and then click a reminder unit: minutes, hours, or days.
11. Type a value for the reminder.
 - If you do not want a reminder, deselect the **Reminder** option (☑ changes to ☐).
12. In the large text box, type notes related to the appointment.
13. Press ⌘+S to save the appointment.
14. Click the **Close** button (●).

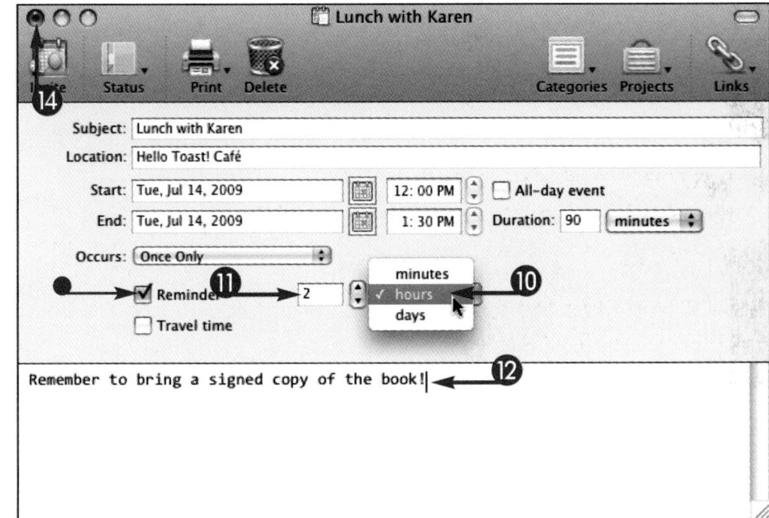

**How do I make changes to an appointment?**

To edit the appointment, navigate to the date and then double-click the appointment block to open the appointment details in a window. Make your changes, press ⌘+S, and then click ●. To remove an appointment, click it, press Del, and then click **Delete**.

**Calendar automatically sets a 15-minute reminder for each new appointment. Can I change this?**

Yes. Click **Entourage** and then click **Preferences** to open the Preferences dialog. Click **Calendar** to display the Calendar preferences. If you want to turn off automatic reminders, deselect the **Set default reminder to occur** option (☑ changes to ☐). Otherwise, click the **Set default reminder to occur** ⬍, click a time unit (hours, minutes, or days), and then type the number of units in the text box.

# Create a Repeating Appointment

If you have an appointment that occurs at a regular interval, such as a daily department meeting or weekly lunch date, you can schedule such an appointment as a *recurring event*. You can set up the appointment to repeat daily, weekly, monthly, yearly, or every weekday.

**You can also set up a custom recurrence pattern to suit your needs.**

## Create a Repeating Appointment

### CREATE A BASIC REPEATING APPOINTMENT

1. Switch to Calendar and create a new appointment.

***Note:** See the section "Create an Appointment"" to learn how to create a new appointment.*

2. Click the **Occurs** ⬍ and then click the recurrence interval you want to use.

- To create your own recurrence interval, click **Custom** or click **Edit** to open the Recurring Event dialog. The rest of this section shows you how to use this dialog.

### CREATE A DAILY REPEATING APPOINTMENT

1. Select the **Daily** option (○ changes to ◉).
2. Select the **Every** option (○ changes to ◉).
3. Type the daily interval you want to use.

- If you want to schedule the appointment on weekdays, select the **Every weekday** option (○ changes to ◉).

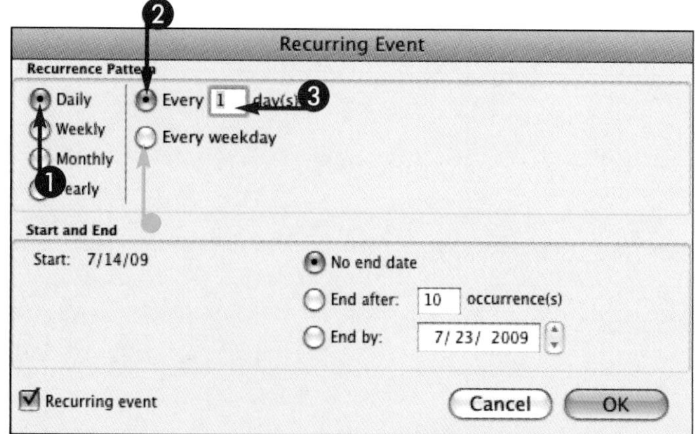

### CREATE A WEEKLY REPEATING APPOINTMENT

1. Select the **Weekly** option (○ changes to ◉).
2. Type the weekly interval you want to use.
3. Select the check box beside each day you want to use (☐ changes to ☑).

### CREATE A MONTHLY REPEATING APPOINTMENT

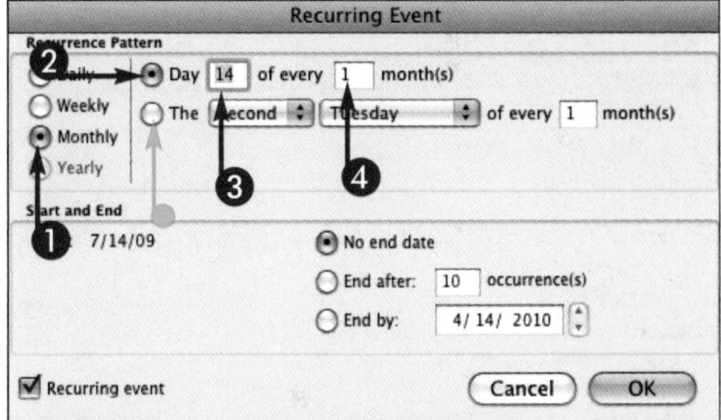


1. Select the **Monthly** option (○ changes to ◉).
2. Select the **Day** option (○ changes to ◉).
3. Type the day of the month you want to use.
4. Type the monthly interval you want to use.

- You can also click here (○ changes to ◉) and then specify a relative interval.

### CREATE A YEARLY REPEATING APPOINTMENT

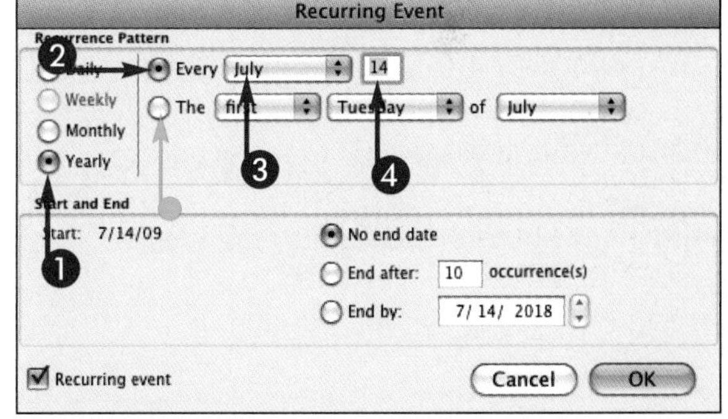


1. Select the **Yearly** option (○ changes to ◉).
2. Select the **Every** option (○ changes to ◉).
3. Click ⬍ and then click a month.
4. Type the day of the month you want to use.

- You can also click here (○ changes to ◉) and then specify a relative interval.

**Can I make changes to one appointment in a series of appointments?**

Yes. Follow these steps:

1. In Calendar, navigate to the date when the appointment occurs.
2. Double-click the appointment.
3. Select **Open this one** (○ changes to ◉).
4. Click **OK**.

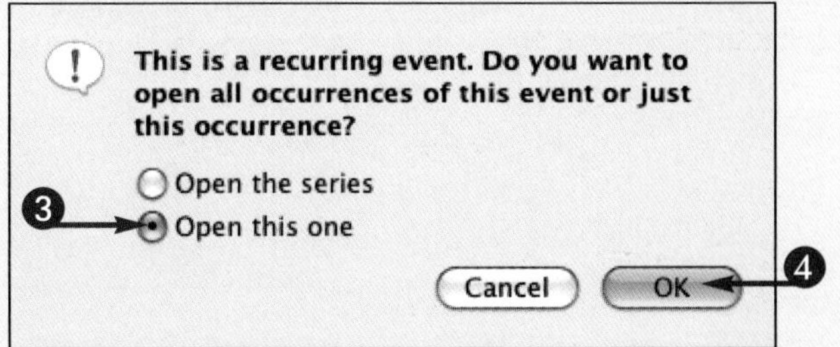


5. Make changes to the appointment and save your work.

# Create an All-Day Event

You can create an all-day event if the event has no set time — for example, a birthday, anniversary, or multiple-day event such as a sales meeting or vacation.

## Create an All-Day Event

1. In Entourage, click the **Calendar** button (▦).
2. Navigate to the date when the event occurs or begins.
3. Click **New**.

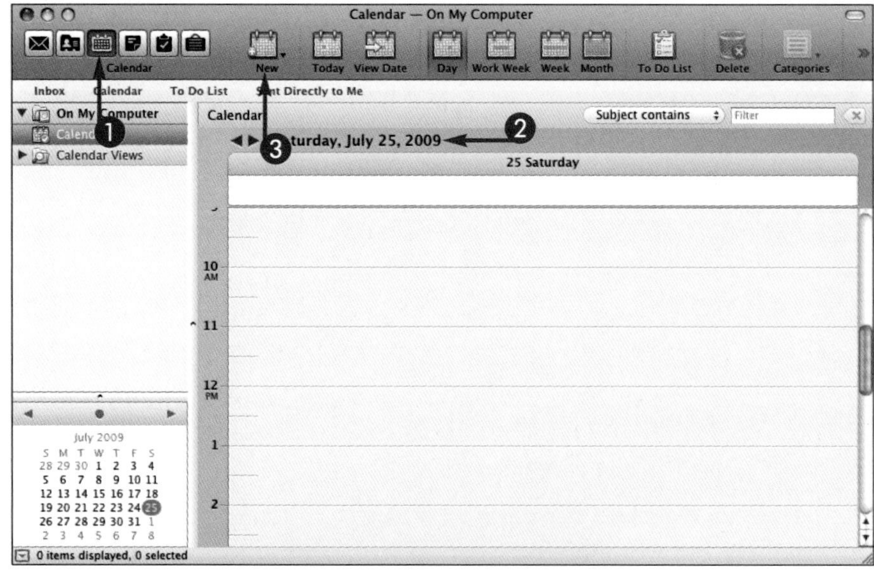


4. Select the **All-day event** option (☐ changes to ☑).
5. If the start date is incorrect, use the Start date navigator to click the correct date.
6. If the event occurs over multiple days, use the End date navigator to click the ending date.

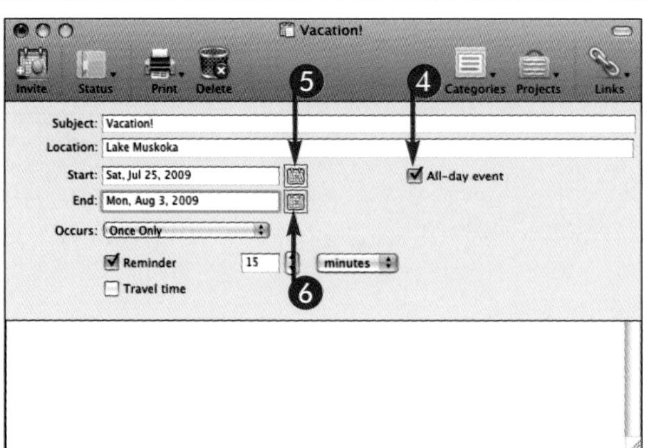

7 Fill in the rest of the event details.

***Note:*** *See the section "Create an Appointment" to learn how to specify appointment details.*

8 Press ⌘+S to save the event.

9 Click the **Close** button (●).

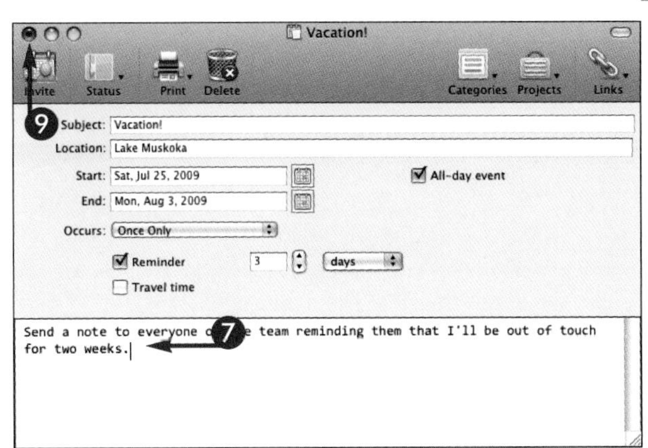


- Calendar adds the event to the top of the appointments list.

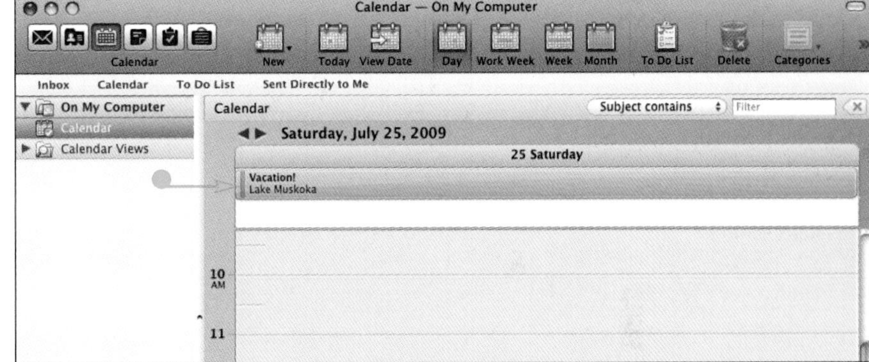


TIP

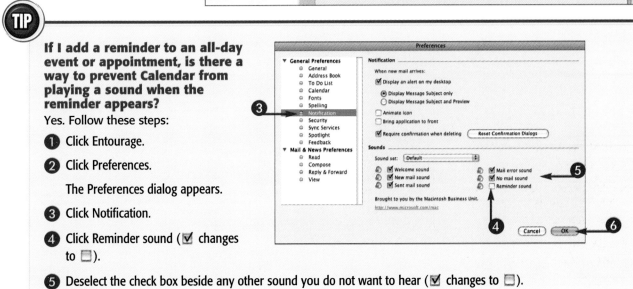

**If I add a reminder to an all-day event or appointment, is there a way to prevent Calendar from playing a sound when the reminder appears?**

Yes. Follow these steps:

1 Click Entourage.

2 Click Preferences.

The Preferences dialog appears.

3 Click Notification.

4 Click Reminder sound (☑ changes to ☐).

5 Deselect the check box beside any other sound you do not want to hear (☑ changes to ☐).

6 Click OK.

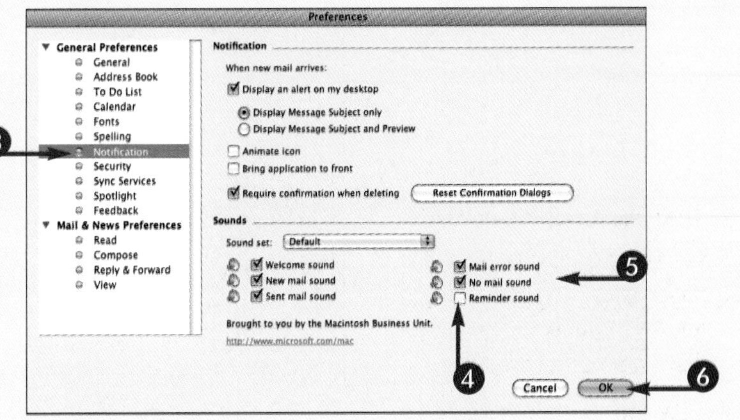

# Invite People to a Meeting

You can use Entourage to send an e-mail message that invites other people to a meeting. You can then use Entourage to monitor the responses and see who accepts or declines the invitation.

**For best results, the people you invite should be using a compatible calendar program, which means a program that supports the iCalendar format. This includes other Entourage users, Mac iCal users, and Microsoft Outlook users.**

## Invite People to a Meeting

1. Switch to Calendar and create a new appointment.

*Note: See the section "Create an Appointment" to learn how to create a new appointment.*

2. Click **Invite**.

   You can also run the Invite command by pressing Shift + ⌘ + I.

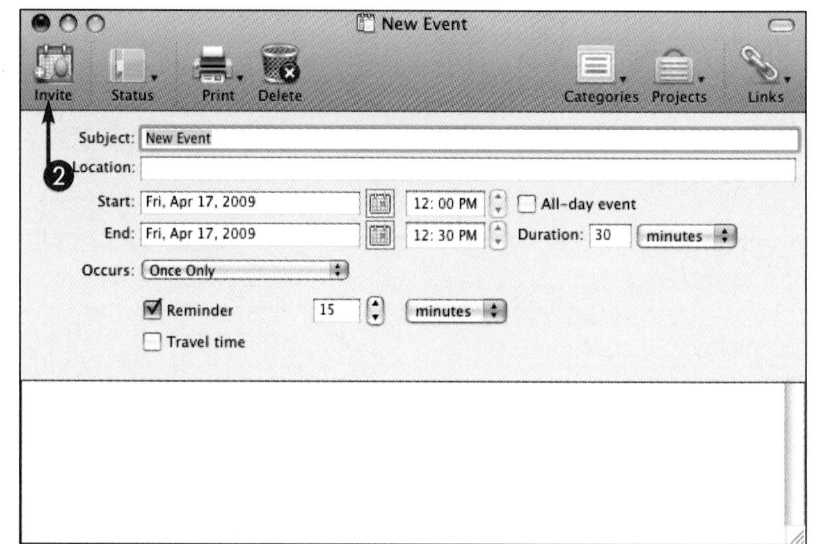


   An addressing dialog appears.

3. Click the **To** field and then type the recipient's address or click the Address Book button and then double-click the recipient in your Address Book list.
4. Click **Add** or press Tab.
5. Repeat Steps **3** and **4** to add all the attendees you want to invite to your meeting.
6. Press Return.

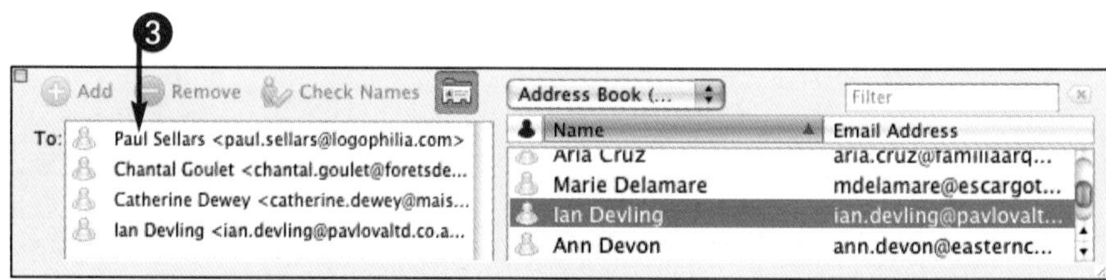

- Entourage adds the attendees to the event window.

7 If you have more than one e-mail account, click the **From** and then click the account you want to use to send the invitation.

8 Fill in the rest of the meeting details.

***Note:*** *See the section "Create an Appointment" to learn how to specify appointment details.*

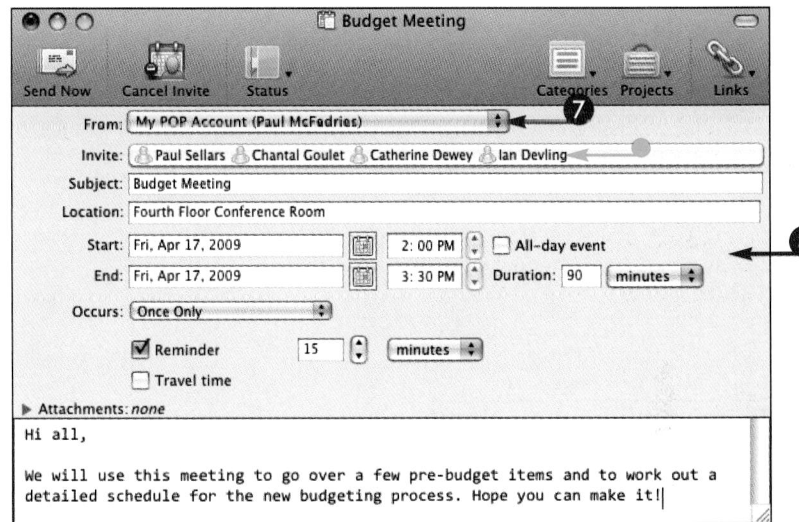


9 Press ⌘ + S to save the meeting.

10 Click **Send Now**.

You can also send the invitation by pressing ⌘ + Return.

Entourage adds the meeting to your calendar and sends the invitation message.

***Note:*** *To check attendee responses, double-click the meeting in Calendar, and then click* ***View attendee status****.*

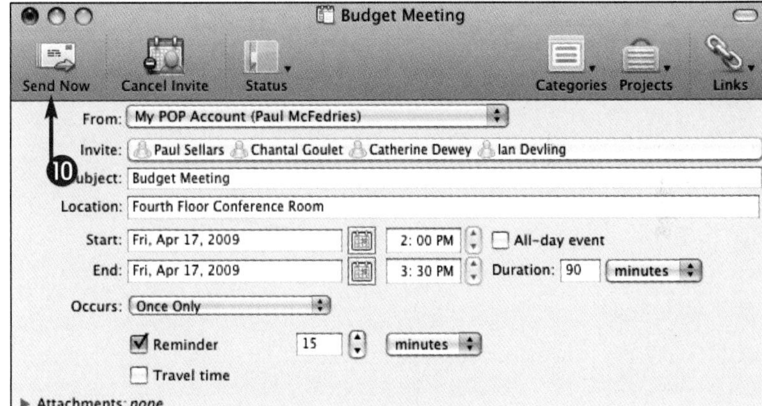

### How do I respond to a meeting invitation?

Double-click the message to open it, and then click one of the following buttons:

- **Accept** if you can attend the meeting.
- **Decline** if you cannot attend the meeting.
- **Tentative** if you are not sure you can attend.

When Entourage asks if you want to send a response, select **Yes, with comments**; **Yes, without comments**; or **No** (○ changes to ◉), and then click **OK**.

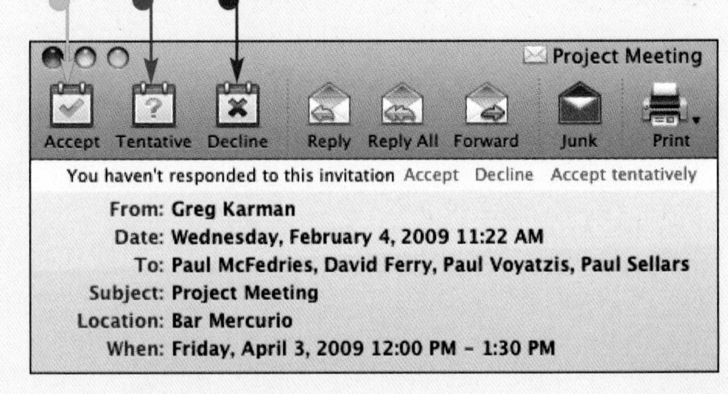

# Create a Task

You can monitor tasks — from large projects such as budgets to basic chores such as returning phone calls — by using Calendar to record your tasks, including when they start and when they are due.

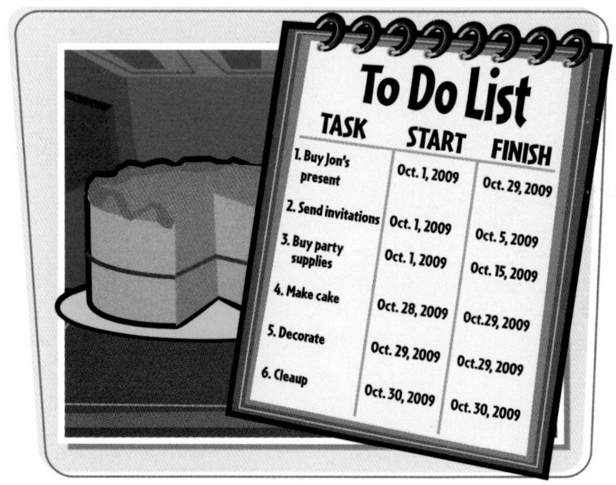


## Create a Task

1. Click the **Tasks** button (☑).

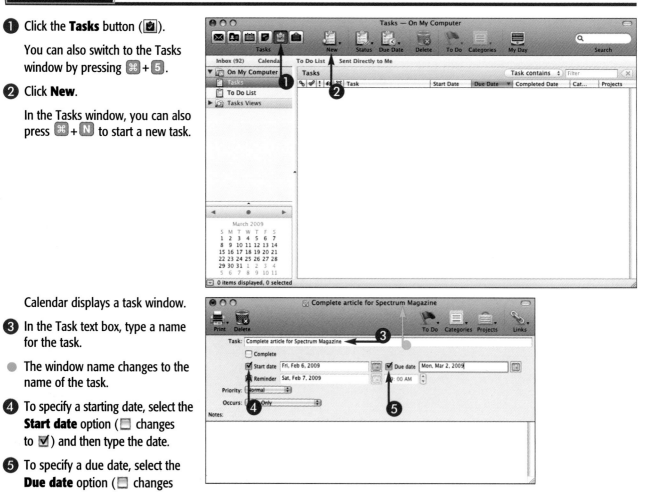

   You can also switch to the Tasks window by pressing ⌘+5.

2. Click **New**.

   In the Tasks window, you can also press ⌘+N to start a new task.

Calendar displays a task window.

3. In the Task text box, type a name for the task.

- The window name changes to the name of the task.

4. To specify a starting date, select the **Start date** option (☐ changes to ☑) and then type the date.

5. To specify a due date, select the **Due date** option (☐ changes to ☑) and then type the date.

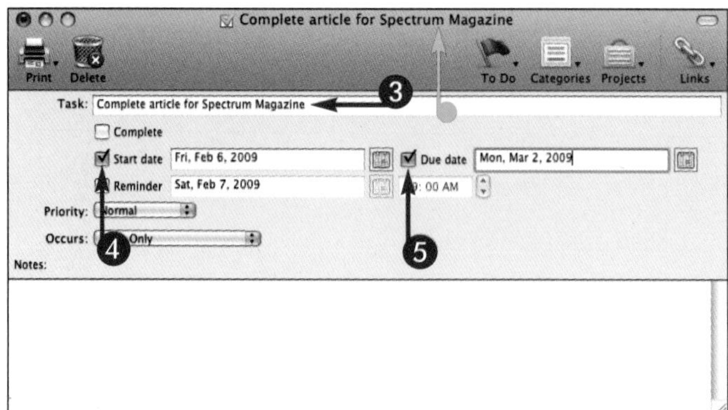

6 Click the **Priority** and then click the priority you want to assign the task.

7 In the large text box, type notes related to the task.

8 Press ⌘+S to save the task.

9 Click the **Close** button ( ).

- Entourage adds the task to the Tasks list.

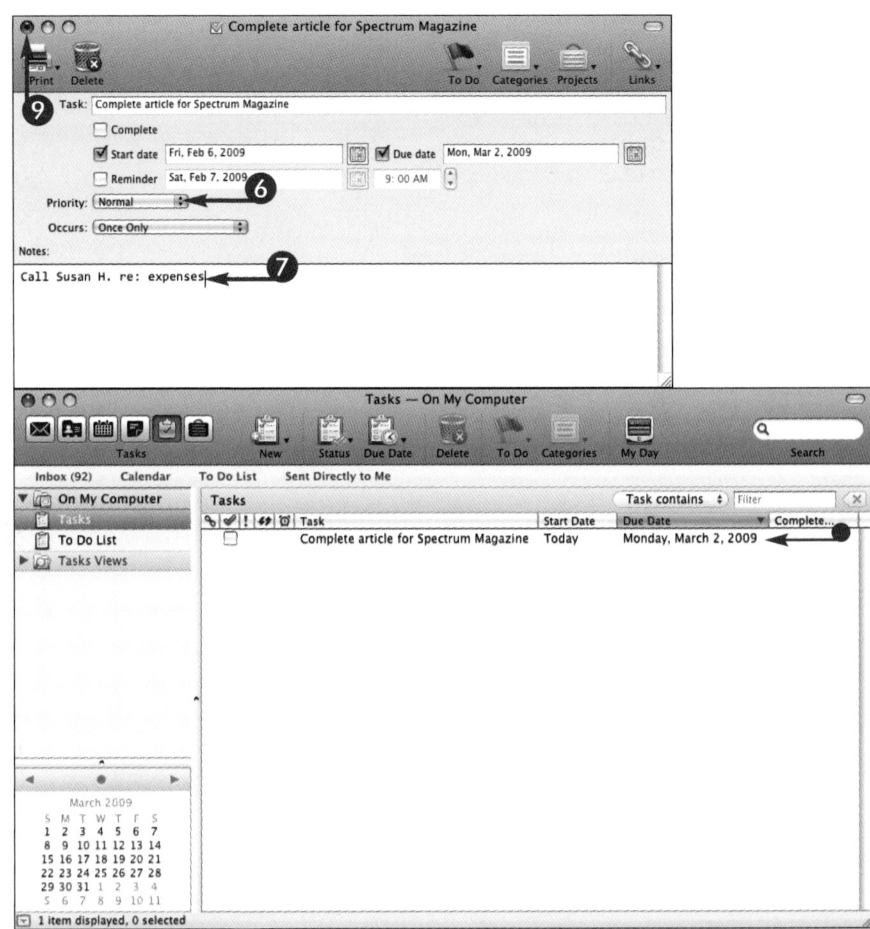

### How do I make changes to a task?

When you save a new task, Calendar adds it to both the Tasks list and the To Do List. To edit the task, click and then click either **Tasks** or **To Do List**. Double-click the task to open the task details in a window. Make your changes, press ⌘+S, and then click . To remove a task, click it, press Del, and then click **Delete**.

### Can Calendar remind me on a specific date and time when a task is due?

Yes. As with an appointment, you can specify a specific date and time that Calendar displays a reminder for the task. Follow Steps **1** to **5** to set up a task. Select the **Reminder** option ( changes to ☑) and then type the date and time when you want the reminder to appear.

# Create a Repeating Task

You can schedule a task that occurs at a regular interval, such as a weekly phone call or a monthly writing assignment as a *recurring task*. You can set up the task to repeat daily, weekly, monthly, yearly, or every weekday.

**You can also set up a custom recurrence pattern to suit your needs.**

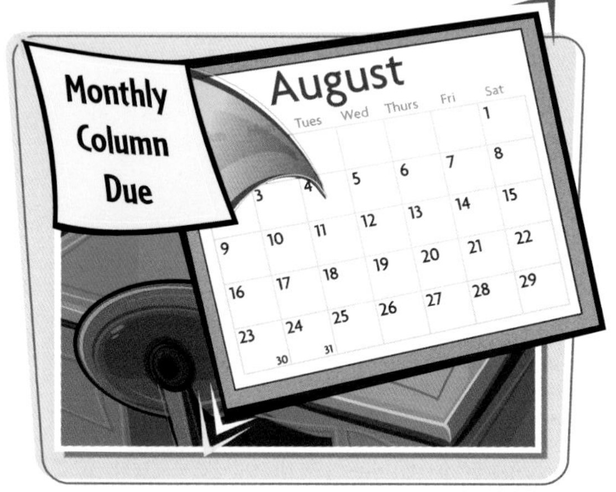


## Create a Repeating Task

### CREATE A BASIC REPEATING TASK

1. Switch to Tasks and create a new task.

***Note:*** *See the section "Create a Task" to learn how to create a new task.*

2. Click the **Occurs** ⬍ and then click the recurrence interval you want to use.

- To create your own recurrence interval, click **Custom** or click **Edit** to open the Recurring Task dialog. The rest of this section shows you how to use this dialog.

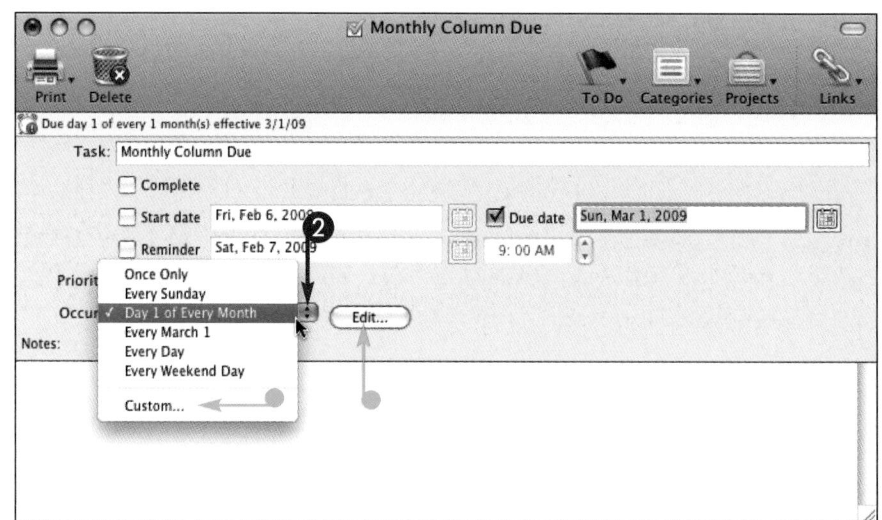


### CREATE A DAILY REPEATING TASK

1. Select the **Daily** option (○ changes to ◉).
2. Select the **Every** option (○ changes to ◉).
3. Type the daily interval you want to use.

- If you want to schedule a new task after you complete the current task, select this option (○ changes to ◉).

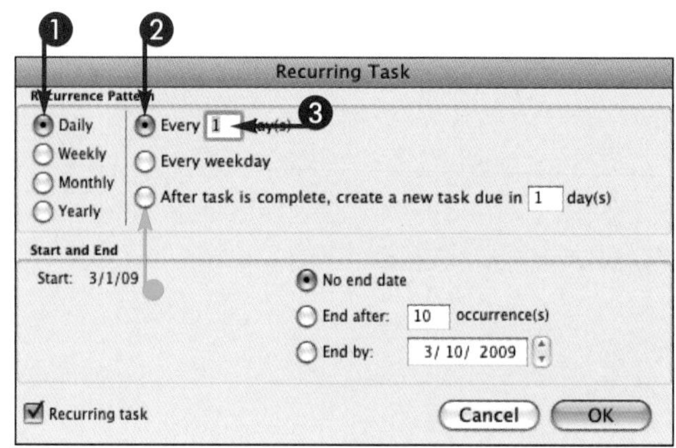

### CREATE A WEEKLY REPEATING TASK

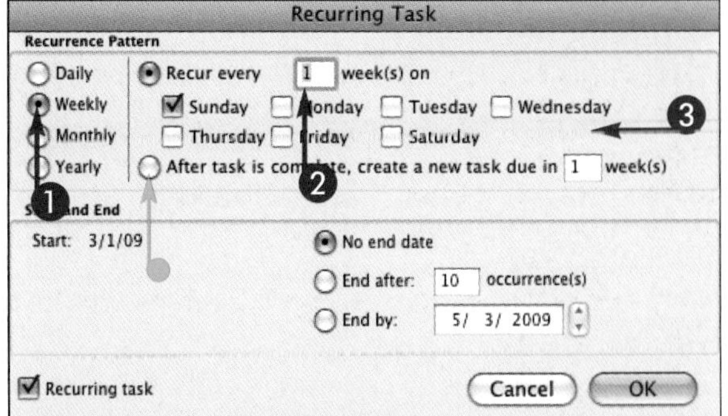


1. Select the **Weekly** option (○ changes to ◉).
2. Type the weekly interval you want to use.
3. Select the check box beside each day you want to use (☐ changes to ☑).

- If you want to schedule a new task after you complete the current task, select this option (○ changes to ◉).

### CREATE A MONTHLY REPEATING TASK

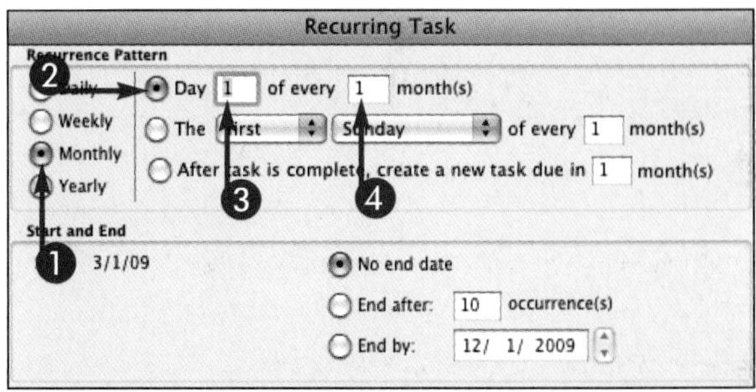


1. Select the **Monthly** option (○ changes to ◉).
2. Select the **Day** option (○ changes to ◉).
3. Type the day of the month you want to use.
4. Type the monthly interval you want to use.

### CREATE A YEARLY REPEATING TASK

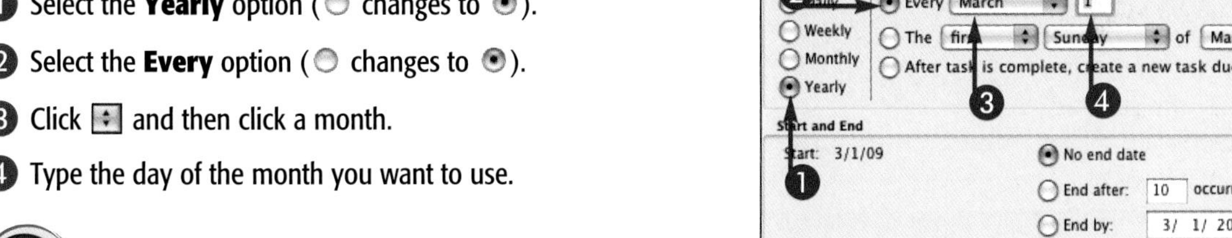

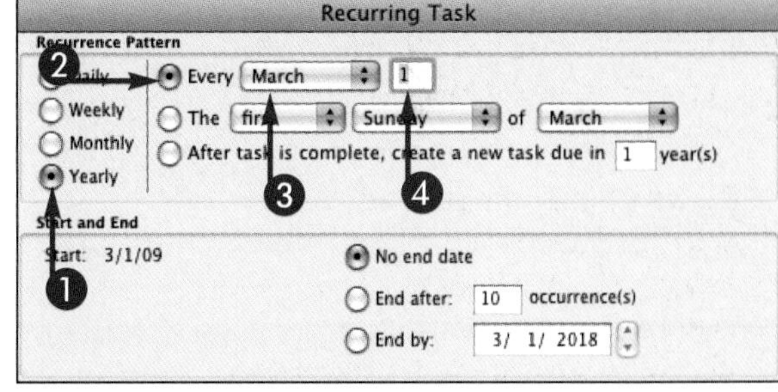


1. Select the **Yearly** option (○ changes to ◉).
2. Select the **Every** option (○ changes to ◉).
3. Click ⬍ and then click a month.
4. Type the day of the month you want to use.

TIP

**Can I create a repeating task that ends after a certain number of occurrences?**

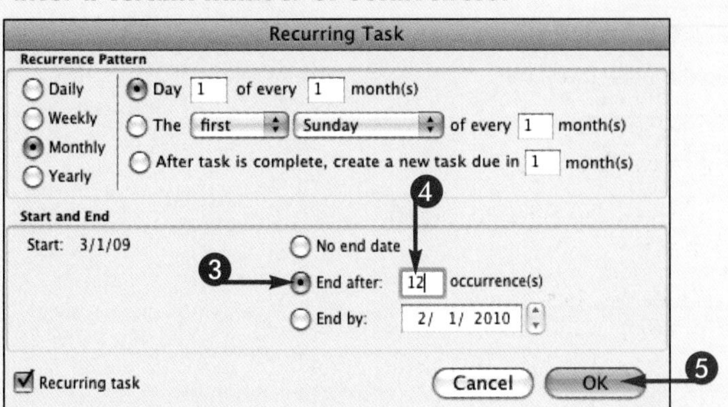


1. Follow the steps in this section to create a repeating task.
2. Double-click the repeating task to open the Recurring Task dialog.
3. Select the **End after** option (○ changes to ◉).
4. Type the total number of occurrences you want Entourage to repeat.
5. Click **OK**.

# Mark a Task as Complete

When you finish a task, you should mark it as complete to keep your list of tasks up-to-date and to avoid accidentally repeating a task.

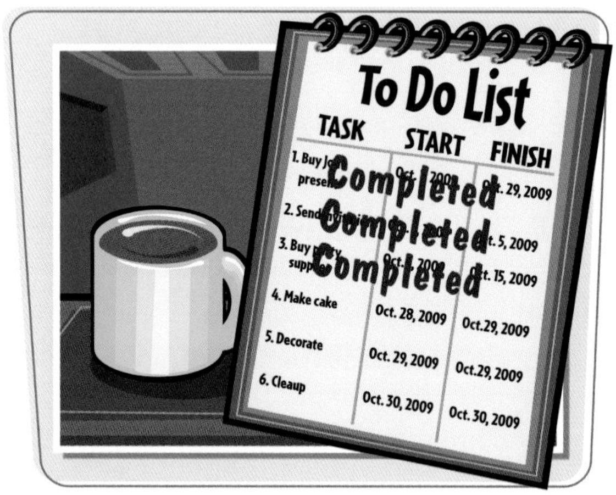


## Mark a Task as Complete

1. Click the **Tasks** button ( ).

   You can also switch to the Tasks window by pressing ⌘+5.

2. Select the check box beside the finished task (☐ changes to ☑).

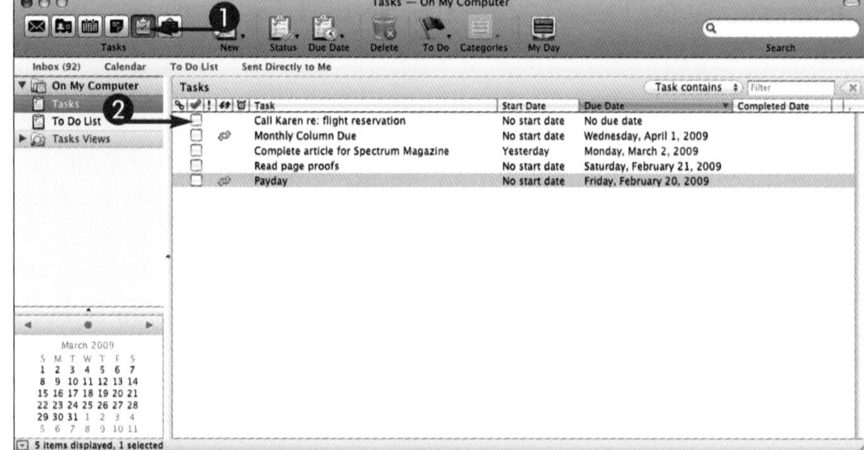


- Entourage adds strikethrough formatting to the task text.
- Entourage inserts the current date and time in the Completed Date field.

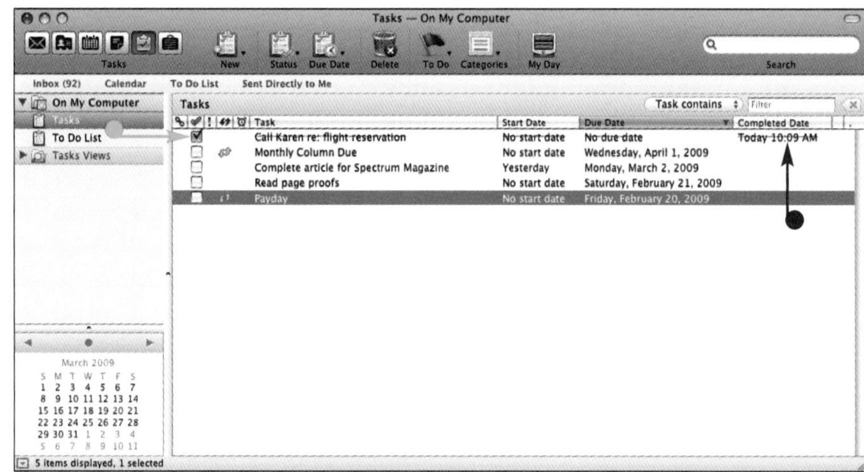

# Display Only Incomplete Tasks

You can make the Tasks list easier to navigate and your pending tasks easier to view by configuring the Tasks list to display only incomplete tasks. This is particularly useful if you have a long list of completed and pending tasks, because it enables you to focus on just those tasks that remain to be done.

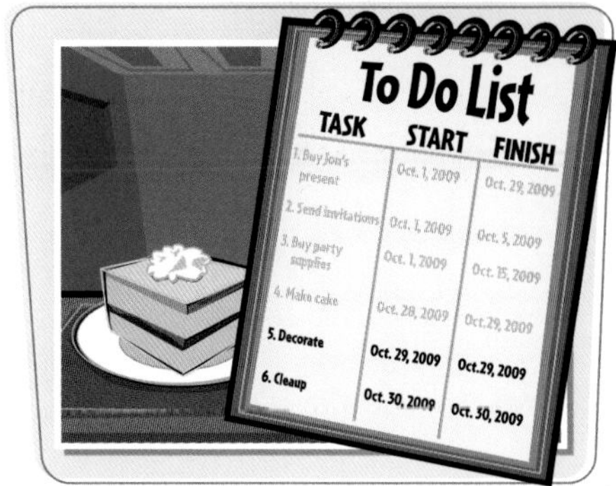


## Display Only Incomplete Tasks

1. Click the **Tasks** button (📋).

   You can also switch to the Tasks window by pressing ⌘ + 5.

2. Click **View**.
3. Click **Incomplete Tasks**.

- Entourage displays only your incomplete tasks in the Tasks list.
- You can also click the **Task Views** ▶ (▶ changes to ▼) and then click **Incomplete**.

# Working with Contacts

Entourage includes the Address Book tool to enable you to manage your contacts, whether they are colleagues or clients, friends or family members. For each person you can store a wide range of information, and you can also organize contacts into groups for easier e-mailing.

# Add a New Contact

You can store contact information for a particular person by creating a card for that person in Address Book. You can store a person's name, work and home addresses, phone numbers, e-mail address, Web page address, and much more.

## Add a New Contact

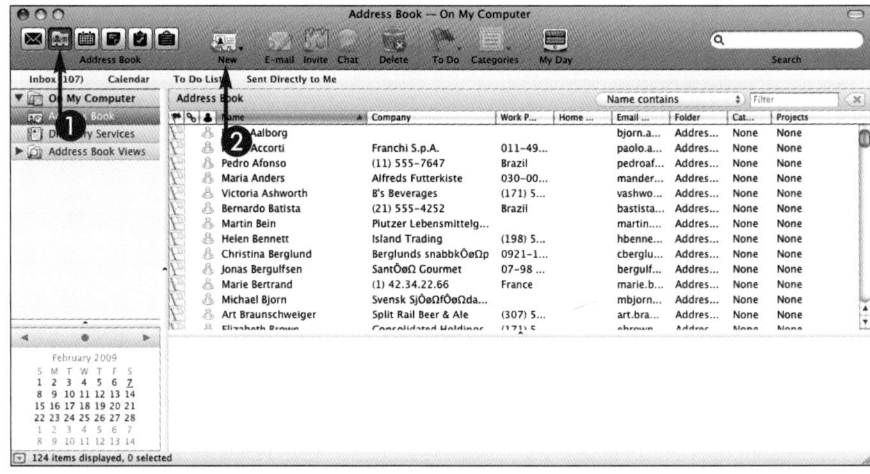


1. In Entourage, click the **Address Book** button (▣).
2. Click **New**.

   In the Address Book window, you can also start a new contact by pressing ⌘ + N.

   Entourage displays the Create Contact window.

3. Type the contact's name and work information in the fields in the Name & E-mail section.

- If you have a second e-mail address for the contact, click ⬍, click the type of e-mail address, and then type the address in the text box.

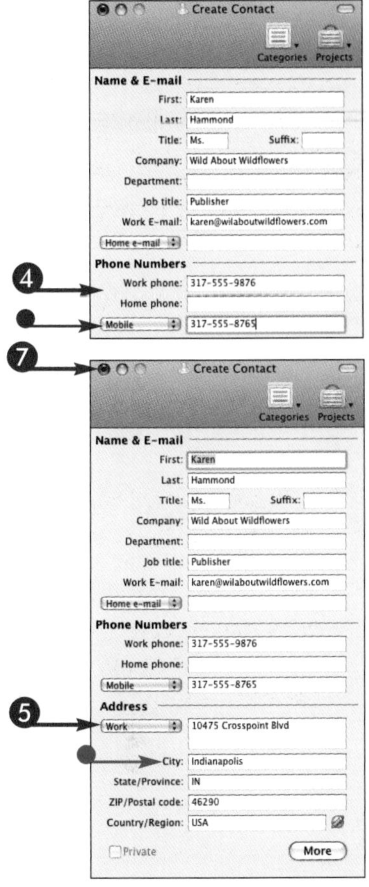


4. Type the contact's phone numbers in the fields in the Phone Numbers section.

- If you have a phone number that is not a mobile number, you can click ⬍ and then click the type of phone number.

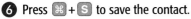

5. Type the contact's work address in the fields in the Address section.

- If you have a home address for the contact, click ⬍ and then click **Home**.

***Note:*** *See the section "Edit a Contact" to learn how to add more data to the card.*

6. Press ⌘ + S to save the contact.

7. Click ●.

   Entourage saves the new contact and adds it to the Address Book.

### Can I add an e-mail correspondent to the Address Book?

Yes. You can use a message that you have received from that person to create a contact. Click **Mail** (✉), click the message from the person you want to add, click **Message**, and then click **Add To Address Book** (or press Option + ⌘ + C). If the person sent you a vCard (VCF) file as an attachment, double-click the file, click **Open**, and press ⌘ + S to save the contact data.

### How do I import messages from another address book program?

First, use the other program to export your contacts to a comma-delimited text file, also called a comma-separated values (CSV) file, and then store that file on your Mac. In Entourage, click **File** and then click **Import** to open the Import dialog. Select the **Contacts or messages from a text file** option (○ changes to ◉), press Return, select the **Import contacts from a tab- or comma-delimited text file** option (○ changes to ◉), press Return, click the file, and then click **Import**.

# Add a Contact for Yourself

You should add an item to the Address Book that includes your contact information. This enables you to easily send your contact data to other people.

## Add a Contact for Yourself

1. In Entourage, click the **Address Book** button (📇).
2. Create a new contact and add your contact information.

***Note:*** *See the section "Add a New Contact" to learn how to create a new contact.*

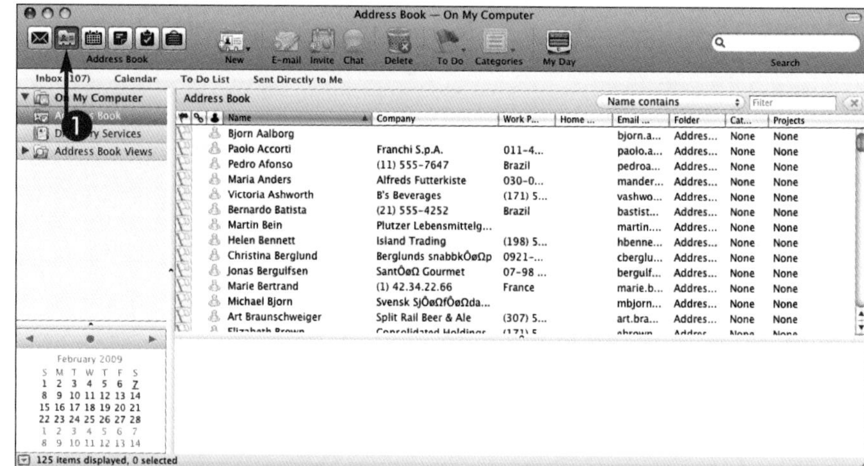


3. In the Address Book list, click your contact.
4. Click **Contact**.
5. Click **This Contact Is Me**.

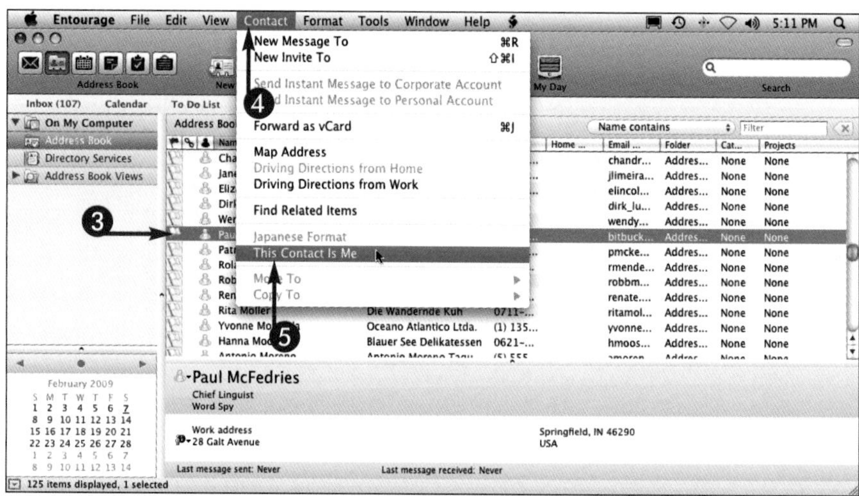

Entourage asks you to confirm that you want this contact to represent you.

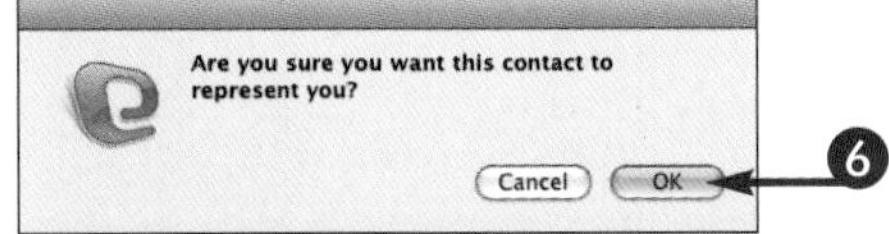


6 Click **OK**.

- Entourage marks your contact with a special icon.

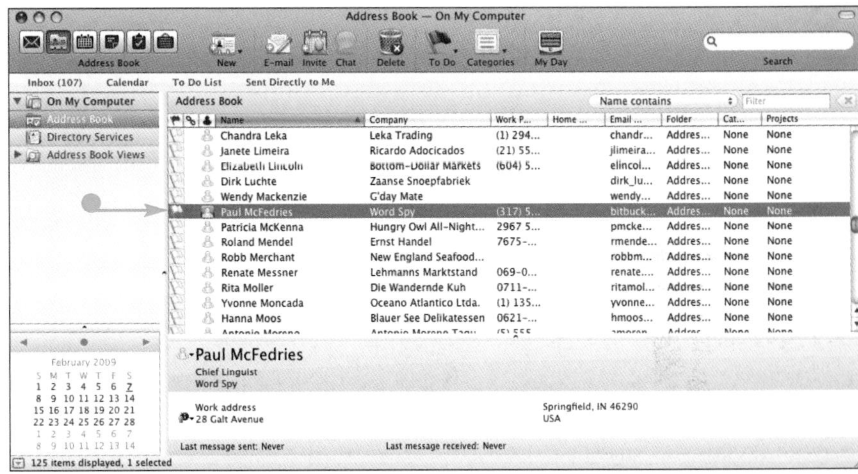

## How do I send my contact information to another person?

Now that you have your contact information in the Entourage Address Book, you can share that information with other people by sending your data as a vCard. This is a standard contact file format that is supported by many address book programs, including Entourage, Apple's Address Book, and Microsoft Outlook.

Click the **Address Book** button (), click your contact, click **Contact**, and then click **Forward as vCard** (or press ⌘ + J). In the address window, type your recipient's address and then press Return. Complete the e-mail message and then click **Send**.

# Edit a Contact

If you need to change a contact's existing information, or if you need to add new information to a contact, you can edit the contact from within the Address Book list.

**If Entourage does not have an existing field that suits the data you need to add to a contact, you can create a custom text or date field.**

## Edit a Contact

### EDIT EXISTING CONTACT FIELDS

❶ In Entourage, click the **Address Book** button (▣).

❷ Double-click the contact you want to edit.

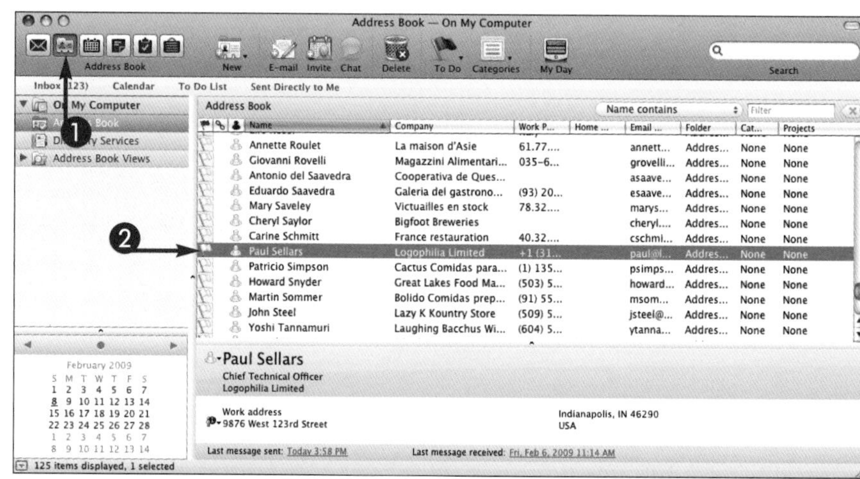


Entourage opens the contact for editing.

❸ Click the tab that contains the data you want to edit.

❹ Edit the existing fields as required.

❺ Repeat Steps **3** and **4** to make all your changes to the contact's data.

❻ Press ⌘ + S to save your work.

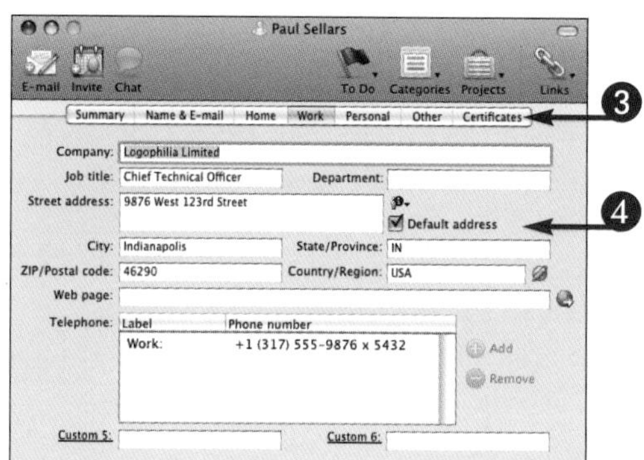

## EDIT CUSTOM CONTACT FIELDS

1. Click the tab that is appropriate to the type of data you want to add.
   - If you want to add a custom date field, click the **Other** tab.
2. Click the label of the custom field you want to use.

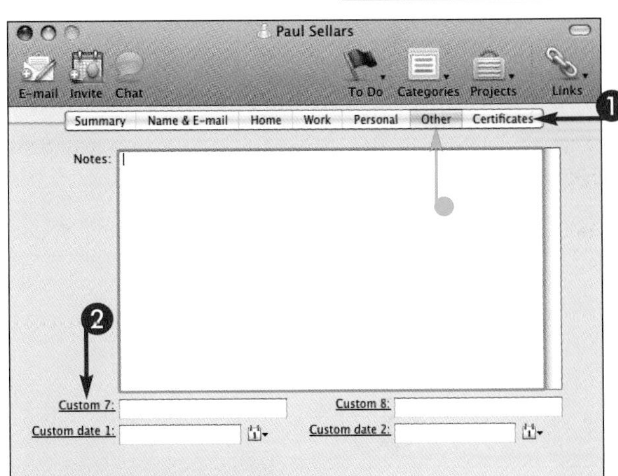


Entourage displays the Edit Custom Label dialog.

3. In the Edit label text box, type a label for the new data.
4. Click **OK**.
   - Entourage updates the label.
5. Type the data into the custom field.
6. Repeat Steps **1** to **5** to edit other custom fields.
7. Press ⌘ + S to save your work.
8. Click the **Close** button (●).

Entourage closes the editing window.

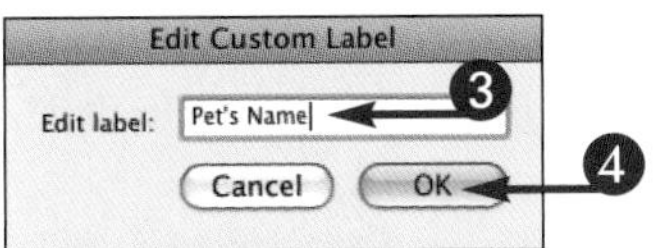


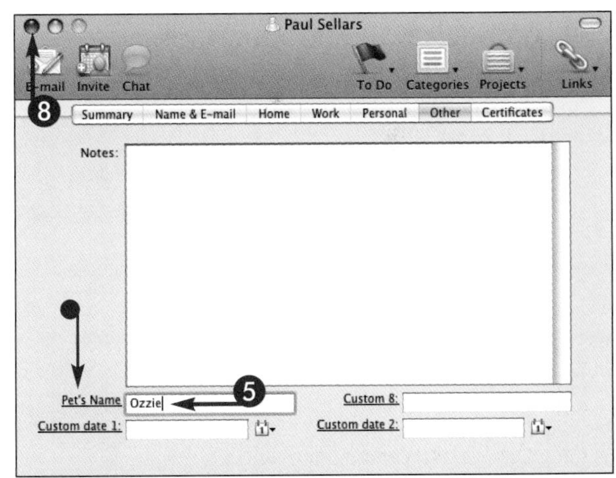

### Multiple people have access to my Address Book. Is there a way to keep track of the edited contacts?

Entourage does not offer any direct way to track changes made to contacts. However, Entourage does offer a special Address Book view that shows only those contacts that have been edited in the past seven days. To switch to this view, click the **Address Book Views** ▶ (▶ changes to ▼) and then click **Changed in the Past 7 Days**.

### I want to edit multiple contacts. Is there an easy way to navigate my contacts?

Fortunately, Entourage offers a couple of keyboard shortcuts that enable you to navigate your contacts without closing the editing window. To move to the next contact in the Address Book list, press ⌘ + ]; to move to the previous contact in the Address Book list, press ⌘ + [.

# Create a Contact Group

You can organize your contacts into one or more groups, which is useful if you want to view just a subset of your contacts. You can create a group first and then add members, or you can select members in advance and then create the group.

## Create a Contact Group

1. In Entourage, click the **Address Book** button (📇).
2. Select the contacts that you want to add to the group.

   To select multiple contacts, hold down ⌘ and click each contact.

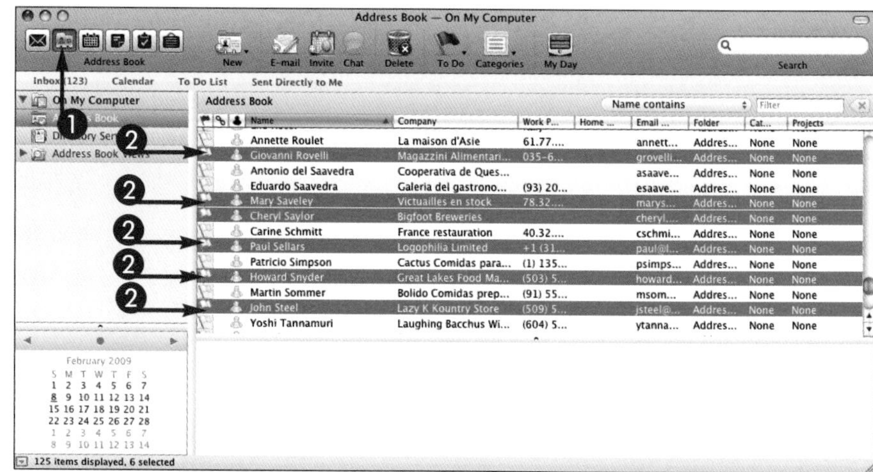


3. Click the **New** ▾.
4. Click **Group**.

   Entourage opens a new group window.

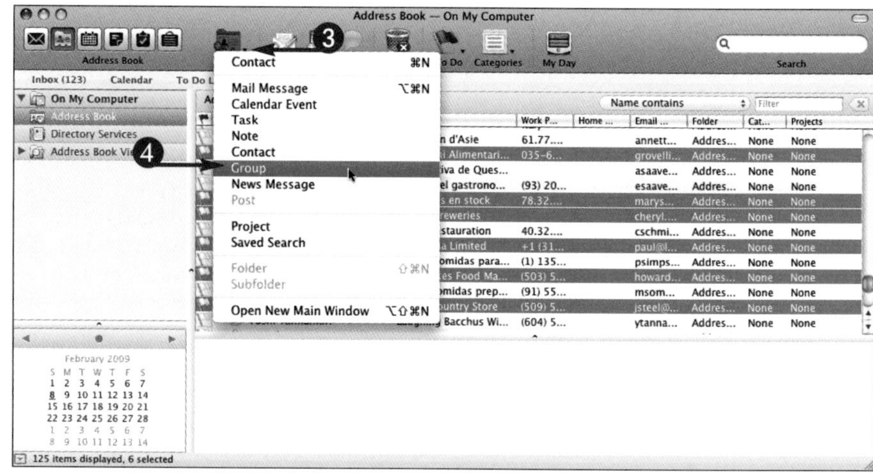

- The contacts you selected appear in the group list.

5. In the Group name text box, type a name for the group.
6. To add another contact to the group, click **Add**.
7. Type the contact's address.

   If the person is in your Address Book, you can also type his or her name.
8. Press ⌘ + S to save your work.
9. Click .

   Entourage closes the editing window.

- Entourage adds the contact group to the Address Book list.

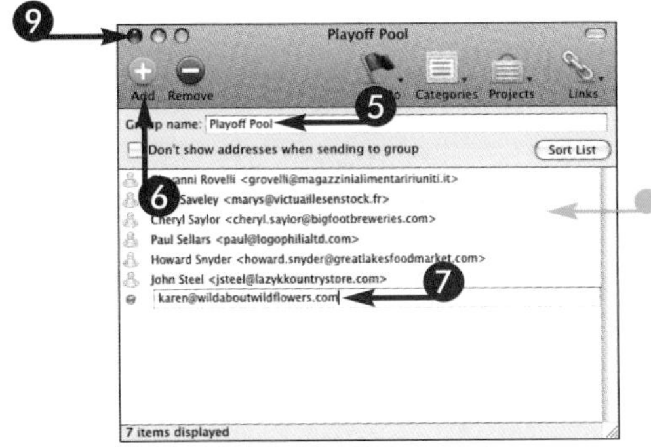

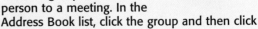

## TIPS

### Can I send an e-mail message to the group?

Yes. This is one of the best reasons to create a group. Normally, sending an e-mail message to multiple contacts involves typing or selecting multiple addresses. With a group, however, you send a single message to the group, and Entourage automatically sends a copy to each member. In the Address Book list, click the group and then click **E-mail** in the toolbar.

### Can I set up a meeting with the group?

Yes. If you often invite the same people to a meeting, create a group that consists of those contacts. You can then use that group to invite each person to a meeting. In the Address Book list, click the group and then click **Invite** in the toolbar.

# Map a Contact's Address

If you have added a contact's home or work address to the Entourage Address Book, you can display a map that shows the location of that address.

**Entourage uses Microsoft MapPoint to display the address on the MSN Maps & Directions Web site.**

## Map a Contact's Address

1. In Entourage, click the **Address Book** button (▣).
2. Double-click the contact you want to work with.

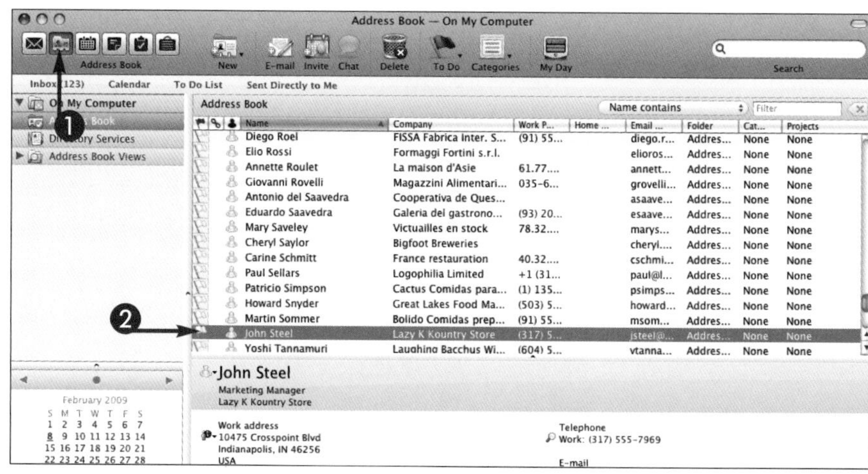


Entourage opens the contact.

3. Click the tab that contains the address you want to map.
4. Click the **Address Actions** icon (▣).

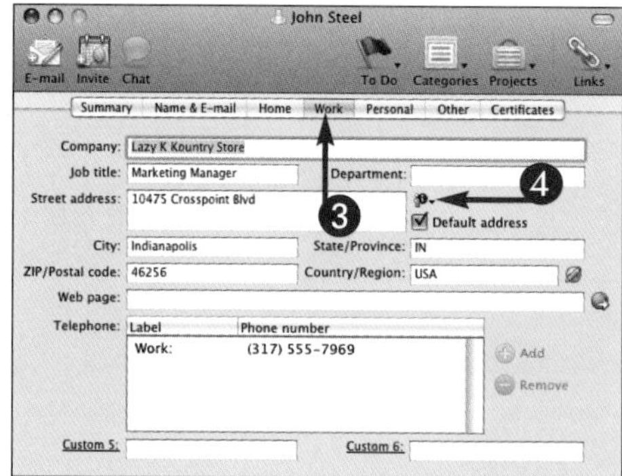

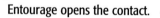

5 Click **Show on Map**.

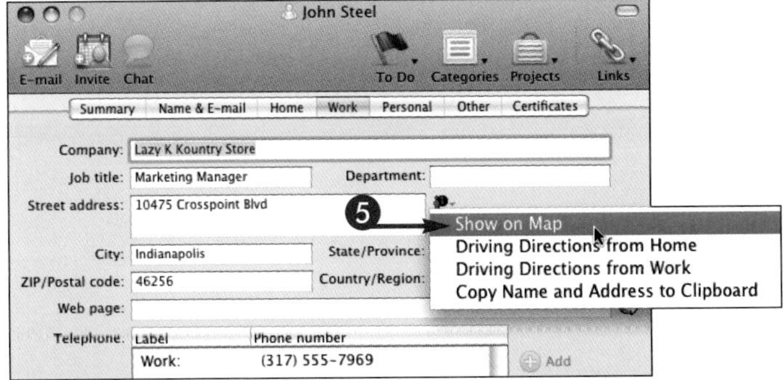


Entourage launches your Web browser, loads the MSN Maps & Directions Web site, and displays a map that shows the address.

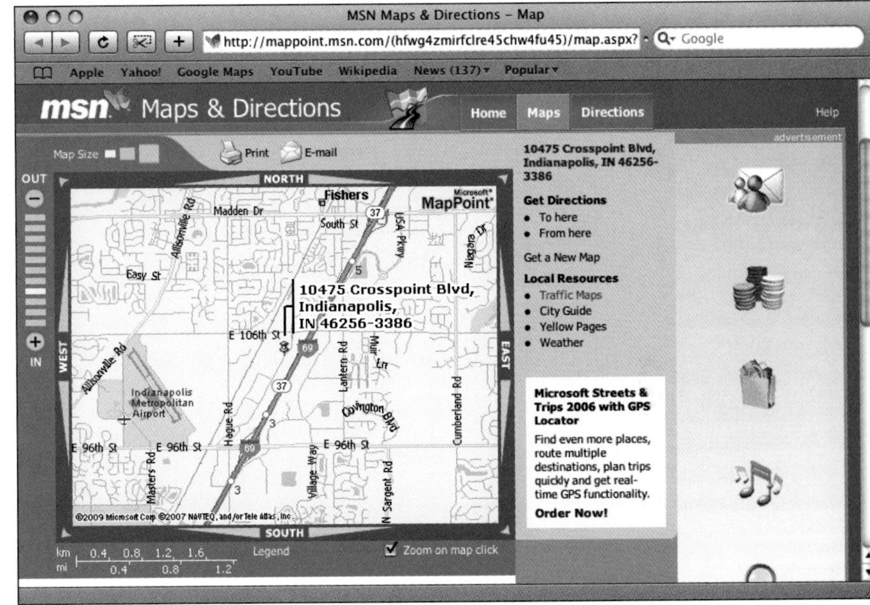


TIP

### How do I display a contact's Web page?

If you added a Web address to the contact's Home or Work tab, follow these steps to load the page into your Web browser:

1. Click [icon].
2. Double-click the contact you want to work with.
3. Click the tab that contains the Web address you want to load.
4. Click the **Open Web Page** icon ([icon]).

   Entourage launches your Web browser and displays the Web page.

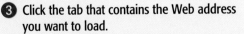

# Get Directions to a Contact's Address

If you add a contact's home or work address to the Entourage Address Book, and you add a home or work address to your own contact, you can get specific directions to the contact's address.

**Entourage uses Microsoft MapPoint to display the driving directions on the MSN Maps & Directions Web site.**

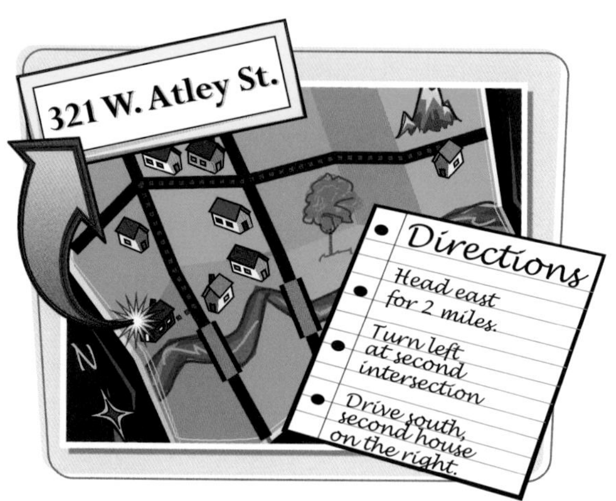


## Get Directions to a Contact's Address

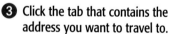

1. In Entourage, click the **Address Book** button ( ).
2. Double-click the contact you want to work with.

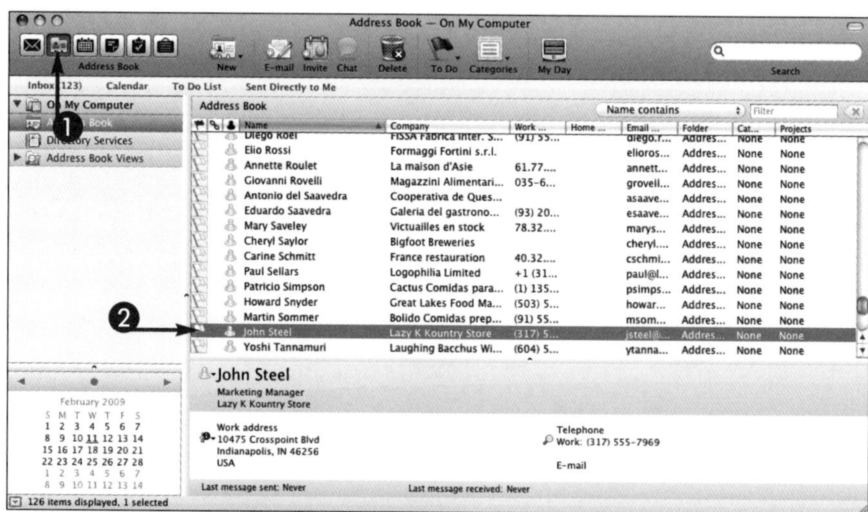


Entourage opens the contact.

3. Click the tab that contains the address you want to travel to.
4. Click the **Address Actions** icon ( ).

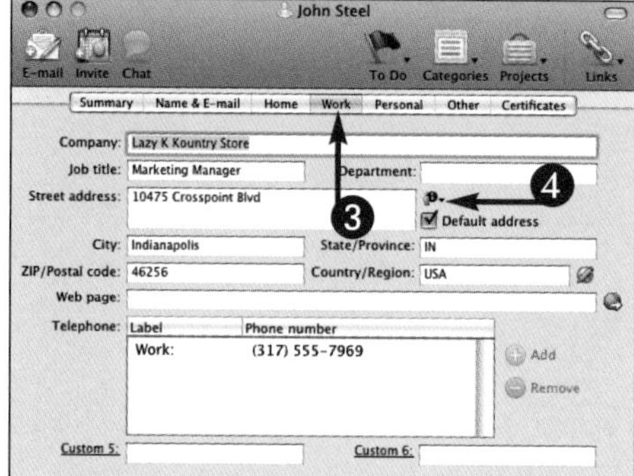

5 Click **Driving Directions from Home**.

- If you are traveling to the contact's address from work, click **Driving Directions from Work**.

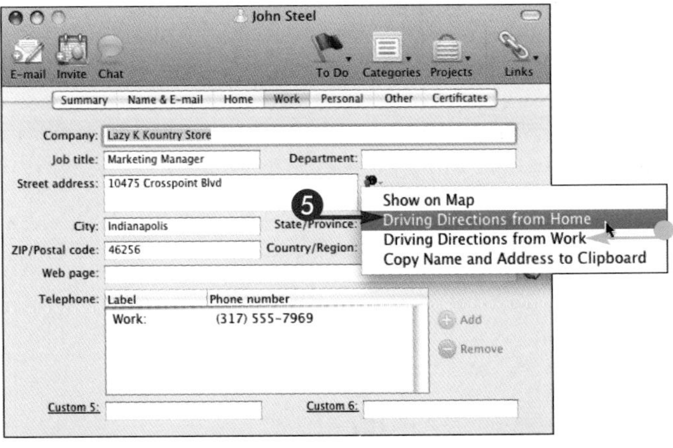


Entourage launches your Web browser, loads the MSN Maps & Directions Web site, and displays the directions.

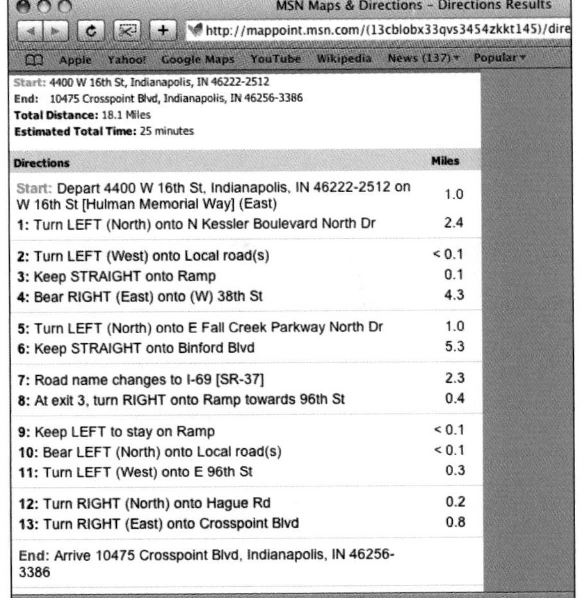

MSN Maps & Directions - Directions Results
http://mappoint.msn.com/(13cblobx33qvs3454zkkt145)/dire
Apple
Yahoo!
Google Maps
YouTube
Wikipedia
News (137)
Popular
Start: 4400 W 16th St, Indianapolis, IN 46222-2512
End: 10475 Crosspoint Blvd, Indianapolis, IN 46256-3386
Total Distance: 18.1 Miles
Estimated Total Time: 25 minutes
Directions
Miles
Start: Depart 4400 W 16th St, Indianapolis, IN 46222-2512 on W 16th St [Hulman Memorial Way] (East) 1.0
1: Turn LEFT (North) onto N Kessler Boulevard North Dr 2.4
2: Turn LEFT (West) onto Local road(s) < 0.1
3: Keep STRAIGHT onto Ramp 0.1
4: Bear RIGHT (East) onto (W) 38th St 4.3
5: Turn LEFT (North) onto E Fall Creek Parkway North Dr 1.0
6: Keep STRAIGHT onto Binford Blvd 5.3
7: Road name changes to I-69 [SR-37] 2.3
8: At exit 3, turn RIGHT onto Ramp towards 96th St 0.4
9: Keep LEFT to stay on Ramp < 0.1
10: Bear LEFT (North) onto Local road(s) < 0.1
11: Turn LEFT (West) onto E 96th St 0.3
12: Turn RIGHT (North) onto Hague Rd 0.2
13: Turn RIGHT (East) onto Crosspoint Blvd 0.8
End: Arrive 10475 Crosspoint Blvd, Indianapolis, IN 46256-3386


TIP

**I want to use a contact's address in a separate document. Is there an easy way to copy the entire address?**

Yes. Entourage has a feature that you can use to copy a contact's name and address to the Mac OS X Clipboard. Follow Steps **1** to **3** to display the tab that contains the address you want to copy. Click [icon] and then click **Copy Name and Address to Clipboard**. Switch to the document you are working on, position the cursor where you want the name and address to appear, and then press ⌘ + V. Mac OS X inserts the name and address into the document.

# Work Faster with the Preview Pane

You can use features found in the preview pane to perform many contact tasks faster and easier. For example, you can use the preview pane to send a contact an e-mail message or meeting invitation, edit a contact, and map a contact's address.

## Work Faster with the Preview Pane

### EXPAND THE PREVIEW PANE

1. In Entourage, click the **Address Book** button (![icon]).
2. Click the contact you want to work with.

- Entourage displays some of the contact's data in the preview pane.

3. Click and drag the divider bar up to show more information in the preview pane.

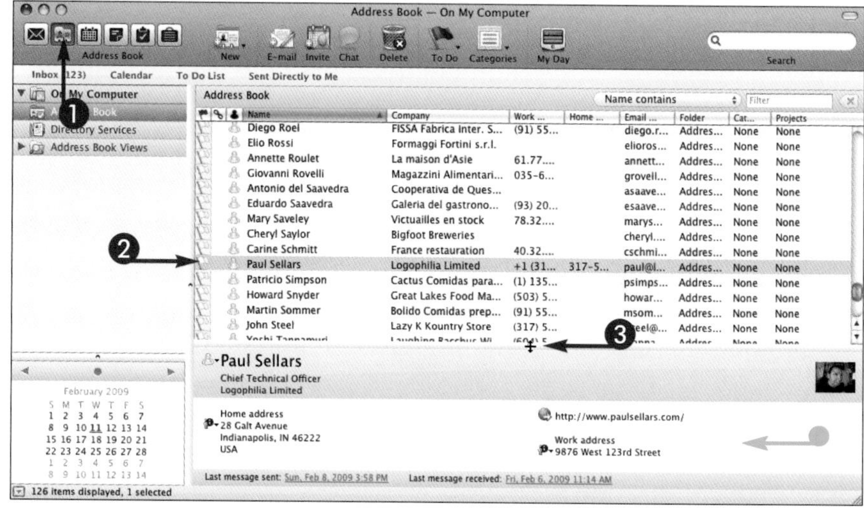


### SEND A MESSAGE TO THE CONTACT

1. Click the **Edit this Contact** icon (![icon]).
2. Click **New Message To**.

- To invite the contact to a meeting, click **New Invite To**.
- You can also send a message by clicking the **Send Mail** button (![icon]).
- Click this link to view the most recent message you sent to the contact.
- Click this link to view the most recent message you received from the contact.

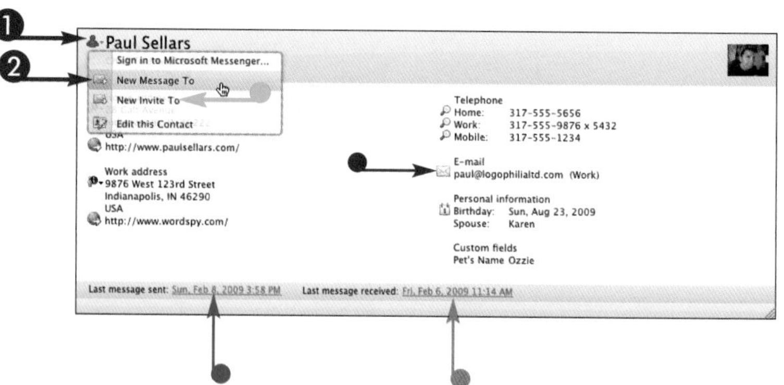

## WORK WITH THE CONTACT'S ADDRESSES

1. Click the **Address Actions** icon ( ) beside the address you want to work with.
2. Click the address action you want to perform.

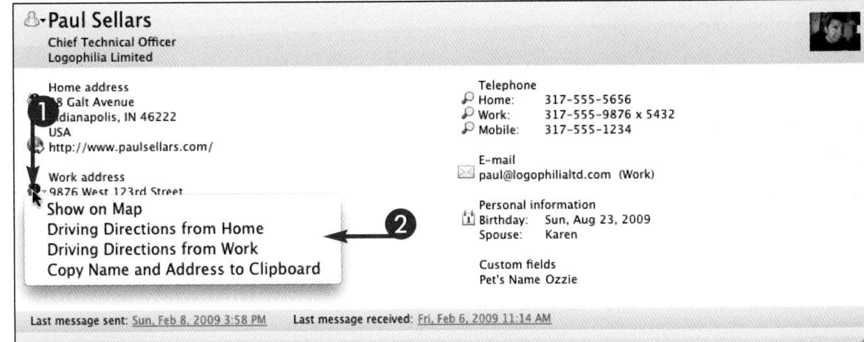


## DISPLAY THE CONTACT'S WEB PAGE

1. Click the **Open Web Page** icon ( ) beside the Web address you want to display.

- You can click the **Add to Calendar** icon ( ) beside any date to add that item to the Entourage Calendar.
- You can click the **Magnify Phone Number** icon ( ) to display a magnified version of any phone number.

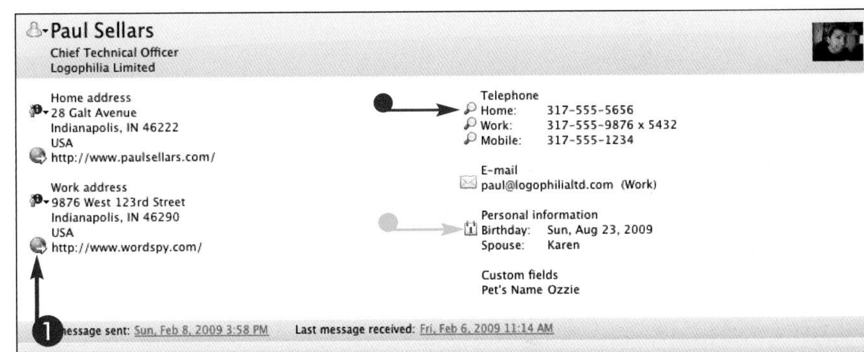


TIP

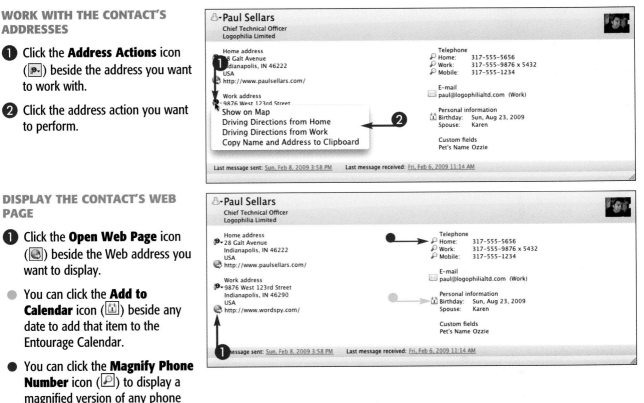

### If I do not use the preview pane, can I turn it off?

Yes. The preview pane can be very handy, but it takes up quite a bit of room, especially if you expand it to show more contact data. If you use the preview pane rarely or not at all, it is a good idea to turn it off to get more room in the Address Book window. To toggle the preview pane off and on, click **View** and then click **Preview Pane**. You can also toggle the preview pane by pressing ⌘ + \.

# Delete a Contact

If you have an Address Book contact that you no longer require, you should delete that contact to make the Address Book list easier to navigate.

**You can also delete any contact groups that you have created.**

## Delete a Contact

### DELETE A CONTACT

1. In Entourage, click the **Address Book** button (📇).
2. Click the contact you want to delete.
3. Click **Edit**.
4. Click **Delete Contact**.

   You can also press Delete.

   Entourage asks you to confirm the deletion.

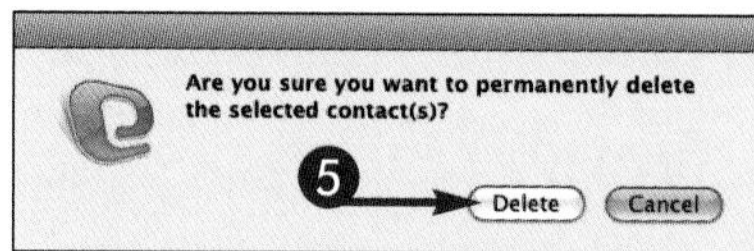


5. Click **Delete**.

   Entourage removes the contact from the Address Book.

## DELETE A CONTACT GROUP

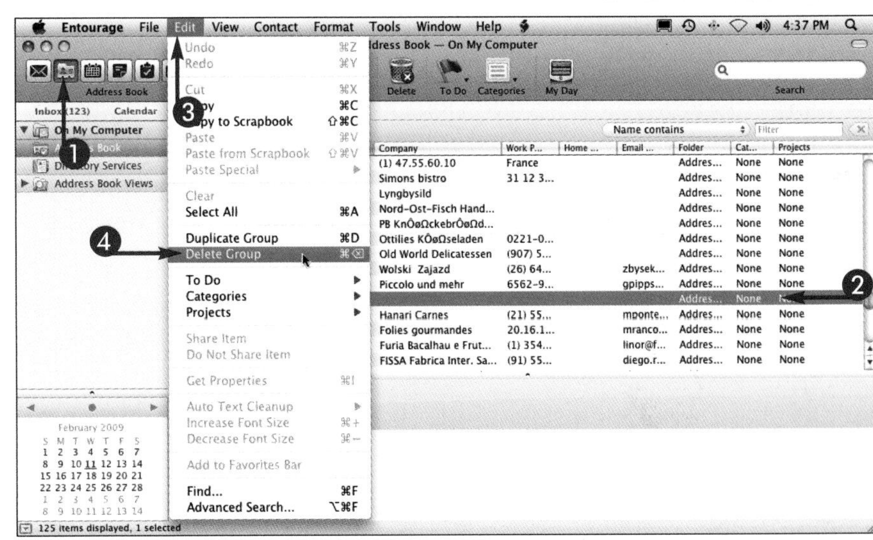


1. Click .
2. Click the contact group you want to delete.
3. Click **Edit**.
4. Click **Delete Group**.

   You can also press ⌘ + Delete.

   Entourage asks you to confirm the deletion.

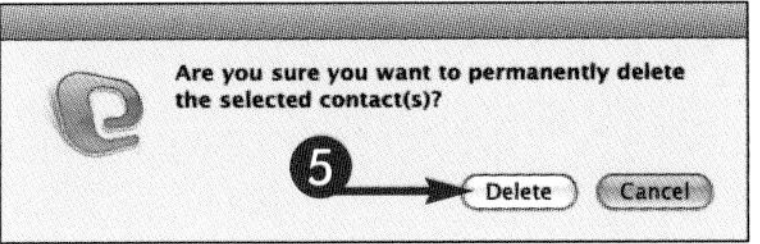


5. Click **Delete**.

   Entourage removes the contact group from the Address Book.

### How do I delete a contact from a group?

To remove just a single contact from a group, click  and then click the contact group you want to work with. In the list of the group's contacts, click the contact you want to delete and then click **Remove**. Press ⌘ + S to save the group, and then click the Close button ().

### When I delete a contact group, does this affect the group's contacts in any way?

No. A contact group is a separate list of contacts, and deleting a group — or deleting a single contact from a group — has no effect on those contacts. In particular, the group's contacts are not removed from the Address Book.

# Index

## Symbols and Numerics



## A



## B



## C

## D



## E

# Index

# Index



## Q



## R



## S

## T

# Index

## Y